Street by Street

TYNE & WEAR

PLUS ASHINGTON, BLYTH, CHESTER-LE-STREET, CONSETT, CRAMLINGTON, MORPETH, PETERLEE, PRUDHOE, SEAHAM, STANLEY

Enlarged Areas Durham, Gateshead, Newcastle upon Tyne, South Shields, Sunderland

2nd edition March 2002
Ist edition May 2001

© Automobile Association Developments Limited 2002

Ordnance Survey® This product includes map data licensed from Ordnance Survey® with the permission of the Controller of Her Majesty's Stationery Office.© Crown copyright 2002. All rights reserved. Licence No: 399221.

Published by AA Publishing (a trading name of Automobile Association Developments Limited, whose registered office is Millstream, Maidenhead Road, Windsor, Berkshire SL4 5GD. Registered number 1878835).

The Post Office is a registered trademark of Post Office Ltd. in the UK and other countries.

Mapping produced by the Cartographic Department of The Automobile Association. A01227

A CIP Catalogue record for this book is available from the British Library.

Printed by G. Canale & C. S.P.A., Torino, Italy

Ref: MX053z

Key to map pages	ii-iii
Key to map symbols	iv-1
Enlarged scale pages	2-17
Street by Street	18-185
Index – towns & villages	186
Index – streets	187-220
Index – featured places	221-226

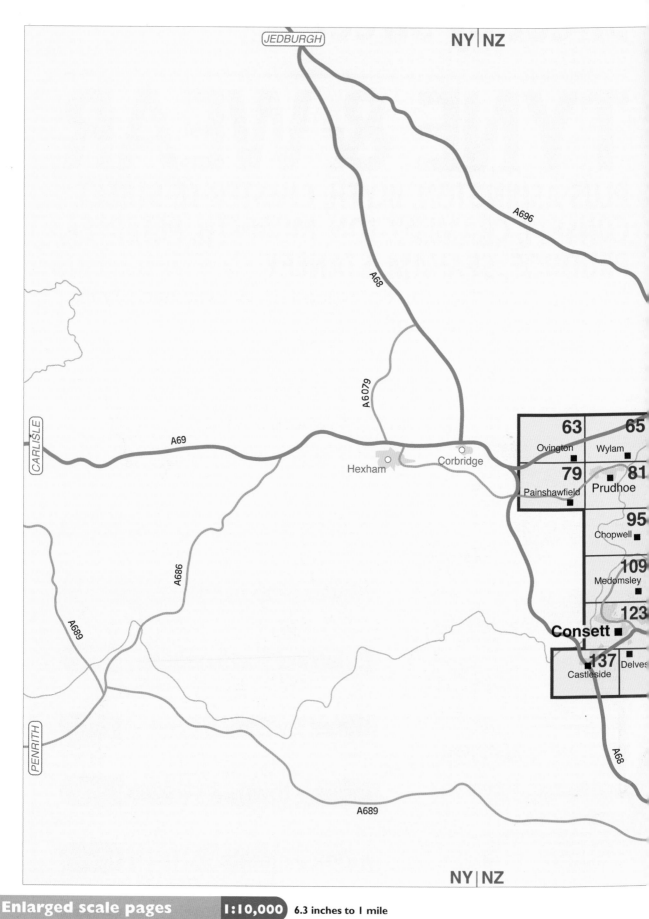

JEDBURGH

A696

A68

A6079

CARLISLE

A69

Hexham

Corbridge

63	65
Ovington	Wylam
79	81
Painshawfield	Prudhoe

95
Chopwell

109
Medomsley

123

Consett

137   Delves
Castleside

A686

A689

PENRITH

A689

A68

NY | NZ

Enlarged scale pages   **1:10,000**   **6.3 inches to 1 mile**

0   1/4   miles   1/2   3/4

0   1/4   1/2   kilometres   3/4   1   1 1/4

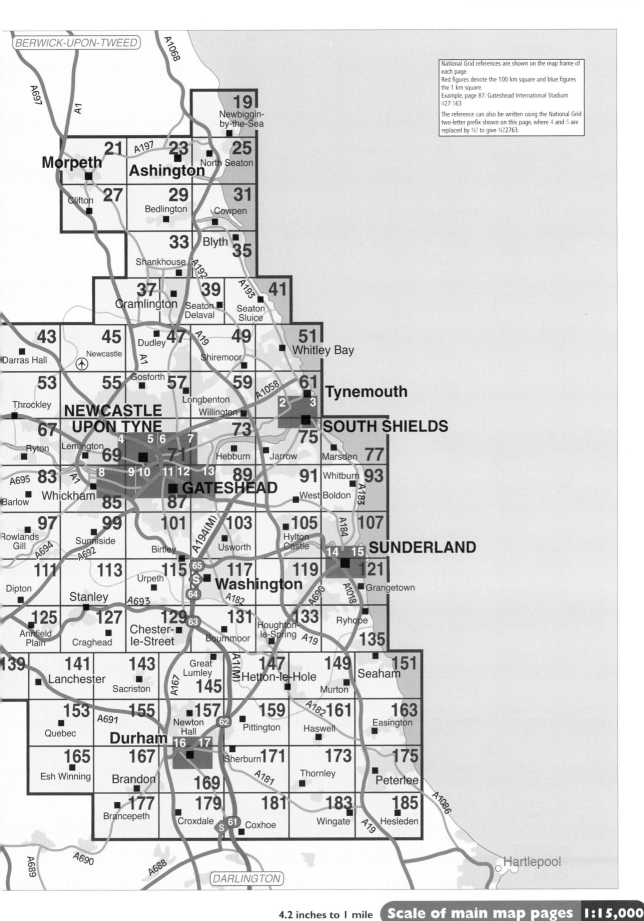

BERWICK-UPON-TWEED

A1068

A697

A1

19
Newbiggin-
by-the-Sea

21
Morpeth

A197

23
Ashington

North Seaton

25

Clifton

27

29
Bedlington

31
Cowpen

33
Shankhouse

Blyth

35

A192

37
Cramlington

A193

39
Seaton
Delaval

Seaton
Sluice

41

A19

43
Darras Hall

45
Newcastle

Dudley

47

A1

Shiremoor

49

A1058

51
Whitley Bay

53
Throckley

55
Gosforth

57
Longbenton
Willington

59

61
Tynemouth

2
3

NEWCASTLE
UPON TYNE

67
Ryton

Lemington

4

5 **6**

69

71

7

73

Hebburn

Jarrow

75
SOUTH SHIELDS

Marsden

77

A695

83
Barlow

Whickham

A1

8

9 **10**

11 **12**

85

87

13

89
GATESHEAD

91
West Boldon

Whitburn

93

A183

97
Rowlands
Gill

A694

99
Sunniside

A692

101
Birtley

A194(M)

103
Usworth

105
Hylton
Castle

A184

107

14 **15**
SUNDERLAND

111
Dipton

113
Stanley

A693

Urpeth

115

65

S

64

117
Washington

A182

119

A690

A1018

121

Grangetown

125
Annfield
Plain

127
Craghead

129
Chester-
le-Street

63

131
Bournmoor

Houghton-
le-Spring

133

A19

Ryhope

135

139

141
Lanchester

143
Sacriston

A167

Great
Lumley

A1(M)

145

147
Hetton-le-Hole

149
Murton

Seaham

151

153
Quebec

A691

155

157
Newton
Hall

62

159
Pittington

Haswell

A182

161

163
Easington

Durham

16 **17**

165
Esh Winning

167
Brandon

Sherburn

171

A181

173
Thornley

175
Peterlee

169

177
Brancepeth

179
Croxdale

S

61

Coxhoe

181

A19

183
Wingate

185
Hesleden

A1086

A689

A690

A668

DARLINGTON

Hartlepool

National Grid references are shown on the map frame of each page.
Red figures denote the 100 km square and blue figures the 1 km square.
Example, page 87: Gateshead International Stadium 427 563

The reference can also be written using the National Grid two-letter prefix shown on this page, where 4 and 5 are replaced by NZ to give NZ2763.

4.2 inches to 1 mile

Scale of main map pages 1:15,000

0   1/4   miles   1/2   3/4   1

0   1/4   1/2   kilometres   3/4   1   1 1/4   1 1/2   1 3/4

Junction 9	Motorway & junction
Services	Motorway service area
	Primary road single/dual carriageway
Services	Primary road service area
	A road single/dual carriageway
	B road single/dual carriageway
	Other road single/dual carriageway
	Minor/private road, access may be restricted
← ←	One-way street
	Pedestrian area
	Track or footpath
	Road under construction
	Road tunnel
AA	AA Service Centre
P	Parking
P+	Park & Ride
	Bus/Coach station
	Railway & main railway station
	Railway & minor railway station

⊖	Underground station
⊖	Light Railway & station
+++++++++	Preserved private railway
LC	Level crossing
•–•–•–•–•	Tramway
-----------	Ferry route
....	Airport runway
–·–·–·–	Boundaries - borough/district
▼▼▼▼▼	Mounds
93	Page continuation 1:15,000
7	Page continuation to enlarged scale 1:10,000
	River/canal, lake, pier
	Aqueduct, lock, weir
465 ▲ Winter Hill	Peak (with height in metres)
	Beach
	Coniferous woodland
	Broadleaved woodland
	Mixed woodland
	Park

Cemetery		Theme Park	
Built-up area		Abbey, cathedral or priory	
Featured building		Castle	
City wall		Historic house or building	
24-hour Accident & Emergency hospital	A&E	National Trust property	Wakehurst Place NT
Post Office	PO	Museum or art gallery	
Public library		Roman antiquity	
Tourist Information Centre	i	Ancient site, battlefield or monument	
Petrol station — Major suppliers only		Industrial interest	
Church/chapel	†	Garden	
Toilet		Arboretum	
Toilet with disabled facilities		Farm or animal centre	
Public house — AA recommended	PH	Zoological or wildlife collection	
Restaurant — AA inspected		Bird collection	
Theatre or performing arts centre		Nature reserve	
Cinema		Visitor or heritage centre	
Golf course		Country park	
Camping — AA inspected		Cave	
Caravan Site — AA inspected		Windmill	
Camping & Caravan Site — AA inspected		Distillery, brewery or vineyard	

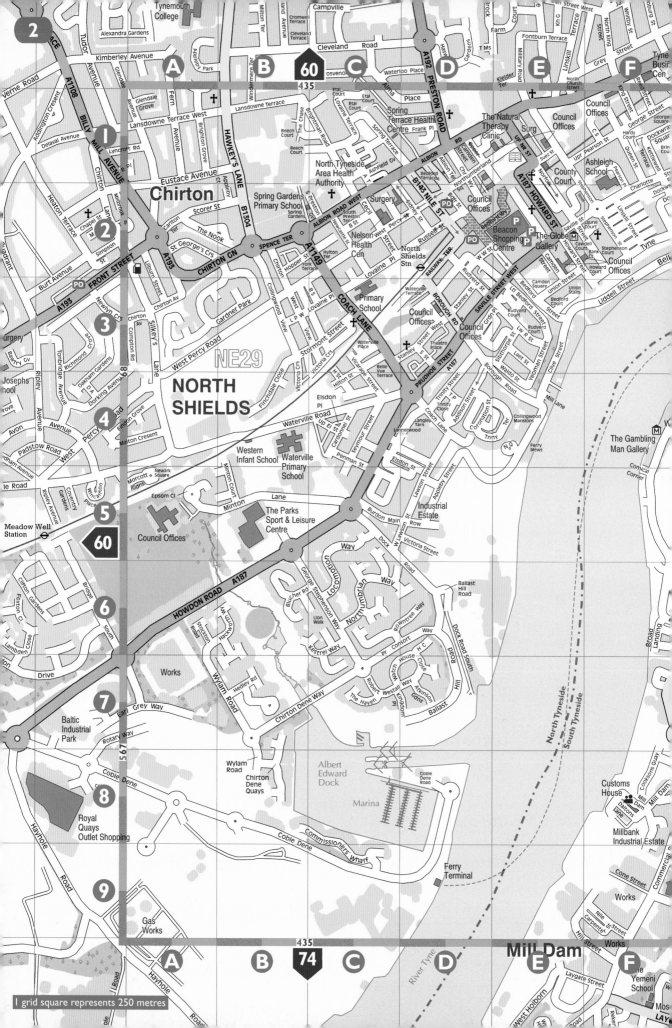

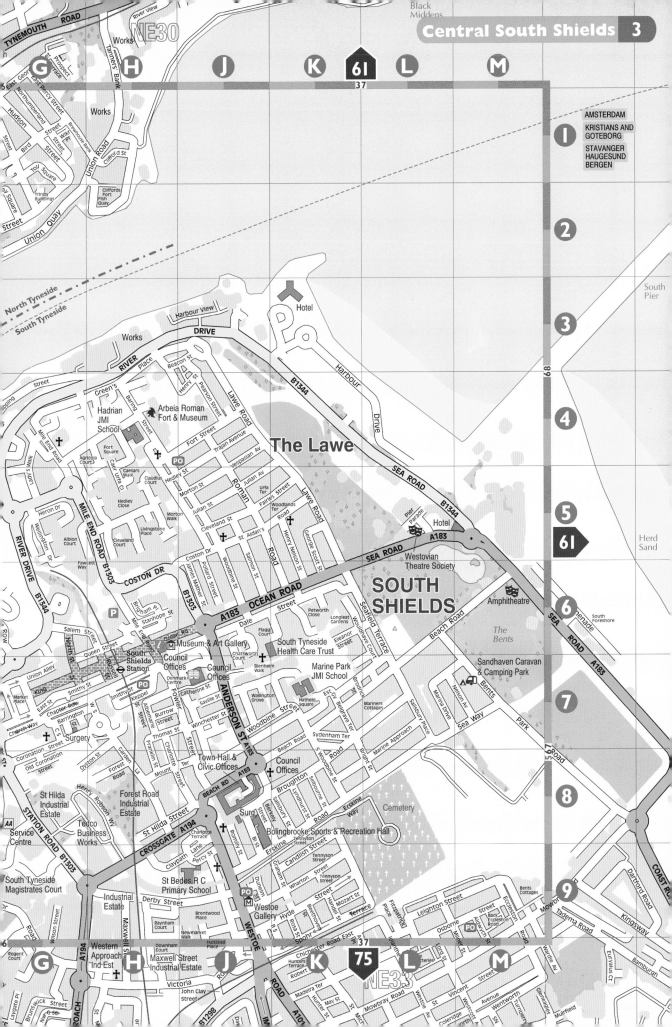

The Lawe

SOUTH SHIELDS

AMSTERDAM

KRISTIANS AND GOTEBORG

STAVANGER HAUGESUND BERGEN

South Pier

Herd Sand

South Foreshore

The Bents

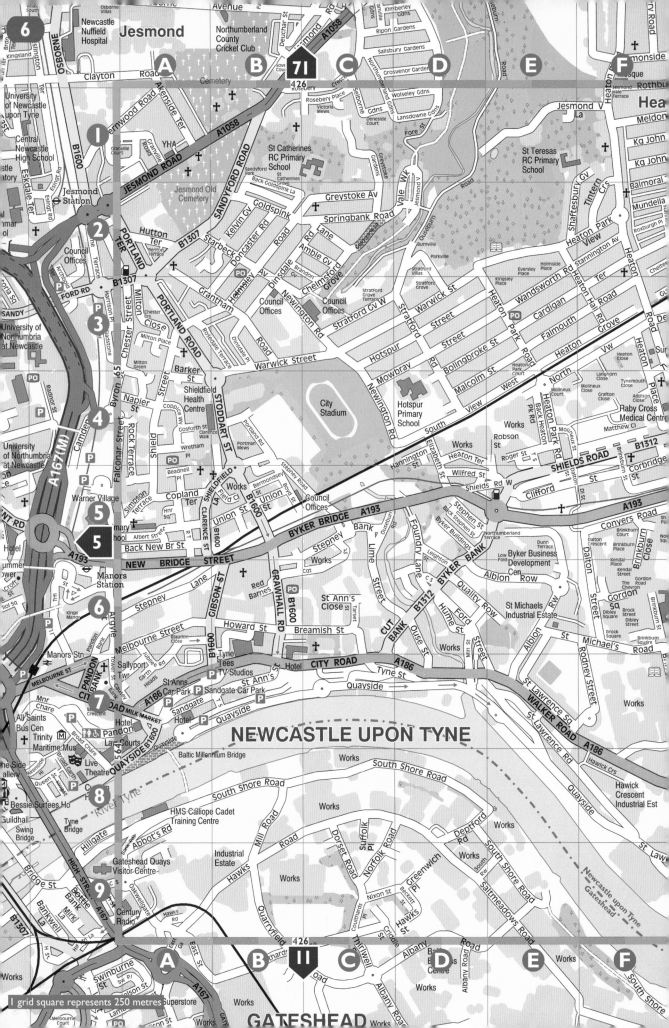

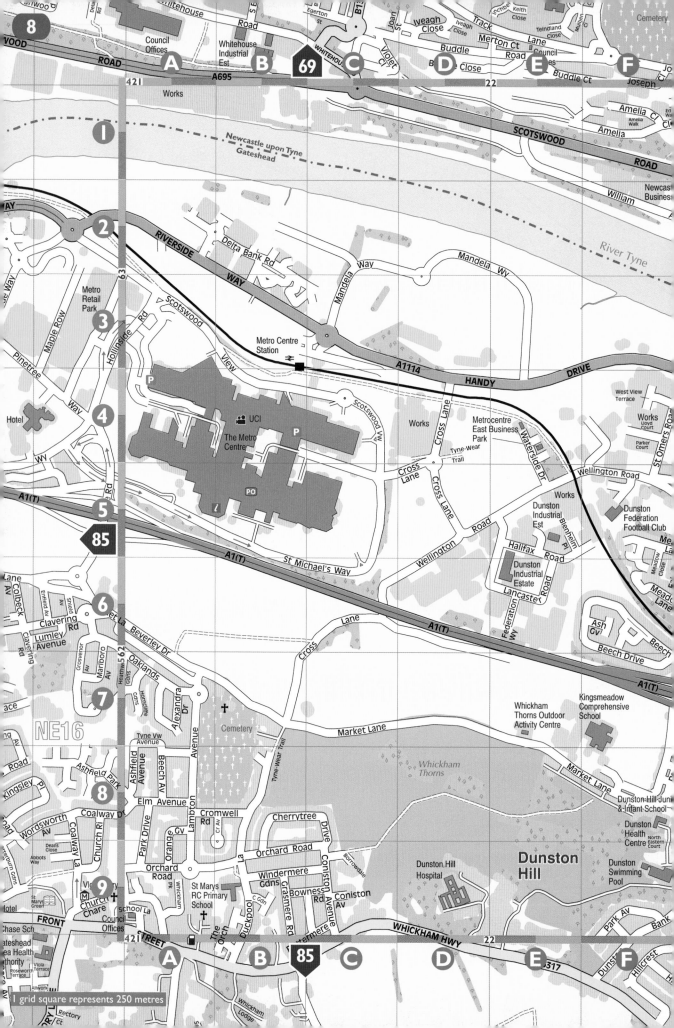

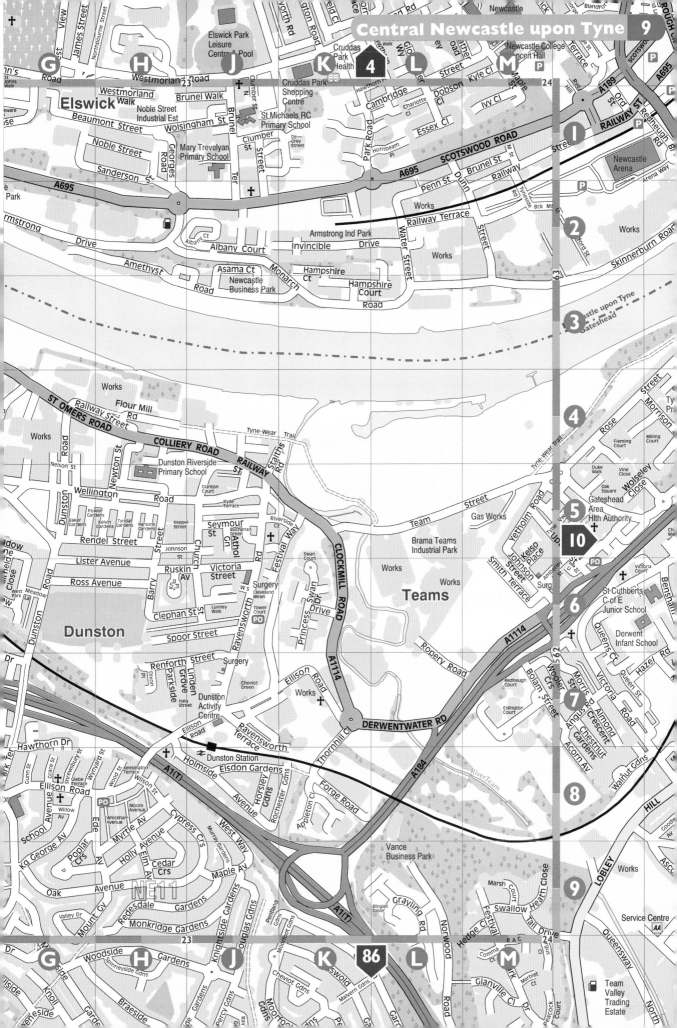

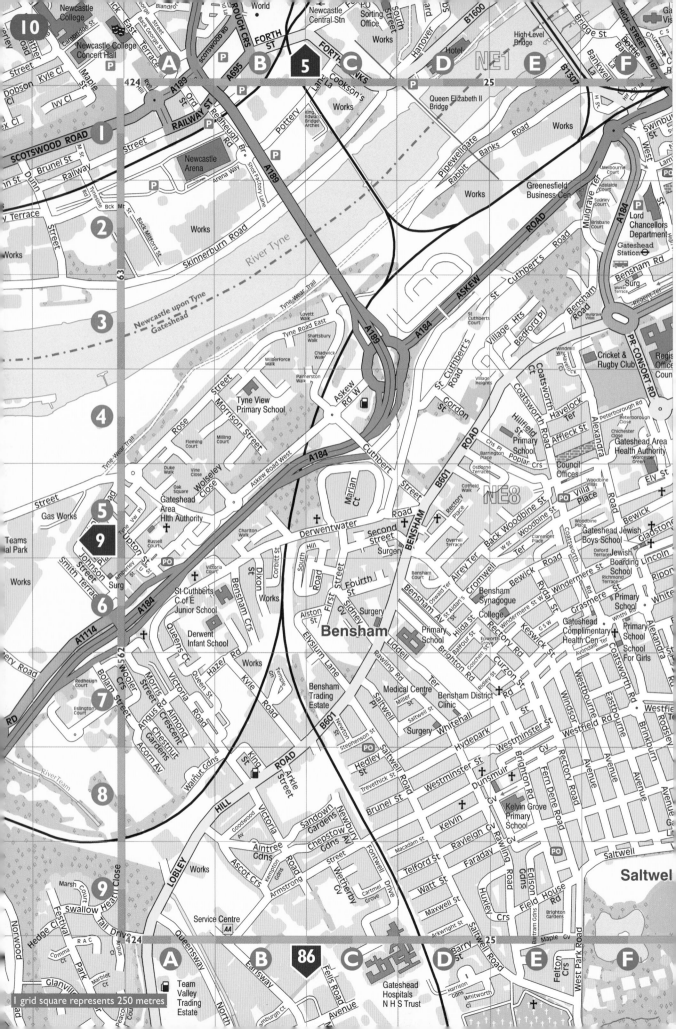

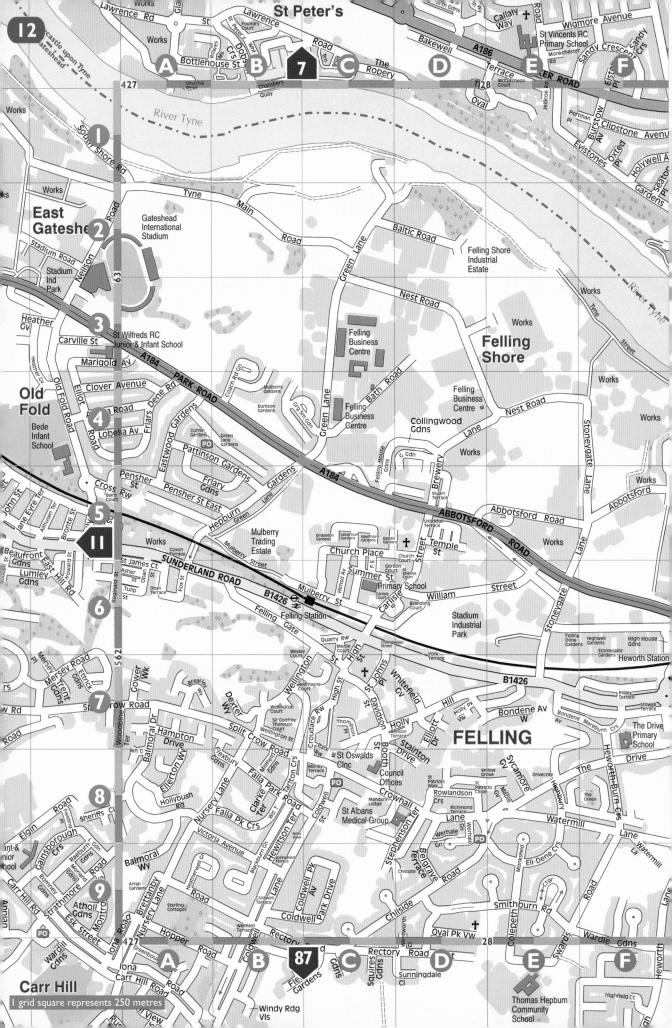

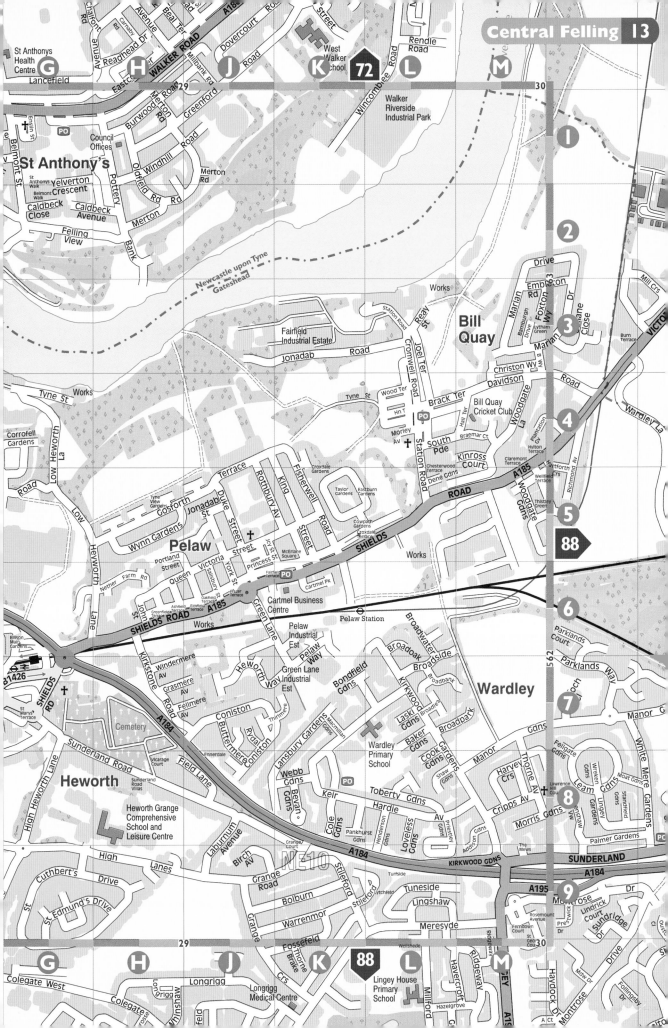

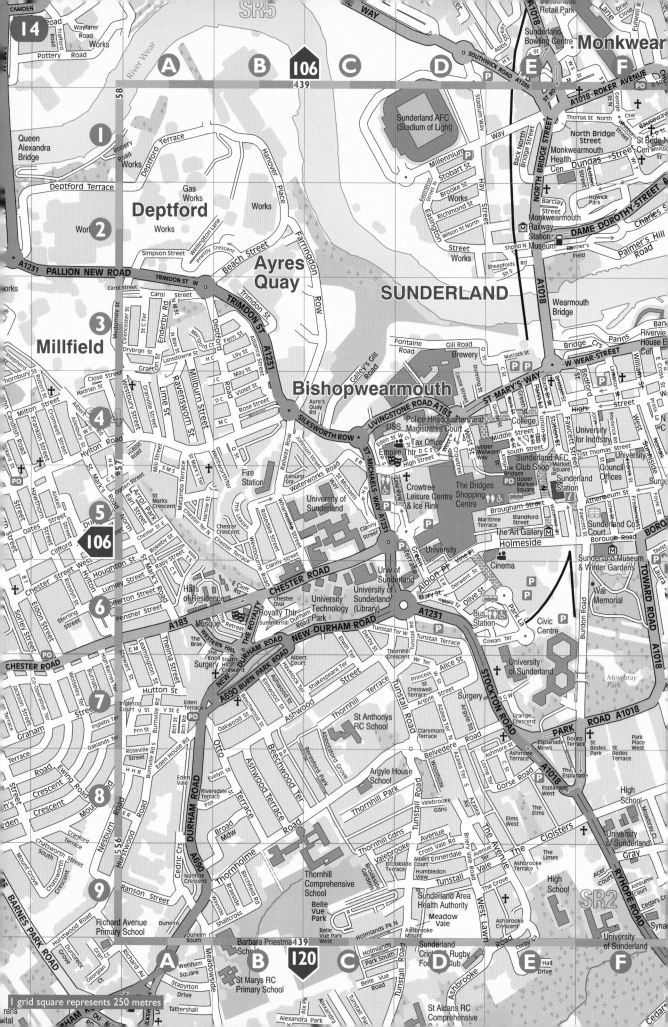

mouth

SR6

G   H   J   K   107   L   M

Roker

Zetland Square

Wickham St East

DAME DOROTHY STREET

Sand

Dame Dorothy Crescent

Liberty Way

Topcliff

Mulgrave

H R

School

North Sands Business Centre

P

National Glass Centre

St Peters' View

Medical

St Peters'

University of Sunderland

Sunderland Harbour

University Halls of Residence

P
P

business

Russell Street

B1293

Cork Street

A1018

Little Villiers St

Villiers Street

SR1

Norfolk

Nile

Villiers Street

Coronation street

Durham St

North

Coronation Close

B1294

Hedworth Terrace

Brg Rd

Smyrna Pl

Hendon Road

South Durham Court

Nicholson Ct

Mandela

LAWRENCE STREET

Minorca Cl

Wear Street

Menvill Place

Hedworth Court

Bunston Ct

Malings Cl

R l S

MOOR TER

B1294

B1522 HENDON ROAD

Barrack Street

Warren Square

St Jnns

Turnbull Street

Silver Street

East Vines

Starford Street

Rickaby

N Ter

M Ct

Mariner Square

Maddison Court

ROW

LC

High Street East

Low

Hartley Street

Havelock

Lucknow Street

Prospect

Church Street East

James Williams St

St E

Lombard St

Afras Lane

Trinity Square

Stamps Lane

School

The Quadrant

Zion St

Lilburne Close

Adelaide Cl

Cousin St

Moor St

Adelaide Pl

Hudson Dock North

South Dock

Hudson Dock South

Works

Works

B1294

Extension Road

Oak St

Hendon Rd East

Fleet St

Sunderland Dock

107

Woodbine Street

Works

Back Lodge

Terrace

Hendon

Avon Street

Glaholm Road

Health Centre

D'Arcy Court

Raine Gv

Wilam Gv

B M G

Chaytor Grove

Works

Henry Street East

Works

Ferguson Street

Hendon Dock

White House Road

Addison Street

The Parade

Gray Road

Old Mill Road

East Back Parade

Stanfield Business Centre

Works

Salisbury Street

Egerton Street

Coxon St

Salem Road

Peel Street

Salem Street

Osman

Lindsay

Un Hse Rd

Morley Close

Findhale Close

Bramwell Road

Crossby Court

Emma

Hendon

Nelson Close

St Vincent Street

Amberley Street

Harrogate St

Bramwell

Gray Road

N B R

Primary

Mowbray

Harold Sq

Salem St S

Deerness Park Medical Cen

S L Cl

Ward Court

Suffolk

Noble St

Tower Street

Ridley Terrace

Mainsforth Terrace

Vane Terrace

B1522

Works

The Parade

P

Works

The Oaks

Athol Ter

Beaumont St

Juniper Close

V B St

Guildford St

Villette Path

Athol Road

Hendon Burn Avenue

Tower Street West

Valley Terrace

Barnabas Way

Lewis Cts

Robinson Terrace

Robinson Terrace

Works

COMMERCIAL ROAD

Raich Carter Sports Centre

Hendon Valley Court

Rosalie Terrace

Mainsforth Ter West

Valley Road Junior School

Preston Road

Valley Road Infant School

Ashburne Medical Centre

PO

Tel

Cairo Street

Percy Terrace

Hunter Ter

Leonard

Corporation Road

Hyde St

Canon

G   H   J   K   121   L   M

1 2 3 4 5 6 7 8 9

58 57 56

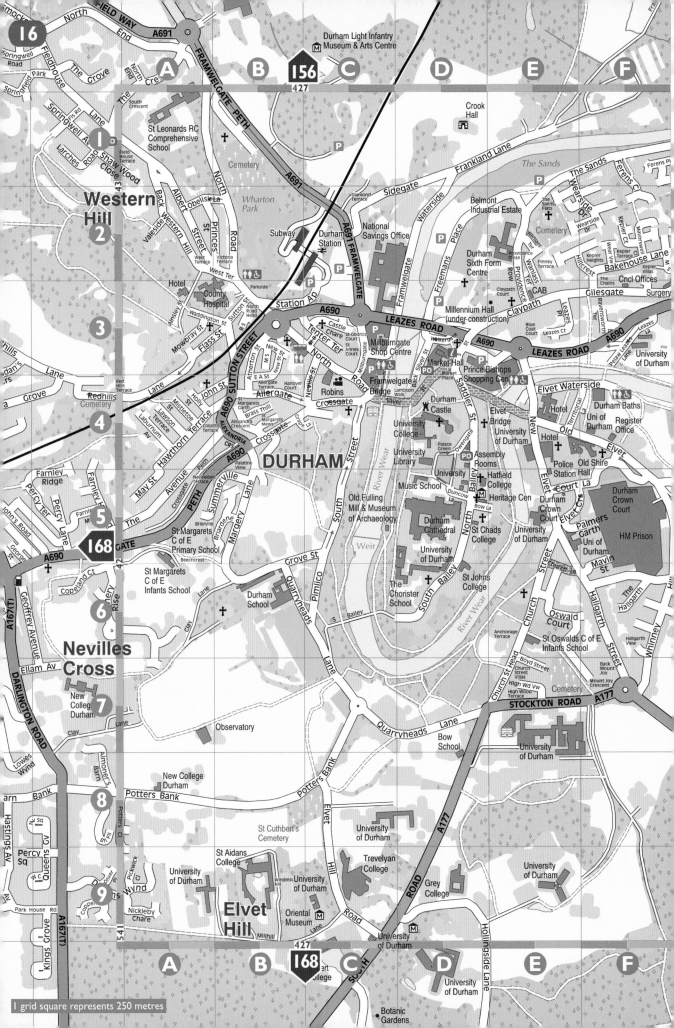

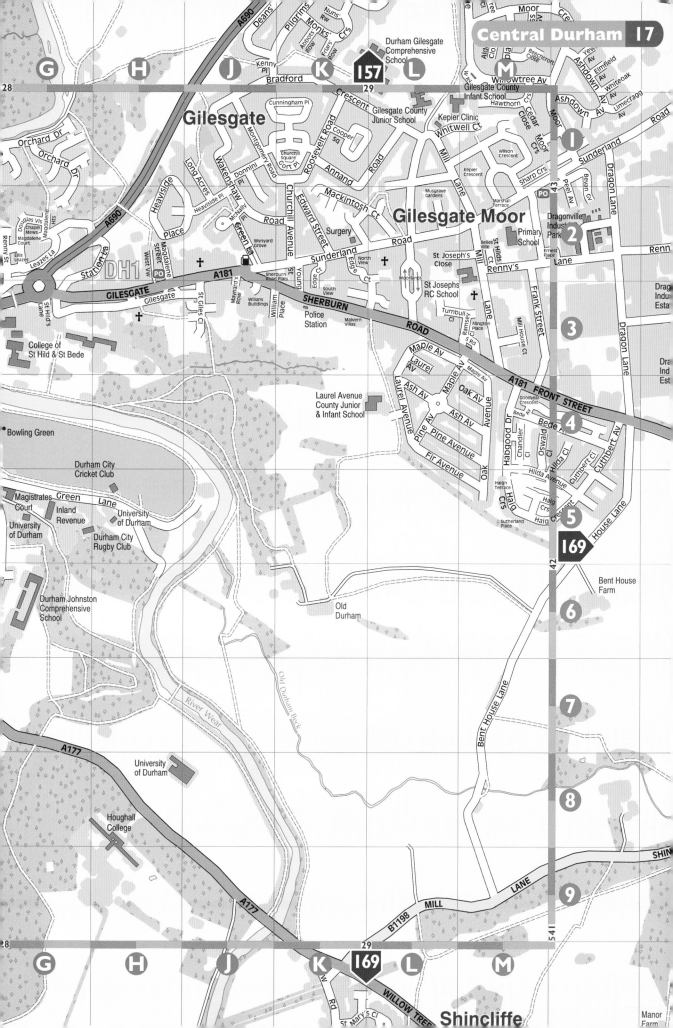

Ellington
18

A   B   C   D   E

428   29   30

Lyne Terrace
Chester Square
Eden Terrace
Briard Road
Dalton Avenue
Albion Terrace
Guilford Square
Henley Square
Jersey Square
Fenham Rd
Kings Rd
Matlock Square
Neville Square
Oakland Ter
PO
W.Mk St

Lynemouth County First School
Sea View

Lynemouth

Park Road
Bridge Road

Albion Terrace

Park Road

Cemetery

Works

Works

Lynefield House

A189

Woodhorn   A197

Woodhorn Church Museum
Cem
A197

Third House Farm

Queen Elizabeth II Country Park

Store Farm

Woodbridge

Woodhorn Colliery Museum

A197

A197   Summerhouse Lane

Deans Av
Pelaw Av

Cheviot View
Woodhorn Road
St Pauls Cl
St Nch Cl
St Brthlm Cl
St Lukes Cl
St Marys Drive

428   29   **24** Wansbeck General Hospital   30

Newbiggin-by-the-Sea County Middle School

Terrace
First
PO

A   B   C   D   E

1 grid square represents 500 metres

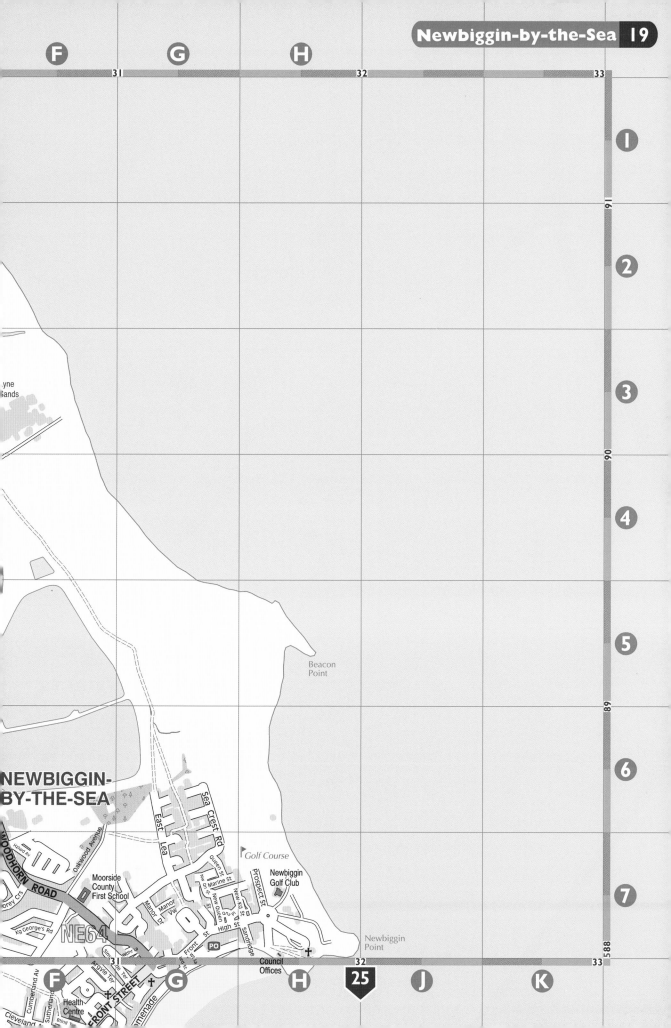

F **G** **H**

31 32 33

1
16
2
3
90
4
5
89
6
7
588

yne
Sands

Beacon
Point

NEWBIGGIN-
BY-THE-SEA

Sea Crest Rd

East Lea

Oakwood Avenue

H2Wd Av

Moorside
County
First School

orey Crs

WOODHORN ROAD

Kg George's Rd

NE64

Simn side Ter

Wohn La

Manor Dr

Manor Vw

Front St

Queen St

Nw on St

New Queen

Marine St

New Kg St

High St

Prospect St

Golf Course

Newbiggin
Golf Club

Sandridge

Brd St

Frw't La

PO

Newbiggin
Point

Council
Offices

31 32 33

F **G** **H** **J** **K**

25

Cumberland Av

Sutherland

Cleveland

Brind Ter

Health
Centre

Argyle Ter

FRONT STREET

Promenade

F G B1337 H J

21 22 23 88

Pegswood

Fawdon House

Pegswood Moor

1

Pegswood County First School

Trentham Gdns

Longhirst Road

Pegswood Industrial Estate

Longleat Gdns

Stowe Gdns

Hebron Av

Morpeth Av

Kirkham

Petworth Gdns

H Gdn Mtf Av

Langwell Terrace

Welbeck Terrace

Lindisfarne

2

Moor Vw Cl

Spencer Dr

Howard Cl

Bamburgh

Whitefield Crs

Shadfen Crs

Charles St

John St

PO

Alnwick Dr

Castleway

Gillian

Belsay Cl

Butterwell Drive

Coquetdale Cl

F C

Bentinck Crs

West View

Wansbeck Crs

Edward St

A197

A197

Cheviot Gv

Stanton Drive

Tranwell Cl

Maplen Rd

Patton Wy

south

South Vw

William St

Pegswood Station

Chevington Cl

Chevington

3 Whitefield

WHORRAL BANK

East Riding Clinic

A197

Climbing Tree Farm

River Wansbeck

4

22

5

Green Lane

Park House

Shadfen Park

Shadfen

Fenway

Windmill Wy

Oram

WC

LC

Coopies Lane

Coopies Lane Industrial Estate

Coopies Field

Coopies Lane

Coopies Haugh

Coopies Way

LC

A196

Dunces House

6

Stobhillgate

Carlisle Lea

5xt Av

LC

Second Av

Charlton Gdns

Beech Av

Broom Cl

Green Lane

A196

Fourth Avenue

Fifth Av

First School

Ninth Av

Eleventh Av

Collingwood School

Third Avenue

Shields Rd

Tenth Av

Choppington Rd

PO

Jobling Crs

Healeywood

Hepscott Red House

7

Thornton Close

Edgehill

Edgington Av

Norham Waterton

Egling Gv

Rnnngtn Cl

F

B192

Acomb Cl

Chatton Cl

Crookham Gv

Northam Dr

Chatton Gv

G

H

27

J LC

K

High Stobhill Farm

21 22 23

22

I
Pegswood Industrial Estate

Langwell Terrace
Welbeck Terrace

Lindisfarne
Dilston

Warkworth Dr
Castleway
Callaly

2

Pegswood Station

Bothal Park

A197

Coney Garth

Bothal Bank
Bothal Barns

Whitefield

3

Bothal

Sheepwash Rd

SHEEPWASH ROAD

A1068

4

21

Bothalhaugh

Sheepwash

5

A196

Paddock Hall Farm

North Choppington

A196

Riverside Avenue
West Av
Pine Av
Welbeck
North Av
Central
Sycamore Av
Sheepwash Avenue
Bothal Av
Morpeth Road

FRONT ST

Police Station

6

Meadow Bank Dr
Gldwll
Overdale Ct
Sarabel
Grnfl Dr
Undrhill Dr
Morpeth Cl
Acreford Court

A1068

High St

Haleywood

7

28

1 grid square represents 500 metres

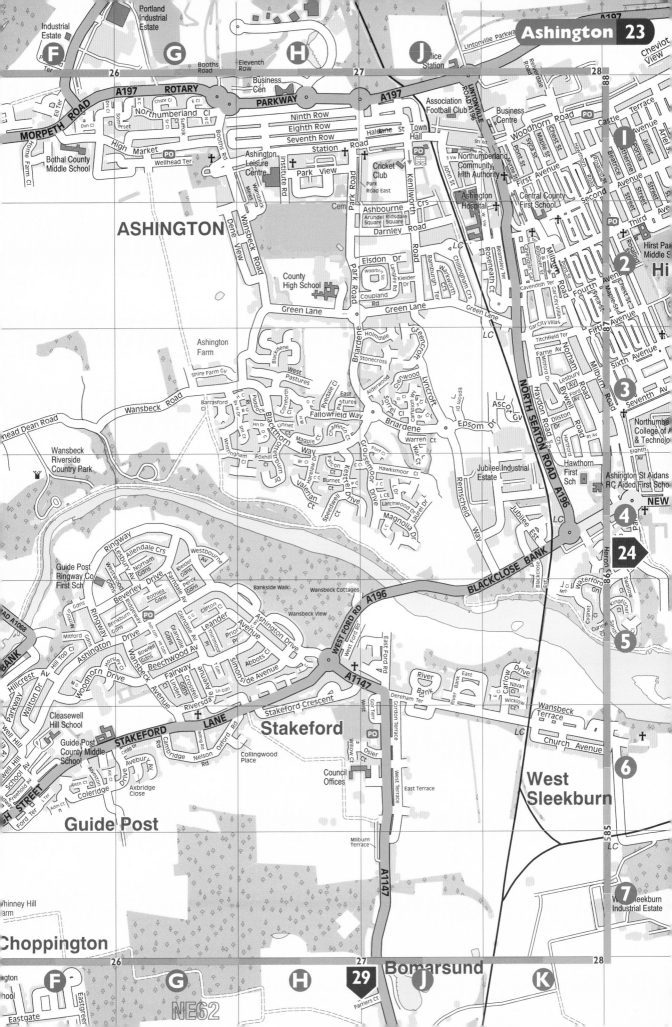

F NE64

G

H

19

J

31

33

88

1

87

2

3

86

4

5

85

6

7

County First School

KG George's

Storey Crs

ROAD

Manor Dr

Manor Vw

Front St

High St

New Kg St

New Queen St

Project St

Sandridge

PO

Council Offices

Newbiggin Point

Health Centre

Brind Ter

Aqua Ter

Wndsr Rd

Windsor County First School

PO

GIBSON ST

FRONT STREET

Promenade

Argyle Ter

Sunnyside Ter

Cumberland Av

Sutherland Av

Cleveland Av

Westmorland Av

Northumberland Av

North View

Seaton Av

Westfield Clt

NORTH SEATON ROAD

Melrose Ter

Beach Ter

Beach Terrace

Newbiggin Bay

Spital Carrs

Spital Point

31

32

33

F

G

H

31

J

K

418

A

B

20
19

C

D

Stobhill

E

Morpeth
Athletics
Football Club

Loansdean

Council
Offices

Churchburn
Drive
Middle Ca

The Crs

The Steads

Merley
Ga

Grove
Lane

Moorf
Rd

Rooksw
Pl

High Stob

20

County Hall

1

High
Common
House

The Avenue

The W

The Turn

Fairway

The Chip

Long
Drive

Fairway

Northumberland
Business Centre

B6524

84

2

Tranwell

Catchburn
Farm

A1(T)

A197

3

83

Catch Burn

Cli

4

Gubeon
Wood

A1(T)

A197

5

Bet's
Lane

Glororum

Well Hill

The Drive

North
Whitehouse
Farm

6

82

Stannington
Children's Hospital

Green
Lane

Dovecote
Farm

7

St Marys
Hospital

Green Lane

581

418

A

19

B

C

19

D

20

E

F
G
H
21
J

Thornton Close

Edgehill

Norham Way
Wooler Cl
Norham

Drive
Crookham Gv
Eglingham
Chatton Cl
Norham Dr
Clanton
Nrm Cl
Acomb Cl

Rnnngtn Cl
Chatton Cl

High Stobhill Farm

A192

Catch Burn

Barmoor Farm

The Orchard

LC

Crofts Park

Fieldhouse Lane
Fieldhouse Cl

Hepscott

I

Coalburn Farm

Coal Burn

Thornlea

Briarlea

Hazeldene

Stoneleigh

A192

Field House Farm

2

3

Hepscott Manor Farm

LC

Clifton Lane

Hepscott Manor

A192

28

4

Park
Drive

High Clifton Farm

Hepscott Park

5

on

Stannington Station Road

The Grange

6

A1(T)

Stannington

Stannington Station
LC

Moor Lane

Netherton Wood

Pegwhistle Burn

7

Stannington Station Road

F
G
H
J
K

Netherton Park

84

83

82

581

28

A   B   22   C   D   E

423   24   25

I

pscott

84

2

Field House
Farm

3

83

Burnt
House

Glebe
Farm

4

27

Netherton

Blue House
Farm

NE22

Knaresborough
Cl

York Gv   Edinburgh
Ripley
Cl   Featherstone Gv
Ayton Ct
Skipton   Octavia
Augustus
Way
Centurian
The Wynding
Richmond Cl
Dunstanburgh Cl
Warwick   Hylton
Cl   Chirton Cl   Bamard Cl   The Crest
Meadow Ct   The W
Dover Close   Northumberland Av

5

82   Lane

Conway Ci   Dunstanburgh C   Hazelmere Av   Rosedale   Forster Avenue   Westmorland Av   Cmbm Av

NETHERTON LANE   B1331   RIDGE TERRACE

North   Ridge   Nth
Meadowdale Cl   Link   Av
The Grange   North
Farm   B1331   Netherton   First   St Benet   Catholi

Oakdale   Lane   School   Biscops RC

6   South   Red House Farm   Cemetery   High School
Hallwood   Farm   Nedderton   Hartfo

A192   Westlea   Hartfo

Bedlingtonlane   Hartfo
Farm   Hartfo

7

A1068

581   TFORD   ROAD   25
423   24

A   B   32   C   D   E

1 grid square represents 500 metres

F   G   H   **25**   J

31   33

I

84

2

3

83

Sleekburn
Business
Centre

West Bridge Street

4

**North
Blyth**

5

Wrs St
Dale St
Gray St

82

Crawford St Ann's Rw
Millfd. Gdns

6

Willow Av
Poplar Av
Sycamore Av
Chestnut Av
Laburnum
Lilac Av
Durban

HODGSON'S ROAD

Thmp St
Balfour St
Osch St
Hmbl St
Goschen St
Stephen St

RECENT STREET

Thmps St

B.C.
S.L.
Station St
Kimberley St
Maddison St
Regent St

Burt
St

Works

W Salisbury St

Disraeli Street

Gladstone St
Beaumont St

**Wright
Waterloo Med Group**

Delaval Ter
Edward St

Works

B1329

Works

Bl Hl

Qysd

S.L.

6

Builder's
South
Retail Park

Way
SW Av

COWPEN ROAD

t. Andrews RC
ided First School

Bolam

Harper St
H St

Bowes St

WATERLOO RD

B1328
Croft
Ter
Wallaw

Coomassie St

Wolsley Rd
Wanley St

smpsn St

Union St

Rink St

**Headway
Thtr.**

BRIDGE ST

Bath La

Pol Stn

LOW Quay

Harper St
Sidney St

Bondicar
Ter

Marine

Cypress Middleton Ter

Street
Collingwood Rd

Surg

**Phoenix
Thtr**

Junior
Sch

First
School

Forster St
Percy St
Crntn St

Bridge St

Forster St

Bath Ter

East PK
View

Park VW

RIDLEY AVENUE

B1329

7

Marrow St
Lynn St
Claremont Ter

Blyth
Sports Centre

Council
Offices

Cypress Dr
Cypress
Crs

RENWICK RD

Winchester Av
Haughton Ter
Rowley St

UNION ST

Richard
Aldborough
Stannington St

Maughan St

Romond St

St Wilfrids
Middle School

Prs Louise
Princess Louise Road
Princess Louise
First School

Prs Louise Rd
Brdw Crs

**Council
Offices**

K Av
Victoria
Rd

Scn Av

Third Av
193 **BROADWAY**

**Blyth Spartans
AFC**

Jubilee

First
School

Kingsway

SEY RD

Dalmatia Ter
Plessey Av

Crofton Mill
Industrial Estate

81

Rosemary Ter
Aller

WENSL

F   G   H   **35**   J   K

31   33

First Av
Sixth Avenue

Seventh

Hunter Av
Grantham St
Z Ter

34

Bebside

30

29

BLYTH

NE24

New
Delaval

South

Golf Course

Golf Course

Blyth
Golf Club

Blyth New
Delaval County
First School

Low Horton
Farm

4

33

Laverock
Hall

Stickley
Farm

North Moor
Farm

A189

A192

A1061

LAVEROCK HALL ROAD

A1061

NEWCASTLE ROAD

SOUTH NEWSHAM ROAD

Laverock Hall Road

Plessey Road

Delaval Crescent

The Oval

Park Dr

Hallside Road

Northumberland
Area Hlth
Authority

Chase
Meadows

Golf Course

I grid square represents 500 metres

428

81

80

79

578

428

29

30

A **B** **C** **D** **E**

A **B** **C** **D** **E**

39

F G H **34** J

28 29 30

I

2

3

North Moor
Farm

A192

Montrose
Close

Hastings Gdns

Melton

Chipchase Ct

Street

Avon Court

Dorchester
Ct

Bristol

Aster

Brunswick Ct

**East
Cramlington**

wood C's

Wdn Rd

B1326

Double Row

Delaval
Trading
Est

77

76

First
School

A192

**SEATON
DELAVAL**

4

Allenheads

40

A192

Wheatridge

Middle
School

ASTLEY ROAD

Blyth St

Prospect Av

Mitford
Av

Rt Gv

Surg

Avel
Farm

Whytrigg Close

Linden Road

Western Avenue

PO

Park Road

Hartley St

Sinclair Gdns

Viewpk

Park
View

5

Wheatridge

Prospect Avenue

Bolam Wy

Clanton Av

AVENUE ROAD

A190

Elsdon
Rd

Bavington
Road

Swinburn
Road

Avenue

**Middle
Farm**

Ancroft Road

Council
Offices

Astley
Community
High School

Krsly

6

LC

Mares Close
Farm

Acomb
Av

Ashkirk Wy

Newbrough
Av

Thornhill
Cl

Derw

Staward

Atkinson House
School

Thornbury Av

Whiteford Pl

Twickenham

Trinity Gv

Kenmere

Dene

Grove

Burnlea

A190

Newbo
Av

Melrose

Durken Business
Park

Front Street

Murrayfield

Hatfield Drive

Trevone Pl

Winton Cl

Kirkwood Ct

Deneside

Hill Av

Burnlea
Gdns

7

Carrington Close

Seghill County
First School

Forest Way

Front St

Mvw Cl

Front Street

Barrass Av

PO

Ind
Estate

STATION ROAD

Es Ct

Bonnivard
Gdns

The Close

Barrowburn
Pl

574

Fox Lea
Walk

Brmo

Ches

WC Cl

The Crescent

Seghill

Reid's Lane

Birch
wood
Cl

Oakfield Way

H2 Pl

MAIN STREET NORTH

F G H **48** J **K**

8 29 30

BACKWO

West Fie

County

F   G   H   J

33   34   35

I
77
2
3
76
4

Seaton Sluice

St Mary's Lighthouse

St Mary's or Bait Island

Hartley

Crag Point

St Mary's Wynd

East End

The Crest

The Rise

NE26

Hartley West Farm

HARTLEY LANE

A193 BLYTH ROAD

5
75
6

B1325

Cemetery

The Crematorium

The Links

Gerrard Road

Garsdale Road

Gerrard Cl

Linton

Brierdene Rd

Craneswater AV

Westley

Westley Avenue

Gorsedene Road

THE LINKS

PO

Hastings Avenue

Brier Dene Farm

574
7

F   G   H   J   K

33   34   35

Brierdene

50

Astley Drive

Br   Crescent

A193

Golf Course

Whitley Bay Golf Club

Whitley Lodge

BANK

Park Field Ter

Easedale

Westlands

The Seaburn Ov

Cresswell

The Links

PH

West Ter

Collywell

A193

Ochtree

Queens Road

Southward

Simon Cl

Clarence St

Elwyn Close

Millfield

Elwin Cl

Budworth AV

Malvern Road

Dereham

Granville AV

Melton Crs

Dereham Rd

Simonside

Rosewood Crs

BERESFORD ROAD

Taylor Gdns

Albert Rd

CC

CC

Bay Rd

Millway

PO

Seaton Burn

F G H J

I

74

Prestwick Mill
Farm

Eland Green

Eland
Hall

Golf Course

2

North Road

North Gra

Stannington
Pl

Elmwood

Thornhill
Road

Ashbrooke
Dr

Twizell
Pl

Rowan Drive

Br Ct

Berwick Hil Rd

The Gn

North Road

Jackson
Avenue

Thm Pl

G Ct

Pont
VW

Ladywell Way

Simonside Vw

Beechwood
Pl

Kirkley Drive

Rothley
Close

**Richard Coates
C of E
Middle School**

Grange Rd

Thornhil Rd

Meadowfield

Ponteland Health
Cen

First School

Tynn Pl

Thornhill
Rd

Eland

Church
Chare

Paddock Hl

Church

Flatt

Carr

Low-

Wood

Eland

Haugh

Eland
Edge

Lane

Church
Fld

PONTELAND

73

Ponteland
Golf Club

Clickemin

Clickemin

**THE
BEECHES**

Fox Covert Lane

WEST ROAD

Meadowfield

Meadowfield
Industrial
Est

Council
Offices

PO

**MAIN
STREET**

Brewery
Lane

Riverside

Cecil
Cl

Fairney

Fairney
Edge

Mayfair Gdns

A696(T)

PONTELAND

A696(T)

Ridgely Drive

3

Ponteland
Leisure Centre

ROAD

Runnymede Road

Kingsway

The
Grove

The Cl

Darras Road

Dungsgreen

Court

Meadow

Way

Eastern

CALLERTON LANE

Ponteland County
Middle School

Ponteland County
High School

Elm

Road

4

Street
Houses

44

72

PH

Cemetery

AS

Oaklands Ct

Collingwood

Crescent

Sycamore

Avenue

The
Wynde

Middle Drive

Ladyrigg

Callerton
Court

Willow
Place

B6545

A696(T)

5

Road

Whinfell

Woodlands

Hawthorn way

Eastern

Way

Willow

Way

**CALLERTON
LANE**

B6323

6

571

Queensway

Whinbank

High View

end

Edge Hill

Edgewood

Deyncourt
Close

Hill
PK

Callerton
Hall

**High
Callerton**

Hold House
Farm

Northumberland County

Newcastle upon Tyne

7

16 17 18

44

A B C D E

74 418 19 20

Carr Grange Farm

1 Prestwick Mill Farm

2 Newcastle upon Tyne
Northumberland County

Dinnington

Moory Spot

73

3 Prestwick Whins

Prestwick Hall

Prestwick

4

72

43

Houses

PH

A696(T)

Cemetery

5

Prestwick Pit Houses

P

Newcastle International Airport

Airport Station

6 Prestwick Industrial Estate

B6918

Works

571

Woolsington Hall

7 A696(T)

Airport Freightway

South Drive

Middle Drive

Hotel

Woolsington Hall

Works

A B C D E

418 19.C 20

54

Callerton Park Station

Low

B691

F G H 36 J

21 22 23

74

Mason

Mason Lodge

North East Mason Farm

I

Oakfield Grange
PO

W Acres   East Acres

North Vw

Beech Avenue

Front   Street

Elm Av   Ash Av   Oak Av   Poplar Av   Pine Av

Ft

Dunsley Gdns

Church Cl

T Wndn

Sycamore Av

NE13

Hartley Burn

Big Waters
Nature Reserve

2

The Crest

Hrt Cl   Hrt Crs   Hrt Crs   Brnsl Cl

Dinnington Village First School

Mitford Way

Castleway   M Dr

Hvn Crs

Main Road

Mill Hill

Waterford Pk

73

Westfield Av

3

Cracken

Way

Sandy   Lane

Hack Hall

Brunswick Park Industrial Estate

Wallington Avenue

Sandson Court

Hawthorn Av

Morley Hill Farm

Brunswick Village

Industrial Est

Sandford Ms

Ma Pl

Arnd Cl

4

Main Road

46

Coach Lane

72

Ls St

En St

St Cl

Works

Bl Av

Newsham Av

5

Hazle

West Brunton Farm

6

Sunnyside

Middle Brunton West Farm

571

Brunton Lane

7

F G Brunton Lane H 55 J K

21 22 23

46

A 423 74

B FRONT STREET   Thorntree Avenue   Brenkley Way

37 Seaton Burn   C   D   E

Blezard Business Park

24   25

1
rth East Mason
rm

North East Mason

Burnbridge   Brenkley Ct   PO

DUDLEY LANE   Cemetery
Patience Av   Nrin Cl   Rookwood Dr   B1321
Meadow Drive
Six-Mile Bridge
Green's Houses Farm

Seaton Burn Hall

2
ers
Reserve

73

BRIDGE STREET   B1318

Russell Sq   McCracken Dr

Rayleigh Drive   Chantry Drive   Gray Av   Morpeth Avenue
Swinhoe Gdns   Warkworth Drive   Taylor Av

3
Brunswick Park
ndustrial Estate

Drysdale Cresent
Westfield Av   Cheviot View   B Gv   Gry St   Special School   PO

Hayes Walk   Havant Gdns   Boulmer Gdns   Eversley   Woodhorn Gdns

Stalks   Road   PO
Darren Street   ElV Cl

Waterford Pk   Wallington Avenue   Hawthorn Av   Brookside Av   Seaton Place   Ad Cl   Astr Pl   H Cl

Hazlewood Community Primary School   Winchester   WK   Brasford Dr
Canterbury   Longhirst   Bar   Harrow Gdns

Wide Open

Sandison Court

Industrial Est   Mayfield Pl   Smn   Prf Pl   Rms Cl   Rms Cl
Sandford Ms   Arnd Cl   Astr Cl   Highfield Pl

Woodlands Park Health Centre

Worcester Way

4
Beacon Drive   Torver Cl   Thrn Cl   Wllws Cl

Birchwood   Emwood Av   Larchwood Av   Av
Limewood Gv   Oakwood

45   72
PO   Melness Road   Hg Rdg
Ashwood Gv   Pinewood Avenue

Coach Lane   High Ridge
Cem   Cem   Pinewood Avenue

SANDY LANE

5
Hazlerigg
571
Newham Av   Arkle St   Fergu   Son Crs   Castle Street

Farm Cottages

Parklands Golfing Complex

6
A1056   North Brunton
Hotel   Newcastle Racecourse
B1318
Northumberland Golf Club

7
Brunton Lane
A1(T)
East Brunton   Greenfield Rd   GREAT NORTH ROAD
Golf Course   High Gosforth Park

423   Queen 24 ay   **56**   Glamis   Sherwood Place   Council Offices
B   Grenville D   Greenfield Rd   Westwood   Norwood Avenue   Easdale Avenue   Polwarth   C   D   E
th Bend

A   B   C   D   E

Gosfort

WHITLEY
BAY

Cullercoats

Marden

A   B   C   D   E

403   Shildonhill   04   05

67

I

66

2   Newton Fell House

Heathery Edge

65

3   Stelling Hall

Well House Farm

Newton Hall

4   Newton High House

Mowden Hall (Newton) School Trust

B6309

5   Newton

A69(T)

564   The Old Forge

PO

6   Shaw House

A69(T)

North Acomb

7   A69(T)

B6309

403   04   05

A   B   78   C   D   E

1 grid square represents 500 metres

Bywell Home Farm

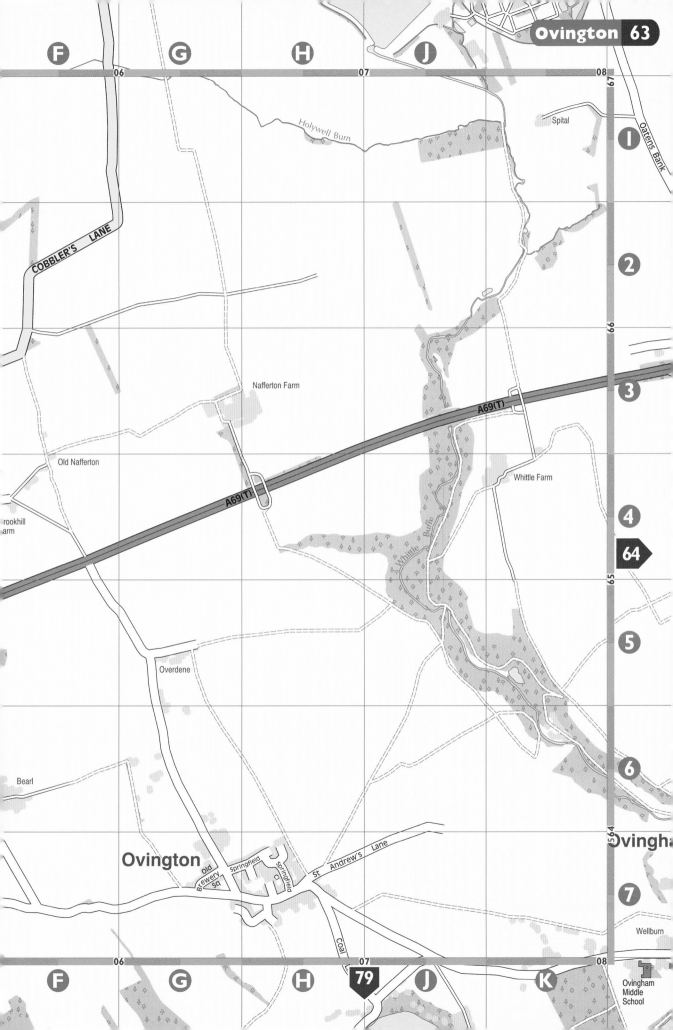

F   G   H   J

06   07   08

67

I

Spital

Oatens Bank

2

Holywell Burn

66

COBBLER'S LANE

3

A69(T)

Nafferton Farm

Old Nafferton

A69(T)

Whittle Farm

rookhill arm

Whittle Burn

4

64

65

5

Overdene

6

Bearl

64

Ovingha

Ovington

Old Brewery Sq

Springfield

Springfield Ct

St Andrew's Lane

7

Wellburn

Coal

Ovingham Middle School

F   G   H   J

Military Road

NARY ROAD   B6318

First School

Taber

A69(T)

Houghton

B6528   Trajan

NE15   Remus   AV

Hill   Aquila   drive   Martius

Head   Campus

Killiebrigs

Heddon Banks

Close Lea   Heddon

Holeyn
Hall

Oakwood
House

High Close   Close
House   House

Holeyn   Acomb Dr

Hall   Rift Farm

Road   George Stephenson's
Birthplace (NT)

Bluebell Cl   DENE ROAD   Wylam County
Penecroft   Tynedale Cl   First School

DENE Road   Bell Rd

Algernon   Hackworth   Parson Road
Gdns

ter   Woodcroft   Hedley Rd

Church Road   The Dene

Main   Falcon Terrace

PO   Road

Ovingham Road   Woodcroft Road   NE41   Station

Surgery   LC   Wylam
Station

Front St   Elm Bank Road   **Wylam**

The Crs

A695   Wylam Wd Rd   Castle Hill
Farm   Crawcrook Lane

Low Prudhoe   Wylam
Industrial   Wood Farm
Estate   Crawcrook Lane

nts Dr   Works

nts Dr

Daniel
Farm

Prudhoe Town
Football Club

house   Eastwood
County Middle   Sled Lane
Rd   School   Golf Course   Bradley   Infa
Crs   Hall Farm   Bradley
Bradley   Hall
Road   Eastw
od Av   Horsley Vw

I

2

3

4

66

5

6

7

67   66   65   564

ARY ROAD B6318

A **B** **52** **C** **D** **E**

413 14 15

Ingleton Drive

Ainderby Road

Throckley
Middle
School

I

First
School

The Towne Gate

PO

Remus Av

Aquila Drive

Campus Martius

Killiebrigs

Walk

Nicholas Gdns

Taberna Cl

Calvus Dr

Civs Dr

Valerian Av

Marius Av

Camilla Rd

Antonine Walk

Centurion Way

Heddon Banks

Station Road

Heddon
Banks Farm

Ollerton Drive

Sheringham Gardens

Horncliffe Place

Hill House Road

The Mount

Coquet

Grove

C C Stuart

Woodlands

Valeside

Wilsway

Coquet Gv

T Brr

Reeth Wy

Wellfield Close

Throckley
First
School

**Heddon-on-
the-Wall**

Bank Top

Hly Rd

Throckley
House

Leaze

Coach Road

Close **2**

Heddon Banks

Heddon

Heddon

Heddon
Hall

se
use **3**

Station Road

Newcastle upon Tyne
Northumberland County

4

Maryside
Hill

Golf Course

Ryton
Golf Club

65

Coach Road

River Lane

LC

5

Clara Vale

Golf Course

Tyneside
Golf Club

Westfield   Lane

Station Bank

Elvaston
Road

Village

Building
Farm

Ryton
Grange

Grange

Barmoor

Lonnen

Blackhouse La

Ryt Hl Dr

C Gv

Ash
Cl

My Av

Hi Av

Cedar Gv

Lime Gv

Park Field

Northumberland Rd

Balgonie Cottages

Orchard Ct

Orchard La

Whitewell Lane

Tower Gdns

6

Hill

Crawcrook Lane

Stannerford Road

Ryton Junior
& Infant School

Ryton Comprehensive
School and Leisure
Centre

Bar Moor

MAIN ROAD

Woodside Rd

Woodside Cl

PO

B6315

Beechwood Av

Grange Rd

RYT

North Cl

Rosby Gdns

Fairfields

Hedgelea

Burnaby Dv

The Mount

Grange
Crs

Western Wy

South
Grange View

The Ridge

Grange
Wy

Crawcrook Lane

Garden House Estate

West Gdns

Emmaville
Primary
School

PO

Beech Gv Ct

Md Gv

Cloverhill Drive

Ryton
Rugby Club

Crawcrook

Heather Pl

F Gdn

Thistle Av

Moss Crs

Works **7**

St Agnes

Infant School

Dale

Gardener's

Crawcrook
Medical Centre

Kepier

Clifford Ter

Lambton Cl

Molyfair

Petty Cl

MAIN ST

A **B** **82** **C** **D** **E**

413 14 15

Westey Gv

Iris Ter

Rosedale

Hill Pl

Clifford St

Chamberlain

Charles

Caplin

Laurel Wy

Bracken

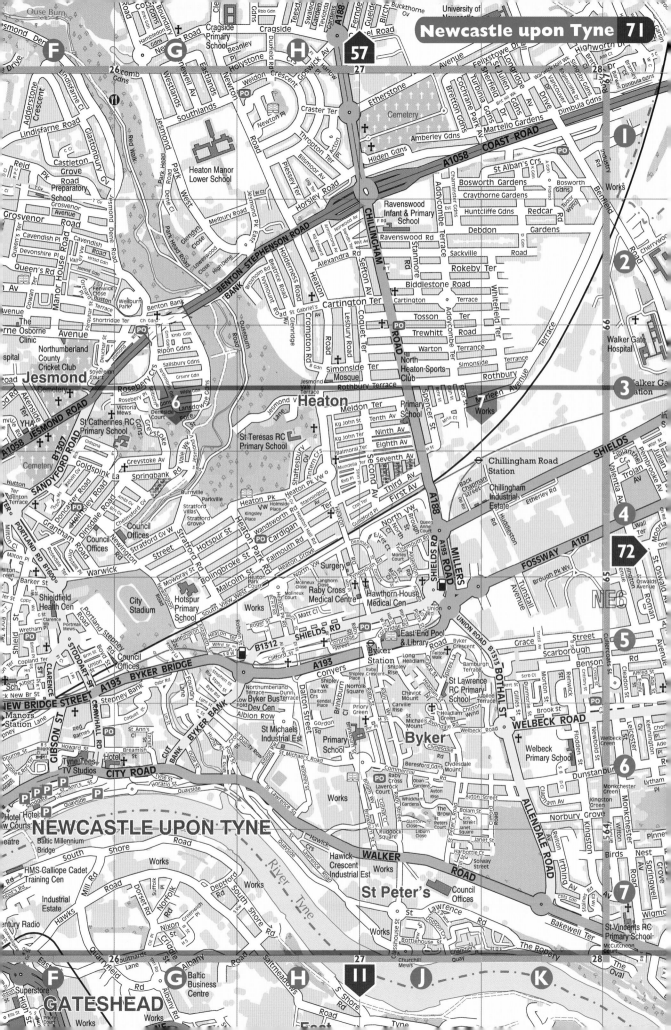

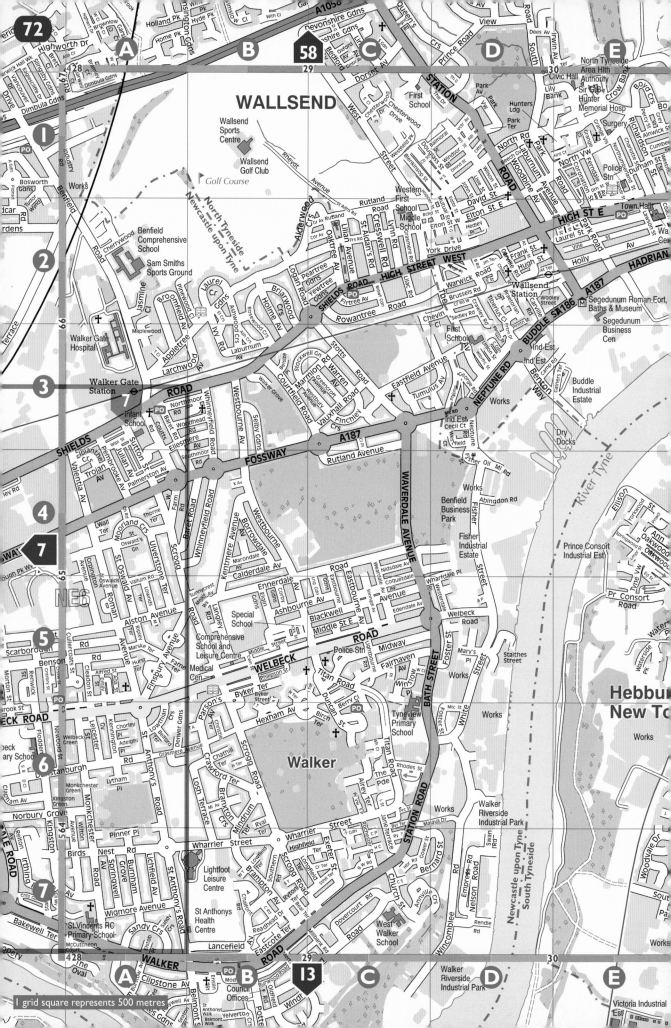

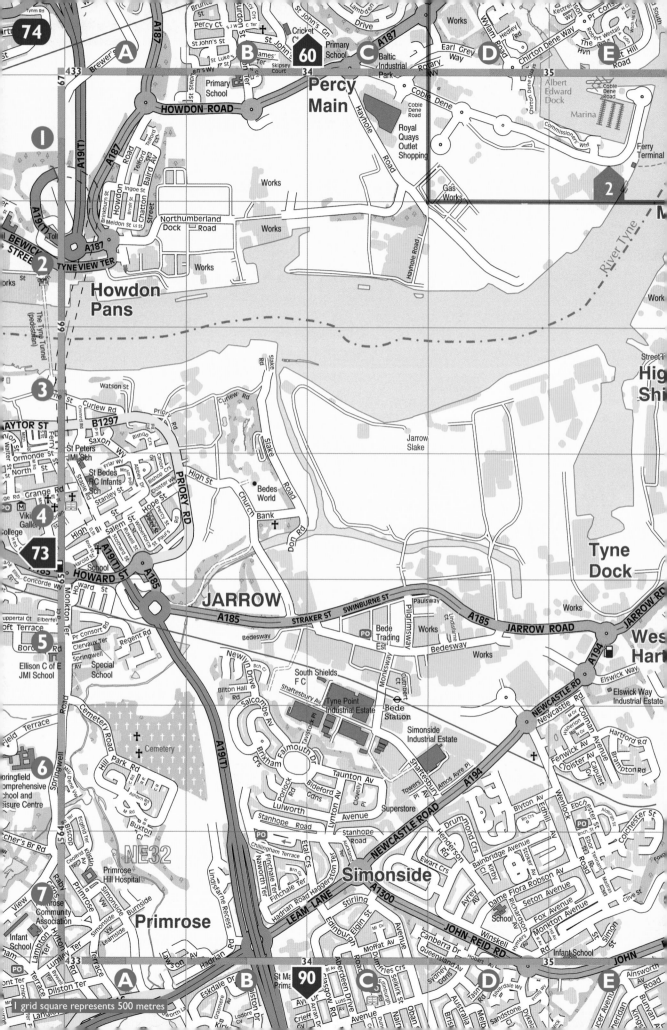

I grid square represents 500 metres

SOUTH SHIELDS

NE33

Westoe

Horsley Hill

West Park

Harton

NE34

Whiteleas

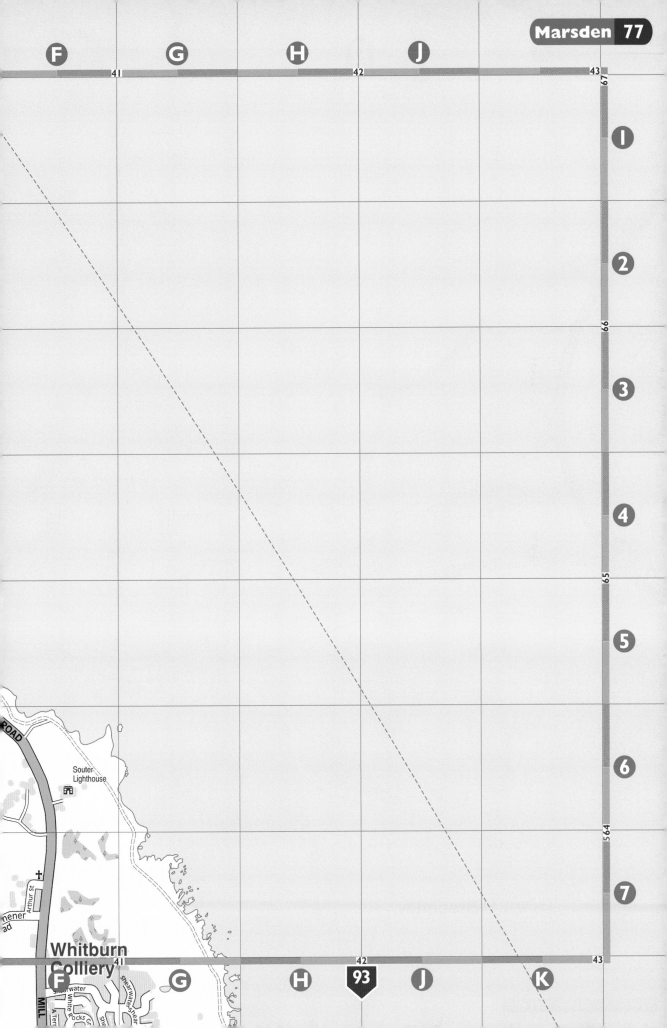

F   G   H   J

41   42   43

67

1

2

66

3

4

65

5

Souter
Lighthouse

6

64

7

Whitburn
Colliery 41

F   G   H **93** J   K

42   43

A **B** 62 **C** **D** **E**

403 04 05

1

Bywell Home
Farm

Bywell Estate
Office

A68

2

Stonyverge Burn

Peepy

Clockey Burn

63

3

62

A68

B6309

4

B6309

N

A695

Bywell

Low
Shilford

Stocksfield
Station

5

A695

River Tyne

61

6

Roe House

7

Broomley

560

403 04 05

A **B** **C** **D** **E**

A695

B6309

Wellburn

F   G   H   **63**   J

06   07   08

Ovingham Middle School

1

River Ty

Short Wood

Station Bank

Eltringham

2

Thomas Bewick Birth Place Museum

Bewick Garth

PO

Mickley Square

Station Bank

3

Riding Dn

A695

River Tyne

Chapel Rw

Eastgate

Cherryburn (NT)

Mickley County First School

Stocksfield Hall

Merry Shield

43

Broomley County First School

Stocksfield Cricket Club

Hall Farm

The Pastures

A695

Oak St

Beech St

Hallyards

Bank

4

80

Stonybank

Way

Brunwell Cr

Stocksfield

Wetherbit Av

PO

A695

Surgery

Branch End

Bowler's   Hill

High Mickley

5

Birches Nook Road

Crabtree Road

Baillol Rd

Nevill Rd

New Ridley Road

Guessburn

Road

Cadehill Road

Ayton Cl

Halton

Welton

Tynedale Gardens

New Ridley Road

6

Stocksfield Burn

Apperley Road

Painshawfield Road

Old Ridley

Ridley Mill

Painshawfield

Ridley Mill Road

Painshawfield Road

Well Road

Meadowfield Road

Meadowfield Pk South

The Paddock

Mickley Grange

7

Batt House Road

Lead Road

F   G   H   J   K

06   07   08

Modigars   Lane

Wellbu   **A**   **B** Prudhoe
                          Station   **C** PRINCESS WAY   A695   Princess Ct   **D** Industrial   **E**   PRINCESS
                                         64   Estate
                                         LC
                                         09

408   LC   **Prudhoe**   Mill
                                         Station   Rl
Ovingham   Ovingham C of E   Works   Works   Prudhoe Castle
Middle   First School   Greenwell
School   Oginel   Dean   Lassell Rigg
                            Works   Station Industrial   Ddebe   Pcy Loh   Adderlāne
                                       Est   Ford   Ct   First
River Tyne   LC   The   Or Hl Appletree Drive   Broomhouse La School
I   Station   Cry Ldy Vw   Br
                              Cherry Gv   Ford   Umfraville   Broomhill Road
63   Holly Grove   Dene Gv   Station   **PRUDHOE**   Dene   Road
              Works   Lime Cv   Road   Surgery Kepwell Ct Cranleid Neale St   Adderlane Dene St
2   Maple Master's Cheyne Rd Western PO   PO Tyne View Ter HI Wylam
          Works   Gv   Cts   Cheyne Rd AV Kepwell Road   Wesley Ter VW **STONYFLAT BANK** Road
                    Prudhoe   Leaway Kepwell Road B6395   Oakfield Cameron Rd Council Waterworld B63
                    Castle   Western   **NE42** Kepwell Bank Top Pk   Offices Stancley Rd
                    First School Rowan Cranbrook Dr Edgewell Grange Cemetery   Swalwell Hillcrest Priestclose Rd Redwell Ro Paddock Cl
       Eltringham Road Sycamore   S C Cl St Thomas Hillcrest Redwell Ct Paddock
3 Gv   **WEST** Milton Gv   Highfield South Ms   Cheviot View Wood
A695   **ROAD** Snowy   Prudhoe West County Lane Highfield Road Orchard Homedale
                    Broom Simonside Milton Gv First School   Highfield   Park Lane Moorlands Valley
              Otter Burn Way Beaumont Edgewell Rd St Matthews RC Highfield   Prudhoe County Park La Av
                          Tennyson Ct First School   Highfield County High School Park La
4   Broom Way   Unnng Cem Middle   Park Lane
              Ovington Vw Ruskin High Shaw School   Cemetery North
79   Grir Ct TCl Cemetery   NHS
                                                    Highfield

                              Edgewell
                              House Farm

5
Bowler's
Hill
igh
ickley   Mickley
                              Moor   Durham
              Lumley's Lane   Riding
6

7

56 408
A   **B** **94** **C**   **D**   **E**

1 grid square represents 500 metres

F
Prudhoe Town
Football Club

Eastwood
County Middle
School

Golf Course

G

H

65
12

J

Daniel
Farm

Sled Lane

Bradley
Hall Farm

Bradley
Hall

Sled Lane

I

B653

Wellfield Ct

Infi

Plo

2

nhouse
Road

Parkwood Av

Horsley Vw

Bradley Road

Eastwoods Road

Coldwell Rd

Prudhoe
Golf Club

Bell View

Sandyford
AV

Woodhead Rd

Scales Crs

y Crs

The
ose

Prudhoe
ealth
entre

63

Coalway Lane

Coalway La

62

Westwood
Farm

Bradley Fell La

B6395

Kyo Bog Lane

Kyo Bog Lane

3

Bradley Fell Road

Frenches
Close

4

te & Prudhoe
ust

Bradley Fell Road

Nook Lane

Buck's Nook

Kyo Lane

Kyo
Hall

Kyo Lane

82

5

The
Guards

Buck's
Nook

Coalburns

Lead Road

61

6

Moor Road

Chirty Burn

Coalburn
Farm

7

Engine Road

Engine Road

Dukeshagg
Farm

Northumberland County
Gateshead

Horsegate Bank

560

F

G

H

95
12

J

K

Clayton T

Horse

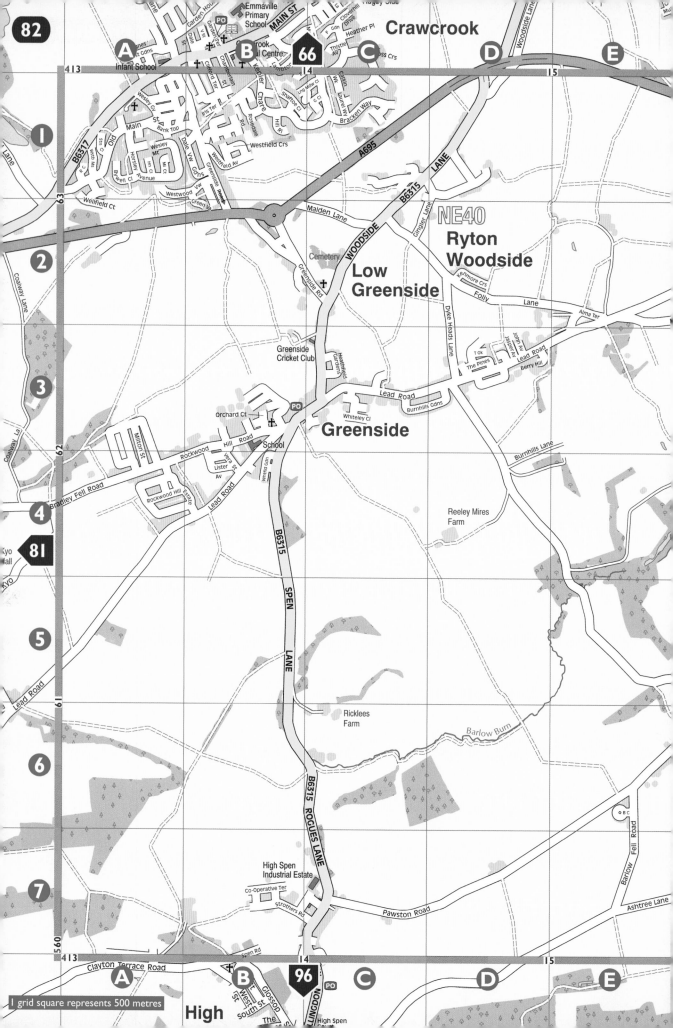

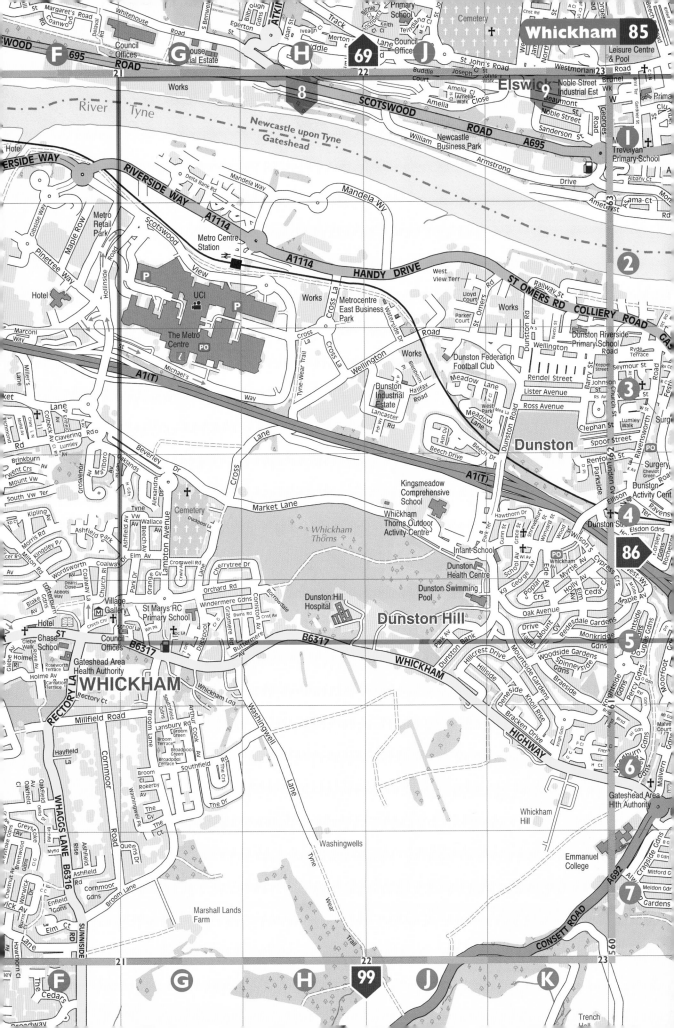

F G H 77 J
42
43

I
93

2

3
62

4

5
61

6

7
560

F 41 G H 42 J 107 K 43

Whitburn Colliery

Shearwater
White Rocks
Shearwater Grove
Shearwater
A Terr
Lilac Av
Lily Crs
Marsden Av
Rose Crs
Rose
Fern Avenue
Wheatall Drive
Outer View
Fulmar Wk
Cedar Gv
Poplar Drive
Birch
Geoffrey St
Rupert St
Sycamore Rd
Maple Gv
High Cft
WHITBURN
Rupert
Bryers
Mr Ter
Myrtle Av
Myrtle Avenue
Larch Av
Larch Av
Elm Dr
Oak Crs
Beech Av
Elm Dr
Ash 2
Whitburn Cem
Bowman St
Rackly Wy
Adolphus Street
Holly Av
Oak Crs
Guards
PO
Whitburn Comprehensive School & Leisure Centre
East Street
East Flds
Whitburn Cricket Club
Church Lane
Newark Dr
Markham Av
Nicholas Av
WHITBURN BENTS ROAD
A183
MILL LANE
EAST STREET
A183
Svaledale
Ryedale
Farndale Av
Eskdale Rd
Whitby Av
Seaburn Centre

F

G

H

81

J

I

Clayton Ter

60

Horse Gate

Garesfield Golf Club

Leadgate

Lead Road

Golf Course

2

59

Broomfield Farm

Greenhead Road

Clayton Terrace Road

Ashtree

3

Ramsay Road

Meadow Brook Drive

Hall Rd

Wear St

PO

South Rd

Surgery

South Rd

Tay St

Mersey St

Hmd St

Whittonstall Rd

Derwent Street

Clyde St

Forth St

East St

William St

Chopwell County Primary School

Chopwell

4

Chopwell W

96

58

Broomfield Crs

Milkwellburn Wood

NE17

Moorland Vw

Mill Road

Valley Dene

5

Carr House

Runnymede Gdns

Gateshead Northumberland County

6

557

Blackhall Mill

Moraine Crs

Riversdale Crs

Mill Race

Nursery Ct

Derwent St

PO

Prtr Braw

Connolly Ter

Chopwell Rd

Armondside Rd

River View

7

Broad Oak Farm

A694

F

G

PO

Dene Ct

Derwent Crs

H

109

sterl

J

K

Derwentco Steel Furnace

Forge Lane

Surgery

Cemetery

96

A B **82** C D E

413 60

I

Iub

Clayton Terrace Road

Spen Rd

East St
West St
South St
Glossop St

High Spen

PO

Collingdon Gn

High Spen Court

Co-Operative Ter

strothers F

Pawston Road

Ashtree La

413 14 15

The Granaries

Bute Dr

Bute Road N

Ashfield Ct

Spen Banks

2

59

Bute Rd S

The Crescent

Greenlea

Fell View

Spen Burn

Hookergate

HOOKERGATE

Firwood Crescent

School Lane

Wendy Ct

Spen Lane

Hookergate
Comprehensive School
and Leisure Centre

Spen Burn

3

Hookergate Lane

LANE

Low Spen
Farm

William Morris Av

Cowell Gv

Smiles Gv

SMAILES LANE

B6315

St Josephs
School

Cemetery

Highfield Junior
& Infant School

Wellfield
Road

Margaret Ter

PO

Highfield Road

Highfi

4

58

95

Chopwell Wood

Whinfield
Industrial
Estate

Woodside Walk

Whi

5

Carr
House

Lintzford Lane

*Lintzford
Wood*

6

Gateshead
Durham County

Lintzford

Lintz Green Lane

LINTZFOR

7

557

Derwentcote
Steel Furnace

**Hamsterley
Mill**

Forge Lane

Lodge Cl

Long Cl

High Hamsterley Road

LINTZFORD ROAD

A694

Mill Farm

High Mill

Lintz Green Lane

Lintz Green

A B **110** C D E

413 14 15

F **G** **H** **85** **J** CONSETT

21 22 23 60

1

Trench Hall

Meldon Gdns

Cornmoor Gdns

Enfield Gdns

Broom Lane

Marshall Lands Farm

Wear

Warwick Dr

SUNNISIDE RD

The Cedars

Broadway

Hawthorn Cl

Wickham Fell

Black Burn

B6316 SUNNISIDE ROAD

Felside

Longwood Cl

Longwood Wy

Stratton Gv

Sunniside Ct

Laburnum Gv

Prieston

Avenue

Granby Close

Sidegate Gallery

GATESHEAD ROAD

Street Ga

Shedton Cottages

Pennyfine Road

The Grynes

A692

2

59

Hill Head Wood

Neill Dr

Prinn Pl

Berkeley

Coronation Road

Fernville Av

Kingsway

Farm Cl

Elm St

Burdon Lea

Bowes Spring Walk

PO

Fell Cl

E Farm Ct

Elm St W St

Queens Dr

Princess St

Street Gate

3

A692

GATESHEAD ROAD

Sunniside

Hill Head Farm

High Park Wood

Marley Hill

A6076

A6076 BURDON PLAIN

Tanfield Railway

4

100

58

5

Old F

Birkland Lane

6

Ravensworth Grange

557

Birkheads Lane

7

A6076

Hedley West House Farm

Hedley Lane

Hotel

Follingsby

Follingsby Lane

LC

F **G** **H** 89 **J**

31 32 33

River Don

NORTHUMBERLAND WAY

I

South Tyneside

Sunderland

2

North Moor Farm

East House

Waterloo Road

Northumbria Sports Centre

Merevale Cl

Barton Cl

Marwell Drive

Usworth Secondary School and Leisure Centre

Stephenson Industrial Estate

Stephenson Road

Gullane

Foxton

Hall

Norfolk

Warwick

Essex Drive

Rutherford

Baird Rd

Wm Cl

Stedman

Usworth Hall Road

Waterloo Road

3

West Moor Farm

NE37

St Bedes RC Primary School

Rainhill Road

Sulgrave

A1290

4

104

Monterey

Inkerman Road

Sulgrave Industrial Estate

Junior School

Trafalgar Road

Brackley

Sharlstone

Usworth Grange Primary School

Marlborough Road

Sulgrave Road

Cherry Blossom Way

Peepy Plantation

60 59 58

worth

Tyne Gardens

Park Gv

Vernon St

Vernon Road

Viola

Sulgrave

Helmdon

Foxley

Silverstone Road

Bamburn

Usworth

Edgecote

Station Rd

Cherwell

Barmston Lane

Works

5

cord

House Ter

CAB

Victoria Rd

PO

Manor

Manor Vw

Mandeville

PO

LC

Cherry Blossom Wy

Nissan Way

VERMONT

GLOVER ROAD

6

Washington Football Club

Hertburn Industrial Estate

Industrial Road

Bridgewater Rd

Tower Rd

Bental Business Park

Glover Industrial Estate

Spire Road

57

Washington Secondary School and Leisure Centre

Spout Lane

Brindley Road

WASHINGTON

A1231

SUNDERLAND HIGHWAY A1231

7

RLAND HIGHWAY

A1231

Washington Village Primary School

Hill Rise

Richmond Av

Valley Forge

Spout Lane

Barmston Way

Stockley Rd

Horsley Road

Pattinson Industrial Estate

Pattinson Road

Village

Council Crs

PO

Washington Old Hall

Cemetery

Thrn Cl

PO

Barmston Medical Centre

Alston Road

Lee Cl

Faraday Cl

Barmston Lane

St Josephs Cof School

F 31 **G** **H** 117 **J** **K**

32 33

Washington Vill

Primary School

NORTHUMBERLAND WAY

Westerhope Dr

Primary School

Burnhope Road

Glebe Road

kerley Road

Avebury Dr

Crescent

Barmston

Walton Road

Walton Road

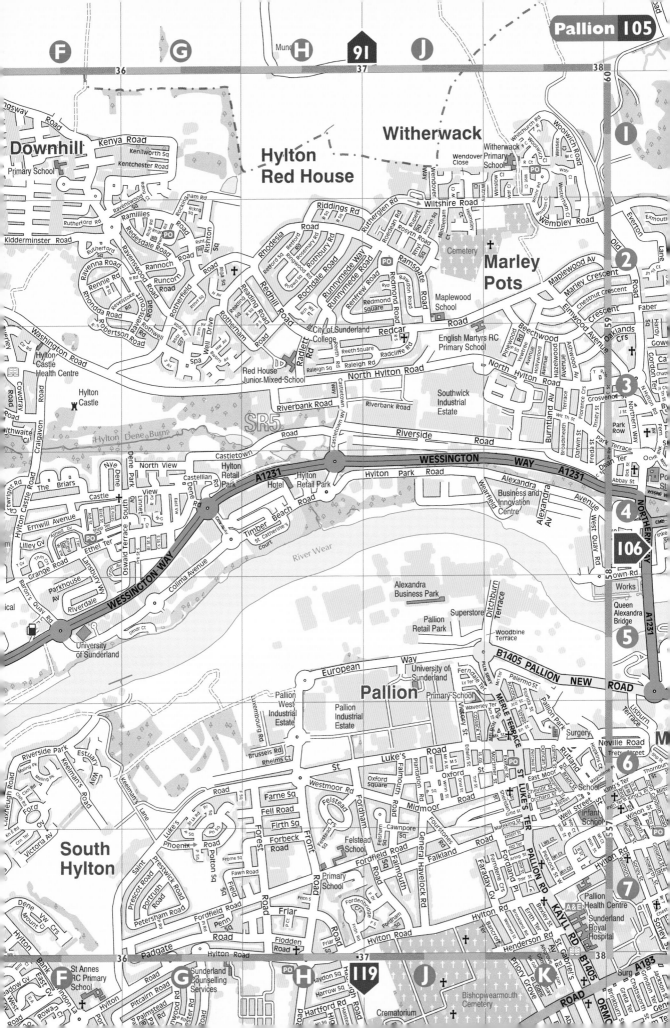

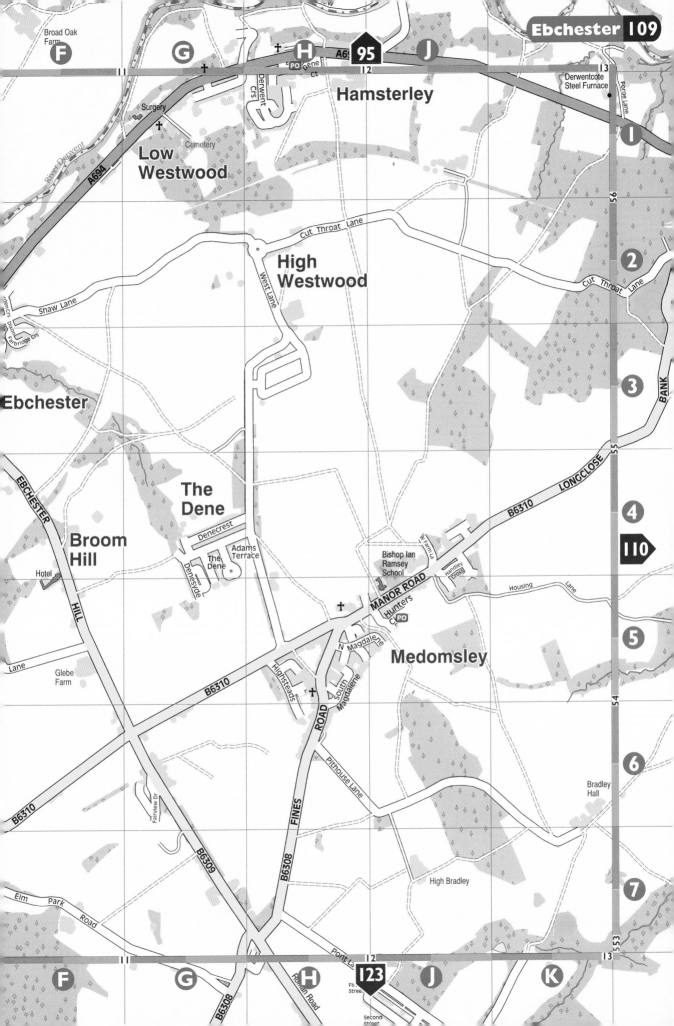

F
G
95
12
H
A69
J
I
13
56

Broad Oak Farm

Derwentcote Steel Furnace

Forge Lane

PO
Dene Ct

† Derwent Crs

Hamsterley

Surgery

† Cemetery

Low Westwood

River Derwent

A694

Cut Throat Lane

High Westwood

Cut Throat Lane

2

West Lane

Shaw Lane

ntten Crs

Dixon

Farbridge Crs

3

BANK

55

Ebchester

LONGCLOSE

B6310

4

110

The Dene

Denecrest

Adams Terrace

W. Farm La

Bishop Ian Ramsey School

Handley Cross

Broom Hill

Deneside

The Dene

Housing

Lane

Hotel

MANOR ROAD

† Hunters

C PO

5

54

EBCHESTER HILL

N Magdalene

Medomsley

Lane

Glebe Farm

Highsteads

† South Magdalene

B6310

6

Bradley Hall

B6310

ROAD

FINES

Pithouse Lane

Fairview Dr

High Bradley

7

553

B6309

B6308

Elm Park Road

Port La

F
11
G
H
123
12
J
K
13

Rough Road

Fli
Stree

Second Street

A   B   **Hamsterley** **96**   C   D   E
    Mill **14**

413

Derwentcote
Steel Furnace

Forge Lane

Hagg House

Long Close Road

Lintzford Road

Lodge Cl

High Hamsterley Rd

Mill Farm Road

High Mill Road

Lintz Green

Lintz Green Lane

1

Tollgate Road

A694

56

B6310

Parklands

B6310

15

2

Cut Throat Lane

BANK

Hamsterley
Hall

Low
Ewehurst

3

55

Southfield

Southfield
Farm

Lane

Ewehurst
Wood

LONGCLOSE

4

◄109

Pont Burn

Collierley

Collierley

5

Lane

54

South Burn

6

Bradley
Hall

Billingside
Wood

Dipton

Surgery

Collierley County
Primary School

Co-Ope

PO

FRONT STREET

7

553

A692

Pikesyde

Pontopsyde

Pontop Pike Lane

413   A   B   **124**   C   D   E
              14

15

Pontop
Pike

1 grid square represents 500 metres

F **G** **H** **J**

97

I

2

3

4

112

5

6

7

High Harelaw

B6310

Briardene

Maple Avenue

Pine Avenue

Birch Crescent

Crescent

PO

Raby Gardens

Lintz Ter

Friars Garden

Albion Gardens

BU OPFIELD

Lintz

Hobson Industrial Est

Mulberry Gv

The Maw

Syke Road

FRONT STREET

Cragleas

Hobson

Hobson Municipal Golf Club

Golf Co

Tanfield Moor

Lintz Hall Farm

Loft House

Lintz Lane

A692

Pickering Nook

Clough Dene

B6173

Straightneck Wood

EWEHURST ROAD

A692

Chapel St

Unity Terrace

PO

B6311

South View

field m

Tantobie

Alder Crs

Bute St

W L

Westhi

Hill Top

A692

Ewehurst Pde

Road

Ht L

Ewehurst Crs

Ewehurst

Fr St

FLINT HILL BANK

FRONT STREET

Palmer Rd

Wyndways Dr

Plunkett Rd

T Mm

Mn Pl

Flint Hill

B6311

WEST ROAD

Larch Terrace

Harperley Lane

White-le-Head

Tanfield Lea County Junior M & Infant School

The Cl

Woodburn

The Paddock

Lane

South Meadow

Lily Gardens

NORTH ROAD

Unity Ter

L Dr

Catchwell Road

Delight Bank

Harelaw Industrial Estate

Bush Blades

Kyo

Fondlyset

Stob House

Bushblades Lane

Peter's Bank

Harperley Lane

Harelaw Gdns

F **G** **H** **J**

B6168

125

Garelaw **Harperley** **E t Kyo**

97

125

16 17 18

56 55 54 53

2 3 4 5 6 7

F   G   H   **99**   J

21   22   23

Causey

A6076

Hedley West House Farm

Hedley Lane

Hedley Hall Farm

Hotel

Coppy La.

Beamishburn Road

Gateshead
Durham County

Coppy Lane

Coppy

Beamish Burn

Beamish Hall

Beamish Park Golf Club

Golf Course

Kibble Comn

Beamish East Moor

Pockerley Buildings

114

Bobby S Caravan

Hammer

Square Ba

High Forge

Beamish, The North of England Open Air Museum

Mount Escob

Birchwood Cl

Shield Row

Station Road

Peggy's Wicket

Abbots Wk

New Ro

A693

Beamish County School

Co-operative Villas

Roseberry St
John Street
Gladstone St
Beamish Hills

Beamish

Bourne Ct
East St
St Heliers
Beamish VW
Broom
Strathmore Ter

HILL TOP

Alda Cl

Spencer Ct
Milton Cl
Ruskin
Masefield Cl
Thorntree Ter
Acton Dene
Ballater Cl
Kinross Dr
Colville Ct
Gulla
Brentwood Cl
Harwick Ct

FRONT ST

PO

Stony

Edenfield

West Pelton

PO

Plantation View

County Junior Middle & Infant

Orchard

F   G   H   **127**   J   K

21   22   23

A693

I   2   3   4   5   6   7

56   55   54   553

Ⓐ   Ⓑ   **100**   Ⓒ   Ⓓ   **Kibbl**Ⓔ**worth**

423   24   25

School

PO

Bank

Grange Est

Ashvale Av

Laburnum Crs

Moorhil

Greenford

Coltspo

Ouselaw

Volvdene

Kibbles

①

56

Kibblesworth
Grange

Cooper House

Riding Lane

River Team

②

Kibblesworth
Common

Riding Farm

③

55

Beamish
East Moor

Bellerby Dr

Bird Gr

Melbeck Dr

Carlton

Bradley Cl

Bradley Cl

Pockerley
Buildings

Abbotside Cl

Bradley
Close

Cl

Walden Cl

④

113

Hammer

Square Bank

Bobby Shafto
Caravan Park

Mill La

Urpe

Ous
Jun
Sch

Leyburn Cl

Middleham Cl

Wensley Cl

Redmires

⑤

River Team

Mount
Escob

High Urpeth

⑥

Perkinsville

Stony   Lane

**High
Handenhold**

New   Road

Sydney St

Arthur St

Baytree

Laurel
Crs

Ter

A693

Fairfield

Mossway

Sandyford

Middlefield

Greenacres

Health
Centre

IVYWAY

Ernest

Constance St

Barbary

PO

⑦

553

A693

†

Edenfield
Bank

Green's

Thornton
Lea

King's Lane

Cemetery

†

Front   Street

Vcrg Cl

Orchard St

Fieldside

Southfie

Wood St

Brackenfield

423   24   25

PO

Ⓐ   Ⓑ   **128**   Ⓒ   Ⓓ   Ⓔ

Pelton

Elm Av

The Pde

Heathmeads

Lovaine St

Pelton Ms

Elwin Cl

Grange St

PELTON

I grid square represents 500 metres

County Junior
Middle & Infant

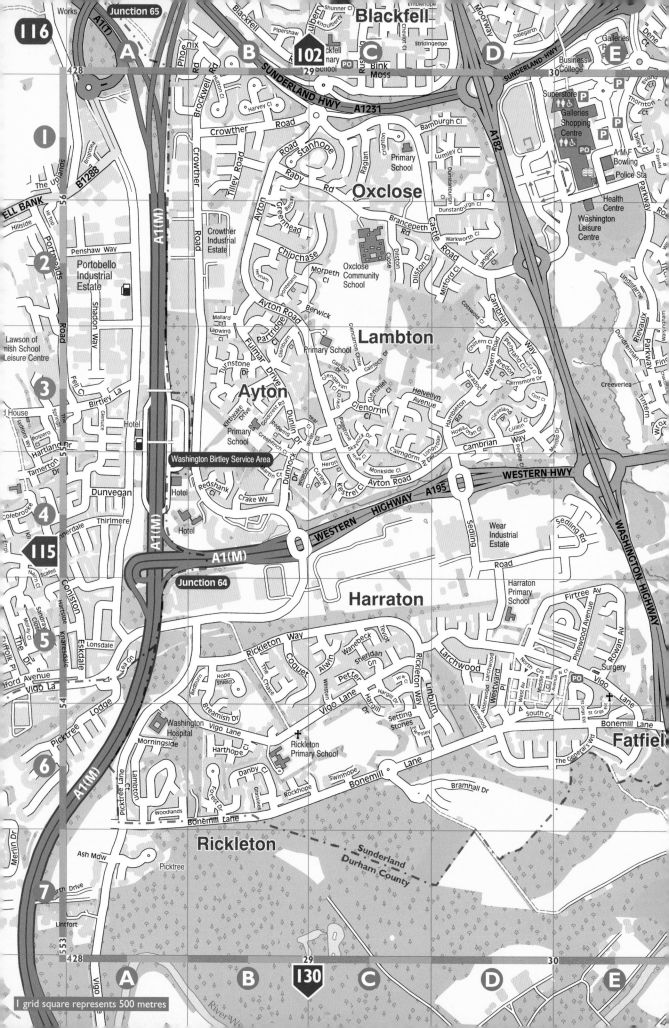

408
53
52
51
550
408

A **B** 108 **C** **D** **E**

1
2
3
4
5
6
7

A **B** 137 **C** **D** **E**

Waskerley

Pike Hill

BURNMILL BANK

B6278

Shotley Hall

Shotley Bridge Junior School

SNOW'S GREEN RD

B6310

School

Shotley Bridge General Hospital

The Elms

Ascot Cl

The Mount

The Woodlands

The Close

The Drive

Woodland Ct

Selborne Gdns

Carnoustie Cl

Links Drive

Turnberry

Lytham Cl

Links Dr

Troon Cl

Muirfield Cl

Benfieldside

Rosedale Av

Golden Acre

Briar Mews

Queen's Road

Cemetery

Redwood Ct

Hope Cl

A691

Park St

Buckham Cl

Manse Street

North Industrial Est

B6322

PARK

Genesis Way

CONSETT

Ponds Court Business Pa

Victoria Cl

Parliamen

Romany Drive

Genesis Way

Ponds Way

A692

Templetow

How Indu Park

Works

A692

A691 CUTLERS' HALL ROAD

Grove Rd

Shotley

Valley View

Gill Side

The Crescent

Bridgehill

Backstone Burn

Broadwood Vw

Queens Wy

West Acre

N Stead Dr

Priory

Nwst Rd

Western Hi

Moorlands

York Rd

Benfieldside Road

Benfield Cl

Benfieldside

Surtees

St Cuthbert's

Greenacres Rd

Ashby Crs

Murray Court

Briarside

Avenue

Princess Av

King's Rd

Beverley Gdns

Ritson's Road

Ravenside Ter

John St

Thomas St

Ritson St

Benfieldside CP School

PO

George St

Newlands

North Vw

M Crs

DURHAM RD A691

PO

St Andrew's Rd

Andrew's Rd

Mary's Crs

St Mary's St

Oxley St

Derwent Ms

Benfieldside Cemetery

Dixon St

Shotley Grove

Pleasant

The Crescent

Maple Gdns

Valley Gdns

Sandford Rd

Barley Mill Crs

West South Vw

Chayton Rd

Cortland Rd

Alston Rd

Alston Ter

Pemberton Road

Highridge

Pheonix Ct

Kilchurn

Braemar Court

Braemar

St Marys Primary Sch

Blackhill

Derwentdale Industrial Est

Park Road Industrial Est

Meadowfield

Hawthorn

Bessemer St

Roger St

Cort St

St Aldan's

Church Rd

Hilfield

Thornhill

Tromill

Park Rd

St George's Pl

Railway Pl

Bridge St

Mortinull St

Edge Ct

Berry Ct

Romany Dr

Crd

Letch Burn

Barley Mill Road

Northumberland County

Durham County

River Derwent

Allensdale Cam Camping Park

Allensford

Pemberton Road

Consett Lane

Hallgarth

Hall

Selby Gdns

Cdr Gdn

The Grove

Oakfield Lane

Priestman Av

Grove County JMI School

The Grove Industrial Estate

St Pius RC School

Pemberton Av

Fell Vw

Evansleigh Rd

Welford Rd

Holly Crs

Hydenside Dr

Moorside Comprehensive School

Dunelm Road

Dunelm Crescent

Dunelm Road

Kent Rd

Chester Road

Lincoln Place

Surrey Road

Sussex Road

Devon

Rutland Road

Lancaster Rd

Derby Dr

PO

Moorside

Shotle Bridge

Front Street

Oley Mdw

Green St

Woods Rd

The Ter

The Briary

Churchill

The Road

Peile Pk

Church Bank

Riverside

The Crescent

Cutler's Av

Woodland

Ashfield

Ms

PO

1 grid square represents 500 metres

F G H **109** J

I

2

3

LEADGAT

4

124

5

6

7

Elm Park Road

High Bradley

Pont Lane

Roman Road

WATLING STREET

B6308 ROAD

B6309

Berry Edge Farm

Bunker Hill

Golf Course

Consett & District Golf Club

MEDOMSLEY

Werdohl

Number One Industrial Est

Way

First Street

Second Street

Crag Works

Third Street

Second Street

Pont Bungalows

Fourth Street

Watling Street Bungalows

Third Street

Second Street

First Street

Eden Avenue

Trent St

Mersey St

Tees Gv

Tweed Avenue

Derwent Crs

Pont Lane

Avenue

Road

Blackfyne Comprehensive School

Fairways

Elsdon Gdns

Cyril St

A691 VILLA REAL ROAD

The Crescent

Bright

Beaconsfield St

East View

Laing St

Balmoral Gv

Consett Business Park

Bradley Workshops Industrial Est

Wansbeck Gv

Wear Gv

SC

MS

Tyne

Rydal MS

Borrowdale

Coniston Wk

Grassmere

Annaside Mews

St Ives

Redwell Hill Clin

Redwell Farm

Dere Pk

Garden Terrace

S Cross St

Surgery

PO St

Brooms RC Primary School

Elm Terrace

Park Terrace

Ash Terrace

Wingrove Terrace

Ridley Ter

Derwentside College

ROAD

The Prom

Cyril St

Balfour

Aynsley Terrace

Br HS Av

B6308

Br Vue

Civic Centre

MEDOMSLEY ROAD

Allison

Park

VW

Belle Vue Leisure Centre

Belle Vue Av

Ashdale

Oakdale Road

School

Elmdale Rd

Beechdale Rd

Front Street

West St

The Hvn

Valley View

Nelson St

Plantation Street

Green Street

DURHAM ROAD

Duneim Walk

Dunelm

Prospect Business Park

Leadgate County Junior Mixed School

Alder Gv

D Willow

Laurel

Lilac Pl

College View

Leadgate Road

Crookhall La

Crookhall Lane

LEADGATE ROAD

A692

Larch

George St

Stanley St

Park Av

Russell St

Hartington Ter

Infant School

Council Offices

Sherburn Ter

Meadow Rise

Crookhall Rd

LEADGATE ROAD

A692

Works

Works

Main St

Consett Medical Centre

Empire

Delves La

Gill Street

A692

Hermiston Retail Park

Gatehouse Industrial Estate

Berry Edge Rd

Front Street

Crookhall

Knitsley Lane

Mickleton Cl

Eggleston Dr

Eggleston Dr

Gloucester Road

Castleglene

Mercatte Rd

Fairfield Rd

Delvedere Rd

Hall Road

Old

Dere Rd

Pontop Vw

Percy Gdns

Stockerley Rd

Iveston Rd

Sharto Cl

Neston Rd

Salem

Sydney Gdns

Lambton Avenue

Delves Lane

Woodside Drive

Lumley Dr

Greencroft Rd

Glenmore Dr

Doval

Briar Dale

Ladywell Rd

Pixley Dell

Greenways

Birch

Broadway

Meadow View

Works

PO

F G H **138** J K

Delves

124

A   B   **110**   C   D   E

53 413   14   15

I

Pontop
Pike

2
Tweed
Avenue
Lane

52

A692

A693

East
Castle

Road

3
Redwell
Hills
Clinic
Redwell Hills
Farm

Brook
Primary School
Elm Terrace
Park Terrace
Wingrove
Terrace
LEADGATE
Ridley Ter

Low Brooms
Farm

Brooms Lane

Stonyheap Lane

**Stony
Heap**

DUNEIM WAY
Duneim Walk
Duneim
Cr

4
URHAM R
ow Crs
Lilac

A692

Hanging
Stone

123

51

Stonyheap
Lane

Hanging

5

A691

Leadgate
Industrial Estate

Back Lane

Sunniside
Farm

550

Iveston Lane

6
Iveston

Lund's Lane

Durham
Hill

Gorecock

Moorside

7

WOODSIDE BANK

Woodside

413   14   15

A   B   **139**   C   D   E

1 grid square represents 500 metres

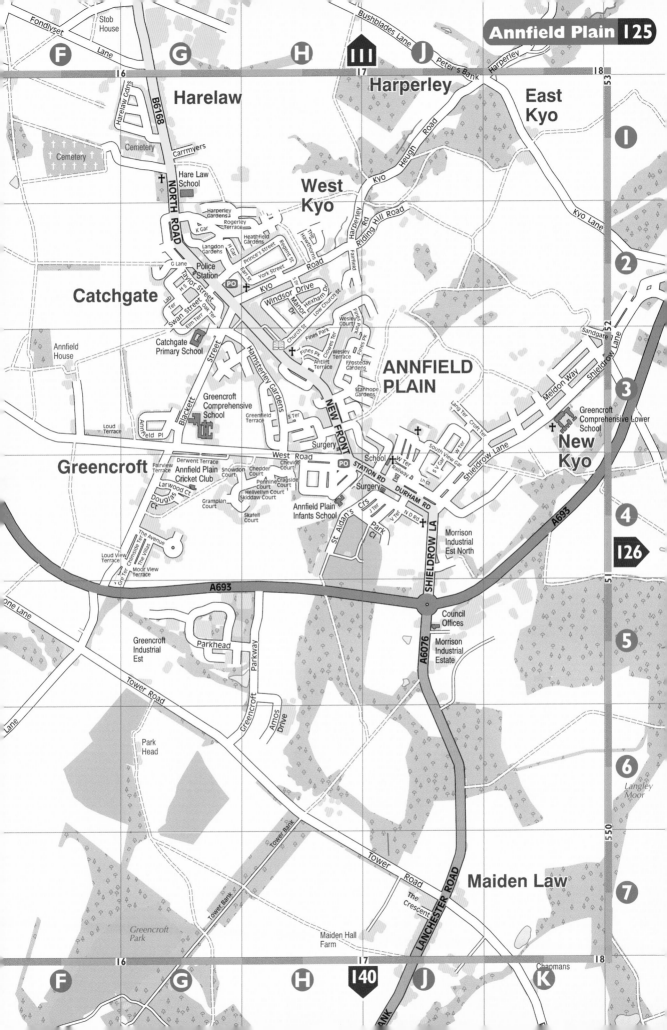

F G H 111 17 J
I

Fondlyset Lane
Stob House
16
Harelaw Gdns
B6168
Bushblades Lane
Peter's Bank
Harperley
18
53

Harelaw
Harperley
East Kyo

Cemetery
Carrmyers
NORTH ROAD
Cemetery
Hare Law School
West Kyo
Kyo Heugh Rd
Riding Hill Road
Harperley Rd
Kyo Lane

2

Harperley Gardens
K Car
Rogerley Terrace
Heathfield Gardens
Langdon Gardens
H Car
Prince's Street
Regent St
The Hawthorns
Road
Fairfield
52
Sandgate

G Lane
Police Station
PO
York Street
Kyo
Windsor Drive
Manor Dr
Hexham Dr
Low Church St
Church St
Fines Park
Wesley Court
Fines Pk
Fines Pk
Meldon Way
Shieldrow Lane

3

Catchgate
Taylor Street
Swan Street
Lab Ter
H S
Oak Ter
Elm Ter
East St
Str
Clowes Ter
Wesley Terrace
Antliff Terrace
Frosteday Gardens
Greencroft Comprehensive Lower School
New Kyo

Annfield House
Catchgate Primary School
Hamsterley Gardens
Blackett Street
Greencroft Comprehensive School
Greenfield Terrace
S Ter
Fines Pk
Stanhope Gardens
ANNFIELD PLAIN
Lang Ter
Croft Ter
Shieldrow Lane

Loud Terrace
Annfield Pl
NEW FRONT STREET
Surgery
South View Car
W Ter
W Ter
A693

4
126

Greencroft
Fairview Terrace
Derwent Terrace
Annfield Plain Cricket Club
Snowdon Court
Chedder Court
Cheviot Court
West Road
Cragside Court
Pennine Court
Hellvellyn Court
Skiddaw Court
School
PO
STATION RD
Surgery
DURHAM RD
Railway
South View Car
W Ter
S V Rd
Ln Ct
SHIELDROW LA
Morrison Industrial Est North

Larwood Ct
Douglas Ct
Grampian Court
Skafell Court
Annfield Plain Infants School
St Aidan's Crs
J Ter
N D Rd
Y Ter
51
5

The Avenue
Loud View Terrace
The Villas
Gre Ter
Chilnside Ter
Moor View Terrace
Park Cl
A6076
Council Offices
Morrison Industrial Estate

Ione Lane
A693
Parkhead
Greencroft Parkway
Amos Drive
6
Langley Moor

Lane
Greencroft Industrial Est
Park Head
Tower Road
Tower Bank
50

7
Maiden Law

Tower Bank
Tower Road
The Crescent
LANCHESTER ROAD
Greencroft Park
Maiden Hall Farm
Chapmans

F 16 G 17 H 140 J BANK K 18

128

114

127

143

A693
Road
Sydney St
Arthur St
Bartree Ter
Laurel Crs
A693

Thornton Lea
King's Lane
Health Centre
IVY way
Front Street
Fieldside
Southfield

Cemetery

Elm Av
The Pde
Pelton
Oak Ter
Heathmeads

PELTON

Station Lane

The Wynd

Elwin Place
Grange St

Plantation View
Edenfield
Green's Bank
Somerfield
PO
423
53

County Junior Middle & Infant School
Orchard Cl

Pelton Ms
Holyoake St
Alexandra St
Provident St
Industrial St
Lovaine St

Golf Course

Roseberry Grange Golf Course

Roseberry Primary School

Pelton Lane
Roseberry Vis
PO
Front Street

Grange Villa

Stone Row
West Street
East Street
Albert St
Queen St
Pine St

Pelton Lane

Newfield

Stella Indust Est

2

52

Newbridge Banks

3

Blindy Burn
Twizell Burn

Grange Ter
New Grange Terrace
Plunkett Ter
Miller Gdns
Surgery

B6313
BEAMISH
VIEW

DH2

Pelton Fell Surgery
Briarwood Av
PO
Whitehill
Crs
Tennyson Rd

BLUEHOUSE BANK

Hett Hills

Valley Rd
Fell Rd
Byron

Shakespere Ter

Wordsworth Avenue
Avenue
Ruskin Av
Henley Av

4

127
51

White Hall Farm

Tribley Farm

5

Waldridge

6

Broomy Holm

Little Burn

Olive St

Beech Grove Farm

550

Humble...

OUSE LANE

Waldridge Lane

7
423

Congburn Bridge

CONGBURN BANK

Waldridge Country

ng Burn

A
B
C
D
E

Edmondsley JMI School

I grid square represents 500 metres

130

North Drive

Lintfort

A **A** B **B** **116** C **C** D **D** E **E**

428
53

Vigo Lane

River Wear

Lambton Park

Lambton Castle

1 A1(M)

Black Drive

Black Drive

A183

Rickleton Av

Cherry Banks

Junction 63

PICKTREE LANE

NEWBRIDGE BANK

A183

Chester le Street

2

A167

A183 CHESTER

ROAD A183

A183

A183

A1052

PARK RD NORTH A167(T)

3

White House

Houghton Gate

Chester le Street Leisure Centre

DH3

Forge Lane

A1(M)

View munity Sch

4

Roman

129

PARK RD CTRL

Forge La

St Cuthberts RC Primary School

Park Centre

Lane

Chester-le-Street Golf Club

5

Latimer Ter

Castle Ct

B1284

LUMLEY

Golf Course

Lumley Park Burn

Beverley Gdns

Durham CCC - County Ground, Riverside

River Wear

Rosery Lane

PARK ROAD SOUTH

Crichton Av

Bradman

Riverside Stadium

NEW ROAD

B1284

A1(M)

6

The Parks

Larwood Cl

Drive

Lumley Thicks

Lumley Riding

550

7

Scorer's

Lumley County Infant School

428
29
30

A **A** B **145** C **C** D **D** E **E**

BEAT LUMLEY

Council Offices

Lane

Scott

134

438

Silksworth Rd
Church View Medical Cen
Silksworth Health Cen

A

Rutland Av
Windsor Rd
Edward
Silksworth Terrace
Trident Rd
Londonderry St
Church Vw
Mill Hill Rd
Hill St
Maria St
Park Av
Alne St
Robert St
Norman
Davison Av
Orr Av
Surrey Rd
Pembroke Av
Quarry Rd

B

Londonderry Rd
Dorset La
Burdon Gv
Myrtle Gv

120
39

B1286

BURDON ROAD

Runswick Cl
Fylingdale

Coathland Cl
Goathland Dr

Tunstall

C

Ryemount Rd
Richmond
Runcorn
Rachel Cl
Rowell
Ravensworth Rd
Ramil
Ridgeway
Rothbury
Rushford
40

D

Brick Rw
Shaftesbury Av
Western Hill
B1286
Cheviot
Back
Bevan Av

RYHOPE

Western

E

Wraith Terrace
Hylton Terrace
Burdock Crescen
Wilkinson Ter
Esdale
Esdale
Burdon

Blyton Avenue
Smith Gv
Bevan
Stewart Av

1

Skye Ct
Bute Ct
Hill Rd
Bute Ct
Aspley Cl
Shalcombe Cl
Staley Ct
Woburn Dr
Hinkley Cl
Gayhurst Crs
Stratus Ct
Ruswarp Cl
Saint Ct
Trool Ct
Laxford Court
Froisher Ct

DOXFORD PARK WAY

Hillside Cl
Brookbank Cl

2
Plough Road
Hall Farm Road
Treecone Cl
Cornbank Cl
Badger Cl
Foxtail Cl
Thornbank Cl

Hallfield Cl
Farm Cl
Lowland
Honeysuckle Cl
The Cheyne
Aylesbury
Berryfield
Silverdale
Fairmile Dr
Burdon Road
Yardley Close
Hoyle

Tunstall Lodge Farm
The Fold

Lodgeside Meadow

Doxford Park

Burdon Lane

East Farm

3
Craigwell Dr
Grleston W
Alnville
Fold

Burdon Lane

The House Farm
4

133

Burdon

Burn Hall Farm

A19(T)

5

**Old
Burdon**

Pacific Hall Farm

6
Sharpley Hall Farm

Sunderland
Durham County

B1404

B1404

SEATON LANE

Blayweston
Uster Cl
Middleton
Hall
Enterprise Cl
Partnership Court

Seaton Crs
Seaton Grove
Hall Cl
Hillrise
Avoncroft Close

Sharpley Dr
Pcfe Hill
Stotfold Close
Sharpley
Waverley Drive
Eppleton Hall Close
Manor Hall Drive

7

Seaton

St RC
Haverley
Westlea Junior School

Seaton Moor House

A

Sea
Bar
Top

149
39

B

C

D

E

Cherry Knowle Hospital

438
39
40

A19(T)

1 grid square represents 500 metres

136

Oak

Northumberland Co

Durham County

Wharnley
Burn

A   406   B   C   07   D   Allensford Bank   E

Combfield
House

Derwent
Grange

Castleside

I

A68

FRONT ST

2

Dean Howl
Farm

Wharnley Way

Hillcrest

CONSE

Moorlan
School

PO

ROWLEY

Horsleyhope Burn

Watergate
Road

3

Healeyfield

Church Street

Healeyfield Lane

48

4

Goldhill Lane

Goldhill

5

Horsleyhope

Honey
Hill

Healeyfield Lane

47

Greenside

6

Whitehall
Moss

Middles
Farm

7

Lindisfarne

5 46   406   A   B   07   C   D   E

1 grid square represents 500 metres

Comprehensive School

Dunelm Road

Kent Road

Kent Rd.

Dunelm Road

Devon Crescent

Dunelm Crescent

Rutland Road

Lincoln Place

Surrey

Sussex Road

PO

F

G

H

122

J

Works

Moorside County School

Chester Road

Lincoln Road

Derby Drive

Lancaster Rd

York Avenue

Warwick Av

Warwick Avenue

Somerset

Road

Cm

Essex

Cumberland Road

Norfolk Road

Avenue

Castleside Industrial Estate

Moorside

Hown's Farm

I

49

Castle Hills

ROAD

A692

Drover

Ter

The Rise

Bil Vw Dr

Drover Road

Wesley Terrace

Wesley Gardens

Hillgarth

Middles Farm

2

Rowley

A68

Middle Heads

3

48

†

Knitsley Lane

Waskerley Way

Whitehall

Longedge Lane

Oliver Ford Lane

High House Lane

Outputs La

138

4

Longedge Lane

5

47

China Hall Farm

6

Mount Pleasant Farm

Whickham Grange

Sheepwalks Farm

Millershill Lane

7

546

F

G

H

09

J

10

K

Lane

Broadmeadows

138

A B 123 C PO D E

411 12

Delves

Greenways Glenmore Doual

Briar Dale College View

Lachwell Road

Pixley Dell

Meadow View

Delves Lane Industrial Estate

Delves Lane

Little Greencroft Farm

Broadway

1

49

Knitsley

2

Backsill Burn

Hownsgill Dr

Butsfield Lane

East Knitsley Grange

3

48

Knitsley Mill

4

Dyke Nook

Outputs Lane

Newbiggin Lane

137 s Lane

New House Farm

5

ngedge Lane

47

Woodlands Park Farm

Woodlands Hall

Longedge Lane

6

Sheepwalks Farm

Eliza Lane

Red Houses

Longedge Lane

7

Knitsley Lane

Rippon Burn

546

Sawmill Wood

411 12

A B C D E

1 grid square represents 500 metres

Broadmeadow

F G H 124 J

A691

Woodside

I

Esp Green

2 A691

Stockerley Lane

Stockerley Bridge

Stockerley Burn

Smallthorpe Burn

Hurbuck Cottages

Low Meadows

3

Lizards

Humberhill Lane

4 140

Newbiggin

Newbiggin Lane

5

L

Yeckhouse Lane

Upper Houses

6

Humber House Farm

Hollinside

Middlewood Farm

7

Colepike Hall

F G H 124 J K

Longedge La

berhill Lane

B6296

Burnhope

142

A   421   B   **127**   C   22   D   E

Holmside Hall

1

Hag Wood

Holmside

Cong Burn

Wheatley Green Farm

Ash Tree Terrace

Holmside Hall Road

49

Warland Green

Holmside Lane

West Edmondsley

Holmside Lane

Warland

Whiteside Farm

2

Whiteside Burn

3

Charlaw Plantation

48

Charlaw Lane

Long Edge

4

141

Long Edge

Broom House

Acornclose Lane

5

Norburn Lane

47

West Hall Cottage

6

Horn's House

Coalpark Gill

Langley Lane

Kay's Burn

Langley

7

546

Langley Lane

A   421   B   **154**   C   22   D   E

A691

Norburn Lane

A691

1 grid square represents 500 metres

144

I

A 426 B **129** C A167(T) D E

Chester
Moor

The Crs
Waldridge Lane
Union Lane
The Gallery

49

2

Bealey
Lane

3

48

Darley Court

Ugly Lane
Nettlesworth
Primary School
PARK VIEW
Hillmeads

4

143

Tanmeads

Tan
Hills

Hawthorn Close

B6312 A167(T)

Mill Lane
Mill House

Plawsworth

Wheatleywell Lane

The Dene
27
Holmhill Lane

The Oval

Holmhill Lane

Southill
Hall

Cedar Avenue
Oak Crescent
Ch
Vw

Sycamore Rd
Briar Cl
Elm Crescent

5

Kimblesworth

Industrial
Estate

6

Kimblesworth
Grange

7

Viewly
Grange

Nag's Fold
Farm

Cocken Road

Bishop's
Grange

Mill Lane

A167(T)

Hag House

Finchale Abbey
Training Centre

Red
House

A 426 B **156** C
Service
Centre
AA
27
Abbeywoods
Business
Park
D
Beaver
Cl
Oatlands Way
E

Rosemount
Newton
Grange

1 grid square represents 500 metres

House

Smithfield
Abbywds
Mercia
Ryelands
Finchale

F G H J

130

GREAT
LUMLEY

Lumley
County
Infant School

Council
Offices

Lumley
JMI School

Fenton
Lumley
Grange

Fenton   Well   Lane   Back   Lane   Front   Street   Scott

Winchester
Cl

Cn Cl

Salisbury
Cl

Cambridge

Gloucester

Exeter

Worcester

Drive

PO

Norwich
Cl

St Alban's

Lcht Cl

Stainmore Drive

Prudenerley

M Cl
Cl

Nenthead
Cl

Brignall Cl

Lartington
Close

Old Mill Lane

Cocken Lane

George   Pit   Lane

Pea Flatts Lane

A1(M)

I

2

3

Harbour House
Farm

River Wear

Charles Pit
Cottages

Cocken White
House Farm

Prior's
Close

48

4

146

Low Cocken
Farm

Cocken Lane

5

River Wear

Finchale Priory

Finchale
Banks

Cocken Road

47

Broom
House

6

Raintonpark
Wood

7

East Moor
Leazes

546

F G H J K

157

Union Hall

Rowan
Dr

Finchale   Avenue

Beech
Close

8   29   30

A1(M)

148

B1404

Law

GILLAS LANE

A   Houghton-Le-Spring Golf Club   B   **133**   C   37   D   E

1

Golf Course

High Sharpley

Sunderland   Durham County

Green Lane

Byer Square

2   Dene St   Low Downs Rd   Henry St   Lindsay Street   Maudlin St   Nicholas Street

Church Road   Oswald Road

Hetton Downs

North Lane

Downs Pit Lane

3   George St   Downs Street   Percy St   Mkt St   Ep RW

DH5

Great Eppleton

Carrhouse Lane

4   Edward Street   Carol   S Market St   The Avenue   Urwin Street

147   John St   St Cl   J St

Carr House Farm

Richard Street

HETTON-LE-HOLE

Salter's Lane

5   Logan St   Wear St   HOUGHTON ROAD STATION RD   Claude St

Hetton Lyons Industrial Estate

Murton Moor Farm   **B1285**

COLLIERY LANE

B1285

6   Hetton Le So   **Lyons**   Eppleton Hall

Redhills Way   Belmont Rise   Lambton Dr

FOUR LANE ENDS   Castle   Gillesgate Road   Bailey   Lyons Avenue   Derwent Street   Bowes   Lyons La   H Ter

LILYWHITE   PEMBERTON BANK   Derwent Way   Neil St   Hartside Gdns

7   Walter Terrace   Bradley   Lawson Ter   Seymour Ter   North View   East View   Willow Crescent

Murton Lane   Cemetery

Easington   **Easington Lane**   37

Brick Garth   Elemore Leisure Cen   PO   HIGH STREET   SOUTH HE

A   436   B   Dorset St   **160**   C   Easington Lane   D   E

Elemore Vale   Cranberry   Easington Lane Primary

Seaton

F   **G**   **H**   134   **J**   40

Westlea Junior School

Seaton Bank Top

Seaton Moor House

Melrose Crescent

PO

B1285

Warkworth Crs

Windermere

Windsor Road

Wycliffe Road

Wesley Way

West Lea

Windermere

Wordsworth Av

Webb Av

Wells Crs

Surgery

I

Wolsey Road

Watling Avenue

Windermere

Walpole

Doreen Av

Stotfold

Bowes Av

Escallond Drive

2

Haverley House

Slingley Hill

Ovrdn

3

B1285

Dalton Moor

4

Truro Avenue

Bude Sq

St Andrew's Square

Sea View Walk

150

D'Arcy Square

Hesledon Walk

Davison Crs

Clarke Terrace

Bevan Square

Webb Av

Burnip Road

Greenhill

Penzance Bungs

Tregoney Av

Glebe Vw

Glebe

Station Est

Stephens

Clarke Ter

Hill Crs

Crs

Toft

Ash Ter

Cedars Crs

Trevone Av

Penryn Av

Claude Terrace

Short N

Gowland Sq

Luke Crs

Council Offices

Primary School

Police Station

Farmer Crs

Barnes Road

Watkin Crs

Watts St

Infant School

Surgery

5

Metcalfe Crs

Wellfield Road

Calvert Ter

Cook Crs

Calvert Ter

Porter Ter

Stphns St

Frdy St

N-H S Clinic

Station Est E

Station Road

Gray Av

Porter

Edison St

Station Est South

PO

Park Lane

Williams Rd

Knaresborough Rd

Ripon Ter

George St

STATION   **ROAD**   B1285

CHURCH LANE

Federation Sq

Wnd's

Council Offices

CHURCH ST   **CHURCH STREET**

47

Winds Lonnen Est

Melrose Avenue

Winds Lane

Cemetery

St Josephs RC School

Cookson Ter

Effe St

B1285

Hawthorne Cl

6

Hesledon Moor East

7

F   **G**   **H**   161   **J**   40   **K**

Little Coop House Farm

A   B   **135**   C   D   E

Westlea Junior School

Melrose Crescent

Seaton Pa

Militate

Windslow Crs

B1285

Melrose Crescent

Enfield Road

Windsor Road

Eastlea Road

Escdale Ro

Eskdale Close

Elgin Av

Emmerdale Cl

Everton Dr

Warky

Windermere Road

Wesley Way

WyCliffe Road

Webb Av

Eastdene Rd

Ryton Crs

Malvern Crs

Wordsworth Av

Watling Av

Wagwood

Windermere Road

Wolsey Road

Walpole

Watling Avenue

Surgery

Essex Crs

Epping Close

Saturn Street

Topaz Street

Lawnside

Malvern Crescent

Eastlea Crescent

Queensbury Road

Oxford Street

Colling Avenue

Portland Avenue

Milton Close

Bethune Avenue

Council Offices

The Avenue

Dalton Av

Exeter Av

Frank Av

Grantham Av

Hexham Av

Ivy Av

Jasper Av

Kingston Av

Ivy Avenue

Hexham Av

Laurel Avenue

The Lawns

Deneside Junior & Infant School

The Drive

Weymouth Drive

THE GRAHAM WAY

Deneside

Dawlish Close

Dorm C

Bmt St

Doreen Av

Waring Ter

Watson Cl

Sidmouth

B1285

B1287

Bowes Av

Escallond Drive

Dene Road

Church Court

PO

Kingfisher Ind Est

Cheviot Court

Easington District Leisure Centre

PO

Easington District Leisure Centre

Deneside Medical Centre

Strangford Rd

NEW STRANGFORD-RD

Dene Road

Maureen Ter

Victoria

Princess

Springfield Crs

Camden Square Secondary School

Junior School

Cemetery

Parkside Crs

Beech Crescent

Cedar Crs

Beech Crs

Daphne Crs

Parkside Crescent

Elmtree Court

PO

Council Offices

Parkside Infant School

Heathway

Jasmine Crs

Lbrm Crs

Fern Crescent

Maple Crs

Parkside

Seaham Golf Club

Golf Course

Golf Course

Fox Cover Industrial Estate

Hesledon East Hous

Seaham Station

Harbour Walk

Community College

Tempest Road

Primary School

Northdene Av

Dene Terrace

Castlereagh Rd

Cornelia Te

Blandford Pl

George St

George St

Sophia St

Viceroy Street

Regency Ct

Frederick St

West St

Alxnd St

Park St

Garron St

Rainton St

Cottages

Fox St

K Edward St

Alexandra

Shrewsbury Street

Longnewton

Mt Pleast

Adelaide Row Med Cen

Railway St

Church S

Ind Est Herbert Ter

Maria St

Maglona Street

Queen

Magiona Street

SR7

South View

Overdene

Ovrdn

B1285

B1285

B1432

A19(T)

A19(T)

A19(T)

A182

Cold Hesledon Industrial Est

Cold Hesledon

Dalton-le-Dale

Walk

149

1

2

3

4

5

6

7

1 grid square represents 500 metres

Service Area

STOCKT

Law

SEAHAM

Police Station

PO

Foundry Road

Primary School

Bottle Works Rd

Albert St

Alfred St

Stewart St

Candlish Ter

Fenwick Row

Gas Works Road

Embankment

Hill Crs

Dawdon

Road

LC

Edith Street

Dawdon Industrial Estate

Nose's Point

A182

Kinley Hill

Chourdon Point

Hawthorn Hive

F Works

G Hopeside Hall

H

141

J

A691

1

8
19
20
46

River Browney

Hedley's Wood

2

Biggen House Farm

Blackburn

45

Davis Crs

The Crescent

Garden Avenue

Cemetery

Low Moor Road

Netherton

Willow Pk

Cedar Ct

Eldon Cl

Staralt

Hawthorn

Middn

Phoenix Cl

Hylton Rd

3

Hamsteels Lane

North Farm

Esh

Esh Bank

4

Esh C of E Aided Primary School

PO

Front Street

154

44

Greenland Road

Front Street

Hall Rd

St Michaels RC School

Low Esh Farm

Esh RC Primary School

5

Laude Bank

Bank

DH7

6

Hag Wood

Hag House Farm

43

7

Flasshall

Bank

Rose Ct

Vale Garth

B6302

Drive

Clifford's Gate

Bailey

Western Av

Willow Rd

Cvt Vw

Rowley

Rw Ln

Crs

Flass Hall

8
19
20

F

G

H

165

J

B6302

K

Hamsteels County Junior & Infant School

New House

Esh Winning Industrial

Rag Path Wood

A   B   142   C   D   E

421   22

Norburn Lane

A691

1

Hedley's Wood

Langley Park Industrial Estate

Stobbilee Farm

Wall Nook

Wallnook Lane

River Browney

2

Riverside Industrial Estate

Dale St

Hawthorne Ter

Bridge St

Palm St

Pine St

Elm St

Bridge Park Close

Bridge Drive

Langley Park

The Crescent

Garden Avenue

Derwentside College

PO

Park

Kingsway

Esh Hillside

Crs

Low Moor Road

Cedar Ct

Eldon

Phoenix Cl

Hylton Cl

Netherton Cl

Hawthorne

Eppleton Cl

Hospital Road

Cherrytree Drive

Maplewood Court

Beech Ct

Linden Ms

Eastern Av

Crossways

Hilltop View

3

Middridge Road

Langley Park Primary School

Springwell Av

East Clere

Esh

4

Hill Top

Front Street

153

44

w Esh m

College Road   College Road

5

Ushaw Farm

Ushaw College

6

Broadgate Road

East Flass Farm

B6302   **COCKHOUSE**

Surgery

Temperance Ter

PO

Whitehouse

Flass Av

7

Flasshall Lane

LANE

Ushaw Moor Infant School

Ushaw Moor

Sta Road

Ushaw Moor Cricket Club

Flass Hall

A   421   B   166   C   D   E

King m Wood

Hare Holme Farm

Map Labels

Witton Gilbert

SACRISTON

Bearpark

Witton Gilbert County School

FRONT ST

A691

Witton Gilbert County School

Fyndoune Cottage

Wellsprings Farm

Potterhouse

Hartside Farm

Trouts Lane School

Durham County N H S Trust

Earls House Hospital

Sniperley Hall

Aden Cottage

Lodge Farm

Stotgate

River Browney

Aldin Grange

Arbour House

Hedley Ct

Hilltop Road

College Vw
Park Wd Av
Beaurepaire
Woodside Av
East Side Av
Quarry Crs
Woodland Close
Cook
Ritson Avenue
Kingston Avenue
Surgery
Auton Stile

Blackburn Cl
Hilltop
Blackcliffe Way

Bearpark Colliery Rd

County Junior & Infant School

Taylor Avenue

Bearpark Colliery Road

Auton Stile

PO

Deerness Valley Comprehensive School

Aldridge Ct
New Acres
Oakridge

Broom Hall

Ushaw Moor Junior School

St. Josephs C School

Cemetery

B6302

Chestnut Gv
Broom Crescent
Deerness Sports Cen

Brancepeth

Baxter

Norburn
Briar La
May Lea
Oak Lea
Dene Ct
View
Fair
Durham Gdns
South
LANE
Brookside
Cragside
Friarside
Glebeside
Brookside
Burnside
Newton St
Chapel Ct

156

Potter H

Grid References

F G H 143 J

I

2

3

4

5

6

7

F G H 167 J K

23 24 25 46 45 44 543

F G H **147** J

High Moorsley

Moorsley Road

Front Street
York St
Coal Bank Farm

Golf Course

Ele Vale

Elemore Golf Course

Lorne St

1

2
Hetton le Hill

Sunderland
Durham County

Elemore Lane

Hillside

3

Lawrence C
St

Newby Lane

4

Elemore Hall School

160

Elemore Grange

Church Vale

5

Coalford Lane

Littletown

Cross Street

Plantation Avenue

Hastings House Farm

Green Lane

6

Littletown House

Littleton Lane

543

Cook's Hold

7

F G H **171** J K

Kell Crs
Jub Crs

The Croft

Local Avenue
Av

Sherburn Hill

Haswell Moor Farm

33 34 35 46

A   B **148**   C   D   E

**Easington
Lane**

Cemetery

Murton
Willow Cresc
High Street
South Hetton Road A182

**Elemore
Vale**

Golf Course

Elemore
Golf Course

Brick Garth
Brick Garth
Dorset St
Lane
Prospect
Crs
Thames
Rydal Av
Cramsit
Coniston
Tyne Street
Tamar St
Tay St

Ulliswater Av
Windermere
Loweswater Av
Buttermere Av
Avenue
White Hill Rd
Sheriff's
Moor
Ruskin Av

Easington Lane
Primary School

Qu Elizabeth
South
View
South
View

Hetton le Hill

Front Street
Industrial Estate

Patrick Crs
Terrace
Conishead
Donald Av
Keswick Ter
Windsor
Dr
Argyle
Pl
Ravensworth
Court
Coldwell Cl
FRONT
STREET

Pinedale Drive

**South
Hetton**

South Hetton
Primary School

B1280
SALTER'S
LANE

159

Coldwell   Burn

Fallowfield

**High
Haswell**

Low Haswell
Farm

Green Lane

Green Lane

Haswell
Lodge

County
Junior & Infant
School

Church St
Faraday Ter
Windsor Terrace
Richmond Ter

B1280
FRONT
STREET

Station Street
George
St
Chapel
Lane
PO
Blossom
Almond
Close
Acre Dr
Hall
Lane

Haswe

Green
Lane

Haswell Moor
Farm

A   B **172**   C **aswell
Plough**   D   E

Hesse ville Crs
Gloucester
Marine
Kent

B1280
SALTER'S
LANE

F G H **149** J

I

2

3

Little Coop House
Farm

We
Far

Hetton
rial Estate

th Hetton
alth Centre

A182

PO

Windermere Road

Bevin Hawthorn Cottages

Greencroft

Coronation
Sq

Sq

Gr T

West Lane

Great Coop House
Farm

45

Ashwood

Oakwood

Maythorne
Drive

West Moor House
Farm

Duncombe
Moor

A182

162

4

44

Hallfield

5

Holy
Cross

Pesspool Lane

Pesspool Lane

Chestnut
Drive

Pesspool
Hall

Low Ling
Close

6

43

II

High Ling
Close

DURHAM LANE

B1283

Moor House
Farm

7

F   G   H   151   J

44   45   46

I

Hawthorn
Hawthorn Hive

Beacon
Point

2

Shippersea
Bay

45

3

White
Lea

Dene Av

East View

Raby Av

West Av

The Crs

4

**EASINGTON
COLLIERY**

Lane

John Street

Thomas St

Thorpe St

Cem

Tower
St

Abbot St

Alan St

Anthony St

Argus St

Argent St

Ascot St

Ashton St

Andrew St

Alfred St

Arthur St

Barwick St

Office Street

Charles St

School
Street

PO

BYRON ST

Browning St

Castle St

B1283

Barwick St

Bradley St

Bolam St

Court St

5

Welfare Close

Blake St

Beatty St

Camp St

Bede
Street

Boyd St

Butler St

Cornwall St

Cardiff St

Memorial Avenue

Baldwin St

Boston St

Corbett St

STATION ROAD

44

Paradise

6

Horden Burn

Springfield Ter

Garfield Terrace

Angus Terrace

Fairport Terrace

Finchcape Terrace

Maritime Crs

Maritime Crs

Horden
Point

Culloden Ter

SUNDERLAND ROAD

543

7

44   45

F   G   H   175   J   K

A1086

Thorpe

Horden & Easington   Kilbur

F **G** **H** **153** **J**

19 20

Flass Hall

I

Valley
Rose Ct
B6302
Vale Garth
Cliffords Gate
Western Av
Willow Rd
Drive
Hamsteels County Junior & Infant School
Rowley Crs
New House
Swallow Close
Cstl vw
Fir Terraces
Prstb Cl
Esh Winning Industrial Estate
B6302
South Terrace
Castlefields

Esh Winning

Osprey Cl
Falcon vw
Woodlands
Newhouse Av
Esh Winning Child Hlth Clinic
Fair View
Hill View
Coppice Hill

2

Osprey Cl
Dene Park
Arbourcourt Av
Road
Evenwood Rd
Brandon Road
Burnell Rd
Acton Road
Pine View Villas

Raven Court
Birch Place
Cypress Park
Arbourcourt Av
Ridding
Riddng Ct
Mckennas Sports Club
STATION VW
NEWHOUSE ROAD
DURHAM ROAD

Merlin Ct
The Oaks
The Larches
Redwood
Ridding
Road
Phntree
The Wynds
Cem
PO
Station Avenue

3

Rowan Court
College View
Waterhouses JMI School
Holburn Wood

4

166

Station Street
Russell Street
River Deerness

Standalone

5

Waterhouses Wood

Brandon Lane

6

West Brandon

Baal Hill

7

Weather Hill Wood

Wols Sham Road

F **G** **H** **J** **K**

19 20

South Brandon

42 41 40 39

A   B   154   C   D   E

Flasshall Lane

Flass Hall

Rag Path Wood

1

Hare Holme Farm

2

Eshwood Hall

Prospect place

PO

Fairfalls Terrace

Rock Ter
Edward Ter
Prospect Ter
Cooperative Ter

Waltons Ter

New Brancepeth

New Brancepeth Primary School

Tuscan Cl

Rowley Cl

Pringle Pl

Doric Road

Pringle Grove

3

Hill House

Pringle Cl

4

165

Stobb House

5

Brandon Lane   Pit Lane

Cemet

40

6

Pithouse Plantation

Morley Farm

7

Maple Court

Brancepeth Vw

Forest

Ashbeck

Scripton

Beech

Whellington Road

421   22

A   B   176   C   D   E
Little White

Brawn's Den

Quarry Hill

Morley Lane

Ushaw Moor Infant School

Temperance Ter

PO

Ushaw Moor

Station Road

Ushaw Moor Cricket Club

Red Burn

42

41

155

F G H J

I

2

3

4

168

5

6

7

Broom
Hall

Usher Moor
Junior School

St. Josephs
R C School

Cemetery

B6302

Oakridge Av
Ash Av
Holly Pk
Lilac Gv
Park Pk
Fir Pk
Broom Crescent
Maple Pk
Pine Pk
Hollywell
Court
Chestnut Gv
Broom
Road
Valley View
Thornley Cl
Deerness Sports Cen
Beech Gv
Elm Gv
Rowley Dr
Elder Dr
H Ct
Broom Hall Dr
Brancpeth Close
Stockley Court
Cst VW

BROOM LANE

Broompark

B6302 **BROOM LANE**

Cooke's Wood

Deerness Valley
Walk

River
Deerness

Mill Lane

Alum
Waters

Baxter
Wood

Stone Bridge

A690

Langley
Hall Farm

Front
Street

Langley Moor
Primary School

N B Cl

Grove Terrace

Langley
Moor

Black Road
PO

Brandon Lane
Lyne's Dr
Langley Crs
Byr
Blair Ct
St Cuthberts Wk

HIGH STREET
High St S Back

Littleburn La

Littleburn
Industrial Est

Stack
Garth

Brandon
United
Football Club

Tiree Cl

Brandon Cricket
Club

Deerness Heights
North
End
Midhill Cl
High Mdw

Pear
Lea
Pine
Lea
Redwood
Rowan Lea
Poplar Lea
Oakgreen
Flats
Holly Lea
Red Firs
Lime Pk
Hw Pk

Meadowfield
Sports Centre

Council
Offices

Mill Road

St Patricks
RC School

Durham
Business
Centre

Bus
Cen

Littleburn Road

Rosebay Road

Littleburn
Industrial
Estate

BRANDON

Sawmill
Lane
Schron Gill
White Ceda
Beech Park
Alder Park
Alder Park
Alder Park
Meadow
Briar
Carvis Cl

Carr Avenue
Victoria Avenue
Station Avenue
Silver Cts
Lowland
PO
Acorn Pl
Chalfont Way
Penny Wy
Arundel Way
Chalfont Way
Brckn
Alston Rd
Strth Cl
Chl Wy
Vcrg
Fts

Brandon Modern
School

Leesfield Gardens
Leesfield Dr

Grove Road
Avenue
Fir Av
Elm Av
Gy Rd
Moor
Edge
Health
Centre

South
View
Central Av
Station Rd

West
View

Dominion Road

Murrayfield
Drive
Cavendish Ct
Lexington Court
Clover Laid
Hazel Av
Winchester Drive

Red Barns

A690

Meadowfield

PO
A690
Meadowfield Clinic

Dominco
Villas

Edwardson Road
St John's Road

Meadowfield
Industrial
Estate

Browney County
Primary School

Durham
Golf

Fm

BROWNEY LANE

Sherburn Grange

GILESGATE

PO

Station Rd

St Giles Cl

Maynards Rw

Willans Buildings

William Place

SHERBURN ROAD

Police Station

Malvern Villas

St Josephs RC School

Frank St

Turnbull Cl

Mill House

Allington Place

Council Offices

157

Dragonville Industrial Estate

F

College of St Hild & St Bede

Church Lane

DH

G

29

H

FRONT STREET

A181

J

Lane

A1(M)

30

B1283

I

Bowling Green

River Wear

Durham City Cricket Club

Magistrates Court

Green

Inland Revenue

University of Durham

Durham City Rugby Club

Laurel Avenue County Junior & Infant School

Maple Av

Laurel Av

Ash Av

Oak Av

Pine Av

Fir Avenue

Oak Avenue

Londonderry Gr

Chandler

Bede Avenue

Oswald

Hilda

Cuthbert

Cuthbert

Avenue

Haigh Terrace

Hilda Av

Walg Cl

Sutherland Place

A181

42

2

Durham Johnston Comprehensive School

Old Durham

Bent House Lane

Bent House Farm

Shincliffe Lane

A177

University of Durham

Houghall College

Old Durham Beck

MILL LANE

B1198

SHINCLIFFE LANE

41

A1(M)

3

I7

WILLOW TREE AVENUE A177

Shincliffe

Low Road

Low Gn

St Mary's Clo

Hill E

Jubil

PH

High Street

Hall Lane

Manor Farm

4

LC

170

High Shincliffe

Hillcrest

Heathways

Lnds

Beal WK

Foxton

Thrpton

Meldon Wy

Mitford Cl

LL

Apperley Av

Whitwell Acres

Whitwell Acres

Shincliffe C of E Junior & Infant School

Hill Mdw

Ancroft Garth

The Lings

Brnly Cl

Whitwell Acres

5

40

West Grange

Strawberry Lane

Telford Close

LC

Low Grange

6

oughall Farm

A177

High Grange

539

7

F

G

High Butterby Farm

H

179

uth range

J

K

A177

Whitw South

Marlene Avenue

Dallymore

F **G** **H** **159** **J**

3 34 35

Haswell Moor Farm

Kell Crs

Jubilee Crs

Sherburn Hill

The Croft

Local Avenue

Local AV

LOCAL AV

PO

FRONT STREET

Pinders Wy

I

42

B1283

Crime Rigg

Crime Rigg

DURHAM LANE

B1283

2

Woodside Bank

Hill House

3

Church Lane

Shadforth

Lu

41

Bridge Court

Chare

Dene Ct

Oliver Crs

George Square

4

172

Ox Close

5

A181

A181

40

6

SILENT BANK

Strawberry Hill

High Croft House

DH6

DUNELM ROA

7

539

Old Cassop

3 34 35

F **G** **H** **181** **J** **K**

D House

B6291

High Ling Close

161

F G H J

Moor House Farm

B1283

DURHAM

I

Council Offices

2

Mill Hill

Cook

Sandy Carrs

Westmoor Farm

B1283

B1280

Burdon Drive

3

Shotton Road

41

Cem
Shotton RC JMI School

Fleming Field

Worton Close
Waverley Cl
Waskerley Dr
Station   Road
Belverdere Gdns
Westgarth
Atkinson Gr
Sutherland Gr
Grove
Thornhill Rd
Winfield
Thornhill Rd
Winfield

Modern Mixed School
Surgery
Shotton Colliery Primary School

Southdene Medical Centre
Ind Est
Arden Street
Jbl Pl

Front-Street Industrial Est

Shotton   Road

Dnlm Pl
Tudor
East St
Shotton
Windsor Pl
Eden
Vw

4

174

Whitworth

Shotton Colliery

SALTER'S LANE

Hawthorne
Lilac
Hazel Terrace
Terrace
West St
West St
Terrace

Surgery
PO
King St
Friar
Victoria Street
Terrace
Milton Grove

Lane

Brack

Shotton

5

Grove Court
Hooper
Ter
Millbank

Council Offices

St
Byron Ter
Burn's Ter

Low Crow's House

PO
Dixon Est
Al cook
Ter
Bruce Terrace
Dixon
Est Glasier

B1280

Dixon Est Bungalows

6

Edder Acres

B1279

Green Hills

Thornley Station Industrial Estate

Watson Cl
CG
CG
Dodds Cl
PATTON WALK
Weardale Park

7

39

183

SALTER'S LANE

40

5 39

Edderacres Plantation

176

166

Woisingham Road

421

22

A

B

C

D

E

1

Brawn's Den

Quarry Hill

Little White

Morley Lane

Woisingham Road

A690

2

Stockley Beck

Goodwell Field

Goodwell Lea

The Old Forge

Golf Course

3

Stockley Fell Plantation

Brancepeth

A690

Brancepeth Castle Golf Club

PO

Brancepeth Castle

4

Hundred Acre Plantation

Stockley

Stockley Lane

A690

5

Oakenshaw

Park House

Ox Close Farm

A690

Whitworth Lane

6

Dunelm Industrial Estate

Lingey Close

7

Works

A690

Old House Beck

Low Willington Industrial Estate

421

A

B

C

22

D

E

39

38

37

421

536

Cemetery

1 grid square represents 500 metres

F
G Red Barns
H
167
J

Carvis Cl
Clover Laid
Hazel Av
Cft Rigg Av
Dominion Road
West View
South Vie
A V
Av
Villas
Browney County Primary School
Littleburn

Murrayfield
Drive
Cavendish Gr
Lexington Cl
Court
Jackson
Winchester Drive
Road

A690
24
25
39

I

Scripton Lane

BROWNEY LANE

B6300

Scripton

2

River

Holywell Beck

Nafferton

Burnigil

38

3

Holywell

Brancepeth
Park

Scripton Lane

4

River Wear

178

37

5

East
Parks

Coldstre
Farm

Spring
Wood

6

536

7

age
Bank
PO

Weardale Way

Works

Lane

Mill

23
24
25

F
G
H Woodhouse
arm
J
K

Esb Ct
E Ct
NWb Ct

F G H 169 J

Croxdale 179

Whitwe
South

A177

South
Grange

High Butterby
Farm

Dallymore drive

Marlene
Avenue

George

Horton Crs

I

Robson
Crs

Phill

Bowburn North
Industrial Estate

Pr Charles

St Mary's Ct

Castle Av

Tweddle Ter

Burn Av

Winn St

Avenue

Edward

2

Burn St

Bow St

Bowburn South
Industrial Estate

PO

Runc

Steave

High
Croxdale

3

DURHAM R

Bowburn

4

Durham Service Area

180

37

Tursdale
House

LC

5

A688

Street

East Street

Hett

West St

CV CT

Leeman's Lane

6

536

Broom Hill
Farm

Works

Ramsay St

School St

Tursdale

7

F G Hett Moor H J K

Old Cassop

F G H **171** J

Dene House Farm

B6291

Dene View

Cassop

PO

Luke Avenue

STREET

Cemetery

FRONT

Church Street

Cassop Primary School

Quarrington Hill

B6291

Quarrington Hill Industrial Estate

PO

Malcolm Av

Hazel Av

Avenue

David Terrace

Carr House

182

wn Kelloe

Cemetery

Ann Av

school

Av

Mary Crs

Kelloe JMI School

Kelloe

Kelloe Beck

Ramona Avenue

Woodland

Crescent

Tate Av

Sharon Avenue

Tate Avenue

PO

Low Raisby

Coxhoe East House

I

2

3

4

5

6

7

F G H J K

Garmondsway

182

A   436   B   **172**   C   37   D   E

1

2

3

4

181

5

6

7

A   436   B   C   37   D   E

1 grid square represents 500 metres

Wheat Hill

Cemetery

Thornley RC School

Health Clinic Industrial Est
Police Stn
Surgery
FRONT STREET
Pcly St
Black La

Quilstyle Road
Henderson Avenue
Quetlaw Road
Cain Terrace
Wheatley Terrace
Wheatley Hill Primary School
Shakespeare Street
Moor St
Brns St
Wordsworth Av
Woodlands Avenue
Cemetery Road
Shinwell Terrace
R Ter
Lindell Terrace
Dalton Ter
PO
Lk T
And Ter
Brn Ct
H B
W S

Wingate Lane

A181

White House

Bankdam Farm

Thornley Hall

B1278

Green Lane

Old Wingate

Nature Reserve

Kelloe Law

Carr House

Cemetery

Town Kelloe

Wingate House

Station Road

Fairlawns

Deaf Hill Primary School
PO

Southern Law

SALTER'S LANE

Windsor St

Rdwll St

The Medical Centre

North Moor Avenue

Barrel Crs

Trimdon Grange Industrial Estate

B1278

Rose Street

Luke Street

Trimdon Grange Health Clinic

Rothbury

Kielder Drive

N P

Harwood Ct

PO

Trimdon Grange

Beech Grove

Cemetery

F G H 173 J

Weardale Park

ON WALK

39 40 39

Edderacres Plantation

I

B1280

A181 A181 2

Durham Road

Taylor Grove

Wingrove

Greenhills Est

The Maltings

Wellfield Road

Walton Terrace

Dodds Ter

North Road

Burdon Crs

Wellfield Comprehensive Sch

Ingram Wy

Glaisby Ct

Roxby Wynd

Stewart

Martindale Wk

Dr

38

King's Road

Coronation Road

Oaklea Sch Obs Ter Clinic

Snaith Ter

Vicarage Est

Vicarage Estate

3

Wingate

B1280

Dawson Rd

Newd Coln Arms Av

Gray Sq

Gully Road

Queen's Road

New Cross Rd

Forest Gate

Woodland View

PO

County Junior Mixed School

Wingate Grange Farm

Moor Lane

4

Wingate Grange Industrial Estate

NORTH ROAD

Wingate RC Junior & Infant School

184

37

Pickering St

FRONT ST

C Sc

PO

Market Crescent

Station Rd

Station Pk

5

Rodrigo St

Lake Vw

Lake Bank

Ter

Church St

Acclom Ct

Vane

Wingate Road

Deaf Hill

Rydale Ct

Malvern Crs

argaret Ter

Beech Gve

Russel Crs

Wood View

Lbmm Sd

Lbnm Crs

sprngdl Av

Station Town

FRONT ST

MILBANK TER

Newholme Est

6

Cnnm St

Trimdon Colliery

West Woodburn

36

Low Dyke Park Street Road

ws St

7

se Lane

Woodlands Close

39 40

Hurworth Bryan Farm

F G H J K

TS28

184

A   B   **174**   C   D   E

Edderacres Plantation

I

Shotton

441

39

Golf Course

A181

The Maltings

2

Castle Eden & Peterlee Golf Club

South Vw

B1281

Roxby Wynd

Martindale Wk

Stewart Dr

38

Vicarage Estate

Gray Sq

3

Road

Thacmyers

A19(T)

Mill Hill

Castle Eden

Lane

Heads Hope

4

183

37

Eden Va

PO

5

STATION RD

Rodridge Pk

Lake Bank

Lake Vw

Church St

Acclom St

Vane St

FRONT ST

Station Town

Ferndale Cl

6

Beachdale Cl

MILBANK TER

Newholme Est

Cem

Hutton Henry

Rodridge Hall

Hutton Henry C of E School

Street

PO

Hutton Crs

The Oaks

Front

Hutton Crs

536

Ambrooke Ct

7

B1280

Rodridge Farm

Blakeley Hill

Leechmire

441

42

TS2   A   B   C   D   E

I grid square represents 500 metres

F
G
H
J
I

185

B1281

Hesleden Road

Hardwick Hall Farm

Hotel

B1281

Castle Eden Dene Nature Reserve

Dene Leazes

Hesleden Road

Sycamore Drive

Hazel Dr
Hazel Dr

Gray Avenue

B1281

Cem

Hesleden County Junior & Infant School

The Elms

Hig
He

Front St

PO

Church St

Harold Wilson Dr

Southfield Farm

Hillcrest Place

Station Rd

Eden Cottages

East Ter

Hesleden

The Bleachery

Monk
Hesle

Hulam

Nesbitt Hall

A19(T)

Hutton House

Bellows Burn Lane

Sheraton Hill

Bellows Burn Lane

Durham Cou
Hartlepool

A19(T)

Fleet Shot

F
G
H
J
K

1
2
3
4
5
6
7

39
38
37
536

3
44
45

Albany 102 D6
Annfield Plain 125 J5
Annitsford 38 D7
Ashington 23 G2
Axwell Park 84 B4
Aykley Heads 156 C5
Ayres Quay 14 B2
Ayton 116 B3
Backworth 48 E5
Bank Top 66 D2
Barley Mow 115 J4
Barlow 83 F6
Bar Moor 66 C6
Barmston 117 H1
Battle Hill 58 E5
Beaconhill 37 K2
Beacon Lough 101 J1
Beamish 113 J7
Bearpark 155 H6
Bebside 29 G4
Bedlington 29 G4
Bedlington Station 29 H4
Bell's Close 68 C5
Belmont 157 K6
Benfieldside 122 C2
Bensham 10 C6
Benton Square 58 C1
Benwell 69 F5
Biddick 117 F2
Biddick Hall 91 F2
Bill Quay 13 M3
Billy Mill 60 B3
Birtley 101 K7
Bishopwearmouth 14 B4
Black Callerton 53 J2
Blackfell 102 C7
Blackhall Mill 95 H6
Blackhill 122 C4
Blakelaw 69 G1
Blaydon 84 B1
Blaydon Burn 83 G3
Blaydon Haughs 68 C7
Blyth 34 E1
Boldon Colliery 90 D2
Bomarsund 29 J1
Bothal 22 B3
Bournmoor 131 G4
Bowburn 179 K3
Brancepeth 176 C3
Branch End 79 H5
Brandon 166 E6
Brenkley 36 B5
Bridgehill 122 C3
Broom Hill 109 F4
Broom Hill 147 K2
Broomley 78 B7
Broompark 167 J2
Brunswick Village 45 K4
Burdon 134 B4
Burnhope 141 H4
Burnopfield 97 H7
Burnside 131 K5
Burradon 47 H4
Byermoor 98 B6
Byker 7 G6
Bywell 78 D4
Callerton 53 K4
Callerton Lane End 53 F3
Cambois 30 E1
Camperdown 47 J4
Carley Hill 106 B2
Carr Hill 87 H5
Carrville 157 K5
Cassop 181 J2
Castle Eden 184 D3
Castleside 136 E1
Castletown 104 E4
Catchgate 125 F2
Causey 113 F1
Chester-le-Street 129 F4
Chester Moor 144 B1
Chilton Moor 146 E1
Chirton 2 A2
Chirton 60 C4
Choppington 23 F7
Chopwell 95 J4
Chowdene 100 D3
Clara Vale 66 B5
Cleadon 92 A4
Cleadon Park 76 A7
Clifton 26 E4
Clough Dene 111 K3
Coalburns 81 J5
Cold Hesledon 150 C6
Colliery Row 132 A7
Collingwood 38 C4
Columbia 117 G2
Concord 102 E5
Consett 122 E5
Cornsay Colliery 152 D6
Cowpen 30 D6
Coxhoe 180 E7
Coxlodge 56 A5
Craghead 127 G6
Cramlington 37 K3
Crawcrook 66 C7
Crookgate Bank 98 A7
Crookhall 123 H6
Crookhill 67 G6
Croxdale 178 C4
Cullercoats 51 H7
Dalton-le-Dale 150 A4

Darras Hall 42 E4
Dawdon 151 F3
Deaf Hill 183 F6
Deckham 11 H8
Delves 138 D1
Deneside 150 B2
The Dene 109 G4
Denton Burn 68 C4
Deptford 14 A2
Deptford 106 A5
Dinnington 44 E2
Dipton 110 E6
Donwell 102 D4
Downhill 105 F1
Doxford Park 134 A3
Dudley 47 G2
Dunston 9 G6
Dunston Hill 8 E9
Durham 16 B4
Earsdon 49 J3
Easington 162 B5
Easington Colliery 163 G4
Easington Lane 148 C7
East Boldon 91 G4
East Cramlington 39 F3
East Denton 68 E3
East Gateshead 11 M2
East Hartford 33 H4
East Herrington 133 H1
East Holywell 49 F2
East Kyo 125 K1
East Law 108 D4
East Rainton 147 G4
East Sleekburn 30 C3
East Stanley 112 E7
Ebchester 109 F3
Eden Vale 184 C4
Edmondsley 143 F2
Eighton Banks 101 K3
Eland Green 43 H1
Elemore Vale 160 A1
Elswick 9 G1
Eltringham 79 K2
Elvet Hill 16 B9
Esh 153 J4
Esh Winning 165 F2
Farringdon 119 J7
Fatfield 116 E6
Fawdon 55 J3
Fellgate 89 J3
Felling 12 D7
Felling Shore 12 E3
Fellside 84 D6
Fence Houses 131 J6
Fenham 69 H4
Fleming Field 173 F3
Flint Hill 111 H5
Follingsby 89 F7
Fordley 47 H2
Forest Hall 57 K1
Framwellgate Moor 156 C4
Fulbeck 20 C2
Fulwell 106 C1
Gateshead 11 H1
Gilesgate 17 H1
Gilesgate 157 F6
Gilesgate Moor 17 L2
Glebe 116 E1
Gosforth 56 B5
Grangetown 120 E5
Grange Villa 128 A2
Grasswell 132 B5
Great Eppleton 148 C3
Great Lumley 145 G1
Greencroft 125 F3
Greenhill 149 H4
Greenside 82 C3
Grindon 119 F3
The Grove 122 B6
Guide Post 23 F6
Hallgarth 158 D5
Hamsterley 109 H1
Hamsterley Mill 96 B7
Harelaw 125 G1
Harlow Green 101 H3
Harperley 125 J1
Harraton 116 C5
Hartley 41 H4
Harton 75 J5
Hasting Hill 118 E4
Haswell 160 E6
Haswell Plough 172 C1
Hawthorn 162 C2
Hazlerigg 46 A5
Healeyfield 136 D3
Heaton 6 F1
Hebburn 73 G6
Hebburn Colliery 73 G3
Hebburn New Town 72 E5
Heddon-on-the-Wall 66 A2
Hedley Hill 164 A2
Hedworth 90 A2
Hendon 15 H7
Hepscott 27 K1
Hepscott Park 27 J5
Hesleden 185 H3
Hett 179 F5
Hetton Downs 148 A3
Hetton-le-Hill 159 K2
Hetton-le-Hole 148 A5
Heworth 13 G8
High Callerton 43 G7

High Church 20 C6
High Dubmire 131 K7
Highfield 96 E4
High Forge 113 J5
High Friarside 97 F7
High Handenhold 114 A7
High Haswell 160 C5
High Mickley 79 K5
High Moorsley 159 G1
High Shields 74 E3
High Shincliffe 169 H5
High Southwick 106 A2
High Spen 96 B1
High Urpeth 114 B6
High Westwood 109 H2
Hill Top 111 G4
Hill Top 154 C4
Hillview 120 C5
Hirst 24 A2
Hobson 111 K2
Holmside 142 C1
Holy Cross 58 E7
Holywell 39 H5
Holywell 40 C6
Hooker Gate 96 B2
Horden 175 F3
Horsley 64 D3
Horsley Hill 75 K3
Horsleyhope 136 A5
Houghton 65 J1
Houghton-le-Spring 132 B7
Howdon 59 J7
Howdon Pans 74 A2
Humbledon 119 K3
Hutton Henry 184 D6
Hylton Castle 104 E3
Hylton Red House 105 H1
Isabella Pit 35 F2
Iveston 124 B6
Jarrow 74 B5
Jesmond 71 F3
Kelloe 181 G6
Kenton 55 H6
Kenton Bankfoot 54 E4
Kenton Bar 55 H6
Kibblesworth 100 E7
Killingworth 47 K7
Killingworth Moor 48 C7
Killingworth Village 48 A5
Kimblesworth 143 K5
Kingston Park 55 H4
Kip Hill 112 E5
Knitsley 138 B2
Lady Park 100 D4
Lambton 116 C3
Lamesley 100 D4
Lanchester 140 A5
Langley Moor 168 A4
Langley Park 154 C3
The Lawe 3 J4
Leadgate 95 G1
Leadgate 123 K3
Leam Lane 88 C6
Leamside 146 B6
Lemington 68 A4
Lintz 111 H1
Lintzford 96 D6
Little Thorpe 162 D7
Littletown 159 H5
Loansdean 26 C1
Lobley Hill 86 B6
Longbenton 57 J2
Low Eighton 101 H5
Lowes Barn 168 A3
Low Fell 87 F7
Low Greenside 82 C2
Low Moorsley 147 J7
Low Prudhoe 64 B7
Low Thornley 83 J7
Low Westwood 109 G1
Ludworth 172 A3
Lumley Thicks 130 E6
Lynemouth 18 B2
Lyons 148 B6
Maiden Law 125 J7
Marden 50 E7
Marley Hill 99 F4
Marley Pots 105 K2
Marsden 76 C6
Mason 45 F1
Mayfield 38 D3
Meadowfield 167 J6
Medburn 42 A7
Medomsley 109 J5
Mickley Square 79 K3
Middle Herrington 119 F6
Middle Rainton 147 F5
The Middles 126 E4
Mill Dam 74 E2
Millfield 106 A6
Monkseaton 50 B3
Monkton 73 J7
Monkwearmouth 106 B4
Moor End 157 K5
Moorside 137 H1
Morpeth 20 D5
Mount Pleasant 11 K7
Murton 49 K7
Murton 149 G4
Nedderton 28 B6
Nelson Village 38 A1
Nettlesworth 143 K4

Nevilles Cross 168 B2
Newbiggin 139 J4
Newbiggin-by-the-Sea 19 F6
Newbiggin Hall Estate 54 D6
Newbottle 132 C4
New Brancepeth 166 D3
Newcastle upon Tyne 6 B7
New Delaval 34 D4
Newfield 128 C2
New Hartley 40 B2
New Herrington 132 C1
New Kyo 125 K3
Newlands 108 D5
Newsham 35 F3
New Silksworth 119 K7
Newton 62 A5
Newton Hall 62 B4
Newton Hall 157 F3
New Town 90 D3
New Town 132 E7
New York 60 A1
North Blyth 31 G4
North End 156 A5
North Hylton 104 C6
Northlea 135 H6
North Seaton 24 D4
North Seaton Colliery 24 B5
North Shields 2 A4
North Walbottle 53 J7
Offerton 118 C3
Old Burdon 134 A5
Old Cassop 171 G7
Old Fold 11 L4
Old Quarrington 180 D5
Old Wingate 182 D3
Ornsby Hill 140 C5
Ouston 115 G4
Ovingham 63 K7
Ovington 63 G7
Oxclose 116 C1
Oxhill 126 B1
Page Bank 176 E7
Painshawfield 79 G6
Pallion 105 H5
Palmersville 58 C1
Parkside 150 D3
Path Head 67 K7
Pegswood 21 J1
Pelaw 13 H5
Pelton 128 D1
Pelton Fell 129 F3
Pennywell 119 F2
Penshaw 118 A7
Percy Main 74 C1
Perkinsville 114 E6
Peterlee 174 C4
Philadelphia 132 B2
Pickering Nook 111 J2
Pittington 158 E3
Pity Me 156 C2
Plawsworth 144 B4
Ponteland 43 J2
Portobello 115 J2
Preston 60 E2
Preston Grange 50 D7
Prestwick 44 B4
Primrose 74 A7
Prudhoe 80 C1
Quaking Houses 126 B5
Quarrington Hill 181 G3
Quebec 152 E5
Rainton Bridge 147 H2
Rainton Gate 146 B7
Rickleton 116 B7
Roker 107 F3
Rosehill 73 G2
Rowlands Gill 97 G3
Rowley 137 G3
Running Waters 170 E5
Ryhope 135 F1
Ryhope Colliery 120 E7
Ryton 66 E6
Ryton Woodside 82 D2
Sacriston 143 G4
St Anthony's 13 G1
St Peter's 7 H9
Saltwell 10 F9
Scotland Gate 29 G1
Scotswood 68 E7
Seaham 151 F1
Seaton 40 D3
Seaton 134 D7
Seaton Burn 37 H7
Seaton Delaval 39 K4
Seaton Sluice 41 F3
Seghill 39 G7
Shadforth 171 H3
Shankhouse 33 J6
Sheep Hill 97 K6
Sheepwash 22 E5
Sherburn 170 D1
Sherburn Hill 171 H1
Sheriff Hill 87 H6
Shield Row 113 F6
Shincliffe 169 H4
Shiney Row 131 K2
Shiremoor 49 J6
Shotley Bridge 108 B7
Shotton 174 B6
Shotton Colliery 173 G4
Simonside 74 C7

South Beach 35 J3
South Bents 92 E6
Southfield 38 C5
South Gosforth 56 D6
South Hetton 160 E2
South Hylton 105 F7
South Moor 126 B3
South Newsham 34 E4
South Pelaw 129 H1
South Shields 3 L6
South Stanley 126 C2
Southwick 106 A4
Spital Tongues 4 C2
Springwell 102 C4
Springwell 119 J3
Stakeford 23 H6
Stanley 126 D1
Stannington 27 G6
Stargate 83 F1
Station Town 183 K6
Stella 67 J7
Stobhill 20 E7
Stobhillgate 21 F5
Stocksfield 79 F5
Stony Gate 132 E3
Stony Heap 124 C4
Street Gate 99 H3
Sulgrave 103 G5
Sunderland 14 C3
Sunderland 106 A5
Sunderland Bridge 178 C3
Sunniside 98 E3
Sunniside 132 A4
Swalwell 84 E3
Tanfield 112 B2
Tanfield Lea 112 B5
Tan Hills 144 A4
Tantobie 111 J4
Teams 9 L6
Team Valley 86 D7
Templetown 122 E6
Thorney Close 119 G5
Thornley 172 B7
Throckley 53 G7
Town Kelloe 182 A5
Tranwell 26 A2
Trimdon Colliery 183 F6
Trimdon Grange 182 D7
Tunstall 134 B1
Tursdale 179 K7
Tyne Dock 74 E4
Tynemouth 61 F2
Urpeth 114 E4
Ushaw Moor 154 E7
Usworth 102 E4
Walbottle 67 G2
Waldridge 128 E6
Walker 72 B6
Wall Nook 154 C2
Wallsend 72 B1
Wardley 13 M7
Washington 103 J7
Washington Village 117 F1
Waterhouses 164 E4
West Allotment 59 G1
West Boldon 90 E4
West Chirton 59 J5
West Denton 68 C2
Westerhope 54 B6
Western Hill 156 B7
West Harton 74 E5
West Herrington 118 D7
West Holywell 49 F3
West Jesmond 70 B1
West Kyo 125 H1
Westlea 28 D6
West Lea 149 K2
West Monkseaton 50 A6
West Moor 57 H1
Westoe 75 J2
West Park 75 G4
West Pelton 113 K7
West Rainton 146 D5
West Sleekburn 23 K6
West Wylam 80 E1
Wheatley Hill 160 B3
Whickham 85 F5
Whitburn 93 F3
Whitburn Colliery 77 F7
Whitehills 87 K7
Whiteleas 91 G1
White-le-Head 111 J5
Whitley Bay 51 G4
Whitley Sands 50 E2
Wickham Fell 99 F1
Wide Open 46 C4
Willington 59 G6
Willington Quay 73 J2
Windy Nook 87 K6
Wingate 183 H3
Winlaton 83 J2
Winlaton Mill 83 K6
Witherwack 105 J1
Witton Gilbert 143 H7
Woodbridge 18 B6
Woodhorn 18 C6
Woolsington 54 B2
Woolsington Hall 44 C7
Wrekenton 101 H2
Wylam 65 H6

USING THE STREET INDEX

Street names are listed alphabetically. Each street name is followed by its postal town or area locality, the Postcode District, the page number, and the reference to the square in which the name is found.

Standard index entries are shown as follows:

Abbay St *SWCK/CAS* SR5 .... **106** A4

Street names and selected addresses not shown on the map due to scale restrictions are shown in the index with an asterisk or with the name of an adjoining road in brackets:

Abingdon Ct *GOS/KPK* * NE3 .... **55** H3

Abbey Ms
  BDN/LAN/SAC
  (off Priory Ct) DH7 .... **143** H6

187

GENERAL ABBREVIATIONS

ACC ACCESS
ALY ALLEY
AP APPROACH
AR ARCADE
ASS ASSOCIATION
AV AVENUE
BCH BEACH
BLDS BUILDINGS
BND BEND
BNK BANK
BR BRIDGE
BRK BROOK
BTM BOTTOM
BUS BUSINESS
BVD BOULEVARD
BY BYPASS
CATH CATHEDRAL
CEM CEMETERY
CEN CENTRE
CFT CROFT
CH CHURCH
CHA CHASE
CHYD CHURCHYARD
CIR CIRCLE
CIRC CIRCUS
CL CLOSE
CLFS CLIFFS
CMP CAMP
CNR CORNER
CO COUNTY
COLL COLLEGE
COM COMMON
COMM COMMISSION
CON CONVENT
COT COTTAGE
COTS COTTAGES
CP CAPE
CPS COPSE
CR CREEK
CREM CREMATORIUM
CRS CRESCENT
CSWY CAUSEWAY
CT COURT
CTRL CENTRAL
CTS COURTS
CTYD COURTYARD
CUTT CUTTINGS
CV COVE
CYN CANYON
DEPT DEPARTMENT
DL DALE
DM DAM
DR DRIVE
DRO DROVE
DRY DRIVEWAY
DWGS DWELLINGS
E EAST
EMB EMBANKMENT
EMBY EMBASSY
ESP ESPLANADE
EST ESTATE
EX EXCHANGE
EXPY EXPRESSWAY
EXT EXTENSION
F/O FLYOVER
FC FOOTBALL CLUB
FK FORK
FLD FIELD
FLDS FIELDS
FLS FALLS
FLS FLATS
FM FARM
FT FORT
FWY FREEWAY
FY FERRY
GA GATE
GAL GALLERY
GDN GARDEN
GDNS GARDENS
GLD GLADE
GLN GLEN
GN GREEN
GND GROUND
GRA GRANGE
GRG GARAGE
GT GREAT
GTWY GATEWAY
GV GROVE
HGR HIGHER
HL HILL
HLS HILLS
HO HOUSE
HOL HOLLOW
HOSP HOSPITAL
HRB HARBOUR
HTH HEATH
HTS HEIGHTS
HVN HAVEN
HWY HIGHWAY
IMP IMPERIAL
IN INLET
IND EST INDUSTRIAL ESTATE
INF INFIRMARY
INFO INFORMATION
INT INTERCHANGE
IS ISLAND
JCT JUNCTION
JTY JETTY
KG KING
KNL KNOLL
L LAKE
LA LANE
LDG LODGE
LGT LIGHT
LK LOCK
LKS LAKES
LNDG LANDING
LTL LITTLE
LWR LOWER
MAG MAGISTRATE
MAN MANSIONS
MD MEAD
MDW MEADOWS
MEM MEMORIAL
MKT MARKET
MKTS MARKETS
ML MALL
ML MILL
MNR MANOR
MS MEWS
MSN MISSION
MT MOUNT
MTN MOUNTAIN
MTS MOUNTAINS
MUS MUSEUM
MWY MOTORWAY
N NORTH
NE NORTH EAST
NW NORTH WEST
O/P OVERPASS
OFF OFFICE
ORCH ORCHARD
OV OVAL
PAL PALACE
PAS PASSAGE
PAV PAVILION
PDE PARADE
PH PUBLIC HOUSE
PK PARK
PKWY PARKWAY
PL PLACE
PLN PLAIN
PLNS PLAINS
PLZ PLAZA
POL POLICE STATION
PR PRINCE
PREC PRECINCT
PREP PREPARATORY
PRIM PRIMARY
PROM PROMENADE
PRS PRINCESS
PRT PORT
PT POINT
PTH PATH
PZ PIAZZA
QD QUADRANT
QU QUEEN
QY QUAY
R RIVER
RBT ROUNDABOUT
RD ROAD
RDG RIDGE
REP REPUBLIC
RES RESERVOIR
RFC RUGBY FOOTBALL CLUB
RI RISE
RP RAMP
RW ROW
S SOUTH
SCH SCHOOL
SE SOUTH EAST
SER SERVICE AREA
SH SHORE
SHOP SHOPPING
SKWY SKYWAY
SMT SUMMIT
SOC SOCIETY
SP SPUR
SPR SPRING
SQ SQUARE
ST STREET
STN STATION
STR STREAM
STRD STRAND
SW SOUTH WEST
TDG TRADING
TER TERRACE
THWY THROUGHWAY
TNL TUNNEL
TOLL TOLLWAY
TPK TURNPIKE
TR TRACK
TRL TRAIL
TWR TOWER
U/P UNDERPASS
UNI UNIVERSITY
UPR UPPER
V VALE
VA VALLEY
VIAD VIADUCT
VIL VILLA
VIS VISTA
VLG VILLAGE
VLS VILLAS
VW VIEW
W WEST
WD WOOD
WHF WHARF
WK WALK
WKS WALKS
WLS WELLS
WY WAY
YD YARD
YHA YOUTH HOSTEL

POSTCODE TOWNS AND AREA ABBREVIATIONS

ASHBK/HED/RY Ashbrooke/Hedon/Ryhope
ASHGTN Ashington
BDLGTN Bedlington
BDN/LAN/SAC Brandon/Lanchester/Sacriston
BLAY Blaydon
BLYTH Blyth
BOL Boldon
BOLCOL Boldon Colliery
BW/LEM/TK/HW Benwell/Lemington/Throckley/Heddon-on-the-Wall
BYK/HTN/WLK Byker/Heaton/Walker
CHPW Chopwell
CLDN/WHIT/ROK Cleadon/Whitburn/Roker
CLS/BIR/GTL Chester-le-Street/Birtley/Great Lumley
CLSW/PEL Chester-le-Street west/Pelton
CNUT Central Newcastle upon Tyne
CON/LDGT Consett/Leadgate
CRAM Cramlington
CRK/WIL Crook/Willington
DHAM Durham
DIN/WO Dinnington/Wide Open
DUN/TMV Dunston/Team Valley
ELS/FEN Elswick/Fenham
FELL Felling
GATE Gateshead
GOS/KPK Gosforth/Kingston Park
HAR/WTLS Harton/Whiteleas
HEBB Hebburn
HLH Hetton-le-Hole
HLS Houghton-le-Spring
JES Jesmond
JRW Jarrow
LGB/HTN Longbenton/Heaton
LGB/KIL Longbenton/Killingworth
LWF/SPW/WRK Low Fell/Springwell/Wrekenton
MLFD/PNYW Millfield/Pennywell
MONK Monkseaton
MPTH Morpeth
NSHW North Shields west
NWBGN Newbiggin-by-the-Sea
PLEE/EAS Peterlee/Easington
PONT/DH Ponteland/Darras Hall
PRUD Prudhoe
PSHWF Painshawfield
RDHAMSE Rural Durham south & east
RHTLP Rural Hartlepool
ROWG Rowlands Gill
RYTON Ryton
SEA/MUR Seaham/Murton
SMOOR Shiremoor
SPEN Spennymoor
SSH South Shields
STKFD/GP Stakefold/Guide Post
STLY/ANP Stanley/Annfield Plain
STMFDH Stamfordham
SUND Sunderland
SUNDSW Sunderland southwest
SWCK/CAS Southwick/Castletown
TRIM Trimdon
TYNE/NSHE Tynemouth/North Shields east
WASHN Washington north
WASHS Washington south
WBAY Whitley Bay
WD/WHPE/BLK West Denton/Westerhope/Blakelaw
WEAR Weardale
WICK/BNPF Wickham/Burnopfield
WLSD/HOW Wallsend/Howdon
WNGT Wingate
WYLAM Wylam

Index - streets

Abb - Ald

A

Abbay St *SWCK/CAS* SR5 106 A4
Abbey Cl *MONK* NE25 50 B5
WASHS NE38 117 F1
Abbey Ct *GATE* NE8 11 H6
Abbey Dr *JRW* NE32 74 A4
TYNE/NSHE NE30 61 H2
WD/WHPE/BLK NE5 53 K6
Abbey Ga *MPTH* NE61 20 B6
Abbey Mdw *MPTH* NE61 20 B6
Abbey Ms
BDN/LAN/SAC
(off Priory Ct) DH7 143 H6
Abbey Rd *DHAM* DH1 156 B1
WASHS NE38 117 F1
Abbeywoods *DHAM* DH1 156 C1
Abbot Ct *GATE* NE8 11 H2
Abbots Cl *STKFD/GP* NE62 23 H5
Abbotsfield Cl *SUNDSW* SR3 133 K2
Abbotsford Gv
ASHBK/HED/RY SR2 14 C7
Abbotsford Pk *MONK* NE25 50 D5
Abbotsford Rd *FELL* NE10 12 C5
Abbotsford Ter *JES* NE2 70 D3
Abbotside Cl *CLSW/PEL* DH2 114 D4
Abbotside Pl
WD/WHPE/BLK NE5 68 A2
Abbotsmeade Cl
WD/WHPE/BLK NE5 69 F3
Abbot's Rd *GATE* NE8 6 A9
Abbots' Rw *DHAM* DH1 157 G6
Abbot St *PLEE/EAS* SR8 163 G4
Abbots Wk *STLY/ANP* DH9 113 K6
Abbots Wy *MPTH* NE61 20 C5
NSHW NE29 60 C2
WICK/BNPF NE16 85 F5
Abbs St *SWCK/CAS* SR5 106 D4
Abercorn Pl *WLSD/HOW* NE28 59 G4
Abercorn Rd
BW/LEM/TK/HW NE15 68 E6
SUNDSW SR3 119 H5
Abercrombie Pl
WD/WHPE/BLK NE5 69 F1
Aberdare Rd *SUNDSW* SR3 119 H7
Aberdeen *CLSW/PEL* DH2 115 F5
Aberdeen Ct *DIN/WO* NE13 55 H2
Aberdeen Dr *JRW* NE32 74 C7
Aberford Cl *WD/WHPE/BLK* NE5 53 K7
Aberfoyle *CLSW/PEL* DH2 115 F5
Aberfoyle Ct *STLY/ANP* DH9 127 F1
Abernethy *CLSW/PEL* DH2 115 F4
Abingdon Ct *GOS/KPK* * NE3 55 H3
Abingdon Rd
BYK/HTN/WLK NE6 72 D4
Abingdon Sq *CRAM* NE23 33 J6
Abingdon St *MLFD/PNYW* SR4 119 K1
Abingdon Wy *BOL* NE36 90 C5
BOLCOL NE35 90 B3
Abinger St *ELS/FEN* NE4 4 F6
Aboyne Sq *SUNDSW* SR3 119 H5
Acacia Av *HLS* DH4 131 J6
PLEE/EAS SR8 175 J4
Acacia Gv *HAR/WTLS* NE34 75 J6
HEBB NE31 73 G7
Acacia Rd *FELL* NE10 11 M4
Acacia St *DUN/TMV* NE11 86 C7
Acanthus Av *ELS/FEN* NE4 69 H4
Acclom St *WNGT* TS28 184 A6
Acer Ct *ASHBK/HED/RY* SR2 14 F9
Acer Dr *RDHAMSE* DH6 160 E6
Acklam Av *ASHBK/HED/RY* SR2 121 F5
Acomb Av *MONK* NE25 40 A6
WLSD/HOW NE28 59 F3
Acomb Cl *MPTH* NE61 27 F1
Acomb Ct *ASHBK/HED/RY* SR2 121 F5
BDLGTN NE22 29 G5
Acomb Crs *GOS/KPK* NE3 55 F4
Acomb Dr *WYLAM* NE41 65 G4
Acomb Gdns
WD/WHPE/BLK NE5 69 G3
Acorn Av *BDLGTN* NE22 29 F6
GATE NE8 10 A7
Acorn Cl *BDN/LAN/SAC* DH7 143 G4
Acornclose La
BDN/LAN/SAC DH7 142 E4
Acorn Pl *BDN/LAN/SAC* DH7 167 G6
Acorn Rd *JES* NE2 70 E1
Acreford Ct *STKFD/GP* NE62 22 E7
Acre Rigg Rd *PLEE/EAS* SR8 174 C3
Acton Dene *STLY/ANP* DH9 127 G1
Acton Dr *NSHW* NE29 60 B2
Acton Pl *LGB/HTN* NE7 71 H1
Acton Rd *BDN/LAN/SAC* DH7 165 H2
WD/WHPE/BLK NE5 68 D3
Adair Av *BW/LEM/TK/HW* NE15 69 G5
Adam St *PLEE/EAS* * SR8 175 J4
Adams Terrace *CON/LDGT* DH8 109 G4
Ada St *BYK/HTN/WLK* NE6 7 L5
SSH NE33 75 H2
Adderlane Rd *PRUD* NE42 80 E1
Adderstone Av *CRAM* NE23 38 C3
Adderstone Crs *JES* NE2 71 F1
Adderstone Gdns *NSHW* NE29 59 K1
Addington Crs *NSHW* NE29 60 C4
Addington Dr *BLYTH* NE24 35 G2
WLSD/HOW NE28 59 F3
Addison Cl *BYK/HTN/WLK* NE6 6 F4
Addison Ct *WLSD/HOW* NE28 73 J2
Addison Gdns *FELL* NE10 13 M9
Addison Rd *BOL* NE36 90 E5
BW/LEM/TK/HW NE15 68 B4
Addison St *ASHBK/HED/RY* SR2 15 J7
NSHW NE29 2 D4
Addycombe Ter
BYK/HTN/WLK NE6 71 J2
Adelaide Cl *SUND* SR1 15 H4
Adelaide Ct *GATE* NE8 10 F2
Adelaide Pl *SUND* SR1 15 J4
Adelaide Rw *SEA/MUR* * SR7 150 E1
Adelaide Ter *ELS/FEN* NE4 69 H6
Adeline Gdns *GOS/KPK* NE3 70 A1
Adelphi Cl *NSHW* NE29 60 A2
Adelphi Pl *BYK/HTN/WLK* NE6 7 L6
Adfrid Pl *PLEE/EAS* SR8 174 E3
Admington Ct *STKFD/GP* NE62 23 F6
Admiral Wy *SUNDSW* SR3 133 G2
Adolphus St
CLDN/WHIT/ROK SR6 93 F3
Adolphus St West
SEA/MUR SR7 150 E1
Adrian Pl *PLEE/EAS* SR8 175 F5
Adventure La *HLS* DH4 146 C5
Affleck St *GATE* NE8 10 E4
Afton Ct *HAR/WTLS* NE34 75 G6
Afton Wy *GOS/KPK* NE3 55 J5
Agar Rd *SUNDSW* SR3 119 H6
Agincourt *HEBB* NE31 73 F4
LGB/KIL NE12 47 K5
Agnes Maria St *GOS/KPK* NE3 56 A5
Agnes St *STLY/ANP* DH9 112 D7
Agricola Ct *SSH* NE33 3 G4
Agricola Gdns *WLSD/HOW* NE28 59 F4
Agricola Rd *ELS/FEN* NE4 4 A5
Aidan Av *WBAY* NE26 40 E2
Aidan Cl *DIN/WO* NE13 46 A3
LGB/KIL NE12 58 E1
STLY/ANP DH9 113 F7
Aidan Wk *GOS/KPK* NE3 56 D5
Aiden Wy *HLH* DH5 147 K3
Ailesbury St *MLFD/PNYW* SR4 106 A6
Ainderby Rd
BW/LEM/TK/HW NE15 66 D1
Ainsdale Gdns
WD/WHPE/BLK NE5 68 A1
Ainsley St *DHAM* DH1 16 A3
Ainslie Pl *WD/WHPE/BLK* NE5 69 F2
Ainsworth Av *HAR/WTLS* NE34 90 A1
Ainthorpe Cl *SUNDSW* SR3 120 B7
Ainthorpe Gdns *LGB/HTN* NE7 57 H6
Aintree Dr *CON/LDGT* DH8 108 D7
Aintree Gdns *GATE* NE8 10 B9
Aintree Rd *SUNDSW* SR3 119 H6
Airedale *WLSD/HOW* NE28 58 B5
Airedale Gdns *HLH* DH5 147 J6
Aireys Cl *HLS* DH4 132 A7
Airey Ter *BYK/HTN/WLK* NE6 72 C6
GATE NE8 10 D6
Airport Freightway
DIN/WO NE13 44 C7
Airville Mt *SUNDSW* SR3 134 A3
Aisgill Cl *CRAM* NE23 38 C2
Aisgill Dr *WD/WHPE/BLK* NE5 68 A2
Aiskell St *MLFD/PNYW* SR4 106 A7
AJ Cook Ter *RDHAMSE* DH6 173 H5
Akeld Cl *CRAM* NE23 38 C3
Akenside Hl *CNUT* NE1 5 L8
Alamein Av *HLH* DH5 132 D7
Alan St *PLEE/EAS* SR8 163 G4
Alansway Gdns *SSH* NE33 75 H3
Albany Av *LGB/KIL* * NE12 57 K2
Albany Ct *ELS/FEN* NE4 9 H2
Albany Rd *GATE* NE8 11 J1
Albany St East *SSH* NE33 75 H3
Albany St West *SSH* NE33 75 H3
Albany Wy *WASHN* NE37 102 E6
Albatross Wy *BLYTH* NE24 35 G4
Albemarle Av *JES* NE2 56 D7
Albemarle St *SSH* NE33 3 H7
Albert Av *WLSD/HOW* NE28 72 D1
Albert Ct *ASHBK/HED/RY* SR2 14 D9
Albert Dr *LWF/SPW/WRK* NE9 100 E1
Albert Pl *LWF/SPW/WRK* NE9 101 F1
WASHS NE38 117 H3
Albert Rd *BDLGTN* NE22 29 K4
CON/LDGT DH8 123 F5
JRW NE32 73 K4
MLFD/PNYW SR4 106 A6
WBAY NE26 41 G2
Albert St *CLS/BIR/GTL* DH3 129 J4
CLSW/PEL DH2 128 A2
DHAM DH1 16 A2
HEBB NE31 73 F4
JES NE2 6 A5
RDHAMSE DH6 172 C6
SEA/MUR SR7 150 E2
Albert Ter *LGB/KIL* NE12 57 J1
Albion Ct *SSH* NE33 3 G5
Albion Gdns *WICK/BNPF* NE16 111 H1
Albion Pl *SUND* SR1 14 D6
Albion Rd *NSHW* NE29 2 D1
Albion Rd West *NSHW* NE29 2 C2
Albion Rw *BYK/HTN/WLK* NE6 6 E6
Albion St *FELL* NE10 87 K6
MLFD/PNYW SR4 104 E7
Albion Ter *MPTH* NE61 18 C1
NSHW NE29 2 D1
Albion Wy *BLYTH* NE24 30 E7
CRAM NE23 33 K6
Albury Park Rd
TYNE/NSHE NE30 61 G3
Albury Pl *WICK/BNPF* NE16 84 E7
Albury Rd *JES* NE2 56 D7
Albyn Gdns *SUNDSW* SR3 120 A3
Alcester Cl *STKFD/GP* NE62 23 F6
Alconbury Cl *BLYTH* NE24 35 G2
Alcote Gv *RDHAMSE* DH6 173 J4
Alcroft Cl *WD/WHPE/BLK* NE5 53 K6
Aldborough St *BLYTH* NE24 31 G7
Aldbrough Cl
ASHBK/HED/RY SR2 135 F1
Aldbrough St *HAR/WTLS* NE34 74 E6
Aldeburgh Av
BW/LEM/TK/HW NE15 68 A3
Aldenham Rd *SUNDSW* SR3 119 J6
Alder Av *ELS/FEN* NE4 69 H3
Alder Cl *HLH* DH5 147 J5
MPTH NE61 20 E5
Alder Crs *STLY/ANP* DH9 111 H4
Alderdene *BDN/LAN/SAC* DH7 140 B5
Alderdene Cl
BDN/LAN/SAC * DH7 167 H1
Alder Gv *CON/LDGT* DH8 123 K4
MONK NE25 50 C3
Alder Lea Cl *DHAM* DH1 157 H6
Alderley Cl *ASHBK/HED/RY* SR2 121 F4
BOLCOL NE35 90 C3
Alderley Dr *LGB/KIL* NE12 48 B5
Alderley Rd *LWF/SPW/WRK* NE9 86 E7
Alderley Wy *CRAM* NE23 33 K6
Alderman Wood Rd
STLY/ANP DH9 112 C6
Alderney Gdns
WD/WHPE/BLK NE5 68 A1
Alder Pk *BDN/LAN/SAC* DH7 167 F6
Alder Rd *NSHW* NE29 59 J3
PLEE/EAS SR8 175 J4
WLSD/HOW NE28 59 G4
Aldershot Rd *SUNDSW* SR3 119 H7
Aldershot Sq *SUNDSW* SR3 119 H7
Alderside Crs
BDN/LAN/SAC DH7 140 B4
Alder St *SWCK/CAS* SR5 105 F4
Alder Wy *LGB/KIL* NE12 47 J5
Alderwood *ASHGTN* NE63 23 J3
WASHS NE38 116 D5
Alderwood Crs
BYK/HTN/WLK NE6 72 B2
Alderwyk *FELL* NE10 88 D6
Aldhome Ct *DHAM* DH1 156 B3
Aldridge Ct *BDN/LAN/SAC* DH7 155 F7
Aldsworth Cl
LWF/SPW/WRK NE9 102 B4
Aldwick Rd
BW/LEM/TK/HW NE15 68 D5
Aldwych Dr *NSHW* NE29 59 K3
Aldwych Rd *SUNDSW* SR3 119 H7

Aldwych Sq *SUNDSW* SR3 ....**133** H1
Aldwych St *SSH* NE33 ....**3** M9
Alexander Dr *HLH* DH5 ....**147** J5
Alexander Ter
  CLDN/WHIT/ROK SR6 ....**106** D2
Alexandra Av *SWCK/CAS* SR5 ....**105** K4
Alexandra Cl *DHAM* DH1 ....**156** B3
Alexandra Crs *DHAM* DH1 ....**16** B4
Alexandra Dr *WICK/BNPF* NE16 ......**8** A7
Alexandra Gdns *NSHW* NE29 ......**60** C4
Alexandra Pk
  ASHBK/HED/RY SR2 ....**120** C3
  SUNDSW SR3 ....**120** B2
Alexandra Rd *ASHGTN* NE63 ....**24** A1
  BYK/HTN/WLK NE6 ....**71** H2
  GATE NE8 ....**10** F6
  MPTH NE61 ....**20** E5
Alexandra Wy *CRAM* NE23 ....**38** C3
Alexandria Crs *DHAM* DH1 ....**16** B4
Alexandrina Dr *SEA/MUR* SR7 ...**150** E1
Alford *CLSW/PEL* DH2 ....**115** F4
Alfred Av *BDLGTN* NE22 ....**29** H5
Alfred St *BYK/HTN/WLK* NE6 ....**7** L5
  HEBB NE31 ....**73** H6
  PLEE/EAS SR8 ....**163** F4
  SEA/MUR SR7 ....**151** F7
Alfreton Cl *BDN/LAN/SAC* DH7 ...**177** H2
Algernon *LGB/KIL* NE12 ....**47** K4
Algernon Cl *BYK/HTN/WLK* NE6 ....**7** G3
Algernon Pl *WBAY* NE26 ....**51** F5
Algernon Rd
  BW/LEM/TK/HW NE15 ....**68** A5
  BYK/HTN/WLK NE6 ....**7** G4
Algernon Ter *TYNE/NSHE* NE30 ....**61** G2
  WYLAM NE41 ....**65** G5
Algiers Rd *SUNDSW* SR3 ....**119** G7
Alice St *ASHBK/HED/RY* SR2 ....**14** D7
  BLAY NE21 ....**83** K3
  CLSW/PEL DH2 ....**115** F6
  SSH NE33 ....**75** G3
Aline St *SEA/MUR* SR7 ....**151** F1
  SUNDSW SR3 ....**120** B7
Alington Pl *DHAM* DH1 ....**17** M3
Alison Dr *BOL* NE36 ....**91** H5
Allandale Av *LGB/KIL* NE12 ....**57** K3
All Church
  BW/LEM/TK/HW NE15 ....**69** F5
Allchurch Dr *ASHGTN* NE63 ....**24** C2
Allendale Av *WLSD/HOW* NE28 ....**58** D6
Allendale Crs *HLS* DH4 ....**117** J6
  SMOOR NE27 ....**49** J6
  STKFD/GP NE62 ....**23** C4
Allendale Dr *HAR/WTLS* NE34 ......**76** A3
Allendale Pl *TYNE/NSHE* NE30 .....**61** H3
Allendale Rd
  BDN/LAN/SAC DH7 ....**167** H6
  BLYTH NE24 ....**35** H1
  BYK/HTN/WLK NE6 ....**7** J7
  SUNDSW SR3 ....**119** H7
Allendale Sq *SUNDSW* SR3 ....**119** J5
Allendale St *HLH* DH5 ....**147** K6
Allendale Ter
  BYK/HTN/WLK NE6 ....**72** B6
Allenhead *WASHS* NE38 ....**117** C5
Allenheads *MONK* NE25 ....**39** K4
  WD/WHPE/BLK NE5 ....**68** C2
Allensford Bank
  CON/LDGT DH8 ....**136** E1
Allensgreen *CRAM* NE23 ....**38** C2
Allen St *CLS/BIR/GTL* DH3 ....**129** J5
Allerdean Cl
  BW/LEM/TK/HW NE15 ....**67** K4
Allerdene Wk *WICK/BNPF* NE16 ...**84** E6
Allergate *DHAM* DH1 ....**16** B4
Allergate Ter *DHAM* DH1 ....**16** B4
Allerhope *CRAM* NE23 ....**38** C3
Allerton Gdns
  BYK/HTN/WLK NE6 ....**71** K1
Allerwash *WD/WHPE/BLK* NE5 ....**68** C2
Allery Banks *MPTH* NE61 ....**20** E5
Allhusen Ter *GATE* NE8 ....**11** M5
Alliance St *MLFD/PNYW* SR4 ....**14** B3
Allingham Ct *LGB/HTN* NE7 ....**57** K7
Allison Ct
  WICK/BNPF
  (off Metrocentre) NE16 ....**85** F3
Allison Gdns *CON/LDGT* DH8 .....**123** F3
Allison St *CON/LDGT* DH8 ....**123** F4
Allnanville *LGB/KIL* NE12 ....**47** J4
Alloa Rd *SUNDSW* SR3 ....**119** H6
Allonby Wy *WD/WHPE/BLK* NE5 ..**69** F3
All Saints Dr *HLH* DH5 ....**147** K2
Allwork Ter *WICK/BNPF * NE16 .....**85** F5
Alma Pl *HLS* DH4 ....**132** A1
  NSHW NE29 ....**60** E4
  WBAY NE26 ....**51** F5
Alma St *MLFD/PNYW* SR4 ....**104** E6
Almond Cl *RDHAMSE* DH6 ....**160** B6
Almond Crs *GATE* NE8 ....**10** A7
Almond Dr *SWCK/CAS* SR5 ....**104** E5
Almond Pl *ELS/FEN* NE4 ....**69** H4
Almoner's Barn *DHAM* DH1 ....**168** B2
Aln Av *GOS/KPK* NE3 ....**56** A4
Aln Ct *BW/LEM/TK/HW* NE15 ....**68** A5
Aln Crs *GOS/KPK* NE3 ....**56** A3
Aln Gv *BW/LEM/TK/HW* NE15 ......**68** A4
Alnham Ct *GOS/KPK* NE3 ....**55** J3
Alnmouth Av *NSHW* NE29 ....**60** B6
Alnmouth Dr *GOS/KPK* NE3 ....**56** E6
Aln St *ASHGTN* NE63 ....**24** A1
  HEBB NE31 ....**73** H5
Aln Wk *GOS/KPK* NE3 ....**56** A4
Alnwick Av *NSHW* NE29 ....**60** B6
Alnwick Cl *CLSW/PEL* DH2 ....**129** G6
  WICK/BNPF NE16 ....**84** E5
Alnwick Gv *JRW* NE32 ....**89** K2
Alnwick Rd *DHAM* DH1 ....**156** D2
  HAR/WTLS NE34 ....**75** G5
  SUNDSW SR3 ....**119** J6
Alnwick St
  BW/LEM/TK/HW NE15 ....**67** H5
  PLEE/EAS SR8 ....**163** F4
  WLSD/HOW NE28 ....**72** E1

Alnwick Ter *DIN/WO* NE13 ....**46** C2
Alpine Ct *CLSW/PEL* DH2 ....**129** J4
Alpine Gv *BOL* NE36 ....**91** F5
Alpine Wy *SUNDSW* SR3 ....**120** A3
Alresford *LGB/KIL* NE12 ....**47** K5
Alston Av *BYK/HTN/WLK* NE6 ....**7** M4
  CRAM NE23 ....**38** E3
Alston Cl *NSHW* NE29 ....**60** A3
  WLSD/HOW NE28 ....**59** J6
Alston Crs *CLDN/WHIT/ROK* SR6 ..**92** C7
Alstone Ct *STKFD/GP* NE62 ....**23** F6
Alston Gdns
  BW/LEM/TK/HW NE15 ....**53** F7
Alston Gv *WBAY* NE26 ....**40** E1
Alston Rd *CON/LDGT* DH8 ....**122** B3
  MONK NE25 ....**40** A2
  WASHS NE38 ....**103** K7
Alston St *GATE* NE8 ....**10** B6
Alston Ter *CON/LDGT* DH8 ....**122** C3
Alston Wk *PLEE/EAS* SR8 ....**175** F5
Alston Wy *BDN/LAN/SAC* DH7 ....**167** H6
Altan Pl *LGB/KIL* NE12 ....**57** H3
Alum Well Rd
  LWF/SPW/WRK NE9 ....**87** F7
Alverston Cl
  BW/LEM/TK/HW NE15 ....**68** A3
Alverstone Av
  LWF/SPW/WRK NE9 ....**100** E1
Alverthorpe St *SSH* NE33 ....**75** H3
Alveston Cl *STKFD/GP* NE62 ....**23** F6
Alvin Gra *JRW* NE32 ....**73** H4
Alwin *WASHS* NE38 ....**116** C5
Alwin Cl *HLS* DH4 ....**131** G4
Alwinton Av *NSHW* NE29 ....**60** B2
Alwinton Cl *BLYTH* NE24 ....**30** E6
  WD/WHPE/BLK NE5 ....**54** E6
Alwinton Dr *CLSW/PEL* DH2 ....**129** G6
Alwinton Gdns *DUN/TMV* NE11 ....**86** A7
Alwinton Rd *SMOOR* NE27 ....**49** J6
Alwinton Ter *GOS/KPK* NE3 ....**56** D5
Amara Sq *SUNDSW* SR3 ....**119** J6
Ambassadors Wy *NSHW* NE29 .....**59** K2
Amber Ct *BLYTH* NE24 ....**34** E1
Ambergate Cl
  WD/WHPE/BLK NE5 ....**54** E7
Amberley Cha *LGB/KIL* NE12 ....**48** A5
Amberley Cl *WLSD/HOW * NE28 ....**59** J6
Amberley Gdns *LGB/HTN* NE7 ......**71** J1
Amberley St
  ASHBK/HED/RY SR2 ....**15** G7
  GATE NE8 ....**9** M6
Amberley St South
  ASHBK/HED/RY SR2 ....**15** G8
Amberley Wy *BLYTH* NE24 ....**35** G2
Amberly Gv *WICK/BNPF* NE16 ......**84** E7
Amble Av *HAR/WTLS* NE34 ....**76** B3
  MONK NE25 ....**51** F6
Amble Cl *BLYTH* NE24 ....**34** E2
Amble Gv *JES* NE2 ....**6** B2
Amble Pl *LGB/KIL* NE12 ....**58** B1
Amble Wy *GOS/KPK* NE3 ....**56** B6
Ambridge Wy *GOS/KPK* NE3 ....**55** K5
Ambrose Pl *BYK/HTN/WLK* NE6 ...**72** B5
Ambrose Rd *SUNDSW* SR3 ....**119** H6
Amec Wy *WLSD/HOW* NE28 ....**73** G2
Amelia Cl *ELS/FEN* NE4 ....**8** F1
Amelia Gdns *SUNDSW* SR3 ....**119** F7
Amelia Wk *ELS/FEN* NE4 ....**8** F1
Amen Cnr
  CNUT
  (off St. Nicholas Chambers) NE1 ...**5** K8
Amersham Crs *PLEE/EAS* SR8 ....**174** E3
Amersham Pl
  WD/WHPE/BLK NE5 ....**69** F1
Amersham Rd *BLYTH* NE24 ....**35** F3
Amesbury Cl
  WD/WHPE/BLK NE5 ....**53** K7
Amethyst Rd *ELS/FEN* NE4 ....**9** H2
Amethyst St *MLFD/PNYW* SR4 ....**105** K6
Amherst St *GOS/KPK* NE3 ....**55** J4
Amos Ayre Pl *HAR/WTLS* NE34 ....**74** D6
Amos Dr *STLY/ANP* DH9 ....**125** H6
Amsterdam Rd *SUNDSW* SR3 .....**119** J6
Amy St *SWCK/CAS* SR5 ....**106** B3
Ancaster Av *LGB/KIL* NE12 ....**57** H4
Ancaster Rd *WICK/BNPF* NE16 ....**84** D7
Anchorage Ter *DHAM* DH1 ....**16** E6
Ancona St *MLFD/PNYW* SR4 ....**105** K5
Ancroft Av *NSHW* NE29 ....**60** D3
Ancroft Garth *DHAM* DH1 ....**169** J6
Ancroft Pl *ASHGTN* NE63 ....**24** B4
  WD/WHPE/BLK NE5 ....**69** F3
Ancroft Rd *MONK* NE25 ....**39** J5
Ancroft Wy *GOS/KPK* NE3 ....**55** K2
Ancrum St *JES* NE2 ....**4** E3
Anderson St *SSH* NE33 ....**3** J7
Andover Pl *WLSD/HOW* NE28 ....**59** G4
Andrew Rd *SUNDSW* SR3 ....**119** G7
Andrew's La *PLEE/EAS* SR8 ....**162** B7
Andrew St *PLEE/EAS* SR8 ....**163** F4
Andrew Ter *RDHAMSE* DH6 ....**182** D2
Anfield Rd *GOS/KPK* NE3 ....**55** J5
Angerton Av *SMOOR* NE27 ....**49** H7
  TYNE/NSHE NE30 ....**60** E1
Angerton Gdns
  WD/WHPE/BLK NE5 ....**69** H3
Anglesey Gdns
  WD/WHPE/BLK NE5 ....**68** A1
Anglesey Pl *ELS/FEN* NE4 ....**4** C1
Anglesey Rd *SUNDSW* SR3 ....**119** H1
Anglesey Sq *SUNDSW* SR3 ....**119** G1
Angle Ter *WLSD/HOW* NE28 ....**73** H1
Angram Dr
  ASHBK/HED/RY SR2 ....**121** G7
Angrove Gdns
  MLFD/PNYW SR4 ....**105** K7
Angus *CLSW/PEL* DH2 ....**115** F4
Angus Cl *LGB/KIL* NE12 ....**47** J6
Angus Crs *NSHW* NE29 ....**60** B6

Angus Rd *GATE* NE8 ....**10** A7
Angus St *PLEE/EAS* SR8 ....**163** F4
Angus Ter *PLEE/EAS* SR8 ....**163** G6
Annand Rd *DHAM* DH1 ....**17** K1
Annaside Ms *CON/LDGT* DH8 .....**123** K3
Anne Dr *LGB/KIL* NE12 ....**58** C2
Ann Av *RDHAMSE* DH6 ....**181** G5
Annfield Pl *STLY/ANP* DH9 ....**125** D3
Annfield Rd *CRAM* NE23 ....**33** H5
Annie St *CLDN/WHIT/ROK* SR6 ....**93** F1
Annitsford Dr *CRAM* NE23 ....**47** H1
Ann's Rw *BLYTH* NE24 ....**31** G5
Ann St *BLAY* NE21 ....**84** A1
  CON/LDGT DH8 ....**123** F5
  GATE NE8 ....**11** G3
  HEBB NE31 ....**72** E4
Annville Crs *BYK/HTN/WLK* NE6 ...**72** C7
Anscomb Gdns *LGB/HTN* NE7 ......**57** G7
Anson Cl *SSH* NE33 ....**75** F3
Anson Pl *WD/WHPE/BLK* NE5 ......**54** D7
Anstead Cl *CRAM* NE23 ....**38** C2
Anthony Rd *SUNDSW* SR3 ....**119** H7
Anthony St *PLEE/EAS* SR8 ....**163** G4
  STLY/ANP DH9 ....**112** C9
Antlett Ter *STLY/ANP* DH9 ....**125** H3
Antonine Wk
  BW/LEM/TK/HW NE15 ....**66** B1
Anton Pl *CRAM* NE23 ....**38** C3
Antrim Cl *WD/WHPE/BLK* NE5 ......**55** G7
Antrim Gdns *SEA/MUR* SR7 ....**135** J7
Antwerp Rd *SUNDSW* SR3 ....**119** G7
Anvil Ct *DHAM* DH1 ....**156** B2
Apperley *WD/WHPE/BLK* NE5 ......**68** C2
Apperley Av *DHAM* DH1 ....**169** K6
Apperley Rd *PSHWF* NE43 ....**79** G6
Appian Pl *BW/LEM/TK/HW* NE15 ..**67** G1
  LWF/SPW/WRK NE9 ....**11** L9
Appleby Ct *HLS* DH4 ....**131** F6
  NSHW NE29 ....**2** B1
Appleby Gdns *WLSD/HOW* NE28 ..**59** J6
Appleby Pk *NSHW* NE29 ....**60** D4
Appleby Rd *SUNDSW* SR3 ....**119** H6
Appleby Sq *NSHW* NE29 ....**2** D5
Appledore Gdns
  CLS/BIR/GTL DH3 ....**129** K2
Appledore Rd *BLYTH* NE24 ....**35** G2
Appleforth Av
  ASHBK/HED/RY SR2 ....**121** G5
Appleton Cl *DUN/TMV* NE11 ....**9** K8
Appleton Dr *PRUD* NE42 ....**80** C1
Appletree Gdns
  BYK/HTN/WLK NE6 ....**72** A3
  MONK NE25 ....**50** C6
Applewood *LGB/KIL* NE12 ....**48** B6
Appley Ter
  CLDN/WHIT/ROK SR6 ....**106** E4
Apsley Crs *GOS/KPK* NE3 ....**55** J5
Aqua Ter *BW/LEM/TK/HW* NE15 ...**65** K1
Aquila Dr *BW/LEM/TK/HW* NE15 ...**65** K1
Arbourcourt Av
  BDN/LAN/SAC DH7 ....**165** C2
Arbroath Rd *SUNDSW* SR3 ....**119** H6
The Arcade
  CLS/BIR/GTL
  (off Front St) DH3 ....**129** J4
  WICK/BNPF
  (off Metrocentre) NE16 ....**8** B4
Arcadia Av *CLS/BIR/GTL* DH3 ......**129** J2
Arcadia Ter *BLYTH* NE24 ....**35** C1
Archbold Ter *JES* NE2 ....**5** M2
Archer Rd *SUNDSW* SR3 ....**119** H6
Archer Sq *SUNDSW* SR3 ....**119** H6
Archer St *WLSD/HOW* NE28 ....**59** G7
Archery Ri *DHAM* DH1 ....**168** B2
Archibald St *GOS/KPK* NE3 ....**56** C5
Arcot Av *CRAM* NE23 ....**37** K1
  MONK NE25 ....**50** C6
Arcot Dr *MONK* NE25 ....**50** C7
  WD/WHPE/BLK NE5 ....**68** C3
Arden Av *GOS/KPK* NE3 ....**56** B1
Arden Cl *WLSD/HOW* NE28 ....**59** F3
Arden Crs *WD/WHPE/BLK* NE5 ....**69** H2
Arden Sq *SUNDSW* SR3 ....**119** J6
Arden St *RDHAMSE* DH6 ....**173** H5
Ardrossan *CLSW/PEL* DH2 ....**115** F5
Ardrossan Rd *SUNDSW* SR3 ......**119** H7
Arena Wy *ELS/FEN* NE4 ....**10** A2
Argent St *PLEE/EAS* SR8 ....**163** F4
Argus Cl *DUN/TMV* NE11 ....**86** B5
Argyle Cl *STLY/ANP* DH9 ....**112** C6
Argyle Pl *NSHW* NE29 ....**60** E2
  RDHAMSE DH6 ....**160** E2
Argyle Sq *ASHBK/HED/RY* SR2 ....**14** D7
Argyle St *ASHBK/HED/RY* SR2 .....**14** D7
  CNUT NE1 ....**5** M6
  HEBB NE31 ....**73** H4
  TYNE/NSHE NE30 ....**61** H2
Argyll Ter *NSHW* NE29 ....**60** E2
  NWBGN NE64 ....**25** F1
Ariel St *ASHGTN* NE63 ....**24** A1
Arisaig *CLSW/PEL* DH2 ....**115** F4
Arklecrag *WASHN* NE37 ....**102** E7
Arkleside Pl *WD/WHPE/BLK* NE5 ..**68** A2
Arkle St *DIN/WO* NE13 ....**46** A5
  GATE NE8 ....**10** B8
Arkwright St *GATE* NE8 ....**86** D5
Arlington Av *GOS/KPK* NE3 ....**55** K7
Arlington Cl
  GOS/KPK (off Kenton Av) NE3 ....**56** A7
Arlington Gv *CRAM* NE23 ....**33** H5
  WICK/BNPF NE16 ....**84** E6
Arlington Rd *HEBB* NE31 ....**50** E5
Arlington St *MLFD/PNYW* SR4 ....**105** K7
Armonside Rd *CHPW* NE17 ....**95** J7
Armstrong Av
  BYK/HTN/WLK NE6 ....**71** H2
  HAR/WTLS NE34 ....**75** J4
  WNGT TS28 ....**183** K3
Armstrong Rd
  BW/LEM/TK/HW NE15 ....**68** D6
  ELS/FEN NE4 ....**69** H7
  PLEE/EAS SR8 ....**174** E2
  WASHN NE37 ....**102** A3

  WLSD/HOW NE28 ....**73** J2
Armstrong St *DUN/TMV* NE11 ......**86** C5
  GATE NE8 ....**10** B9
Armstrong Ter *SSH* NE33 ....**75** C3
Arncliffe Gdns
  WD/WHPE/BLK NE5 ....**68** A1
Arndale Houses
  CLS/BIR/GTL
  (off Durham Rd) DH3 ....**115** J2
Arnham Gv *MLFD/PNYW* SR4 .....**118** D4
Arnold Cl *STLY/ANP* DH9 ....**126** E1
Arnold Rd *SUNDSW* SR3 ....**119** H6
Arnold St *BOLCOL* NE35 ....**90** D4
Arran Ct *SUNDSW * SR3 ....**134** A1
Arran Dr *JRW* NE32 ....**90** C1
Arran Gdns *FELL* NE10 ....**12** A9
Arran Pl *NSHW* NE29 ....**60** A2
Arras La *SUND* SR1 ....**15** H4
Arrol Pk *MLFD/PNYW* SR4 ....**14** A5
Arrow Cl *LGB/KIL* NE12 ....**47** H7
Arther Ter *CLDN/WHIT/ROK* SR6 ..**93** F1
Arthur Av *ASHBK/HED/RY* SR2 ...**135** C1
Arthur Cook Av
  WICK/BNPF NE16 ....**85** C5
Arthur Pl *BLYTH* NE24 ....**31** C6
  CLDN/WHIT/ROK SR6 ....**77** F7
  GATE NE8 ....**11** C4
  JRW NE32 ....**73** K5
  STLY/ANP DH9 ....**114** A7
Arun Cl *PLEE/EAS* SR8 ....**174** D5
Arundel Cl *WD/WHPE/BLK* NE5 ....**54** D7
  DIN/WO NE13 ....**46** A4
Arundel Dr
  BW/LEM/TK/HW NE15 ....**68** C4
  MONK NE25 ....**49** K5
Arundel Gdns
  LWF/SPW/WRK NE9 ....**87** G7
  SUNDSW SR3 ....**119** G7
Arundel Ct *GOS/KPK * NE3 ....**55** C3
Arundel Rd *SUNDSW* SR3 ....**119** H6
Arundel Sq *ASHGTN* NE63 ....**23** J2
Arundel Wy *BDN/LAN/SAC* DH7 ..**167** H6
Asama Ct *ELS/FEN* NE4 ....**9** J2
Ascot Cl *WLSD/HOW* NE28 ....**59** F4
Ascot Ct *GOS/KPK* NE3 ....**55** C3
  SUNDSW SR3 ....**119** H7
Ascot Crs *GATE* NE8 ....**10** B9
Ascot Gv *ASHGTN* NE63 ....**23** K3
Ascot Pl *CLSW/PEL* DH2 ....**115** F7
Ascot Rd *CON/LDGT* DH8 ....**108** E7
Ascot St *PLEE/EAS* SR8 ....**163** G5
Ash Av *BDN/LAN/SAC* DH7 ....**155** F7
  DHAM DH1 ....**17** L4
  DIN/WO NE13 ....**45** F2
Ash Banks *MPTH* NE61 ....**20** E6
Ashberry Gv
  CLDN/WHIT/ROK SR6 ....**106** D4
Ashbourne Av
  BYK/HTN/WLK NE6 ....**72** B5
Ashbourne Cl *SMOOR* NE27 ....**48** E4
Ashbourne Crs *ASHGTN* NE63 .....**23** J2
Ashbourne Rd *JRW* NE32 ....**74** A6
Ashbrook Cl
  BDN/LAN/SAC DH7 ....**166** E7
Ashbrooke *MONK* NE25 ....**50** C4
Ashbrooke Ct *RHTLP* TS27 ....**184** D7
Ashbrooke Crs
  ASHBK/HED/RY SR2 ....**14** E9
Ashbrooke Cross
  *ASHBK/HED/RY * SR2 ....**120** C3
Ashbrooke Dr *PONT/DH* NE20 ....**43** C2
Ashbrooke Gdns
  WLSD/HOW NE28 ....**59** G7
Ashbrooke Mt
  ASHBK/HED/RY SR2 ....**14** D9
Ashbrooke Range
  ASHBK/HED/RY SR2 ....**120** C3
Ashbrooke Rd
  ASHBK/HED/RY SR2 ....**120** C3
Ashbrooke St
  WD/WHPE/BLK NE5 ....**55** J7
Ashbrooke Ter
  ASHBK/HED/RY SR2 ....**14** E9
Ashburne Ct
  ASHBK/HED/RY SR2 ....**14** F9
Ashburn Rd *WLSD/HOW* NE28 .....**59** G4
Ashburton Rd *GOS/KPK* NE3 ....**56** A6
Ashbury *MONK* NE25 ....**50** A3
Ashby Crs *CON/LDGT* DH8 ....**122** D2
Ashby La *CON/LDGT* DH8 ....**122** D3
Ashby St *ASHBK/HED/RY* SR2 ....**121** F3
Ash Crs *SEA/MUR* SR7 ....**150** D3
Ashcroft Dr *LGB/KIL* NE12 ....**58** A3
Ashdale *HLS* DH4 ....**117** C6
  PONT/DH NE20 ....**42** E6
Ashdale Rd *CON/LDGT* DH8 ....**123** F4
Ashdown Av *DHAM* DH1 ....**157** J6
Ashdown Cl *LGB/KIL* NE12 ....**57** H3
Ashdown Rd *SUNDSW* SR3 ....**119** H6
Ashdown Wy *LGB/KIL* NE12 ....**57** H3
Asher St *GATE* NE8 ....**11** M6
Ashfield *CON/LDGT* DH8 ....**122** D1
  JRW NE32 ....**90** B3
Ashfield Av *WICK/BNPF* NE16 ......**84** A8
Ashfield Cl *ELS/FEN* NE4 ....**4** D8
Ashfield Ct
  CON/LDGT
  (off Benfieldside Rd) DH8 ....**122** D1
  ROWG NE39 ....**96** C1
Ashfield Gdns *WLSD/HOW* NE28 ..**58** B7
Ashfield Gv *NSHW* NE29 ....**2** C1
  WBAY NE26 ....**50** E5
Ashfield Pk *WICK/BNPF* NE16 ......**85** F4
Ashfield Ri *WICK/BNPF* NE16 ....**85** F7
Ashfield Rd *GOS/KPK* NE3 ....**56** A6
  WICK/BNPF NE16 ....**84** A8
Ashfield Ter *FELL* NE10 ....**13** H6
  ASHBK/HED/RY SR2 ....**135** C1
Ash Gv *CLDN/WHIT/ROK* SR6 ......**93** C3
  DUN/TMV NE11 ....**8** F6
  MPTH NE61 ....**20** C6
RYTON NE40 ....**66** E5
  TRIM TS29 ....**183** F6
  WLSD/HOW NE28 ....**73** F1
Ashgrove Av *HAR/WTLS* NE34 ......**75** K7
Ashgrove Ter *GATE * NE8 ....**10** F5
Ashington Dr *STKFD/GP* NE62 .....**23** F5
Ashkirk *CRAM* NE23 ....**47** C1
Ashkirk Cl *CLSW/PEL* DH2 ....**129** C6
Ashkirk Wy *MONK* NE25 ....**40** A6
Ashleigh Av *DHAM* DH1 ....**156** C4
Ashleigh Cl *BLAY* NE21 ....**84** B3
Ashleigh Crs
  WD/WHPE/BLK NE5 ....**68** E3
Ashleigh Gv *BDN/LAN/SAC* DH7 ..**140** A4
  CLDN/WHIT/ROK SR6 ....**106** C1
  JES NE2 ....**70** D1
  LGB/KIL NE12 ....**57** K3
  TYNE/NSHE NE30 ....**61** G2
Ashleigh Rd *WD/WHPE/BLK* NE5 ..**68** E3
Ashley Cl *LGB/KIL* NE12 ....**48** B5
  WASHS NE38 ....**117** F3
Ashley Gdns *STKFD/GP* NE62 ......**23** C4
Ashley Rd *HAR/WTLS* NE34 ....**75** C5
Ashley Ter *CLS/BIR/GTL* DH3 ......**129** J3
Ashmead Cl *LGB/KIL* NE12 ....**48** A5
Ash Mdw *CLS/BIR/GTL* DH3 ....**116** A7
Ashmore St *ASHBK/HED/RY* SR2 ..**14** E8
Ashmore Ter
  ASHBK/HED/RY SR2 ....**14** E8
Asholme *WD/WHPE/BLK* NE5 ......**68** C2
Ashridge Cl *HAR/WTLS* NE34 ....**76** B6
Ashridge Ct *FELL* NE10 ....**88** D5
Ash St *BLAY* NE21 ....**84** A3
  CON/LDGT DH8 ....**123** F5
  SEA/MUR SR7 ....**149** H5
Ashton Ct *RYTON* NE40 ....**67** F7
Ashton Ri *CLSW/PEL* DH2 ....**129** J5
  PLEE/EAS SR8 ....**175** F5
Ashton St *PLEE/EAS* SR8 ....**163** G5
Ashton Wy *SUNDSW* SR3 ....**133** G1
  WBAY NE26 ....**50** B2
Ashtree Cl *ROWG* NE39 ....**97** H2
Ash Tree Dr *BDLGTN* NE22 ....**29** F4
Ashtree La *BLAY* NE21 ....**82** E7
Ashtrees Gdns
  LWF/SPW/WRK NE9 ....**11** H9
Ash Tree Ter
  BDN/LAN/SAC DH7 ....**142** C1
Ashvale Av *DUN/TMV* NE11 ....**100** C7
Ashwell Rd *SUNDSW* SR3 ....**119** H6
Ashwood Av *SWCK/CAS* SR5 ......**105** K3
Ashwood Cl *CRAM* NE23 ....**33** H5
  LGB/KIL NE12 ....**58** A2
Ashwood Crs
  BYK/HTN/WLK NE6 ....**72** B2
Ashwood Cft *HEBB* NE31 ....**73** F4
Ashwood Gdns
  LWF/SPW/WRK NE9 ....**101** G3
Ashwood Gv *DIN/WO* NE13 ....**46** B4
  SWCK/CAS SR5 ....**105** K4
Ashwood St
  ASHBK/HED/RY SR2 ....**14** B7
Ashwood Ter
  ASHBK/HED/RY SR2 ....**14** B8
Askern Av *ASHBK/HED/RY* SR2 ...**121** G5
Askerton Dr *PLEE/EAS* SR8 ....**174** B7
Askew Rd *GATE* NE8 ....**10** D3
Askew Rd West *GATE* NE8 ....**10** C4
Askrigg Av *ASHBK/HED/RY* SR2 ..**121** F5
  WLSD/HOW NE28 ....**59** F5
Aspen Av *PLEE/EAS* SR8 ....**175** J4
Aspen Cl *DHAM * DH1 ....**17** M1
Aspen Ct *SUNDSW * SR3 ....**133** J1
Aspen Ter *WD/WHPE/BLK* NE5 .....**69** J2
Aspley Cl *SUNDSW* SR3 ....**134** A1
Asquith St *RDHAMSE* DH6 ....**172** D6
Association Rd
  CLDN/WHIT/ROK SR6 ....**106** C3
Aster Pl *ELS/FEN* NE4 ....**69** G4
Astley Dr *WBAY* NE26 ....**50** C1
Astley Gdns *MONK* NE25 ....**39** K5
  WBAY NE26 ....**40** E1
Astley Gv *WBAY* NE26 ....**40** E1
Astley Rd *MONK* NE25 ....**39** K4
Astley Vis *WBAY* NE26 ....**40** E1
Aston Sq *SUNDSW* SR3 ....**119** H7
Aston St *SSH* NE33 ....**75** H4
Athelhampton *WASHS* NE38 ....**117** J1
Athelstan Rigg
  ASHBK/HED/RY SR2 ....**121** G7
Athenaeum St *SUND* SR1 ....**14** F5
Atherton Dr *ELS/FEN* NE4 ....**69** J7
  HLS DH4 ....**146** D1
Atherton St *DHAM* DH1 ....**16** B4
Athlone Pl *CLS/BIR/GTL* DH3 .....**115** K5
Athol Gdns
  ASHBK/HED/RY SR2 ....**135** G1
  MONK NE25 ....**50** B6
Athol Gn *DUN/TMV* NE11 ....**9** J5
Athol Gv *SUNDSW* SR3 ....**120** A1
Atholl Gdns *LWF/SPW/WRK* NE9 ..**11** M9
Athol Pk *ASHBK/HED/RY* SR2 ......**15** H9
Athol Rd *ASHBK/HED/RY* SR2 ......**15** H8
Athol St *DUN/TMV * NE11 ....**9** J5
Athol Ter *ASHBK/HED/RY* SR2 ......**15** H8
Athull *CLSW/PEL* DH2 ....**115** F4
Atkinson Gdns *NSHW* NE29 ....**2** D1
Atkinson Gv *RDHAMSE* DH6 ....**173** G3
Atkinson Rd
  CLDN/WHIT/ROK SR6 ....**106** C1
  CLS/BIR/GTL DH3 ....**129** K2
  ELS/FEN NE4 ....**69** H7
Atkinson St *WLSD/HOW* NE28 ......**72** D2
Atkinson Ter *ELS/FEN* NE4 ....**69** H6
  WLSD/HOW NE28 ....**72** D1
Atkin St *LGB/KIL* NE12 ....**47** H5
Atlantis Rd *SUNDSW* SR3 ....**119** G6
Atley Wy *CRAM* NE23 ....**32** C5
Attlee Cl *CRAM* NE23 ....**35** G2
Attlee Gv *ASHBK/HED/RY* SR2 ....**120** C8
Attwood Gv *SWCK/CAS* SR5 ....**106** B4
Aubone Av
  BW/LEM/TK/HW NE15 ....**69** C5
Auburn Cl *WLSD/HOW* NE28 ....**73** J1
Auburn Gdns *ELS/FEN* NE4 ....**69** J3
Auckland *CLSW/PEL* DH2 ....**129** F5

Auckland Av HAR/WTLS NE34 76 B5
Auckland Rd DHAM DH1 156 E2
HEBB NE31 73 H4
Auckland Ter JRW NE32 74 C7
Auden Gv ELS/FEN NE4 69 J5
Audley Gdns SUNDSW SR3 120 B3
Audley Rd GOS/KPK NE3 56 E6
Augusta Ct WLSD/HOW NE28 59 G4
Augusta Sq SUNDSW SR3 119 H7
Augustine Cl DHAM DH1 156 B3
August Pl SSH NE33 3 K9
Augustus Dr BDLGTN NE22 28 E4
Austen Av HAR/WTLS NE34 91 F1
Austen Pl STLY/ANP DH9 126 E3
Austin Sq SWCK/CAS SR5 106 B3
Australia Gv HAR/WTLS NE34 90 D1
Austral Pl DIN/WO NE13 46 A4
Auton Stile BDN/LAN/SAC DH7 155 F6
Autumn Cl WASHS NE38 103 F7
Avalon Dr
BW/LEM/TK/HW NE15 68 C3
Avalon Rd SUNDSW SR3 119 H6
Avebury Av STKFD/GP NE62 23 G6
Avebury Dr WASHS NE38 117 G1
Avebury Pl CRAM NE23 33 J6
Avenue Rd GATE NE8 11 G8
MONK NE25 39 K5
Avenue Ter ASHBK/HED/RY SR2 14 D9
The Avenue ASHBK/HED/RY SR2 14 D8
BDN/LAN/SAC DH7 141 H3
BLAY NE21 84 C2
CLS/BIR/GTL DH3 115 J2
CLS/BIR/GTL DH3 131 G2
CLSW/PEL DH2 129 H4
DHAM DH1 16 A5
HLH DH5 148 A4
LWF/SPW/WRK NE9 87 G5
MONK NE25 40 A4
MPTH NE61 26 D1
PONT/DH NE20 52 A1
RDHAMSE DH6 180 D7
ROWG NE39 97 H2
SEA/MUR SR7 150 B1
STLY/ANP DH9 125 G4
WASHS NE38 117 G1
WBAY NE26 50 D4
WLSD/HOW NE28 72 D2
Avenue Vivian HLS DH4 131 H6
Aviemore Rd BOL NE36 91 F5
Avis Av NWBGN NE64 24 E2
Avision St ELS/FEN NE4 4 E6
Avison Pl ELS/FEN NE4 4 E5
Avison St ELS/FEN NE4 4 E5
Avocet Cl BLYTH NE24 35 G4
Avolon Ct ELS/FEN NE4 4 E5
Avolon Pl ELS/FEN NE4 4 E5
Avolon Wk ELS/FEN NE4 4 E5
Avon Av JRW NE32 90 A2
NSHW NE29 60 C6
Avon Cl ROWG NE39 97 H2
WLSD/HOW NE28 59 F4
Avon Ct MONK NE25 40 A3
Avon Crs HLS DH4 131 J7
Avoncroft Cl SEA/MUR SR7 134 D7
Avondale MLFD/PNYW SR4 118 E1
Avondale Av BLYTH NE24 30 A6
HLS DH4 117 K7
LGB/KIL NE12 57 K2
Avondale Cl BLYTH NE24 30 B6
Avondale Gdns ASHGTN NE63 24 C4
BOL NE36 90 E5
Avondale Ri BYK/HTN/WLK NE6 7 G6
Avondale Rd BYK/HTN/WLK NE6 7 H6
CON/LDGT DH8 123 F4
PONT/DH NE20 42 C6
Avondale Ter CLSW/PEL DH2 129 J4
GATE NE8 10 E7
Avonlea Wy WD/WHPE/BLK NE5 55 G7
Avonmouth Rd SUNDSW SR3 119 G7
Avonmouth Sq SUNDSW SR3 119 H7
Avon Rd HEBB NE31 73 G7
PLEE/EAS SR8 174 D5
STLY/ANP DH9 126 D2
Avon St GATE NE8 11 K6
PLEE/EAS SR8 163 F4
SUND SR1 15 J6
Awnless Ct HAR/WTLS NE34 75 G6
Axbridge Cl STKFD/GP NE62 23 G6
Axbridge Gdns ELS/FEN NE4 69 J7
Axminster Cl CRAM NE23 33 J6
Axwell Dr BLYTH NE24 30 D7
Axwell Park Cl
WICK/BNPF * NE16 84 E5
Axwell Park Rd BLAY NE21 84 C3
Axwell Park Vw
BW/LEM/TK/HW NE15 69 F6
Axwell Ter WICK/BNPF * NE16 84 E3
Axwell Vw BLAY NE21 84 A3
WICK/BNPF NE16 84 E5
Aycliffe Av LWF/SPW/WRK NE9 101 K1
Aycliffe Crs
LWF/SPW/WRK NE9 101 K1
Aydon Gv JRW NE32 89 K1
Aykley Ct DHAM DH1 156 B5
Aykley Gn DHAM DH1 156 B5
Aykley Rd DHAM DH1 156 C3
Aykley V DHAM DH1 156 B4
Aylesbury Dr SUNDSW SR3 134 A2
Aylesbury Pl LGB/KIL NE12 57 H3
Aylesford Sq BLYTH NE24 35 G2
Aylsham Cl WD/WHPE/BLK NE5 53 K6
Aylsham Ct SUNDSW SR3 134 A3
Aylyth Pl GOS/KPK NE3 55 K7
Aynsley Ter CON/LDGT DH8 123 F4
Ayr Dr JRW NE32 90 B1
Ayre's Quay Rd SUND SR1 14 C4
Ayre's Ter NSHW NE29 2 C1
Ayrey Av HAR/WTLS NE34 74 D7
Aysgarth Av
ASHBK/HED/RY SR2 121 F4
WLSD/HOW NE28 59 F3
Ayton Av ASHBK/HED/RY SR2 121 F5
Ayton Cl PSHWF NE43 79 H6
WD/WHPE/BLK NE5 54 C7
Ayton Ct BDLGTN NE22 28 D4
Ayton Ri BYK/HTN/WLK NE6 7 H7
Ayton Rd WASHS NE38 116 B2
Ayton St BYK/HTN/WLK NE6 7 H7
Azalea Av ASHBK/HED/RY SR2 14 D8
Azalea Ter North
ASHBK/HED/RY SR2 14 D7
Azalea Ter South
ASHBK/HED/RY SR2 14 D8

B

Back
JES (off Osborne Ter) NE2 5 M2
Back Bridge St SUND SR1 14 E4
Back Croft Rd BLYTH NE24 31 G7
Back East Pde CON/LDGT DH8 123 G5
Back Eccleston Rd SSH NE33 3 M9
Back George St ELS/FEN NE4 5 G9
Back Goldspink La JES NE2 6 B1
Back Heaton Park Rd
BYK/HTN/WLK NE6 6 E4
Back La BLAY NE21 83 K2
CLS/BIR/GTL DH3 145 H1
CON/LDGT DH8 124 B5
HLS DH4 117 K6
MONK NE25 50 C4
Back Lodge Ter SUND SR1 15 K5
Back Mitford St ELS/FEN NE4 9 M2
Back Mount Joy DHAM DH1 16 F7
Back New Bridge St CNUT NE1 6 A5
Back North Bridge St
SWCK/CAS SR5 14 E1
Back North Railway
St SEA/MUR SR7 135 K7
Back North Ter SEA/MUR SR7 135 K7
Back Palmerston St
CON/LDGT DH8 123 F5
Back Percy Gdns
TYNE/NSHE NE30 61 H2
Back Rw WICK/BNPF NE16 84 E5
Back Ryhope St
ASHBK/HED/RY SR2 120 E7
Back Silver St DHAM DH1 16 D4
Back South Railway St
SEA/MUR SR7 150 E1
Back Stephen St
BYK/HTN/WLK NE6 6 D5
Backstone Burn
CON/LDGT DH8 122 C2
Backstone Rd CON/LDGT DH8 122 B3
Back St BLAY NE21 83 J3
Back Walker Rd
BYK/HTN/WLK NE6 72 C7
Back Western Hl DHAM DH1 16 A2
Back Woodbine St GATE NE8 10 D5
Backworth La CRAM NE23 48 B1
Baden Crs SWCK/CAS SR5 104 E2
Baden Powell St
LWF/SPW/WRK NE9 11 J9
Baden St CLS/BIR/GTL DH3 129 J5
Badger Cl SUNDSW SR3 134 A2
Badgers Gn MPTH NE61 20 B3
Badger's Wd STLY/ANP DH9 112 E5
Badminton Cl BOLCOL NE35 90 C3
Baffin Ct SUNDSW SR3 133 K1
Baildon Cl WLSD/HOW NE28 58 E6
Bailey Ri PLEE/EAS SR8 174 E2
Bailey Sq SWCK/CAS SR5 104 E1
Bailey Wy HLH DH5 148 A6
Bainbridge Av HAR/WTLS NE34 74 D7
SUNDSW SR3 120 B3
Bainbridge Holme Cl
SUNDSW SR3 120 B3
Bainbridge Holme Rd
SUNDSW SR3 120 C3
Bainbridge St DHAM DH1 158 A4
Bainford Av
BW/LEM/TK/HW NE15 68 E5
Baird Av WLSD/HOW NE28 74 A1
Baird Cl WASHN NE37 103 G3
Baird Ct GATE NE8 11 M5
Baird St SWCK/CAS SR5 104 E2
Bakehouse La DHAM DH1 16 F2
Baker Gdns DUN/TMV NE11 9 G5
FELL NE10 13 L7
Baker Rd CRAM NE23 32 D6
Baker St HLH DH5 132 C6
SWCK/CAS SR5 104 E2
Bakewell Ter BYK/HTN/WLK NE6 7 K9
Baldersdale Gdns SUNDSW SR3 120 B4
Baldwin Av BOL NE36 91 H5
ELS/FEN NE4 4 A3
Baldwin St PLEE/EAS SR8 163 G5
Balfour Rd
BW/LEM/TK/HW NE15 68 E6
Balfour St BLYTH NE24 31 F5
CON/LDGT DH8 123 F3
GATE NE8 10 D7
HLH DH5 132 C6
Balgonie Cottages RYTON NE40 66 E6
Baliol Rd PSHWF NE43 79 G5
Baliol Sq DHAM DH1 168 B3
Balkwell Av NSHW NE29 60 B5
Balkwell Gn NSHW NE29 60 C4
Ballast Hl BLYTH NE24 31 H6
Ballast Hill Rd NSHW NE29 2 D6
Ballater Cl STLY/ANP DH9 127 F1
Balliol Av LGB/KIL NE12 57 J1
Balliol Cl PLEE/EAS SR8 174 C4
Balliol Gdns LGB/HTN NE7 57 H5
Balmain Rd GOS/KPK NE3 55 J6
Balmoral Av GOS/KPK NE3 56 E6
JRW NE32 90 C1
Balmoral Cl BDLGTN NE22 29 J4
Balmoral Ct SWCK/CAS SR5 104 E2
Balmoral Crs HLH DH5 147 J1
Balmoral Dr FELL NE10 12 A8
PLEE/EAS SR8 174 B7
Balmoral Gdns NSHW NE29 60 D3
Balmoral Gv CON/LDGT DH8 123 G3
Balmoral St WLSD/HOW NE28 72 D1
Balmoral Ter
ASHBK/HED/RY SR2 121 F4
BYK/HTN/WLK NE6 6 F2
GOS/KPK NE3 56 E6
SUNDSW SR3 119 G7
Balmoral Wy FELL NE10 12 A9
Balroy Ct LGB/KIL NE12 58 A2
Baltic Millennium Br CNUT NE1 6 A8
Baltic Rd FELL NE10 12 C2
Baltimore Av SWCK/CAS SR5 104 C1
Baltimore Sq SWCK/CAS SR5 104 D2
Bamborough Ct CRAM NE23 47 F1
Bamborough Ter
TYNE/NSHE NE30 60 E3
Bambro' St ASHBK/HED/RY SR2 15 H8
Bamburgh Av SSH NE33 75 K2
Bamburgh Cl BLYTH NE24 30 E7
WASHS NE38 116 C1
Bamburgh Ct DUN/TMV NE11 86 C6
Bamburgh Dr FELL NE10 13 M3
MPTH NE61 21 K2
WLSD/HOW NE28 73 H1
Bamburgh Gdns SUNDSW SR3 120 B3
Bamburgh Gv HAR/WTLS NE34 76 B3
Bamburgh Rd DHAM DH1 156 D2
LGB/KIL NE12 58 B2
WD/WHPE/BLK NE5 68 C1
Bamburgh Ter ASHGTN NE63 23 J2
BYK/HTN/WLK NE6 7 H5
Bampton Av
CLDN/WHIT/ROK SR6 92 C7
Banbury WASHN NE37 103 G5
Banbury Gdns WLSD/HOW NE28 59 F5
Banbury Rd GOS/KPK NE3 55 K4
Banbury Ter SSH NE33 75 H3
Banbury Wy BLYTH NE24 35 F2
NSHW NE29 60 B6
Bancroft Ter MLFD/PNYW SR4 105 K7
Banesley La DUN/TMV NE11 100 B4
Banff St SWCK/CAS SR5 104 E1
Bank Av WICK/BNPF NE16 84 E5
Bank Ct TYNE/NSHE NE30 2 F2
Bankdale Gdns BLYTH NE24 30 C7
Bankhead Rd
BW/LEM/TK/HW NE15 67 H2
Bankhead Ter HLS DH4 131 J6
Bank Rd GATE NE8 6 A9
Banks Holt CLSW/PEL DH2 129 F5
Bankside MPTH NE61 20 E5
Bankside Cl
ASHBK/HED/RY SR2 120 E7
Bankside La HAR/WTLS NE34 75 G6
Bankside Rd
BW/LEM/TK/HW NE15 68 D6
Bankside Wk STKFD/GP NE62 23 H5
Bank Top RYTON NE40 82 A1
Bank Top Hamlet
WICK/BNPF * NE16 84 E5
Bankwell La GATE NE8 5 M9
Bannister Dr LGB/KIL NE12 58 B2
Bannockburn LGB/KIL NE12 47 K5
Barbara St ASHBK/HED/RY SR2 121 F3
Barbary Cl CLSW/PEL DH2 114 E7
Barbary Dr
CLDN/WHIT/ROK SR6 107 F3
Barbondale Lonnen
WD/WHPE/BLK NE5 68 A2
Barbour Av HAR/WTLS NE34 76 A4
Barclay Pl WD/WHPE/BLK NE5 69 F2
Barclay St SWCK/CAS SR5 14 E2
Barcusclose La
WICK/BNPF NE16 98 A7
Bardolph Rd NSHW NE29 60 B4
Bardon Cl WD/WHPE/BLK NE5 54 D6
Bardon Crs MONK NE25 40 C6
Bardsey Pl LGB/KIL NE12 57 H4
Barehirst St SSH NE33 75 F4
Barents Cl WD/WHPE/BLK * NE5 68 D1
Baret Rd BYK/HTN/WLK NE6 7 M1
Barford Dr CLSW/PEL DH2 129 G6
Bargate Bank
BDN/LAN/SAC DH7 140 C7
Baring St SSH NE33 3 H4
Barker St JES NE2 6 A4
Barking Crs SWCK/CAS SR5 104 D2
Barking Sq SWCK/CAS SR5 104 D2
Barkwood Rd ROWG NE39 97 F3
Barleycorn Pl
SUND (off Laura St) SR1 14 F6
Barley Mill Crs CON/LDGT DH8 122 B3
Barley Mill Rd CON/LDGT DH8 122 B3
Barlow Crs BLAY NE21 82 E6
Barlow Fell Rd BLAY NE21 82 E7
Barlowfield Cl BLAY NE21 83 J4
Barlow La BLAY NE21 83 F6
Barmoor La RYTON NE40 66 D6
Barmouth Cl WLSD/HOW NE28 59 F5
Barmouth Rd NSHW NE29 60 A5
Barmouth Wy NSHW NE29 60 B6
Barmston La WASHN NE37 104 A7
WASHS NE38 117 K1
Barmston Rd WASHS NE38 117 J2
Barmston Wy WASHS NE38 103 H7
Barnard Av RDHAMSE DH6 172 B3
Barnard Cl BDLGTN NE22 28 D5
DHAM DH1 156 E2
Barnard Crs HEBB NE31 73 G4
Barnard Gv JRW NE32 74 B7
Barnard St BLYTH NE24 31 G7
MLFD/PNYW SR4 119 K1
Barnard Wynd PLEE/EAS SR8 174 C7
Barnesbury Rd ELS/FEN NE4 69 J6
Barnes Park Rd
MLFD/PNYW SR4 120 A2
Barnes Rd SEA/MUR SR7 149 G5
SSH NE33 75 F3
Barnes St HLH DH5 147 K4
Barnes Vw MLFD/PNYW SR4 119 K2
Barnett Ct SWCK/CAS SR5 106 B3
Barn Hl STLY/ANP DH9 112 C7
Barn Hollows SEA/MUR SR7 162 D2
Barningham WASHS NE38 117 J2
Barningham Cl SUNDSW SR3 120 B4
Barns Cl JRW NE32 73 J7
Barnstaple Cl WLSD/HOW NE28 58 E5
Barnstaple Rd NSHW NE29 60 A1
The Barns STLY/ANP DH9 112 C6
Barnston ASHGTN NE63 24 D2
Barnton Rd FELL NE10 88 A6
Barnwood Cl WLSD/HOW NE28 58 E5
Baroness Dr
BW/LEM/TK/HW NE15 68 E4
Baron's Quay Rd
SWCK/CAS SR5 105 F5
Baronswood GOS/KPK NE3 56 B6
Barrack Rd ELS/FEN NE4 4 E3
Barrack St SUND SR1 15 J2
Barras Av BLYTH NE24 35 F2
CRAM NE23 38 C7
Barras Av West BLYTH NE24 34 E3
Barras Br CNUT NE1 5 K4
Barras Dr SUNDSW SR3 120 B4
Barrasford Cl ASHGTN NE63 23 G3
GOS/KPK NE3 56 A6
Barrasford Dr DIN/WO NE13 46 C4
Barrasford Rd CRAM NE23 38 D2
DHAM DH1 156 E3
Barrasford St WLSD/HOW NE28 74 A2
Barrass Av CRAM NE23 39 F7
Barr Cl WLSD/HOW NE28 59 G5
Barr Hills CON/LDGT DH8 123 F4
Barr House Av CON/LDGT DH8 123 F4
Barrie Sq SWCK/CAS SR5 106 B3
Barrington Av TYNE/NSHE NE30 50 D7
Barrington Ct BDLGTN NE22 29 G6
Barrington Dr WASHS NE38 117 F1
Barrington Pk BDLGTN NE22 30 B3
Barrington Pl ELS/FEN NE4 4 E4
GATE NE8 10 D4
Barrington Rd BDLGTN NE22 29 J3
STKFD/GP NE62 29 F3
Barrington St SSH NE33 3 G7
Barrington Ter HLH DH5 147 K3
Barrington Wy RDHAMSE DH6 180 A2
Barron St South SWCK/CAS SR5 105 G4
Barrowburn Pl CRAM NE23 39 H7
Barrow St SWCK/CAS SR5 104 D1
Barry St DUN/TMV NE11 9 H6
GATE NE8 86 D5
Barsloan Gv PLEE/EAS SR8 174 C2
Barton Cl TYNE/NSHE NE30 61 F1
WASHN NE37 103 G3
WLSD/HOW NE28 59 F5
Barton Ct
CLDN/WHIT/ROK * SR6 92 C7
Bartram St SWCK/CAS SR5 106 C2
Barwell Cl WLSD/HOW NE28 59 F5
Barwell Ct LGB/HTN NE7 58 A7
Barwick St PLEE/EAS SR8 163 G5
Basildon Gdns WLSD/HOW NE28 58 E5
Basil Wy HAR/WTLS NE34 91 J1
Basingstoke Pl LGB/KIL NE12 57 J3
Basingstoke Rd PLEE/EAS SR8 174 D3
Baslow Gdns SUNDSW SR3 120 B3
Bassington Av CRAM NE23 37 K1
Bassington Dr CRAM NE23 32 D7
Bassington La CRAM NE23 32 D7
Bates La BLAY NE21 84 D2
Bath Cl WLSD/HOW NE28 59 G5
Bathgate Cl WLSD/HOW NE28 59 G5
Bathgate Sq SWCK/CAS SR5 104 D2
Bath La BLYTH NE24 31 H7
CNUT NE1 5 H7
CON/LDGT DH8 123 F4
Bath Lane Ter ELS/FEN NE4 4 F7
Bath Rd FELL NE10 12 C4
HEBB NE31 89 G1
Bath St BYK/HTN/WLK NE6 72 C6
Bath Ter BLYTH NE24 31 H7
GOS/KPK NE3 56 D5
TYNE/NSHE NE30 61 H3
Batley St SWCK/CAS SR5 104 D2
Batt House Rd PSHWF NE43 79 F7
Battle Hill Dr WLSD/HOW NE28 58 E6
Baugh Cl WASHN NE37 102 C7
Baulkham Hills HLS DH4 131 K1
Bavington FELL NE10 88 C7
Bavington Dr
WD/WHPE/BLK NE5 69 G2
Bavington Gdns
TYNE/NSHE NE30 60 E1
Bavington Rd MONK NE25 40 A5
Bawtry Gv NSHW NE29 60 C5
Baxter Av ELS/FEN NE4 69 J5
Baxter Rd SWCK/CAS SR5 104 D1
Baxter Sq SWCK/CAS SR5 104 D1
Baxterwood Gv ELS/FEN NE4 4 D5
Bay Av PLEE/EAS SR8 175 J4
Baybridge Rd
WD/WHPE/BLK NE5 54 C7
Bayfield Gdns GATE NE8 11 L6
Baysdale HLS DH4 117 G6
Bayswater Av SWCK/CAS SR5 104 E2
Bayswater Rd GATE NE8 11 L7
JES NE2 70 E1
Bayswater Sq SWCK/CAS SR5 104 E2
Baytree Gdns MONK NE25 50 C6
Baytree Ter STLY/ANP DH9 114 B7
Baywood Gv WLSD/HOW NE28 58 E5
Beach Av WBAY NE26 50 E4
Beach Croft Av
TYNE/NSHE NE30 51 F7
Beachcross Rd
ASHBK/HED/RY SR2 14 A7
Beachdale Cl WNGT TS28 184 A6
Beach Gv PLEE/EAS SR8 175 H4
Beach Rd NSHW NE29 60 C3
SSH NE33 3 J8
TYNE/NSHE NE30 60 E2
Beach St MLFD/PNYW SR4 14 B2
Beach Ter NWBGN NE64 25 F2
Beachville St MLFD/PNYW SR4 14 A7
Beachway BLYTH NE24 35 H3
Beach Wy TYNE/NSHE NE30 60 E1
Beacon Dr
CLDN/WHIT/ROK SR6 107 F4
DIN/WO NE13 46 A4
Beacon Gld HAR/WTLS NE34 76 C5
Beacon La CRAM NE23 37 J2
Beacon Lough Rd
LWF/SPW/WRK NE9 101 G1
Beaconsfield Av
LWF/SPW/WRK NE9 87 G7
Beaconsfield Cl MONK NE25 50 B2
Beaconsfield Crs
LWF/SPW/WRK NE9 87 G7
Beaconsfield Rd
LWF/SPW/WRK NE9 87 F7
Beaconsfield St BLYTH NE24 31 H7
CON/LDGT DH8 123 F3
ELS/FEN NE4 4 D5
STLY/ANP DH9 112 D7
Beaconside HAR/WTLS NE34 76 C5
Beacon St LWF/SPW/WRK NE9 87 F7
SSH NE33 3 H3
TYNE/NSHE NE30 2 F1
Beadling Gdns ELS/FEN NE4 69 J5
Beadnell Av NSHW NE29 60 B6
Beadnell Cl BLAY NE21 83 J4
Beadnell Gdns SMOOR NE27 49 H6
Beadnell Pl JES NE2 6 A5
Beadnell Rd BLYTH NE24 34 D2
Beadnell Wy GOS/KPK NE3 56 A5
Beal Cl BLYTH NE24 30 E7
Beal Dr LGB/KIL NE12 58 B2
Beal Gdns WLSD/HOW NE28 59 H5
Beal Rd SMOOR NE27 49 H6
Beal Ter BYK/HTN/WLK NE6 72 B7
Beal Wk DHAM DH1 169 J5
Beal Wy GOS/KPK NE3 56 B5
Beaminster Wy GOS/KPK NE3 55 G5
WD/WHPE/BLK NE5 55 G5
Beamishburn Rd
STLY/ANP DH9 112 E5
Beamish Cl BDN/LAN/SAC DH7 154 A3
WLSD/HOW NE28 58 E5
Beamish Gdns
LWF/SPW/WRK NE9 101 K1
Beamish Hills STLY/ANP DH9 113 H7
Beamish St STLY/ANP DH9 112 C7
Beamish Vw CLSW/PEL DH2 128 B4
STLY/ANP DH9 113 F7
Beamsley Ter ASHGTN NE63 23 K2
Beaney La CLSW/PEL DH2 144 A2
Beanley Av HEBB NE31 73 F7
Beanley Crs TYNE/NSHE NE30 61 G3
Beanley Pl LGB/HTN NE7 57 G7
Bearpark Colliery Rd
BDN/LAN/SAC DH7 155 G5
Beatrice Av BLYTH NE24 34 D3
Beatrice Gdns BOL NE36 91 H5
HAR/WTLS NE34 75 J5
Beatrice St ASHGTN NE63 24 A1
CLDN/WHIT/ROK SR6 106 E4
Beatrice Ter HLS DH4 117 G5
Beattie St HAR/WTLS NE34 75 F6
Beatty Av JES NE2 56 E7
Beatty Rd BDLGTN NE22 29 H6
Beatty St PLEE/EAS SR8 163 G5
Beaufort Cl HLS DH4 131 K2
WD/WHPE/BLK NE5 55 H7
Beaufort Gdns
WLSD/HOW NE28 59 F5
Beaufront Cl FELL NE10 88 D6
Beaufront Gdns GATE NE8 11 L5
WD/WHPE/BLK NE5 69 G3
Beaufront Ter JRW NE32 89 K1
SSH NE33 75 G3
Beauly WASHS NE38 117 F3
Beaumaris Gdns SUNDSW SR3 119 G7
Beaumaris Wy
WD/WHPE/BLK NE5 55 F6
Beaumont Cl DHAM DH1 156 B2
RDHAMSE DH6 180 A3
Beaumont Crs PLEE/EAS SR8 175 F1
Beaumont Dr MONK NE25 50 A2
WASHS NE38 117 F2
Beaumont Mnr BLYTH NE24 30 B7
Beaumont Pl PLEE/EAS SR8 175 F5
Beaumont St
ASHBK/HED/RY SR2 15 G9
BLYTH NE24 31 F6
ELS/FEN NE4 9 G1
NSHW NE29 2 C2
SEA/MUR SR7 150 E2
SWCK/CAS SR5 106 A2
Beaumont Ter GOS/KPK NE3 56 D5
JRW NE32 73 J6
WD/WHPE/BLK NE5 68 D1
Beaumont Wy PRUD NE42 80 B3
Beaurepaire
BDN/LAN/SAC DH7 155 F6
Beaver Cl DHAM DH1 156 D1
Bebdon Ct BLYTH NE24 34 E1
Bebside Furnace Rd
BLYTH NE24 29 K6
Bebside Rd BLYTH NE24 29 J7
Beckenham Av BOL NE36 91 H4
Beckenham Cl BOL NE36 91 J4
Beckenham Gdns
WLSD/HOW NE28 58 E6
Beckett St GATE NE8 6 D9
Beckfoot Cl WD/WHPE/BLK NE5 69 F2
Beckford WASHS NE38 117 J2
Beckford Cl WLSD/HOW NE28 58 E5
Beck Pl PLEE/EAS SR8 174 E3
Beckside Gdns
WD/WHPE/BLK NE5 67 K2
Beckwith Rd SUNDSW SR3 119 G6
Beda Hl BLAY NE21 84 A1
Bedale Cl DHAM DH1 158 A5
WLSD/HOW NE28 58 E5
Bedale Crs SWCK/CAS SR5 104 E2
Bedale Dr MONK NE25 50 D6
Bedale Gn WD/WHPE/BLK NE5 55 H7
Bedale St HLH DH5 147 K6
Bedburn WASHS NE38 116 B5
Bede Av DHAM DH1 17 M4
Bede Burn Rd JRW NE32 73 K5
Bedeburn Rd
WD/WHPE/BLK NE5 54 D5
Bede Burn Vw JRW NE32 73 K6
Bede Cl LGB/KIL NE12 58 D2
Bede Ct CLS/BIR/GTL DH3 129 J4
GATE NE8 11 J4
Bede Crs WASHS NE38 102 E7
WLSD/HOW NE28 59 F6
Bede St CLDN/WHIT/ROK SR6 106 E3
PLEE/EAS SR8 163 G5
Bedesway JRW NE32 74 B5
Bede Ter BOL NE36 91 H5
CLSW/PEL DH2 129 H4
JRW NE32 73 K6
RDHAMSE DH6 180 A2
Bede Wk HEBB NE31 73 H6
Bede Wy DHAM DH1 156 C3
PLEE/EAS SR8 174 E4
Bedford Av CLS/BIR/GTL DH3 115 K5
SSH NE33 75 G2
WLSD/HOW NE28 58 C7
Bedford Ct NSHW NE29 2 E3
Bedford Pl GATE NE8 10 E3

SUNDSW SR3 120 A6
WD/WHPE/BLK NE5 68 A2
Bedfordshire Dr DHAM DH1 158 A7
Bedford St NSHW NE29 2 D2
SUND SR1 14 F3
Bedford Ter NSHW NE29 2 D1
Bedford Wy NSHW NE29 2 D2
Bedlington Bank BDLGTN NE22 29 G6
Beech Av CLDN/WHIT/ROK SR6 93 G3
CRAM NE23 38 E3
DIN/WO NE13 45 F2
GOS/KPK NE3 55 K4
HLS DH4 132 B6
MPTH NE61 21 F6
WICK/BNPF NE16 8 A8
Beech Cl DHAM DH1 157 F1
GOS/KPK NE3 56 C1
Beech Ct BDN/LAN/SAC DH7 154 B3
NSHW NE29 2 B1
PONT/DH NE20 52 C1
Beech Crs SEA/MUR SR7 150 D2
Beechcrest DHAM DH1 16 A5
Beechcroft Av
BDN/LAN/SAC DH7 166 E7
GOS/KPK NE3 56 A7
Beechcroft Cl DHAM DH1 157 H6
Beechdale Rd CON/LDGT DH8 123 G4
Beech Dr DUN/TMV NE11 8 F6
Beecher St BLYTH NE24 30 D5
Beeches La
CON/LDGT (off Church St) DH8 136 E2
The Beeches
ELS/FEN (off Clumber St) NE4 9 J1
LGB/KIL (off Eastfield Rd) NE12 57 K4
PONT/DH NE20 43 F3
Beechfield Gdns
WLSD/HOW NE28 58 C7
Beechfield Ri RDHAMSE DH6 180 D6
Beechfield Rd GOS/KPK NE3 56 B6
Beech Gv BDN/LAN/SAC DH7 141 G4
BDN/LAN/SAC DH7 167 G1
HAR/WTLS NE34 75 K7
LGB/KIL NE12 57 K4
LWF/SPW/WRK NE9 102 B4
TRIM TS29 183 F6
WBAY NE26 50 D4
WLSD/HOW NE28 72 D1
Beech Grove Ct RYTON NE40 66 B7
Beech Grove Rd ELS/FEN NE4 4 C8
Beech Pk BDN/LAN/SAC DH7 167 F7
Beech Rd CON/LDGT DH8 123 K4
DHAM DH1 156 C4
RDHAMSE DH6 158 C7
Beech Sq WASHS NE38 117 G2
Beech St ELS/FEN NE4 69 J7
GATE NE8 11 L5
JRW NE32 73 J4
PSHWF NE43 79 J4
Beech Ter BLAY NE21 84 A3
STLY/ANP DH9 127 F4
Beech Wy LGB/KIL NE12 47 J5
Beechways DHAM DH1 156 A6
Beechwood Av
LWF/SPW/WRK NE9 101 G2
MONK NE25 50 B5
RYTON NE40 66 E6
STKFD/GP NE62 23 G5
Beechwood Cl JRW NE32 74 B5
Beechwood Crs SWCK/CAS SR5 105 K3
Beechwood Gdns
DUN/TMV NE11 86 B7
Beechwood Pl PONT/DH NE20 43 G2
Beechwoods CLSW/PEL DH2 129 H2
Beechwood St
ASHBK/HED/RY SR2 14 B7
Beechwood Ter
ASHBK/HED/RY SR2 14 B7
HLS DH4 132 A5
Beeston Av SWCK/CAS SR5 104 D2
Beetham Crs
WD/WHPE/BLK NE5 68 E3
Beethoven St SSH NE33 3 K9
Begonia Cl HEBB NE31 89 G1
Bek Rd DHAM DH1 156 D3
Beldene Dr MLFD/PNYW SR4 119 J2
Belford Av SMOOR NE27 49 H6
Belford Cl ASHBK/HED/RY SR2 120 D3
WLSD/HOW NE28 59 F5
Belford Ct
BLYTH
(off Devonworth Pl) NE24 30 D7
Belford Gdns DUN/TMV NE11 86 A7
Belford Rd ASHBK/HED/RY SR2 120 E3
Belford St PLEE/EAS SR8 175 G2
Belford Ter BYK/HTN/WLK NE6 7 M6
TYNE/NSHE NE30 60 E3
The Belfry HLS DH4 131 J3
Belgrade Crs SWCK/CAS SR5 104 D1
Belgrade Sq SWCK/CAS SR5 104 D2
Belgrave Crs BLYTH NE24 31 H7
Belgrave Gdns ASHGTN NE63 24 C3
Belgrave Pde ELS/FEN NE4 4 E9
Belgrave Ter FELL NE10 12 D9
SSH NE33 3 K7
Bellburn Ct CRAM NE23 33 J7
Belle Grove Pl JES NE2 4 E2
Belle Grove Ter JES NE2 4 F2
Belle Grove Vls JES NE2 4 F2
Belle Gv West JES NE2 4 E2
Bellerby Dr CLSW/PEL DH2 114 E3
Belle St STLY/ANP DH9 112 D7
Belles Ville DHAM DH1 17 M2
Belle View Dr CON/LDGT DH8 137 F2
Belle Vue Av GOS/KPK NE3 56 D5
Belle Vue Bank
LWF/SPW/WRK NE9 86 E7
Belle Vue Ct
DHAM (off Claypath) DH1 16 E3
Bellevue Crs CRAM NE23 33 H5
Belle Vue Crs SSH NE33 75 F5
Belle Vue Gdns CON/LDGT DH8 123 F4
Belle Vue Gv
LWF/SPW/WRK * NE9 87 F7
Belle Vue Pk
ASHBK/HED/RY SR2 14 C9
Belle Vue Pk West
ASHBK/HED/RY SR2 14 C9
Belle Vue Rd
ASHBK/HED/RY SR2 120 C2
Belle Vue Ter NSHW NE29 2 C3
Bellfield Av GOS/KPK NE3 55 K4
Bellgreen Av GOS/KPK NE3 56 D1
Bell Gv LGB/KIL NE12 47 J5
Bell House Rd SWCK/CAS SR5 92 A7
Bellingham Cl WLSD/HOW NE28 59 F6
Bellingham Ct BDLGTN NE22 29 H5
GOS/KPK* NE3 55 H5
Bellingham Dr LGB/KIL NE12 58 B3
Bellister Gv WD/WHPE/BLK NE5 69 G3
Bellister Pk PLEE/EAS SR8 175 F6
Bellister Rd NSHW NE29 60 B4
Bell Meadow
BDN/LAN/SAC DH7 167 F7
Belloc Av HAR/WTLS NE34 91 F1
Bellows Burn La RHTLP TS27 185 G6
Bell Rd WYLAM NE41 65 H5
Bellsburn Ct ASHGTN NE63 23 H3
Bells Cl BLYTH NE24 30 B6
BW/LEM/TK/HW NE15 68 C6
Bell's Folly DHAM DH1 168 B3
Bellshill Cl WLSD/HOW NE28 59 G4
Bell's Pl BDLGTN NE22 29 G6
Bell St HEBB NE31 73 F5
HLS DH4 117 K6
MLFD/PNYW SR4 105 K7
TYNE/NSHE NE30 2 F2
WASHS NE38 117 H2
Bell Vw PRUD NE42 81 F1
Belmont FELL NE10 88 C7
Belmont Av MONK NE25 50 B5
SEA/MUR SR7 162 C1
Belmont Cl WLSD/HOW NE28 59 F5
Belmont Ri HLH DH5 147 K7
Belmont Rd MLFD/PNYW SR4 119 K1
Belmont St BYK/HTN/WLK NE6 13 G1
Belmont Wk BYK/HTN/WLK NE6 13 G2
Belmount Av GOS/KPK NE3 56 D1
Belper Cl WLSD/HOW NE28 58 E5
Belsay WASHS NE38 116 B2
Belsay Av DIN/WO NE13 46 A5
HAR/WTLS NE34 76 A4
MONK NE25 51 F5
Belsay Cl MPTH NE61 21 K2
WLSD/HOW NE28 58 E5
Belsay Ct BLYTH NE24 30 E7
Belsay Gdns DUN/TMV NE11 86 A7
GOS/KPK NE3 55 K2
MLFD/PNYW SR4 119 K1
Belsay Gv BDLGTN NE22 29 J3
Belsay Pl ELS/FEN NE4 4 C5
Belsfield Gdns JRW NE32 73 K7
Belsize Pl BYK/HTN/WLK NE6 72 B3
Beltingham WD/WHPE/BLK NE5 68 C2
Belvedere NSHW NE29 60 D3
Belvedere Av MONK NE25 50 D5
Belvedere Ct BYK/HTN/WLK NE6 7 G4
Belvedere Gdns LGB/KIL NE12 57 K4
Belvedere Pkwy GOS/KPK * NE3 55 G4
Belvedere Rd
ASHBK/HED/RY SR2 14 D8
Belverdere Gdns
RDHAMSE DH6 173 G3
Bemersyde Dr JES NE2 56 E7
Benbrake Av NSHW NE29 60 C1
Bendigo Av HAR/WTLS NE34 90 D1
Benedict Rd
CLDN/WHIT/ROK SR6 107 F3
Benevente St SEA/MUR SR7 150 E2
Benfield Cl CON/LDGT DH8 122 C1
Benfield Gv WBAY NE26 40 E1
Benfield Rd BYK/HTN/WLK NE6 71 K1
Benfieldside Rd
CON/LDGT DH8 122 C2
Benjamin Rd WLSD/HOW NE28 59 J7
Bennett's Wk MPTH NE61 20 E5
Benridge Bank HLS DH4 146 C6
Bensham Av GATE NE8 10 D6
Bensham Ct GATE NE8 10 D6
HAR/WTLS NE34 75 G6
Bensham Crs GATE NE8 10 B6
Bensham Rd GATE NE8 10 C5
Benson Pl BYK/HTN/WLK NE6 7 H5
Benson Rd BYK/HTN/WLK NE6 7 K5
Benson St CLS/BIR/GTL DH3 129 J5
STLY/ANP DH9 112 C7
Benson Ter FELL NE10 12 C7
Bent House La DHAM DH1 17 M7
Bentinck Crs ELS/FEN * NE4 4 B8
MPTH NE61 21 J2
Bentinck Rd ELS/FEN NE4 4 B8
Bentinck St ELS/FEN NE4 4 B8
Bentinck Vls ELS/FEN NE4 4 B6
Benton Bank JES NE2 71 G2
LGB/HTN NE7 71 G2
Benton Cl LGB/HTN NE7 57 H5
Benton Hall Wk LGB/HTN NE7 71 K1
Benton La LGB/KIL NE12 57 H2
Benton Lodge Av LGB/HTN NE7 57 H5
Benton Park Rd LGB/HTN NE7 57 F5
Benton Rd HAR/WTLS NE34 91 G2
LGB/HTN NE7 57 J5
SMOOR NE27 49 F7
Benton Ter JES NE2 6 A2
Benton Wy WLSD/HOW NE28 72 D3
Bents Cottages SSH NE33 3 M9
Bents Park Rd SSH NE33 3 M7
Benwell Cl
BW/LEM/TK/HW
(off Benwell Gra) NE15 69 H6
Benwell Dene Ter
BW/LEM/TK/HW NE15 69 G6
Benwell Grange Av
BW/LEM/TK/HW NE15 69 H6
Benwell Grange Rd
BW/LEM/TK/HW NE15 69 G6
Benwell Grange Ter
BW/LEM/TK/HW NE15 69 G6
Benwell Gv ELS/FEN NE4 69 J6
Benwell Hall Dr
BW/LEM/TK/HW NE15 69 F5
Benwell Hill Gdns
WD/WHPE/BLK NE5 69 G4
Benwell Hill Rd
WD/WHPE/BLK NE5 69 F4
Benwell La
BW/LEM/TK/HW NE15 69 F6
Benwell Village
BW/LEM/TK/HW NE15 69 F5
Benwell Village Ms
BW/LEM/TK/HW NE15 69 G5
Beresford Av HEBB NE31 89 G1
Beresford Gdns
BYK/HTN/WLK NE6 7 G7
Beresford Pk A
SHBK/HED/RY SR2 14 B8
Beresford Rd TYNE/NSHE NE30 50 E6
WBAY NE26 41 G3
Bergen Cl NSHW NE29 59 K6
Bergen Sq SWCK/CAS SR5 104 D1
Bergen St SWCK/CAS SR5 104 D1
Berkdale Rd
LWF/SPW/WRK NE9 100 E3
Berkeley Cl BOLCOL NE35 90 C3
LGB/KIL NE12 48 A5
SUNDSW SR3 119 G7
Berkeley Sq GOS/KPK NE3 56 B3
Berkely St SSH NE33 3 J8
Berkhamstead Ct FELL * NE10 88 E5
Berkley Av BLAY NE21 84 C2
Berkley Cl WLSD/HOW NE28 59 F5
Berkley Rd NSHW NE29 60 B4
Berkley St
BW/LEM/TK/HW NE15 67 H3
Berkley Wy HEBB NE31 73 H3
Berkshire Cl DHAM DH1 157 K6
WD/WHPE/BLK NE5 68 D1
Berkshire Rd PLEE/EAS SR8 174 D2
Bermondsey St JES NE2 6 B5
Bernard St BYK/HTN/WLK NE6 72 C7
HLS DH4 132 B7
Berrington Dr
WD/WHPE/BLK NE5 55 F7
Berrishill Gv MONK NE25 50 A3
Berry Cl BYK/HTN/WLK NE6 72 C6
WLSD/HOW NE28 58 E5
Berry Edge Rd CON/LDGT DH8 123 F5
Berry Edge Vw CON/LDGT DH8 122 E4
Berryfield Cl SUNDSW SR3 134 A2
Berry Hl RYTON NE40 66 C7
Berryhill Cl BLAY NE21 84 B3
Berrymoor ASHGTN NE63 24 A1
Bertha St CON/LDGT DH8 123 F4
Bertram Crs
BW/LEM/TK/HW NE15 69 G5
Bertram St SSH NE33 75 G3
Bertram Ter ASHGTN NE63 23 K2
Berwick WASHS NE38 116 B2
Berwick Av SWCK/CAS SR5 104 D1
Berwick Cha PLEE/EAS SR8 174 C7
Berwick Cl
BW/LEM/TK/HW NE15 67 J4
Berwick Ct PONT/DH NE20 43 H2
Berwick Dr WLSD/HOW NE28 59 F5
Berwick Hill Rd PONT/DH NE20 43 G2
Berwick Sq SWCK/CAS SR5 104 D1
Berwick Ter NSHW NE29 60 B6
Besford Gv SUND SR1 15 H5
Bessemer St CON/LDGT DH8 122 E4
Bethnell Av BYK/HTN/WLK * NE6 7 J2
Bethune Av SEA/MUR SR7 150 B1
Betjeman Cl STLY/ANP DH9 126 E1
Bet's La MPTH NE61 26 B5
Betts Av BW/LEM/TK/HW NE15 69 F6
Beumaris HLS DH4 131 F4
Bevan Av ASHBK/HED/RY SR2 120 E7
Bevan Crs RDHAMSE DH6 182 D2
Bevan Gdns FELL NE10 13 K8
Bevan Gv DHAM DH1 157 J6
Bevan Sq SEA/MUR SR7 149 H4
Beverley Cl GOS/KPK NE3 46 B7
Beverley Crs
LWF/SPW/WRK NE9 87 G7
Beverley Dr BLAY NE21 83 H4
STKFD/GP NE62 23 G5
WICK/BNPF NE16 8 A6
Beverley Gdns
CLS/BIR/GTL DH3 129 K5
CON/LDGT DH8 122 D2
TYNE/NSHE NE30 51 G6
Beverley Pk MONK NE25 50 C5
Beverley Pl WLSD/HOW NE28 73 H1
Beverley Rd
ASHBK/HED/RY SR2 121 F4
LWF/SPW/WRK NE9 87 G6
MONK NE25 50 D5
Beverley Ter BYK/HTN/WLK NE6 72 C6
TYNE/NSHE NE30 51 G6
Beverley Wy PLEE/EAS SR8 174 D3
Bevin Sq RDHAMSE DH6 161 G2
Beweshill Crs BLAY NE21 83 J3
Bewick Cl CLSW/PEL DH2 129 G7
Bewick Crs
BW/LEM/TK/HW NE15 68 B4
Bewicke Rd WLSD/HOW NE28 73 J2
Bewicke St WLSD/HOW NE28 73 K2
Bewick Garth PSHWF NE43 79 J3
Bewick La PRUD NE42 64 B7
Bewick Pk WLSD/HOW NE28 59 H4
Bewick Rd GATE NE8 10 E6
Bewick St CNUT NE1 5 H8
SSH NE33 75 G3
Bewley Gdns WLSD/HOW NE28 59 F5
Bewley Gv PLEE/EAS SR8 174 B7
Bexhill Rd SWCK/CAS SR5 104 D2
Bexhill Sq BLYTH NE24 35 G2
SWCK/CAS SR5 104 D2
Bexley Av
BW/LEM/TK/HW NE15 68 E5
Bexley Pl WICK/BNPF NE16 84 E7
Bexley St MLFD/PNYW SR4 105 K7
Bickington Ct HLS * DH4 132 A4
Biddick Hall Dr HAR/WTLS NE34 75 F7
Biddick La WASHS NE38 117 F3
Biddick Vw WASHS NE38 117 G3
Biddick Vls WASHS NE38 117 G3
Biddlestone Crs NSHW NE29 60 B5
Biddlestone Rd
BYK/HTN/WLK NE6 71 J2
Bideford Gdns HAR/WTLS NE34 76 A2
JRW NE32 74 B6
LWF/SPW/WRK NE9 101 F2
WBAY NE26 50 D3
Bideford Gv WICK/BNPF NE16 84 E7
Bideford Rd GOS/KPK NE3 55 J6
Bideford St
ASHBK/HED/RY SR2 121 F4
Bigbury Cl HLS DH4 132 A3
Bigges Gdns WLSD/HOW NE28 58 B6
Bigg Market CNUT NE1 5 K7
Bilbrough Gdns ELS/FEN NE4 69 H7
Billy Mill Av NSHW NE29 60 C4
Billy Mill La NSHW NE29 60 B3
Bilsdale CLDN/WHIT/ROK SR6 93 F5
Bilsdale Pl LGB/KIL NE12 57 F4
Bilsmoor Av LGB/HTN NE7 71 H1
Bilton Hall Rd JRW NE32 74 B5
Binchester St HAR/WTLS NE34 74 E7
Bingfield Gdns
WD/WHPE/BLK NE5 69 G3
Bingley Cl WLSD/HOW NE28 59 G5
Bingley St SWCK/CAS SR5 104 D2
Bink Moss WASHN NE37 102 C7
Binswood Av
WD/WHPE/BLK NE5 69 F2
Bircham Dr BLAY NE21 84 B2
Bircham St STLY/ANP DH9 126 B2
Birch Av CLDN/WHIT/ROK SR6 93 F3
FELL NE10 13 J9
Birch Ct SUNDSW SR3 133 J1
Birch Crs WICK/BNPF NE16 97 H7
Birches Nook Rd PSHWF NE43 79 G5
The Birches STLY/ANP DH9 112 D6
WICK/BNPF NE16 99 G2
Birchfield WICK/BNPF NE16 85 F6
Birchfield Gdns
BW/LEM/TK/HW NE15 68 C4
LWF/SPW/WRK NE9 101 G3
Birchfield Rd
ASHBK/HED/RY SR2 14 B9
Birchgate Cl BLAY NE21 83 J3
Birch Gv CON/LDGT DH8 138 D1
WLSD/HOW NE28 58 E5
Birchgrove Av DHAM DH1 157 J6
Birchington Av SSH NE33 75 G4
Birch Pl BDN/LAN/SAC DH7 165 G2
Birch Rd BLAY NE21 84 B2
Birch St CON/LDGT DH8 123 F5
JRW NE32 73 J4
Birch Ter BYK/HTN/WLK NE6 72 C6
Birchvale Av
WD/WHPE/BLK NE5 68 E1
Birchwood Av DIN/WO NE13 46 B4
LGB/HTN NE7 57 J7
WICK/BNPF NE16 84 E7
Birchwood Cl CRAM NE23 39 F7
STLY/ANP DH9 113 J6
Birdhill Pl HAR/WTLS NE34 75 G6
Birds Nest Rd BYK/HTN/WLK NE6 7 K8
Bird St TYNE/NSHE NE30 3 G1
Birkdale MONK NE25 50 B4
SSH NE33 75 J2
Birkdale Av
CLDN/WHIT/ROK SR6 92 E5
Birkdale Cl LGB/HTN NE7 57 J6
WLSD/HOW NE28 58 D6
Birkdale Dr HLS DH4 131 J3
Birkdale Gdns DHAM DH1 158 A6
Birkdene PSHWF NE43 79 H6
Birkheads La DUN/TMV NE11 99 J7
Birkland La WICK/BNPF NE16 99 H5
Birks Rd BW/LEM/TK/HW NE15 52 D5
Birling Pl WD/WHPE/BLK NE5 69 H1
Birnam Gv JRW NE32 90 C2
Birney Edge PONT/DH NE20 52 E1
Birnie Cl ELS/FEN NE4 69 J7
Birrell Sq SWCK/CAS SR5 104 D1
Birrell St SWCK/CAS SR5 104 D1
Birtley Av TYNE/NSHE NE30 61 H2
Birtley Cl GOS/KPK NE3 56 A6
Birtley La CLS/BIR/GTL DH3 115 J2
Birtwistle Av HEBB NE31 89 F1
Biscop Ter JRW NE32 73 K6
Bishop Crs JRW NE32 74 A3
Bishopdale HLS DH4 117 G6
WLSD/HOW NE28 58 B5
Bishopdale Av BLYTH NE24 34 C1
Bishop Morton Gv SUND SR1 15 H6
Bishop Ramsay Ct
HAR/WTLS NE34 76 A5
Bishop Rock Dr LGB/KIL NE12 57 G4
Bishop Rock Rd LGB/KIL NE12 57 G4
Bishop's Av ELS/FEN NE4 4 C6
Bishops Cl WLSD/HOW NE28 73 G1
Bishops Dr RYTON NE40 83 F1
Bishops Meadow BDLGTN NE22 28 E5
Bishop's Rd ELS/FEN NE4 69 H7
Bishops Wy DHAM DH1 156 C2
SUNDSW SR3 133 K2
Bishopton St
ASHBK/HED/RY SR2 15 G7
Bisley Dr HAR/WTLS NE34 75 H4
Bittern Cl WLSD/HOW NE28 59 J4
Biverfield Rd PRUD NE42 80 E1
Black Boy Rd HLS DH4 146 B1
Blackburn Cl
BDN/LAN/SAC DH7 155 F5
Blackburn Gn FELL NE10 12 B9
Blackcliffe Wy
BDN/LAN/SAC DH7 155 F5
Blackclose Bank ASHGTN NE63 23 J5
Blackclose Est ASHGTN NE63 23 K5
Blackdene ASHGTN NE63 23 H3
Blackdown Cl LGB/KIL NE12 57 G4
PLEE/EAS SR8 174 C5
Black Dr CLS/BIR/GTL DH3 130 E1
Blackettbridge
CNUT (off Eldon Sq) NE1 5 J6
Blackett St CNUT NE1 5 J6
HEBB NE31 73 H3
STLY/ANP DH9 125 G3
Blackfell Rd WASHN NE37 102 B6
Blackfriars CNUT NE1 5 H7
Blackfriars Ct CNUT * NE1 5 H7
Blackfriars Wy LGB/KIL NE12 57 G3
Blackheath Cl WASHN NE37 102 E3
Blackheath Ct
WD/WHPE/BLK NE5 55 F5
Blackhill Av WLSD/HOW NE28 59 G3
Blackhill Crs
LWF/SPW/WRK NE9 101 K1
Blackhills Rd PLEE/EAS SR8 175 H2
Black House La
BDN/LAN/SAC DH7 127 K7
Blackhouse La RYTON NE40 66 D6
Black La BLAY NE21 83 J2
LWF/SPW/WRK NE9 101 H4
RDHAMSE DH6 172 E7
Black Rd ASHBK/HED/RY SR2 121 F7
BDN/LAN/SAC DH7 167 K4
HEBB NE31 73 H4
Blackrow La
BW/LEM/TK/HW NE15 52 C6
Blackstone Ct BLAY NE21 83 J2
Blackthorn Dr WLSD/HOW NE28 58 E5
Blackthorn Wy ASHGTN NE63 23 H3
BLYTH NE24 34 E3
HLS DH4 131 J5
Blackwood Rd SWCK/CAS SR5 104 E2
Bladen St JRW NE32 73 J4
Blagdon Av HAR/WTLS NE34 75 J3
Blagdon Cl CNUT NE1 6 A6
MPTH NE61 20 C5
Blagdon Ct BDLGTN NE22 29 J4
Blagdon Crs CRAM NE23 32 E7
Blagdon Dr BLYTH NE24 34 E5
Blaidwood Dr DHAM DH1 168 B5
Blair Cl RDHAMSE DH6 170 C1
Blair Ct BDN/LAN/SAC DH7 167 K5
Blake Av WICK/BNPF NE16 85 F5
Blakelaw Rd
WD/WHPE/BLK NE5 69 F1
Blakemoor Pl
WD/WHPE/BLK NE5 69 G2
Blakes Cl STLY/ANP DH9 126 E1
Blake St PLEE/EAS SR8 163 G5
Blake Wk GATE NE8 11 J4
Blanche Gv PLEE/EAS SR8 174 E5
Blanchland WASHS NE38 117 G5
Blanchland Av
BW/LEM/TK/HW NE15 67 K4
DHAM DH1 157 F3
DIN/WO NE13 46 B3
Blanchland Cl WLSD/HOW NE28 59 F6
Blanchland Dr MONK NE25 40 C6
SWCK/CAS SR5 106 C2
Blanchland Ter
TYNE/NSHE NE30 61 F3
Blandford Pl SEA/MUR SR7 150 E1
Blandford Rd NSHW NE29 60 B2
Blandford Sq CNUT NE1 5 G8
Blandford St CNUT NE1 5 G9
SUND SR1 14 E5
Blaxton Pl WICK/BNPF NE16 84 D7
Blaydon Bank BLAY NE21 83 K2
Blaydon Hwy BLAY NE21 84 A1
Blaykeston Cl SEA/MUR SR7 134 E6
Bleachfeld FELL NE10 88 B6
Bleasdale Crs HLS DH4 117 K7
Blencathra WASHN NE37 102 E6
Blenheim LGB/KIL NE12 47 K5
Blenheim Dr BDLGTN NE22 29 J3
Blenheim Gdns MPTH NE61 21 J1
Blenheim Pl DUN/TMV NE11 8 E5
Blenheim St CNUT NE1 5 G9
Blenheim Wk SSH NE33 3 J7
Blenkinsop Gv JRW NE32 89 J1
Blenkinsopp Ct PLEE/EAS SR8 184 C1
Blenkinsop St WLSD/HOW NE28 72 C1
Blind La CLS/BIR/GTL DH3 129 K1
HLS DH4 131 K4
SUNDSW SR3 120 A6
Blindy La HLH DH5 148 B7
Bloomfield Dr HLH DH5 147 G5
Bloomsbury Ct GOS/KPK NE3 56 B6
Blossomfield Wy
RDHAMSE DH6 160 E6
Blossom Gv HLS DH4 131 K3
Blount St BYK/HTN/WLK NE6 7 K5
Blucher Rd LGB/KIL NE12 57 J1
NSHW NE29 2 B6
Blue Anchor Ct CNUT * NE1 5 M8
Bluebell Cl LWF/SPW/WRK NE9 87 H7
WYLAM NE41 65 G4
Bluebell Dene
WD/WHPE/BLK NE5 54 E5
Bluebell Wy HAR/WTLS NE34 75 F6
Blueburn Dr LGB/KIL NE12 48 B5
Blue Coat Ct DHAM DH1 16 E3
Bluehouse Bank
STLY/ANP DH9 127 K4
Blue House Buildings
DHAM (off High St) DH1 157 K5
Blue House Ct WASHN NE37 102 D5
Blue House La
CLDN/WHIT/ROK SR6 91 K5
WASHN NE37 102 D5
Blue House Rd HEBB NE31 89 F1
Blue Quarries Rd
LWF/SPW/WRK NE9 87 H6
Blyth Cl CRAM NE23 47 F1
Blyth Ct BW/LEM/TK/HW NE15 68 A4
HAR/WTLS NE34 75 G6
Blyth Rd WBAY NE26 41 H5
Blyth Sq SWCK/CAS SR5 104 E2
Blyth St MONK NE25 39 K4
SWCK/CAS SR5 104 E2
Blyth Ter ASHGTN NE63 24 A1
Blyton Av ASHBK/HED/RY SR2 120 E7
HAR/WTLS NE34 74 D6
Bodlewell La SUND SR1 15 H3
Bodley Cl GOS/KPK NE3 55 H5
Bodmin Cl WLSD/HOW NE28 59 G5
Bodmin Rd NSHW NE29 60 A2
Bodmin Sq SWCK/CAS SR5 104 E2
Bodmin Wy GOS/KPK NE3 55 K4
Bognor St SWCK/CAS SR5 104 D1
Bohemia Ter BLYTH NE24 35 G1
Boker La BOL NE36 91 F4
Bolam Av BLYTH NE24 31 F7
TYNE/NSHE NE30 60 E1
Bolam Dr ASHGTN NE63 24 A3
Bolam Gdns WLSD/HOW NE28 59 K7
Bolam Gv TYNE/NSHE NE30 60 E1
Bolam Rd LGB/KIL NE12 47 J6
Bolam St BYK/HTN/WLK NE6 7 H7
GATE NE8 9 M7
PLEE/EAS SR8 163 G5
Bolam Wy BYK/HTN/WLK NE6 7 G7

MONK NE25 .....39 K5
Boland Rd MPTH NE61 .....18 C1
Bolbec Rd ELS/FEN NE4 .....69 J4
Bolburn FELL NE10 .....13 K9
Boldon Cl WLSD/HOW NE28 .....59 F5
Boldon Dr BOL NE36 .....90 D5
Boldon Gdns
  LWF/SPW/WRK NE9 .....101 K1
Boldon La CLDN/WHIT/ROK SR6 .....91 J3
  HAR/WTLS NE34 .....75 G7
Boldon North Br BOL NE36 .....91 G4
Bolingbroke Rd NSHW NE29 .....60 B4
Bolingbroke St
  BYK/HTN/WLK NE6 .....6 C4
  SSH NE33 .....3 J8
Bollihope Dr SUNDSW SR3 .....120 B4
Bolsover St ASHGTN NE63 .....23 K2
Bolsover Ter ASHGTN NE63 .....23 K2
Bolton Cl DHAM DH1 .....156 D2
Bonchester Cl BDLGTN NE22 .....29 F4
Bonchester Pl CRAM NE23 .....33 J7
Bond Cl SWCK/CAS SR5 .....106 C4
Bond Ct ELS/FEN * NE4 .....69 H6
Bondene Av FELL NE10 .....12 E7
Bondene Av West FELL NE10 .....12 E7
Bondene Wy CRAM NE23 .....33 H5
Bondfield Gdns FELL NE10 .....13 K7
Bondicarr Pl
  WD/WHPE/BLK NE5 .....69 H2
Bondicar Ter BLYTH NE24 .....31 F7
Bond St ELS/FEN * NE4 .....69 H6
Bonemill La CLS/BIR/GTL DH3 .....116 E4
  WASHS NE38 .....116 E6
Bonington Wy
  WD/WHPE/BLK NE5 .....69 F1
Bonner's Fld
  CLDN/WHIT/ROK SR6 .....14 E2
Bonnivard Gdns CRAM NE23 .....39 H7
Booths Rd ASHGTN NE63 .....23 C1
Booth St FELL NE10 .....12 C7
  MLFD/PNYW SR4 .....106 A6
Bootle St SWCK/CAS SR5 .....104 E1
Bordeaux Cl SUNDSW SR3 .....133 J1
Border Rd WLSD/HOW NE28 .....72 D2
Boreham Cl WLSD/HOW NE28 .....59 F5
Borodin Av SWCK/CAS SR5 .....104 D1
Borough Rd HAR/WTLS NE34 .....75 K6
  JRW NE32 .....73 K5
  NSHW NE29 .....2 D3
  SUND SR1 .....14 F5
Borrowdale CON/LDGT DH8 .....123 K3
  WICK/BNPF NE16 .....8 C9
Borrowdale Av BLYTH NE24 .....30 C6
  BYK/HTN/WLK NE6 .....72 B4
  CLDN/WHIT/ROK SR6 .....92 C1
Borrowdale Cl BOL NE36 .....91 G4
  DHAM DH1 .....158 B5
  HLS DH4 .....131 J6
Borrowdale Crs BLAY NE21 .....83 K4
Borrowdale Dr DHAM DH1 .....157 K5
Borrowdale Gdns
  LWF/SPW/WRK NE9 .....101 H2
Borrowdale St HLH DH5 .....147 K6
Boscombe Dr WLSD/HOW NE28 .....58 E6
Boston Av LGB/HTN NE7 .....57 H5
  WASHS NE38 .....102 E7
Boston Cl WLSD/HOW NE28 .....59 F5
Boston Crs BOL NE36 .....104 C1
  SWCK/CAS SR5 .....104 C1
Boston St PLEE/EAS SR8 .....163 G5
  SWCK/CAS SR5 .....104 C1
Boswell Av HAR/WTLS NE34 .....91 F1
Bosworth LGB/KIL NE12 .....47 J5
Bosworth Gdns
  BYK/HTN/WLK NE6 .....71 J1
Bothal Av STKFD/GP NE62 .....22 E6
Bothal Bank MPTH NE61 .....22 C3
Bothal Cl MPTH NE61 .....21 J2
Bothal St BYK/HTN/WLK NE6 .....7 J5
Bothal Ter ASHGTN * NE63 .....23 F1
Botha Ter STKFD/GP * NE62 .....23 H5
Bottle Bank GATE NE8 .....5 M9
Bottlehouse St
  BYK/HTN/WLK NE6 .....7 H1
Bottle Works Rd SEA/MUR SR7 .....151 F1
Boulby Cl SUNDSW SR3 .....120 C1
The Boulevard
  WICK/BNPF
  (off Metrocentre) NE16 .....8 B4
Boulmer Av CRAM NE23 .....33 H5
Boulmer Cl GOS/KPK NE3 .....55 K2
Boulmer Ct CLSW/PEL DH2 .....129 J5
Boulmer Gdns DIN/WO NE13 .....46 B3
Boulsworth Rd NSHW NE29 .....60 C1
Boundary Dr MPTH NE61 .....20 E6
Boundary Gdns LGB/HTN NE7 .....57 J2
Boundary St SWCK/CAS SR5 .....106 C3
Bourne Av ELS/FEN NE4 .....69 J4
Bourne Ct STLY/ANP DH9 .....112 E7
Bournemouth Dr
  SEA/MUR SR7 .....150 A2
Bournemouth Gdns WBAY NE26 .....50 D3
  WD/WHPE/BLK NE5 .....54 D7
Bournemouth Rd NSHW NE29 .....60 A5
Bourn Lea HLS DH4 .....131 J2
Bourtree Rd WLSD/HOW NE28 .....58 E6
Bowbank Cl SUNDSW SR3 .....120 B4
Bowburn Av SWCK/CAS SR5 .....105 C3
Bowburn Cl FELL NE10 .....88 E5
Bower St CLDN/WHIT/ROK SR6 .....106 D1
The Bower JRW NE32 .....89 K4
Bowes Av SEA/MUR SR7 .....149 K2
Bowes Cl WICK/BNPF NE16 .....99 F3
Bowes Lea HLS DH4 .....131 H3
Bowes Lyon Cl ROWG NE39 .....97 F5
Bowes St BLYTH NE24 .....31 F7
  GOS/KPK NE3 .....56 E5
Bowfell Av WD/WHPE/BLK NE5 .....55 H7
Bowfell Cl WD/WHPE/BLK NE5 .....55 H7
Bowfield Av SWCK/CAS SR5 .....104 D1
Bow La DHAM DH1 .....16 D5
Bowler's Hl PSHWF NE43 .....79 K5
Bowlynn Cl SUNDSW SR3 .....133 J1
Bowman Av CRAM NE23 .....47 H1
Bowman Pl SSH NE33 .....75 G2
Bowman St
  CLDN/WHIT/ROK SR6 .....93 F3

Bowmont Dr CRAM NE23 .....33 K7
  STLY/ANP DH9 .....112 A6
Bowness Av WLSD/HOW NE28 .....59 G4
Bowness Cl BOL NE36 .....91 G5
  PLEE/EAS SR8 .....175 F3
Bowness Pl
  LWF/SPW/WRK NE9 .....101 H1
Bowness Rd WD/WHPE/BLK NE5 .....68 C2
  WICK/BNPF NE16 .....8 B9
Bowness St SWCK/CAS SR5 .....104 E1
Bowsden Ct GOS/KPK NE3 .....56 E5
Bowsden Ter GOS/KPK NE3 .....56 E5
Bow St RDHAMSE DH6 .....172 C6
  RDHAMSE DH6 .....180 A2
Boyd Crs WLSD/HOW NE28 .....72 E1
Boyd Rd WLSD/HOW NE28 .....72 E1
Boyd St BW/LEM/TK/HW NE15 .....67 G3
  DHAM DH1 .....16 E7
  JES NE2 .....6 B5
  PLEE/EAS SR8 .....163 G5
Boyne Ct BDN/LAN/SAC DH7 .....167 J5
Brabourne St HAR/WTLS NE34 .....75 G5
Bracken Av WLSD/HOW NE28 .....58 E5
Brackenbeds Cl CLSW/PEL DH2 .....114 E7
Bracken Cl DIN/WO NE13 .....44 E3
  STLY/ANP DH9 .....126 B1
Brackendene Dr
  LWF/SPW/WRK NE9 .....86 E7
Bracken Dr DUN/TMV NE11 .....85 K6
Bracken Field Rd DHAM DH1 .....156 C4
Brackenfield Rd GOS/KPK NE3 .....56 B6
Bracken Hl PLEE/EAS SR8 .....174 A5
Bracken Rdg MPTH NE61 .....20 A3
Brackenridge WICK/BNPF NE16 .....97 G7
Brackenside GOS/KPK NE3 .....55 K4
Bracken Wy RYTON NE40 .....82 C1
Brackenwood Gv
  ASHBK/HED/RY SR2 .....120 C4
Brackley WASHN NE37 .....103 C4
Bracknell Cl SUNDSW SR3 .....120 C6
Bracknell Gdns
  WD/WHPE/BLK NE5 .....67 K2
Brack Ter FELL NE10 .....13 L4
Bradbury Cl FELL NE10 .....88 E5
  STLY/ANP DH9 .....112 A6
Bradbury Ct MONK NE25 .....40 A2
Bradford Av SWCK/CAS SR5 .....104 E1
  WLSD/HOW NE28 .....59 F5
Bradley Av HAR/WTLS NE34 .....76 A6
  HLH DH5 .....147 H2
Bradley Cl CLSW/PEL DH2 .....114 D4
Bradley Fell La WYLAM NE41 .....81 J2
Bradley Fell Rd PRUD NE42 .....81 H4
Bradley Lodge Dr
  STLY/ANP DH9 .....111 G6
Bradley Rd PRUD NE42 .....81 F1
Bradley St CON/LDGT DH8 .....123 J3
  PLEE/EAS SR8 .....163 G5
Bradley Ter HLH DH5 .....148 A7
Bradman Dr CLS/BIR/GTL DH3 .....130 A5
Bradman Sq SWCK/CAS SR5 .....104 E1
Bradman St SWCK/CAS SR5 .....104 E1
Bradshaw St SWCK/CAS SR5 .....104 E2
Bradwell Wy HLS DH4 .....131 K2
Brady Sq WASHS NE38 .....117 H1
Brady St MLFD/PNYW SR4 .....105 K6
Braebridge Pl GOS/KPK NE3 .....55 K6
Braemar Ct CON/LDGT DH8 .....122 C4
  FELL NE10 .....13 M4
Braemar Dr HAR/WTLS NE34 .....76 A3
Braemar Gdns SUNDSW SR3 .....120 B3
  SUNDSW SR3 .....133 G1
Braeside BW/HED/RY SR2 .....14 B9
  BDN/LAN/SAC DH7 .....141 G4
  DUN/TMV NE11 .....86 A6
The Brae MLFD/PNYW SR4 .....14 A6
Brahman Av NSHW NE29 .....60 B6
Braintree Gdns GOS/KPK NE3 .....55 K6
Braithwaite Rd FELL NE10 .....175 G4
Brakespeare Pl PLEE/EAS SR8 .....175 F3
Bramble Dykes
  BW/LEM/TK/HW NE15 .....69 F6
Bramhall Dr WASHS NE38 .....116 D6
Bramley Cl MLFD/PNYW SR4 .....118 E4
Bramley Ct LGB/HTN NE7 .....58 A7
Brampton Av
  BYK/HTN/WLK NE6 .....72 B7
Brampton Ct PLEE/EAS SR8 .....162 C6
Brampton Gdns
  BW/LEM/TK/HW NE15 .....67 F1
  LWF/SPW/WRK NE9 .....101 G2
  WLSD/HOW NE28 .....59 J6
Brampton Pl NSHW NE29 .....60 B5
Brampton Rd HAR/WTLS NE34 .....74 E6
Bramwell Rd
  ASHBK/HED/RY SR2 .....15 J7
  HLS DH4 .....131 J6
Brancepeth Av ELS/FEN NE4 .....69 J7
Brancepeth Chare
  PLEE/EAS SR8 .....174 C7
Brancepeth Cl
  BW/LEM/TK/HW NE15 .....68 A3
  DHAM DH1 .....157 F3
Brancepeth Rd HEBB NE31 .....73 H3
  WASHS NE38 .....116 C2
Brancepeth Ter JRW NE32 .....89 K1
Brancepeth Vw
  BDN/LAN/SAC DH7 .....166 E7
Branch St BLAY * NE21 .....83 K3
Brancpeth Cl
  BDN/LAN/SAC DH7 .....167 H1
Brand Av ELS/FEN NE4 .....69 J4
Brandling Ct FELL NE10 .....75 K7
  HAR/WTLS NE34 .....75 K7
Brandling Pk JES NE2 .....5 K1
Brandling Pl JES * NE2 .....5 L1
Brandling Pl South JES NE2 .....5 L1
Brandling St
  CLDN/WHIT/ROK SR6 .....106 E3
Brandling St South
  CLDN/WHIT/ROK SR6 .....106 E4
Brandlings Wy PLEE/EAS SR8 .....174 E3
Brandon Av SMOOR NE27 .....49 G6

Brandon Cl BLAY NE21 .....83 J4
  BLYTH NE24 .....30 D6
  HLS DH4 .....132 B7
Brandon Gdns
  LWF/SPW/WRK NE9 .....101 K2
Brandon Gv JES NE2 .....6 B2
Brandon La BDN/LAN/SAC DH7 .....167 J5
  CRK/WIL DL15 .....165 J6
Brandon Rd BDN/LAN/SAC DH7 .....165 H2
  GOS/KPK NE3 .....55 K4
  NSHW NE29 .....60 B6
Brandy La WASHN NE37 .....102 D6
Brannen St NSHW NE29 .....2 B3
Bransdale HLS DH4 .....117 G6
Bransdale Av
  CLDN/WHIT/ROK SR6 .....92 C5
Branston St SWCK/CAS SR5 .....106 B3
Branton Av HEBB NE31 .....89 F1
Brantwood CLSW/PEL DH2 .....129 F4
Brantwood Av MONK NE25 .....50 B5
Branxton Crs
  BYK/HTN/WLK NE6 .....72 B6
Brass Thill DHAM DH1 .....16 B4
Bray Cl WLSD/HOW NE28 .....59 F5
Braydon Dr NSHW NE29 .....60 B7
Brayside Dr WBAY NE26 .....50 B3
Breamish Dr WASHS NE38 .....116 B6
Breamish St CNUT NE1 .....6 B6
  JRW NE32 .....73 J6
Brearley Wy FELL NE10 .....12 A7
Breckenbeds Rd
  LWF/SPW/WRK NE9 .....100 E1
Brecken Wy FELL NE10 .....12 A7
Breckon Cl ASHGTN NE63 .....24 A4
Brecon Cl PLEE/EAS SR8 .....174 C5
  WD/WHPE/BLK NE5 .....55 F6
Brecon Pl CLSW/PEL DH2 .....115 F6
Brecon Rd DHAM DH1 .....157 F2
Bredon Cl WASHS NE38 .....116 D3
Brendale Av
  WD/WHPE/BLK NE5 .....54 A7
Brendon Pl PLEE/EAS SR8 .....174 C3
Brenkley Av SMOOR NE27 .....49 G7
Brenkley Cl DIN/WO NE13 .....45 F2
Brenkley Ct DIN/WO NE13 .....46 B1
Brenkley Wy DIN/WO NE13 .....37 G7
Brenlynn Cl SUNDSW SR3 .....133 J1
Brennan Cl ASHGTN NE63 .....24 C2
  BW/LEM/TK/HW NE15 .....69 F5
Brentford Av SWCK/CAS SR5 .....104 E2
Brentford Sq SWCK/CAS SR5 .....104 E2
Brentwood Av JES NE2 .....70 D1
Brentwood Cl MONK NE25 .....40 B7
Brentwood Gdns STLY/ANP DH9 .....127 G1
Brentwood Gdns SUNDSW SR3 .....120 B3
  WICK/BNPF NE16 .....85 F7
Brentwood Gv
  WLSD/HOW NE28 .....73 F2
Brentwood Pl SSH NE33 .....3 J9
Brentwood Rd HLS DH4 .....131 J2
Brettanby Rd FELL NE10 .....12 A9
Brett Cl LGB/HTN NE7 .....57 K7
Brettonby Av PSHWF NE43 .....79 H5
Bretton Gdns LGB/HTN NE7 .....71 J1
Brewer's La NSHW NE29 .....60 A7
Brewer Ter
  ASHBK/HED/RY SR2 .....135 G1
Brewery Bank WICK/BNPF NE16 .....84 E3
Brewery La FELL NE10 .....12 D5
  PONT/DH NE20 .....43 G3
  SSH* NE33 .....2 F8
  WICK/BNPF* NE16 .....84 E3
Brewhouse Bank
  TYNE/NSHE NE30 .....3 G1
Briar Av BDN/LAN/SAC DH7 .....167 J5
  HLS DH4 .....132 B7
  WBAY NE26 .....50 D2
Briar Cl CLSW/PEL DH2 .....144 A5
  HLS DH4 .....131 H3
  WLSD/HOW NE28 .....58 E5
Briar Dl CON/LDGT DH8 .....123 J7
Briar Di CON/LDGT DH8 .....123 J7
Briardale Rd BLYTH NE24 .....30 C7
Briardene ASHGTN NE63 .....23 J3
  BDN/LAN/SAC DH7 .....140 B5
  DHAM DH1 .....16 B5
  WICK/BNPF NE16 .....97 G7
Briardene Cl SUNDSW SR3 .....133 G1
Briardene Crs GOS/KPK NE3 .....56 A7
Briardene Dr FELL NE10 .....89 F5
Briar Edge LGB/KIL NE12 .....57 K2
Briar Fld WASHS NE38 .....117 F5
Briarfield Rd GOS/KPK NE3 .....56 B6
Briarhill CLSW/PEL DH2 .....129 G2
Briar La BW/LEM/TK/HW NE15 .....67 G2
Briar Lea BDN/LAN/SAC DH7 .....143 C7
  HLS DH4 .....131 H3
Briarlea MPTH NE61 .....21 J2
Briar Ms CON/LDGT DH8 .....122 C2
Briar Pl BW/LEM/TK/HW NE15 .....68 E6
Briar Rd DHAM DH1 .....158 A5
  ROWG NE39 .....97 F3
Briarside CON/LDGT DH8 .....122 C2
Briarsyde Cl WICK/BNPF NE16 .....84 C7
Briarwood CRAM NE23 .....47 H1
Briarwood Av CLSW/PEL DH2 .....128 C4
  GOS/KPK NE3 .....56 A4
Briarwood Crs
  BYK/HTN/WLK NE6 .....72 B2
Briarwood Rd BLYTH NE24 .....35 H1
Briary Gdns CON/LDGT DH8 .....122 C1
The Briary
  BW/LEM/TK/HW NE15 .....66 E1
  CON/LDGT DH8 .....122 C1
Brick Garth HLH DH5 .....148 A7
Brick Rw ASHBK/HED/RY SR2 .....120 C5
Bridge Cottages CRAM NE23 .....47 H1
Bridge Crs SUND SR1 .....14 E3
Bridge Ct RDHAMSE DH6 .....171 H3
Bridge Crs SUND SR1 .....14 E3
Bridgemere Dr DHAM DH1 .....156 B3
Bridge Pk GOS/KPK NE3 .....56 C2
Bridge Rd MPTH NE61 .....18 C2
Bridge Rd South NSHW NE29 .....60 C5
The Bridges SUND SR1 .....14 E5

Bridge St BDN/LAN/SAC DH7 .....154 B2
  BLAY NE21 .....67 K7
  BLYTH NE24 .....31 H6
  CON/LDGT DH8 .....122 D4
  DHAM DH1 .....16 B3
  DIN/WO NE13 .....46 B1
  GATE NE8 .....5 L9
  MPTH NE61 .....20 D5
  NWBGN NE64 .....19 G7
  STLY/ANP DH9 .....126 B3
  SUND SR1 .....14 G4
Bridge Ter STKFD/GP * NE62 .....23 H7
Bridgewater Cl
  BW/LEM/TK/HW NE15 .....68 A4
  WLSD/HOW NE28 .....58 E6
Bridgewater Rd WASHN NE37 .....103 G6
Bridge Wy GOS/KPK NE3 .....56 C3
Bridle Pth BOL NE36 .....91 G3
  SUNDSW SR3 .....119 G6
The Bridle SMOOR NE27 .....49 K7
Bridlington WLSD/HOW NE28 .....59 F5
Bridlington Av
  LWF/SPW/WRK NE9 .....101 F2
Bridport Rd NSHW NE29 .....60 B1
Brier Av PLEE/EAS SR8 .....175 G2
Brier Dene Crs WBAY NE26 .....50 C1
Brierdene Rd WBAY NE26 .....41 J7
Brierfield Gv MLFD/PNYW SR4 .....119 H2
Brierley Rd BLYTH NE24 .....30 C7
Briermede Av
  LWF/SPW/WRK NE9 .....101 F1
Brierville DHAM DH1 .....16 A5
Brieryside WD/WHPE/BLK NE5 .....69 H1
Briery Vale Rd
  ASHBK/HED/RY SR2 .....14 D8
Brigham Av WD/WHPE/BLK NE5 .....55 J7
Brigham Pl SSH NE33 .....3 H6
Brightlea CLS/BIR/GTL DH3 .....116 A1
Brightman Rd NSHW NE29 .....2 B1
Brighton Cl WLSD/HOW NE28 .....59 G5
Brighton Gdns GATE NE8 .....10 E9
Brighton Gv ELS/FEN NE4 .....4 C5
  NSHW NE29 .....2 A1
  WBAY NE26 .....50 D2
Brighton Rd GATE NE8 .....10 E9
Bright St CLDN/WHIT/ROK SR6 .....106 E4
  CON/LDGT DH8 .....123 F3
  SSH NE33 .....3 K7
Brignall Cl CLS/BIR/GTL DH3 .....145 J2
Brignall Gdns
  BW/LEM/TK/HW NE15 .....68 C4
Brignall Ri SUNDSW SR3 .....120 B3
Brindley Rd PLEE/EAS SR8 .....174 A4
  WASHN NE37 .....103 C7
Brinkburn CLSW/PEL DH2 .....129 G4
  WASHS NE38 .....117 C4
Brinkburn Av BLYTH NE24 .....35 H1
  CRAM NE23 .....38 D2
  GATE NE8 .....10 F7
  GOS/KPK NE3 .....56 B4
  WICK/BNPF NE16 .....84 E4
Brinkburn Cl BLAY NE21 .....83 J4
  BYK/HTN/WLK NE6 .....6 F5
Brinkburn Crs ASHGTN NE63 .....24 A2
  HLS DH4 .....132 A5
Brinkburn Gdns STKFD/GP NE62 .....23 F5
Brinkburn La
  BYK/HTN/WLK * NE6 .....6 F5
Brinkburn Pl BYK/HTN/WLK NE6 .....6 F5
Brinkburn Sq BYK/HTN/WLK NE6 .....6 F5
Brinkburn St
  HAR/WTLS NE34 .....75 F5
  MLFD/PNYW SR4 .....120 A1
  WLSD/HOW NE28 .....74 A2
Brinkburn St South 7 G7
Brisbane Av HAR/WTLS NE34 .....90 D1
Brisbane Ct GATE NE8 .....10 F2
Brisbane St SWCK/CAS SR5 .....104 E2
Brislee Av TYNE/NSHE NE30 .....61 C3
Bristlecone SUNDSW SR3 .....133 J2
Bristol Av WASHN NE37 .....102 D5
Bristol Dr WLSD/HOW NE28 .....59 F5
Bristol St MONK NE25 .....39 K3
Bristol Ter ELS/FEN NE4 .....4 C8
Britannia Ct ELS/FEN NE4 .....4 C8
Britannia Pl ELS/FEN NE4 .....4 C7
Britannia Rd SUNDSW SR3 .....120 A7
Brixham Av
  LWF/SPW/WRK NE9 .....101 F2
Brixham Cl SEA/MUR SR7 .....150 B2
Brixham Crs JRW NE32 .....74 B6
Brixham Gdns SUNDSW SR3 .....120 B4
Broadbank FELL NE10 .....13 L7
Broad Chare CNUT NE1 .....5 M7
Broadfield Pl HAR/WTLS NE34 .....75 H6
Broad Garth CNUT NE1 .....5 M8
Broadgate Rd
  BDN/LAN/SAC DH7 .....154 B6
Broad Landing SSH NE33 .....2 F6
Broadlands
  CLDN/WHIT/ROK SR6 .....92 A5
Broadlea FELL NE10 .....13 L7
Broadmayne Av
  MLFD/PNYW SR4 .....119 H2
Broadmayne Gdns
  MLFD/PNYW SR4 .....119 H2
Broad Mdw ASHBK/HED/RY SR2 .....14 D8
Broadmeadows
  RDHAMSE DH6 .....180 B2
  SUNDSW SR3 .....133 F1
  WASHS NE38 .....117 G4
Broadmead Wy
  BW/LEM/TK/HW NE15 .....68 E6
Broadoak FELL NE10 .....13 L6
Broadoak Dr
  BDN/LAN/SAC DH7 .....140 B5
Broadpark FELL NE10 .....13 L7
Broadpool Gn WICK/BNPF NE16 .....85 G6
Broadpool Ter WICK/BNPF NE16 .....85 G6
Broadsheath Ter
  SWCK/CAS SR5 .....105 A4
Broadside FELL NE10 .....13 L7
Broadstairs Ct
  MLFD/PNYW SR4 .....119 H2

Broadstone Gv
  WD/WHPE/BLK NE5 .....68 A2
Broadwater FELL NE10 .....13 L6
Broadway BLYTH NE24 .....35 G1
  BW/LEM/TK/HW NE15 .....68 B3
  CLS/BIR/GTL DH3 .....129 K2
  CON/LDGT DH8 .....138 C1
  LWF/SPW/WRK NE9 .....11 L9
  PONT/DH NE20 .....42 E6
  STKFD/GP NE62 .....22 E6
  TYNE/NSHE NE30 .....61 G2
  WICK/BNPF NE16 .....84 D7
Broadway Cl MONK NE25 .....51 F6
Broadway Crs BLYTH NE24 .....35 G1
Broadway East GOS/KPK NE3 .....56 C3
The Broadway HLS DH4 .....132 C4
  MLFD/PNYW SR4 .....119 G2
  TYNE/NSHE NE30 .....51 F7
Broadway Vls
  BW/LEM/TK/HW NE15 .....69 F6
Broadway West GOS/KPK NE3 .....56 B3
Broadwell Ct GOS/KPK NE3 .....57 F6
Broadwood Rd
  BW/LEM/TK/HW NE15 .....68 D4
Broadwood Vw 122 C2
Brockenhurst Dr
  MLFD/PNYW SR4 .....118 E4
Brock Farm Ct
  TYNE/NSHE NE30 .....60 E4
Brockhampton Cl BOLCOL NE35 .....90 C2
Brock La BDLGTN NE22 .....30 B3
  STKFD/GP NE62 .....24 B7
Brockley Av HAR/WTLS NE34 .....74 E7
Brockley Cl SWCK/CAS SR5 .....104 E2
Brock Sq BYK/HTN/WLK NE6 .....6 F6
Brockwell RHTLP TS27 .....175 K7
Brockwell Cl BLAY NE21 .....83 J5
Brockwell Ct BLYTH NE24 .....34 E3
Brockwell Dr ROWG NE39 .....97 G2
Brockwell Rd WASHS NE38 .....116 B1
Brockwood Cl ASHGTN NE63 .....23 H4
Brodie Cl HAR/WTLS NE34 .....91 G1
Brodrick Cl GOS/KPK NE3 .....55 H5
Brodrick St SSH NE33 .....3 K7
Brokenheugh
  WD/WHPE/BLK NE5 .....68 D2
Bromford Rd GOS/KPK NE3 .....55 C6
Bromley Av MONK NE25 .....50 C6
Bromley Cl DHAM DH1 .....169 J6
Bromley Ct GOS/KPK NE3 .....55 H3
Bromley Gdns BLYTH NE24 .....35 G2
  WLSD/HOW NE28 .....59 F5
Brompton Pl DUN/TMV * NE11 .....9 J7
Bromsgrove Cl
  WLSD/HOW NE28 .....59 G5
Bronte Pl STLY/ANP DH9 .....127 F3
Bronte St GATE NE8 .....11 M5
Brookbank Cl SUNDSW SR3 .....133 K2
Brookdale DHAM DH1 .....158 B6
Brooke Av WICK/BNPF NE16 .....84 E4
Brooke St SWCK/CAS SR5 .....14 D2
Brookfield Crs
  WD/WHPE/BLK NE5 .....68 A2
Brookfield Ter FELL * NE10 .....13 K6
Brookland Dr LGB/KIL NE12 .....48 A6
Brookland Rd
  MLFD/PNYW SR4 .....105 K7
Brooklands PONT/DH NE20 .....42 C6
Brooklands Wy BOLCOL NE35 .....90 B4
Brookside BDN/LAN/SAC DH7 .....143 H4
  BDN/LAN/SAC DH7 .....155 C1
  CRAM NE23 .....47 G1
Brookside Av BLYTH NE24 .....30 D7
  DIN/WO NE13 .....46 A4
Brookside Crs
  WD/WHPE/BLK NE5 .....69 H2
Brookside Gdns
  ASHBK/HED/RY SR2 .....14 C9
Brookside Ter
  ASHBK/HED/RY SR2 .....14 C9
Brookside Vls
  SEA/MUR
  (off Dene House Rd) SR7 .....135 K7
Brookside Wd WASHS NE38 .....117 F5
Brooksmead WLSD/HOW NE28 .....58 B6
Brook St WBAY NE26 .....51 F4
Brookvale Av GOS/KPK NE3 .....55 K6
Brook Vw BDN/LAN/SAC DH7 .....146 B5
Broom Cl MPTH NE61 .....21 G6
  STLY/ANP DH9 .....113 F7
  WICK/BNPF NE16 .....85 G6
Broom Ct LWF/SPW/WRK NE9 .....102 B4
Broom Crs BDN/LAN/SAC DH7 .....167 F1
Broome Cl GOS/KPK NE3 .....56 A4
Broome Rd DHAM DH1 .....158 A5
Broomfield JRW NE32 .....90 A3
Broomfield Av
  BYK/HTN/WLK NE6 .....72 A2
  WLSD/HOW NE28 .....58 E5
Broomfield Crs CHPW NE17 .....95 H5
Broomfield Rd GOS/KPK NE3 .....56 B6
Broom Gn WICK/BNPF NE16 .....85 G6
Broom Hall Dr
  BDN/LAN/SAC DH7 .....167 G1
Broomhill Rd PRUD NE42 .....80 E1
Broomhill Ter HLH DH5 .....147 J3
Broomhouse La PRUD NE42 .....80 E1
Broomhouse Rd PRUD NE42 .....80 E1
Broom La BDN/LAN/SAC DH7 .....167 F1
  WICK/BNPF NE16 .....85 F7
Broomlea NSHW NE29 .....59 K1
Broomlee ASHGTN NE63 .....24 A3
Broomlee Rd LGB/KIL NE12 .....47 K6
Broomley Wk GOS/KPK NE3 .....55 K3
Broomridge Av
  BW/LEM/TK/HW NE15 .....69 H6
Broomshields Av
  SWCK/CAS SR5 .....106 B2
Broomshields Cl
  SWCK/CAS SR5 .....106 B2
Broomside La DHAM DH1 .....158 A5
Brooms La CON/LDGT DH8 .....124 C4

Broom Ter WICK/BNPF NE16 85 G6
WICK/BNPF NE16 97 K7
Broom Wood Ct PRUD NE42 80 B2
Broomy Hill Rd
BW/LEM/TK/HW NE15 67 F1
Brotherlee Rd GOS/KPK NE3 55 K3
Brougham Ct PLEE/EAS SR8 174 B7
Brougham St SUND SR1 14 E5
Brough Ct BYK/HTN/WLK * NE6 7 G3
Brough Gdns WLSD/HOW NE28 59 J6
Brough Park Wy
BYK/HTN/WLK NE6 7 K4
Brough St BYK/HTN/WLK NE6 7 G3
Broughton Rd SSH NE33 3 K8
Brough Wy BYK/HTN/WLK NE6 7 G3
Browbank BDN/LAN/SAC DH7 143 J6
Browne Rd
CLDN/WHIT/ROK SR6 106 D2
Browney La BDN/LAN/SAC DH7 167 J7
Browning Cl HAR/WTLS NE34 91 F2
STLY/ANP DH9 112 E7
Browning Hl RDHAMSE DH6 180 D7
Browning St PLEE/EAS SR8 163 G5
Brownlow Cl LGB/HTN NE7 58 A7
Brownlow Rd HAR/WTLS NE34 75 G5
Brownney Ct
BDN/LAN/SAC DH7 154 B2
Brownrigg Dr CRAM NE23 38 D3
Browns Cl RDHAMSE DH6 180 D6
Brownsea Pl
LWF/SPW/WRK NE9 11 K9
Browntop Pl HAR/WTLS NE34 75 G6
The Brow BYK/HTN/WLK NE6 7 H7
Broxburn Cl WLSD/HOW NE28 59 G5
Broxburn Ct
WD/WHPE/BLK NE5 55 F7
Broxholm Rd
BYK/HTN/WLK NE6 71 H2
Bruce Cl HAR/WTLS NE34 75 G7
WD/WHPE/BLK* NE5 68 D1
Bruce Gdns WD/WHPE/BLK NE5 69 G4
Bruce Glasier Ter
RDHAMSE DH6 173 H5
Bruce Kirkup Rd PLEE/EAS SR8 175 F2
Bruce Pl PLEE/EAS SR8 174 D2
Bruce St BDN/LAN/SAC DH7 143 G2
Brumell Dr MPTH NE61 20 B4
Brumwell Ct PSHWF NE43 79 F5
Brundon Av WBAY NE26 50 D2
Brunel Dr CLDN/WHIT/ROK SR6 107 F4
Brunel St ELS/FEN NE4 9 M1
GATE NE8 10 C8
Brunel Ter ELS/FEN NE4 9 J1
Brunel Wk ELS/FEN NE4 9 H1
Brunswick Gv DIN/WO NE13 46 A3
Brunswick Rd SMOOR NE27 49 H7
SWCK/CAS SR5 104 E1
Brunswick St SSH NE33 75 G2
Brunton Av GOS/KPK NE3 55 K4
WLSD/HOW NE28 59 K7
Brunton Cl SMOOR NE27 49 H7
Brunton Gv GOS/KPK NE3 55 K4
Brunton La DIN/WO NE13 46 A7
GOS/KPK NE3 55 G3
Brunton Rd DIN/WO NE13 55 F3
Brunton St NSHW NE29 60 B7
Brunton Ter MLFD/PNYW SR4 106 A7
Brunton Wy CRAM NE23 33 H5
FELL NE10 13 M3
Brussels Rd MLFD/PNYW SR4 105 H6
WLSD/HOW NE28 72 D2
Bryden Ct HAR/WTLS NE34 75 H6
Bryers St CLDN/WHIT/ROK SR6 93 F3
Bryon St PLEE/EAS SR8 163 G5
Buchanan Gn DUN/TMV NE11 9 J5
Buckham St CON/LDGT DH8 122 E3
Buckingham SUNDSW SR3 119 J6
Buckingham Cl
CLDN/WHIT/ROK SR6 93 F4
Buckingham Rd PLEE/EAS SR8 174 C2
Buckinghamshire Rd
DHAM DH1 157 K6
Buckingham St ELS/FEN NE4 4 F7
Buckland Cl HLS DH4 132 A5
WASHS NE38 117 F3
Buck's Nook La RYTON NE40 81 J5
Buckthorne Gv LGB/HTN NE7 57 J7
Buddle Cl ELS/FEN NE4 69 H7
PLEE/EAS SR8 174 E2
Buddle Ct ELS/FEN NE4 69 J7
Buddle Rd ELS/FEN NE4 69 H7
Buddle St WLSD/HOW NE28 72 D3
Buddle Ter ASHBK/HED/RY SR2 15 H8
Bude Gdns LWF/SPW/WRK NE9 101 F2
Bude Gv NSHW NE29 60 B1
Bude Sq SEA/MUR SR7 149 J4
Budle Cl BLYTH NE24 30 E7
Budleigh Rd GOS/KPK NE3 55 K5
Budworth Av WBAY NE26 41 G3
Buford Ct
DHAM (off Western Hl) DH1 16 A4
Bullers Gn MPTH NE61 20 C4
Bullfinch Dr WICK/BNPF NE16 84 E6
Bullion La CLSW/PEL DH2 129 H4
Bulman's La NSHW NE29 60 E2
Bulmer Rd HAR/WTLS NE34 76 A4
The Bungalows
CLS/BIR/GTL
(off Lansbury Dr) DH3 101 H7
PLEE/EAS
(off Sunderland Rd) SR8 175 G2
RDHAMSE (off Dixon Est) DH6 173 H5
STLY/ANP DH9 112 A6
WLSD/HOW NE28 59 H7
Bunyan Av HAR/WTLS NE34 90 E1
Burdale Av WD/WHPE/BLK NE5 68 E2
Burdoch Crs
ASHBK/HED/RY SR2 134 E1
Burdon Av CRAM NE23 38 A1
HLH DH5 132 E7
Burdon Cl CLDN/WHIT/ROK SR6 91 J3
Burdon Crs
CLDN/WHIT/ROK SR6 91 J3
SEA/MUR SR7 135 F6
WNGT TS28 183 J2
Burdon Dr PLEE/EAS SR8 173 K3
Burdon Gv SUNDSW SR3 120 B7
Burdon Hall Pk
SUNDSW (off Burdon) SR3 134 B4
Burdon La ASHBK/HED/RY SR2 134 E1
SUNDSW SR3 134 A3
Burdon Ldg WICK/BNPF NE16 99 G3
Burdon Main Rw NSHW NE29 2 C5
Burdon Pk WICK/BNPF NE16 99 G3
Burdon Pl PLEE/EAS SR8 175 F4
Burdon Pln WICK/BNPF NE16 99 F6
Burdon Rd ASHBK/HED/RY SR2 14 F6
CLDN/WHIT/ROK SR6 91 J3
SUNDSW SR3 134 B2
Burdon St NSHW NE29 60 B7
Burdon Ter JES NE2 70 D3
Burford Ct LGB/HTN NE7 57 G6
Burford Gdns SUNDSW SR3 120 B4
Burghley Rd FELL NE10 87 J6
Burke St SWCK/CAS SR5 104 E2
Burlawn Cl ASHBK/HED/RY SR2 121 F6
Burleigh St SSH NE33 3 J9
Burlington Cl
ASHBK/HED/RY SR2 15 H7
Burlington Ct WLSD/HOW NE28 59 G3
Burlington Gdns
BYK/HTN/WLK NE6 71 H3
Burlison Gdns FELL NE10 12 B4
Burnaby Dr RYTON NE40 66 D7
Burnaby St MLFD/PNYW SR4 120 A1
Burn Av LGB/KIL NE12 57 K2
Burnbank Av MONK NE25 49 K4
Burnbridge DIN/WO NE13 46 B1
Burn Crook HLH DH5 147 G2
Burnden Gv HLS DH4 131 H2
Burnell Rd BDN/LAN/SAC DH7 165 H2
Burnet Cl WLSD/HOW NE28 58 E5
Burnet Ct ASHGTN NE63 23 H4
Burney Vls GATE NE8 11 J6
Burnfoot Wy GOS/KPK NE3 55 J7
Burn Gdns PLEE/EAS SR8 162 D5
Burnhall Dr SEA/MUR SR7 135 G6
Burnham Av
BW/LEM/TK/HW NE15 67 J4
Burnham Cl BLYTH NE24 35 G2
Burnham Gv BOL NE36 91 H5
BYK/HTN/WLK NE6 7 M8
Burnham St HAR/WTLS NE34 75 G5
Burn Heads Rd HEBB NE31 73 F7
Burnhills Gdns RYTON NE40 82 C3
Burnhills La RYTON NE40 82 D4
Burnhope Dr SWCK/CAS SR5 106 B2
Burnhope Rd WASHS NE38 103 G7
Burnhopeside Av
BDN/LAN/SAC DH7 140 D5
Burnhope Wy PLEE/EAS SR8 174 C4
Burnip Rd SEA/MUR SR7 149 H4
Burn La HLH DH5 147 K5
Burnlea Gdns CRAM NE23 39 H6
Burnley St BLAY NE21 84 A2
Burnmill Bank CON/LDGT DH8 122 A1
Burnmoor Gdns
LWF/SPW/WRK NE9 101 K2
Burnopfield Gdns
BW/LEM/TK/HW NE15 68 E5
Burnopfield Rd ROWG NE39 97 H4
Burn Park Rd
ASHBK/HED/RY SR2 14 B7
HLS DH4 132 A7
Burn Prom HLS DH4 132 B7
Burn Rd BLAY NE21 83 H3
Burns Av BLYTH NE24 34 E2
BOLCOL NE35 91 F4
Burns Av South HLH DH5 147 H1
Burns Cl HAR/WTLS NE34 91 F1
HLS DH4 146 D6
STLY/ANP DH9 126 E1
WICK/BNPF NE16 85 F7
Burns Crs WICK/BNPF NE16 84 E4
Burnside ASHGTN NE63 24 C2
BDLGTN NE22 29 K3
BDN/LAN/SAC DH7 140 B4
BDN/LAN/SAC DH7 155 G1
BOL NE36 91 J5
JES NE2 4 F2
JRW NE32 74 A7
MONK (off Hesleyside Rd) NE25 49 K4
PLEE/EAS SR8 174 D4
PONT/DH NE20 42 D6
Burnside Av CRAM NE23 47 H1
HLS DH4 132 A6
PLEE/EAS SR8 175 H4
Burnside Cl BLYTH NE24 30 D6
PRUD NE42 64 A7
WICK/BNPF NE16 98 E1
Burnside Rd GOS/KPK NE3 56 C3
ROWG NE39 97 F4
TYNE/NSHE NE30 51 F6
The Burnside
WD/WHPE/BLK NE5 68 C2
Burnside Vw CRAM NE23 39 F7
Burns St JRW NE32 73 K4
RDHAMSE DH6 182 D1
Burn's Ter RDHAMSE DH6 173 J5
Burnstones WD/WHPE/BLK NE5 68 C2
Burn St RDHAMSE DH6 180 A2
Burn Ter HEBB NE31 88 E2
Burnthouse Bank
CLSW/PEL DH2 129 F3
Burnthouse Cl BLAY NE21 83 J4
Burnthouse La
WICK/BNPF NE16 84 E7
Burnt House Rd MONK NE25 50 C6
Burntland Av SWCK/CAS SR5 105 K3
Burn Vw
BOLCOL (off Foxhomes) NE35 90 B4
CRAM NE23 47 H1
Burnville BYK/HTN/WLK NE6 6 D2
Burnville Rd MLFD/PNYW SR4 14 A7
Burnville Rd South
MLFD/PNYW SR4 14 A8
Burradon Rd CRAM NE23 47 H3
Burrow St SSH NE33 3 H7
Burscough Crs
CLDN/WHIT/ROK SR6 106 D3
Burstow Av BYK/HTN/WLK NE6 12 F1
Burt Av NSHW NE29 60 C5
Burt Cl PLEE/EAS SR8 174 E2
Burt Crs CRAM NE23 47 H1
Burt Rd BDLGTN NE22 30 A3
Burt St BLYTH NE24 31 G6
Burwell Av WD/WHPE/BLK NE5 68 D3
Burwood Rd BYK/HTN/WLK NE6 13 H1
NSHW NE29 60 A2
Bushblades La STLY/ANP DH9 111 H7
Buston Ter JES NE2 71 F2
Busty Bank WICK/BNPF NE16 97 J5
Butcher's Bridge Rd JRW NE32 73 K7
Bute Ct SUNDSW SR3 133 K1
Bute Dr ROWG NE39 96 B1
Buteland Rd
BW/LEM/TK/HW NE15 68 D4
Buteland Ter NWBGN NE64 25 F1
Bute Rd North ROWG NE39 96 B1
Bute Rd South ROWG NE39 96 B2
Bute St STLY/ANP DH9 111 J4
Butler St PLEE/EAS SR8 163 G5
Butsfield Gdns SUNDSW SR3 120 B4
Butsfield La CON/LDGT DH8 138 D2
Butterburn Cl LGB/HTN NE7 58 A6
Butterfield Cl RYTON NE40 82 B1
Buttermere
CLDN/WHIT/ROK SR6 92 A3
FELL NE10 13 J7
PLEE/EAS SR8 174 B7
Buttermere Av HLH DH5 160 B1
WICK/BNPF NE16 85 G5
Buttermere Cl
WD/WHPE/BLK NE5 69 F2
Buttermere Crs BLAY NE21 83 K4
Buttermere Gdns
HAR/WTLS NE34 75 J5
LWF/SPW/WRK NE9 87 G7
Buttermere Rd
TYNE/NSHE NE30 50 E7
Buttermere St
ASHBK/HED/RY SR2 120 E4
Buttermere Wy BLYTH NE24 30 D5
Butterwell Dr MPTH NE61 21 H2
Button's Bank
BDN/LAN/SAC DH7 164 E5
Buxton Cl JRW NE32 74 A6
WLSD/HOW NE28 59 F5
Buxton Gdns SUNDSW SR3 120 B3
WD/WHPE/BLK NE5 54 D7
Buxton Rd JRW NE32 74 A6
Byers Ct SUNDSW SR3 120 B6
Byer Sq HLH DH5 147 K2
Byer St HLH DH5 147 K2
The Bye CON/LDGT DH8 122 C7
The Byeways LGB/KIL NE12 57 H4
Bygate Cl WD/WHPE/BLK NE5 55 J7
Bygate Rd MONK NE25 50 B6
Byker Bank BYK/HTN/WLK NE6 6 D6
Byker Br CNUT NE1 6 B5
Byker Buildings
BYK/HTN/WLK NE6 6 D5
Byker Crs BYK/HTN/WLK NE6 7 H4
Byker St BYK/HTN/WLK NE6 72 B5
Byker Ter BYK/HTN/WLK NE6 72 B5
Byland Cl HLS DH4 132 A5
Byland Ct BDN/LAN/SAC DH7 155 G6
WASHS NE38 116 E1
Byland Rd LGB/KIL NE12 57 F4
Byony Toft
ASHBK/HED/RY SR2 121 G7
Byrness WD/WHPE/BLK NE5 68 C2
Byrness Cl GOS/KPK NE3 55 G6
Byron Av BLYTH NE24 34 E2
BOLCOL NE35 90 E4
CLSW/PEL DH2 128 E4
HEBB NE31 73 H5
Byron Cl CLSW/PEL DH2 115 G5
STKFD/GP NE62 22 E6
Byron Ct WICK/BNPF NE16 84 E4
Byron Pl ASHGTN NE63 24 B3
Byron Rd SWCK/CAS SR5 106 A3
Byron St JES NE2 5 M4
SWCK/CAS SR5 106 B4
Byron Ter RDHAMSE DH6 173 J4
Byron Wk GATE NE8 11 J4
The By-Way
BW/LEM/TK/HW NE15 67 F2
Bywell Av
BW/LEM/TK/HW NE15 68 C4
GOS/KPK NE3 55 K2
HAR/WTLS NE34 76 A4
SWCK/CAS SR5 106 C2
Bywell Cl RYTON NE40 82 A1
Bywell Dr PLEE/EAS SR8 174 D7
Bywell Gdns DUN/TMV NE11 86 A7
LWF/SPW/WRK NE9 87 H6
Bywell Rd ASHGTN NE63 23 K3
CLDN/WHIT/ROK SR6 91 K4
Bywell St BYK/HTN/WLK NE6 7 K6
Bywell Ter JRW NE32 89 K1

C

Cadehill Rd PSHWF NE43 79 F6
Cadger Bank
BDN/LAN/SAC DH7 140 B5
Cadleston Ct CRAM NE23 33 K7
Cadwell La PLEE/EAS SR8 162 C5
Caernarvon Cl
WD/WHPE/BLK NE5 55 F6
Caernarvon Dr SUNDSW SR3 133 G1
Caer Urfa Cl SSH NE33 3 H4
Caesars Wk SSH NE33 3 H5
Cain Ter RDHAMSE DH6 182 D1
Cairncross SWCK/CAS SR5 104 E4
Cairnglass Gn CRAM NE23 33 K7
Cairngorm Av WASHS NE38 116 C3
Cairnsmore Cl CRAM NE23 38 C4
Cairnsmore Dr WASHS NE38 116 D3
Cairns Rd SEA/MUR SR7 149 F5
SWCK/CAS SR5 106 C1
Cairns Sq SWCK/CAS SR5 106 C1
Cairns Wy GOS/KPK NE3 55 K3
Cairo St ASHBK/HED/RY SR2 120 E2
Caithness Rd SWCK/CAS SR5 104 D3
Caithness Sq SWCK/CAS SR5 104 D3
Calais Rd SWCK/CAS SR5 104 D4
Caldbeck Av BYK/HTN/WLK NE6 13 G2
Caldbeck Cl BYK/HTN/WLK NE6 13 G2
Calderbourne Av
CLDN/WHIT/ROK SR6 106 E1
Calderdale WLSD/HOW NE28 58 B5
Calderdale Av
BYK/HTN/WLK NE6 72 B5
Calder Wk WICK/BNPF NE16 98 E3
Calderwood Crs
LWF/SPW/WRK NE9 101 G2
Caldew Ct HLH DH5 148 A6
Caldew Crs WD/WHPE/BLK NE5 68 E3
Caldwell Rd GOS/KPK NE3 55 K2
Caledonian St HEBB NE31 73 F4
Caledonia St BYK/HTN/WLK NE6 72 C7
Calf Close Dr JRW NE32 89 K2
Calfclose La JRW NE32 90 A2
Calf Close Wk JRW NE32 89 K1
California BLAY NE21 83 K3
Callaley Av WICK/BNPF NE16 84 D6
Callaly Av CRAM NE23 38 D2
Callaly Cl MPTH NE61 21 K2
Callaly Wy BYK/HTN/WLK NE6 7 K9
Callander CLSW/PEL DH2 115 G4
Callerdale Rd BLYTH NE24 30 C6
Callerton LGB/KIL NE12 47 K4
Callerton Av NSHW NE29 60 A3
Callerton Cl ASHGTN NE63 24 A3
Callerton Ct PONT/DH NE20 43 G5
WD/WHPE/BLK
(off Marsden La) NE5 54 E7
Callerton La PONT/DH NE20 43 G4
WD/WHPE/BLK NE5 53 G2
Callerton Pl ELS/FEN NE4 4 C6
Callerton Rd
BW/LEM/TK/HW NE15 67 G1
Callerton Vw
WD/WHPE/BLK NE5 53 K6
Calley Cl PLEE/EAS SR8 174 D7
Callington Dr
ASHBK/HED/RY SR2 121 F7
Calthwaite Cl SWCK/CAS SR5 104 E3
Calvert Ter SEA/MUR SR7 149 G5
Calvus Dr BW/LEM/TK/HW NE15 66 B1
Camberley Cl SUNDSW SR3 120 C6
Camberley Dr
BDN/LAN/SAC DH7 166 E7
Camberley Rd WLSD/HOW NE28 59 J6
Camberwell Cl DUN/TMV NE11 86 B6
Camberwell Wy SUNDSW SR3 133 H2
Cambo Av BDLGTN NE22 29 J5
MONK NE25 50 B6
Cambo Cl BLYTH NE24 30 E7
GOS/KPK NE3 56 D5
WLSD/HOW NE28 59 F4
Cambo Dr CRAM NE23 38 D3
Cambo Gn WD/WHPE/BLK NE5 69 G1
Cambo Pl TYNE/NSHE NE30 60 E1
Camborne Gv GATE NE8 11 G6
Camborne Pl GATE NE8 11 G6
Cambourne Av
CLDN/WHIT/ROK SR6 106 E1
Cambria Gn MLFD/PNYW SR4 104 E7
Cambrian St JRW NE32 73 K4
Cambrian Wy WASHS NE38 116 D2
Cambria St MLFD/PNYW SR4 104 E7
Cambridge Av CON/LDGT DH8 137 F2
HEBB NE31 73 H6
LGB/KIL NE12 57 K2
WASHN NE37 102 D5
WLSD/HOW NE28 58 C7
Cambridge Dr
CLS/BIR/GTL DH3 145 H2
Cambridge Pl
CLS/BIR/GTL DH3 115 J5
Cambridge Rd PLEE/EAS SR8 174 D2
STKFD/GP NE62 23 G6
SUNDSW SR3 120 A7
Cambridgeshire Dr DHAM DH1 157 K7
Cambridge St ELS/FEN NE4 9 K1
Cambridge Ter GATE * NE8 10 F6
Camden Sq NSHW NE29 2 E3
Camden St JES NE2 5 M4
SWCK/CAS SR5 106 A4
TYNE/NSHE NE30 2 E2
Camelford Ct
BW/LEM/TK/HW NE15 68 A3
Camelot Cl SEA/MUR SR7 135 J7
Cameron Cl HAR/WTLS NE34 91 G1
Cameron Rd PRUD NE42 80 D2
Cameron Wk
WICK/BNPF
(off Metrocentre) NE16 8 B4
Camerton Pl WLSD/HOW NE28 59 G3
Camilla Rd
BW/LEM/TK/HW NE15 66 B1
Camilla St GATE NE8 11 H5
Campbell Park Rd HEBB NE31 73 G5
Campbell Pl ELS/FEN NE4 4 D6
Campbell Rd SWCK/CAS SR5 104 D3
Campbell St HEBB NE31 73 F4
Camperdown
WD/WHPE/BLK NE5 68 D2
Camperdown Av
CLS/BIR/GTL DH3 129 K2
Campion Dr STLY/ANP DH9 112 B6
Campion Gdns FELL NE10 87 K7
Campion Wy ASHGTN NE63 23 J3
Camp Rd WLSD/HOW NE28 72 D3
Campsie Cl WASHS NE38 116 D3
Campsie Crs TYNE/NSHE NE30 60 E1
Camp St PLEE/EAS SR8 163 G5
Camp Ter NSHW NE29 60 E4
Campus Martius
BW/LEM/TK/HW NE15 65 K1
Campville NSHW NE29 60 E4
Camsey Cl LGB/KIL NE12 57 F4
Canberra Av MONK NE25 50 B6
Canberra Dr HAR/WTLS NE34 74 C7
Canberra Rd MLFD/PNYW SR4 119 H2
Candelford Cl LGB/HTN NE7 57 K7
Candlish St SSH NE33 3 K9
Candlish Ter SEA/MUR SR7 151 F2
Canning St ELS/FEN NE4 69 H6
HEBB NE31 73 G6
Cannock CLSW/PEL DH2 115 F4
LGB/KIL NE12 47 K5
Cannock Dr LGB/HTN NE7 57 G6
Cannon St GATE NE8 5 M9
Cann Rd PLEE/EAS SR8 174 E2
Canon Gv JRW NE32 74 A4
Canonsfield Cl SUNDSW SR3 133 K2
Canterbury Av
WLSD/HOW NE28 59 F4
Canterbury Cl ASHGTN NE63 24 B3
CLS/BIR/GTL DH3 145 H2
LGB/KIL NE12 57 G4
Canterbury Rd DHAM DH1 156 E1
SWCK/CAS SR5 104 E3
Canterbury St
BYK/HTN/WLK NE6 7 K5
SSH NE33 75 H3
Canterbury Wy DIN/WO NE13 46 C3
Capetown Rd SWCK/CAS SR5 104 D3
Caplestone Cl WASHS NE38 116 D3
The Captains Rw SSH NE33 75 F3
Capulet Gv HAR/WTLS NE34 74 E6
Capulet Ter ASHBK/HED/RY SR2 15 H9
Caradoc Cl WASHS NE38 116 D3
Caragh Rd CLSW/PEL DH2 129 J6
Caraway Wk HAR/WTLS NE34 91 J1
Carden Av HAR/WTLS NE34 76 B6
Cardiff Sq SWCK/CAS SR5 104 D4
Cardiff St PLEE/EAS SR8 163 G5
Cardigan Gv TYNE/NSHE NE30 50 E6
Cardigan Rd SWCK/CAS SR5 104 D3
Cardigan Ter BYK/HTN/WLK NE6 6 E3
Cardinal Cl LGB/KIL NE12 57 G4
WD/WHPE/BLK NE5 53 K7
Cardinals Cl SUNDSW SR3 133 K2
Cardonnel St NSHW NE29 2 C4
Cardwell St
CLDN/WHIT/ROK SR6 106 E4
Careen Crs SUNDSW SR3 119 F7
Carey Cl RDHAMSE DH6 180 A3
Carham Av CRAM NE23 38 D2
Carham Cl GOS/KPK NE3 56 D4
Carisbrooke BDLGTN NE22 29 F4
Caris St GATE NE8 11 J8
Carlby Wy CRAM NE23 33 F5
Carlcroft Pl CRAM NE23 38 D3
Carley Hill Rd SWCK/CAS SR5 106 B2
Carley Rd SWCK/CAS SR5 106 B3
Carlingford Rd CLSW/PEL DH2 129 H6
Carlington Ct
BLAY (off Factory Rd) NE21 68 C7
Carliol Sq CNUT NE1 5 L6
Carliol St CNUT NE1 5 L6
Carlisle Ct FELL NE10 12 C6
Carlisle Crs HLS DH4 117 J7
Carlisle Lea MPTH NE61 20 E6
Carlisle Rd DHAM DH1 157 F2
Carlisle St FELL NE10 12 C6
Carlisle Vw MPTH NE61 20 D5
Carlisle Wy LGB/KIL NE12 58 E1
Carlow Dr STKFD/GP NE62 23 K5
Carlton Av BLYTH NE24 34 E4
Carlton Cl CLSW/PEL DH2 114 E4
GOS/KPK* NE3 56 A7
Carlton Ct DUN/TMV NE11 86 C7
Carlton Crs SUNDSW SR3 119 G7
Carlton Gdns
BW/LEM/TK/HW NE15 68 C4
Carlton Gv ASHGTN NE63 24 B4
Carlton House
BDLGTN (off Glebe Rd) NE22 29 F6
Carlton Rd LGB/KIL NE12 57 K4
Carlton St BLYTH NE24 31 H7
Carlton Ter LWF/SPW/WRK NE9 86 E7
NSHW NE29 2 A2
PLEE/EAS SR8 162 C6
Carlyle Ct WLSD/HOW NE28 73 J2
Carlyle Crs WICK/BNPF NE16 84 E4
Carlyle St WLSD/HOW NE28 73 J2
Carlyon St ASHBK/HED/RY SR2 14 E8
Carmel Gv CRAM NE23 33 G6
Carmel Rd STLY/ANP DH9 126 B1
Carnaby Rd BYK/HTN/WLK NE6 72 B7
Carnation Av HLS DH4 131 F4
Carnation Ter WICK/BNPF NE16 85 F5
Carnegie Cl HAR/WTLS NE34 75 G7
Carnegie St
ASHBK/HED/RY SR2 121 F4
Carnforth Cl WLSD/HOW NE28 59 F3
Carnforth Gdns
LWF/SPW/WRK NE9 101 H1
ROWG NE39 97 G2
Carnforth Gn GOS/KPK NE3 55 J6
Carnoustie CLSW/PEL DH2 115 F5
HAR/WTLS NE34 91 K1
WASHN NE37 102 E2
Carnoustie Cl CON/LDGT DH8 122 E2
LGB/HTN NE7 57 J6
Carnoustie Ct MONK NE25 50 A4
Carnoustie Dr HAR/WTLS NE34 91 K1
Carol Gdns LGB/HTN NE7 57 H7
Caroline Gdns WLSD/HOW NE28 59 J7
Caroline St ELS/FEN NE4 69 J7
HLH DH5 147 K4
JRW NE32 73 J4
SEA/MUR SR7 150 E1
Carol St MLFD/PNYW SR4 14 A3
Carolyn Cl LGB/KIL NE12 57 J4
Carolyn Crs WBAY NE26 50 C2
Carolyn Wy WBAY NE26 50 C2
Carpenter St SSH NE33 2 F9
Carr Av BDN/LAN/SAC DH7 167 G6
Carr Fld PONT/DH NE20 43 H2
Carrfield Rd GOS/KPK NE3 55 K4
Carr Hill Rd LWF/SPW/WRK NE9 11 J8
Carr House Dr DHAM DH1 156 D3
Carrhouse La HLH DH5 148 D3
Carrick Dr BLYTH NE24 35 F2
Carrigill Pl LGB/KIL NE12 57 G4
Carrington Cl CRAM NE23 39 G7
Carrmere Rd
ASHBK/HED/RY SR2 120 E5
Carrmyers STLY/ANP DH9 125 G1
Carrock Cl PLEE/EAS SR8 174 E7
Carrowmore Rd
CLSW/PEL DH2 129 J6
Carrs Cl PRUD NE42 81 F1
Carrsdale DHAM DH1 158 A4
The Carrs
DHAM (off Old Pit La) DH1 156 D2
Carr St BLYTH NE24 34 E3
HEBB NE31 73 F4
Carrsway DHAM DH1 158 A4

Carrsyde Cl WICK/BNPF NE16 ......84 D7
Carsdale Rd GOS/KPK NE3 ......55 H5
Cartington Av SMOOR NE27 ......49 C7
Cartington Cl PLEE/EAS SR8 ...174 E7
Cartington Ct GOS/KPK NE3 ......55 J3
Cartington Rd DHAM DH1 .....156 D4
 NSHW NE29 ......60 C5
Cartington Ter
 BYK/HTN/WLK NE6 ......71 J2
Cartmel Ct CLSW/PEL DH2 ...129 C5
Cartmel Gv GATE NE8 ......10 C9
Cartmel Pk FELL NE10 ......13 K6
Cartwright Rd SWCK/CAS SR5 ...105 F4
Carville Ri BYK/HTN/WLK NE6 ......7 C5
Carville Rd WLSD/HOW NE28 ......72 C2
Carville St FELL NE10 ......11M3
Carvill Gdns WLSD/HOW NE28 ......72 C3
Carvis Cl BDN/LAN/SAC DH7 ...167 F7
Carwarding Pl
 WD/WHPE/BLK NE5 ......69 C2
Caseton Cl MONK NE25 ......50 A3
Caspian Cl JRW * NE32 ......74 A6
Caspian Rd SWCK/CAS SR5 ...104 D4
Caspian Sq SWCK/CAS SR5 ...104 D4
Castellian Rd SWCK/CAS SR5 ...105 C4
Casterton Gv
 WD/WHPE/BLK NE5 ......53 K7
Castle Av RDHAMSE DH6 ...179 K2
Castle Bank MPTH NE61 ......20 E5
Castle Chare DHAM DH1 ......16 C3
Castle Cl CLS/BIR/GTL DH3 ...129 K5
 GOS/KPK NE3 ......55 H5
 HLH DH5 ......148 A6
 MPTH NE61 ......20 D5
 WICK/BNPF NE16 ......84 E5
Castledale Av BLYTH NE24 ......34 C1
Castledene Ct GOS/KPK NE3 ......57 F6
Castle Dene Gv HLS DH4 .....132 B7
Castledene Rd CON/LDGT DH8 ...123 H6
Castlefields BDN/LAN/SAC DH7 ...165 J1
Castleford Rd SWCK/CAS SR5 ...104 C3
Castlegate Gdns GATE * NE8 ......9 K6
Castle Hills CON/LDGT DH8 ...137 F2
Castle Leazes JES NE2 ......4 F3
Castle Mdw MPTH NE61 ......20 C6
Castlenook Pl
 BW/LEM/TK/HW NE15 ......68 D4
Castlereagh Rd SEA/MUR SR7 ...150 E1
Castlereagh St SUNDSW SR3 ...120 A7
Castlereigh Cl HLS DH4 .....131 F4
Castle Riggs CLSW/PEL DH2 ...129 H4
Castle Rd PRUD NE42 ......80 B2
 WASHS NE38 .....116 C2
Castles Farm Rd LGB/HTN NE7 ......56 E6
Castles Gn LGB/KIL NE12 ......48 A6
Castleside Rd
 BW/LEM/TK/HW NE15 ......68 C5
Castle Sq SMOOR NE27 ......48 D5
Castle St DIN/WO NE13 ......46 A5
 PLEE/EAS SR8 ......163 C5
 SUND SR1 ......14 D3
Castle St South SWCK/CAS SR5 ...105 C4
Castle Ter ASHGTN NE63 ......23 K1
 JES NE2 ......71 F1
Castleton Cl CRAM NE23 ......33 C6
 JES NE2 ......71 F1
Castleton Gv JES NE2 ......71 F1
Castleton Rd JRW NE32 ......74 A6
Castletown Rd SWCK/CAS SR5 ...105 C4
Castletown Wy SWCK/CAS SR5 ...105 H3
Castle Vw BDN/LAN/SAC DH7 ...165 G1
 BDN/LAN/SAC DH7 ...167 H1
 CLS/BIR/GTL DH3 ...129 J2
 PRUD NE42 ......64 B7
 SWCK/CAS SR5 ...105 F4
Castle Wk MPTH NE61 ......20 C4
Castleway DIN/WO NE13 ......45 F3
 MPTH NE61 ......21 K2
Castlewood Cl
 WD/WHPE/BLK NE5 ......68 B1
Catchside Cl WICK/BNPF NE16 ...84 E7
Catchwell Rd STLY/ANP DH9 ...111 F6
Cateran Wy CRAM NE23 ......38 C4
Caterhouse Rd DHAM DH1 ...156 C2
Catharine St West
 MLFD/PNYW SR4 .....106 A7
Cathedral Ct GATE NE8 ......11 J2
Cathedral Vw
 BDN/LAN/SAC DH7 ...143 J6
 HLS DH4 .....132 B4
Catherine Cookson Ct
 SSH NE33 ......75 J2
Catherine Rd HLS DH4 .....132 B1
Catherine St SSH NE33 ......3 J7
Catherine Ter STLY/ANP DH9 ...112 D6
Catholic Rw BDLGTN NE22 ......28 E6
Catkin Wk RYTON NE40 ......66 C7
Cato Sq SWCK/CAS SR5 ...106 A3
Cato St SWCK/CAS SR5 ...106 A3
Catton Gv WICK/BNPF NE16 ...99 F2
Catton Pl WLSD/HOW NE28 ......59 C4
Cauldwell Av HAR/WTLS NE34 ...75 J4
 MONK NE25 ......50 B6
Cauldwell Cl MONK NE25 ......50 C5
Cauldwell La MONK NE25 ......50 B5
Cauldwell Pl HAR/WTLS NE34 ...75 J4
Cauldwell Vls HAR/WTLS NE34 ...75 J4
Causeway CLDN/WHIT/ROK SR6 ...14 F1
 LWF/SPW/WRK NE9 ......87 H6
The Causeway
 BW/LEM/TK/HW NE15 ......67 C2
 LWF/SPW/WRK NE9 ......11 K8
Causey Bank CNUT NE1 ......5 M7
Causey Dr STLY/ANP DH9 ...112 C5
Causey Rd STLY/ANP DH9 ...112 C4
Causey St GOS/KPK NE3 ......56 C6
Causey Wy STLY/ANP DH9 ...112 D5
Cavalier Wy HEBB NE31 ......73 F4
Cavalier Wy SUNDSW SR3 ...119 K7
Cavell Sq PLEE/EAS SR8 ...162 E4
Cavendish Ct
 BDN/LAN/SAC DH7 ...167 F7
Cavendish Gdns ASHGTN NE63 ...23 K2
Cavendish Pl JES NE2 ......71 F2
 SUNDSW SR3 ...119 K7
Cavendish Rd JES NE2 ......71 F2
Cavendish Sq MPTH NE61 ......21 J7
Cavendish Ter ASHGTN NE63 ...23 K2

Caversham Rd
 WD/WHPE/BLK NE5 ......53 K7
Cawburn Cl LGB/HTN NE7 ......58 A7
Cawdell Rd TYNE/NSHE NE30 ...2 E2
Cawnpore Sq MLFD/PNYW SR4 ...105 J7
Cawthorne Ter NSHW * NE29 ...60 C2
Caynham Cl DIN/WO NE13 ......46 A4
Cayton Gv WD/WHPE/BLK NE5 ...67 K1
Cecil Ct PONT/DH NE20 ......43 H3
 WLSD/HOW NE28 ......72 D5
Cecil St NSHW NE29 ......2 C2
Cedar Av CLSW/PEL DH2 ...144 A4
 DHAM DH1 .....17M1
Cedar Cl BDLGTN NE22 ......29 F4
 DHAM DH1 .....17M1
Cedar Ct BDN/LAN/SAC DH7 ...153 K3
Cedar Crs DUN/TMV NE11 ......9 H9
 LWF/SPW/WRK NE9 .....101 F1
 SEA/MUR SR7 .....150 D2
Cedar Dr DHAM DH1 .....168 C5
Cedar Gdns CON/LDGT DH8 ...122 C6
Cedar Gv CLDN/WHIT/ROK SR6 ...93 F2
 HAR/WTLS NE34 ......75 K6
 HEBB NE31 ......89 C1
 RYTON NE40 ......66 E6
 WLSD/HOW NE28 ......73 F2
Cedar Rd BLAY NE21 ......84 A2
 ELS/FEN NE4 ......69 H4
Cedars Ct ASHBK/HED/RY SR2 ...14 F9
Cedars Crs SEA/MUR SR7 .....149 J5
Cedars Gn LWF/SPW/WRK NE9 ...101 C2
Cedars Pk ASHBK/HED/RY SR2 ...120 E3
The Cedars
 ASHBK/HED/RY SR2 .....120 D2
 ELS/FEN (off Park Rd) NE4 ......9 L1
 WICK/BNPF NE16 ......99 F1
Cedar St PLEE/EAS SR8 ...175 J4
Cedartree Gdns MONK NE25 ......50 C6
Cedarway FELL NE10 ......88 A7
Cedar Wy LGB/KIL * NE12 ......58 A2
Cedarwood Av
 BYK/HTN/WLK NE6 ......72 C2
Cedarwood Gv
 ASHBK/HED/RY SR2 .....120 C4
Cedric Crs ASHBK/HED/RY SR2 ...14 A9
Celadon Cl
 BW/LEM/TK/HW NE15 ......68 A3
Celandine Cl GOS/KPK NE3 ......56 D3
Celandine Cl ASHGTN NE63 ......23 H4
Celandine Wy FELL NE10 ......87 K6
Celtic Cl CLDN/WHIT/ROK SR6 ...91 J3
Cemetery Ap HAR/WTLS NE34 ...75 J3
Cemetery Rd GATE NE8 ......11 H5
 JRW NE32 ......74 A6
 RDHAMSE DH6 .....182 E2
 STLY/ANP DH9 .....112 D7
Centenary Av HAR/WTLS NE34 ...76 A5
Central Av BDN/LAN/SAC DH7 ...167 H7
 CLDN/WHIT/ROK SR6 ......92 A4
 HAR/WTLS NE34 ......75 K5
 NSHW NE29 ......60 C5
 STKFD/GP NE62 ......22 E6
Central Gdns HAR/WTLS NE34 ...75 K5
Central Station
 CNUT (off Neville St) NE1 ......5 J8
Centurian Wy BDLGTN NE22 ...28 E4
Centurion Rd
 BW/LEM/TK/HW NE15 ......68 C3
Centurion Wy
 BW/LEM/TK/HW NE15 ......66 A1
 LWF/SPW/WRK NE9 ......87 H6
Ceolfrid Ter JRW NE32 ......74 A7
Chacombe WASHS NE38 .....116 C3
Chadderton Dr
 WD/WHPE/BLK NE5 ......53 K7
Chadwick St WLSD/HOW NE28 ...72 D2
Chadwick Wk GATE NE8 ......10 C3
Chaffinch Ct ASHGTN NE63 ...23 H5
Chaffinch Wy LGB/KIL NE12 ......47 K4
Chainbridge Rd BLAY NE21 ......84 B1
Chain Bridge Rd BLAY NE21 ......84 D1
The Chains DHAM DH1 ......16 F2
Chair La SPEN DL16 .....178 B6
Chalfont Gv MLFD/PNYW SR4 ...118 D4
Chalfont Rd BYK/HTN/WLK NE6 ...72 B7
Chalfont Wy
 BDN/LAN/SAC DH7 ...167 J6
Challoner's Gdns MPTH NE61 ...20 C4
Chamberlain St BLYTH NE24 ...35 H1
 RYTON NE40 ......66 B7
Chandler Cl DHAM DH1 .....17M1
Chandlers Ford HLS DH4 .....117 H6
Chandlers Quay
 BYK/HTN/WLK NE6 ......12 B1
Chandos SUNDSW SR3 .....134 A3
Chandos St GATE NE8 ......11 H7
Chandra Pl WD/WHPE/BLK NE5 ...69 F1
Chantry Cl SUNDSW SR3 .....133 J2
Chantry Dr DIN/WO NE13 ......46 B2
Chantry Ms
 MPTH (off Bridge St) NE61 ......20 D5
Chantry Pl MPTH NE61 ......20 D5
Chapel Av WICK/BNPF NE16 ...97 K7
Chapel Cl GOS/KPK NE3 ......56 D1
Chapel Ct BDN/LAN/SAC DH7 ...155 F1
 RDHAMSE DH6 .....170 D1
Chapel Hill Rd PLEE/EAS SR8 ...175 J4
Chapel House Dr
 WD/WHPE/BLK NE5 ......68 A2
Chapel House Gv
 BW/LEM/TK/HW NE15 ......68 A2
Chapel La RDHAMSE DH6 .....160 E6
 WYLAM NE41 ......65 C5
Chapel Ms DHAM DH1 ......17 C2
Chapel Rd JRW NE32 ......73 K4
Chapel Rw HLS DH4 .....132 A2
 PSHWF NE43 ......79 J3
Chapel St HLH DH5 .....147 K4
 NSHW NE29 ......60 C5
 STLY/ANP DH9 .....111 J4
 WNGT TS28 .....183 K5
Chapel Vw HLS DH4 .....146 C7
 ROWG NE39 ......97 C2

The Chare CNUT * NE1 ......5 J5
Charlaw Cl BDN/LAN/SAC DH7 ...143 G4
Charlaw La BDN/LAN/SAC DH7 ...142 D3
Charlbury Cl
 LWF/SPW/WRK NE9 .....102 B4
Charlcote Crs BOL NE36 ......91 H5
Charles Av GOS/KPK NE3 ......55 J4
 LGB/KIL NE12 ......57 K2
Charles Baker Wk
 HAR/WTLS NE34 ......76 B5
Charles Ct BYK/HTN/WLK NE6 ...7 C3
Charles Dr CRAM NE23 ......47 H1
Charles St BOLCOL NE35 ......90 D4
 CLDN/WHIT/ROK SR6 ......14 F2
 DIN/WO NE13 ......46 A4
 GATE NE8 ......11 C3
 MPTH NE61 ......21 K2
 PLEE/EAS SR8 .....163 G5
 SEA/MUR SR7 .....150 E1
 STLY/ANP DH9 .....126 C3
 SUND SR1 ......14 F3
Charleswood GOS/KPK NE3 ......56 D2
Charlotte Cl ELS/FEN NE4 ......9 L1
Charlotte Ms CNUT * NE1 ......5 H7
Charlotte St CNUT NE1 ......5 H7
 SSH NE33 ......3 H7
 STLY/ANP DH9 .....126 C3
 TYNE/NSHE NE30 ......2 F2
 WLSD/HOW NE28 ......72 E1
Charlotte Ter SSH NE33 ......3 J8
Charlton Gdns MPTH NE61 ......21 F6
Charlton Gv
 CLDN/WHIT/ROK SR6 ......92 A4
Charlton Rd SWCK/CAS SR5 ...106 C2
Charlton St
 BW/LEM/TK/HW NE15 ......68 B5
Charlton Wk GATE NE8 ......10 B5
Charman St SUND SR1 ......14 E4
Charminster Gdns
 BYK/HTN/WLK NE6 ......71 J1
Charnwood STLY/ANP DH9 ...112 C6
Charnwood Av LGB/KIL NE12 ...57 G4
Charnwood Ct
 SSH (off Leighton St) NE33 ......3M9
Charter Dr SUNDSW SR3 .....119 G7
Chartwell Pl DHAM DH1 .....123 F3
Chasedale Crs BLYTH NE24 ......30 C7
Chase Farm Dr BLYTH NE24 ...30 B6
Chase Mdw BLYTH NE24 ......34 B1
Chase Ms BLYTH NE24 ......30 B7
The Chase LGB/KIL NE12 ......47 G7
 NSHW NE29 ......2 B1
 WASHS NE38 .....116 B3
Chatham Cl MONK NE25 ......40 A7
Chatham Rd SWCK/CAS SR5 ...104 E3
Chathill Cl MONK NE25 ......50 A4
 MPTH NE61 ......26 E1
Chathill Ter BYK/HTN/WLK NE6 ...72 B6
Chatsworth Cl SSH NE33 ......3 J6
Chatsworth Crs
 MLFD/PNYW SR4 .....120 A2
Chatsworth Dr BDLGTN NE22 ...29 J3
Chatsworth Gdns
 BYK/HTN/WLK NE6 ......7 G9
 WD/WHPE/BLK NE5 ......69 J1
Chatsworth Pl WICK/BNPF NE16 ...84 E7
Chatsworth Rd JRW NE32 ......74 A6
Chatsworth St
 MLFD/PNYW SR4 .....120 A1
Chatsworth St South
 MLFD/PNYW SR4 .....120 A1
Chatterton St SWCK/CAS SR5 ...106 A3
Chatton Av CRAM NE23 ......38 D3
 HAR/WTLS NE34 ......76 B3
Chatton Cl CLSW/PEL DH2 ...129 G6
 MPTH NE61 ......27 F1
Chatton Rd WLSD/HOW NE28 ...74 A2
Chatton Wynd GOS/KPK NE3 ...56 A3
Chaucer Av HAR/WTLS NE34 ...90 E1
Chaucer Cl GATE NE8 ......11 J3
 STLY/ANP DH9 .....126 E1
Chaucer Rd WICK/BNPF NE16 ...84 E4
Chaytor Gv SUND SR1 ......15 H6
Chaytor Rd CON/LDGT DH8 ...122 C3
Chaytor St JRW NE32 ......73 K5
Cheadle Av CRAM NE23 ......33 G6
 WLSD/HOW NE28 ......59 F4
Cheadle Rd SWCK/CAS SR5 ...104 E3
Cheam Cl WICK/BNPF NE16 ...85 F7
Cheam Rd SWCK/CAS SR5 ...104 E3
Chedder Ct STLY/ANP DH9 ...125 H4
Cheeseburn Gdns
 WD/WHPE/BLK NE5 ......69 G3
Cheldon Cl MONK NE25 ......50 A3
Chelford Cl WLSD/HOW NE28 ...59 G3
Chelmsford Gv JES NE2 ......6 C3
Chelmsford Rd SWCK/CAS SR5 ...104 E3
Chelmsford Sq SWCK/CAS SR5 ...104 E3
Chelsea Gdns GATE NE8 ......11 L7
Chelsea Gv ELS/FEN NE4 ......4 C5
Cheltenham Dr BOLCOL NE35 ...90 C2
Cheltenham Rd SWCK/CAS SR5 ...104 E3
Cheltenham Sq SWCK/CAS SR5 ...104 E3
Cheltenham Ter
 BYK/HTN/WLK NE6 ......6 F2
Chelton Cl DIN/WO NE13 ......46 B5
Chepstow Cl CON/LDGT DH8 ...108 D7
Chepstow Gdns GATE NE8 ......10 C9
Chepstow Rd
 BW/LEM/TK/HW NE15 ......68 D5
Chepstow St MLFD/PNYW SR4 ...14 A4
Cherry Banks CLS/BIR/GTL DH3 ...129 K2
Cherry Blossom Wy
 WASHN NE37 .....103 K5
Cherry Gv LGB/KIL NE12 ......47 J5
 PRUD NE42 ......80 B1
Cherry Pk BDN/LAN/SAC DH7 ...167 F7
Cherrytree Cl LGB/KIL NE12 ......48 B7
Cherrytree Ct BDLGTN NE22 ...29 K4
Cherry Tree Dr BDLGTN NE22 ...29 F5
Cherrytree Dr
 BDN/LAN/SAC DH7 .....154 A3
 WICK/BNPF NE16 ......8 D7
Cherry Tree Gdns
 BW/LEM/TK/HW NE15 ......64 C3
Cherrytree Gdns
 LWF/SPW/WRK NE9 .....101 G1

MONK NE25 ......50 D6
Cherry Trees BLYTH NE24 ......35 F1
Cherry Tree Sq
 ASHBK/HED/RY SR2 .....120 E6
Cherry Wy HLS DH4 .....131 K6
Cherrywood BYK/HTN/WLK NE6 ...72 A2
Cherrywood Gdns
 SUNDSW SR3 .....120 B7
Cherwell WASHN NE37 .....103 H5
Cherwell Rd PLEE/EAS SR8 ...174 C5
Chesham Gdns
 WD/WHPE/BLK NE5 ......67 K1
Cheshire Av CLS/BIR/GTL DH3 ...115 J5
Cheshire Cl ASHGTN NE63 ......23 C1
Cheshire Dr DHAM DH1 .....157 K7
Cheshire Gdns WLSD/HOW NE28 ...58 C7
Cheshire Gv HAR/WTLS NE34 ...76 B4
The Chesils LGB/KIL NE12 ......57 C5
Chesmond Dr BLAY NE21 ......83 K1
Chessar Av WD/WHPE/BLK NE5 ...69 F1
Chester Av WLSD/HOW NE28 ...59 H7
Chester Cl PONT/DH NE20 ......42 D5
Chester Ct LGB/KIL NE12 ......57 H4
Chester Crs JES NE2 ......6 A3
 SUND SR1 ......14 B5
Chesterfield Rd ELS/FEN NE4 ......4 A9
Chester Gdns HAR/WTLS NE34 ...75 J4
Chester Gv BLYTH NE24 ......34 E1
 CRAM NE23 ......39 F7
Chester Ms MLFD/PNYW SR4 ...14 A6
Chester Ov ASHBK/HED/RY SR2 ...14 D6
Chester Pl GATE NE8 ......10 D4
 PLEE/EAS SR8 .....174 C2
Chester Rd CLS/BIR/GTL DH3 ...130 C3
 CON/LDGT DH8 .....137 F1
 HLS DH4 .....131 F4
 MLFD/PNYW SR4 .....118 C4
 STLY/ANP DH9 .....112 E7
Chester Road Est
 STLY/ANP DH9 .....112 E7
Chesters Av LGB/KIL NE12 ......57 G4
Chesters Dene CON/LDGT DH8 ...108 E3
Chesters Pk LWF/SPW/WRK NE9 ...87 F6
Chester Sq MPTH NE61 ......18 B1
The Chesters CON/LDGT DH8 ...108 E3
 MONK NE25 ......50 B3
 WD/WHPE/BLK NE5 ......68 A2
Chester St HLS DH4 .....132 B5
 JES NE2 ......6 A3
 MLFD/PNYW SR4 .....106 A7
Chester St East
 MLFD/PNYW SR4 ......14 A5
Chester St West
 MLFD/PNYW SR4 .....106 A7
Chester Ter North
 MLFD/PNYW SR4 ......14 A5
Chesterton Rd HAR/WTLS NE34 ...75 F7
Chesterwood Dr
 WLSD/HOW NE28 ......72 C1
Chesterwood Ter FELL NE10 ...13 L5
 MONK NE25 ......50 D5
 WD/WHPE/BLK NE5 ......69 J1
 WICK/BNPF NE16 ......85 F7
Chestnut Av BLYTH NE24 ......31 F5
 WD/WHPE/BLK NE5 ......69 J1
 WICK/BNPF NE16 ......85 F7
Chestnut Cl JRW NE32 ......90 B3
 LGB/KIL NE12 ......47 H5
Chestnut Crs SWCK/CAS SR5 ...105 K2
Chestnut Dr RDHAMSE DH6 ...161 F6
Chestnut Gdns GATE NE8 ......10 A7
Chestnut Gv
 BDN/LAN/SAC DH7 ...167 F1
 HAR/WTLS NE34 ......75 K7
Chestnut St ASHGTN NE63 ......23 K1
 WLSD/HOW NE28 ......72 E2
Cheswick Dr GOS/KPK NE3 ......56 D4
Cheveley Wk DHAM DH1 .....158 A6
Chevin Cl BYK/HTN/WLK NE6 ...72 C2
Chevington FELL NE10 ......88 C3
Chevington Cl MPTH NE61 ......21 H2
Chevington Gdns
 WD/WHPE/BLK NE5 ......69 H2
Chevington Gv MONK NE25 ...50 B2
Cheviot Cl WASHN NE37 .....102 C7
Cheviot Cl SEA/MUR SR7 .....135 G7
 STLY/ANP DH9 .....125 H4
Cheviot Gdns DUN/TMV NE11 ...86 A5
 SEA/MUR SR7 .....135 G7
Cheviot Gra CRAM NE23 ......47 J5
Cheviot Gn DUN/TMV NE11 ......9 J7
Cheviot Gv MPTH NE61 ......21 H2
Cheviot La ASHBK/HED/RY SR2 ...120 E7
Cheviot Mt BYK/HTN/WLK NE6 ...7 J7
Cheviot Pl PLEE/EAS SR8 ...174 C4
Cheviot Rd BLAY NE21 ......84 A3
 HAR/WTLS NE34 ......76 A3
 JRW NE32 ......73 H7
Cheviot St MLFD/PNYW SR4 ...105 K6
Cheviot Vw ASHGTN NE63 ......18 A7
 CLSW/PEL DH2 .....129 C7
 DIN/WO NE13 ......46 A3
 PRUD NE42 ......80 C2
 SMOOR (off West St) NE27 ......59 F1
 STLY/ANP (off Front St) DH9 ...110 E7
Cheviot Wy STKFD/GP NE62 ...23 H5
The Chevron BYK/HTN/WLK NE6 ...6 A
Chevy Cha
 CNUT (off Eldon Sq) NE1 ......5 J5
Chevychase Ct SEA/MUR SR7 ...135 F5
Cheyne Rd PRUD NE42 ......80 C1
The Cheyne SUNDSW SR3 ...134 A3
Chichester Av CRAM NE23 ......33 F7
Chichester Cl ASHGTN NE63 ...24 C3
 GATE NE8 ......10 F4
 GOS/KPK NE3 ......55 C3
Chichester Gv BDLGTN NE22 ...29 F4
Chichester Pl SSH NE33 ......75 C3
Chichester Rd
 CLDN/WHIT/ROK SR6 .....106 C1
 DHAM DH1 .....156 E2
 SSH NE33 ......75 H2
Chichester Rd East SSH NE33 ...75 J3
Chicken Rd WLSD/HOW NE28 ...58 C7
Chick's La CLDN/WHIT/ROK SR6 ...92 E3
Chigwell Cl HLS DH4 .....117 K7
Chilcote FELL NE10 ......12 D9
Chilcrosse FELL NE10 ......88 B5
Chilham Ct NSHW NE29 ......59 K2

Chillingham Cl BLYTH NE24 ......34 D2
Chillingham Ct
 BYK/HTN/WLK NE6 ......7 G3
Chillingham Crs ASHGTN NE63 ...23 J2
Chillingham Dr CLSW/PEL DH2 ...129 J7
 NSHW NE29 ......60 B6
Chillingham Gv PLEE/EAS SR8 ...174 B6
Chillingham Rd
 BYK/HTN/WLK NE6 ......71 J2
 DHAM DH1 .....156 E3
Chillingham Ter JRW NE32 ......74 B7
Chilside Rd FELL NE10 ......12 C9
Chiltern Cl ASHGTN NE63 ......24 A4
 WASHS NE38 .....116 D3
Chiltern Dr LGB/KIL NE12 ......57 H1
Chiltern Gdns DUN/TMV NE11 ...86 A5
Chiltern Rd NSHW NE29 ......50 D7
Chilton Gdns HLS DH4 .....131 J7
Chilton Garth PLEE/EAS SR8 ...175 C5
Chilton St SWCK/CAS SR5 ...106 C4
Chimside Ter STLY/ANP DH9 ...125 G4
China St ASHBK/HED/RY SR2 ...120 E2
Chingford Cl HLS DH4 .....118 A7
Chipchase Av CRAM NE23 ......38 C3
Chipchase Cl BDLGTN NE22 ...28 D5
 MPTH NE61 ......21 K2
Chipchase Ct HLS DH4 .....131 F6
 MONK NE25 ......39 K2
 SEA/MUR SR7 .....135 F5
Chipchase Crs
 WD/WHPE/BLK NE5 ......54 C7
Chipchase Ter STLY/ANP DH9 ...89 K1
Chippendale Pl JES NE2 ......4 E1
The Chip MPTH NE61 ......26 D1
Chirton Av HAR/WTLS NE34 ...76 C5
 NSHW NE29 ......2 A2
Chirton Dene Quays NSHW NE29 ...2 B8
Chirton Dene Wy NSHW NE29 ...2 B7
Chirton Gn NSHW NE29 ......2 A2
Chirton Gv HAR/WTLS NE34 ...76 C5
Chirton Hill Dr NSHW NE29 ...60 A3
Chirton La NSHW NE29 ......60 C4
Chirton West Vw NSHW NE29 ...2 B2
Chirton Wynd
 BYK/HTN/WLK NE6 ......7 H6
Chislehurst Rd HLS DH4 .....117 K7
Chiswick Gdns GATE NE8 ......11 L8
Chiswick Rd MONK NE25 ......40 A6
 SWCK/CAS SR5 ...104 E3
Chollerford Av MONK NE25 ...51 F5
 NSHW NE29 ......60 A4
Chollerford Cl GOS/KPK NE3 ...56 A6
Chollerford Ms MONK NE25 ...50 A6
Chollerton Dr BDLGTN NE22 ...29 C5
 LGB/KIL NE12 ......58 C2
Choppington Rd MPTH NE61 ...21 F7
 STKFD/GP NE62 ......29 F3
Chopwell Rd CHPW NE17 ......95 J7
Chorley Pl BYK/HTN/WLK NE6 ...7 L6
Chowdene Bank
 DUN/TMV NE11 .....100 E3
 LWF/SPW/WRK NE9 .....101 F2
Christal Ter
 CLDN/WHIT/ROK SR6 .....106 D2
Christchurch Pl PLEE/EAS SR8 ...174 D5
Christie Ter BYK/HTN/WLK NE6 ...72 B6
Christon Cl GOS/KPK NE3 ......56 E5
Christon Rd GOS/KPK NE3 ......56 E5
Christon Wy FELL NE10 ......13M4
Chudleigh Gdns
 WD/WHPE/BLK NE5 ......67 K1
Church Av GOS/KPK NE3 ......56 D5
 STKFD/GP NE62 ......23 K6
Church Bank
 BW/LEM/TK/HW NE15 ......67 H4
 CON/LDGT DH8 .....122 C1
 JRW NE32 ......74 B4
 STLY/ANP DH9 .....112 D7
 SWCK/CAS SR5 .....106 A4
 WLSD/HOW NE28 ......73 F1
Churchburn Dr MPTH NE61 ......20 C5
Church Chare PONT/DH NE20 ...43 H2
 WICK/BNPF NE16 ......85 F5
Church Cl BDLGTN NE22 ......29 F6
 CON/LDGT DH8 .....108 E3
 DIN/WO NE13 ......45 F2
 MONK NE25 ......50 B3
 PLEE/EAS SR8 .....175 F5
 SEA/MUR SR7 .....135 J7
Church Ct BDLGTN NE22 ......29 F6
 FELL NE10 ......12 D5
 SEA/MUR SR7 .....135 G7
Churchdown Cl BOLCOL NE35 ...90 C2
Church Dr LWF/SPW/WRK NE9 ...87 C6
Churcher Gdns
 WLSD/HOW NE28 ......58 C6
Church Flatt PONT/DH NE20 ...43 H2
Church Gn SEA/MUR SR7 .....135 J7
Churchill Av DHAM DH1 ......17 K1
 MONK NE25 ......50 B3
 SWCK/CAS SR5 .....106 A3
Churchill Cl CON/LDGT DH8 ...122 C1
Churchill Gdns JES NE2 ......71 G2
Churchill Ms BYK/HTN/WLK NE6 ...7 J2
Churchill Sq DHAM DH1 ......17 K1
 HLS DH4 .....132 B4
Churchill St SUND SR1 ......15 G6
 WLSD/HOW NE28 ......59 H6
Church La BDLGTN NE22 ......29 G6
 CLDN/WHIT/ROK SR6 ......93 F4
 DHAM DH1 ......16 E6
 GOS/KPK NE3 ......56 D5
 LWF/SPW/WRK NE9 ......87 H6
 RDHAMSE DH6 .....171 H3
 SEA/MUR SR7 .....149 G5
Church Pk RDHAMSE DH6 ...172 E7
Church Pl FELL NE10 ......12 C5
Church Ri RYTON NE40 ......67 G6
 WICK/BNPF NE16 ......85 F5
Church Rd
 BW/LEM/TK/HW NE15 ......67 H4
 CON/LDGT DH8 .....122 D3
 GOS/KPK NE3 ......56 D5
 HLH DH5 .....147 K2
 LWF/SPW/WRK NE9 .....101 F1
 SMOOR NE27 ......48 E4

WYLAM NE41 .....65 G5
Church St BDN/LAN/SAC DH7 .....143 G5
  BLAY NE21 .....83 J3
  BYK/HTN/WLK NE6 .....72 C7
  CON/LDGT DH8 .....123 J3
  CON/LDGT DH8 .....125 F5
  CON/LDGT DH8 .....136 E3
  DHAM DH1 .....16 E6
  DUN/TMV NE11 .....9 J5
  GATE NE8 .....5 M9
  HEBB NE31 .....73 F4
  HLH DH5 .....132 C7
  HLS DH4 .....132 C7
  HLS DH4 .....146 D6
  MLFD/PNYW SR4 .....104 E7
  RDHAMSE DH6 .....160 D6
  RDHAMSE DH6 .....172 C7
  RHTLP TS27 .....185 H2
  SEA/MUR SR7 .....149 J6
  SEA/MUR SR7 .....150 E1
  STLY/ANP DH9 .....112 D7
  STLY/ANP DH9 .....125 H3
  SWCK/CAS SR5 .....106 B3
  TYNE/NSHE NE30 .....2 F1
  WICK/BNPF NE16 .....98 E5
  WNGT DH8 .....184 A5
Church St East SUND SR1 .....15 H3
Church St Head DHAM DH1 .....16 E7
Church St North
  CLDN/WHIT/ROK SR6 .....106 D4
Church V RDHAMSE DH6 .....159 F5
Church Vw BOLCOL NE35 .....90 C3
  CLSW/PEL DH2 .....144 B5
  SUNDSW SR3 .....120 A7
  WLSD/HOW NE28 .....73 F1
Church Wk MPTH NE61 .....20 D5
  PLEE/EAS SR8 .....162 B6
Church Wy MONK NE25 .....49 J3
  NSHW NE29 .....2 D1
  SSH NE33 .....3 G7
Church Wynd RDHAMSE DH6 .....170 C1
Churston Rd HLS DH4 .....132 A3
Chyll Edge MPTH NE61 .....20 A4
Cinderford CI BOLCOL NE35 .....90 B2
Cirencester St LWF/SPW/WRK SR4 .....14 A3
Citadel East LGB/KIL NE12 .....47 K6
Citadel West LGB/KIL NE12 .....47 K6
City Rd CNUT NE1 .....5 M7
City Wy SUNDSW SR3 .....133 F2
Civic Ct HEBB NE31 .....73 H6
Clacton Rd SWCK/CAS SR5 .....104 D4
Clanfield CI LGB/HTN NE7 .....57 F6
Clanny St SUND SR1 .....14 B6
Clanton CI FELL NE10 .....88 E5
Clapham Av BYK/HTN/WLK NE6 .....7 K7
Clappersgate PLEE/EAS SR8 .....162 B6
Clara St ELS/FEN NE4 .....69 H7
  SEA/MUR SR7 .....135 H7
Clare Lea PSHWF NE43 .....94 A2
Claremont Av
  BW/LEM/TK/HW NE15 .....68 B3
  CLDN/WHIT/ROK NE6 .....106 E2
Claremont Dr HLS DH4 .....131 J1
Claremont Gdns BOL NE36 .....91 H5
  WBAY NE26 .....
Claremont North Av GATE * NE8 .....10 E4
Claremont PI GATE NE8 .....10 E5
  JES* NE2 .....5 H2
Claremont Rd
  CLDN/WHIT/ROK SR6 .....106 E2
  JES NE2 .....70 A3
  WBAY NE26 .....50 C1
Claremont South Av GATE * NE8 .....10 E4
Claremont St JES NE2 .....5 G2
Claremont Ter
  ASHBK/HED/RY SR2 .....14 D7
  BLYTH NE24 .....31 F7
  FELL NE10 .....13 M4
  JES NE2 .....5 G2
Claremount Ct BOL NE36 .....91 F5
Clarence St JES NE2 .....6 A5
  RDHAMSE DH6 .....180 A3
  SEA/MUR SR7 .....150 E1
  SWCK/CAS SR5 .....106 A3
  WBAY NE26 .....41 G3
Clarence Ter CLS/BIR/GTL DH3 .....129 J4
Clarence Wk JES NE2 .....6 A4
Clarendon Sq SWCK/CAS SR5 .....106 B2
Clarendon St CON/LDGT DH8 .....123 F4
Clare Rd PLEE/EAS SR8 .....174 C5
Clarewood Av ELS/FEN NE4 .....76 A3
Clarewood Gn ELS/FEN NE4 .....4 C1
Clarewood PI WD/WHPE/BLK NE5 .....69 G3
Clarke Ter FELL NE10 .....12 B8
  SEA/MUR SR7 .....149 H4
Clarks Fld MPTH NE61 .....20 C5
Clarks Hill Wk
  BW/LEM/TK/HW NE15 .....67 H4
Clasper Wy WICK/BNPF NE16 .....84 E1
Claude St HLH DH5 .....147 K5
Claude Ter SEA/MUR SR7 .....149 J5
Claudius Ct SSH NE33 .....3 H5
Claverdon St
  WD/WHPE/BLK NE5 .....53 K6
Clavering PI CNUT NE1 .....5 K8
Clavering Rd WICK/BNPF NE16 .....85 F3
Clavering St WLSD/HOW NE28 .....73 K2
Clavering Wy BLAY NE21 .....84 C3
Claverley Dr SMOOR NE27 .....48 E4
Claxheugh Rd
  MLFD/PNYW SR4 .....105 F6
Claxton St PLEE/EAS SR8 .....175 H3
Clay La DHAM DH1 .....168 B2
Claymere Rd
  ASHBK/HED/RY SR2 .....120 E5
Claypath DHAM DH1 .....16 E5
Claypath Ct DHAM DH1 .....16 E5
Claypath La SSH NE33 .....3 H9
Claypool Rd HLH DH5 .....147 K6
Claypool Ct HAR/WTLS NE34 .....75 G6
Claypool Farm CI RHTLP TS27 .....184 E6
Clayton Park Sq JES NE2 .....5 L1
Clayton Rd JES NE2 .....5 K1
Clayton St BDLGTN NE22 .....29 K4

CNUT NE1 .....5 J7
JRW NE32 .....73 K4
Clayton St West CNUT NE1 .....5 H8
Clayton Ter FELL * NE10 .....12 A5
Clayton Terrace Rd CHPW NE17 .....95 J3
Clayworth Rd GOS/KPK NE3 .....56 B1
Cleadon Hill Dr HAR/WTLS NE34 .....92 A1
Cleadon Hill Rd HAR/WTLS NE34 .....76 B7
Cleadon La BOL NE36 .....91 J4
  CLDN/WHIT/ROK SR6 .....
Cleadon Lea
  CLDN/WHIT/ROK SR6 .....91 K3
Cleadon Mdw
  CLDN/WHIT/ROK SR6 .....92 A3
Cleadon St BYK/HTN/WLK NE6 .....7 L5
Cleadon Towers
  HAR/WTLS
  (off the Lonnen) NE34 .....76 B6
Cleasby Gdns
  LWF/SPW/WRK NE9 .....87 F6
Cleasewell Ter STKFD/GP * NE62 .....23 G5
Cleaside Av HAR/WTLS NE34 .....76 A7
Cleaswell HI STKFD/GP NE62 .....22 E6
Cleehill Dr NSHW NE29 .....60 C2
Cleeve Ct WASHS NE38 .....116 E1
Cleghorn St BYK/HTN/WLK NE6 .....71 J3
Clement Av BDLGTN NE22 .....29 J5
Clementina CI
  ASHBK/HED/RY SR2 .....15 H7
Clement St LWF/SPW/WRK NE9 .....87 F7
Clennel Av HEBB NE31 .....73 F6
Clent Wy LGB/KIL NE12 .....57 G4
Clephan St DUN/TMV NE11 .....9 H6
Clervaux Ter JRW NE32 .....74 A5
Cleveland Av CLSW/PEL DH2 .....129 H5
  NSHW NE29 .....60 D3
  NWBGN NE64 .....25 F1
Cleveland Ct SSH NE33 .....3 H5
Cleveland Crs NSHW NE29 .....60 E4
Cleveland Dr WASHS NE38 .....116 D3
Cleveland Gdns LGB/HTN NE7 .....57 G6
Cleveland PI PLEE/EAS SR8 .....174 C4
Cleveland Rd MLFD/PNYW SR4 .....119 K2
Cleveland St NSHW NE29 .....60 E4
Cleveland Ter NSHW NE29 .....60 E4
  CLDN/WHIT/ROK SR6 .....92 A6
Cleveland Vw
  CLDN/WHIT/ROK SR6 .....92 A6
Clickemin PONT/DH NE20 .....43 J3
Clifford's Bank
  BDN/LAN/SAC DH7 .....152 E6
Cliffords Fort TYNE/NSHE NE30 .....3 H2
Cliffords Ga BDN/LAN/SAC DH7 .....165 F1
Clifford St BLAY NE21 .....84 A1
  BYK/HTN/WLK NE6 .....6 E5
  CLS/BIR/GTL DH3 .....129 J6
  MLFD/PNYW SR4 .....106 A7
  TYNE/NSHE NE30 .....3 H1
Clifford Ter CLS/BIR/GTL DH3 .....129 J6
  RYTON NE40 .....66 B7
Cliff Rd ASHBK/HED/RY SR2 .....135 G1
Cliff Rw WBAY NE26 .....51 G5
Cliffside HAR/WTLS NE34 .....76 C5
Clifton Av HAR/WTLS NE34 .....75 J4
  WLSD/HOW NE28 .....72 D1
Cliftonbourne Av
  CLDN/WHIT/ROK SR6 .....106 E1
Clifton CI RYTON NE40 .....67 G7
  STKFD/GP NE62 .....23 G5
Clifton Ct GOS/KPK NE3 .....55 H3
Clifton Gdns BLYTH NE24 .....35 F3
  LWF/SPW/WRK NE9 .....87 F5
  NSHW NE29 .....60 C7
Clifton Gv MONK NE25 .....50 C3
Clifton La MPTH NE61 .....27 F5
Clifton Rd
  CLDN/WHIT/ROK SR6 .....106 E2
  CRAM NE23 .....38 D3
  ELS/FEN NE4 .....69 J6
Clifton Sq PLEE/EAS SR8 .....174 E3
Clifton Ter LGB/KIL NE12 .....57 K3
  SSH NE33 .....75 G4
  WBAY NE26 .....51 F4
Cliftonville Av ELS/FEN NE4 .....69 J6
Cliftonville Gdns WBAY NE26 .....50 E3
Clinton PI GOS/KPK NE3 .....46 B7
Clipsham CI LGB/KIL NE12 .....47 J5
Clipstone Av BYK/HTN/WLK NE6 .....12 F1
Clipstone CI
  BW/LEM/TK/HW NE15 .....66 E1
Clive St HAR/WTLS NE34 .....74 E7
  NSHW NE29 .....2 E4
Clockburn Lonnen
  WICK/BNPF NE16 .....84 B7
Clockburnsyde CI
  WICK/BNPF NE16 .....84 C7
Clockmill Rd GATE NE8 .....9 K5
Clockstand CI
  CLDN/WHIT/ROK SR6 .....106 E3
Clock Tower Flats
  MPTH (off Oldgate) NE61 .....20 D5
Clockwell St SWCK/CAS SR5 .....105 K4
Cloister Av HAR/WTLS NE34 .....74 E6
Cloister Ct GATE NE8 .....11 H2
Cloister Garth LGB/HTN NE7 .....57 F5
The Cloisters
  ASHBK/HED/RY SR2 .....14 E9
  LGB/HTN NE7 .....57 F5
Cloister Wk JRW NE32 .....74 A4
Closeburn Sq SUNDSW SR3 .....134 B1
Closefield Gv MONK NE25 .....50 C5
Close St MLFD/PNYW SR4 .....106 A6
  SWCK/CAS* SR5 .....106 B4
The Close BDN/LAN/SAC DH7 .....140 B4
  BLAY NE21 .....83 J3
  CLDN/WHIT/ROK SR6 .....91 K3
  CON/LDGT DH8 .....122 D1
  CRAM NE23 .....39 G7
  HLH DH5 .....132 D7
  PONT/DH NE20 .....43 G4
  PRUD NE42 .....80 E1
  WD/WHPE/BLK NE5 .....68 C3
  WICK/BNPF NE16 .....98 A6
Cloth Market CNUT NE1 .....5 K7
Clousden Dr LGB/KIL NE12 .....58 A1
Clousden Gra LGB/KIL NE12 .....58 A1

Clovelly Av ELS/FEN NE4 .....69 J6
Clovelly Gdns BDLGTN NE22 .....29 F6
  WBAY NE26 .....
Clovelly PI JRW NE32 .....74 C6
  PONT/DH NE20 .....42 E7
Clovelly Rd SWCK/CAS SR5 .....104 D2
Clover Av BLAY NE21 .....84 A6
  FELL NE10 .....11 M4
Cloverdale BDLGTN NE22 .....28 E5
Cloverdale Gdns LGB/HTN NE7 .....57 H7
  WICK/BNPF NE16 .....85 F7
Cloverfield Av GOS/KPK NE3 .....55 K4
Clover HI WICK/BNPF NE16 .....98 E3
Cloverhill Av HEBB NE31 .....89 F1
Cloverhill CI CRAM NE23 .....38 B7
Cloverhill Dr RYTON NE40 .....66 C7
Clover Laid BDN/LAN/SAC DH7 .....167 F1
Clowes Ter STLY/ANP DH9 .....125 H3
Club La DHAM DH1 .....156 B6
Clumber St BYK/HTN/WLK NE6 .....9 J1
Clumber St North ELS/FEN NE4 .....4 C9
Clyde Av HEBB NE31 .....89 G1
Clydedale Av LGB/KIL NE12 .....57 J3
Clydesdale Av HLS DH4 .....117 K5
Clydesdale Garth DHAM DH1 .....156 E1
Clydesdale Mt
  BYK/HTN/WLK NE6 .....7 H7
Clydesdale Rd
  BYK/HTN/WLK NE6 .....7 H6
Clydesdale St HLH DH5 .....147 K6
Clyde St CHPW NE17 .....95 J4
  GATE NE8 .....11 K7
Clyvedon Ri HAR/WTLS NE34 .....92 A1
Coach La DIN/WO NE13 .....45 J5
  LGB/HTN NE7 .....57 J5
  NSHW NE29 .....2 C3
Coach Open WLSD/HOW NE28 .....73 K2
Coach Rd BW/LEM/TK/HW NE15 .....67 F2
  DUN/TMV NE11 .....86 B7
  WASHN NE37 .....102 E3
  WLSD/HOW NE28 .....72 E2
Coach Road Gn FELL NE10 .....12 B4
Coalbank Rd HLH DH5 .....147 J6
Coaley La HLS DH4 .....132 A4
Coalford La RDHAMSE DH6 .....158 E3
Coalford Rd RDHAMSE DH6 .....158 C7
Coal La PRUD NE42 .....63 H7
Coalway Dr WICK/BNPF NE16 .....85 F4
Coalway La WICK/BNPF NE16 .....85 F4
Coalway La North
  WICK/BNPF NE16 .....85 F3
Coanwood Dr CRAM NE23 .....38 C3
Coanwood Gdns
  DUN/TMV NE11 .....86 B7
Coanwood Rd
  BW/LEM/TK/HW NE15 .....69 F7
Coanwood Wy
  WICK/BNPF NE16 .....99 F2
Coast Rd BYK/HTN/WLK NE6 .....71 J1
  HAR/WTLS NE34 .....76 D4
  NSHW NE29 .....60 B4
  PLEE/EAS SR8 .....175 J4
  SSH NE33 .....75 K2
  WLSD/HOW NE28 .....59 H6
Coatsworth Ct GATE NE8 .....10 E3
Coatsworth Rd GATE NE8 .....10 E3
Cobalt BW/LEM/TK/HW NE15 .....68 A3
Cobbett Crs HAR/WTLS NE34 .....91 F1
Cobbler's La PSHWF NE43 .....63 F2
Cobden Rd CRAM NE23 .....38 D4
Cobden St CON/LDGT DH8 .....123 C5
  GATE NE8 .....11 K6
  WLSD/HOW NE28 .....72 C1
Cobden Ter GATE NE8 .....11 J6
Cobham PI BYK/HTN/WLK NE6 .....72 C7
Cobham Sq SWCK/CAS SR5 .....106 B3
Coble Dene NSHW NE29 .....74 C1
Coble Dene Rd NSHW NE29 .....74 C1
Coburg St BLYTH NE24 .....31 H7
  GATE NE8 .....11 L4
  TYNE/NSHE NE30 .....61 F4
Cochrane Ct ELS/FEN * NE4 .....69 J6
Cochrane Park Av LGB/HTN NE7 .....71 J1
Cochran St BLAY * NE21 .....84 A1
Cockburn Ter NSHW NE29 .....60 B7
Cocken La CLS/BIR/GTL DH3 .....145 J3
  DHAM DH1 .....145 J5
Cocken Rd CLS/BIR/GTL DH3 .....144 E5
  DHAM DH1 .....145 K3
Cockermouth Rd
  SWCK/CAS SR5 .....104 D2
Cockhouse La
  BDN/LAN/SAC DH7 .....154 C7
Cockshott Dean PRUD NE42 .....80 C7
Cohort CI CON/LDGT DH8 .....108 E5
Colbeck Av WICK/BNPF NE16 .....85 F5
Colbeck Ter TYNE/NSHE NE30 .....61 G5
Colbourne Av CRAM NE23 .....32 E6
Colbourne Crs
  CRAM (off Nelson Pk) NE23 .....32 E6
Colbury CI CRAM NE23 .....33 G6
Colby Ct ELS/FEN NE4 .....4 E8
Colchester St HAR/WTLS NE34 .....74 E7
Colchester Ter
  MLFD/PNYW SR4 .....119 K1
Coldbeck Ct CRAM NE23 .....38 D3
Coldingham Ct
  BDN/LAN/SAC DH7 .....143 G3
Coldingham Gdns
  WD/WHPE/BLK NE5 .....69 H1
Coldside Gdns
  WD/WHPE/BLK NE5 .....67 K1
Coldstream CLSW/PEL DH2 .....115 F4
Coldstream Av SWCK/CAS SR5 .....106 B3
Coldstream CI HLS DH4 .....131 K2
Coldstream Dr BLAY NE21 .....83 J4
Coldstream Gdns
  WLSD/HOW NE28 .....59 H7
Coldstream Rd
  BW/LEM/TK/HW NE15 .....69 F5
Coldstream Wy NSHW NE29 .....60 A2
Coldwell La RDHAMSE DH6 .....160 D2
Coldwell La FELL NE10 .....87 J5
Coldwell Park Av FELL NE10 .....12 B9
Coldwell Park Dr FELL NE10 .....12 B9
Coldwell Rd PRUD NE42 .....81 F1
  FELL NE10 .....13 J7

Coldwell St FELL NE10 .....12 C8
Coldwell Ter FELL NE10 .....12 B9
Colebridge CI
  WD/WHPE/BLK NE5 .....55 G7
Colebrooke CLS/BIR/GTL DH3 .....115 K4
Cole Gdns FELL NE10 .....13 K6
Colegate FELL NE10 .....88 B5
Colegate West FELL NE10 .....88 A5
Colepike Rd BDN/LAN/SAC DH7 .....140 B5
Coleridge Av
  LWF/SPW/WRK NE9 .....100 E1
  SSH NE33 .....75 J2
Coleridge Dr STKFD/GP NE62 .....23 C6
Coleridge Rd SWCK/CAS SR5 .....105 F3
Coleridge Sq HEBB NE31 .....73 G5
Coley Hill CI WD/WHPE/BLK NE5 .....54 A6
Coley Ter CLDN/WHIT/ROK SR6 .....106 E2
Colgrove Wy GOS/KPK NE3 .....55 K5
Colima Av SWCK/CAS SR5 .....105 G4
Colin CI BYK/HTN/WLK NE6 .....72 C3
Colin Ter ASHBK/HED/RY SR2 .....135 F1
Colin Av HAR/WTLS NE34 .....76 B6
Colling Av SEA/MUR SR7 .....150 B1
Collingdon Gn ROWG NE39 .....82 B7
Collingdon Rd ROWG NE39 .....96 C1
Collingwood Av
  WLSD/HOW NE28 .....58 D6
Collingwood Crs
  PONT/DH NE20 .....43 F5
Collingwood Dr HLS DH4 .....131 J1
Collingwood Gdns FELL NE10 .....12 D4
Collingwood Man NSHW NE29 .....2 E4
Collingwood PI STKFD/GP NE62 .....23 H6
Collingwood St CNUT NE1 .....5 K8
  FELL NE10 .....12 C6
  HEBB NE31 .....73 J5
  HLH DH5 .....147 K2
  SSH NE33 .....75 G3
  SWCK/CAS SR5 .....106 B3
Collingwood Ter BLYTH NE24 .....31 G7
  TYNE/NSHE NE30 .....61 J3
Collingwood Vw NSHW NE29 .....2 B3
Collison St CON/LDGT DH8 .....123 F4
Collywell Bay Rd WBAY NE26 .....41 G2
Collywell Ct MONK NE25 .....41 G2
Colman Av HAR/WTLS NE34 .....74 E6
Colnbrook CI GOS/KPK NE3 .....55 H3
Colombo Rd SWCK/CAS SR5 .....104 D4
Colpitts Ter DHAM DH1 .....16 A4
Colston Ri ELS/FEN NE4 .....174 D3
Colston St ELS/FEN NE4 .....69 H6
Colston Wy MONK NE25 .....50 B2
Coltere Av BOL NE36 .....91 J5
Colton Gdns
  LWF/SPW/WRK NE9 .....101 G2
Coltpark WD/WHPE/BLK * NE5 .....68 D2
Coltsfoot Gdns FELL NE10 .....87 H7
Coltspool DUN/TMV NE11 .....100 D7
Columba St SWCK/CAS SR5 .....106 B3
Columba Wk GOS/KPK NE3 .....56 D5
Columbia Gra GOS/KPK NE3 .....55 J5
Columbia Ter BLYTH NE24 .....35 G1
Colville Ct STLY/ANP DH9 .....127 F1
Colwell PI WD/WHPE/BLK NE5 .....69 F4
Colwell Rd ASHGTN NE63 .....24 B4
  NSHW NE29 .....60 D1
Colwyne PI WD/WHPE/BLK NE5 .....69 F1
Combe Dr
  BW/LEM/TK/HW NE15 .....67 K4
Comet PLEE/EAS SR8 .....162 D5
Comet Rw LGB/KIL NE12 .....47 J7
Comet Sq SUNDSW SR3 .....120 A7
Comical Cnr SSH NE33 .....3 H4
Comma Ct DUN/TMV NE11 .....86 B5
Commercial Rd
  ASHBK/HED/RY SR2 .....121 F2
  BYK/HTN/WLK NE6 .....7 G7
  GOS/KPK NE3 .....56 E5
  JRW NE32 .....74 A3
  SSH NE33 .....75 F2
Commercial St
  BDN/LAN/SAC DH7 .....152 D5
  BLAY NE21 .....83 K3
  TRIM TS29 .....182 E6
Commissioners' Whf NSHW NE29 .....2 B8
Compton Av HAR/WTLS NE34 .....75 H4
Compton Rd NSHW NE29 .....2 A3
Concorde Wy JRW NE32 .....73 K5
Condercum Ct
  BW/LEM/TK/HW NE15 .....69 G6
Condercum Rd ELS/FEN NE4 .....69 H6
Conel CI PRUD NE42 .....80 D1
Cone St SSH NE33 .....2 F9
Congburn Bank
  BDN/LAN/SAC DH7 .....128 B7
Congburn Br
  BDN/LAN/SAC DH7 .....128 A7
Conhope La
  BW/LEM/TK/HW NE15 .....69 H6
Conifer Av FELL NE10 .....88 C1
Conifer Ct DHAM DH1 .....157 H6
Conifer Ct
  RYTON (off Lead Rd) NE40 .....82 D3
Coniscliffe Rd STLY/ANP DH9 .....126 B2
Conishead Ter RDHAMSE DH6 .....160 E1
Coniston CLS/BIR/GTL DH3 .....115 K5
  FELL NE10 .....13 J7

Coniston Av HEBB NE31 .....73 H6
  HLH DH5 .....160 E1
  JES NE2 .....70 E1
  NWBGN NE64 .....24 E2
  SWCK/CAS SR5 .....106 C1
  WICK/BNPF NE16 .....8 C9
Coniston CI DHAM DH1 .....158 B5
  LGB/KIL NE12 .....47 J6
  PLEE/EAS SR8 .....175 F4
Coniston Crs BLAY NE21 .....83 K4
Coniston Dr BDN/LAN/SAC DH7 .....143 G4
  JRW NE32 .....90 B1
Coniston Gdns
  LWF/SPW/WRK NE9 .....87 H7
Coniston PI LWF/SPW/WRK NE9 .....87 H7
Coniston Rd BLYTH NE24 .....30 B5
  TYNE/NSHE NE30 .....50 D7
  WLSD/HOW NE28 .....59 H6
Coniston Wy CON/LDGT DH8 .....123 K3
Connaught CI HLS DH4 .....132 A2
Connaught Ter JRW NE32 .....73 K5
Conningsby CI GOS/KPK NE3 .....56 D2
Connolly Ter CHPW NE17 .....95 J7
Consett La CON/LDGT DH8 .....122 B5
Consett Rd CON/LDGT DH8 .....136 E2
  DUN/TMV NE11 .....85 K7
Constable CI RYTON NE40 .....67 G7
  STLY/ANP DH9 .....126 D1
Constable Gdns
  HAR/WTLS NE34 .....91 G1
Constance St CLSW/PEL DH2 .....114 E7
  CON/LDGT DH8 .....123 F5
Content St BLAY NE21 .....84 A3
Convent Rd ELS/FEN NE4 .....69 H4
Conway Av BDLGTN NE22 .....28 D5
  RYTON NE40 .....83 F1
Conway Dr LGB/HTN NE7 .....57 G6
Conway Gdns SUNDSW SR3 .....119 G7
  WLSD/HOW NE28 .....58 C6
Conway Gv WBAY NE26 .....40 E1
Conway PI CLSW/PEL DH2 .....115 F6
Conway Rd SWCK/CAS SR5 .....105 F3
Conway Sq LWF/SPW/WRK NE9 .....11 J8
  SWCK/CAS SR5 .....104 D3
Conyers Av CLSW/PEL DH2 .....129 H2
Conyers Crs PLEE/EAS SR8 .....175 F1
Conyers Gdns CLSW/PEL DH2 .....129 H2
Conyers PI CLSW/PEL DH2 .....129 H2
Conyers Rd BYK/HTN/WLK NE6 .....7 G6
  CLSW/PEL DH2 .....129 H2
Cook CI BDN/LAN/SAC DH7 .....155 F6
Cook Crs SEA/MUR SR7 .....149 G5
Cooke's Wd BDN/LAN/SAC DH7 .....167 H2
Cook Gdns FELL NE10 .....13 L8
Cookshold La RDHAMSE DH6 .....158 E7
Cookson CI ELS/FEN NE4 .....4 E6
Cookson PI STLY/ANP DH9 .....127 F2
Cookson's La CNUT NE1 .....5 J9
Cookson Ter CLSW/PEL DH2 .....129 H4
  SEA/MUR SR7 .....149 J6
Cook Sq SWCK/CAS SR5 .....104 E3
Cooks Wd WASHS NE38 .....117 F3
Cook Wy PLEE/EAS SR8 .....173 K3
Coomassie Rd BLYTH NE24 .....31 G7
Coomside CRAM NE23 .....38 D4
Co-operative Ter
  BDN/LAN/SAC DH7 .....141 H3
  BDN/LAN/SAC DH7 .....166 D2
  MLFD/PNYW SR4 .....120 A1
  ROWG NE39 .....82 B7
  STLY/ANP DH9 .....110 E6
Cooper's CI RDHAMSE DH6 .....172 C6
Cooper Sq DHAM DH1 .....17 H1
Cooper's Ter RDHAMSE DH6 .....172 C6
Cooper St
  CLDN/WHIT/ROK SR6 .....106 E4
Coopies Fld MPTH NE61 .....21 G6
Coopies Haugh MPTH NE61 .....21 G6
Coopie's La MPTH NE61 .....21 F5
Coopies Wy MPTH NE61 .....21 G6
Copeland Ct DHAM DH1 .....168 B2
Copland Ter JES NE2 .....6 A5
Copley Av HAR/WTLS NE34 .....91 G2
Copley Dr SUNDSW SR3 .....120 B4
Copperas La
  BW/LEM/TK/HW NE15 .....68 D4
Copper Chare MPTH NE61 .....20 D4
Copperfield DHAM * DH1 .....168 B3
Coppergate Ct HEBB NE31 .....73 H4
Coppice HI BDN/LAN/SAC DH7 .....165 J2
Coppice Wy JES NE2 .....6 A4
Coppy La STLY/ANP DH9 .....113 G3
  WICK/BNPF NE16 .....113 F1
The Copse BLAY NE21 .....84 D2
  PRUD NE42 .....81 F2
  WICK/BNPF NE16 .....97 H7
Coquet WASHS NE38 .....116 B5
Coquet Av BLYTH NE24 .....35 G2
  GOS/KPK NE3 .....56 B4
  HAR/WTLS NE34 .....76 A3
  WBAY NE26 .....50 E4
Coquetdale Av
  BYK/HTN/WLK NE6 .....72 C5
Coquetdale CI MPTH NE61 .....21 H2
Coquetdale Vis
  CLDN/WHIT/ROK
  (off Roker Baths Rd) SR6 .....106 E4
Coquet Dr CLSW/PEL DH2 .....114 C7
Coquet Gdns STLY/ANP DH9 .....126 C3
Coquet Gv
  BW/LEM/TK/HW NE15 .....66 E1
Coquet St CNUT NE1 .....6 C6
  HEBB NE31 .....73 F5
  JRW NE32 .....73 J6
Coquet Ter BYK/HTN/WLK NE6 .....71 H2
  CRAM NE23 .....47 F1
Corbett St PLEE/EAS SR8 .....163 G5
Corbiere CI SUNDSW SR3 .....133 J1
Corbitt St GATE NE8 .....10 B6
Corbridge Rd WLSD/HOW NE28 .....59 G4
Corbridge Rd BYK/HTN/WLK NE6 .....7 G4
Corbridge St BYK/HTN/WLK NE6 .....72 B5
Corby Gdns BYK/HTN/WLK NE6 .....72 B5
Corby Ga ASHBK/HED/RY SR2 .....120 D2
Corby Gv PLEE/EAS SR8 .....174 B7

Corby Hall Dr
  ASHBK/HED/RY SR2 ....120 D2
Corchester Rd BDLGTN NE22 ......28 E4
Corchester Wk LGB/HTN NE7 ......57 H6
Corinthian Sq SWCK/CAS SR5 ....104 E3
Cork St SUND SR1 ....15 G4
Cormorant CI ASHGTN NE63 ....24 A4
  BLYTH NE24 ....35 H3
Cornbank CI SUNDSW SR3 ....134 A2
Corndean WASHS NE38 ....117 J2
Cornelia Ter SEA/MUR SR7 ....150 D1
Cornel Rd LGB/HTN NE7 ....57 H7
Corney St SSH NE33 ....75 F4
The Cornfields HEBB NE31 ....73 C5
Cornforth CI ASHGTN NE63 ....23 H3
  FELL NE10 ....88 E6
Cornhill Av GOS/KPK NE3 ....55 J3
Cornhill Crs NSHW NE29 ....60 B3
Cornhill Rd CRAM NE23 ....38 C2
  SWCK/CAS SR5 ....106 B3
Corn Mill Dr HLH DH5 ....147 G2
Cornmoor Gdns
  WICK/BNPF NE16 ....85 F7
Cornmoor Rd WICK/BNPF NE16 ...85 F6
Cornthwaite Dr
  CLDN/WHIT/ROK SR6 ....92 E3
Cornwallis Sq SSH NE33 ....75 F2
Cornwallis St SSH NE33 ....3 G7
Cornwall Rd HEBB NE31 ....89 H1
Cornwall St PLEE/EAS SR8 ....163 G5
Cornwell Ct LGB/HTN NE7 ....57 F6
Cornwell Crs BDLGTN NE22 ....29 H6
Coronation Av
  ASHBK/HED/RY SR2 ....135 F1
  DHAM DH1 ....158 A5
Coronation Bungalows
  GOS/KPK (off Church Rd) NE3 ...56 D5
Coronation CI SUND SR1 ....15 G4
Coronation Gn HLH DH5 ....160 C1
Coronation Rd
  WD/WHPE/BLK NE5 ....53 K7
  WICK/BNPF NE16 ....99 F3
  WNGT TS28 ....183 J2
Coronation St RDHAMSE DH6 ......161 G2
Coronation St
  CLS/BIR/GTL DH3 ....129 K5
  NSHW NE29 ....2 D4
  SSH NE33 ....3 G8
  SUND SR1 ....15 G4
  WLSD/HOW NE28 ....72 E1
Coronation Ter ASHGTN * NE63 ...23 K4
  MLFD/PNYW SR4 ....105 F7
Corporation Rd
  ASHBK/HED/RY SR2 ....121 F2
Corporation St ELS/FEN NE4 ....5 G7
Corporation Yd MPTH NE61 ....20 D5
Corriedale CI DHAM * DH1 ....156 D1
Corrofell Gdns FELL NE10 ....13 G4
Corry Ct MLFD/PNYW SR4 ....119 J2
Corsair WICK/BNPF NE16 ....84 D6
Corsenside WD/WHPE/BLK NE5 ....68 D2
Corstorphine Town SSH NE33 ....75 F3
Cortina Av MLFD/PNYW SR4 ....119 H2
Cortland Rd CON/LDGT DH8 ....122 C4
Cort St CON/LDGT DH8 ....122 E4
Cossack Ter MLFD/PNYW SR4 ......105 J6
Cosserat PI HEBB NE31 ....73 F4
Cosser St BLYTH * NE24 ....34 D3
Coston Dr SSH NE33 ....3 H6
Cosyn St BYK/HTN/WLK NE6 ....6 D6
Cotehill Dr PONT/DH NE20 ....42 D5
Cotehill Rd WD/WHPE/BLK NE5 ....69 F2
Cotemede FELL NE10 ....88 C7
Cotfield Wk GATE NE8 ....10 D5
The Cotgarth FELL NE10 ....12 E9
Cotherstone Ct SUNDSW SR3 ......120 B4
Cotherstone Rd DHAM DH1 ....156 D1
Cotman Gdns HAR/WTLS NE34 .....91 H2
Cotsford Est PLEE/EAS SR8 ....175 J4
Cotsford La PLEE/EAS SR8 ....175 J4
Cotswold Av LGB/KIL NE12 ....57 H1
Cotswold CI WASHS NE38 ....116 D2
Cotswold Dr ASHGTN NE63 ....24 A4
  MONK NE25 ....30 A6
Cotswold Gdns DUN/TMV NE11 ....86 A5
  LGB/HTN NE7 ....57 G7
Cotswold La BOLCOL NE35 ....90 C2
Cotswold PI PLEE/EAS SR8 ....174 C3
Cotswold Rd NSHW NE29 ....50 C7
  SWCK/CAS SR5 ....104 E2
Cotswold Sq SWCK/CAS SR5 ......104 E2
Cotswold Ter STLY/ANP DH9 ....126 E2
Cottage La WD/WHPE/BLK NE5 .....69 H2
Cottages Rd SEA/MUR SR7 ....150 C4
Cottenham St BYK/HTN/WLK NE4 ...9 F1
Cotterdale WLSD/HOW NE28 ....58 B5
Cotterdale Av GATE NE8 ....11 G8
Cotter Riggs PI
  WD/WHPE/BLK NE5 ....67 K1
Cottersdale Gdns
  WD/WHPE/BLK NE5 ....53 K7
Cottingham CI PLEE/EAS SR8 ......174 C3
Cottinglea MPTH NE61 ....20 D4
Cottingvale MPTH NE61 ....20 D3
Cottingwood Gdns ELS/FEN NE4 .....4 E5
Cottingwood Gn BLYTH NE24 ....34 D4
Cottingwood La MPTH NE61 ....20 D3
Cottonwood HLS DH4 ....131 H1
  SUNDSW SR3 ....133 J2
Coulthards La GATE NE8 ....11 H1
Coulthards PI GATE NE8 ....6 C9
Coulton Dr BOL NE36 ....91 H5
Council Av HLS DH4 ....131 H1
Counden Rd
  WD/WHPE/BLK NE5 ....54 C7
Countess Av WBAY NE26 ....50 E4
Countess CI SEA/MUR SR7 ....135 J7
Countess Dr
  BW/LEM/TK/HW NE15 ....68 E4
Coupland Gv JRW NE32 ....89 J1
Coupland Rd ASHGTN NE63 ....23 J2
Courtfield Rd
  BYK/HTN/WLK NE6 ....72 B5
Court La DHAM DH1 ....16 E5
Courtney Ct GOS/KPK NE3 ....55 J5
Courtney Dr SUNDSW SR3 ....119 K6
Court Rd BDLGTN NE22 ....29 F5
Court St PLEE/EAS SR8 ....163 G5

The Court WICK/BNPF NE16 ....85 G6
The Courtyard STLY/ANP DH9 ......112 A6
Cousin St SUND SR1 ....15 H4
Coutts Rd BYK/HTN/WLK NE6 ....7 M1
Coventry Gdns ELS/FEN NE4 ....5 J7
  NSHW NE29 ....60 C6
Coventry Rd DHAM DH1 ....156 E2
Coverdale FELL NE10 ....88 C6
  WLSD/HOW NE28 ....58 B5
Coverdale Av BLYTH NE24 ....30 C7
Coverley Rd SWCK/CAS SR5 ....104 E2
The Covers LGB/KIL NE12 ....58 A4
  MPTH NE61 ....20 E6
The Cove HLS DH4 ....131 K1
Cowan CI BLAY NE21 ....67 J7
Cowans Av LGB/KIL NE12 ....47 J5
Cowan Ter ASHBK/HED/RY SR2 ....14 D6
Cowdray Ct SSH NE33 ....55 G3
Cowdray Rd SWCK/CAS SR5 ....105 F3
Cowell Gv ROWG NE39 ....96 E3
Cowell St PLEE/EAS SR8 ....175 G3
Cowen Gdns
  LWF/SPW/WRK NE9 ....101 G4
Cowen Rd BLAY NE21 ....84 B1
Cowen St BYK/HTN/WLK NE6 ....72 B5
Cowley PI BLYTH NE24 ....30 D6
Cowley Rd BLYTH NE24 ....30 D5
Cowley St RDHAMSE DH6 ....173 J4
Cowpath Gdns FELL NE10 ....13 K5
Cowpen Hall Rd BLYTH NE24 ....30 C6
Cowpen Rd BLYTH NE24 ....30 B6
Coxfoot CI HAR/WTLS NE34 ....91 J2
Coxgreen Rd HLS DH4 ....117 J6
Coxlodge Rd GOS/KPK NE3 ....56 A5
Coxlodge Ter GOS/KPK NE3 ....56 A5
Coxon St ASHBK/HED/RY SR2 ......15 G6
Coxon Ter FELL NE10 ....12 A5
Crabtree Rd PSHWF NE43 ....79 G5
Cradock Av HEBB NE31 ....73 F7
Craggyknowe WASHN NE37 ....102 B7
Craghall Dene JES NE2 ....56 E6
Craghall Dene Av JES NE2 ....56 E6
Craghead La STLY/ANP DH9 ....127 J4
Cragleas WICK/BNPF NE16 ....111 J2
Cragside BDN/LAN/SAC DH7 ......155 G1
  CLSW/PEL DH2 ....129 G3
  CRAM NE23 ....38 C4
  HAR/WTLS NE34 ....76 B6
  LGB/HTN NE7 ....57 H7
  WBAY NE26 ....50 E4
Cragside Av NSHW NE29 ....60 B2
Cragside Ct STLY/ANP DH9 ....125 H4
Cragside Gdns DUN/TMV NE11 ....86 A7
  LGB/KIL NE12 ....48 B5
  WLSD/HOW NE28 ....59 H7
Cragside Rd WASHN NE37 ....102 C6
Cragston Av
  WD/WHPE/BLK NE5 ....55 G7
Cragston CI
  WD/WHPE/BLK NE5 ....69 G1
Cragton Gdns BLYTH NE24 ....30 D7
Craigavon Rd SWCK/CAS SR5 .....105 F4
Craig Crs CRAM NE23 ....47 C1
Craighill HLS DH4 ....131 J1
Craigmillar Av
  WD/WHPE/BLK NE5 ....55 G7
Craigmillar CI
  WD/WHPE/BLK NE5 ....55 F7
Craigmill Pk BLYTH NE24 ....30 C6
Craigshaw Rd SWCK/CAS SR5 ....104 D2
Craig Ter PLEE/EAS SR8 ....162 C6
Craigwell Dr SUNDSW SR3 ....134 A3
Craik Av HAR/WTLS NE34 ....75 F6
Crake Wy WASHS NE38 ....116 B4
Cramer St GATE NE8 ....11 H6
Cramlington Rw SWCK/CAS SR5 ..104 D4
Cramlington Sq SWCK/CAS SR5 ..104 D3
Cramlington Ter BLYTH NE24 ....34 E3
Cramond Ct
  LWF/SPW/WRK NE9 ....100 E2
Cramond Wy CRAM NE23 ....38 C4
Cranberry Rd SWCK/CAS SR5 .....104 E3
Cranberry Sq SWCK/CAS SR5 .....104 E3
Cranbrone SUNDSW SR3 ....133 G1
Cranbourne Gv
  TYNE/NSHE NE30 ....51 F6
Cranbrook Av GOS/KPK NE3 ....56 C3
Cranbrook Ct GOS/KPK NE3 ....55 J3
Cranbrook Dr PRUD NE42 ....80 B2
Cranbrook PI
  BW/LEM/TK/HW NE15 ....69 F7
Cranbrook Rd
  BW/LEM/TK/HW NE15 ....69 F7
Cranemarsh CI ASHGTN NE63 ......23 H4
Craneswater Av WBAY NE26 ....41 J7
Cranfield Ct
  BW/LEM/TK/HW NE15 ....68 A4
Cranford St HAR/WTLS NE34 ....75 C5
Cranford Ter MLFD/PNYW SR4 ....120 A1
Cranham CI LGB/KIL NE12 ....48 B5
Cranleigh Av DIN/WO NE13 ....55 F3
Cranleigh Gv PRUD NE42 ....80 D1
Cranleigh PI MONK NE25 ....50 B2
Cranleigh Rd SWCK/CAS SR5 ......104 E3
Cranshaw PI CRAM NE23 ....38 D3
Crantock Rd GOS/KPK NE3 ....55 K5
Cranwell Ct GOS/KPK NE3 ....55 J5
Cranwell Dr DIN/WO NE13 ....46 B3
Craster Av HAR/WTLS NE34 ....76 B3
  LGB/KIL NE12 ....58 B1
  SMOOR NE27 ....49 G6
Craster CI BLYTH NE24 ....30 E7
  CLSW/PEL DH2 ....129 F6
  MONK NE25 ....50 B3
Craster Gdns WLSD/HOW NE28 ....59 H7
Craster Rd NSHW NE29 ....60 B5
Craster Sq GOS/KPK NE3 ....56 A4
Craster Ter LGB/HTN NE7 ....71 H1
Craven La CLDN/WHIT/ROK SR6 ..107 F4
Crawford Av PLEE/EAS SR8 ....174 E2
Crawford CI RDHAMSE DH6 ....170 C1
Crawford PI MONK NE25 ....50 C5
Crawford St BLYTH NE24 ....31 F5
Crawford Ter
  BYK/HTN/WLK NE6 ....72 B6
Crawhall Crs MPTH NE61 ....20 C6

Crawhall Rd CNUT NE1 ....6 B6
Crawlaw Rd PLEE/EAS SR8 ....162 E4
Crawley Av HEBB NE31 ....89 F1
Crawley Gdns WICK/BNPF NE16 .....8 B9
Crawley Rd WLSD/HOW NE28 ....72 D2
Crawley Sq HEBB NE31 ....89 F1
Craythorne Gdns
  BYK/HTN/WLK NE6 ....71 J1
Creeverlea WASHS NE38 ....116 E3
Creighton Av GOS/KPK NE3 ....55 F9
Creland Wy WD/WHPE/BLK NE5 ...55 G7
Crescent CI RDHAMSE DH6 ....170 C1
The Crescent
  BDN/LAN/SAC DH7 ....125 J7
  BDN/LAN/SAC DH7 ....143 G2
  BDN/LAN/SAC DH7 ....153 K3
  BW/LEM/TK/HW NE15 ....67 F1
  CLDN/WHIT/ROK SR6 ....91 K4
  CLSW/PEL DH2 ....129 H4
  CLSW/PEL DH2 ....144 B1
  CON/LDGT DH8 ....122 B3
  CON/LDGT DH8 ....123 F3
  CRAM NE23 ....39 G7
  DHAM DH1 ....156 B6
  DIN/WO NE13 ....55 F4
  HAR/WTLS NE34 ....75 K7
  HLS DH4 ....131 J2
  HLS DH4 ....132 B3
  HLS DH4 ....146 C6
  JRW NE32 ....73 J7
  LGB/HTN NE7 ....57 H5
  MPTH NE61 ....20 D7
  PLEE/EAS SR8 ....163 F4
  PONT/DH NE20 ....42 C6
  RDHAMSE DH6 ....170 C1
  ROWG NE39 ....96 B2
  ROWG NE39 ....97 H3
  RYTON NE40 ....67 F6
  STLY/ANP DH9 ....112 B6
  SUNDSW SR3 ....120 A5
  TYNE/NSHE NE30 ....61 G2
  WICK/BNPF NE16 ....85 G6
  WLSD/HOW NE28 ....58 D7
  WYLAM NE41 ....65 H6
Crescent Wy North
  LGB/KIL NE12 ....58 A2
Crescent Wy South
  LGB/KIL NE12 ....58 A2
Cressbourne Av
  CLDN/WHIT/ROK SR6 ....106 E1
Cresswell Av LGB/KIL NE12 ....58 A1
  NSHW NE29 ....60 D3
  PLEE/EAS SR8 ....175 H4
  WBAY NE26 ....41 F2
Cresswell CI BLAY NE21 ....83 H4
  MONK NE25 ....50 C6
Cresswell Dr BLYTH NE24 ....34 D2
  GOS/KPK NE3 ....55 J3
Cresswell Rd WLSD/HOW NE28 ....72 C2
Cresswell St BYK/HTN/WLK NE6 .....7 K5
Cresswell Ter
  ASHBK/HED/RY SR2 ....14 D7
The Crest BDLGTN NE22 ....28 E5
  DIN/WO NE13 ....45 F2
  WBAY NE26 ....41 G4
Crichton Av CLS/BIR/GTL DH3 .....129 K6
Cricklewood Dr HLS DH4 ....117 K7
Cricklewood Rd SWCK/CAS SR5 ..104 D4
Criddle St GATE NE8 ....6 C9
Crieff Gv JRW NE32 ....90 B1
Crieff Sq SWCK/CAS SR5 ....104 D3
Crigdon HI WD/WHPE/BLK NE5 .....68 D2
Crighton WASHS NE38 ....116 C1
Crimdon Gv HLS DH4 ....147 F1
Crime Rigg Bank
  RDHAMSE DH6 ....171 G2
Crindledykes WASHS NE38 ....117 G4
Cripps Av FELL NE10 ....13 M8
Croft Av LGB/KIL NE12 ....58 A3
  WLSD/HOW NE28 ....72 E1
Croft CI RYTON NE40 ....67 F7
Croftdale Rd BLAY NE21 ....83 K2
Crofter CI CRAM NE23 ....38 B7
Crofthead Dr CRAM NE23 ....38 C4
Crofton St BLYTH NE24 ....31 G7
  HAR/WTLS NE34 ....75 C5
Crofton Wy
  BW/LEM/TK/HW NE15 ....67 K4
Croft PI
  CON/LDGT (off Delves La) DH8 ...123 H7
Croft Rigg BDN/LAN/SAC DH7 ....167 F7
Croft Rd BLYTH NE24 ....31 G7
Croftside Av
  CLDN/WHIT/ROK SR6 ....93 F4
Croft's La
  BW/LEM/TK/HW NE15 ....64 C3
Crofts Pk MPTH NE61 ....27 J1
Croft St CNUT NE1 ....5 L6
Croftsway ELS/FEN NE4 ....4 A8
Croft Ter JRW NE32 ....73 K5
  STLY/ANP DH9 ....125 J3
The Croft GOS/KPK NE3 ....56 A6
  LGB/KIL NE12 ....48 A5
  RDHAMSE DH6 ....171 G1
Cromarty CLSW/PEL DH2 ....115 F4
Cromarty St
  CLDN/WHIT/ROK SR6 ....106 D3
Cromdale PI
  WD/WHPE/BLK NE5 ....69 F2
Cromer Av LWF/SPW/WRK NE9 ...101 F2
Cromer Gdns WBAY NE26 ....50 E3
Crompton Rd
  BYK/HTN/WLK NE6 ....71 H2
Cromwell Av BLAY NE21 ....83 K2
Cromwell Ct BLAY NE21 ....67 J7
  FELL* NE10 ....88 E2
Cromwell Rd FELL NE10 ....13 L3
  WICK/BNPF NE16 ....8 A8
Cromwell St GATE NE8 ....11 J6
  MLFD/PNYW SR4 ....106 A6
Cromwell Ter GATE NE8 ....10 D6
  NSHW NE29 ....60 D4
Crondall St SSH NE33 ....75 H4
Cronin Av HAR/WTLS NE34 ....74 E7
Crookhall La CON/LDGT DH8 ....123 J3
Crookhall Rd CON/LDGT DH8 .....123 G4
Crookham Gv MPTH NE61 ....27 F1
Crookham Wy CRAM NE23 ....38 D4

Cropthorne FELL NE10 ....88 D6
Cross Av WLSD/HOW NE28 ....58 B5
Crossbank
  WD/WHPE/BLK NE5 ....55 H7
Crossbrook Rd
  WD/WHPE/BLK NE5 ....69 H1
Crossby St ASHBK/HED/RY SR2 ...15 J7
Crossfell PONT/DH NE20 ....42 E6
Crossfell Gdns STKFD/GP NE62 ...123 C5
Crossfield BDN/LAN/SAC DH7 .....143 H6
Crossfield Pk FELL NE10 ....87 J6
Crossfield Ter
  BYK/HTN/WLK NE6 ....72 C7
Crossgate DHAM DH1 ....16 B4
  SSH NE33 ....3 H9
Crossgate Moor Gdns
  DHAM DH1 ....156 A7
Crossgate Peth DHAM DH1 ....16 A5
Crossgate Rd HLH DH5 ....147 K6
Crosshill Rd
  BW/LEM/TK/HW NE15 ....69 F1
Cross Keys La
  LWF/SPW/WRK NE9 ....87 F7
Cross La BDN/LAN/SAC DH7 ....143 H4
  DUN/TMV NE11 ....8 D5
  DUN/TMV NE11 ....100 A2
  WICK/BNPF NE16 ....8 B7
Crosslaw WD/WHPE/BLK NE5 ......68 C2
Crossleaw Av SUNDSW SR3 ....120 B3
Crossley Ter ELS/FEN NE4 ....4 B5
  LGB/KIL NE12 ....58 B1
Cross Pde ELS/FEN NE4 ....4 E8
Cross PI SUND SR1 ....15 G4
Cross Rigg CI HLS DH4 ....117 H7
Cross Rw GATE NE8 ....11 M5
Cross St CNUT NE1 ....5 H7
  CON/LDGT DH8 ....122 D3
  GATE NE8 ....11 H6
  HLS DH4 ....131 J7
  HLS DH4 ....132 B6
  RDHAMSE DH6 ....159 G6
  RDHAMSE DH6 ....178 C4
Cross Ter ROWG NE39 ....97 F4
Cross Vale Rd
  ASHBK/HED/RY SR2 ....14 D9
Crossway HAR/WTLS NE34 ....76 A6
  JES NE2 ....56 E7
  LWF/SPW/WRK NE9 ....87 F7
  STKFD/GP* NE62 ....23 F6
  TYNE/NSHE NE30 ....61 G2
Crossways BDN/LAN/SAC DH7 ....154 B3
  BOL NE36 ....91 J5
  SUNDSW SR3 ....119 K7
The Crossway
  BW/LEM/TK/HW NE15 ....68 C3
The Cross Wy GOS/KPK NE3 ....55 K6
  MPTH NE61 ....20 C7
Croudace Rw FELL NE10 ....12 C7
Crow Bank WLSD/HOW NE28 ....72 E1
Crow Hall La CRAM NE23 ....33 F7
Crowhall La FELL NE10 ....12 C8
Crow Hall Rd CRAM NE23 ....33 F6
Crow La SUNDSW SR3 ....119 F7
Crowley Av WICK/BNPF NE16 ....8 B8
Crowley Gdns BLAY NE21 ....84 A2
Crowley Rd WICK/BNPF NE16 ....84 E3
Crowley Vis WICK/BNPF* NE16 .....84 E3
Crown Rd SWCK/CAS SR5 ....106 A5
Crown St SSH NE33 ....31 H7
Crowther Rd WASHS NE38 ....116 A3
Crowtree Rd SUND SR1 ....14 D4
Crow Trees La RDHAMSE DH6 .....180 A3
Croxdale Gdns FELL NE10 ....13 K5
Croxdale Ter FELL NE10 ....13 K5
Croydon Rd ELS/FEN NE4 ....4 C3
Crozier St SWCK/CAS SR5 ....106 C4
Cruddas Pk
  ELS/FEN
  (off Westmorland Rd) NE4 ....4 D9
Crudwell La BOLCOL NE35 ....90 C2
Crummock Av
  CLDN/WHIT/ROK SR6 ....106 C1
Crummock Rd
  WD/WHPE/BLK NE5 ....69 F3
Crumstone Ct LGB/KIL NE12 ....48 B5
Cuba St ASHBK/HED/RY SR2 ......120 E2
Cuillin CI WASHS NE38 ....116 D3
Culford PI WLSD/HOW NE28 ....73 K2
Cullercoats Rd SWCK/CAS SR5 ...104 D4
Cullercoats St BYK/HTN/WLK NE6 ...7 L5
Culloden Ter PLEE/EAS SR8 ....163 G6
Culloden Wk LGB/KIL NE12 ....47 K5
Culzean Ct CON/LDGT* DH8 ....122 D3
Cumberland Av BDLGTN NE22 ......28 E5
  NWBCN NE64 ....25 F1
Cumberland PI
  CLS/BIR/GTL DH3 ....115 K5
  HAR/WTLS NE34 ....76 B4
Cumberland Rd
  CON/LDGT DH8 ....137 F2
  NSHW NE29 ....59 K3
  SUNDSW SR3 ....120 A6
Cumberland St SUND SR1 ....14 E3
  WLSD/HOW NE28 ....72 E1
  WLSD/HOW NE28 ....73 K2
Cumberland Wk LGB/HTN NE7 .....57 H6
Cumberland Wy WASHN NE37 .....103 F2
Cumbrian Av
  CLDN/WHIT/ROK SR6 ....92 C7
Cumbrian Gdns DUN/TMV NE11 ...86 A6
Cumbrian Wy PLEE/EAS SR8 ....175 F4
Cumbria Wk STLY/ANP DH9 ....112 C7
Cumbria Wk ELS/FEN NE4 ....4 D7
Cummings Av RDHAMSE DH6 .....158 C7
Cummings St BLYTH * NE24 ....31 G6
Cunningham PI DHAM DH1 ....17 J1
Curlew CI ASHGTN NE63 ....23 K5
  LGB/KIL NE12 ....48 B5
  RYTON NE40 ....67 G7
Curlew HI MPTH NE61 ....20 B3
Curlew Rd JRW NE32 ....74 A3
Curlew Wy BLYTH NE24 ....35 G5
Curly Kews MPTH NE61 ....20 D3
Curren Gdns FELL NE10 ....12 A4
Curtis Rd ELS/FEN NE4 ....4 A3
Curzon PI WD/WHPE/BLK NE5 .....69 F1

Curzon Rd West
  WLSD/HOW NE28 ....72 D2
Curzon St GATE NE8 ....10 E7
Cushat CI BYK/HTN/WLK NE6 ....7 F7
Cushy Cow La RYTON NE40 ....67 F7
Cut Bank CNUT NE1 ....5 J5
Cuthbert CI DHAM DH1 ....169 J1
Cuthbert Ct JRW NE32 ....74 C5
Cuthbertson Ct
  CLDN/WHIT/ROK SR6 ....92 E7
Cuthbert St GATE NE8 ....10 C4
  WICK/BNPF NE16 ....98 E4
Cutler's Av SSH NE33 ....75 G3
Cutlers' Hall Rd CON/LDGT DH8 ..122 C2
Cut Throat La CHPW NE17 ....109 H2
Cygnet CI ASHGTN NE63 ....23 K5
  WD/WHPE/BLK NE5 ....54 B6
Cyncopa Wy
  WD/WHPE/BLK NE5 ....69 H1
Cypress Av ELS/FEN NE4 ....69 H3
Cypress Ct BDN/LAN/SAC DH7 ...167 G7
Cypress Crs BLYTH NE24 ....31 G7
  DUN/TMV NE11 ....9 H6
Cypress Dr BLYTH NE24 ....31 G7
Cypress Gdns BLYTH NE24 ....31 G7
Cypress Gv DHAM DH1 ....157 H6
  RYTON NE40 ....66 E5
Cypress Pk BDN/LAN/SAC DH7 ...165 G2
Cypress Rd BLAY NE21 ....84 A2
  LWF/SPW/WRK NE9 ....101 K3
Cypress Sq SUNDSW SR3 ....120 A6
Cyprus Gdns
  LWF/SPW/WRK NE9 ....87 G6
Cyril St CON/LDGT DH8 ....123 F3

D

Dachet Rd MONK NE25 ....50 B2
Dacre Rd CLDN/WHIT/ROK SR6 ..106 D1
Dacre St MPTH NE61 ....20 D4
  SSH NE33 ....75 G3
Dahlia Ct MLFD/PNYW SR4 ....14 B4
Dahlia PI ELS/FEN NE4 ....69 H3
Dahlia Wy HEBB NE31 ....73 G7
Dairy La HLS DH4 ....132 A3
Dalden Gv SEA/MUR SR7 ....135 K7
Dalegarth WASHN NE37 ....102 D7
Dalegarth Gv
  CLDN/WHIT/ROK SR6 ....92 C7
Dale Rd MONK NE25 ....50 B5
Daleside BDN/LAN/SAC DH7 ....143 H4
Dale St BDN/LAN/SAC DH7 ....154 B2
  BLYTH NE24 ....31 G5
  CON/LDGT DH8 ....122 D4
  RYTON NE40 ....66 B7
  SSH NE33 ....3 J6
Dale Ter CLDN/WHIT/ROK SR6 ....106 E2
Dale Top MONK NE25 ....40 B7
Dale View Gdns RYTON NE40 ....82 A1
Dalla St MLFD/PNYW SR4 ....104 E6
Dallymore Dr RDHAMSE DH6 ......179 K1
Dalmahoy WASHN NE37 ....103 F2
Dalmatia Ter BLYTH NE24 ....35 G1
Dalston PI BLYTH NE24 ....35 G3
Dalton Av MPTH NE61 ....18 C1
  SEA/MUR SR7 ....150 C1
Dalton CI CRAM NE23 ....38 C2
Dalton Ct WLSD/HOW NE28 ....58 B5
Dalton Crs BYK/HTN/WLK NE6 ....6 F5
Dalton PI
  MLFD/PNYW
  (off St. Marks Rd) SR4 ....14 A6
  WD/WHPE/BLK NE5 ....54 A7
Daltons La SSH NE33 ....2 F8
Dalton St BYK/HTN/WLK NE6 ....6 F5
Dalton Ter RDHAMSE DH6 ....182 D2
Dame Dorothy Crs
  CLDN/WHIT/ROK * SR6 ....106 E4
Dame Dorothy St
  CLDN/WHIT/ROK * SR6 ....14 E2
Dame Flora Robson Av
  HAR/WTLS NE34 ....74 D7
Danby CI SUNDSW SR3 ....134 B1
  WASHS NE38 ....116 B6
Danby Gdns BYK/HTN/WLK NE6 ...71 K2
Danville Rd
  CLDN/WHIT/ROK SR6 ....106 E1
Daphne Crs SEA/MUR SR7 ....150 D3
D'arcy CI SUND SR1 ....15 H6
D'arcy Sq SEA/MUR SR7 ....149 K4
Darden CI LGB/KIL NE12 ....48 B5
Darden Lough
  WD/WHPE/BLK NE5 ....68 C2
Darien Av CLDN/WHIT/ROK SR6 ..106 D1
Dark La MPTH NE61 ....20 E4
Darley Ct CLSW/PEL DH2 ....144 B3
Darley PI BW/LEM/TK/HW NE15 ...68 E6
Darlington Rd DHAM DH1 ....168 B2
Darnell PI ELS/FEN NE4 ....4 E5
Darnley Rd ASHGTN NE63 ....23 J2
Darras Dr NSHW NE29 ....75 H2
Darras Dr NSHW NE29 ....60 A3
Darras Rd PONT/DH NE20 ....42 D6
Darrell St DIN/WO NE13 ....46 A3
Dartford Rd
  CLDN/WHIT/ROK SR6 ....106 D1
  SSH NE33 ....75 K1
Dartmouth Av
  LWF/SPW/WRK NE9 ....101 F2
Dartmouth CI SEA/MUR SR7 ....150 B2
Dart Rd PLEE/EAS SR8 ....174 C5
Darvall CI MONK NE25 ....50 B2
Darwin Crs GOS/KPK NE3 ....55 H1
Darwin St SWCK/CAS SR5 ....105 K4
Daryl CI BLAY NE21 ....83 J5
Daryl Wy FELL * NE10 ....89 F5
Davenport Dr GOS/KPK NE3 ....56 B1
David Gdns
  CLDN/WHIT/ROK SR6 ....107 F2
Davidson Rd FELL NE10 ....13 M4
Davidson St HLS DH4 ....12 C7
David St WLSD/HOW NE28 ....72 D4
David Ter RDHAMSE DH6 ....180 A1
  RDHAMSE DH6 ....181 G4

Davies Hall
HEBB (off Ellison St) NE31 ....73 F4
Davies Crs *BDN/LAN/SAC DH7* 153 K2
Davison Av *SUNDSW SR3* 120 B7
Davison Crs *SEA/MUR SR7* 149 G4
Davison St *BLYTH* * *NE24* 31 G5
BOLCOL NE35 ....90 C3
BW/LEM/TK/HW NE15 ....67 G3
Davis Ter *PLEE/EAS SR8* 162 E6
Davis Wk *PLEE/EAS SR8* 175 F2
Davy Bank *WLSD/HOW NE28* 73 F2
Davy Dr *PLEE/EAS SR8* 174 A2
Dawdon Crs *SEA/MUR SR7* 150 E2
Dawlish CI *SEA/MUR SR7* 150 B2
Dawlish Gdns
LWF/SPW/WRK NE9 ....101 F2
Dawlish PI *WD/WHPE/BLK NE5* 54 A7
Dawson Dr *MPTH NE61* 20 D4
Dawson Rd *WNGT S28* 183 K3
Dawson Sq *TYNE/NSHE NE30* 61 H5
Dawson Ter *MLFD/PNYW SR4* 104 E6
Daylesford Dr *LGB/HTN NE7* 57 F6
Daylesford Rd *CRAM NE23* 33 G5
Dayshield *WD/WHPE/BLK NE5* 68 D2
Deacon CI *WD/WHPE/BLK NE5* 67 K1
Deacon Ct *LGB/KIL NE12* 57 G3
Deaconsfield CI *SUNDSW SR3* 133 K2
Deal CI *BLYTH NE24* 35 G3
Dean CI *PLEE/EAS SR8* 175 G5
Deanery St *BDLGTN NE22* 28 E5
Deanham Gdns
WD/WHPE/BLK NE5 ....69 G3
Dean Rd *SSH NE33* 75 H3
Deans Av *NWBGN NE64* 18 E7
Deans CI *WICK/BNPF NE16* 85 F5
Deansfield CI *SUNDSW SR3* 133 K2
Dean St *CNUT NE1* 5 L7
LWF/SPW/WRK NE9 ....87 F7
Deans' Wk *DHAM DH1* 157 C6
SWCK/CAS SR5 ....105 K4
Dean View Dr *BLYTH NE24* 30 D6
Dearham Gv *CRAM NE23* 33 G5
Debdon Gdns
BYK/HTN/WLK NE6 ....71 J2
Debdon PI *CRAM NE23* 38 C2
Debdon Rd *ASHGTN NE63* 24 B3
Deckham Ter *GATE NE8* 11 J7
Deepbrook Rd
WD/WHPE/BLK NE5 ....69 G2
Deepdale *WLSD/HOW NE28* 58 B5
Deepdale CI *WICK/BNPF NE16* 98 D1
Deepdale Crs
WD/WHPE/BLK NE5 ....69 H1
Deepdale Gdns *LGB/KIL NE12* 57 J4
Deepdale Rd *TYNE/NSHE NE30* 51 F7
Deepdale St *HLH DH5* 147 K7
Deepdene Gv
CLDN/WHIT/ROK SR6 ....92 D7
Deepdene Rd
CLDN/WHIT/ROK SR6 ....92 D7
Deerbolt PI *LGB/KIL NE12* 57 J5
Deer Park Wy *BLAY NE21* 84 C3
Dees Av *WLSD/HOW NE28* 58 D7
Deerfell CI *ASHGTN NE63* 23 H3
Deerness Ct
BDN/LAN/SAC
(off Station Av) *DH7* 167 H6
Deerness Rd
BDN/LAN/SAC DH7 ....165 G1
Deerness Hts
BDN/LAN/SAC DH7 ....167 G5
Deerness Rd
ASHBK/HED/RY SR2 ....15 H7
Deerness Valley Wk
CRK/WIL DL15 ....164 C6
Dee Rd *HEBB NE31* 89 G1
Dee St *JRW NE32* 74 A4
Defender Ct *SWCK/CAS SR5* 105 G5
Defoe Av *HAR/WTLS NE34* 91 F1
De Grey St *ELS/FEN NE4* 9 K1
Deighton Wk
WD/WHPE/BLK NE5 ....68 D2
Delacour Rd *BLAY NE21* 84 A1
Delamere Ct *SUNDSW* * *SR3* 134 A1
Delamere Crs *CRAM NE23* 33 G5
Delamere Rd *GOS/KPK NE3* 55 K5
Delaval Av *NSHW NE29* 60 C4
Delaval Ct *BDLGTN NE22* 29 J4
SSH NE33 ....75 H2
Delaval Crs *BLYTH NE24* 34 D3
Delaval La *PLEE/EAS SR8* 175 G5
Delaval Gdns
BW/LEM/TK/HW NE15 ....69 F7
Delaval Rd
BW/LEM/TK/HW NE15 ....69 F7
LGB/KIL NE12 ....57 K2
WBAY NE26 ....51 G5
Delaval St *BLYTH NE24* 31 F6
GOS/KPK NE3 ....56 A6
Delight Bank *STLY/ANP DH9* 111 F7
Dellfield Dr *MLFD/PNYW SR4* 118 E2
The Dell *HLS DH4* 132 B4
MPTH NE61 ....20 C2
Delta Bank Rd *WICK/BNPF NE16* ...8 B2
Delvedene *CON/LDGT DH8* 123 H6
Delves La *CON/LDGT DH8* 123 H7
De Merley Rd *MPTH NE61* 20 B3
The Demesne *ASHGTN NE63* 24 D3
De Mowbray Wy *MPTH NE61* 20 B3
Dempsey Rd *DIN/WO NE13* 46 B4
Denbeigh PI *LGB/KIL NE12* 57 J3
Denbigh Av
CLDN/WHIT/ROK SR6 ....106 D1
WLSD/HOW NE28 ....59 J6
Denby CI *CRAM NE23* 33 G5
The Dene *CON/LDGT DH8* 109 G4
Dene Av *BW/LEM/TK/HW NE15* 68 B5
DIN/WO NE13 ....46 A3
GOS/KPK NE3 ....56 E6
HLH DH5 ....132 E7
LGB/KIL NE12 ....57 F6
PLEE/EAS SR8 ....163 F4
ROWG NE39 ....97 F4

Denebank *MONK NE25* 50 C4
Dene Bank Av *PLEE/EAS SR8* 175 H4
Dene Bank Vw *GOS/KPK NE3* 55 J7
Dene CI *LGB/HTN NE7* 71 G1
PRUD NE42 ....64 B6
RYTON NE40 ....67 F6
Dene Ct *BDN/LAN/SAC DH7* 143 G7
CHPW NE17 ....95 H1
CLS/BIR/GTL DH3 ....101 J7
RDHAMSE DH6 ....171 H4
WASHS NE38 ....102 E7
Denecrest *CON/LDGT DH8* 109 G4
Dene Gv *CRAM NE23* 39 H6
GOS/KPK NE3 ....56 E6
PRUD NE42 ....80 B1
Deneholm *MONK NE25* 50 C3
WLSD/HOW NE28 ....59 F7
Denewood
LGB/HTN NE7 ....57 H7
Derwent Gdns
LGB/HTN NE7 ....57 H7
Derwent Gdns
WLSD/HOW NE28 ....59 J6
Derwenthaugh Marina
BLAY NE21 ....84 E1
Derwenthaugh Rd *BLAY NE21* 84 E1
Derwent Ms *CON/LDGT DH8* 122 D3
Derwent PI *CON/LDGT DH8* 122 C1
Derwent Rd *PLEE/EAS SR8* 175 F3
TYNE/NSHE NE30 ....51 F7
WBAY NE26 ....40 E7
Derwentside
WICK/BNPF
(off Woodhouse La) *NE16* 84 E4
Derwent St *CHPW NE17* 95 H4
CHPW NE17 ....95 H1
CON/LDGT DH8 ....122 D5
HLH DH5 ....148 A6
SUND SR1 ....14 D6
Derwent Ter *STLY/ANP DH9* 125 C4
Derwent Vw *BLAY NE21* 83 K3
Derwent Wk *WICK/BNPF NE16* 84 D4
Derwentwater Ct *GATE* * *NE8* 10 C5
Derwentwater Rd *GATE NE8* 9 K7
NWBGN NE64 ....24 E1
Derwent Wy *BLAY NE21* 84 C3
LGB/KIL NE12 ....47 J6
Deuchar St *JES NE2* 71 F3
Devon CI *ASHGTN NE63* 23 F1
Devon Crs *CLS/BIR/GTL DH3* 101 H7
CON/LDGT DH8 ....137 C1
Devon Dr *SUNDSW SR3* 120 A6
LWF/SPW/WRK NE9 ....11 H9
Devonport *HLS DH4* 132 A4
Devon Rd *HEBB NE31* 89 H1
NSHW NE29 ....60 B1
Devonshire Dr *SMOOR NE27* 58 E1
Devonshire Gdns
WLSD/HOW NE28 ....58 B7
Devonshire PI *JES NE2* 71 F2
Devonshire Rd *DHAM DH1* 157 K7
Devonshire St *SSH NE33* 75 F4
SWCK/CAS SR5 ....106 C4
Devon St *HLS DH4* 132 A1
Devonworth PI *BLYTH NE24* 30 C7
De Walden Sq *MPTH NE61* 21 J2
Dewberry CI *BLYTH NE24* 34 E3
Dewley *CRAM NE23* 38 C3
Dewley PI *WD/WHPE/BLK NE5* 54 C7
Dewley Rd *WD/WHPE/BLK NE5* 68 C2
Dewsgreen *CRAM NE23* 38 C2
Dexter Wy *FELL NE10* 12 B7
PONT/DH NE20 ....43 F7
Deyncourt *DHAM DH1* 168 B4
Deyncourt CI *PONT/DH NE20* 53 F1
Diamond Ct *GOS/KPK NE3* 55 C5
Diamond St *WLSD/HOW NE28* 72 C1
Diamond Ter *DHAM DH1* 16 C2
Diana St *ELS/FEN NE4* 4 F6
Dibley Sq *BYK/HTN/WLK NE6* 6 F7
Dibley St *BYK/HTN/WLK NE6* 6 F7
Dickens Av *HAR/WTLS NE34* 91 F1
WICK/BNPF NE16 ....84 E4
Dickens St *HLS DH4* 132 B7
SWCK/CAS SR5 ....106 A4
Dickens Wynd *DHAM DH1* 168 B3
Didcot Av *NSHW NE29* 60 C6
Didcot Wy *BOL NE36* 90 D5
BOLCOL NE35 ....90 A4
Dillon St *JRW NE32* 73 J6
SEA/MUR SR7 ....150 E1
Dilston Av *MONK NE25* 51 F5
MPTH NE61 ....22 A2
PLEE/EAS SR8 ....174 D7
SMOOR NE27 ....49 H7
WASHS NE38 ....116 C2
Dilston Dr *ASHGTN NE63* 23 K3
WD/WHPE/BLK NE5 ....54 C7
Dilston Gdns *MLFD/PNYW SR4* 119 K1
Dilston Rd *DHAM DH1* 156 E5
ELS/FEN NE4 ....4 C5
Dilston Ter *JRW NE32* 89 K1
Dimbula Gdns *LGB/HTN NE7* 71 K1
Dinsdale Av *WLSD/HOW NE28* 58 E5
Dinsdale Dr *DHAM DH1* 158 A5
Dinsdale PI *JES NE2* 6 B3
Dinsdale Rd
CLDN/WHIT/ROK SR6 ....106 D3
JES NE2 ....6 B3
Dinsdale St
ASHBK/HED/RY SR2 ....135 F1
Dinsdale St South
ASHBK/HED/RY SR2 ....135 F1
Dinting CI *PLEE/EAS SR8* 174 C5
Dipe La *BOL NE36* 90 D4
Dipton Gdns *SUNDSW SR3* 120 B4
Dipton Rd *MONK NE25* 50 B2
Dipwood Rd *ROWG NE39* 97 F4
Dipwood Wy *ROWG NE39* 97 F5
Disraeli St *BLYTH NE24* 31 F6
HLS DH4 ....131 K7
Dissington PI
WD/WHPE/BLK NE5 ....69 G3
WICK/BNPF NE16 ....84 E7
Ditchburn Ter
MLFD/PNYW SR4 ....105 K5
Dixon Av *BW/LEM/TK/HW NE15* 68 A3
Dixon Est *RDHAMSE DH6* 109 F2
Dixon Estate Bungalows
RDHAMSE DH6 ....173 H5
Dixon PI *DUN/TMV NE11* 9 H7

Dixon Ri *PLEE/EAS SR8* 175 J4
Dixon Rd *HLH DH5* 147 G2
Dixon's Sq
CLDN/WHIT/ROK SR6 ....106 D4
Dixon St *CON/LDGT DH8* 122 E3
GATE NE8 ....10 B6
SSH NE33 ....75 G2
Dock Rd *NSHW NE29* 2 C3
Dock Rd South *NSHW NE29* 2 D6
Dock St *CLDN/WHIT/ROK SR6* 15 G1
Dockwray CI *TYNE/NSHE NE30* 3 F2
Dockwray Sq *TYNE/NSHE NE30* 3 F2
Doddfell CI *WASHN NE37* 102 C7
Dodds Farm
GOS/KPK
(off Princes Meadow) *NE3* 56 A7
Dodds Ter *WNGT S28* 183 J1
Dogger Bank *MPTH NE61* 20 C4
Dolphin Ct *ELS/FEN* * *NE4* 69 H6
Dolphin Quay
NSHW (off Clive St) NE29 ....2 E3
TYNE/NSHE (off Liddell St) NE30 ...2 F3
Dolphin St *ELS/FEN NE4* 69 H6
Dominies CI *ROWG NE39* 97 H2
Dominion Rd
BDN/LAN/SAC DH7 ....167 G7
Donald Av *RDHAMSE DH6* 160 D1
Donald St *GOS/KPK NE3* 56 E5
Doncaster Rd *JES NE2* 6 B2
Doncrest Rd *WASHN NE37* 102 C4
Don Dixon Dr *JRW NE32* 73 J7
Donerston Gv *PLEE/EAS SR8* 174 B7
Don Gdns *BOL NE36* 90 D5
Donkin Rd *WASHN NE37* 102 B6
Donkin Ter *TYNE/NSHE NE30* 61 G3
Donnington CI *SWCK/CAS SR5* 104 E4
Donnington Gdns *GOS/KPK NE3* ...57 F6
Donnini PI *DHAM DH1* 17 J1
Donnison Gdns *SUND SR1* 15 H4
Donvale Rd *WASHN NE37* 102 C4
Don Vw *BOL NE36* 90 D5
Dorcas Av
BW/LEM/TK/HW NE15 ....69 G6
Dorchester CI
WD/WHPE/BLK NE5 ....53 K7
Dorchester Ct *MONK NE25* 39 K2
Dorchester Gdns
LWF/SPW/WRK NE9 ....101 F3
Doreen Av *SEA/MUR SR7* 150 A2
Doric Rd *BDN/LAN/SAC DH7* 166 E3
Dorking Av *NSHW NE29* 60 C6
Dorking CI *BLYTH NE24* 35 G3
Dorking Rd
CLDN/WHIT/ROK SR6 ....106 D1
Dorlonco Vls
BDN/LAN/SAC DH7 ....167 H7
Dormand Dr *PLEE/EAS SR8* 174 D7
Dornoch Crs *FELL NE10* 88 A6
Dorrington Rd *GOS/KPK NE3* 55 J4
Dorset Av
CLDN/WHIT/ROK SR6 ....106 E1
CLS/BIR/GTL DH3 ....115 J5
HAR/WTLS NE34 ....76 B4
HEBB NE31 ....73 H6
WLSD/HOW NE28 ....72 C1
Dorset CI *ASHGTN NE63* 23 F1
Dorset Gv *NSHW NE29* 60 B1
Dorset La *SUNDSW SR3* 120 B7
Dorset Rd
BW/LEM/TK/HW NE15 ....68 D5
GATE NE8 ....6 C8
Dorset St *HLH DH5* 160 B1
Douai Dr *CON/LDGT DH8* 123 J7
Double Rw *MONK NE25* 39 J3
Douglas Av *HAR/WTLS NE34* 76 C7
Douglas Gdns *DUN/TMV NE11* 86 A3
Douglas Rd
CLDN/WHIT/ROK SR6 ....106 E1
Douglass St *WLSD/HOW NE28* 72 C1
Douglas St *WLSD/HOW NE28* 73 J2
Douglas Ter *ELS/FEN NE4* 4 F6
HLS DH4 ....117 K6
Douglas Vls *DHAM DH1* 17 G2
Douglas Wy
CNUT (off Eldon Sq) NE1 ....5 J5
Doulting CI *LGB/KIL NE12* 57 H4
Douro Ter *ASHBK/HED/RY SR2* 14 E7
Dove Av *JRW NE32* 90 A1
Dove CI *BDN/LAN/SAC DH7* 167 F6
Dovecote CI *MONK NE25* 50 A3
Dovecote Rd *LGB/KIL NE12* 58 C3
Dovedale Av *BLYTH NE24* 30 C7
Dovedale Gdns *LGB/HTN NE7* 57 G7
LWF/SPW/WRK NE9 ....101 G1
Dovedale Rd
CLDN/WHIT/ROK SR6 ....92 C7
Dover CI *BDLGTN NE22* 28 D5
WD/WHPE/BLK NE5 ....54 A7
Dovercourt Rd
BYK/HTN/WLK NE6 ....72 A1
Dowling Av *MONK NE25* 50 D5
Downe CI *BLYTH NE24* 35 G3
Downend Rd
WD/WHPE/BLK NE5 ....54 B7
Downfield *WASHN NE37* 103 F2
Downham *WD/WHPE/BLK NE5* 68 D2
Downham Ct *SSH NE33* 75 G2
Downhill La *BOL NE36* 104 C1
WASHN NE37 ....104 B1
Downs La *HLH DH5* 148 A3
Downs Pit La *HLH DH5* 148 C3
Downswood CI *LGB/KIL NE12* 48 B6
Dowsey Rd *RDHAMSE DH6* 158 C2
Dowson Sq *SEA/MUR SR7* 149 F5
Doxford Av *HLH DH5* 147 J2

Doxford Dr *PLEE/EAS SR8* 174 A4
Doxford Gdns
WD/WHPE/BLK NE5 ....69 H2
Doxford Park Wy
SUNDSW SR3 ....133 J1
Doxford PI *CRAM NE23* 38 C5
Doxford Ter *HLH DH5* 147 J2
Dragon La *DHAM DH1* 157 J7
Drake CI *HEBB NE31* 75 F3
Drawback CI *PRUD NE42* 80 D2
The Dray *PONT/DH NE20* 42 D6
Drayton Rd
CLDN/WHIT/ROK SR6 ....106 D1
GOS/KPK NE3 ....55 J6
Drivecote *FELL NE10* 12 E8
The Drive *CLS/BIR/GTL DH3* 115 K5
CON/LDGT DH8 ....122 D1
FELL NE10 ....12 E8
GOS/KPK NE3 ....56 C7
LGB/HTN NE7 ....57 H6
LWF/SPW/WRK NE9 ....87 F6
MPTH NE61 ....26 B5
TYNE/NSHE NE30 ....61 H2
WASHN NE37 ....102 E4
WD/WHPE/BLK NE5 ....68 D5
WICK/BNPF NE16 ....85 G6
WLSD/HOW NE28 ....72 D1
Dronfield CI *CLSW/PEL DH2* 129 F6
Drove Rd *BW/LEM/TK/HW NE15* 52 D7
Drover Rd *CON/LDGT DH8* 137 F2
Drover Ter *CON/LDGT DH8* 137 F2
Drummond Crs *HAR/WTLS NE34* ...74 D6
Drummond Rd *GOS/KPK NE3* 55 K7
Drummond Ter
TYNE/NSHE NE30 ....61 F3
Drumoyne CI *SUNDSW SR3* 133 J1
Drumoyne Gdns *MONK NE25* 50 B6
Drum Rd *CLSW/PEL DH2* 115 H6
Drumsheugh PI
WD/WHPE/BLK NE5 ....69 G1
Druridge Av
CLDN/WHIT/ROK SR6 ....92 D7
Druridge Crs *BLYTH NE24* 34 C2
HAR/WTLS NE34 ....76 B3
Druridge Dr *BLYTH NE24* 34 C2
WD/WHPE/BLK NE5 ....69 H2
Drury La *NSHW NE29* 60 A3
SUND SR1 ....15 G4
Drybeck Ct *CRAM NE23* 33 K7
ELS/FEN NE4 ....4 E7
Drybeck Sq *SUNDSW SR3* 134 B1
Drybeck Wk *CRAM NE23* 33 K7
Dryborough St
MLFD/PNYW SR4 ....14 A3
Dryburgh *WASHS NE38* 116 C1
Dryburgh CI *NSHW NE29* 60 C2
Dryburn HI *DHAM DH1* 156 B5
Dryburn Rd *DHAM DH1* 156 B4
Dryden CI *HAR/WTLS NE34* 91 F2
STLY/ANP DH9 ....126 E1
Dryden Rd *LWF/SPW/WRK NE9* 11 H8
Dryden St *SWCK/CAS SR5* 106 A3
Drysdale Ct *DIN/WO NE13* 46 A3
Drysdale Crs *DIN/WO NE13* 46 A3
Dubmire Cottages *HLS DH4* 131 H7
Dubmire Ct *HLS DH4* 131 J7
Duchess Crs *JRW NE32* 89 K1
Duchess Crs East *JRW NE32* 89 K1
Duchess Dr
BW/LEM/TK/HW NE15 ....68 A3
Duchess St *WBAY NE26* 50 E4
Duckets *PRUD NE42* 80 C7
Duckpool La *WICK/BNPF NE16* 85 G5
Duddon CI *PLEE/EAS SR8* 175 F4
Duddon PI *LWF/SPW/WRK NE9* 101 H1
Dudley Av
CLDN/WHIT/ROK SR6 ....106 D1
Dudley Dr *CRAM NE23* 47 G1
Dudley Gdns *SUNDSW SR3* 133 G1
Dudley La *CRAM NE23* 38 B5
DIN/WO NE13 ....46 C1
Dugdale Rd *GOS/KPK NE3* 55 H5
Duke's Av *HEBB NE31* 73 F7
Dukes Ct *PRUD NE42* 64 E7
Dukes Dr *GOS/KPK NE3* 56 B1
Dukesfield *CRAM NE23* 38 C2
Dukes Meadow *DIN/WO NE13* 54 C2
Duke St *FELL NE10* 13 J5
MLFD/PNYW SR4 ....106 A7
SEA/MUR SR7 ....135 F4
WBAY NE26 ....50 E4
Duke St North
CLDN/WHIT/ROK SR6 ....106 D3
Dukes Wk
WBAY
(off Northern Prom) *NE26* 50 E2
Dukesway *DUN/TMV NE11* 86 B7
Dukes Wy *PRUD NE42* 64 E7
Duke Wk *GATE NE8* 10 A5
Dulverton Ct
WD/WHPE/BLK NE5 ....54 A7
Dulverton Av *SSH NE33* 75 F4
Dumfries Crs *JRW NE32* 74 C7
Dunbar St *WD/WHPE/BLK NE5* 54 A7
Dunbar St *MLFD/PNYW SR4* 119 K1
Dunblane Crs
WD/WHPE/BLK NE5 ....68 D3
Dunblane Dr *BLYTH NE24* 35 G3
Dunblane Rd
CLDN/WHIT/ROK SR6 ....106 E1
Dunbreck Gv *MLFD/PNYW SR4* 120 A2
Duncan St *BYK/HTN/WLK NE6* 72 C5
MLFD/PNYW SR4 ....105 K6
Duncombe Crs *STLY/ANP DH9* 112 D6
Duncow La *DHAM DH1* 16 D5
Dun Cow St *SUND SR1* 14 D4
Dundas St *CLDN/WHIT/ROK SR6* ..14 E1
Dundee Ct *JRW NE32* 90 C1
Dundrennan *WASHS NE38* 116 C3
Dunedin
STLY/ANP (off Kyo Rd) DH9 ....125 H2
Dunelm *ASHBK/HED/RY SR2* 14 A9
Dunelm Dr *MPTH NE61* 20 B6
Dunelm Rd
CLS/BIR/GTL
(off Jones St) *DH3* 115 J2
CON/LDGT DH8 ....123 K4

Dunelm Ct
  DHAM (off South St) DH1 .....16 C4
Dunelm Dr *BOL* NE36 .....91 F5
  HLS DH4 .....132 A7
Dunelm Pl *RDHAMSE* DH6 .....173 J4
Dunelm Rd *CON/LDGT* DH8 .....122 B7
  HLH DH5 .....147 J4
  RDHAMSE DH6 .....172 A7
Dunelm South
  ASHBK/HED/RY SR2 .....14 A9
Dunelm St *SSH* NE33 .....3 J1
Dunelm Wk *CON/LDGT* DH8 .....123 K4
  PLEE/EAS SR8 .....174 E5
Dunelm Wy *CON/LDGT* DH8 .....123 K3
Dunford Gdns
  WD/WHPE/BLK NE5 .....54 B6
Dunholm Cl *HLH* DH5 .....147 J1
Dunholme Cl *DHAM* DH1 .....156 C4
Dunholme Rd *ELS/FEN* NE4 .....4 A7
Dunira Cl *JES* NE2 .....71 F1
Dunkeld Cl *BLYTH* NE24 .....35 C3
Dunkirk Av *HLH* DH5 .....147 J1
Dunlin Cl *RYTON* NE40 .....67 G7
Dunlin Dr *BLYTH* NE24 .....35 G3
  WASHS NE38 .....116 B3
Dunlop Cl *LGB/HTN* NE7 .....57 J6
Dunlop Crs *HAR/WTLS* NE34 .....76 A5
Dunmoor Cl *GOS/KPK* NE3 .....56 A6
Dunmore Av
  CLDN/WHIT/ROK SR6 .....92 C2
Dunmorlie St *BYK/HTN/WLK* NE6 ..7 J5
Dunn Av *SUNDSW* SR3 .....120 A5
Dunning St *SUND* SR1 .....14 D3
Dunnlynn Cl *SUNDSW* SR3 .....133 J1
Dunnock Dr *WASHS* NE38 .....116 B4
  WICK/BNPF NE16 .....98 C2
Dunn Rd *PLEE/EAS* SR8 .....174 E1
Dunn's Ter *ELS/FEN* NE4 .....4 E1
Dunn St *ELS/FEN* NE4 .....9 L1
Dunn Ter *BYK/HTN/WLK* NE6 .....6 A4
Dunnykirk Av *GOS/KPK* NE3 .....55 H5
Dunsdale Dr *CRAM* NE23 .....33 K7
Dunsdale Rd *MONK* NE25 .....40 B6
Dunsgreen *PONT/DH* NE20 .....43 C4
Dunsley Gdns *DIN/WO* NE13 .....45 F1
Dunsmuir Gv *GATE* NE8 .....10 D8
Dunstable Pl
  WD/WHPE/BLK NE5 .....53 K7
Dunstanburgh *BDLGTN* NE22 .....28 D5
Dunstanburgh Cl *BDLGTN* NE22 ..28 D5
  WASHS NE38 .....116 D2
Dunstanburgh Rd
  BYK/HTN/WLK NE6 .....7 K7
Dunstan Cl *CLSW/PEL* DH2 .....129 G6
Dunston Bank *DUN/TMV* NE11 ....85 J1
Dunston Pl *BLYTH* NE24 .....30 D7
Dunston Rd *DUN/TMV* NE11 .....9 H8
Dunvegan *CLS/BIR/GTL* DH3 .....116 A4
Dunvegan Av *CLSW/PEL* DH2 ....129 H6
Durant Rd *CNUT* NE1 .....5 K5
Durban St *BLYTH* NE24 .....31 F5
Durham Av *PLEE/EAS* SR8 .....175 G2
  WASHN NE37 .....102 D5
Durham Cl *BDLGTN* NE22 .....28 D4
Durham Dr *BOLCOL* NE35 .....89 K4
  JRW NE32 .....89 K2
Durham Gdns
  BDN/LAN/SAC DH7 .....143 G7
Durham Gv *JRW* NE32 .....89 J2
Durham La *PLEE/EAS* SR8 .....162 A6
  RDHAMSE DH6 .....171 J2
  RDHAMSE DH6 .....173 C1
Durham Pl *CLS/BIR/GTL* DH3 ....115 J5
  GATE NE8 .....11 H6
Durham Rd *ASHBK/HED/RY* SR2 ..14 B6
  BDN/LAN/SAC DH7 .....140 C5
  BDN/LAN/SAC DH7 .....143 H6
  BDN/LAN/SAC DH7 .....165 H2
  CLS/BIR/GTL DH3 .....115 J1
  CON/LDGT DH8 .....122 C3
  CRAM NE23 .....33 J5
  GATE NE8 .....11 C6
  HLH DH5 .....147 G2
  HLS DH4 .....132 C7
  LWF/SPW/WRK NE9 .....101 F1
  RDHAMSE DH6 .....180 A3
  STLY/ANP DH9 .....125 J4
  SUNDSW SR3 .....120 A3
  WNGT TS28 .....183 J2
Durham St *ELS/FEN* NE4 .....4 B8
  HLS DH4 .....131 J7
  SEA/MUR SR7 .....135 H7
  WLSD/HOW NE28 .....72 E1
Durham St West
  WLSD/HOW NE28 .....72 E1
Durham Ter *SUNDSW* SR3 .....120 A5
Durham Vw *PLEE/EAS* SR8 .....174 C7
Duxfield Rd *LGB/HTN* NE7 .....57 H7
Dwyer Crs *ASHBK/HED/RY* SR2 ..135 F1
Dyer Sq *SWCK/CAS* SR5 .....106 B3
Dykefield Av *GOS/KPK* NE3 .....55 J3
Dyke Heads La *RYTON* NE40 .....82 D2
Dykelands Rd
  CLDN/WHIT/ROK SR6 .....106 D1
Dykelands Wy *HAR/WTLS* NE34 ...90 D1
Dykenook Cl *WICK/BNPF* NE16 ..98 E1
Dykes Wy *FELL* NE10 .....87 K7
Dymock Ct *WD/WHPE/BLK* NE5 ..55 F5

E

Eaglescliffe Dr *LGB/HTN* NE7 .....57 K7
Eaglesdene *HLH* DH5 .....147 K4
Eagle St *DUN/TMV* NE11 .....86 B6
Ealing Cl *DIN/WO* NE13 .....55 F4
Ealing Dr *TYNE/NSHE* NE30 .....61 G1
Eardulph Av *CLS/BIR/GTL* DH3 ..129 K4
Earlington Ct *LGB/KIL* NE12 .....58 A1
Earls Ct *PRUD* .....
Earl's Dr *BW/LEM/TK/HW* NE15 ...68 E4
  LWF/SPW/WRK NE9 .....101 F1
Earl's Gdns *BLYTH* NE24 .....30 E6
Earls Gn *HLH* DH5 .....147 G5
Earl St *MLFD/PNYW* SR4 .....14 A5
  SEA/MUR SR7 .....135 G7
  STLY/ANP DH9 .....125 G7

Earlsway *DUN/TMV* NE11 .....86 C5
Earlswood Av
  LWF/SPW/WRK NE9 .....101 K1
Earlswood Gv *BLYTH* NE24 .....35 F4
Earnshaw Wy *MONK* NE25 .....50 B2
Earsdon Cl *WD/WHPE/BLK* NE5 ..68 E1
Earsdon Rd *GOS/KPK* NE3 .....55 J7
  HLH DH5 .....132 D7
  MONK NE25 .....50 B5
  SMOOR NE27 .....49 H5
Earsdon Vw *SMOOR* NE27 .....49 H5
Easby Cl *GOS/KPK* NE3 .....56 D2
Easby Rd *WASHS* NE38 .....117 F2
Easdale Av *GOS/KPK* NE3 .....56 C1
Easdale Gdns
  LWF/SPW/WRK NE9 .....101 G1
Easington Av *CRAM* NE23 .....33 J5
  LWF/SPW/WRK NE9 .....101 J2
Easington St *PLEE/EAS* SR8 .....162 B5
  SWCK/CAS SR5 .....14 D2
Easington St North
  SWCK/CAS SR5 .....84 B2
East Acre *BLAY* NE21 .....
East Acres *DIN/WO* NE13 .....45 F1
East Atherton St *DHAM* DH1 .....16 B4
East Av *HAR/WTLS* NE34 .....76 A5
  LGB/KIL NE12 .....57 K4
  WASHS NE38 .....116 E5
East Back Pde
  ASHBK/HED/RY SR2 .....14 B6
East Bailey *LGB/KIL* NE12 .....47 K6
East Boldon Rd
  CLDN/WHIT/ROK SR6 .....91 J4
Eastbourne Av
  BYK/HTN/WLK NE6 .....72 C4
  GATE NE8 .....10 F7
Eastbourne Gdns
  BYK/HTN/WLK NE6 .....72 C5
  WBAY NE26 .....50 D3
Eastbourne Gv *SSH* NE33 .....3 K7
Eastburn Gdns *FELL* NE10 .....13 G5
Eastcheap *BYK/HTN/WLK* NE6 ....71 J2
East Cleft Rd
  ASHBK/HED/RY SR2 .....14 B6
East Clere *BDN/LAN/SAC* DH7 ...154 B5
Eastcliffe Av *GOS/KPK* NE3 .....56 A7
East Cl *HAR/WTLS* NE34 .....76 A5
Eastcombe Cl *BOLCOL* NE35 .....90 C2
Eastcote Ter *BYK/HTN/WLK* NE6 ..13 H1
East Crs *BDLGTN* NE22 .....29 K4
East Cross St *SUND* SR1 .....14 F3
Eastdene Rd *SEA/MUR* SR7 .....150 A1
Eastdene Wy *PLEE/EAS* SR8 .....175 F7
East Dr *BLYTH* NE24 .....34 C3
  CLDN/WHIT/ROK SR6 .....91 J4
East End *WBAY* NE26 .....41 H4
Easten Gdns *FELL* NE10 .....12 C5
Easterfield Ct *MPTH* NE61 .....20 E4
Eastern Av *BDN/LAN/SAC* DH7 ..154 B3
  DUN/TMV NE11 .....100 D1
Eastern Vls
  LGB/KIL
  (off Station Rd North) NE12 ...57 K2
Eastern Wy *PONT/DH* NE20 .....43 H1
  WD/WHPE/BLK NE5 .....69 H1
East Farm Ct *WICK/BNPF* NE16 ..99 C3
East Farm Ms
  CON/LDGT (off Manor Rd) DH8 ..109 J4
Eastfield Av *BYK/HTN/WLK* NE6 ..72 C3
  MONK NE25 .....50 B5
Eastfield Rd *HAR/WTLS* NE34 .....75 K2
  LGB/KIL NE12 .....57 J4
East Flds *CLDN/WHIT/ROK* SR6 ..93 F4
Eastfield St *MLFD/PNYW* SR4 ...119 K1
Eastfield Ter *LGB/KIL* NE12 .....57 K4
East Ford Rd *STKFD/GP* NE62 .....23 J5
East Forest Hall Rd
  LGB/KIL NE12 .....58 A2
East Front *JES* NE2 .....5 L1
Eastgarth *WD/WHPE/BLK* NE5 ...54 E5
East Ga *GATE* NE8 .....11 C1
Eastgate *STKFD/GP* NE62 .....29 F1
Eastgate Bank *PSHWF* NE43 .....79 K4
East George Potts St *SSH* NE33 ..75 H2
East Gra *MONK* NE25 .....40 C6
  SWCK/CAS SR5 .....106 C2
East Grange Ct *PLEE/EAS* * SR8 ..162 C6
East Gn *RDHAMSE* DH6 .....173 J4
Eastgreen *STKFD/GP* NE62 .....29 F1
East Gv *MLFD/PNYW* SR4 .....119 F1
East Hill Rd *GATE* NE8 .....11 M5
Eastlands *BLAY* NE21 .....83 K3
  LGB/HTN NE7 .....57 G7
East Lea *BLAY* NE21 .....84 A4
  NWBGN NE64 .....19 C6
  RDHAMSE DH6 .....172 B5
Eastlea Crs *SEA/MUR* SR7 .....150 B3
Eastlea Rd *SEA/MUR* SR7 .....150 A1
Eastleigh Cl *BOLCOL* NE35 .....90 C4
East Moffett St *SSH* NE33 .....75 H2
East Moor *MLFD/PNYW* SR4 ....105 K6
East Pde *CON/LDGT* DH8 .....123 C5
East Park Gdns *BLAY* NE21 .....84 A3
East Park Rd
  LWF/SPW/WRK NE9 .....87 F6
East Pk Vw *BLYTH* NE24 .....31 H7
East Pastures *ASHGTN* NE63 .....23 H5
East Percy St *TYNE/NSHE* NE30 ..61 G2
East Riggs *BDLGTN* NE22 .....29 F6
East Side Av
  BDN/LAN/SAC DH7 .....155 F6
East Stevenson St *SSH* NE33 ....75 H2
East Stoneycroft *LGB/KIL* NE12 ..48 A7
East St *CHPW* NE17 .....95 K4
  CLDN/WHIT/ROK SR6 .....93 F4
  CLSW/PEL DH2 .....128 A2
  GATE NE8 .....11 C1
  RDHAMSE DH6 .....172 D6
  RDHAMSE DH6 .....179 F5
  ROWG NE39 .....96 B1
  SSH NE33 .....3 G7
  STLY/ANP DH9 .....113 F7
  TYNE/NSHE NE30 .....61 J2
East Ter *RHTLP* TS27 .....185 H3
  STKFD/GP NE62 .....23 J6

  WNGT TS28 .....184 A6
East Thorp *WD/WHPE/BLK* NE5 ..54 D5
East Vw *CLDN/WHIT/ROK* SR6 ...106 E2
  CON/LDGT DH8 .....123 F5
  HEBB NE31 .....73 F7
  MPTH NE61 .....20 E5
  PLEE/EAS SR8 .....163 F3
  STLY/ANP (off Flint Hl) DH9 ...111 C5
  SWCK/CAS SR5 .....105 G4
  WICK/BNPF NE16 .....97 J7
East View Ter *WICK/BNPF* NE16 ..85 F4
East Vines *SUND* SR1 .....15 J3
Eastward Gn *MONK* NE25 .....50 B5
Eastway *BYK/HTN/WLK* NE6 .....76 B6
Eastwood *BDN/LAN/SAC* DH7 ...143 H6
Eastwood Av *BYK/HTN/WLK* NE24 ..35 F4
Eastwood Cl *CRAM* NE23 .....47 J4
Eastwood Gdns *FELL* NE10 .....12 A5
  GOS/KPK NE3 .....55 K6
  LWF/SPW/WRK NE9 .....87 G6
Eastwood Pl *CRAM* NE23 .....33 J5
Eastwoods Rd *PRUD* NE42 .....81 F1
Eaton Pl *ELS/FEN* NE4 .....4 B6
Eavers Ct *HAR/WTLS* NE34 .....75 C6
Ebba Wk *GOS/KPK* NE3 .....56 D5
Ebchester Ct *GOS/KPK* NE3 .....55 G5
Ebchester Hl *CON/LDGT* DH8 ...109 F4
Ebchester St *HAR/WTLS* NE34 ...74 E6
Ebor St *BYK/HTN/WLK* NE6 .....71 J3
  HAR/WTLS NE34 .....74 E7
Eccleston Cl *SMOOR* NE27 .....48 E5
Eccleston Rd *SSH* NE33 .....3 M9
Ecgfrid Ter *JRW* NE32 .....74 A4
Eddison Rd *WASHS* NE38 .....117 H2
Eddleston Av *GOS/KPK* NE3 .....56 A7
Eddrington Gv
  WD/WHPE/BLK NE5 .....54 A7
Ede Av *DUN/TMV* NE11 .....9 G8
  HAR/WTLS NE34 .....76 B5
Eden Av *CON/LDGT* DH8 .....123 K2
  WICK/BNPF NE16 .....97 J7
Edenbridge Crs *LGB/KIL* NE12 ...57 H3
Eden Cl *WD/WHPE/BLK* NE5 .....68 A1
Eden Cottages
  CON/LDGT
  (off Watling St) DH8 .....123 J2
  RHTLP TS27 .....185 H2
Edendale Av *BLYTH* NE24 .....30 D6
  BYK/HTN/WLK NE6 .....72 C5
Edendale Ter *GATE* NE8 .....11 C8
  PLEE/EAS SR8 .....175 C4
Edenfield *STLY/ANP* DH9 .....114 A7
Eden Gv *MPTH* NE61 .....20 E7
Edenhill Rd *PLEE/EAS* SR8 .....175 F5
Eden House Rd
  MLFD/PNYW SR4 .....14 A8
Eden La *PLEE/EAS* SR8 .....174 E2
Eden Pl *TYNE/NSHE* NE30 .....60 E1
Eden Rd *DHAM* DH1 .....156 D3
Eden St *PLEE/EAS* SR8 .....175 H3
  WLSD/HOW NE28 .....72 D2
Eden St West *SUND* SR1 .....14 C4
Eden Ter *MLFD/PNYW* SR4 .....14 A8
  MPTH NE61 .....18 C1
Eden V *MLFD/PNYW* SR4 .....14 A8
Eden Vw *RDHAMSE* DH6 .....173 J4
Edgar St *GOS/KPK* NE3 .....57 F5
Edgecote *WASHN* NE37 .....103 H5
Edge Ct *DHAM* DH1 .....17 K2
Edgefield Av *GOS/KPK* NE3 .....55 K5
Edgefield Dr *CRAM* NE23 .....33 J5
Edgehill *MPTH* NE61 .....21 F7
Edge Hl *PONT/DH* NE20 .....52 D1
Edgehill Cl *PONT/DH* NE20 .....52 E1
Edge La *BDN/LAN/SAC* DH7 ....140 E1
Edge Mt *LGB/KIL* NE12 .....47 K5
Edgeware Wk *ELS/FEN* NE4 .....8 F1
Edgewell Gra *PRUD* NE42 .....80 B2
Edgewell House Rd
  PSHWF NE43 .....80 A5
Edgewell Rd *PRUD* NE42 .....80 B2
Edgewood *PONT/DH* NE20 .....43 F7
Edgewood Av *BDLGTN* NE22 .....29 J5
Edgeworth Cl *BOLCOL* NE35 .....90 C2
Edgeworth Crs
  CLDN/WHIT/ROK SR6 .....106 E2
Edgmond Ct
  ASHBK/HED/RY SR2 .....120 E3
Edgware Rd *GATE* NE8 .....11 K7
Edhill Av *HAR/WTLS* NE34 .....74 D6
Edinburgh Ct *DIN/WO* * NE13 ...55 H2
Edinburgh Dr *BDLGTN* NE22 .....28 D4
Edinburgh Rd *JRW* NE32 .....74 C7
Edington Gv *TYNE/NSHE* NE30 ..60 E1
Edington Rd *TYNE/NSHE* NE30 ..60 E1
Edison Gdns *GATE* NE8 .....10 E9
Edison St *SEA/MUR* SR7 .....149 H5
Edith Av *BLAY* NE21 .....84 A2
Edith St *ASHBK/HED/RY* SR2 .....15 H9
  CON/LDGT DH8 .....123 F5
  JRW NE32 .....73 J4
  SEA/MUR SR7 .....151 F3
  SWCK/CAS SR5 .....106 B3
  TYNE/NSHE NE30 .....61 G2
Edith Ter *WICK/BNPF* * NE16 ....84 E5
Edlingham Cl *GOS/KPK* NE3 .....57 F6
Edlingham Ct *HLH* * DH5 .....132 D7
Edlingham Rd *DHAM* DH1 .....156 D4
Edmondsley La
  BDN/LAN/SAC DH7 .....143 G5
Edmund Pl *LWF/SPW/WRK* NE9 ..87 F7
Edna Ter *WD/WHPE/BLK* NE5 ....54 E7
Edward Av *PLEE/EAS* SR8 .....175 G3
  RDHAMSE DH6 .....180 A2
Edward Burdis St
  SWCK/CAS SR5 .....106 B3
Edward Cain Ct *PLEE/EAS* SR8 ..175 H6
Edwardia Ct *CON/LDGT* * DH8 ..122 E5
Edward Pl *ELS/FEN* NE4 .....4 E6
Edward Rd *BDLGTN* * NE22 .....29 K4
  CLS/BIR/GTL DH3 .....115 H1
  WLSD/HOW NE28 .....59 H7
Edwardson Rd
  BDN/LAN/SAC DH7 .....167 J7
Edwards Rd *WBAY* NE26 .....51 G5
Edward St *BLYTH* NE24 .....31 F6
  DHAM DH1 .....17 K2

  GOS/KPK NE3 .....56 C5
  HEBB NE31 .....72 E4
  HLH DH5 .....147 K4
  MPTH NE61 .....21 K2
  SEA/MUR SR7 .....150 D2
  STLY/ANP DH9 .....127 G5
  SUNDSW SR3 .....120 A7
Edward's Wk *CNUT* NE1 .....5 J4
Edward Ter *BDN/LAN/SAC* DH7 ..166 E2
Edwin Gv *WLSD/HOW* NE28 .....59 J7
Edwins Av *LGB/KIL* NE12 .....58 A2
Edwin's Av South *LGB/KIL* NE12 ..58 A2
Edwin St *HLH* DH5 .....132 C6
  MLFD/PNYW SR4 .....105 J6
Egerton Rd *HAR/WTLS* NE34 .....75 G5
Egerton St *ASHBK/HED/RY* SR2 ...15 G7
  BW/LEM/TK/HW NE15 .....69 G7
Eggleston Cl *CLS/BIR/GTL* DH3 ..145 J2
  DHAM DH1 .....157 F3
Eggleston Dr *CON/LDGT* DH8 ...123 F6
  SUNDSW SR3 .....120 A4
Egham Rd *WD/WHPE/BLK* NE5 ..68 A1
Eglesfield Rd *SSH* NE33 .....75 J3
Eglingham Pl *MPTH* NE61 .....21 F7
Eglingham Wy *MPTH* NE61 .....21 F7
Eglinton St *SWCK/CAS* SR5 .....106 C4
Eglinton St North
  SWCK/CAS SR5 .....106 C4
Egremont Dr
  LWF/SPW/WRK NE9 .....87 G6
Egremont Gdns
  LWF/SPW/WRK NE9 .....87 G6
Egremont Gv *PLEE/EAS* SR8 .....174 B7
Egremont Pl *WBAY* NE26 .....51 F5
Eider Cl *BLYTH* NE24 .....35 G4
Eider Gv *HAR/WTLS* NE34 .....75 K7
  LWF/SPW/WRK NE9 .....87 F7
Eighteenth Av *BLYTH* NE24 .....34 E2
Eighth Av *ASHGTN* NE63 .....24 A4
  BLYTH NE24 .....35 F1
  BYK/HTN/WLK NE6 .....7 G1
  CLSW/PEL DH2 .....129 H4
  MPTH NE61 .....21 F6
Eighth Rw *ASHGTN* NE63 .....23 H1
Eighth St *PLEE/EAS* SR8 .....175 J1
Eighton Ter
  LWF/SPW/WRK NE9 .....101 K2
Eishort Wy *LGB/KIL* NE12 .....57 H4
Eland Cl *GOS/KPK* NE3 .....55 H5
Eland Edge *PONT/DH* NE20 .....43 H5
Eland La *PONT/DH* NE20 .....43 H2
Elberfeld Ct *JRW* NE32 .....73 K5
Elder Cl *BDN/LAN/SAC* DH7 .....167 G1
Elder Gv *HAR/WTLS* NE34 .....75 K7
  LWF/SPW/WRK NE9 .....87 F7
Elderwood Gdns
  DUN/TMV NE11 .....86 B7
Eldon Cl *BDN/LAN/SAC* DH7 .....153 K3
Eldon Ct
  CNUT (off Percy St) NE1 .....5 J5
Eldon Gdns *CNUT* * NE1 .....5 K6
Eldon Pl *BW/LEM/TK/HW* NE15 ..68 B4
Eldon Rd *BW/LEM/TK/HW* NE15 ..68 B4
Eldon Sq *CNUT* NE1 .....5 K5
Eldon St *GATE* NE8 .....11 J5
  MLFD/PNYW SR4 .....106 A7
  SSH NE33 .....75 F2
  WLSD/HOW NE28 .....73 J1
Eldon Wy
  CNUT (off Eldon Sq) NE1 .....5 K5
Eleanor St *SSH* NE33 .....3 K6
  TYNE/NSHE NE30 .....51 C5
Eleanor Ter *WICK/BNPF* NE16 ...84 E5
Elemore Cl *BDN/LAN/SAC* DH7 ..166 E2
Elemore La *HLH* DH5 .....160 A1
  RDHAMSE DH6 .....159 H3
Elemore St *RDHAMSE* DH6 .....158 E4
Elemore Vw *RDHAMSE* DH6 .....160 D2
Elenbel Av *BDLGTN* NE22 .....29 J5
Eleventh Av *BLYTH* NE24 .....35 G1
  MPTH NE61 .....21 F6
Eleventh St *PLEE/EAS* SR8 .....175 G3
  RHTLP TS27 .....175 K6
Elford Cl *MONK* NE25 .....50 A4
Elfordleigh *HLS* DH4 .....132 A3
Elgar Av *WD/WHPE/BLK* NE5 ....68 A1
Elgar Cl *STLY/ANP* DH9 .....126 E2
Elgin Av *SEA/MUR* SR7 .....150 A1
  WLSD/HOW NE28 .....59 H6
Elgin Cl *NSHW* NE29 .....60 A2
Elgin Gdns *BYK/HTN/WLK* NE6 ...72 B5
Elgin Gv *STLY/ANP* DH9 .....127 F1
Elgin Rd *LWF/SPW/WRK* NE9 ....11 L8
Elgin St *JRW* NE32 .....74 C7
Elgy Rd *GOS/KPK* NE3 .....56 B7
Elisabeth Av *CLS/BIR/GTL* DH3 ..101 H7
Elizabeth Ct *LGB/KIL* NE12 .....58 C2
Elizabeth Crs *CRAM* NE23 .....47 G1
Elizabeth Diamond Gdns
  SSH NE33 .....75 F3
Elizabeth Dr *LGB/KIL* NE12 .....58 C2
Elizabeth Rd *WLSD/HOW* NE28 ..59 J7
Elizabeth St *BYK/HTN/WLK* NE6 ..6 D4
  HLH DH5 .....132 C6
  SEA/MUR * SR7 .....150 D1
  SWCK/CAS SR5 .....105 F4
  SWCK/CAS SR5 .....106 C2
Eliza La *CON/LDGT* DH8 .....168 B2
Ellam Av *DHAM* DH1 .....168 B2
Ell-Dene Crs *FELL* NE10 .....12 E9
Ellersmere Gdns
  TYNE/NSHE NE30 .....51 F2
Ellerton Wy *CRAM* NE23 .....33 J5
  FELL NE10 .....12 A8
Ellesmere *HLS* DH4 .....131 F4
Ellesmere Av *BYK/HTN/WLK* NE6 ..7 M2
  WD/WHPE/BLK NE5 .....68 C1
Ellesmere Ct
  ASHBK/HED/RY SR2 .....120 E3
Ellesmere Dr *SEA/MUR* SR7 .....150 A1
Ellesmere Rd *ELS/FEN* NE4 .....69 J6
Ellington Cl
  ASHBK/HED/RY SR2 .....135 F2
  BW/LEM/TK/HW NE15 .....67 K4
Ellington Ter *ASHGTN* NE63 .....23 F1
Elliot Cl *HLS* DH4 .....117 K7
Elliot Rd *FELL* * NE10 .....11 M5

Elliot St *RDHAMSE* DH6 .....172 C6
Elliott Dr *FELL* NE10 .....12 D7
Elliott Gdns *WLSD/HOW* NE28 ...58 C6
Elliott Rd *PLEE/EAS* SR8 .....174 E3
Elliott St *BLYTH* NE24 .....34 D5
Ellis Leazes *DHAM* DH1 .....17 G2
Ellison Main Gdns *FELL* NE10 ....13 H6
Ellison Pl *CNUT* NE1 .....5 L5
  JRW NE32 .....73 K3
  LWF/SPW/WRK NE9 .....101 F1
Ellison Rd *DUN/TMV* NE11 .....9 G8
  PLEE/EAS SR8 .....175 F3
Ellison St *GATE* NE8 .....11 C2
  HEBB NE31 .....73 F5
  JRW NE32 .....73 K4
Ellison Vls *GATE* NE8 .....11 K7
Ellis Rd *SWCK/CAS* SR5 .....106 A2
Ellis Sq *SWCK/CAS* SR5 .....106 B2
Ellwood Gdns
  LWF/SPW/WRK NE9 .....11 H8
Elm Av *BDN/LAN/SAC* DH7 .....167 G2
  CLSW/PEL DH2 .....128 C1
  DIN/WO NE13 .....45 F2
  DUN/TMV NE11 .....9 H9
  HAR/WTLS NE34 .....65 H6
  WICK/BNPF NE16 .....8 A8
Elm Bank Rd *WYLAM* NE41 .....65 H6
Elm Cl *CRAM* NE23 .....33 J5
Elm Crs *CLSW/PEL* DH2 .....144 A5
Elm Croft Rd *LGB/KIL* NE12 .....58 A3
Elmdale Rd *CON/LDGT* DH8 .....123 G4
Elm Dr *BDLGTN* NE22 .....29 G5
  CLDN/WHIT/ROK SR6 .....93 G3
Elmfield *BDN/LAN/SAC* DH7 .....140 B4
  DHAM DH1 .....157 J6
Elmfield Cl *SUNDSW* SR3 .....133 F1
Elmfield Gdns *WLSD/HOW* NE28 ..58 B4
Elmfield Gv *GOS/KPK* NE3 .....56 B7
Elmfield Pk *GOS/KPK* NE3 .....56 B7
Elmfield Rd
  BW/LEM/TK/HW NE15 .....67 G1
  CON/LDGT DH8 .....123 F3
  GOS/KPK NE3 .....56 B7
  HEBB NE31 .....89 H1
Elmfield Ter *FELL* NE10 .....12 A8
  HEBB NE31 .....73 H7
Elm Gv *BDN/LAN/SAC* DH7 .....167 G1
  GOS/KPK NE3 .....55 K3
  HAR/WTLS NE34 .....75 K7
  LGB/KIL NE12 .....133 J2
  WICK/BNPF NE16 .....97 H7
Elm Park Rd *CON/LDGT* DH8 ....109 F7
Elm Rd *BLAY* NE21 .....84 B2
  NSHW NE29 .....59 K3
  PONT/DH NE20 .....43 J4
Elmsford Gv *LGB/KIL* NE12 .....57 J4
Elmsleigh Gdns
  CLDN/WHIT/ROK SR6 .....92 E1
The Elms *ASHBK/HED/RY* SR2 .....14 B8
  CON/LDGT DH8 .....108 E7
  GOS/KPK (off Elmfield Rd) NE3 ....56 B7
  HLH DH5 .....148 C7
  RHTLP TS27 .....185 K2
Elm St *BDN/LAN/SAC* DH7 .....154 B3
  CLS/BIR/GTL DH3 .....129 J4
  CON/LDGT DH8 .....123 F3
  DUN/TMV NE11 .....86 B6
  JRW NE32 .....73 J4
  STLY/ANP DH9 .....126 B3
  WICK/BNPF NE16 .....99 F3
Elm St West *WICK/BNPF* NE16 ...99 F3
Elms West *ASHBK/HED/RY* SR2 ...14 E8
Elm Ter *CON/LDGT* DH8 .....123 K3
  STLY/ANP DH9 .....125 G3
Elmtree Ct *SEA/MUR* SR7 .....150 D3
Elmtree Gdns *MONK* NE25 .....50 C6
Elmtree Gv *GOS/KPK* NE3 .....56 B7
Elm Trees *BLYTH* NE24 .....35 F1
Elmway *CLSW/PEL* DH2 .....129 G2
Elmwood
  BW/LEM/TK/HW NE15 .....68 A3
Elmwood Av *DIN/WO* NE13 .....46 B2
  SWCK/CAS SR5 .....105 K2
Elmwood Crs
  BYK/HTN/WLK NE6 .....72 B2
Elmwood Dr *PONT/DH* NE20 .....43 G2
Elmwood Gdns *DUN/TMV* NE11 ..86 B6
Elmwood Gv *WBAY* NE26 .....50 D5
Elmwood Rd *MONK* NE25 .....50 C5
Elmwood St
  ASHBK/HED/RY SR2 .....14 B7
  HLS DH4 .....131 G6
Elrick Cl *WD/WHPE/BLK* NE5 ....68 A1
Elrington Gdns
  WD/WHPE/BLK NE5 .....69 F3
Elsdon Av *MONK* NE25 .....40 A5
Elsdonburn Rd *SUNDSW* SR3 ...133 J2
Elsdon Cl *BLYTH* NE24 .....30 E7
  PLEE/EAS SR8 .....175 H5
Elsdon Ct *WICK/BNPF* NE16 .....84 E7
Elsdon Dr *ASHGTN* NE63 .....23 J2
  LGB/KIL NE12 .....58 B2
Elsdon Gdns *CON/LDGT* DH8 ....123 F3
  DUN/TMV NE11 .....9 J8
Elsdon Ms
  HEBB (off High Lane Rw) NE31 ..73 H4
Elsdon Pl *NSHW* NE29 .....2 C4
Elsdon Rd *DHAM* DH1 .....156 D3
  GOS/KPK NE3 .....56 C5
  WICK/BNPF NE16 .....84 E6
Elsing Cl *WD/WHPE/BLK* NE5 ...55 F6
Elstob Pl *BYK/HTN/WLK* NE6 ....7 M9
  SUNDSW SR3 .....120 A1
Elston Cl *WD/WHPE/BLK* NE5 ...68 A1
Elstree Ct *DIN/WO* NE13 .....55 F3
Elstree Gdns *BLYTH* NE24 .....35 F4
Elswick East Ter *ELS/FEN* NE4 .....4 C6
Elswick Rd *ELS/FEN* NE4 .....69 J7
Elswick Rw *ELS/FEN* NE4 .....4 E7
Elswick Wy *HAR/WTLS* NE34 .....74 E5
Elterwater Rd *CLSW/PEL* DH2 ...129 H6
Elton St East *WLSD/HOW* NE28 ..72 C2
Elton St West *WLSD/HOW* NE28 ..72 C2
Eltringham Cl *WLSD/HOW* NE28 ..72 C1

Eltringham Rd *PRUD* NE42 ....80 A2
Elvaston Rd *RYTON* NE40 ....66 E5
Elvet Br *DHAM* DH1 ....16 E4
Elvet Cl *BYK/HTN/WLK* NE6 ....7 G3
DIN/WO NE13 ....46 A3
Elvet Crs *DHAM* DH1 ....16 E5
Elvet Gn *CLSW/PEL* DH2 ....129 J5
HLH DH5 ....147 K7
Elvet Hill Rd *DHAM* DH1 ....16 C8
Elvet Waterside *DHAM* DH1 ....16 E4
Elvet Wy *BYK/HTN/WLK* * NE6 ....7 G3
Elvington St
CLDN/WHIT/ROK SR6 ....106 E2
Elwin Cl *WBAY* NE26 ....41 G3
Elwin Pl *CLSW/PEL* DH2 ....128 E1
Elwin Ter *ASHBK/HED/RY* SR2 ....14 C6
Elwyn Cl *WBAY* NE26 ....41 G3
Ely Cl *LGB/KIL* NE12 ....57 K6
Ely Rd *DHAM* DH1 ....156 E1
Elysium La *GATE* NE8 ....10 B6
Ely St *GATE* NE8 ....10 F5
Embankment Rd
SEA/MUR SR7 ....135 H6
Embassy Gdns
BW/LEM/TK/HW NE15 ....69 F5
Emblehope *WASHN* NE37 ....102 C7
Emblehope Dr *GOS/KPK* NE3 ....56 A6
Embleton Av *GOS/KPK* NE3 ....56 A4
HAR/WTLS NE34 ....76 B3
WLSD/HOW NE28 ....59 G5
Embleton Cl *DHAM* DH1 ....156 E2
Embleton Crs *NSHW* NE29 ....60 A2
Embleton Dr *BLYTH* NE24 ....34 E2
CLSW/PEL DH2 ....129 F7
Embleton Gdns *FELL* NE10 ....12 C5
WD/WHPE/BLK NE5 ....69 H2
Embleton Rd *FELL* NE10 ....13 M3
NSHW NE29 ....60 A2
Embleton St *SEA/MUR* SR7 ....150 E3
Emden Rd *GOS/KPK* NE3 ....55 J4
Emerson Chambers
CNUT (off Blackett St) NE1 ....5 K6
Emily Davison Av *MPTH* NE61 ....20 C5
Emily St *BYK/HTN/WLK* NE6 ....7 L5
GATE NE8 ....11 M5
Emily St East *SEA/MUR* SR7 ....150 E1
Emlyn Rd *HAR/WTLS* NE34 ....75 G5
Emma Ct *ASHBK/HED/RY* SR2 ....15 H7
Emmbrook Cl *HLH* DH5 ....147 G4
Emmerson Pl *SMOOR* NE27 ....49 G6
Emperor Wy *SUNDSW* SR3 ....133 F2
Empress Rd *BYK/HTN/WLK* NE6 ....72 D7
Empress St *SWCK/CAS* SR5 ....106 C4
Emsworth Rd *SWCK/CAS* SR5 ....106 A2
Enderby Rd *MLFD/PNYW* SR4 ....14 A3
Enfield Av *WICK/BNPF* NE16 ....85 F3
Enfield Gdns *WICK/BNPF* NE16 ....85 F7
Enfield Rd *LWF/SPW/WRK* NE9 ....11 G8
SEA/MUR SR7 ....150 A1
Enfield St *MLFD/PNYW* SR4 ....105 K6
Engine Inn Rd *WLSD/HOW* NE28 ....59 H6
Engine La *LWF/SPW/WRK* NE9 ....101 F1
Engine Rd *CHPW* NE17 ....94 E1
PRUD NE42 ....81 F7
Englefield Cl *GOS/KPK* NE3 ....55 H3
Englemann Wy *SUNDSW* SR3 ....133 J3
Enid Av *CLDN/WHIT/ROK* SR6 ....106 D2
Enid St *DIN/WO* NE13 ....46 A5
Ennerdale *ASHBK/HED/RY* SR2 ....14 D9
CLS/BIR/GTL DH3 ....115 K4
FELL NE10 ....13 J8
Ennerdale Cl *DHAM* DH1 ....158 B5
SEA/MUR SR7 ....150 A1
Ennerdale Crs *BLAY* NE21 ....83 K4
HLS DH4 ....117 J6
Ennerdale Gdns
LWF/SPW/WRK NE9 ....87 G7
WLSD/HOW NE28 ....59 J6
Ennerdale Rd *BLYTH* NE24 ....30 B5
BYK/HTN/WLK NE6 ....72 B5
TYNE/NSHE NE30 ....50 E7
Ennerdale St *HLH* DH5 ....147 H6
Ennis Cl *STKFD/GP* NE62 ....23 K5
Enslin St *BYK/HTN/WLK* NE6 ....13 G1
Enterprise Ct
CRAM (off Crosland Pk) NE23 ....33 F6
SEA/MUR SR7 ....134 E5
Enterprise House
DUN/TMV (off Kingsway) NE11 ....100 D1
Epping Cl *SEA/MUR* SR7 ....150 A2
Eppleton Cl *BDN/LAN/SAC* DH7 ....154 A3
Eppleton Hall Cl *SEA/MUR* SR7 ....134 E7
Eppleton Rw *HLH* DH5 ....148 A4
Epsom Cl *CON/LDGT* DH8 ....108 E7
NSHW NE29 ....2 A5
Epsom Ct *GOS/KPK* NE3 ....55 G3
Epsom Dr *ASHGTN* NE63 ....23 J3
Epsom Wy *BLYTH* NE24 ....35 F4
Epwell Gv *CRAM* NE23 ....33 J5
Epworth *STLY/ANP* DH9 ....112 A6
Epworth Gv *GATE* NE8 ....10 D6
Equitable St *WLSD/HOW* NE28 ....72 D1
Erick St *CNUT* NE1 ....5 L6
Erith Ter *MLFD/PNYW* SR4 ....105 K7
Ernest Pl *DHAM* DH1 ....17 M2
Ernest St *ASHBK/HED/RY* SR2 ....15 H9
BOLCOL NE35 ....90 E4
CLSW/PEL DH2 ....114 E7
Ernest Ter *STLY/ANP* DH9 ....112 D6
Ernwill Av *SWCK/CAS* SR5 ....105 F4
Errington Cl *PONT/DH* NE20 ....42 D7
Errington Dr *STLY/ANP* DH9 ....112 A6
Errington Rd *PONT/DH* NE20 ....42 E6
Errington Ter *LGB/KIL* NE12 ....58 A1
Errol Pl *CLS/BIR/GTL* DH3 ....115 K4
Erskine Rd *SSH* NE33 ....3 J9
Erskine Wy *SSH* NE33 ....3 K8
Escallond Dr *SEA/MUR* SR7 ....150 A2
Esdale *ASHBK/HED/RY* SR2 ....134 E1
Esh Bank *BDN/LAN/SAC* DH7 ....153 H4
Esher Ct *GOS/KPK* NE3 ....55 G3
Esher Gdns *BLYTH* NE24 ....35 F4
Esh Hillside *BDN/LAN/SAC* DH7 ....154 C3
Eshmere Crs
WD/WHPE/BLK NE5 ....68 A1
Eshott Cl *GOS/KPK* NE3 ....56 A4
WD/WHPE/BLK NE5 ....68 E2
Eskdale *CLS/BIR/GTL* DH3 ....116 A5
HLS DH4 ....117 J6
Eskdale Av *BLYTH* NE24 ....30 C6
WLSD/HOW NE28 ....58 E6
Eskdale Cl *SEA/MUR* SR7 ....150 A1
Eskdale Ct *HAR/WTLS* NE34 ....75 G5
Eskdale Dr *JRW* NE32 ....90 B1
Eskdale Gdns
LWF/SPW/WRK NE9 ....101 G1
Eskdale Rd
CLDN/WHIT/ROK SR6 ....93 F6
Eskdale St *HAR/WTLS* * NE34 ....75 G6
HLH DH5 ....147 J6
Eskdale Ter *JES* NE2 ....5 L1
WBAY NE26 ....51 G5
Eskdale Wk *PLEE/EAS* SR8 ....175 F4
Esk St *LWF/SPW/WRK* NE9 ....11 M9
Eslington Ct *GATE* NE8 ....9 M7
Eslington Rd *JES* NE2 ....5 M2
Eslington Ter *JES* NE2 ....70 E3
Esmaralda Gdns *CRAM* NE23 ....39 G7
Esplanade *WBAY* NE26 ....51 F4
Esplanade Ms
ASHBK/HED/RY SR2 ....14 E7
The Esplanade
ASHBK/HED/RY SR2 ....14 E8
Esplanade West
ASHBK/HED/RY SR2 ....14 E8
Espley Cl *LGB/KIL* NE12 ....58 C2
Espley Ct *GOS/KPK* NE3 ....55 J3
Essen Wy *SUNDSW* SR3 ....120 B3
Essex Av *CON/LDGT* DH8 ....137 F2
Essex Cl *ASHGTN* NE63 ....23 G1
ELS/FEN NE4 ....9 L1
Essex Crs *SEA/MUR* SR7 ....150 A1
Essex Dr *WASHN* NE37 ....103 F4
Essex Gdns *HAR/WTLS* NE34 ....76 C4
LWF/SPW/WRK NE9 ....11 H9
WLSD/HOW NE28 ....59 G7
Essex Gv *SUNDSW* SR3 ....120 A6
Essex Pl *PLEE/EAS* SR8 ....174 D2
Essington Wy *PLEE/EAS* SR8 ....174 D1
Est Vw *HLH* DH5 ....148 C7
Esther Campbell Ct
JES (off Richardson Rd) NE2 ....5 G2
Esther Sq *WASHS* NE38 ....117 G2
Esthwaite Av *CLSW/PEL* DH2 ....129 H6
Eston Ct *BLYTH* NE24 ....30 D6
WLSD/HOW NE28 ....58 B5
Eston Gv *SWCK/CAS* SR5 ....106 C2
Estuary Wy *MLFD/PNYW* SR4 ....105 F6
Etal Av *MONK* NE25 ....51 F5
NSHW NE29 ....60 B6
Etal Ct *NSHW* NE29 ....2 C1
Etal Crs *JRW* NE32 ....74 B7
SMOOR NE27 ....49 H6
Etal La *WD/WHPE/BLK* NE5 ....54 E7
Etal Pl *GOS/KPK* NE3 ....56 A3
Etal Rd *BLYTH* NE24 ....34 D4
Etal Wy *WD/WHPE/BLK* NE5 ....55 F6
Ethel Av *ASHBK/HED/RY* SR2 ....135 G1
BLAY NE21 ....84 A2
Ethel St *CRAM* NE23 ....47 G3
ELS/FEN NE4 ....69 H7
Ethel Ter *HAR/WTLS* NE34 ....75 F6
SWCK/CAS SR5 ....105 F4
Etherley Cl *DHAM* DH1 ....156 E2
Etherley Rd *BYK/HTN/WLK* NE6 ....7 J2
Etherstone Av *LGB/HTN* NE7 ....71 J1
Eton Cl *CRAM* NE23 ....33 J5
Eton Sq *HEBB* NE31 ....73 H5
Ettrick Cl *LGB/KIL* NE12 ....47 J5
Ettrick Gdns *GATE* NE8 ....11 M7
MLFD/PNYW SR4 ....119 J2
Ettrick Gv *MLFD/PNYW* SR4 ....119 K2
SUNDSW SR3 ....119 K3
Ettrick Rd *JRW* NE32 ....73 J6
European Wy
MLFD/PNYW SR4 ....105 H5
Euryalus Ct *SSH* NE33 ....75 K2
Eustace Av *NSHW* NE29 ....2 A2
Evanlade *FELL* NE10 ....88 D6
Evansleigh Rd *CON/LDGT* DH8 ....122 C7
Eva St *BW/LEM/TK/HW* NE15 ....68 A5
Evelyn St *ASHBK/HED/RY* SR2 ....14 A8
Evelyn Ter *STLY/ANP* DH9 ....126 C1
Evenwood Gdns
LWF/SPW/WRK NE9 ....87 H7
Evenwood Rd
BDN/LAN/SAC DH7 ....165 H2
Everard St *CRAM* NE23 ....33 H4
Everest Gv *BOL* NE36 ....91 F5
Eversleigh Pl
BW/LEM/TK/HW NE15 ....67 G1
Eversley Pl *BYK/HTN/WLK* NE6 ....6 E2
WLSD/HOW NE28 ....59 H7
Everton Dr *SEA/MUR* SR7 ....150 A1
Everton La *SWCK/CAS* SR5 ....106 A2
Evesham *MLFD/PNYW* SR4 ....104 E7
Evesham Av *WBAY* NE26 ....50 D3
Evesham Cl *BOLCOL* NE35 ....90 D3
Evesham Garth *GOS/KPK* NE3 ....55 J7
Evesham Rd *SEA/MUR* SR7 ....150 A1
Eve St *PLEE/EAS* SR8 ....175 J4
Evistones Gdns
BYK/HTN/WLK NE6 ....12 E1
Evistones Rd
LWF/SPW/WRK NE9 ....87 F6
Ewart Crs *HAR/WTLS* NE34 ....74 C7
Ewbank Av *ELS/FEN* NE4 ....69 J4
Ewehurst Crs *STLY/ANP* DH9 ....111 G5
Ewehurst Pde *STLY/ANP* DH9 ....111 G5
Ewehurst Rd *STLY/ANP* DH9 ....111 G5
WICK/BNPF NE16 ....111 H4
Ewen Ct *NSHW* NE29 ....59 K2
Ewesley *WASHS* NE38 ....116 C6
Ewesley Cl *WD/WHPE/BLK* NE5 ....68 E1
Ewesley Gdns *DIN/WO* NE13 ....46 B3
Ewesley Rd *MLFD/PNYW* SR4 ....119 K1
Ewing Rd *MLFD/PNYW* SR4 ....14 A8
Exebly Cl *GOS/KPK* NE3 ....56 C2
Exeter Av *SEA/MUR* SR7 ....150 C1
Exeter Cl *ASHGTN* NE63 ....24 C3
CLS/BIR/GTL DH3 ....145 H2
Exeter Rd *WLSD/HOW* NE28 ....58 C5
Exeter St *BYK/HTN/WLK* NE6 ....72 C7
GATE NE8 ....10 F6
MLFD/PNYW SR4 ....105 K6
Exmouth Cl *SEA/MUR* * SR7 ....150 B2
Exmouth Rd *NSHW* NE29 ....60 A5
Exmouth Sq *SWCK/CAS* SR5 ....106 A2
Extension Rd *SUND* SR1 ....15 K5
Eyemouth La *SWCK/CAS* SR5 ....106 A2
Eyemouth Rd *NSHW* NE29 ....60 A5
Eyre St *STLY/ANP* DH9 ....126 B2

F

Faber Rd *SWCK/CAS* SR5 ....106 A2
Factory Rd *BLAY* NE21 ....68 B7
Fairbairn Rd *PLEE/EAS* SR8 ....174 E2
Fairburn Av *HLH* DH5 ....147 H2
LGB/HTN NE7 ....57 J6
Fairclough Clough
PLEE/EAS SR8 ....174 C5
Fairdale Av *LGB/HTN* NE7 ....57 J6
Fairfalls Ter *BDN/LAN/SAC* DH7 ....166 D2
Fairfield *CLSW/PEL* DH2 ....114 D7
CON/LDGT DH8 ....123 H6
LGB/KIL NE12 ....57 F4
STLY/ANP DH9 ....125 H2
Fairfield Av *BLYTH* NE24 ....35 F3
WICK/BNPF NE16 ....84 E7
Fairfield Cl *DUN/TMV* NE11 ....9 G6
Fairfield Dr *ASHGTN* NE63 ....24 C3
CLDN/WHIT/ROK SR6 ....92 E2
MONK NE25 ....50 A5
TYNE/NSHE NE30 ....51 F7
Fairfield Gn *MONK* NE25 ....50 A5
Fairfield Rd *JES* NE2 ....70 D2
Fairfields *RYTON* NE40 ....66 D7
Fairfield Ter *FELL* NE10 ....13 J6
Fair Gn *MONK* NE25 ....50 A5
Fairgreen Cl *SUNDSW* SR3 ....134 A2
Fairhaven *LWF/SPW/WRK* NE9 ....102 B3
Fairhaven Av
BYK/HTN/WLK NE6 ....72 C5
Fairhill Cl *LGB/HTN* NE7 ....57 J6
Fairholme Av *HAR/WTLS* NE34 ....75 K5
Fairholme Rd *SUNDSW* SR3 ....120 C3
Fairholm Rd *ELS/FEN* NE4 ....69 J6
Fairlands East
CLDN/WHIT/ROK SR6 ....106 D3
Fairlands West *SWCK/CAS* SR5 ....106 D3
Fairlawn Gdns
MLFD/PNYW SR4 ....119 J2
Fairlawns Cl *TRIM* TS29 ....182 E5
Fairles St *SSH* NE33 ....3 J5
Fairmead Wy *MLFD/PNYW* SR4 ....118 E1
Fairmile Dr *SUNDSW* SR3 ....134 A2
Fairmont Wy *LGB/HTN* NE7 ....57 J6
Fairney Cl *PONT/DH* NE20 ....43 H3
Fairney Edge *PONT/DH* NE20 ....43 H3
Fairport Ter *PLEE/EAS* SR8 ....163 G6
Fairspring *WD/WHPE/BLK* NE5 ....68 E1
Fair Vw *BDN/LAN/SAC* DH7 ....143 F7
BDN/LAN/SAC DH7 ....165 H1
Fairview Av *HAR/WTLS* NE34 ....75 K4
Fairview Dr *CON/LDGT* DH8 ....109 G6
Fairview Gn *LGB/HTN* NE7 ....57 J6
Fairview Ter *STLY/ANP* DH9 ....125 G4
Fairville Cl *CRAM* NE23 ....33 H5
Fairville Crs *LGB/HTN* NE7 ....57 J6
Fairway *MPTH* NE61 ....26 D1
STKFD/GP NE62 ....23 G5
Fairway Cl *GOS/KPK* NE3 ....56 B2
Fairways *CON/LDGT* DH8 ....123 F2
MONK NE25 ....50 A4
SUNDSW SR3 ....120 B7
Fairways Av *LGB/HTN* NE7 ....57 J5
The Fairways *BOL* * NE36 ....90 E5
STLY/ANP DH9 ....126 B5
The Fairway *BLAY* NE21 ....67 J7
GOS/KPK NE3 ....56 B2
WASHN NE37 ....103 F2
Falconar's Ct *CNUT* NE1 ....5 J7
Falconar St *JES* NE2 ....5 M5
Falcon Ct *ASHGTN* NE63 ....23 H4
Falcon Hl *MPTH* NE61 ....20 B6
Falcon Pl *LGB/KIL* NE12 ....57 G3
Falcon Ter *WYLAM* NE41 ....65 H5
Falcon Wy *BDN/LAN/SAC* DH7 ....165 F1
HAR/WTLS NE34 ....75 F7
Faldonside *BYK/HTN/WLK* NE6 ....71 K1
Falkirk *LGB/KIL* NE12 ....47 K5
Falkland Av *GOS/KPK* NE3 ....55 K7
HEBB NE31 ....73 G5
Falkland Rd *MLFD/PNYW* SR4 ....105 J7
Falla Park Crs *FELL* NE10 ....12 B8
Falla Park Rd *FELL* NE10 ....12 B8
Falloden Av *GOS/KPK* NE3 ....55 K2
Fallodon Gdns
WD/WHPE/BLK NE5 ....69 H1
Fallodon Rd *NSHW* NE29 ....60 B5
Fallowfeld *FELL* NE10 ....88 C5
Fallowfield *WASHS* NE38 ....117 G5
Fallowfield Av *GOS/KPK* NE3 ....55 K4
Fallowfield Wy *ASHGTN* NE63 ....23 H3
WASHS NE38 ....117 F4
Fallow Park Av *BLYTH* NE24 ....34 E1
Fallow Rd *HAR/WTLS* NE34 ....76 D5
Fallsway *DHAM* DH1 ....158 A4
Falmouth Cl *SEA/MUR* SR7 ....150 B2
Falmouth Dr *JRW* NE32 ....74 B6
Falmouth Rd *BYK/HTN/WLK* NE6 ....6 E3
MLFD/PNYW SR4 ....105 J6
NSHW NE29 ....60 A5
NSHW NE29 ....60 B1
Falmouth Sq *MLFD/PNYW* SR4 ....105 J7
Falsgrave Pl *WICK/BNPF* NE16 ....84 E6
Falstaff Rd *NSHW* NE29 ....60 B4
Falstone *FELL* NE10 ....88 B7
WASHS NE38 ....117 G4
Falstone Av
BW/LEM/TK/HW NE15 ....68 C3
HAR/WTLS NE34 ....76 A5
Falstone Cl *LGB/KIL* NE12 ....58 C2
Falstone Crs *ASHGTN* NE63 ....24 A4
Falstone Dr *CLSW/PEL* DH2 ....129 F6
Falstone Sq *GOS/KPK* NE3 ....56 A4
Falston Rd *BLYTH* NE24 ....34 E2
Faraday Cl *WASHS* NE38 ....117 K1
Faraday Gv *GATE* NE8 ....10 D9
MLFD/PNYW SR4 ....105 J7
Faraday Rd *PLEE/EAS* SR8 ....175 F1
Faraday St *SEA/MUR* SR7 ....149 H5
Faraday Ter *RDHAMSE* DH6 ....160 D6
Farbridge Crs *CON/LDGT* DH8 ....109 F3
Fareham Gv *BOLCOL* NE35 ....90 B4
Farlam Av *TYNE/NSHE* NE30 ....60 E1
Farlam Rd *WD/WHPE/BLK* NE5 ....69 F3
Farleigh Ct *NSHW* NE29 ....59 K2
Farm Cl *WASHN* NE37 ....102 D4
WICK/BNPF NE16 ....99 F3
Farm Ct *BLAY* NE21 ....84 D2
SPEN DL16 ....178 A7
Farmer Crs *SEA/MUR* SR7 ....149 G5
Farm Hill Rd
CLDN/WHIT/ROK SR6 ....92 A2
Farm Rd *DHAM* DH1 ....168 E5
Farm St *SWCK/CAS* SR5 ....106 B4
Farnborough Cl *CRAM* NE23 ....33 H7
Farnborough Dr *SUNDSW* SR3 ....120 B6
Farn Ct *DIN/WO* NE13 ....55 H2
Farndale *WLSD/HOW* NE28 ....58 B5
Farndale Av
CLDN/WHIT/ROK SR6 ....93 F6
STKFD/GP NE62 ....23 G4
Farndale Cl *BLAY* NE21 ....83 H4
DIN/WO NE13 ....45 F2
Farndale Rd *ELS/FEN* NE4 ....69 J6
Farne Av *ASHGTN* NE63 ....23 K3
GOS/KPK NE3 ....56 A2
HAR/WTLS NE34 ....76 B4
Farne Rd *LGB/KIL* NE12 ....58 A2
SMOOR NE27 ....49 H6
Farne Sq *MLFD/PNYW* SR4 ....105 H6
Farne Ter *BYK/HTN/WLK* NE6 ....7 M5
Farnham Cl *DHAM* DH1 ....156 D4
Farnham Gv *BLYTH* NE24 ....35 F3
Farnham Ldg
LGB/KIL (off Bardsey Pl) NE12 ....57 H3
Farnham Rd *DHAM* DH1 ....156 D3
HAR/WTLS NE34 ....75 G5
Farnham St
BW/LEM/TK/HW NE15 ....68 B5
Farnham Ter *MLFD/PNYW* SR4 ....119 K1
Farnley Hey Rd *DHAM* DH1 ....168 B1
Farnley Mt *DHAM* DH1 ....168 B1
Farnley Rdg *DHAM* DH1 ....168 B1
Farnley Rd *BYK/HTN/WLK* NE6 ....71 J2
Farnon Rd *GOS/KPK* NE3 ....56 A5
Farquhar St *JES* NE2 ....71 F3
Farrier Cl *WASHS* NE38 ....117 G4
Farriers Ct *STKFD/GP* NE62 ....29 H1
Farringdon Rd
TYNE/NSHE NE30 ....50 E7
Farringdon Rw
MLFD/PNYW SR4 ....14 B2
Farrington Av *SUNDSW* SR3 ....119 G6
Farrow Dr *CLDN/WHIT/ROK* SR6 ....92 E3
The Farthings *WASHN* NE37 ....102 D3
Fatfield Pk *WASHS* NE38 ....117 F5
Fatfield Rd *WASHS* NE38 ....117 G2
Faversham Ct *GOS/KPK* NE3 ....55 H3
Faversham Pl *CRAM* NE23 ....33 H7
Fawcett St *SUND* SR1 ....14 E4
Fawcett Ter
ASHBK/HED/RY SR2 ....135 G1
Fawcett Wy *SSH* NE33 ....3 G6
Fawdon Cl *GOS/KPK* NE3 ....55 J2
Fawdon Gv *MPTH* NE61 ....21 H2
Fawdon La *GOS/KPK* NE3 ....55 H3
Fawdon Park Rd *GOS/KPK* NE3 ....55 J3
Fawdon Pl *NSHW* NE29 ....60 A4
Fawley Cl *BOLCOL* NE35 ....90 C3
Fawn Rd *MLFD/PNYW* SR4 ....105 G7
Feather Bed La
ASHBK/HED/RY SR2 ....135 G1
Featherstone Gv *BDLGTN* NE22 ....28 D4
JRW NE32 ....89 J1
Featherstone Rd *DHAM* DH1 ....156 E4
Featherstone St
CLDN/WHIT/ROK SR6 ....107 F3
Federation Sq *SEA/MUR* SR7 ....149 H6
Federation Wy *DUN/TMV* NE11 ....8 E6
Fee Ter *ASHBK/HED/RY* SR2 ....134 E1
Feetham Av *LGB/KIL* NE12 ....58 B2
Felixstowe Dr *LGB/HTN* NE7 ....57 J7
Fell Bank *CLS/BIR/GTL* DH3 ....115 K2
Fell Cl *CLS/BIR/GTL* DH3 ....116 A3
WICK/BNPF NE16 ....99 F3
Felldyke *FELL* NE10 ....88 B7
Fellgate Av *JRW* NE32 ....90 A3
Fellgate Gdns *FELL* NE10 ....88 E4
Felling Dene Gdns *FELL* NE10 ....12 E6
Felling Ga *FELL* NE10 ....12 B6
Felling House Gdns *FELL* NE10 ....12 C5
Felling Vw *BYK/HTN/WLK* NE6 ....13 G2
Fellmere Av *FELL* NE10 ....13 H7
Fell Rd *CLSW/PEL* DH2 ....128 E4
LWF/SPW/WRK NE9 ....102 B4
MLFD/PNYW SR4 ....105 H6
Fellside *HAR/WTLS* NE34 ....76 B6
PONT/DH NE20 ....52 D1
Fellside Av *WICK/BNPF* NE16 ....99 F2
Fellside Cl *PONT/DH* NE20 ....52 D1
Fellside Ct *WICK/BNPF* NE16 ....84 E5
Fellside Gdns *DHAM* DH1 ....157 K5
Fellside Rd *WICK/BNPF* NE16 ....84 D7
The Fell Side *GOS/KPK* NE3 ....55 K6
Fells Rd *DUN/TMV* NE11 ....86 D5
Fell Vw *CON/LDGT* DH8 ....122 C6
ROWG NE39 ....96 C2
The Fell Wy *WD/WHPE/BLK* NE5 ....68 B2
Felsham Sq *MLFD/PNYW* SR4 ....105 J7
Felstead Crs *MLFD/PNYW* SR4 ....105 H6
Felstead Pl *BLYTH* NE24 ....35 F3
Felstead Sq *MLFD/PNYW* SR4 ....105 H7
Felton Av *GOS/KPK* NE3 ....56 A4
HAR/WTLS NE34 ....76 A5
MONK NE25 ....51 F5
Felton Cl *MPTH* NE61 ....21 F7
SMOOR NE27 ....49 H6
Felton Crs *GATE* NE8 ....86 E5
Felton Dr *LGB/KIL* NE12 ....58 B1
Felton Gn *BYK/HTN/WLK* NE6 ....7 H5
Felton Wk *BYK/HTN/WLK* NE6 ....7 H5
Fencer Ct *GOS/KPK* NE3 ....56 C2
Fence Rd *CLS/BIR/GTL* DH3 ....131 G1
Fenhall Pk *BDN/LAN/SAC* DH7 ....140 B4
Fenham Cha *ELS/FEN* NE4 ....69 H3
Fenham Hall Dr *ELS/FEN* NE4 ....69 H3
Fenham Rd *ELS/FEN* NE4 ....4 B4
MPTH NE61 ....18 B2
Fenkle St *CNUT* NE1 ....5 H7
Fennel Gv *HAR/WTLS* NE34 ....91 J1
PLEE/EAS SR8 ....162 C5
Fenside Rd
ASHBK/HED/RY SR2 ....121 F6
Fenton Cl *CLSW/PEL* DH2 ....129 G6
Fenton Sq *MLFD/PNYW* SR4 ....105 H7
Fenton Ter *HLS* DH4 ....132 B1
Fenton Well La
CLS/BIR/GTL DH3 ....145 F1
Fenwick Av *BLYTH* NE24 ....35 F2
HAR/WTLS NE34 ....74 E6
Fenwick Cl *CLSW/PEL* DH2 ....129 F6
HLS DH4 ....117 K6
JES NE2 ....71 F2
Fenwick Gv *MPTH* NE61 ....20 E4
Fenwick Rw *SEA/MUR* SR7 ....151 F2
Fenwick St *HLS* DH4 ....117 K6
Fenwick Ter
NSHW (off Preston Rd) NE29 ....2 D1
Ferens Cl *DHAM* DH1 ....16 F1
Ferens Pk *DHAM* DH1 ....16 F1
Ferguson Crs *DIN/WO* NE13 ....46 A5
Ferguson's La
BW/LEM/TK/HW NE15 ....68 E5
Ferguson St
ASHBK/HED/RY SR2 ....15 K6
Fern Av *CLDN/WHIT/ROK* SR6 ....93 F2
CRAM NE23 ....33 H5
GOS/KPK NE3 ....56 A3
JES NE2 ....70 E2
NSHW NE29 ....2 A1
SWCK/CAS SR5 ....106 A3
Fern Ct *STKFD/GP* * NE62 ....22 E6
Fern Crs *SEA/MUR* SR7 ....150 D4
Ferndale *DHAM* DH1 ....158 A6
Ferndale Av *BOL* NE36 ....91 H5
GOS/KPK NE3 ....56 D1
WLSD/HOW NE28 ....72 E1
Ferndale Cl *BLYTH* NE24 ....30 C7
WNGT TS28 ....184 A6
Ferndale Gv *BOL* NE36 ....91 H5
Ferndale La *BOL* NE36 ....91 H5
Ferndale Rd *HLS* DH4 ....117 J6
Ferndale Ter *MLFD/PNYW* SR4 ....105 J5
Fern Dene
WLSD/HOW
(off Simonside Av) NE28 ....59 G6
Ferndene Crs *MLFD/PNYW* SR4 ....105 K7
Ferndene Gv *LGB/HTN* NE7 ....57 H7
Fern Dene Rd *GATE* NE8 ....10 E8
Ferndown Ct *FELL* NE10 ....13 M9
RYTON NE40 ....67 F7
Fern Dr *CLDN/WHIT/ROK* SR6 ....91 K3
CRAM NE23 ....47 G1
Fernhill Av *WICK/BNPF* NE16 ....84 E5
Fernlea Cl *WASHS* NE38 ....117 G4
Fernlea Gdns *RYTON* NE40 ....66 C7
Fernley Vls *CRAM* NE23 ....38 E2
Fern Rd *BDN/LAN/SAC* DH7 ....143 J5
Fern St *CON/LDGT* DH8 ....123 F4
MLFD/PNYW SR4 ....14 B3
Fernsway *SUNDSW* SR3 ....120 B3
Fernville Av *WICK/BNPF* NE16 ....99 F3
Fernville Rd *GOS/KPK* NE3 ....56 B7
Fernville St *MLFD/PNYW* SR4 ....14 A7
Fernway *MPTH* NE61 ....21 F5
Fernwood Av *GOS/KPK* NE3 ....56 D4
Fernwood Cl *SUNDSW* * SR3 ....134 A2
Fernwood Rd
BW/LEM/TK/HW NE15 ....68 B5
JES NE2 ....5 M1
Ferrand Dr *HLS* DH4 ....132 B7
Ferriby Cl *GOS/KPK* NE3 ....56 D2
Ferrisdale Wy *GOS/KPK* NE3 ....55 K3
Ferryboat La *SWCK/CAS* SR5 ....104 D4
Ferrydene Av *GOS/KPK* NE3 ....55 K6
Ferry Ms *NSHW* NE29 ....2 E4
Ferry St *JRW* NE32 ....73 K3
SSH NE33 ....2 F7
Festival Park Dr *DUN/TMV* NE11 ....9 M9
Festival Wy *DUN/TMV* NE11 ....9 J6
Fetcham Ct *GOS/KPK* NE3 ....55 G3
Field Cl *JES* NE2 ....6 B5
Field Fare Ct *WICK/BNPF* NE16 ....112 A1
Fieldhouse Cl *MPTH* NE61 ....27 J1
Fieldhouse La *DHAM* DH1 ....156 B6
MPTH NE61 ....27 J1
Field House Rd *GATE* NE8 ....10 E9
Fielding Ct *WD/WHPE/BLK* NE5 ....54 E6
Fielding Pl *LWF/SPW/WRK* NE9 ....11 M8
Field La *FELL* NE10 ....13 H8
Fieldside *CLDN/WHIT/ROK* SR6 ....92 E3
CLSW/PEL DH2 ....114 E7
HLH DH5 ....147 F5
Field Sq *MLFD/PNYW* SR4 ....105 G7
Field St *FELL* NE10 ....12 C6
GOS/KPK NE3 ....56 E5
Field Ter *JRW* NE32 ....73 K6
Fieldway *BOLCOL* NE35 ....90 A4
JRW NE32 ....90 B3
Fife Av *JRW* NE32 ....90 C1
Fife St *GATE* NE8 ....11 J6
SEA/MUR SR7 ....149 J6
Fifteenth Av *BLYTH* NE24 ....35 F1
Fifth Av *ASHGTN* NE63 ....23 K3
BYK/HTN/WLK NE6 ....7 G2
DUN/TMV NE11 ....86 D7
MPTH NE61 ....21 F6
Fifth St *PLEE/EAS* SR8 ....175 H3
Filby Dr *DHAM* DH1 ....158 A4
Filey Cl *CRAM* NE23 ....33 H7
Filton Cl *CRAM* NE23 ....33 H7
Finchale *WASHS* NE38 ....116 E3
Finchale Av *DHAM* DH1 ....157 G1
Finchale Cl *ASHBK/HED/RY* SR2 ....15 H7
DUN/TMV NE11 ....85 K6
HLS DH4 ....132 B7
Finchale Gdns
BW/LEM/TK/HW NE15 ....53 F7
Finchale Rd *DHAM* DH1 ....156 E1
HEBB NE31 ....89 G1
Finchale Ter *BYK/HTN/WLK* NE6 ....7 G7
JRW NE32 ....74 B7
Finchale Vw *DHAM* DH1 ....156 C2
HLS DH4 ....146 B6

Finchdale Cl NSHW NE29 ......2 B4
Finchley Crs BYK/HTN/WLK NE6 ...72 C3
Findon BDN/LAN/SAC DH7 ...143 G7
Findon Gv NSHW NE29 ....60 C6
Findon Hl BDN/LAN/SAC DH7 ...143 H6
Fine La CON/LDGT DH8 ....108 B3
Fines Pk STLY/ANP DH9 ....125 H3
Fines Rd CON/LDGT DH8 ....109 H6
Finney Ter DHAM DH1 ....16 E2
Finsbury Av BYK/HTN/WLK NE6 ...7 M5
Finsbury St SWCK/CAS SR5 .....106 C1
Finsmere Av
  WD/WHPE/BLK NE5 ....69 F2
Finsmere Pl WD/WHPE/BLK NE5 ...69 F2
Finstock Cl LGB/HTN NE7 ....57 F6
Fir Av BDN/LAN/SAC DH7 ....167 G7
  DHAM DH1 ....17 L4
Firbank Av TYNE/NSHE NE30 .....51 F7
Firbanks JRW NE32 ....90 B3
Firfield Rd WD/WHPE/BLK NE5 ...69 F1
Fir Gv HAR/WTLS NE34 ....75 K6
Fir Pk BDN/LAN/SAC DH7 ....155 C7
First Av ASHGTN NE63 ....23 K1
  BLYTH NE24 ....35 F1
  BYK/HTN/WLK NE6 ....7 G2
  CLSW/PEL DH2 ....115 H6
  DUN/TMV NE11 ....86 C6
  MPTH NE61 ....21 F6
  NSHW NE29 ....59 K6
The Firs GOS/KPK NE3 ....56 B6
Fir St JRW NE32 ....73 J4
First St CON/LDGT DH8 ....123 J2
  GATE NE8 ....10 C6
  PLEE/EAS SR8 ....175 H3
Fir Terraces BDN/LAN/SAC DH7 ...165 G1
Firth Sq MLFD/PNYW SR4 ....105 H7
Firtree Av BYK/HTN/WLK NE6 ...72 C2
  LGB/KIL NE12 ....57 K1
  WASHS NE38 ....116 E5
Fir Tree Cl DHAM * DH1 ....157 H5
Firtree Crs LGB/KIL NE12 ....57 J1
Firtree Gdns MONK NE25 ....50 D6
Firtree Rd WICK/BNPF NE16 .....84 E6
Firtrees CLSW/PEL DH2 ....129 H2
  FELL NE10 ....88 A7
Firtrees Wy WLSD/HOW NE28 ...59 K7
Firwood Gdns DUN/TMV NE11 ...86 B7
Fisher La CRAM NE23 ....32 C7
  DIN/WO NE13 ....37 C5
Fisher Rd SMOOR NE27 ....48 D3
Fisher St BYK/HTN/WLK NE6 .....72 D4
  WLSD/HOW NE28 ....72 D4
Fisherwell Rd FELL NE10 ....13 K4
Fish Market CNUT NE1 ....5 J6
Fish Quay TYNE/NSHE NE30 .....3 H2
Fitzpatrick Pl SSH NE33 ....3 L9

Fordfield Rd MLFD/PNYW SR4 ...105 G7
Ford Gv GOS/KPK NE3 ....56 B5
Fordhall Dr MLFD/PNYW SR4...105 J7
Fordham Rd DHAM DH1 ....156 D4
  MLFD/PNYW SR4 ....105 J7
Fordham Sq MLFD/PNYW SR4 ...105 J7
Fordland Pl MLFD/PNYW SR4 ...105 K7
Ford Ov MLFD/PNYW SR4 ....105 F6
Ford Rd BDN/LAN/SAC DH7 ....140 C5
  DHAM DH1 ....156 E2
Ford St BDN/LAN/SAC DH7 .....140 C5
  BYK/HTN/WLK NE6 ....6 D6
  GATE NE8 ....11 M5
Ford Ter STKFD/GP NE62 ....23 F6
  WLSD/HOW NE28 ....73 G1
The Ford PRUD NE42 ....80 C1
Ford Vw CRAM NE23 ....38 B7
Forest Dr WASHS NE38 ....116 B6
Forest Ga WNGT TS28 ....183 J3
Forest Hall Rd LGB/KIL NE12 .....58 A1
Fore St JES NE2 ....6 D1
Forest Rd
  BW/LEM/TK/HW NE15 ....69 F7
  MLFD/PNYW SR4 ....105 H6
  SSH NE33 ....3 H8
Forest Vw BDN/LAN/SAC DH7 ...166 E7
Forest Wy CRAM NE23 ....39 G7
Forfar St SWCK/CAS SR5 ....106 D3
Forge Cl CHPW NE17 ....95 H7
Forge La CHPW NE17 ....110 A1
  CLS/BIR/GTL DH3 ....130 D4
Forge Rd DUN/TMV NE11 ....9 K8
Forrest Ct STLY/ANP DH9 ....127 F1
Forres Pl CRAM NE23 ....33 H7
Forrest Rd WLSD/HOW NE28 ...72 C2
Forster Av BDLGTN NE22 ....28 E5
  HAR/WTLS NE34 ....75 J4
  RDHAMSE DH6 ....158 D7
Forster Ct
  LWF/SPW/WRK
  (off Durham Rd) NE9 ....101 F1
Forster St BLAY NE21 ....31 H7
  CLDN/WHIT/ROK SR6 ....106 E4
Forsyth Rd JES NE2 ....70 D2
Forth Banks CNUT NE1 ....5 J9
Forth Ct PLEE/EAS SR8 ....174 E5
Forth Ct HAR/WTLS NE34 ....75 C6
Forth Pl CNUT NE1 ....5 H8
Forth St CHPW NE17 ....95 J4
  CNUT NE1 ....5 H9
Fortrose Av SUNDSW SR3.......120 A3
Fort Sq SSH NE33 ....3 H4
Fort St SSH NE33 ....3 J4
Forum Ct BDLGTN NE22 ....29 F5
The Forum
  BW/LEM/TK/HW NE15 ....68 D4
Forum Wy CRAM NE23 ....38 B2
Fossdyke FELL NE10 ....88 B7
Fossefeld FELL NE10 ....88 C5
Fosse Law
  BW/LEM/TK/HW NE15 ....67 G2
Fosse Ter LWF/SPW/WRK NE9 ...87 H6
Fossway BYK/HTN/WLK NE6 .....7 K3
Foss Wy CON/LDGT DH8 ....108 E3
Foster St BYK/HTN/WLK NE6 ...72 D6
Foundry Ct BYK/HTN/WLK NE6 ...7 H9
Foundry La BYK/HTN/WLK NE6 ...6 D5
Foundry Rd SEA/MUR SR7 .....151 F1
Fountain Cl BDLGTN NE22 ....29 F5
Fountain Gv HAR/WTLS NE34 ...75 K3
Fountain Head Bank
  WBAY NE26 ....40 E2
Fountain La BLAY NE21 ....67 K7
Fountain Rw JES NE2 ....4 E2
Fountains Cl DUN/TMV NE11 .....85 K6
  WASHS NE38 ....117 F2
Fountains Crs HEBB NE31 ....89 C1
  HLS DH4 ....132 A5
Fountain Vw
  GATE (off Armstrong St) NE8 ...10 C9
Fouracres Rd
  WD/WHPE/BLK NE5 ....69 J1
Four Lane Ends HLH DH5 ....148 A6
Fourstones WD/WHPE/BLK NE5 ...68 C1
Fourstones Cl GOS/KPK NE3 ....55 H5
Fourstones Rd
  MLFD/PNYW SR4 ....105 J6
Fourth Av ASHGTN NE63 ....23 K2
  BLYTH NE24 ....35 F1
  BYK/HTN/WLK NE6 ....7 G2
  CLSW/PEL DH2 ....129 H4
  DUN/TMV NE11 ....86 C7
  MPTH NE61 ....21 F6
Fourth St CON/LDGT DH8 ....123 J2
  GATE NE8 ....10 C6
  PLEE/EAS SR8 ....175 H3
Fourway St WNGT TS28 ....183 K2
Fowberry Crs ELS/FEN NE4 .....69 J4
Fowberry Rd
  BW/LEM/TK/HW NE15 ....68 D7
Fowler Cl HLS DH4 ....132 A3
Fowler Gdns DUN/TMV NE11.....9 G5
Foxglove Cl BLYTH NE24 ....34 E3
Foxglove Ct HAR/WTLS NE34....74 E7
Foxhill Cl ASHGTN NE63 ....23 H4
Foxhills Cl WASHS NE38 ....117 G4
Foxhills Covert
  WICK/BNPF NE16 ....84 C7
Fox Hills Crs
  BDN/LAN/SAC DH7 ....140 A4
The Foxhills WICK/BNPF NE16...84 C6
Foxhunters Rd MONK NE25......50 D6
Fox Lea Wk CRAM NE23 ....39 F7
Foxley WASHN NE37 ....103 G5
Foxley Cl LGB/KIL NE12 ....48 B5
Fox St ASHBK/HED/RY SR2......14 A8
  FELL NE10 ....12 A6

  SEA/MUR SR7 ....150 E2
Foxton Av GOS/KPK NE3 ....55 K3
  TYNE/NSHE NE30 ....51 F6
Foxton Cl NSHW NE29 ....60 C7
Foxton Hall WASHN NE37 ....103 F2
Foxton Wy DHAM DH1 ....169 J5
  FELL NE10 ....13 M3
Foyle St SUND SR1 ....14 F5
Framlingham Pl JES NE2 ....5 H2
Framwelgate DHAM DH1 ....16 C2
Framwelgate Br DHAM DH1 .....16 C4
Framwelgate Peth DHAM DH1 ...156 C6
Framwelgate Waterside
  DHAM DH1 ....16 B3
Frances St BLAY NE21 ....83 J2
Francis St
  CLDN/WHIT/ROK SR6 ....106 D3
Frank Av SEA/MUR SR7 ....150 C1
Frankham St
  WD/WHPE/BLK NE5 ....68 D1
Frankland Dr MONK NE25 ....50 C6
Frankland La DHAM DH1 ....16 D1
Frankland Rd DHAM DH1 ....156 C4
Franklin St MLFD/PNYW SR4 ...106 A6
  SSH NE33 ....3 H7
Franklyn Av WBAY NE26 ....40 E1
Franklyn Rd PLEE/EAS SR8 .....174 C3
Frank Pl NSHW NE29 ....2 D1
Frank St DHAM DH1 ....17 M3
  SWCK/CAS SR5 ....106 B3
  WLSD/HOW NE28 ....72 C2
Fraser Cl SSH NE33 ....75 F3
Frazer Ter FELL NE10 ....13 J6
Freda St SWCK/CAS SR5 ....105 K4
Frederick Gdns HLS DH4 ....117 J7
Frederick Rd SUND SR1 ....14 F4
Frederick St MLFD/PNYW SR4 ...104 E7
  SEA/MUR SR7 ....150 E1
  SSH NE33 ....75 C3
  SUND SR1 ....14 F4
Frederick Ter RDHAMSE DH6 ...160 E3
Freehold Av STKFD/GP NE62 ...23 F6
Freeman Rd GOS/KPK NE3 ......57 F6
  LGB/HTN NE7 ....57 F6
Freemans Pl DHAM DH1 ....16 D3
Freeman Wy ASHGTN NE63 ....24 B4
Freesia Gra WASHS NE38 ....117 G5
Freezemoor Rd HLS DH4 ....132 B1
Fremantle Rd HAR/WTLS NE34 ...76 B6
Frenchman's Wy
  HAR/WTLS NE34 ....76 B4
French St BLYTH NE24 ....31 C6
Frensham WASHS NE38 ....117 J3
Frensham
  BDN/LAN/SAC DH7 ....167 H5
Frenton Cl WD/WHPE/BLK NE5 ...68 A1
Friarage Av
  CLDN/WHIT/ROK SR6 ....106 D2
Friar Rd MLFD/PNYW SR4 ......105 H7
Friars CNUT NE1 ....5 H7
Friars Dene Rd FELL NE10 ......12 A4
Friarsfield Cl SUNDSW SR3 .....133 J2
Friars Ga MPTH NE61 ....20 B6
Friarside BDN/LAN/SAC DH7 ...155 C1
Friarside Crs ROWG NE39 ......97 F5
Friarside Gdns WICK/BNPF NE16...84 E6
  WICK/BNPF NE16 ....97 H7
Friarside Rd ELS/FEN NE4 ......69 J3
Friar Sq MLFD/PNYW SR4 ......105 H7
Friars' Rw DHAM DH1 ....157 C6
Friars St CNUT NE1 ....5 H7
Friar St RDHAMSE DH6 ....173 J4
Friars Wy WD/WHPE/BLK NE5 ...69 G3
Friar Wy JRW NE32 ....74 A4
Friary Gdns FELL NE10 ....12 A5
Frobisher Ct SUNDSW SR3 .....133 K2
Frobisher St HEBB NE31 ....73 H5
Frome Gdns
  LWF/SPW/WRK NE9 ....101 F3
Frome Pl CRAM NE23 ....33 H7
Frome Sq MLFD/PNYW SR4 ....105 C7
Front Rd MLFD/PNYW SR4 .....105 H7
Front St BDN/LAN/SAC DH7 ...140 B4
  BDN/LAN/SAC DH7 ....143 G5
  BDN/LAN/SAC DH7 ....152 E5
  BDN/LAN/SAC DH7 ....155 F1
  BDN/LAN/SAC DH7 ....167 K4
  BLAY NE21 ....83 K3
  BLYTH NE24 ....29 K7
  BOL NE36 ....91 C5
  BOLCOL NE35 ....90 C3
  CLDN/WHIT/ROK SR6 ....92 A3
  CLDN/WHIT/ROK SR6 ....92 E4
  CLS/BIR/GTL DH3 ....129 J4
  CLS/BIR/GTL DH3 ....145 H1
  CLSW/PEL DH2 ....114 C7
  CLSW/PEL DH2 ....128 C2
  CON/LDGT DH8 ....122 C1
  CON/LDGT DH8 ....123 J3
  CON/LDGT DH8 ....123 F5
  CON/LDGT DH8 ....136 E1
  CRAM NE23 ....38 C7
  CRAM NE23 ....39 G6
  CRAM NE23 ....39 H7
  DHAM DH1 ....17 M4
  DIN/WO NE13 ....37 C7
  DIN/WO NE13 ....45 F2
  HLH DH5 ....147 H7
  HLH DH5 ....147 K4
  HLS DH4 ....132 B4
  LGB/HTN NE7 ....57 J5
  LGB/KIL NE12 ....47 H4
  MONK NE25 ....49 J4
  MONK NE25 ....50 C5
  NSHW NE29 ....60 C5
  NSHW NE29 ....60 D2
  NWBGN NE64 ....25 F1
  PRUD NE42 ....80 C2
  RDHAMSE DH6 ....158 D3
  RDHAMSE DH6 ....160 E6
  RDHAMSE DH6 ....160 D1
  RDHAMSE DH6 ....171 H2
  RDHAMSE DH6 ....172 E7
  RDHAMSE DH6 ....178 C5
  RDHAMSE DH6 ....181 G3
  RHTLS TS27 ....184 D6
  RHTLS TS27 ....185 G2

  STKFD/GP NE62 ....22 E6
  STLY/ANP DH9 ....111 K4
  STLY/ANP DH9 ....112 B2
  STLY/ANP DH9 ....112 E7
  STLY/ANP DH9 ....126 C1
  STLY/ANP DH9 ....127 G4
  TYNE/NSHE NE30 ....51 C6
  TYNE/NSHE NE30 ....61 H7
  WASHN NE37 ....103 F5
  WICK/BNPF NE16 ....84 E5
  WICK/BNPF NE16 ....97 C7
  WICK/BNPF NE16 ....111 J2
  WNGT TS28 ....183 K5
  WYLAM NE41 ....65 G7
Front St East BDLGTN NE22 ....29 C6
Frosteday Gdns STLY/ANP DH9 ...125 H3
Frosterley Cl CLS/BIR/GTL DH3 ...145 J1
  DHAM DH1 ....156 E2
  HLH DH5 ....148 C7
Frosterley Gdns SUNDSW SR3 ...120 B4
Frosterley Pl ELS/FEN NE4 ......4 D5
Froude Av HAR/WTLS NE34 .....91 F1
Fuchia Gdns HEBB NE31 ....89 G1
Fuchsia Pl WD/WHPE/BLK NE5 ...69 H1
Fulbrook Rd GOS/KPK NE3 ......55 K5
Fulforth Cl BDN/LAN/SAC DH7 ...152 E5
Fullerton Pl LWF/SPW/WRK NE9 ...11 J8
Fulmar Dr BLYTH NE24 ....35 G3
  WASHS NE38 ....116 B3
Fulmar Wk
  CLDN/WHIT/ROK SR6 ....93 F2
Fulwell Av HAR/WTLS NE34 .....76 B4
Fulwell Ct
  CLDN/WHIT/ROK SR6 ....106 D2
Fulwell Gn WD/WHPE/BLK NE5 ...69 F2
Fulwell Rd
  CLDN/WHIT/ROK SR6 ....106 D1
  PLEE/EAS SR8 ....175 C5
Furnace Bank BDLGTN NE22 ...29 K5
Furness Cl PLEE/EAS SR8 ....174 E4
Furrowfield FELL * NE10 ....87 J6
Furzefield Rd GOS/KPK NE3 ....56 B6
Fylingdale Dr SUNDSW SR3 .....120 C7
Fyndoune Wy
  BDN/LAN/SAC DH7 ....143 G7
Fynes Cl PLEE/EAS SR8 ....174 E2
Fynway BDN/LAN/SAC DH7 .....143 H6

G

The Gables BDN/LAN/SAC DH7 ...141 G4
  DIN/WO NE13 ....55 F4
Gadwall Rd HLS DH4 ....146 E2
Gainers Ter WLSD/HOW NE28 ...72 E3
Gainford CLSW/PEL DH2 ....129 G4
Gainsborough Av
  HAR/WTLS NE34 ....91 H1
  WASHS NE38 ....117 G2
Gainsborough Cl MONK NE25 ...50 A2
Gainsborough Crs HLS DH4 .....131 H2
  LWF/SPW/WRK NE9 ....11 M9
Gainsborough Gv ELS/FEN * NE4 ...4 B4
Gainsborough Pl CRAM NE23 ...38 C5
Gainsborough Rd
  MLFD/PNYW SR4 ....119 G4
  STLY/ANP DH9 ....126 D2
Gainsbro Gv ELS/FEN NE4 ......4 B4
Gairloch Cl CRAM NE23 ....33 H6
Gairloch Dr CLSW/PEL DH2......115 F7
  WASHS NE38 ....116 C3
Gairloch Rd MLFD/PNYW SR4 ...119 C5
Galashiels Gv HLS DH4 ....131 K3
Galashiels Rd MLFD/PNYW SR4 ...119 F3
Galashiels Sq MLFD/PNYW SR4 ...119 F3
Gale St STLY/ANP DH9 ....126 B2
Galfrid Cl SEA/MUR SR7 ....150 A2
Gallalaw Ter GOS/KPK NE3 .....57 F5
The Galleria
  WICK/BNPF
  (off Metrocentre) NE16 ....8 B4
The Galleries
  WASHS
  (off Washington Centre) NE38 ...116 E1
Galley's Gill Rd SUND SR1 ......14 C4
Galloping Green Rd
  LWF/SPW/WRK NE9 ....101 K3
Galloway Rd PLEE/EAS SR8 ....174 E3
Gallowgate CNUT NE1 ....5 H6
  ELS/FEN NE4 ....5 G5
Gallowhill La PRUD NE42 ....64 B5
Galsworthy Rd HAR/WTLS NE34 ...90 E1
  MLFD/PNYW SR4 ....119 G3
Galt St RDHAMSE DH6 ....172 C6
Galway Rd MLFD/PNYW SR4 ...119 F3
Gambia Rd MLFD/PNYW SR4 ...119 F4
Gambia Sq MLFD/PNYW SR4 ...119 F4
Ganton Av CRAM NE23 ....38 C4
Ganton Cl WASHN NE37 ....102 E3
Ganton Ct HAR/WTLS NE34 .....91 K1
Garasdale Cl BLYTH NE24 ....35 F3
Garden Av BDN/LAN/SAC DH7 ...154 A3
Garden City Vls ASHGTN NE63 ...23 K3
Garden Cl DIN/WO NE13 ....46 B1
Garden Crs CON/LDGT DH8......108 E2
Garden Cft LGB/KIL NE12 ....58 A2
Garden Dr HEBB NE31 ....73 F7
Garden House Est RYTON NE40 ...66 B7
Garden La SSH NE33 ....3 H7
Garden Pk WLSD/HOW NE28 ...59 H6
Garden Pl HLS DH4 ....117 K7
  SUND SR1 ....14 D4
The Gardens CLSW/PEL DH2 ...114 D9
  MONK NE25 ....50 D5
Garden St HLS DH4 ....132 B4
Garden Ter CON/LDGT DH8......123 J5
  MONK NE25 ....49 J4
  RYTON NE40 ....66 B7
Garden Wk
  WICK/BNPF
  (off Metrocentre) NE16 ....8 B5
Gardiner Rd MLFD/PNYW SR4 ...118 C3
Gardiner Sq MLFD/PNYW SR4 ...119 F3
Gardner Pk NSHW NE29 ....2 B3
Gardner Pl NSHW NE29 ....2 D3
Garesfield Gdns ROWG NE39 ...97 G2
Garesfield La BLAY NE21 ....83 H5

Gareston Cl BLYTH NE24 ....30 D7
Garfield St CLS/BIR/GTL DH3 ...115 J1
Garforth Cl CRAM NE23 ....38 B4
Garleigh Cl LGB/KIL NE12 ....48 B6
Garmondsway
  BYK/HTN/WLK NE6 ....7 G8
Garner Cl WD/WHPE/BLK NE5 ...54 B7
Garnet St MLFD/PNYW SR4 ....105 K6
Garrick Cl NSHW NE29 ....60 A3
Garrick St SSH NE33 ....75 G3
Garrigill WASHS NE38 ....117 H5
Garron St SEA/MUR SR7 ....150 E2
Garsdale Av WASHN NE37 ......102 E5
Garsdale Rd WBAY NE26 ....41 H7
Garside Av CLS/BIR/GTL DH3 ...115 J1
Garside Gv PLEE/EAS SR8 ......174 C2
Garsin Cl LGB/HTN NE7 ....58 A7
Garth Cornfield PLEE/EAS SR8 ...175 G5
Garth Crs BLAY NE21 ....83 K3
  HAR/WTLS NE34 ....76 A2
Garth Farm Rd BLAY NE21 ......83 K3
Garthfield Crs
  WD/WHPE/BLK NE5 ....68 E1
Garth Heads CNUT NE1 ....5 L7
Garth Six LGB/KIL NE12 ....47 J6
Garth Sixteen LGB/KIL NE12 ....47 K5
The Garth
  BLAY (off Front St) NE21 ......83 K3
  GOS/KPK NE3 ....55 K6
  WD/WHPE/BLK NE5 ....47 J5
Garth Thirteen LGB/KIL NE12 ...47 J5
  LGB/KIL NE12 ....47 K6
Garth Thirty Three
  LGB/KIL NE12 ....47 K6
Garth Thirty Two LGB/KIL NE12 ...47 J6
Garth Twelve LGB/KIL NE12 .....47 J5
Garth Twenty LGB/KIL NE12 ....48 A6
Garth Twenty Five
  LGB/KIL NE12 ....48 B6
Garth Twenty Four
  LGB/KIL NE12 ....48 B6
Garth Twenty Seven
  LGB/KIL NE12 ....48 B6
Garth Twenty Two
  LGB/KIL NE12 ....48 A6
Gartland Rd MLFD/PNYW SR4 ...118 C3
Garvey Vls LWF/SPW/WRK NE9 ...87 G7
Garwood Rd SSH NE33 ....75 F3
Gas House La MPTH NE61 ......20 E5
Gaskell Av HAR/WTLS NE34 .....91 F1
Gas La BLAY NE21 ....68 A7
Gas Works Rd SEA/MUR SR7 ...151 F2
Gatacre St BLYTH NE24 ....31 G6
Cateley Av BLYTH NE24 ....35 F3
Gatesgarth LWF/SPW/WRK NE9 ...87 G7
Gatesgarth Gv
  CLDN/WHIT/ROK SR6 ....92 C7
Gateshead Hwy GATE NE8 .....11 H1
Gateshead Rd WICK/BNPF NE16 ...99 C2
Gatwick Ct GOS/KPK NE3 ....55 C3
Gatwick Rd MLFD/PNYW SR4 ...119 F3
Gayfield Ter PLEE/EAS SR8 .....163 G6
Gayhurst Crs SUNDSW SR3 ....134 A1
Gayton Rd WASHN NE37 ....103 G4
Geddes Rd MLFD/PNYW SR4 ...119 F3
Gelt Crs HLH DH5 ....148 A6
General Graham St
  MLFD/PNYW SR4 ....119 K1
General Havelock Rd
  MLFD/PNYW SR4 ....105 J7
The General's Wd WASHS NE38 ...116 E6
Genesis Wy CON/LDGT DH8 ....122 E4
Geneva Rd MLFD/PNYW SR4 ...119 F3
Genister Pl ELS/FEN NE4 ....69 H5
Geoffrey Av DHAM DH1 ....168 B2
Geoffrey St
  CLDN/WHIT/ROK SR6 ....93 F3
Geoffrey Ter STLY/ANP DH9 ....126 B2
George Pit La
  CLS/BIR/GTL DH3 ....145 K2
George Rd BDLGTN * NE22 .....29 K4
  WLSD/HOW NE28 ....72 D3
George Scott St SSH NE33 ......3 K5
George Smith Gdns FELL NE10 ...12 B4
George Sq RDHAMSE DH6 ......171 H4
  TYNE/NSHE NE30 ....2 F1
Georges Rd ELS/FEN NE4 ....4 B3
George Stephenson Wy
  NSHW NE29 ....2 B6
George St ASHBK/HED/RY SR2 ...135 G1
  BLAY NE21 ....84 B1
  BLYTH NE24 ....35 G1
  CLS/BIR/GTL DH3 ....115 H2
  CLS/BIR/GTL DH3 ....129 K5
  CON/LDGT DH8 ....123 F4
  DHAM DH1 ....168 B1
  ELS/FEN NE4 ....5 G9
  GOS/KPK NE3 ....56 A5
  HLH DH5 ....147 K3
  RDHAMSE DH6 ....160 E6
  RDHAMSE DH6 ....170 C1
  RDHAMSE DH6 ....179 K1
  SEA/MUR SR7 ....149 H6
  SEA/MUR SR7 ....150 D1
  TYNE/NSHE NE30 ....2 F1
  WD/WHPE/BLK NE5 ....67 H1
  WICK/BNPF NE16 ....84 E5
  WLSD/HOW NE28 ....73 K2
George St North
  CLDN/WHIT/ROK SR6 ....14 F1
Georgia Ct CON/LDGT DH8 .....122 E6
Georgian Cl LGB/KIL NE12 ......57 H1
  MLFD/PNYW SR4 ....120 A2
Gerald St ELS/FEN NE4 ....69 H7
  HAR/WTLS NE34 ....91 G1
Gerrard Cl CRAM NE23 ....38 C4
  WBAY NE26 ....41 H7
Gerrard Rd MLFD/PNYW SR4 ...119 F3
  WBAY NE26 ....41 H7
Gertrude St HLS DH4 ....132 B5
Ghyll Field Rd DHAM DH1 ....156 C4
Gibside CLSW/PEL DH2 ....129 G4
Gibside Cl STLY/ANP DH9 ....113 F7
Gibside Ct DUN/TMV NE11 .....85 G2
Gibside Gdns
  BW/LEM/TK/HW NE15 ....69 G5
Gibside Vw BLAY NE21 ....83 K4
Gibside Wy WICK/BNPF NE16...85 F2
Gibson Ct BOLCOL NE35 ....90 D4

Gibson St CNUT NE1 6 B6
CON/LDGT DH8 123 F4
NWBGN NE64 25 F1
WLSD/HOW NE28 59 G6
Gifford Sq MLFD/PNYW SR4 119 G2
Gilbert Rd MLFD/PNYW SR4 119 F3
PLEE/EAS SR8 174 D3
Gilbert St SSH * NE33 75 G3
Gilderdale HLS DH4 117 G6
Gilderdale Wy CRAM NE23 38 B5
Gilesgate DHAM DH1 16 F3
Gilesgate Ct DHAM * DH1 16 F3
Gilesgate Rd HLH DH5 148 A6
Gilhurst Gra SUND SR1 14 B5
Gillas La HLH DH5 147 K1
Gillas La East HLH DH5 147 J1
Gillas La West HLH DH5 147 H2
Gill Burn ROWG NE39 97 G2
Gillies St BYK/HTN/WLK NE6 7 J5
Gillingham Rd
MLFD/PNYW SR4 119 G3
Gill Rd SUND SR1 14 D3
Gill Side Gv
CLDN/WHIT/ROK SR6 106 E3
Gill Side Vw CON/LDGT DH8 122 C3
Gill St CON/LDGT DH8 123 G6
ELS/FEN NE4 69 J6
Gilmore Cl WD/WHPE/BLK NE5 54 B7
Gilpin St HLS DH4 132 B7
Gilsland Av WLSD/HOW NE28 59 H7
Gilsland Gv CRAM NE23 33 H6
Gilsland St MLFD/PNYW SR4 106 A6
Gilwell Wy GOS/KPK NE3 56 B1
Gingler La RYTON NE40 82 C2
Girtin Rd HAR/WTLS NE34 91 H2
Girton Cl PLEE/EAS SR8 174 C5
Girvan Cl STLY/ANP DH9 127 F1
Gisburn Ct CRAM NE23 33 H6
Gishford Wy
WD/WHPE/BLK NE5 69 F1
Givens St CLDN/WHIT/ROK SR6 106 E3
Gladeley Wy WICK/BNPF NE16 98 E3
The Glade JRW NE32 89 K3
WD/WHPE/BLK NE5 67 J1
Gladewell Ct STKFD/GP NE62 22 E7
Gladstonbury Pl LGB/KIL NE12 57 J4
Gladstone St BLYTH NE24 31 F6
BW/LEM/TK/HW NE15 68 A5
CLDN/WHIT/ROK SR6 106 D4
CON/LDGT DH8 123 G4
HEBB NE31 73 H5
HLS DH4 131 K7
STLY/ANP DH9 113 H7
STLY/ANP DH9 126 B2
WLSD/HOW NE28 73 K2
Gladstone Ter GATE NE8 11 G5
JES NE2 5 M3
Gladstone Ter West GATE NE8 10 F5
Gladwyn Rd MLFD/PNYW SR4 119 F4
Glaholm Rd ASHBK/HED/RY SR2 15 J6
Glaisdale Dr
CLDN/WHIT/ROK SR6 92 E6
Glaisdale Rd LGB/HTN NE7 57 G5
Glamis Av GOS/KPK NE3 46 C7
MLFD/PNYW SR4 119 G2
Glamis Ct HAR/WTLS NE34 91 K1
Glamis Crs ROWG NE39 97 J1
Glamis Vls CLS/BIR/GTL DH3 101 J7
Glanmore Rd MLFD/PNYW SR4 119 F3
Glantlees WD/WHPE/BLK NE5 68 E1
Glanton Av MONK NE25 39 K5
Glanton Cl BYK/HTN/WLK NE6 7 G8
CLSW/PEL DH2 129 G5
MPTH NE61 27 F1
Glanton Ct DUN/TMV NE11 9 J5
Glanton Rd NSHW NE29 60 B3
Glanton Sq MLFD/PNYW SR4 119 G3
Glanton Wynd GOS/KPK NE3 56 B3
Glanville Cl DUN/TMV NE11 86 B5
Glanville Rd SUNDSW SR3 133 H2
Glasbury Av MLFD/PNYW SR4 119 G2
Glasgow Rd JRW NE32 90 C1
Glasshouse St BYK/HTN/WLK NE6 7 G9
Glastonbury WASHS NE38 117 F2
Glastonbury Gv JES NE2 71 F1
Glazebury Wy CRAM NE23 33 H6
Gleaston Ct PLEE/EAS SR8 174 C7
Glebe Av LGB/KIL NE12 57 K3
WICK/BNPF NE16 85 F5
Glebe Cl WD/WHPE/BLK NE5 54 B7
Glebe Crs LGB/KIL NE12 57 K1
WASHS NE38 103 G7
Glebe Farm MPTH NE61 22 E5
Glebe Ms BDLGTN NE22 28 E5
Glebe Ri WICK/BNPF NE16 84 E5
Glebe Rd BDLGTN NE22 29 F5
LGB/KIL NE12 57 K1
Glebeside BDN/LAN/SAC DH7 155 G1
HLH (off Church Rd) DH5 147 K3
Glebe St ELS/FEN NE4 69 H5
Glebe Ter DUN/TMV NE11 9 G8
LGB/KIL NE12 57 K1
PLEE/EAS SR8 162 D5
Glebe Vw SEA/MUR SR7 149 K4
Glebe Vls LGB/KIL NE12 57 J1
Glebe Wk WICK/BNPF NE16 85 F5
Glenallen Gdns
TYNE/NSHE NE30 61 G1
Glen Barr CLSW/PEL DH2 129 H3
Glenbrooke Ter
LWF/SPW/WRK NE9 101 F1
Glenburn Cl WASHS NE38 116 B3
Glencarron Cl WASHS NE38 116 C2
Glen Cl ROWG NE39 97 G2
Glencoe LGB/KIL NE12 47 K5
Glencoe Av CLSW/PEL DH2 129 H3
CRAM NE23 38 C5
Glencoe Rd MLFD/PNYW SR4 119 F4
Glencourse BOL NE36 91 J5
Glendale Av BLYTH NE24 30 A6
GOS/KPK NE3 56 A6
NSHW NE29 60 C4
STKFD/GP NE62 23 G5
WBAY NE26 50 E2
WICK/BNPF NE16 84 E6
WLSD/HOW NE28 58 D6
Glendale Cl BLAY NE21 83 H4
SUNDSW SR3 133 G1
WD/WHPE/BLK NE5 54 B6
Glendale Gdns
LWF/SPW/WRK NE9 87 H7
STKFD/GP NE62 23 G5
Glendale Gv NSHW NE29 2 A1
Glendale Rd ASHGTN NE63 24 C3
SMOOR NE27 49 J6
Glendale Ter BYK/HTN/WLK NE6 7 G4
Glendford Pl BLYTH NE24 35 F3
Glendower Av NSHW NE29 60 B4
Glendyn Cl LGB/HTN NE7 71 G2
Gleneagle Cl
WD/WHPE/BLK NE5 54 B7
Gleneagles SSH NE33 75 J2
Gleneagles Cl LGB/HTN NE7 57 J5
Gleneagles Dr WASHN NE37 102 D3
Gleneagles Rd
LWF/SPW/WRK NE9 100 E2
MLFD/PNYW SR4 119 F4
Gleneagles Sq
MLFD/PNYW SR4 119 F4
Glenesk Gdns
ASHBK/HED/RY SR2 120 C4
Glenesk Rd
ASHBK/HED/RY SR2 120 C3
Glenfield Av CRAM NE23 33 H6
Glenfield Rd LGB/KIL NE12 57 J3
Glengarvan Cl WASHS NE38 116 C3
Glenhurst Dr
WD/WHPE/BLK NE5 54 B7
WICK/BNPF NE16 98 D1
Glenhurst Gv HAR/WTLS NE34 75 K5
Glenhurst Rd PLEE/EAS SR8 162 E5
Glenkerry Cl WASHS NE38 116 C3
Glenleigh Dr MLFD/PNYW SR4 119 G3
Glen Luce Dr
ASHBK/HED/RY SR2 121 F4
Glenluce Dr CRAM NE23 38 B5
Glenmoor HEBB NE31 73 F4
Glenmore CON/LDGT DH8 123 J7
Glenmore Av CLSW/PEL DH2 129 H3
Glenmuir Av CRAM NE23 38 B5
Glenorrin Cl WASHS NE38 116 C3
Glen Pth ASHBK/HED/RY SR2 120 D3
Glenridge Av BYK/HTN/WLK NE6 71 H2
Glenroy Gdns CLSW/PEL DH2 129 H3
Glenshiel Cl WASHS NE38 116 C3
Glenside CON/LDGT DH8 122 D1
Glen St HEBB NE31 73 F6
Glen Ter CLSW/PEL DH2 129 G3
The Glen ASHBK/HED/RY SR2 120 D3
Glenthorn Rd JES NE2 70 E1
Glenuce CLS/BIR/GTL DH3 116 A3
Glenwood ASHGTN NE63 23 J3
Gloria Av MONK NE25 40 A2
Glossop St ROWG NE39 96 B1
Gloucester Av
CLDN/WHIT/ROK SR6 106 E1
Gloucester Cl CLS/BIR/GTL DH3 145 H2
Gloucester Ct DIN/WO NE13 55 G2
Gloucester Pl HAR/WTLS NE34 76 A6
PLEE/EAS SR8 174 C3
Gloucester Rd CON/LDGT DH8 123 G6
ELS/FEN NE4 4 D6
NSHW NE29 59 K3
Gloucestershire Dr DHAM DH1 157 K6
Gloucester Ter ELS/FEN NE4 4 D8
RDHAMSE DH6 172 D1
Gloucester Wy ELS/FEN NE4 4 E9
Glover Rd MLFD/PNYW SR4 119 F4
WASHN NE37 103 H5
Glynfellis FELL NE10 88 B7
Glynwood Cl CRAM NE23 33 H6
Glynwood Gdns
LWF/SPW/WRK NE9 87 G7
Goalmouth Cl
CLDN/WHIT/ROK SR6 106 E3
Goathland Av LGB/KIL NE12 57 J3
Goathland Cl SUNDSW SR3 120 C7
Goathland Dr SUNDSW SR3 120 B7
Godfrey Rd MLFD/PNYW SR4 118 E3
Goldcrest Rd WASHS NE38 116 B3
Golden Acre CON/LDGT DH8 122 D2
Goldlynn Dr SUNDSW SR3 133 H1
Goldsborough Ct WNGT TS28 183 K2
Goldsbrough Ct
JES (off Richardson Rd) NE2 5 G2
Goldsmith Rd MLFD/PNYW SR4 119 F4
Goldspink La JES NE2 6 B2
Goldstone
LWF/SPW/WRK
(off Pimlico Ct) NE9 101 F1
Goldthorpe Cl CRAM NE23 33 H6
Golf Course Rd HLS DH4 131 H3
Gompertz Gdns SSH NE33 75 F3
Goodrich Cl HLS DH4 132 A3
Good St STLY/ANP DH9 112 C6
Goodwell Lea
BDN/LAN/SAC DH7 176 D2
Goodwood LGB/KIL NE12 48 B6
Goodwood Av GATE NE8 10 B8
Goodwood Cl CON/LDGT DH8 122 E1
WD/WHPE/BLK NE5 54 B7
Goodwood Rd
MLFD/PNYW SR4 118 E3
Goodyear Crs DHAM DH1 17 M4
Goole Rd MLFD/PNYW SR4 119 G3
Goose Hl MPTH NE61 20 E5
Gordon Av GOS/KPK NE3 56 C6
SWCK/CAS SR5 104 E5
Gordon Ct FELL NE10 12 C6
Gordon Dr BOL NE36 91 H5
Gordon Rd BYK/HTN/WLK NE6 6 F6
HAR/WTLS NE34 75 G5
MLFD/PNYW SR4 118 E4
Gordon Sq BYK/HTN/WLK NE6 6 F6
WBAY NE26 51 G5
Gordon St GATE NE8 10 D4
SSH NE33 75 G3
Gordon Ter SWCK/CAS SR5 106 A3
Gordon Ter West
STKFD/GP NE62 23 J5
Gorecock La STLY/ANP DH9 124 E6
Gore Hill Est RDHAMSE DH6 172 B6
Gorleston Wy SUNDSW SR3 133 K3
Gorse Av HAR/WTLS NE34 76 A6
Gorsedale Gv DHAM DH1 158 A6
Gorsedene Rd WBAY NE26 41 J7
Gorse Rd ASHBK/HED/RY SR2 14 E8
Gorseway MPTH NE61 20 B6
Gort Pl DHAM DH1 17 K1
Goschen St BLYTH NE24 31 F6
GATE NE8 10 D7
SWCK/CAS SR5 106 A3
Gosforth Av HAR/WTLS NE34 91 G1
Gosforth Park Wy LGB/KIL NE12 57 F3
Gosforth St
CLDN/WHIT/ROK SR6 106 E4
JES NE2 6 A4
Gosforth Ter FELL NE10 13 H5
Gosport Wy BLYTH NE24 35 F3
Gossington WASHS NE38 117 J1
Goswick Av LGB/HTN NE7 71 H1
Goswick Dr GOS/KPK NE3 55 K2
Goundry Av
ASHBK/HED/RY SR2 135 G1
Gowanburn CRAM NE23 38 B5
WASHS NE38 117 G4
Gowan Ter JES NE2 71 F2
Gower Rd SWCK/CAS SR5 106 A3
Gower St BYK/HTN/WLK NE6 72 C7
Gower Wk FELL NE10 12 A7
Gowland Av ELS/FEN NE4 69 J4
Gowland Sq SEA/MUR SR7 149 G5
Gracefield Cl
WD/WHPE/BLK NE5 54 B7
Grace Gdns WLSD/HOW NE28 58 C6
Grace St BYK/HTN/WLK NE6 7 H5
DUN/TMV NE11 9 G8
Grafton Cl BYK/HTN/WLK NE6 6 F4
Grafton Rd WBAY NE26 51 G5
Grafton St MLFD/PNYW SR4 14 A3
Graham Av WICK/BNPF NE16 84 E4
Graham Ct BDN/LAN/SAC DH7 143 H5
Graham Park Rd GOS/KPK NE3 56 C7
Grahamsley St GATE NE8 11 G3
Graham St SSH NE33 3 K9
The Graham Wy SEA/MUR SR7 150 B2
Grainger Ar CNUT * NE1 5 K6
Grainger Market CNUT * NE1 5 J6
Grainger Park Rd ELS/FEN NE4 4 A8
Grainger St CNUT NE1 5 J7
Graingerville North
ELS/FEN (off Westgate Rd) NE4 4 C6
Graingerville South
ELS/FEN (off Westgate Rd) NE4 4 C6
Grampian Ct STLY/ANP DH9 125 G4
Grampian Dr PLEE/EAS SR8 174 C5
Grampian Gv BOL NE36 91 F5
Grampian Pl LGB/KIL NE12 57 H1
The Granaries ROWG NE39 96 B1
Granby Cl SUNDSW SR3 120 B3
WICK/BNPF NE16 99 F2
Granby Ter WNGT TS28 183 K2
Grand Pde TYNE/NSHE NE30 61 H2
The Grandstand
MPTH
(off North Common) NE61 20 B7
Grange Av BDLGTN NE22 29 K3
HLS DH4 131 J6
LGB/KIL NE12 58 A4
PLEE/EAS SR8 162 C6
SMOOR NE27 49 H5
Grange Cl BLYTH NE24 35 F3
MONK NE25 50 B5
PLEE/EAS SR8 174 D2
TYNE/NSHE NE30 51 F7
WLSD/HOW NE28 72 E1
Grange Ct FELL NE10 13 K8
PRUD NE42 80 D2
Grange Crs ASHBK/HED/RY SR2 14 E7
FELL NE10 13 J9
RDHAMSE DH6 180 D7
RYTON NE40 66 E7
Grange Dr RYTON NE40 66 E7
Grange Est DUN/TMV NE11 100 C7
Grange Farm Dr
WICK/BNPF NE16 84 E7
Grange La WICK/BNPF NE16 84 E7
Grange Lonnen RYTON NE40 66 D6
Grangemere Cl
ASHBK/HED/RY SR2 121 F4
Grange Nook WICK/BNPF NE16 84 E7
Grange Pk MONK NE25 50 A6
Grange Park Av BDLGTN NE22 29 K3
SWCK/CAS SR5 106 C2
Grange Park Crs
RDHAMSE DH6 180 B3
Grange Pl JRW NE32 73 K4
Grange Rd
BW/LEM/TK/HW NE15 67 G3
DHAM DH1 157 K5
ELS/FEN NE4 69 H5
FELL NE10 13 J9
GOS/KPK NE3 56 C3
JRW NE32 73 K4
MPTH NE61 20 E6
PONT/DH NE20 43 G2
RYTON NE40 66 E6
STLY/ANP DH9 126 B1
SWCK/CAS SR5 104 E6
Grange Rd West JRW NE32 73 J4
Grange St CLSW/PEL DH2 128 E1
Grange St South
ASHBK/HED/RY SR2 121 F4
Grange Ter BOL NE36 91 H5
CLSW/PEL DH2 128 C3
LWF/SPW/WRK NE9 11 K8
SWCK/CAS SR5 106 B3
The Grange BDLGTN NE22 28 A6
BOL (off Front St) NE36 91 H5
STLY/ANP DH9 112 A6
Grange Vw HLH DH5 147 G3
HLS DH4 132 B4
RYTON NE40 66 E7
SWCK/CAS SR5 106 C2
Grange Vls WLSD/HOW NE28 72 E1
Grantham Av SEA/MUR SR7 150 C2
Grantham Dr
LWF/SPW/WRK NE9 100 E1
Grantham Pl CRAM NE23 38 B4
Grantham Rd
CLDN/WHIT/ROK SR6 106 E3
JES NE2 6 A3
Grantham St BLYTH NE24 35 H1
Grants Crs SEA/MUR SR7 150 E1
Grant St JRW NE32 73 J4
PLEE/EAS SR8 175 H3
Granville Av LGB/KIL NE12 58 A1
WBAY NE26 41 G3
Granville Ct JES NE2 5 M1
Granville Crs LGB/KIL NE12 58 A4
Granville Dr HLS DH4 132 A2
LGB/KIL NE12 58 A2
WD/WHPE/BLK NE5 54 B7
Granville Gdns JES NE2 71 G3
STKFD/GP NE62 23 G5
Granville Rd GOS/KPK NE3 56 C3
JES NE2 6 A1
PLEE/EAS SR8 175 G5
Granville St GATE NE8 11 G5
MLFD/PNYW SR4 14 A4
Grape La DHAM DH1 16 B4
Grasmere CLDN/WHIT/ROK SR6 92 A3
Grasmere Av BYK/HTN/WLK NE6 7 M6
FELL NE10 13 H7
HLH DH5 160 B1
JRW NE32 90 B1
Grasmere Ct LGB/KIL NE12 47 J6
Grasmere Crs BLAY NE21 83 K4
SWCK/CAS SR5 106 C2
WBAY NE26 50 D2
Grasmere Gdns HAR/WTLS NE34 75 J5
Grasmere Pl GOS/KPK NE3 56 B3
Grasmere Rd CLSW/PEL DH2 129 H6
HEBB NE31 73 H6
PLEE/EAS SR8 175 F3
WICK/BNPF NE16 8 B9
WLSD/HOW NE28 72 C2
Grasmere St GATE NE8 10 E6
Grasmere St West GATE NE8 10 E6
Grasmere Ter
NSHW (off Hawkeys La) NE29 60 D4
RDHAMSE DH6 161 G2
SEA/MUR SR7 149 J6
Grasmoor Pl
BW/LEM/TK/HW NE15 67 K4
Grassdale DHAM DH1 158 A6
Grassholme Mdw SUNDSW SR3 120 B4
Grassholm Pl LGB/KIL NE12 57 G3
Grassington Dr CRAM NE23 38 B4
Grasslees WASHS NE38 116 B6
Grassmere Ms CON/LDGT DH8 123 K3
Grassmere Ter STLY/ANP DH9 126 B3
Grasswell Dr
WD/WHPE/BLK NE5 55 H7
Gravel Wks HLH DH5 132 C6
Gravesend Rd
MLFD/PNYW SR4 119 F4
Gravesend Sq
MLFD/PNYW SR4 119 G4
Gray Av DHAM DH1 156 B4
DIN/WO NE13 46 C2
RDHAMSE DH6 158 C7
RHTLP TS27 185 G2
SEA/MUR SR7 149 H5
Grayling Ct SUNDSW SR3 133 G2
Grayling Rd DUN/TMV NE11 9 L9
Gray Rd ASHBK/HED/RY SR2 15 K7
Grays Cross SUND SR1 15 H4
Gray Sq WNGT TS28 183 K3
Grays Ter BOLCOL NE35 90 C3
Graystones FELL NE10 88 D5
Gray St BLYTH NE24 31 G5
Graythwaite CLSW/PEL DH2 129 F4
Greathead St SSH NE33 75 F4
Great Lime Rd DIN/WO NE13 47 G4
LGB/KIL NE12 57 J1
Great North Forest Trail
HAR/WTLS NE34 76 D4
Great North Rd GOS/KPK NE3 56 C3
Grebe Cl ASHGTN NE63 24 A4
BLYTH NE24 35 G2
Greely Rd WD/WHPE/BLK NE5 68 D1
Greenacres CLSW/PEL DH2 114 D7
Green Acres MPTH NE61 20 C6
PONT/DH NE20 42 E7
Greenacres Cl RYTON NE40 82 C1
Greenacres Rd CON/LDGT DH8 122 D2
Green Av HLS DH4 132 B3
Greenbank BLAY NE21 84 A2
JRW NE32 73 K4
Greenbank Dr
MLFD/PNYW SR4 118 E1
Greenbourne Gdns FELL NE10 87 J5
Green Cl TYNE/NSHE NE30 61 F1
Green Crs CRAM NE23 47 F1
RDHAMSE DH6 180 D7
Greencroft ASHGTN NE63 23 J3
RDHAMSE DH6 161 G2
Greencroft Av
BYK/HTN/WLK NE6 72 C3
Greencroft Pkwy
STLY/ANP DH9 125 H6
Greencroft Rd CON/LDGT DH8 123 J7
Greencroft Ter STLY/ANP DH9 125 F5
Greendale Cl BLYTH NE24 30 C6
Greendale Gdns HLH DH5 147 J6
Greener Ct PRUD NE42 80 B3
Greenfield Av
WD/WHPE/BLK NE5 68 E1
Greenfield Dr STKFD/GP NE62 22 E7
Greenfield Pl ELS/FEN NE4 5 G7
Greenfield Rd DIN/WO NE13 46 B7
GOS/KPK NE3 56 B1
Greenfields
CLSW/PEL (off Ross) DH2 115 G4
Greenfield Ter FELL NE10 13 H6
STLY/ANP DH9 125 H3
Greenfinch Cl WASHS NE38 116 B3
Greenford DUN/TMV NE11 100 D7
Greenford La DUN/TMV NE11 100 E6
Greenford Rd
BYK/HTN/WLK NE6 13 J1
Greenhaugh LGB/KIL NE12 57 H1
Greenhead WASHS NE38 116 B2
Greenhead Rd CHPW NE17 95 H2
Greenhills LGB/KIL NE12 47 K4
Greenhills Est WNGT TS28 183 K2
Greenhill Vw
WD/WHPE/BLK NE5 69 J1
Green Hill Wk HAR/WTLS NE34 76 C5
Greenholme Cl CRAM NE23 33 H6
Greenhow Cl
ASHBK/HED/RY SR2 135 F2
Greenland Rd
BDN/LAN/SAC DH7 153 F5
Greenlands STLY/ANP DH9 126 B3
Greenlands Ct MONK NE25 40 A4
Green La ASHGTN NE63 23 J2
BDN/LAN/SAC DH7 141 K2
BOL NE36 91 H6
DHAM DH1 17 J2
DHAM DH1 17 G5
DIN/WO NE13 54 D2
FELL NE10 12 C4
FELL NE10 13 J6
HAR/WTLS NE34 75 F7
LGB/KIL NE12 48 A6
MPTH NE61 21 F5
MPTH NE61 26 A7
RDHAMSE DH6 160 C5
SEA/MUR SR7 148 D2
STLY/ANP DH9 126 C7
TRIM TS29 182 D3
Green Lane Gdns FELL NE10 12 B4
Greenlaw WD/WHPE/BLK NE5 68 C3
Greenlaw Rd CRAM NE23 38 B5
Green Lea BDN/LAN/SAC DH7 143 G7
Greenlea NSHW NE29 59 K1
Greenlea Cl MLFD/PNYW SR4 119 G3
ROWG NE39 96 C1
Greenlee ASHGTN NE63 24 A3
Greenlee Dr LGB/HTN NE7 57 K7
Greenmarket CNUT * NE1 5 J6
Greenock Rd MLFD/PNYW SR4 119 F4
Green Pk WLSD/HOW NE28 58 A7
Greenrigg Gdns SUNDSW SR3 120 B3
Green's Bank STLY/ANP DH9 114 A7
Greenshields Rd
MLFD/PNYW SR4 119 F4
Greenside Av PLEE/EAS SR8 175 G3
WLSD/HOW NE28 59 H7
Greenside Crs
BW/LEM/TK/HW NE15 68 E4
Greenside Rd RYTON NE40 82 B1
Green's Pl SSH NE33 3 H4
Green St CON/LDGT DH8 108 C7
CON/LDGT DH8 123 J4
SEA/MUR SR7 150 E1
SUND SR1 14 E4
Green Ter SUND SR1 14 D5
The Green
BW/LEM/TK/HW NE15 67 H2
DHAM DH1 169 J6
FELL NE10 12 F8
GOS/KPK NE3 55 K7
HLH DH5 132 D6
MONK NE25 50 C3
PLEE/EAS SR8 174 B6
PONT/DH NE20 43 H1
RDHAMSE
(off Woodland Crs) DH6 181 G6
SWCK/CAS SR5 106 A4
Greentree La STLY/ANP DH9 125 G2
Green Va RYTON NE40 82 B2
Greenway ELS/FEN NE4 69 H3
WD/WHPE/BLK NE5 54 A6
Greenways CON/LDGT DH8 123 J7
The Greenway
MLFD/PNYW SR4 119 G2
Greenwell Cl BLAY NE21 83 J3
Greenwell Dr PRUD NE42 80 D1
Greenwell Pk
BDN/LAN/SAC DH7 140 C5
Greenwich Pl GATE NE8 6 D9
Greenwood LGB/KIL NE12 48 B6
Greenwood Av BDLGTN NE22 29 K3
BDN/LAN/SAC DH7 141 G5
BYK/HTN/WLK NE6 72 C2
HLS DH4 132 A7
Greenwood Cl RDHAMSE DH6 173 F7
Greenwood Gdns
DUN/TMV NE11 86 A7
FELL NE10 12 D4
Greenwood Rd
MLFD/PNYW SR4 119 F3
Greetlands Rd
ASHBK/HED/RY SR2 120 C3
Gregson St BDN/LAN/SAC DH7 143 H5
Gregson Ter SEA/MUR SR7 135 F6
Grenada Cl WBAY NE26 50 D1
Grenada Dr WBAY NE26 50 D1
Grenada Pl WBAY NE26 50 D1
Grenfell Sq MLFD/PNYW SR4 119 F4
Grenville Ct
CRAM (off Megstone Av) NE23 38 B3
PONT/DH NE20 42 C5
Grenville Dr GOS/KPK NE3 56 B1
Grenville Wy WBAY NE26 50 C2
Gresford St SSH NE33 75 G5
Gresham Cl CRAM NE23 38 C4
Gresley Rd PLEE/EAS SR8 174 B4
Greta Gdns SSH NE33 75 H3
Greta Ter MLFD/PNYW SR4 120 A1
Gretna Dr HAR/WTLS NE34 90 D1
Gretna Rd
BW/LEM/TK/HW NE15 69 F4
Gretton Pl LGB/HTN NE7 57 G7
Grey Av CRAM NE23 38 B5
Greybourne Gdns
ASHBK/HED/RY SR2 120 C4
Greyfriars La LGB/KIL NE12 57 G4
Grey Lady Wk PRUD NE42 80 D1
Greystead Cl
WD/WHPE/BLK NE5 54 B7
Greystead Rd MONK NE25 49 K4
Greystoke Av
ASHBK/HED/RY SR2 120 C4
JES NE2 6 C2
WICK/BNPF NE16 85 F6
Greystoke Gdns
ASHBK/HED/RY SR2 120 C3
JES NE2 6 C1
LWF/SPW/WRK NE9 101 H3
WICK/BNPF NE16 85 F7
Greystoke Pk GOS/KPK NE3 56 B2
Greystoke Wk WICK/BNPF NE16 85 F6
Grey St CNUT NE1 5 K6
DIN/WO NE13 46 A3
HLS DH4 132 B6

TYNE/NSHE NE30 61 F4
WLSD/HOW NE28 72 E1
Greywood Av ELS/FEN NE4 69 J4
Grieves' Rw CRAM NE23 47 G1
Grieve St BLYTH NE24 31 F5
Grimsby St BLYTH NE24 35 G1
Grindon Av MLFD/PNYW SR4 119 F1
Grindon Cl CRAM NE23 38 B5
MONK NE25 50 C7
Grindon Ct MLFD/PNYW SR4 119 G3
Grindon Gdns
MLFD/PNYW SR4 119 G3
Grindon La MLFD/PNYW SR4 119 F1
SUNDSW SR3 119 H3
Grindon Pk MLFD/PNYW SR4 119 G3
Grindon Ter MLFD/PNYW SR4 120 A1
Grinstead Cl HAR/WTLS NE34 75 K4
Grinstead Wy DHAM DH1 158 A4
Grisedale Gdns
LWF/SPW/WRK NE9 101 G1
Grisedale Rd PLEE/EAS SR8 175 F4
Grizedale WASHN NE37 102 D7
Grizedale Ct
CLDN/WHIT/ROK SR6 92 C6
Groat Market CNUT NE1 5 K7
Grosvenor Av JES NE2 71 F2
WICK/BNPF NE16 85 F4
Grosvenor Cl CRAM NE23 38 B5
Grosvenor Ct
WD/WHPE/BLK NE5 54 B7
Grosvenor Crs HEBB NE31 89 H1
Grosvenor Dr
CLDN/WHIT/ROK SR6 91 J3
HAR/WTLS NE34 75 K3
MONK NE25 50 E5
Grosvenor Gdns
HAR/WTLS NE34 75 K5
JES NE2 71 G3
WLSD/HOW NE28 59 J7
Grosvenor Pl JES NE2 71 F2
NSHW NE29 60 E4
Grosvenor Rd HAR/WTLS NE34 75 J3
JES NE2 71 F2
Grosvenor St SWCK/CAS SR5 105 K3
Grosvenor Wy
WD/WHPE/BLK NE5 68 B1
Grotto Gdns HAR/WTLS NE34 76 D4
Grotto Rd HAR/WTLS NE34 76 D5
Grousemoor Dr ASHGTN NE63 23 J3
Grove Av GOS/KPK NE3 56 C6
Grove Ct RDHAMSE DH6 173 H5
RDHAMSE DH6 179 F6
Grove Rd BDN/LAN/SAC DH7 167 G7
BW/LEM/TK/HW NE15 67 H2
LWF/SPW/WRK NE9 87 G6
Grove St DHAM DH1 16 B6
Grove Ter BDN/LAN/SAC DH7 167 K4
The Grove ASHBK/HED/RY SR2 14 D9
ASHBK/HED/RY SR2 121 F7
BDN/LAN/SAC DH7 141 G4
DHAM DH1 156 B6
GOS/KPK NE3 56 D6
HLH DH5 147 H2
JES NE2 71 F1
JRW NE32 89 K3
LGB/KIL NE12 57 K4
MONK NE25 50 D5
PLEE/EAS SR8 162 B5
PONT/DH NE20 43 F4
ROWG NE39 97 H4
SWCK/CAS SR5 105 F4
TYNE/NSHE (off Front St) NE30 61 J3
WD/WHPE/BLK NE5 68 B2
WICK/BNPF NE16 85 G6
Guardians Ct PONT/DH NE20 43 H2
Guelder Rd LGB/HTN NE7 57 J7
Guernsey Rd MLFD/PNYW SR4 119 F4
Guernsey Sq MLFD/PNYW SR4 119 F4
Guessburn PSHWF NE43 79 F6
Guildford Pl BYK/HTN/WLK NE6 6 F3
Guildford St
ASHBK/HED/RY SR2 15 H9
Guilford Sq MPTH NE61 18 C1
Guillemot Cl BLYTH NE24 35 G2
Guisborough Dr NSHW NE29 59 K2
Guisborough St
MLFD/PNYW SR4 119 K1
Gullane WASHN NE37 103 F2
Gullane Cl FELL NE10 88 E2
STLY/ANP DH9 127 F1
Gully Rd WNGT TS28 183 K3
Gunnerston Gv GOS/KPK NE3 55 H5
Gunnerton Cl CRAM NE23 38 C4
Gunnerton Pl NSHW NE29 60 B4
Gunn St DUN/TMV NE11 9 G8
Gut Rd WLSD/HOW NE28 73 H1
Guyzance Av GOS/KPK NE3 56 A4

H

Habgood Dr DHAM DH1 17 M4
Hackworth Gdns WYLAM NE41 65 H5
Hackworth Rd PLEE/EAS SR8 174 A1
Hackworth Wy NSHW NE29 2 B6
Haddington Rd MONK NE25 50 A2
Haddon Cl MONK NE25 49 K4
Haddon Gn MONK NE25 49 K4
Haddricksmill Rd GOS/KPK NE3 56 E6
Hadleigh Rd MLFD/PNYW SR4 119 H1
Hadrian Av CLS/BIR/GTL DH3 129 K2
Hadrian Ct
LGB/KIL
(off Garth Thirtythree) NE12 47 K6
PONT/DH NE20 52 D1
Hadrian Gdns BLAY NE21 84 B3
Hadrian Pl
BW/LEM/TK/HW NE15 67 F1
LWF/SPW/WRK NE9 87 H5
Hadrian Rd BLYTH NE24 34 E4
ELS/FEN NE4 69 J5
JRW NE32 74 B7
WLSD/HOW NE28 72 E2
Hadrians Ct DUN/TMV NE11 100 D1
Hadrian St MLFD/PNYW SR4 106 A6
Hadrians Wy CON/LDGT DH8 108 E3
Hadstone Pl
WD/WHPE/BLK NE5 69 G2
Haggerston Cl
WD/WHPE/BLK NE5 55 F6
Haggerston Ct
WD/WHPE/BLK NE5 55 F6
Haggerston Crs
WD/WHPE/BLK NE5 55 F6
Haggerstone Dr
SWCK/CAS SR5 104 E5
Haggerston Ter JRW NE32 74 C7
Haggie Av WLSD/HOW NE28 59 F7
Haig Av MONK NE25 50 D5
Haig Crs BW/LEM/TK/HW NE15 68 E6
DHAM DH1 17 M5
Haigh Ter DHAM DH1 17 M5
Haig Rd BDLGTN NE22 29 H6
Haig St DUN/TMV NE11 9 H7
Hailsham Av LGB/KIL NE12 57 J3
Haininghead WASHS NE38 117 G4
Haininngwood Ter FELL NE10 13 L4
Haldane Ct JES * NE2 70 E3
Haldane St ASHGTN NE63 23 J1
Haldane Ter JES NE2 70 E3
Haldon Pl PLEE/EAS SR8 174 C5
Hale Ri PLEE/EAS SR8 174 E4
Halewood Av GOS/KPK NE3 55 J6
Half Fields Rd BLAY NE21 83 K3
Half Moon La GATE NE8 10 F1
Half Moon St STKFD/GP NE62 23 H5
Halfway House La
ASHBK/HED/RY SR2 121 G3
Halidon Rd
ASHBK/HED/RY SR2 120 D5
Halidon Sq
ASHBK/HED/RY SR2 120 D5
Halifax Rd DUN/TMV NE11 8 E5
Halkirk Wy CRAM NE23 33 G6
Hallam Rd PLEE/EAS SR8 174 E3
Hall Av BDN/LAN/SAC DH7 154 E7
Hall Cl HLS DH4 146 D6
SEA/MUR SR7 134 D7
Hall Dene Wy SEA/MUR SR7 134 E5
Hall Dr LGB/KIL NE12 47 J4
LGB/KIL NE12 47 H4
Halleypike Cl LGB/HTN NE7 57 K7
Hall Farm DHAM DH1 169 G4
Hall Farm Cl PSHWF NE43 79 F5
Hall Farm Rd SUNDSW SR3 133 K2
Hallfield Cl SUNDSW SR3 134 A2
Hallfield Dr PLEE/EAS SR8 162 B6
Hall Gdns BOL NE36 90 E5
FELL NE10 87 K5
Hallgarth CON/LDGT DH8 122 C6
Hallgarth La RDHAMSE DH6 158 E5
Hallgarth Rd BLAY NE21 83 K2
Hallgarth St DHAM DH1 16 F6
RDHAMSE DH6 158 C7
The Hallgarth DHAM DH1 16 F6
Hallgarth Vw DHAM DH1 16 F6
Hallgarth Vls RDHAMSE DH6 170 D1
Hall Gn BLYTH NE24 30 D7
Halling Cl BYK/HTN/WLK NE6 72 C7
Hallington Dr MONK NE25 40 A5
Halliwell St HLS DH4 132 B6
Hall La DHAM DH1 169 G5
HLH DH5 147 H1
HLS DH4 146 D6
RDHAMSE DH6 160 E6
Hallow Dr
BW/LEM/TK/HW NE15 67 F2
Hall Pk BLAY NE21 67 J7
Hall Rd BDN/LAN/SAC DH7 153 J5
CHPW NE17 95 J3
CON/LDGT DH8 122 C6
HEBB NE31 73 G6
WASHN NE37 103 G5
Hallside Rd BLYTH NE24 34 D1
Hall Ter FELL NE10 13 M4
Hall Vw CLDN/WHIT/ROK SR6 93 F4
Hall Wks PLEE/EAS SR8 162 B6
Hallwood Cl BDLGTN NE22 28 A6
Halstead Pl SSH NE33 75 H2
Halstead Sq MLFD/PNYW SR4 119 H1
Halterburn Cl GOS/KPK NE3 56 B6
Halton Cl PSHWF NE43 79 G6
Halton Dr WLSD/HOW NE28 58 B7
Halton Rd DHAM DH1 156 E4
Hamar Cl NSHW NE29 60 A6
Hambard Wy WASHS NE38 117 F2
Hambledon Av
TYNE/NSHE NE30 50 E6
Hambledon Cl BOLCOL NE35 90 B4
Hambledon Gdns LGB/HTN NE7 57 G7
Hambledon Pl PLEE/EAS SR8 174 B5
Hambledon St BLYTH NE24 31 F6
Hambleton Ct ASHGTN NE63 24 B4
Hambleton Dr SEA/MUR SR7 135 H7
Hambleton Rd WASHS NE38 116 D3
Hamilton Ct GATE NE8 11 J7
RDHAMSE DH6 173 H4
Hamilton Crs ELS/FEN NE4 4 E5
NSHW NE29 60 A2
Hamilton Dr WBAY NE26 50 D1
Hamilton Pl ELS/FEN NE4 4 E5
Hamilton Rw
BDN/LAN/SAC DH7 164 E4
Hamilton St PLEE/EAS SR8 175 G3
Hamilton Ter
BDN/LAN/SAC DH7 143 G2
BOL NE36 90 E5
Hammer Square Bank
STLY/ANP DH9 113 K5
Hampden Rd
CLDN/WHIT/ROK SR6 106 E3
Hampden St SSH NE33 75 G3
Hampshire Ct ELS/FEN NE4 9 K2
Hampshire Pl WASHN NE37 103 F4
Hampshire Rd DHAM DH1 157 K6
Hampshire Wy
HAR/WTLS * NE34 76 C4
Hampstead Cl BLYTH NE24 34 E4
Hampstead Rd ELS/FEN NE4 69 J6
MLFD/PNYW SR4 119 H2
Hampstead Sq
MLFD/PNYW SR4 119 G2
Hampton Cl CRAM NE23 38 E1
Hampton Ct CLS/BIR/GTL DH3 115 K7
WICK/BNPF
(off Coalway La North) NE16 85 F3
Hampton Dr FELL NE10 12 A7
Hampton Rd TYNE/NSHE NE30 50 E7
Hamsteels Bank
BDN/LAN/SAC DH7 152 D3
Hamsteels La
BDN/LAN/SAC DH7 153 G4
Hamsterley Cl
CLS/BIR/GTL DH3 145 J1
Hamsterley Ct SUNDSW * SR3 134 A1
Hamsterley Crs
BW/LEM/TK/HW NE15 67 K4
DHAM DH1 156 E3
LWF/SPW/WRK NE9 101 J2
Hamsterley Dr LGB/KIL NE12 47 J5
Hamsterley Gdns
STLY/ANP DH9 125 H3
Hanby Gdns SUNDSW SR3 120 A3
Hancock St CNUT NE1 5 K3
Handel St MLFD/PNYW SR4 106 A6
SSH NE33 3 K9
Handley Cross CON/LDGT DH8 109 J5
Handley St PLEE/EAS SR8 175 G3
Handy Dr DUN/TMV NE11 8 D4
Hangingstone La
STLY/ANP DH9 124 E5
Hangmans La HLH DH5 133 J4
Hanlon Ct JRW NE32 73 H4
Hannington St
BYK/HTN/WLK NE6 6 C5
Hanover Ct CRAM NE23 38 C7
DHAM DH1 16 B4
Hanover Dr BLAY NE21 83 J3
Hanover Pl CRAM NE23 33 G6
MLFD/PNYW SR4 14 B1
Hanover Sq CNUT NE1 5 K9
Harbottle Av GOS/KPK NE3 56 A4
SMOOR NE27 49 H7
Harbottle Ct BYK/HTN/WLK NE6 7 H8
Harbottle Crs JRW NE32 89 K2
Harbour Dr SSH NE33 3 K3
The Harbour HLS DH4 131 K1
Harbour Vw
CLDN/WHIT/ROK SR6 107 F4
SSH NE33 3 H3
Harbour Wk SEA/MUR SR7 135 J7
Harcourt Rd
ASHBK/HED/RY SR2 120 D5
Harcourt St
LWF/SPW/WRK * NE9 87 G7
Hardgate Rd
ASHBK/HED/RY SR2 120 E5
Hardie Av WICK/BNPF NE16 84 E4
Hardie Dr BOL NE36 90 E5
Hardwick Ct GATE NE8 11 K5
Hardwick Pl GOS/KPK NE3 56 A7
Hardwick Ri
CLDN/WHIT/ROK SR6 15 H1
Hardwick St PLEE/EAS SR8 175 H4
RHTLP TS27 175 K7
Hardyards Ct HAR/WTLS NE34 75 G6
Hardy Av HAR/WTLS NE34 91 F1
Hardy Ct TYNE/NSHE NE30 2 F1
Hardy Gv WLSD/HOW NE28 58 C5
Hardy Sq SWCK/CAS SR5 106 A2
Hardy St SEA/MUR SR7 150 E1
Harebell Rd
LWF/SPW/WRK NE9 101 J1
Harehills Av WD/WHPE/BLK NE5 55 H7
Harelaw Dr ASHGTN NE63 23 H4
Harelaw Gdns STLY/ANP DH9 125 F1
Harelaw Gv WD/WHPE/BLK NE5 68 B2
Hareside CRAM NE23 38 B3
Harewood Cl WICK/BNPF NE16 98 E1
Harewood Crs MONK NE25 49 K5
Harewood Dr BDLGTN NE22 29 J4
Harewood Gdns MPTH NE61 21 J1
SUNDSW SR3 120 A3
Harewood Rd GOS/KPK NE3 56 C4
Hareydene WD/WHPE/BLK NE5 54 D5
Hargill Dr WASHS NE38 116 C5
Hargrave Ct BLYTH NE24 34 E1
Harland Wy WASHS NE38 117 F1
Harle Cl WD/WHPE/BLK NE5 68 C2
Harlequin Ldg FELL * NE10 12 C8
Harle Rd SMOOR NE27 49 F5
Harleston Wy FELL NE10 88 A6
Harle St WLSD/HOW NE28 72 D1
Harley Ter GOS/KPK NE3 56 D5
Harlow Av GOS/KPK NE3 55 K3
SMOOR NE27 49 F6
Harlow Green La
LWF/SPW/WRK NE9 101 G3
Harlow Pl LGB/HTN NE7 57 H7
Harlow St MLFD/PNYW SR4 14 A5
Harnham Av NSHW NE29 60 A5
Harnham Gdns
WD/WHPE/BLK NE5 69 G3
Harnham Gv CRAM NE23 38 B3
Harold Sq ASHBK/HED/RY SR2 15 G8
Harold St JRW NE32 74 A4
Harold Wilson Dr RHTLP TS27 185 G2
Harper Bglws RDHAMSE DH6 182 D2
Harperley Dr SUNDSW SR3 120 B4
Harperley Gdns STLY/ANP DH9 125 G2
Harperley La STLY/ANP DH9 111 K7
Harperley Rd STLY/ANP DH9 125 H2
Harper St BLYTH NE24 31 F7
Harras Bank CLS/BIR/GTL DH3 115 J3
Harraton Ter
CLS/BIR/GTL
(off Durham Rd) DH3 115 J3
Harriet Pl BYK/HTN/WLK * NE6 7 H5
Harriet St BLAY NE21 84 A2
BYK/HTN/WLK NE6 7 J5
Harrington Gdns
STKFD/GP * NE62 23 J5
Harrington St WLSD/HOW NE28 72 D1
Harriot Dr LGB/KIL NE12 47 G7
Harrison Cl PLEE/EAS SR8 175 F5
Harrison Gdns GATE NE8 86 D5
Harrison Garth RDHAMSE DH6 158 C7
Harrison Pl JES NE2 5 M3
Harrison Rd WLSD/HOW NE28 59 J7
Harrogate St
ASHBK/HED/RY SR2 15 G7
Harrogate Ter SEA/MUR SR7 149 H5
Harrow Gdns DIN/WO NE13 46 C4
Harrow Sq MLFD/PNYW SR4 119 H1
Hartburn FELL NE10 88 C7
Hartburn Dr
WD/WHPE/BLK NE5 54 B7
Hartburn Pl ELS/FEN NE4 4 A2
Hartburn Rd TYNE/NSHE NE30 60 D1
Hartburn Wk GOS/KPK NE3 55 H5
Hartford Bank CRAM NE23 32 C3
Hartford Br BDLGTN NE22 32 C3
Hartford Ct BDLGTN NE22 28 E6
Hartford Crs ASHGTN NE63 23 K3
BDLGTN NE22 28 E6
Hartford Dr BDLGTN NE22 32 C2
Hartford Rd BDLGTN NE22 32 D1
GOS/KPK NE3 56 D3
HAR/WTLS NE34 74 E6
MLFD/PNYW SR4 119 H1
Hartforth Crs FELL NE10 13 M4
Harthope Av SWCK/CAS SR5 105 G2
Harthope Cl WASHS NE38 116 B6
Harthope Dr NSHW NE29 60 C7
Hartington Rd
TYNE/NSHE NE30 60 E1
Hartington St
CLDN/WHIT/ROK SR6 106 E3
CON/LDGT DH8 123 F4
ELS/FEN NE4 4 C7
GATE NE8 11 G6
Hartington Ter SSH NE33 75 H3
Hartland Dr CLS/BIR/GTL DH3 115 K4
Hartlands BDLGTN NE22 28 E6
Hartleigh Pl BLYTH NE24 30 D7
Hartlepool Av PLEE/EAS SR8 175 G2
Hartlepool St RDHAMSE DH6 172 C6
Hartley Av WBAY NE26 50 C4
Hartleyburn Av HEBB NE31 89 F1
Hartley La MONK NE25 49 K3
Hartley St MONK NE25 39 K5
SUND SR1 15 J3
Hartley Ter BLYTH NE24 34 E3
Hartoft Cl HLS DH4 132 B3
Harton Gv HAR/WTLS NE34 75 J4
Harton House Rd
HAR/WTLS NE34 75 K4
Harton House Rd East
HAR/WTLS NE34 76 A4
Harton La HAR/WTLS NE34 75 G6
Harton Ri HAR/WTLS NE34 75 K4
Hartside BW/LEM/TK/HW NE15 68 A4
CLS/BIR/GTL DH3 115 K5
Hartside Crs BLAY NE21 83 H4
CRAM NE23 33 G5
SMOOR NE27 49 F5
Hartside Gdns HLH DH5 148 B7
JES NE2 71 F2
Hartside Pl GOS/KPK NE3 56 C1
Hartside Vw
BDN/LAN/SAC DH7 155 F5
DHAM DH1 156 B2
Hart Sq MLFD/PNYW SR4 119 H1
Hart Ter CLDN/WHIT/ROK SR6 93 F6
Harvard Rd GOS/KPK NE3 55 J5
Harvest Cl SUNDSW SR3 133 K2
Harvey Cl ASHGTN NE63 24 C2
PLEE/EAS SR8 174 E3
WASHS NE38 116 B1
Harvey Combe LGB/KIL NE12 47 H6
Harvey Crs FELL NE10 13 M8
Harwick Ct STLY/ANP DH9 127 G1
Harwood Cl CRAM NE23 38 B3
WASHS NE38 116 C5
Harwood Ct TRIM TS29 182 D7
Harwood Dr LGB/KIL NE12 48 B6
Hascombe Cl MONK NE25 50 B3
Haslemere Dr SUNDSW SR3 120 A3
Hassop Wy BDLGTN NE22 29 F4
Hastings Av DHAM DH1 168 B3
GOS/KPK NE3 55 H3
LGB/KIL NE12 57 K3
WBAY NE26 40 E1
WBAY NE26 50 C1
Hastings Ct BDLGTN NE22 29 J4
Hastings Dr TYNE/NSHE NE30 61 G2
Hastings Gdns MONK NE25 40 A2
Hastings St
ASHBK/HED/RY SR2 120 E2
CRAM NE23 38 D3
Hastings Ter
ASHBK/HED/RY SR2 121 F3
CRAM NE23 33 K5
MONK NE25 40 A1
Haswell Cl FELL NE10 89 F5
Haswell Gdns TYNE/NSHE NE30 60 E4
Hatfield Av HEBB NE31 73 H5
Hatfield Cl DHAM DH1 156 B3
Hatfield Dr CRAM NE23 39 G6
Hatfield Gdns MONK NE25 49 K5
SUNDSW SR3 120 A3
Hatfield Pl PLEE/EAS SR8 175 F5
Hatfield Sq SSH NE33 3 K7
Hathaway Gdns SUNDSW SR3 120 A3
Hatherton Av TYNE/NSHE NE30 51 F6
Hathery La BLYTH NE24 33 K4
Haugh La RYTON NE40 67 G5
The Haughs PRUD NE42 80 D1
Haughton Crs JRW NE32 89 K2
WD/WHPE/BLK NE5 68 C2
Haughton Ter BLYTH NE24 31 G7
Hautmont Rd HEBB NE31 73 H7
Hauxley LGB/KIL NE12 47 K4
Hauxley Dr CLSW/PEL DH2 129 F7
CRAM NE23 33 G5
GOS/KPK NE3 55 J3
Hauxley Gdns
WD/WHPE/BLK NE5 69 H1
Havanna LGB/KIL NE12 47 K4
Havannah Crs DIN/WO NE13 45 F3
Havannah Rd WASHN NE37 102 D6
Havant Gdns DIN/WO NE13 46 B2
Havelock Cl GATE NE8 10 E3
Havelock Crs BDLGTN NE22 30 B3
Havelock Ms BDLGTN NE22 30 B2
Havelock Pl ELS/FEN NE4 4 E7
Havelock Rd SMOOR NE27 49 F6
Havelock St SSH NE33 75 G2
SUND SR1 15 H3
Havelock Ter
ASHBK/HED/RY SR2 14 B7
GATE NE8 10 E4
JRW NE32 73 K6
Haven Ct BLYTH NE24 34 E1
DHAM DH1 156 D1
The Haven BDN/LAN/SAC DH7 141 G4
CON/LDGT DH8 123 J3
HLS DH4 131 K1
NSHW NE29 2 C7
PRUD NE42 80 D2
Havercroft FELL NE10 88 D5
Haverley Dr SEA/MUR SR7 134 E7
Haversham Pk SWCK/CAS SR5 92 C7
Haversham Rd LGB/HTN NE7 57 G5
Hawarden Crs
MLFD/PNYW SR4 120 A1
Hawes Av CLSW/PEL DH2 129 J6
Hawes Ct CLDN/WHIT/ROK SR6 92 C7
Hawes Rd PLEE/EAS SR8 174 E3
Haweswater Cl HAR/WTLS NE34 75 H5
Haweswater Crs NWBGN NE64 24 E1
Hawick Ct STLY/ANP DH9 127 F1
Hawick Crs BYK/HTN/WLK NE6 6 F8
Hawkey's La NSHW NE29 2 B1
Hawkhill Cl CLSW/PEL DH2 129 G7
Hawkhurst WASHS NE38 117 G4
Hawkins Ct SUNDSW SR3 133 K1
Hawksbury WICK/BNPF NE16 84 E5
Hawkshead Ct DIN/WO NE13 55 H3
Hawkshead Pl
LWF/SPW/WRK NE9 87 H7
Hawksley WD/WHPE/BLK NE5 68 D1
Hawksmoor Cl ASHGTN NE63 23 J4
Hawks Rd GATE NE8 6 A9
Hawks St GATE NE8 6 D9
Hawkwell Ri
BW/LEM/TK/HW NE15 67 F2
Hawsker Cl SUNDSW SR3 120 C7
Hawthorn Av DIN/WO NE13 46 A4
SUNDSW SR3 120 B6
Hawthorn Cl CLSW/PEL DH2 144 A5
WICK/BNPF NE16 85 F7
Hawthorn Cottages
RDHAMSE DH6 161 G2
Hawthorn Crs DHAM DH1 17 M1
Hawthorn Dr DUN/TMV NE11 9 G8
JRW NE32 90 B2
Hawthorne Av HAR/WTLS NE34 75 K7
HEBB NE31 73 H5
Hawthorne Cl
BDN/LAN/SAC DH7 154 A3
SEA/MUR SR7 149 J6
Hawthorne Rd BLYTH NE24 35 H1
Hawthorne Ter
BDN/LAN/SAC DH7 154 B2
RDHAMSE DH6 173 H4
Hawthorn Gdns FELL NE10 12 C5
GOS/KPK NE3 55 K6
NSHW NE29 60 D3
WBAY NE26 50 D4
Hawthorn Ms
ASHGTN
(off Hawthorn Rd) NE63 24 A3
Hawthorn Pk
BDN/LAN/SAC DH7 167 G6
Hawthorn Pl ELS/FEN NE4 9 K1
LGB/KIL* NE12 47 J5
Hawthorn Rd ASHGTN NE63 23 K1
BLAY NE21 84 A2
DHAM DH1 158 A4
GOS/KPK NE3 56 C6
Hawthorn Rd West
GOS/KPK NE3 56 C6
The Hawthorns BOL NE36 91 H5
ELS/FEN (off Park Rd) NE4 9 K1
STLY/ANP DH9 125 H2
Hawthorn St CON/LDGT DH8 122 D3
JRW NE32 73 J4
MLFD/PNYW SR4 106 A7
PLEE/EAS SR8 162 E4
Hawthorn Ter
CLDN/WHIT/ROK SR6 92 E6
CON/LDGT DH8 122 D3
DHAM DH1 16 A4
ELS/FEN NE4 4 D8
WD/WHPE/BLK NE5 67 J1
Hawthorn Vls CRAM NE23 38 D2
Hawthorn Wk ELS/FEN NE4 4 E9
Hawthorn Wy PONT/DH NE20 43 F6
Haydock Dr FELL NE10 88 D5
Haydon WASHS NE38 117 G5
Haydon Pl WD/WHPE/BLK NE5 68 E3
Haydon Rd ASHGTN NE63 23 K3
Haydon Sq MLFD/PNYW SR4 119 H1
Hayes Wk DIN/WO NE13 46 B3
Hayfield La WICK/BNPF NE16 85 F6
Hayhole Rd NSHW NE29 74 C1
Hayleazes Rd
BW/LEM/TK/HW NE15 68 D4
Haymarket CNUT NE1 5 K5
The Hayricks STLY/ANP DH9 112 B2
Hay St SWCK/CAS SR5 14 D1
Hayton Av HAR/WTLS NE34 76 A6
Hayton Cl CRAM NE23 38 D1
Hayton Rd TYNE/NSHE NE30 60 D1
Hazard La HLH DH5 147 H5
Hazel Av BDN/LAN/SAC DH7 167 F7
NSHW NE29 60 D3
RDHAMSE DH6 181 G4
SUNDSW SR3 120 B6
Hazeldene MONK NE25 50 B4
Hazeldene Av GOS/KPK NE3 55 G6
Hazeldene Ct TYNE/NSHE NE30 61 G3
Hazel Dr RHTLP TS27 185 G2
Hazeley Gv GOS/KPK NE3 55 H5
Hazeley Wy GOS/KPK NE3 55 H5
Hazel Gv CLSW/PEL DH2 129 G2
Hazelgrove FELL NE10 88 D5
Hazel Gv HAR/WTLS NE34 75 K7
LGB/KIL NE12 47 H7
Hazel Leigh CLS/BIR/GTL DH3 145 H1
Hazelmere Av BDLGTN NE22 28 E5
Hazelmere Crs CRAM NE23 33 J7
Hazelmere Dene CRAM NE23 39 F7
Hazelmoor HEBB NE31 73 F4
Hazel Rd BLAY NE21 84 B2
GATE NE8 10 A7

Hazel St *JRW* NE32......73 J4
Hazel Ter *RDHAMSE* DH6......173 H4
STLY/ANP DH9......127 F4
Hazelwood Av *JES* NE4......70 E1
NWBGN NE64......19 F7
SWCK/CAS SR5......105 K3
Hazelwood Cl
LWF/SPW/WRK NE9......101 K3
Hazelwood Rd
BDN/LAN/SAC DH7......154 B3
Hazelwood Ter
WLSD/HOW NE28......73 J1
Hazledene Ter
MLFD/PNYW SR4......105 K7
Hazlitt Av *HAR/WTLS* NE34......91 F1
Hazlitt Pl *CRAM* NE23......39 G7
Headlam Gn *BYK/HTN/WLK* NE6......7 H6
Headlam St *BYK/HTN/WLK* NE6......7 G5
Headlam Vw *WLSD/HOW* NE28......73 J1
Healey Dr *SUNDSW* SR3......120 B4
Healeyfield La *CON/LDGT* DH8......136 A5
Heartsbourne Dr
HAR/WTLS NE34......91 K1
Heath Cl *DUN/TMV* NE11......9 M9
PLEE/EAS SR8......175 F5
Heath Crs
BW/LEM/TK/HW NE15......68 C7
Heathdale Gdns *LGB/HTN* NE7......57 H7
Heather Cl *CLDN/WHIT/ROK* SR6......92 A2
Heatherdale Crs *DHAM* DH1......158 A6
Heather Dr *HLH* DH5......147 K3
Heather Gv *FELL* NE10......11 L3
Heather Lea *STLY/ANP* DH9......111 G4
Heatherlea Gdns *SUNDSW* SR3......120 B3
Heather Lea La *PRUD* NE42......80 D1
Heatherlee Gdns
STKFD/GP NE62......23 C5
Heather Pl *ELS/FEN* NE4......69 J3
RYTON NE40......66 C7
Heatherslaw Rd
WD/WHPE/BLK NE5......69 G3
Heather Wy *STLY/ANP* DH9......126 B1
Heatherwell Gn *FELL* NE10......12 A9
Heathery La *GOS/KPK* NE3......56 E3
Heathfield *ASHBK/HED/RY* SR2......120 C1
MPTH NE61......20 E7
Heathfield Crs
WD/WHPE/BLK NE5......55 H7
Heathfield Gdns *RYTON* NE40......82 C3
STLY/ANP DH9......125 G2
Heathfield Pl *GOS/KPK* NE3......56 D1
Heathfield Rd
LWF/SPW/WRK NE9......87 F6
Heath Gra *HLH* DH5......132 C6
Heathmeads *CLSW/PEL* DH2......128 C1
Heath Sq *MLFD/PNYW* SR4......119 J1
Heathway *JRW* NE32......90 A2
SEA/MUR SR7......150 D3
Heathways *DHAM* DH1......169 J5
Heathwell Gdns
WICK/BNPF NE16......85 F4
Heathwell Rd
BW/LEM/TK/HW NE15......68 D4
Heathwood Av
WICK/BNPF NE16......84 E5
Heaton Cl *BYK/HTN/WLK* NE6......6 E2
Heaton Gdns *HAR/WTLS* NE34......91 G2
Heaton Gv *BYK/HTN/WLK* NE6......6 E3
Heaton Hall Rd
BYK/HTN/WLK NE6......6 E2
Heaton Park Ct
BYK/HTN/WLK NE6......6 E3
Heaton Park Rd
BYK/HTN/WLK NE6......6 E3
Heaton Park Vw
BYK/HTN/WLK NE6......6 E2
Heaton Pl *BYK/HTN/WLK* NE6......6 F3
Heaton Rd *BYK/HTN/WLK* NE6......6 F2
Heaton Ter *BYK/HTN/WLK* NE6......6 D4
NSHW NE29......60 C4
Heaton Wk *BYK/HTN/WLK* NE6......6 F4
Heaviside Pl *DHAM* DH1......17 J2
Heber St *ELS/FEN* NE4......5 C6
Hebron Av *MPTH* NE61......21 J1
Hebron Pl *ASHGTN* NE63......24 A2
Hebron Wy *CRAM* NE23......38 B5
Hector St *SMOOR* NE27......49 H5
Heddon Banks
BW/LEM/TK/HW NE15......66 A2
Heddon Cl *GOS/KPK* NE3......56 A4
Heddon Vw *BLAY* NE21......83 K2
Heddon Wy *HAR/WTLS* NE34......75 F5
Hedgefield Ct
BLAY (off Stella Rd) NE21......67 H6
Hedgefield Rd *BLYTH* NE24......34 E4
Hedgefield Vw *CRAM* NE23......38 B7
Hedgehope Rd
WD/WHPE/BLK NE5......54 E6
Hedgelea *RYTON* NE40......66 D6
Hedgelea Rd *HLH* DH5......147 F5
Hedgeley Rd *HEBB* NE31......73 C5
NSHW NE29......60 B3
WD/WHPE/BLK NE5......68 C3
Hedgeley Ter
BYK/HTN/WLK NE6......72 B5
Hedgerow Ms *ASHGTN* NE63......23 H3
Hedley Cl *SSH* NE33......3 H5
Hedley Ct *BDN/LAN/SAC* DH7......155 F5
Hedleyhill La
BDN/LAN/SAC DH7......164 A1
Hedley La *WICK/BNPF* NE16......99 G7
Hedley Pl *WLSD/HOW* NE28......72 C1
Hedley Rd *MONK* NE25......40 B6
NSHW NE29......2 B7
WYLAM NE41......65 H5
Hedley St *GATE* NE8......10 C8
GOS/KPK NE3......56 C5
SSH NE33......3 J5
Hedley Ter *ASHBK/HED/RY* SR2......135 C3
GOS/KPK NE3......56 C5
Hedworth Av *HAR/WTLS* NE34......74 D7
Hedworth Ct *SUND* SR1......15 H5
Hedworth La *BOLCOL* NE35......90 B3
JRW NE32......90 B2
Hedworth Ter *SUND* SR1......15 H5
Heighley St
BW/LEM/TK/HW NE15......68 D6

Helen St *BLAY* NE21......83 J2
CLDN/WHIT/ROK SR6......106 E1
Helford Rd *PLEE/EAS* SR8......174 D6
Hellvellyn Ct *STLY/ANP* DH9......125 H4
Helmdon *WASHS* NE37......103 G5
Helmsdale Av *FELL* NE10......12 C6
Helmsdale Rd
MLFD/PNYW SR4......119 H1
Helmsley Cl *HLS* DH4......131 J1
Helmsley Ct *SWCK/CAS* SR5......105 J2
Helmsley Dr *WLSD/HOW* NE28......73 H1
Helmsley Rd *DHAM* DH1......156 D2
JES NE2......6 B3
Helston Ct
BW/LEM/TK/HW NE15......67 K4
Helvellyn Av *WASHS* NE38......116 C4
Helvellyn Rd
ASHBK/HED/RY SR2......120 D4
Hemlington Cl
ASHBK/HED/RY SR2......135 F2
Hemmel Cts
BDN/LAN/SAC DH7......167 H5
Hemming St
ASHBK/HED/RY SR2......121 F4
Hemsley Rd *HAR/WTLS* NE34......75 K2
Henderson Av *RDHAMSE* DH6......182 D1
WICK/BNPF NE16......84 E4
Henderson Gdns *FELL* NE10......13 L9
Henderson Rd *HAR/WTLS* NE34......74 D6
MLFD/PNYW SR4......119 K1
WLSD/HOW NE28......58 D7
Hendersyde Cl
WD/WHPE/BLK NE5......55 F7
Hendon Burn Av
ASHBK/HED/RY SR2......15 H8
Hendon Burn Av West
ASHBK/HED/RY* SR2......15 H9
Hendon Cl *NSHW* NE29......2 D6
SUND SR1......15 H5
Hendon Gdns *JRW* NE32......90 B2
Hendon Rd *LWF/SPW/WRK* NE9......11 L8
SUND SR1......15 H4
Hendon Rd East *SUND* SR1......15 K5
Hendon St *SUND* SR1......15 J6
Hendon Valley Ct
ASHBK/HED/RY SR2......15 H9
Hendon Valley Rd
ASHBK/HED/RY SR2......15 G8
Henley Av *CLSW/PEL* DH2......128 E4
Henley Cl *CRAM* NE23......38 E1
Henley Gdns *WLSD/HOW* NE28......59 K6
Henley Rd *MLFD/PNYW* SR4......119 H1
TYNE/NSHE NE30......61 F1
Henley Sq *MPTH* NE61......18 C1
Henley Wy *BOLCOL* NE35......90 C4
Henlow Rd
BW/LEM/TK/HW NE15......68 A4
Henry Nelson St *SSH* NE33......3 K5
Henry Robson St *SSH* NE33......3 C8
Henry Sq *JES* NE2......6 A5
Henry St *CON/LDGT* * DH8......122 E4
GOS/KPK NE3......56 C5
HLH DH5......132 C6
NSHW NE29......2 C3
SEA/MUR SR7......135 K7
SSH NE33......3 J4
Henry St East
ASHBK/HED/RY SR2......15 J6
Hensby St *HLS* DH4......55 F6
Henshaw Ct *ASHGTN* NE63......23 H3
Henshaw Gv *MONK* NE25......40 C6
Henshaw Pl *WD/WHPE/BLK* NE5......68 E4
Henshelwood Ter *JES* NE2......70 E2
Henson Cl *WASHS* NE38......117 F2
Hepburn Gdns *FELL* NE10......12 A5
Hepburn Gv *SWCK/CAS* SR5......104 D4
Hepple Cl *BLYTH* NE24......34 E1
Hepple Rd *NWBGN* NE64......24 E2
Hepple Wy *GOS/KPK* NE3......56 A4
Hepscott Dr *MONK* NE25......50 B3
Hepscott Ter *HAR/WTLS* NE34......75 H4
Herbert St *CON/LDGT* * DH8......123 F4
GATE NE8......11 K5
Herbert Ter *SEA/MUR* SR7......150 E1
Herd Cl *BLAY* NE21......83 J3
Herd House La *BLAY* NE21......83 H3
Herdinghill *WASHN* NE37......102 B7
Herdlaw *CRAM* NE23......38 B2
Hereford Ct
ASHBK/HED/RY SR2......120 D5
DIN/WO NE13......55 H2
Hereford Rd
ASHBK/HED/RY SR2......120 D5
Herefordshire Dr *DHAM* DH1......157 K6
Hereford Sq
ASHBK/HED/RY SR2......120 D5
Hermiston *MONK* NE25......50 C4
Hermitage Gdns
CLSW/PEL DH2......129 H6
Heron Cl *ASHGTN* NE63......24 A4
BLYTH NE24......35 G4
WASHS NE38......116 C4
Heron Dr *SSH* NE33......3 C5
Heron Pl *LGB/KIL* NE12......57 G3
Herrick St *WD/WHPE/BLK* NE5......54 E7
Herring Gull Cl *BLYTH* NE24......35 G4
Herrington Rd *HLS* DH4......132 D1
SUNDSW SR3......119 F7
Hersham Cl *DIN/WO* NE13......55 G2
GOS/KPK NE3......55 F3
Hertford *LWF/SPW/WRK* NE9......101 K3
Hertford Av *HAR/WTLS* NE34......76 B4
Hertford Cl *MONK* NE25......50 A3
Hertford Crs *HLS* DH4......147 J4
Hertford Gv *CRAM* NE23......38 D1
Herton Cl *PLEE/EAS* SR8......174 D3
Hesket Ct *GOS/KPK* NE3......55 J3
Hesleden Rd *RHTLP* TS27......175 K7
Hesledon Wk *SEA/MUR* SR7......149 K4
Hesleyside *ASHGTN* NE63......24 B3
Hesleyside Dr
WD/WHPE/BLK NE5......69 F3
Hesleyside Rd *MONK* NE25......49 K4
Hessewelle Crs *RDHAMSE* DH6......172 C1
Hester Av *MONK* NE25......40 A2
Hett La *RDHAMSE* DH6......178 D3
Hetton Rd *HLH* DH5......147 H1
Heugh Hl *LWF/SPW/WRK* NE9......102 C5

Hewitson Ter *FELL* NE10......12 B9
Hewitt Av *ASHBK/HED/RY* SR2......120 E6
Hewley Crs
BW/LEM/TK/HW NE15......67 F2
Heworth Burn Crs *FELL* NE10......12 F7
Heworth Dene Gdns
FELL * NE10......12 F6
Heworth Gv *WASHN* NE37......102 E5
Heworth Rd *WASHN* NE37......103 F3
Heworth Wy *FELL* NE10......13 J7
Hewson Pl *LWF/SPW/WRK* NE9......87 H6
Hexham *WASHS* NE38......116 B2
Hexham Av *BYK/HTN/WLK* NE6......72 B6
CRAM NE23......38 E1
HEBB NE31......89 C2
SEA/MUR SR7......150 B2
Hexham Cl *NSHW* NE29......60 A3
Hexham Ct *HAR/WTLS* NE34......85 K6
Hexham Dr *STLY/ANP* DH9......125 H2
Hexham Old Rd *RYTON* NE40......66 E6
Hexham Rd *BLAY* NE21......84 D3
BW/LEM/TK/HW NE15......65 J1
MLFD/PNYW SR4......119 H1
WICK/BNPF NE16......84 E3
Hextol Gdns
BW/LEM/TK/HW NE15......68 D4
Heybrook Av *NSHW* NE29......60 D2
Heyburn Gdns
BW/LEM/TK/HW NE15......69 H6
Hibernian Rd *JRW* NE32......73 K4
Hibernia Rd *BYK/HTN/WLK* NE6......72 C7
Hickling Ct *WD/WHPE/BLK* NE5......55 F6
Hickstead Cl *WLSD/HOW* NE28......59 G3
Hickstead Gv *CRAM* NE23......38 E1
Hiddleston Av *LGB/HTN* NE7......57 H5
Higham Pl *CNUT* NE1......5 L5
High Back Cl *JRW* NE32......73 J7
High Barnes Ter
MLFD/PNYW SR4......120 A1
High Br *CNUT* NE1......5 K7
Highbury *FELL* NE10......12 E8
JES NE2......70 D1
MONK NE25......50 C4
Highbury Av
LWF/SPW/WRK NE9......102 C3
Highbury Cl
LWF/SPW/WRK NE9......102 C3
High Carr Cl *DHAM* DH1......156 C4
High Chare *CLS/BIR/GTL* DH3......129 J4
Highcliffe Gdns *GATE* NE8......11 K7
High Cl *PRUD* NE42......81 F1
High Cft *CLDN/WHIT/ROK* SR6......93 F3
WASHN NE37......102 C4
High Croft Cl *HEBB* NE31......73 F7
Highcroft Dr
CLDN/WHIT/ROK SR6......92 E3
Highcross Rd *TYNE/NSHE* NE30......50 E6
High Dene *LGB/HTN* NE7......71 G2
Highfield *BDN/LAN/SAC* DH7......143 H5
PRUD NE42......80 C3
WICK/BNPF NE16......99 F2
Highfield Cl *WD/WHPE/BLK* NE5......54 D7
Highfield Ct *FELL* NE10......88 A5
Highfield Crs *CLS/BIR/GTL* DH3......129 J2
Highfield Dr *ASHGTN* NE63......24 B3
HAR/WTLS NE34......75 K3
HLS DH4......131 K7
Highfield Gra *HLS* DH4......146 E1
Highfield La *PRUD* NE42......80 C3
Highfield Pl *DIN/WO* NE13......46 A4
Highfield Ri *CLS/BIR/GTL* DH3......129 J2
Highfield Rd *GATE* NE8......11 K6
HAR/WTLS NE34......75 K3
HLS DH4......131 J1
ROWG NE39......96 E4
WD/WHPE/BLK NE5......68 D1
Highfield Ter
BYK/HTN/WLK NE6......72 B7
High Flatworth *NSHW* NE29......59 K5
High Friars
CNUT (off Eldon Sq) NE1......5 J6
Highgate Gdns *JRW* NE32......90 B2
Highgate Rd *MLFD/PNYW* SR4......119 H1
The High Ga *GOS/KPK* NE3......55 J6
Highgreen Cha
WICK/BNPF NE16......98 E1
High Gv *ELS/FEN* NE4......4 D7
RYTON NE40......67 F7
Highgrove *WD/WHPE/BLK* NE5......68 B1
High Hamsterley Rd
ROWG NE39......110 C1
Highheath *WASHN* NE37......102 C7
High Heworth La *FELL* NE10......13 G8
High Horse Cl *ROWG* NE39......97 J1
High Horse Close Wd
ROWG NE39......97 J1
High House Gdns *FELL* NE10......12 F6
High House La *CON/LDGT* DH8......137 K5
Highland Rd
WD/WHPE/BLK NE5......55 H7
High La *HLS* DH4......132 D3
High Lane Rw *HEBB* NE31......73 H3
High La *FELL* NE10......13 H9
High Laws *GOS/KPK* NE3......57 F6
High Level Br *GATE* NE8......5 L9
High Market *ASHGTN* NE63......23 F1
High Meadow *HAR/WTLS* NE34......75 K3
High Mdw *BDN/LAN/SAC* DH7......167 F5
High Mill Rd *ROWG* NE39......110 C1
Highmoor *MPTH* NE61......20 B6
High Moor Pl *HAR/WTLS* NE34......75 J4
High Pk *MPTH* NE61......20 E6
High Park La
MPTH (off Station Bank) NE61......20 E6
High Pasture *WASHS* NE38......117 G5
Highridge *CON/LDGT* DH8......122 C4
High Rdg *DIN/WO* NE13......46 B4
The High Rd *HAR/WTLS* NE34......75 K5
High Rw *BW/LEM/TK/HW* NE15......68 A5
High Sandgrove
CLDN/WHIT/ROK SR6......92 A3
High Shaw *PRUD* NE42......80 B3
Highside Dr *SUNDSW* SR3......120 A3
High Spen Ct *ROWG* NE39......96 C1
Highstead Av *CRAM* NE23......33 G6
Highsteads *CON/LDGT* DH8......109 H5
High Stobhill *MPTH* NE61......20 E7
High St *BDN/LAN/SAC* DH7......167 K5

BLYTH NE24......31 F7
BW/LEM/TK/HW NE15......67 H4
DHAM DH1......157 K5
DHAM DH1......169 H4
FELL NE10......12 C7
GATE NE8......5 M9
GOS/KPK NE3......56 C5
HLH DH5......148 B7
JRW NE32......74 A4
MLFD/PNYW SR4......104 E7
NWBGN NE64......19 F7
RDHAMSE DH6......158 E3
RDHAMSE DH6......172 B6
STKFD/GP NE62......22 E7
STLY/ANP DH9......112 D7
WLSD/HOW NE28......72 C2
High Street South Back
BDN/LAN/SAC DH7......167 K5
High St West
BYK/HTN/WLK NE6......72 C2
SUND SR1......14 D5
Hightree Cl *SUNDSW* SR3......133 K2
High Vw *PONT/DH* NE20......43 F7
WD/WHPE/BLK NE5......58 D7
High Vw North
WD/WHPE/BLK NE5......58 D6
Highwell Gdns *FELL* NE10......12 F6
Highwell La *WD/WHPE/BLK* NE5......68 C2
High West St *GATE* NE8......10 F2
Highwood Rd
BW/LEM/TK/HW NE15......68 D4
High Wood Ter *DHAM* DH1......16 E7
High Wood Vw *DHAM* DH1......16 E7
Highworth Dr *LGB/HTN* NE7......57 H5
LWF/SPW/WRK NE9......102 B3
Hilda Av *DHAM* DH1......17 M5
Hilda Cl *DHAM* DH1......169 J1
Hilda Pk *CLSW/PEL* DH2......129 H2
Hilda St *CLDN/WHIT/ROK* SR6......106 D2
GATE NE8......10 D6
STLY/ANP DH9......125 G2
Hilden Gdns *LGB/HTN* NE7......71 J1
Hillary Av *LGB/KIL* NE12......57 J2
Hillary Pl *WD/WHPE/BLK* NE5......54 E7
Hill Av *CRAM* NE23......39 H6
Hill Crs *SEA/MUR* SR7......149 H5
SEA/MUR SR7......151 F3
Hill Crest *BDN/LAN/SAC* DH7......143 H6
WICK/BNPF NE16......97 K7
Hillcrest *ASHGTN* NE63......24 C3
CON/LDGT DH8......136 E2
DHAM DH1......16 E2
DHAM DH1......169 J5
HAR/WTLS NE34......76 B7
JRW NE32......90 B2
MONK NE25......50 C4
PRUD NE42......80 D2
SUNDSW SR3......119 F7
Hillcrest Av *STKFD/GP* NE62......23 F5
Hillcrest Dr *DUN/TMV* NE11......85 J5
Hill Crest Gdns *JES* * NE2......56 E6
Hillcrest Pl *RHTLP* TS27......185 G2
Hillcroft *LWF/SPW/WRK* NE9......87 G6
Hill Dyke *LWF/SPW/WRK* NE9......101 J3
Hillfield *CON/LDGT* DH8......122 D4
Hillfield Gdns *SUNDSW* SR3......120 B3
GATE NE8......10 E4
Hillgarth *CON/LDGT* DH8......137 G2
Hillgate *GATE* NE8......5 M9
Hill Ga *MPTH* NE61......20 E5
Hill Head Dr *WD/WHPE/BLK* NE5......68 B2
Hillheads *MONK* NE25......50 D6
Hillhead La *WICK/BNPF* NE16......98 B4
Hillhead Pkwy
WD/WHPE/BLK NE5......54 A7
Hill Head Rd
WD/WHPE/BLK NE5......68 B1
Hillheads Rd *MONK* NE25......50 D6
Hillhead Wy
WD/WHPE/BLK NE5......54 C7
Hill House Rd
BW/LEM/TK/HW NE15......66 D1
Hillingdon Gv *MLFD/PNYW* SR4......118 E4
Hill La *HLS* DH4......118 A5
Hill Mdw *DHAM* DH1......169 H5
Hillmeads *CLSW/PEL* DH2......144 A4
Hill Pk *PONT/DH* NE20......43 F7
Hill Park Rd *JRW* NE32......74 A6
Hill Ri *RYTON* NE40......82 B1
WASHS NE38......103 G7
Hillrise Crs *SEA/MUR* SR7......134 D7
Hillsden Rd *MONK* NE25......50 B2
Hillside *BDN/LAN/SAC* DH7......143 G7
BLAY NE21......83 K2
BOL NE36......90 E5
CLS/BIR/GTL DH3......115 K2
CLS/BIR/GTL DH3......129 J3
DUN/TMV NE11......85 J5
HAR/WTLS NE34......76 B7
MPTH NE61......20 D6
PONT/DH NE20......52 D1
SUNDSW SR3......120 C3
Hillsview Av *GOS/KPK* NE3......55 K5
Hill Ter *HLS* DH4......132 C5
Hillthorne Cl *WASHS* NE38......117 H2
Hill Top *BLAY* NE21......83 K3
CLS/BIR/GTL DH3......115 K2
STLY/ANP DH9......113 F7
Hill Top Av *LWF/SPW/WRK* NE9......87 G7
Hill Top Cl *STKFD/GP* NE62......23 F5

Hill Top Gdns
LWF/SPW/WRK NE9......87 G7
Hilltop Gdns *SUNDSW* SR3......120 C7
Hilltop Rd *BDN/LAN/SAC* DH7......155 F5
Hilltop Vw *BDN/LAN/SAC* DH7......154 C3
Hill Vw *BDN/LAN/SAC* DH7......165 H2
Hillview *SUNDSW* SR3......119 F7
Hillview Crs *HLS* DH4......132 B4
Hill View Gdns *SUNDSW* SR3......120 B3
Hillview Gv *HLS* DH4......132 B4
Hill View Rd
ASHBK/HED/RY SR2......120 E4
Hillview Rd *HLS* DH4......132 B4
Hill View Sq
ASHBK/HED/RY SR2......120 D4
Hilsyde Cres *RDHAMSE* DH6......172 B6
Hilton Av *WD/WHPE/BLK* NE5......69 F1
Hilton Cl *CRAM* NE23......33 G5
Hilton Dr *PLEE/EAS* SR8......174 E1
Hindley Cl *RYTON* NE40......82 A1
Hindley Gdns *ELS/FEN* NE4......69 H4
Hindmarch Dr *BOL* NE36......90 E5
Hind St *SUND* SR1......14 C5
Hinkley Cl *SUNDSW* SR3......134 A1
Hipsburn Dr *SUNDSW* SR3......120 A3
Hiram Dr *BOL* NE36......91 H5
Histon Wy *WD/WHPE/BLK* NE5......55 F7
Hither Gn *JRW* NE32......90 B2
Hobart *WBAY* NE26......50 D2
Hobart Av *HAR/WTLS* NE34......74 D7
Hodgkin Park Crs
BW/LEM/TK/HW NE15......69 G5
Hodgkin Park Rd
BW/LEM/TK/HW NE15......69 G6
Hodgson's Rd *BLYTH* NE24......31 F6
Hodgson Gdns
LWF/SPW/WRK NE9......87 H6
Hogarth Dr *WASHS* NE38......117 G3
Hogarth Rd *HAR/WTLS* NE34......91 G2
Holbein Rd *HAR/WTLS* NE34......91 G1
Holborn Pl
WD/WHPE/BLK * NE5......68 C2
Holborn Rd *MLFD/PNYW* SR4......119 H1
Holborn Sq *MLFD/PNYW* SR4......119 H2
Holburn Cl *RYTON* NE40......67 F6
Holburn Ct *BDN/LAN/SAC* DH7......167 G1
RYTON NE40......67 F5
Holburn Crs *RYTON* NE40......67 G6
Holburn Gdns *RYTON* NE40......67 G6
Holburn La *RYTON* NE40......67 F6
Holburn Wk *RYTON* NE40......67 F6
Holburn Wy *RYTON* NE40......67 F6
Holden Pl *WD/WHPE/BLK* NE5......69 H1
Holder House La
HAR/WTLS NE34......91 J1
Holderness Rd
BYK/HTN/WLK NE6......71 H7
WLSD/HOW NE28......59 J7
Hole La *WICK/BNPF* NE16......98 D1
Holeyn Hall Rd *WYLAM* NE41......65 G4
Holeyn Rd
BW/LEM/TK/HW NE15......66 E2
Holland Dr *JES* NE2......4 E3
Holland Pk
JES (off Holland Dr) NE2......4 E2
WLSD/HOW NE28......58 A7
Holland Park Dr *JRW* NE32......90 B2
The Hollies
RYTON
(off King Edward Rd) NE40......67 G7
Hollinghill Rd *MONK* NE25......40 B6
Hollings Crs *WLSD/HOW* NE28......58 D6
Hollingside La *DHAM* DH1......16 D9
Hollington Av *LGB/KIL* NE12......57 H4
Hollinhill *ROWG* NE39......83 J7
Hollinhill La *ROWG* NE39......97 H1
Hollinside Cl *WICK/BNPF* NE16......84 E7
Hollinside Gdns
BW/LEM/TK/HW NE15......69 F5
Hollinside Rd *MLFD/PNYW* SR4......119 H2
WICK/BNPF NE16......85 F2
Hollinside Sq *MLFD/PNYW* SR4......119 G1
Hollinside Ter *ROWG* NE39......97 F3
Hollon St *MPTH* NE61......20 C4
Hollowdene *HLH* DH5......147 K5
The Hollows *ASHGTN* NE63......24 D3
Holly Av *HLS* DH4......84 A6
CLDN/WHIT/ROK SR6......93 F4
DUN/TMV NE11......9 H9
GOS/KPK NE3......55 K4
HAR/WTLS NE34......76 A6
HLH DH5......132 C7
JES NE2......70 E2
LGB/KIL NE12......57 K1
MONK NE25......49 K4
MPTH NE61......20 D6
RYTON NE40......66 E5
SUNDSW SR3......120 B6
WBAY NE26......50 E4
WLSD/HOW NE28......72 E2
Holly Av West *JES* * NE2......70 E2
Hollybush Rd *FELL* NE10......12 A3
Hollycarrside Rd
ASHBK/HED/RY SR2......120 E6
Holly Crs *BDN/LAN/SAC* DH7......143 H6
Hollydene *DUN/TMV* NE11......100 D7
ROWG NE39......97 H3
Holly Gdns *CON/LDGT* DH8......122 C7
Holly Gv *PRUD* NE42......80 B1
Holly Hvn *HLH* DH5......147 G4
Holly Hl *FELL* NE10......12 C7
Holly Hill Gdns *STLY/ANP* DH9......126 D3
Holly Hill Gdns East
STLY/ANP DH9......126 E2
Holly Hill Gdns West
STLY/ANP DH9......126 D3
Hollyhock *HEBB* NE31......89 G1
Hollymount Sq *BDLGTN* NE22......29 G6
Holly Pk *BDN/LAN/SAC* DH7......167 F1
Holly Park Vw *FELL* NE10......12 D7
Holly Rd *NSHW* NE29......60 D3
The Hollys *CLS/BIR/GTL* DH3......101 H6
Holly St *ASHGTN* * NE63......23 K2
DHAM DH1......16 A4
JRW NE32......73 J4
Holly Vw *FELL* NE10......12 B8
Hollywell Ct *BDN/LAN/SAC* DH7......167 G1

Hollywell Gv *DIN/WO* NE13 ....54 D2
Hollywell Rd *NSHW* NE29 ....60 B4
Hollywood Av *GOS/KPK* NE3 .....56 D4
  SWCK/CAS SR5 ....105 K3
Hollywood Crs *GOS/KPK* NE3 ....56 D4
Holmdale
  DUN/TMV NE11 ....86 B7
Holmdale *ASHGTN* NE63 ....23 J3
Holme Av *BYK/HTN/WLK* NE6 ...72 B2
  WICK/BNPF NE16 ....85 F5
Holme Gdns *SUNDSW* SR3 .....120 B3
  WLSD/HOW NE28 ....73 J1
Holme Ri *WICK/BNPF* NE16 ......85 F5
Holmesdale Rd
  WD/WHPE/BLK NE5 ......69 H2
Holmeside *SUND* SR1 ....14 E5
Holmewood Dr *ROWG* NE39 .....97 F5
Holmfield Av *HAR/WTLS* NE34 ...75 J4
Holmfield Vls *RDHAMSE* DH6 ...180 B5
Holm Gn *MONK* NE25 ....50 B5
Holmhill La *CLS/BIR/GTL* DH5 ..144 D1
  PLEE/EAS SR8 ....162 E4
Holmland
  BW/LEM/TK/HW NE15 ....69 G7
Holmlands *MONK* NE25 ....50 C4
Holmlands Pk North
  ASHBK/HED/RY SR2 ......120 C2
Holmlands Pk South
  ASHBK/HED/RY SR2 ......120 C2
Holmlea *BDN/LAN/SAC* DH7 ....141 G4
Holmside Av
  BDN/LAN/SAC DH7 ....140 C5
  DUN/TMV NE11 ....9 H8
Holmside Hall Rd
  BDN/LAN/SAC DH7 ....127 F7
Holmside La
  BDN/LAN/SAC DH7 ....141 G4
  BDN/LAN/SAC DH7 ....141 K2
Holmside Pl *BYK/HTN/WLK* NE6 ...6 E2
Holmwood Av *MONK* NE25 ......50 B5
Holmwood Gv *JES* NE2 ....70 D1
Holwick Cl *WASHS* NE38 ....116 C4
Holyfields *SMOOR* NE27 ....49 F7
Holy Jesus Bungalows *JES* NE2 ...4 E1
Holylake Sq *MLFD/PNYW* SR4 ..119 H1
Holyoake Gdns
  CLS/BIR/GTL DH3 ....115 J2
  LWF/SPW/WRK NE9 ......11 H8
Holyoake St *CLSW/PEL* DH2 ....128 C1
  PRUD NE42 ....80 D1
Holystone Av *GOS/KPK* NE3 ....56 B4
  MONK NE25 ....51 F5
Holystone Cl *BLYTH* NE24 ....34 E2
  HLS DH4 ....131 K5
Holystone Ct
  GATE (off Fourth St) NE8 ....10 C6
Holystone Crs *LGB/HTN* NE7 ....57 G7
Holystone Dr *SMOOR* NE27 .....48 E7
Holystone Gdns *NSHW* NE29 ....60 B3
Holystone Gra *LGB/KIL* NE12 ....58 E1
Holystone St *HEBB* NE31 ....73 F5
Holywell Av *BYK/HTN/WLK* NE6 .12 F1
  MONK NE25 ....40 C6
  WBAY NE26 ....50 C3
Holywell Cl *ELS/FEN* * NE4 ....4 F4
  MONK NE25 ....40 C6
Holywell Dene Rd *MONK* NE25 ...40 C7
Home Av *LWF/SPW/WRK* NE9 ...101 F1
Homedale *PRUD* NE42 ....80 E2
Homedale Ri *PRUD* NE42 ....80 E2
Home Farm Cl *ASHGTN* NE63 ....23 F1
Home Pk *WLSD/HOW* NE28 .....54 B3
Homestall Cl *HAR/WTLS* NE34 ...75 H6
Honeycomb Cl *CHPW* NE17 ......81 K7
Honeycrook Dr *LGB/HTN* NE7 ....58 A7
Honeysuckle Av
  HAR/WTLS NE34 ....75 F7
Honeysuckle Cl *SUNDSW* SR3 ..134 A2
Honister Av *JES* NE2 ....56 E7
Honister Cl
  BW/LEM/TK/HW NE15 ....68 B4
Honister Dr *SWCK/CAS* SR5 ....106 C2
Honister Pl
  BW/LEM/TK/HW NE15 ....68 B4
Honister Rd *TYNE/NSHE* NE30 ...51 F7
Honister Wy *BLYTH* NE24 ....34 E4
Honiton Cl *HLS* DH4 ....132 A3
Honiton Ct *WD/WHPE/BLK* NE5 .55 F4
Honiton Wy *NSHW* NE29 ....59 K2
Hood Cl *SWCK/CAS* SR5 ....106 C4
Hood St *CNUT* NE1 ....5 K6
  MPTH NE61 ....20 D4
  WICK/BNPF NE16 ....84 E3
Hookergate La *ROWG* NE39 .....96 C2
Hooper Ter *RDHAMSE* DH6 .....173 H4
Hopedene *FELL* NE10 ....88 C1
Hope Shield *WASHS* NE38 .....116 B5
Hope St *CON/LDGT* DH8 ....122 E3
  HAR/WTLS NE34 ....75 F6
  JRW NE32 ....74 A4
  RDHAMSE DH6 ....170 C1
Hope Vw *ASHBK/HED/RY* SR2 ..121 F7
Hopgarth Gdns
  CLS/BIR/GTL DH3 ....129 K3
Hopkins Ct *MLFD/PNYW* SR4 ..105 K6
Hopper Pl *GATE* NE8 ....11 G2
Hopper Rd *FELL* NE10 ....12 A9
Hopper St *GATE* NE8 ....11 G2
  NSHW NE29 ....2 B2
  WLSD/HOW NE28 ....72 C1
Horatio St
  CLDN/WHIT/ROK SR6 ....106 C4
Hornbeam Pl *ELS/FEN* NE4 ......9 L1
Horncliffe Gdns
  WICK/BNPF NE16 ....8 A7
Horncliffe Pl
  BW/LEM/TK/HW NE15 ....66 D1
Hornsea Cl *DIN/WO* NE13 ....46 A4
Hornsey Ter *HLS* DH4 ....148 A7
Horse Crofts *BLAY* NE21 ....84 A1
Horsegate Bank *CHPW* NE17 ....81 K7
Horsham Gdns *SUNDSW* SR3 ..120 A3
Horsley Av *RYTON* NE40 ....82 A1
  SMOOR NE27 ....49 H7
Horsley Cl *STKFD/GP* NE62 .....23 F5
Horsley Ct *GOS/KPK* NE3 ....55 J4
Horsley Gdns *DUN/TMV* NE11 ....9 J8

Horsley Gv *SUNDSW* SR3 ....120 A3
Horsley Hill Rd *HAR/WTLS* NE34 ..75 J2
Horsley Hill Sq *HAR/WTLS* NE34 ..76 B4
Horsley Rd *LGB/HTN* NE7 ....71 H2
  PRUD NE42 ....64 A6
  WASHS NE38 ....103 J7
Horsley Ter *BYK/HTN/WLK* NE6 ..72 B6
  TYNE/NSHE NE30 ....61 H3
Horsley V *HAR/WTLS* NE34 .....75 K4
Horsley Vw *PRUD* NE42 ....81 F1
Horton Av *BDLGTN* NE22 ....29 F6
  HAR/WTLS NE34 ....91 H1
  SMOOR NE27 ....49 H7
Horton Crs *DIN/WO* NE13 ....45 F2
  RDHAMSE DH6 ....180 A1
Hortondale Gv *BLYTH* NE24 .....30 D7
Horton Dr *CRAM* NE23 ....33 G6
Horton Pl *BLYTH* NE24 ....34 D3
Horton Rd *BLYTH* NE24 ....33 J1
Horwood Av
  WD/WHPE/BLK NE5 ......68 B1
Hospital Dr *HEBB* NE31 ....73 F7
Hospital La
  BW/LEM/TK/HW NE15 ....67 K4
Hospital Rd *BDN/LAN/SAC* DH7 .154 A3
Hotch Pudding Pl
  WD/WHPE/BLK NE5 ......68 D3
Hotspur Av *BDLGTN* NE22 ....29 F6
  HAR/WTLS NE34 ....75 J4
  MONK NE25 ....50 E5
Hotspur Rd *WLSD/HOW* NE28 ...58 C5
Hotspur St *BYK/HTN/WLK* NE6 ...6 C3
  TYNE/NSHE NE30 ....61 H2
Hotspur Wy
  CNUT (off Eldon Sq) NE1 ....5 J6
Houghton Av *TYNE/NSHE* NE30 ..51 F6
  WD/WHPE/BLK NE5 ......55 H7
Houghton Cut *HLH* DH5 ....132 C6
Houghton Rd *HLH* DH5 ....147 J2
  HLS DH4 ....132 B4
Houghton St *MLFD/PNYW* SR4 ..106 A7
Houlet Garth *BYK/HTN/WLK* NE6 .7 C7
Houlskye Cl *SUNDSW* SR3 .....120 C7
Hoults Est
  BYK/HTN/WLK
  (off Walker Rd) NE6 ....6 F7
Houndelee Pl
  WD/WHPE/BLK NE5 ......69 G2
Houndslow Dr *ASHGTN* NE63 ...23 H3
Hounslow Gdns *JRW* NE32 .....90 B2
House Ter *WASHN* NE37 ....103 F5
Housing La *CON/LDGT* DH8 ....109 K5
Houston Ct *ELS/FEN* NE4 ....4 F8
Houston St *ELS/FEN* NE4 ....4 F8
Houxty Rd *MONK* NE25 ....49 K4
Hovingham Cl *PLEE/EAS* SR8 ..175 F5
Hovingham Gdns *SUNDSW* SR3 .120 A3
Howard Cl *LGB/KIL* NE12 ....58 E1
Howard Ct *TYNE/NSHE* NE30 ....2 F7
Howard Gv *MPTH* NE61 ....21 J2
Howardian Cl *WASHS* NE38 ....116 D3
Howard Rd *MPTH* NE61 ....20 E4
Howard St *CNUT* NE1 ....6 B6
  FELL NE10 ....87 J6
  GATE NE8 ....11 M6
  JRW NE32 ....74 A5
  *MPTH** NE61 ....20 E5
  SWCK/CAS SR5 ....106 D4
  TYNE/NSHE NE30 ....2 F7
Howard Ter
  TYNE/NSHE (off Albion Rd) NE30 ..2 E1
Howarth St *MLFD/PNYW* SR4 ..106 A7
Howat Av *WD/WHPE/BLK* NE5 ...69 J2
Howburn Crs *MPTH* NE61 ....21 J2
Howden Bank
  BDN/LAN/SAC DH7 ....140 D1
Howdene Rd
  BW/LEM/TK/HW NE15 ....68 D5
Howden Gdns *WNGT* TS28 ....183 K3
Howdon La *WLSD/HOW* NE28 ...59 J7
Howdon Rd *NSHW* NE29 ....2 A6
  WLSD/HOW NE28 ....74 A1
Howe Sq *MLFD/PNYW* SR4 ....119 G1
Howe St *GATE* NE8 ....11 L6
  HEBB NE31 ....73 J5
Howick Av *GOS/KPK* NE3 ....56 A3
Howick Pk *CLDN/WHIT/ROK* SR6 .14 F2
Howletch La *PLEE/EAS* SR8 ....174 D4
Howlett Hall Rd
  BW/LEM/TK/HW NE15 ....68 D5
Howley Av *SWCK/CAS* SR5 .....105 C5
Hownam Cl *GOS/KPK* * NE3 ....56 A6
Hownsgill Dr *CON/LDGT* DH8 ..138 D2
Hoy Crs *SEA/MUR* SR7 ....135 F6
Hoylake Av *LGB/HTN* NE7 ......57 J5
Hoyle Av *ELS/FEN* NE4 ....69 J5
Hoyle Fold *SUNDSW* SR3 ......134 A3
Hubert St *BOLCOL* NE35 ....90 C7
Huddleston Ri
  CLDN/WHIT/ROK SR6 .....15 H1
Huddleston Rd
  BYK/HTN/WLK NE6 ....7 J2
Hudson Av *BDLGTN* NE22 ....29 H5
  CRAM NE23 ....47 H1
Hudson Rd *SUND* SR1 ....15 G5
Hudson St *GATE* NE8 ....10 F1
  HAR/WTLS NE34 ....75 F5
  TYNE/NSHE NE30 ....3 G1
Hudspeth Crs *DHAM* DH1 .....156 B2
Hugh Gdns *ELS/FEN* NE4 ....69 J7
Hugh St *CLDN/WHIT/ROK* SR6 .106 C2
  WASHS NE38 ....117 H1
  WLSD/HOW NE28 ....72 D2
Hull St *ELS/FEN* NE4 ....4 B8
Hulme Av *TYNE/NSHE* NE30 ....61 G3
Humber Gdns *GATE* NE8 ....11 L6
Humber Hl *STLY/ANP* DH9 .....126 E2
Humberhill Dr
  BDN/LAN/SAC DH7 ....140 D5
Humberhill La
  BDN/LAN/SAC DH7 ....139 F3
Humber St *CHPW* NE17 ....95 J4
Humbert St *JRW* NE32 ....73 K5
Humbleburn La
  BDN/LAN/SAC DH7 ....127 J6

Humbledon Vw
  ASHBK/HED/RY SR2 ....14 D9
Hume St *BYK/HTN/WLK* NE6 .....6 D6
  MLFD/PNYW SR4 ....106 A6
Humford Gn *BLYTH* NE24 ....30 D7
Humford Wy *BDLGTN* NE22 .....29 C7
Humsford Gv *CRAM* NE23 ....33 J7
Hunstanton Ct
  LWF/SPW/WRK NE9 ......100 E2
Huntcliffe Av
  CLDN/WHIT/ROK SR6 ......92 E6
Huntcliffe Gdns
  BYK/HTN/WLK NE6 ....71 J2
Hunter Av *BDN/LAN/SAC* DH7 ..154 E7
  BLYTH NE24 ....35 H1
Hunter Cl *BOL* NE36 ....91 H6
Hunter Memorial Homes
  MPTH (off Oldgate) NE61 ...20 D5
Hunter Rd *PLEE/EAS* SR8 ......174 B5
Hunters Cl *CON/LDGT* DH8 .....109 J5
  NSHW NE29 ....60 B7
Hunters Ct *WLSD/HOW* NE28 ...72 E1
Hunters Hall Rd
  MLFD/PNYW SR4 ....14 A8
Hunters Ldg *WLSD/HOW* NE28 ..72 D1
Hunter's Moor Cl *JES* NE2 ....4 E1
Hunter's Pl *JES* NE2 ....4 E1
Hunter's Rd *GOS/KPK* NE3 ......57 F5
  JES NE2 ....4 D2
Hunter Ter *ASHBK/HED/RY* SR2 .120 E3
Hunter St *HLS* DH4 ....131 J2
  SSH NE33 ....75 H2
Huntingdon Cl *DIN/WO* NE13 ...55 G2
Huntingdon Gdns
  SUNDSW SR3 ....120 A3
Huntingdon Pl
  TYNE/NSHE NE30 ....61 H3
Huntingdon Rd *PLEE/EAS* SR8 ..174 D2
Huntingdonshire Dr
  DHAM DH1 ....158 A6
Huntington Dr *CRAM* NE23 .....38 D1
Hunt Lea *WICK/BNPF* NE16 .....84 C7
Huntley Av *SEA/MUR* SR7 .....149 C5
Huntley Crs *BLAY* NE21 ....83 J4
Huntley Sq *MLFD/PNYW* SR4 ..119 H1
Huntly Rd *MONK* NE25 ....50 A2
Hurst Ter *BYK/HTN/WLK* NE6 ....7 M5
Hurstwood Rd
  MLFD/PNYW SR4 ....120 A2
Hurworth Av *HAR/WTLS* NE34 ...76 A5
Hurworth Pl *JRW* NE32 ....73 K5
Hustledown Gdns
  STLY/ANP DH9 ....126 D3
Hustledown Rd *STLY/ANP* DH9 .126 C3
Hutchinson Av
  CON/LDGT * DH8 ....123 F4
Hutton Cl *HLS* DH4 ....132 A7
  WASHS NE38 ....116 B1
Hutton Crs *RHTLP* TS27 ....184 E6
Hutton St *BOLCOL* NE35 ....90 C3
  MLFD/PNYW SR4 ....14 A7
Hutton Ter *JES* NE2 ....6 A2
  LWF/SPW/WRK NE9 ......101 F1
Huxley Crs *GATE* NE8 ....10 D9
Hyacinth Ct *MLFD/PNYW* SR4 ...14 A3
Hydenside Gv *CON/LDGT* DH8 .122 C7
Hyde Pk *WLSD/HOW* NE28 ......58 B7
Hydepark St *GATE* NE8 ....10 D8
Hyde St *ASHBK/HED/RY* SR2 .....3 K9
  SSH NE33 ....75 J2
Hyde Ter *GOS/KPK* NE3 ....56 D5
Hylton Av *HAR/WTLS* NE34 .....76 B5
Hylton Bank *MLFD/PNYW* SR4 ..105 F7
Hylton Castle Rd
  SWCK/CAS SR5 ....105 F4
Hylton Cl *BDLGTN* NE22 ....28 D5
  BDN/LAN/SAC DH7 ....154 A3
Hylton Gra *SWCK/CAS* SR5 ....104 D6
Hylton La *BOL* NE36 ....90 E6
  SWCK/CAS SR5 ....104 E2
Hylton Park Rd *SWCK/CAS* SR5 .105 H6
Hylton Rd *DHAM* DH1 ....156 D3
  JRW NE32 ....73 K7
  MLFD/PNYW SR4 ....14 A4
Hylton St *GATE* NE8 ....11 L1
  HLS DH4 ....132 B5
  MLFD/PNYW SR4 ....106 A7
  NSHW NE29 ....2 C4
Hylton Ter *ASHBK/HED/RY* SR2 .134 E1
  FELL NE10 ....13 M4
  NSHW NE29 ....2 C2
Hylton Wk *MLFD/PNYW* SR4 ...118 E1
Hymers Av *HAR/WTLS* NE34 ....74 D7
Hyperion Av *HAR/WTLS* NE34 ..74 E5

I

Ilchester St *SEA/MUR* SR7 .....150 E2
Ilderton Pl *WD/WHPE/BLK* NE5 ..68 C3
Ilex Av *DUN/TMV* NE11 ....86 C6
Ilford Av *CRAM* NE23 ....33 G6
Ilford Pl *GATE* NE8 ....11 K8
Ilford Rd *JES* NE2 ....56 D7
  WLSD/HOW NE28 ....59 H7
Ilfracombe Av *ELS/FEN* NE4 ....69 J6
Ilminster Ct *GOS/KPK* NE3 .....55 G5
Imeary Gv *SSH* NE33 ....75 H2
Imeary St *SSH* NE33 ....75 H2
Inchberry Cl *ELS/FEN* NE4 ......69 J7
Inchbury Cl *ELS/FEN* NE4 ......69 J7
Inchcape Ter *PLEE/EAS* SR8 ...163 G6
Inchcliffe Crs
  WD/WHPE/BLK NE5 ......69 G5
Indigo St *DUN/TMV* NE11 ....86 C6
Industrial Rd *WASHN* NE37 ....103 G6
Industrial St *CLSW/PEL* DH2 ...128 C1
Industry Rd *BYK/HTN/WLK* NE6 .71 K1
Ingham Gra *SSH* NE33 ....75 J2
Ingham St *CRAM* NE23 ....33 G6
Ingleby Ter *MLFD/PNYW* SR4 ..120 A7
Ingleby Wy *BLYTH* NE24 ....35 F4
Inglemere Pl
  BW/LEM/TK/HW NE15 ....68 E5

Ingleside *WICK/BNPF* NE16 .....84 D6
Ingleside Rd *NSHW* NE29 ......60 D3
Ingleton Ct *MLFD/PNYW* SR4 ..120 A1
Ingleton Dr
  BW/LEM/TK/HW NE15 ....66 D1
Ingleton Gdns *BLYTH* NE24 .....34 E4
Inglewood Cl *BLYTH* NE24 ......30 B7
Inglewood Pl *GOS/KPK* NE3 ....56 C1
Ingoe Av *GOS/KPK* NE3 ....55 K3
Ingoe Cl *BLYTH* NE24 ....30 E7
Ingoe St *BW/LEM/TK/HW* NE15 .68 A5
  WLSD/HOW NE28 ....74 A1
Ingoldsby Ct *MLFD/PNYW* SR4 .119 J2
Ingram Av *GOS/KPK* NE3 ....55 K2
Ingram Cl *CLSW/PEL* DH2 .....129 G6
  WLSD/HOW NE28 ....59 H5
Ingram Dr *BLYTH* NE24 ....30 D7
  WD/WHPE/BLK NE5 ......54 B6
Ingram Ter *BYK/HTN/WLK* NE6 ..72 C5
Ingram Wy *WNGT* TS28 ....183 K2
Inkerman Rd *WASHN* NE37 ....103 F4
Inkerman St *SWCK/CAS* SR5 ...106 A4
Inleborough Dr *RYTON* NE40 ...67 F7
Innesmoor *HEBB* NE31 ....73 F6
Inskip Ter *GATE* NE8 ....11 H8
Institute Ter East
  CLSW/PEL DH2 ....115 F6
Institute Ter West
  CLSW/PEL DH2 ....115 F6
Inverness Rd *JRW* NE32 ....90 C1
Inverness St
  CLDN/WHIT/ROK SR6 ....106 D3
Invincible Dr *ELS/FEN* NE4 ....9 K2
Iolanthe Crs *BYK/HTN/WLK* NE6 ..7 L2
Iolanthe Ter *SSH* NE33 ....3 L9
Iona Pl *BYK/HTN/WLK* * NE6 .....7 K2
Iona Rd *FELL* NE10 ....87 H5
  JRW NE32 ....90 C1
Irene Av *ASHBK/HED/RY* SR2 ..121 F5
Iris Crs *CLSW/PEL* DH2 ....115 F4
Iris Pl *ELS/FEN* NE4 ....69 H4
Iris St *DUN/TMV* NE11 ....86 C6
Iris Ter *RYTON* NE40 ....82 B1
Iroko St *DUN/TMV* NE11 ....86 C6
Ironside St *HLH* DH5 ....132 C6
Irthing Av *BYK/HTN/WLK* NE6 ....7 K8
Irton St *GOS/KPK* NE3 ....56 C5
Irwin Av *WLSD/HOW* NE28 .....58 D7
Isabella Rd *BLYTH* NE24 ....34 E1
Isabella Wk
  BW/LEM/TK/HW NE15 ....67 F2
Isis Rd *PLEE/EAS* SR8 ....174 D5
Islestone
  LWF/SPW/WRK
  (off Pimlico Ct) NE9 ....101 F1
Ivanhoe *MONK* NE25 ....50 C4
Ivanhoe Crs *ASHBK/HED/RY* SR2 .14 A9
Ivanhoe Vw
  LWF/SPW/WRK NE9 ......101 H3
Iveagh Cl *ELS/FEN* NE4 ....69 H7
Ivesley La *BDN/LAN/SAC* DH7 .164 C1
Iveson Rd *BDN/LAN/SAC* DH7 ..164 A3
Iveston La *CON/LDGT* DH8 ....124 B6
Iveston Rd *CON/LDGT* DH8 ....123 H6
Iveston Ter *STLY/ANP* DH9 .....112 D7
Ivor St *ASHBK/HED/RY* SR2 ...121 G4
Ivy Av *RYTON* NE40 ....66 E5
  SEA/MUR SR7 ....150 C2
Ivy Cl *ELS/FEN* NE4 ....9 M1
Ivy La *LWF/SPW/WRK* NE9 ....101 G2
Ivymount Rd
  BYK/HTN/WLK NE6 ....71 H2
Ivy Rd *BYK/HTN/WLK* NE6 ......72 B3
  GOS/KPK NE3 ....56 E4
  LGB/KIL NE12 ....58 A2
Ivy St *DUN/TMV* NE11 ....86 C6
Ivyway *CLSW/PEL* DH2 ....114 E7
Ixia St *DUN/TMV* NE11 ....86 C6

J

Jack Lawson Ter
  RDHAMSE * DH6 ....182 D1
Jackson Av *PONT/DH* NE20 .....43 H2
Jackson Rd *WYLAM* NE41 ......65 H5
Jackson St *BYK/HTN/WLK* NE6 ..72 B5
  GATE NE8 ....11 G2
  MLFD/PNYW SR4 ....120 A1
  TYNE/NSHE NE30 ....61 F4
Jackson St West
  TYNE/NSHE NE30 ....61 F4
Jack's Ter *HAR/WTLS* NE34 .....75 G6
Jacobins Chare *CNUT* * NE1 .....5 H7
Jacques St *MLFD/PNYW* SR4 ..105 K6
Jacques Ter *CLSW/PEL* DH2 ...129 H4
Jade Cl *BW/LEM/TK/HW* NE15 ..68 A3
James Armitage St
  SWCK/CAS SR5 ....106 A3
James Mather St *SSH* NE33 ......3 J6
Jameson St *CON/LDGT* DH8 ...123 F4
James St *ELS/FEN* NE4 ....4 A9
  PLEE/EAS SR8 ....162 E4
  SEA/MUR SR7 ....150 E2
  SWCK/CAS SR5 ....106 A3
  WD/WHPE/BLK NE5 ......68 D1
  WICK/BNPF * NE16 ....84 E5
James Ter *HLH* DH5 ....160 A1
  HLS DH4 ....131 J7
  WLSD/HOW NE28 ....72 D2
James Williams St *SUND* SR1 ...15 H3
Jane Eyre Ter *GATE* NE8 ....11 L5
Jane Ter *BYK/HTN/WLK* NE6 ....72 C6
Janet Sq *BYK/HTN/WLK* NE6 ....7 H8
Janet St *BYK/HTN/WLK* NE6 .....7 H8
Janus Cl *WD/WHPE/BLK* NE5 ...54 A6
Jarrow Rd *HAR/WTLS* NE34 .....74 E5
  JRW NE32 ....74 E5
Jarvis Rd *PLEE/EAS* SR8 ....174 E2
Jasmin Av *WD/WHPE/BLK* NE5 .54 A6
Jasmine Cl *BYK/HTN/WLK* NE6 ..72 A2
Jasmine Crs *SEA/MUR* SR7 ....150 D3
Jasmine Ct *ASHGTN* NE63 .....23 J4
Jasper Av *RYTON* NE40 ....82 C1
  SEA/MUR SR7 ....150 C2

Jaycroft Ct
  TYNE/NSHE
  (off Stephenson St) NE30 ......2 F2
Jedburgh Cl *GATE* * NE8 ....11 H6
  NSHW NE29 ....60 C2
  WD/WHPE/BLK NE5 ......54 A6
Jedburgh Gdns
  BW/LEM/TK/HW NE15 ....69 F5
Jedburgh Rd *HLS* DH4 ....131 K1
Jedmoor *HEBB* NE31 ....73 F4
Jefferson Pl *ELS/FEN* NE4 ....4 F5
Jellicoe Rd *BYK/HTN/WLK* NE6 ..12 C1
Jenifer Gv *LGB/HTN* NE7 ....57 G7
Jenison Av
  BW/LEM/TK/HW NE15 ....69 G6
Jennifer Av *SWCK/CAS* SR5 ....105 C4
Jersey Sq *MPTH* NE61 ....18 C1
Jervis St *HEBB* NE31 ....73 F6
Jesmond Dene Rd *JES* NE2 .....70 D1
Jesmond Gdns *JES* NE2 ....71 F2
Jesmond Pk East *LGB/HTN* NE7 .71 H1
Jesmond Pk West *LGB/HTN* * NE7 .71 H2
Jesmond Rd *JES* NE2 ....6 A2
Jesmond Rd West *JES* NE2 ......5 K3
Jesmond Ter *WBAY* NE26 ......50 E5
Jesmond V *BYK/HTN/WLK* NE6 ..6 D2
Jesmond Vale La
  BYK/HTN/WLK NE6 ....6 E1
Jesmond Vale Ter
  BYK/HTN/WLK NE6 ....6 F1
Jessel St *LWF/SPW/WRK* NE9 ..101 F1
Joan Av *ASHBK/HED/RY* SR2 ..121 F5
Joannah St *SWCK/CAS* SR5 ...106 C2
Joan St *ELS/FEN* NE4 ....69 H7
Jobling Av *BLAY* NE21 ....83 J2
Jobling Crs *MPTH* NE61 ....21 F6
Joel Ter *FELL* NE10 ....13 L3
John Av *RYTON* NE40 ....82 D3
John Brown Ct *BDLGTN* * NE22 .29 F5
John Candlish Rd
  MLFD/PNYW SR4 ....106 A6
John Clay St *SSH* NE33 ....75 H2
John Dobson St *CNUT* NE1 ......5 K5
John Reid Rd *HAR/WTLS* NE34 ..74 D7
Johnson Cl *PLEE/EAS* SR8 .....174 E2
Johnson's St *WNGT* TS28 .....183 K5
Johnson St
  BW/LEM/TK/HW NE15 ....68 A5
  DUN/TMV NE11 ....9 H5
  GATE NE8 ....9 M5
  SSH NE33 ....75 C4
  SUND SR1 ....14 B4
Johnson Ter *STLY/ANP* DH9 ....125 J4
John St *ASHGTN* NE63 ....23 J1
  BDN/LAN/SAC DH7 ....143 H5
  BLYTH NE24 ....30 D6
  CON/LDGT DH8 ....122 D3
  CON/LDGT DH8 ....123 F5
  DHAM DH1 ....16 A4
  FELL NE10 ....13 L6
  GATE NE8 ....11 L1
  GOS/KPK NE3 ....56 A5
  HLH DH5 ....132 D7
  HLH DH5 ....147 K5
  HLS DH4 ....131 J7
  MLFD/PNYW SR4 ....104 E6
  MONK NE25 ....49 J4
  MPTH NE61 ....21 K2
  PLEE/EAS SR8 ....163 F4
  STLY/ANP DH9 ....113 H7
  STLY/ANP DH9 ....126 B3
  STLY/ANP DH9 ....127 G5
  SUND SR1 ....14 F4
  WBAY NE26 ....51 G5
  WLSD/HOW NE28 ....72 D1
John Street Sq *CON/LDGT* DH8 .123 F4
John Taylor Ct *SWCK/CAS* SR5 .106 A2
John Wesley Ct *PRUD* NE42 .....80 D2
John Williamson St *SSH* NE33 ...75 F4
John Wilson Ct *PLEE/EAS* SR8 .175 H3
Joicey Gdns *STLY/ANP* DH9 ...112 D7
Joicey Rd *LWF/SPW/WRK* NE9 ..87 F3
Joicey St *FELL* NE10 ....13 J5
Jolliffe St *CLS/BIR/GTL* DH3 ...129 K6
Jonadab Rd *FELL* NE10 ....13 K3
Jonadab St *FELL* NE10 ....13 J5
Jones St *RDHAMSE* DH6 ....180 A2
Jones St *CLS/BIR/GTL* DH3 ....115 H2
Jonquil Cl *WD/WHPE/BLK* NE5 ..54 A6
Joseph Cl *ELS/FEN* NE4 ....69 J7
Joseph Hopper
  CLS/BIR/GTL
  (off Aged Miners Homes) DH3 ..101 J6
Joseph St *STLY/ANP* DH9 ......126 C2
Jowett Sq *SWCK/CAS* SR5 .....106 A2
Joyce Cl *FELL* NE10 ....88 C4
Joyce Gv *PLEE/EAS* SR8 ......174 D7
Joyce Ter *SWCK/CAS* SR5 .....105 F4
Jubilee Av *LWF/SPW/WRK* NE9 .101 J1
Jubilee Cl *BDN/LAN/SAC* DH7 .143 G5
Jubilee Crs *GOS/KPK* NE3 .....56 A4
  RDHAMSE DH6 ....171 G1
Jubilee Est *ASHGTN* NE63 ......23 K4
Jubilee Pl *DHAM* DH1 ....169 H4
  RDHAMSE DH6 ....173 H3
Jubilee Rd *BLYTH* NE24 ....35 G1
  CNUT NE1 ....6 A6
  GOS/KPK NE3 ....56 A5
Jubilee Sq *HLH* DH5 ....148 B7
Jubilee Ter *BYK/HTN/WLK* NE6 ...7 J5
  WICK/BNPF NE16 ....84 E3
Jude Pl *PLEE/EAS* SR8 ....174 D2
Judson Rd *PLEE/EAS* SR8 .....174 A3
Julian Av *BYK/HTN/WLK* NE6 ....7 L2
  SSH NE33 ....3 J5
Julian Rd *FELL* NE10 ....89 F4
Julian St *SSH* NE33 ....3 J5
Juliet Av *NSHW* NE29 ....60 B4
Juliet St *ASHGTN* NE63 ....24 A1
Julius Caesar St *SWCK/CAS* SR5 .106 A3
June Av *BLAY* NE21 ....84 A6
Juniper Cl *ASHBK/HED/RY* SR2 ...
  BLYTH NE24 ....34 E5
  GOS/KPK NE3 ....56 A5
Jupiter Ct *PLEE/EAS* SR8 ......162 D5
Jutland Av *HEBB* NE31 ....73 G5
Jutland Ter *STLY/ANP* DH9 .....112 B6

K

Kalmia St *DUN/TMV* NE11 ....86 C7
Kane Gdns *FELL* NE10 ....87 J6
Katherine St *ASHGTN* NE63 ....24 A1
Katrine Cl *CLSW/PEL* DH2 ....129 H5
Katrine Ct *SUNDSW* SR3 ....134 A2
Kayll Rd *MLFD/PNYW* SR4 ....105 K7
Kay St *STLY/ANP* DH9 ....112 D7
Kearsley Cl *MONK* NE25 ....40 A5
Kearton Av *WD/WHPE/BLK* NE5 ...34 E2
Keats Av *BLYTH* NE24 ....34 E2
  BOLCOL NE35 ....91 H4
  SWCK/CAS SR5 ....106 A3
Keats Cl *STLY/ANP* DH9 ....126 E1
Keats Gv *ASHGTN* NE63 ....24 B2
Keats Rd *BW/LEM/TK/HW* NE15 ...67 J5
Keats Wk *GATE* NE8 ....11 K4
Keeble Ct *ASHGTN* NE63 ....24 D2
Keebledale Av
  BYK/HTN/WLK NE6 ....72 B4
Keelman's La *MLFD/PNYW* SR4 ...105 F6
Keelman's Rd
  MLFD/PNYW SR4 ....105 F6
  STLY/ANP DH9 ....126 D3
Keir Hardie Av *FELL* NE10 ....13 K8
  STLY/ANP DH9 ....126 D3
Keir Hardie St *HLS* DH4 ....131 K7
Keir Hardie Wy *SWCK/CAS* SR5 ..106 E4
Keith Cl *ELS/FEN* NE4 ....69 J7
Keldane Gdns *ELS/FEN* NE4 ....69 J6
Kelfield Av *CRAM* NE23 ....33 H5
Kelfield Av *LWF/SPW/WRK* NE9 ...87 G6
Kelfield Rd *LWF/SPW/WRK* NE9 ...87 G7
Kell Rd *PLEE/EAS* SR8 ....175 G4
Kells La *LWF/SPW/WRK* NE9 ....87 F7
Kellsway *FELL* NE10 ....88 B7
Kell's Wy *ROWG* NE39 ....97 G4
Kelly Rd *HEBB* NE31 ....89 G1
Kelsey Wy *CRAM* NE23 ....33 H5
Kelso Cl *WD/WHPE/BLK* NE5 ......54 A6
Kelso Dr *NSHW* NE29 ....60 C2
Kelso Gdns
  BW/LEM/TK/HW NE15 ....69 F5
  WLSD/HOW NE28 ....59 J6
Kelso Gv *HLS* DH4 ....131 J1
Kelso Pl *GATE* NE8 ....9 M6
Kelston Wy *WD/WHPE/BLK* NE5 ..69 G1
Kelvin Gdns *DUN/TMV* NE11 ....9 H5
  CLDN/WHIT/ROK SR6 ....106 C3
Kelvin Gv *CLDN/WHIT/ROK* SR6 ..91 J5
  GATE NE8 ....10 D8
  HAR/WTLS NE34 ....75 K2
  JES NE2 ....6 B2
  NSHW NE29 ....60 E2
Kemble Cl *CRAM* NE23 ....33 H5
Kemp Rd *PLEE/EAS* SR8 ....174 D3
Kempton Cl *CON/LDGT* DH8 ......108 D7
Kempton Gdns *GATE* NE8 ....10 B9
Kendal Av *BLYTH* NE24 ....35 F1
  TYNE/NSHE NE30 ....51 F7
Kendal Cl *PLEE/EAS* SR8 ....174 B7
Kendal Dr *BOL* NE36 ....91 G5
  CRAM NE23 ....33 J7
Kendal Wk *WD/WHPE/BLK* NE5 ..54 C7
Kendal Gdns *WLSD/HOW* NE28 ...59 J6
Kendal Gn *BYK/HTN/WLK* NE6 .....6 F5
Kendal Pl *BYK/HTN/WLK* NE6 ......6 F6
Kendal St *BYK/HTN/WLK* NE6 .....6 F6
Kendor Gv *MPTH* NE61 ....20 D7
Kenilworth *LGB/KIL* NE12 ....47 K5
Kenilworth Rd *ASHGTN* NE63 ......23 J1
  ELS/FEN NE4 ....4 F9
  MONK NE25 ....50 D5
Kenilworth Sq *SWCK/CAS* SR5 ...105 G1
Kenilworth Vw
  LWF/SPW/WRK NE9 ....101 G3
Kenley Rd *WD/WHPE/BLK* NE5 ....68 E3
Kenmoor Wy
  WD/WHPE/BLK NE5 ....54 A7
Kenmore Crs *RYTON* NE40 ....82 D2
Kennersdene *TYNE/NSHE* NE30 ...61 G2
Kennet Av *JRW* NE32 ....90 A1
Kennington Gv
  BYK/HTN/WLK NE6 ....7 L6
Kenny Pl *DHAM* DH1 ....157 G6
Kensington Av *GOS/KPK* NE3 .....56 C3
Kensington Ct
  FELL (off Nursery La) NE10 ....12 A8
Kensington Gdns
  TYNE/NSHE NE30 ....61 F4
  WLSD/HOW NE28 ....58 A7
Kensington Gv
  TYNE/NSHE NE30 ....61 F3
Kensington Ter *DUN/TMV* NE11 ...9 H8
  JES NE2 ....5 J2
Kent Av *DUN/TMV* * NE11 ....9 J7
  HEBB NE31 ....73 F6
  WLSD/HOW NE28 ....73 H1
Kentchester Rd *SWCK/CAS* SR5 ..105 F1
Kent Cl *ASHGTN* NE63 ....23 C1
Kent Ct *DIN/WO* NE13 ....55 H2
Kent Gdns *HLS* DH5 ....147 J4
Kentmere Av
  BYK/HTN/WLK NE6 ....72 B5
  CLDN/WHIT/ROK SR6 ....92 C7
Kentmere Cl *CRAM* NE23 ....39 H6
Kentmere Pl *PLEE/EAS* SR8 ....175 F4
Kenton Av *GOS/KPK* NE3 ....56 A7
Kenton Ct *SSH* NE33 ....75 H2
Kenton Crs *GOS/KPK* NE3 ....55 K6
Kenton Gv
  CLDN/WHIT/ROK SR6 ....106 D4
Kenton La *GOS/KPK* NE3 ....55 J6
  WD/WHPE/BLK NE5 ....55 J6
Kenton Rd *GOS/KPK* NE3 ....55 J6
  NSHW NE29 ....60 A3
Kent Pl *HAR/WTLS* NE34 ....75 K5
Kent Rd *CON/LDGT* DH8 ....122 C4
Kent St *JRW* NE32 ....73 J5
Kent Ter *RDHAMSE* DH6 ....172 D1
Kentucky Rd *SWCK/CAS* SR5 .....104 E1
Kenya Rd *SWCK/CAS* SR5 ....105 F1
Kepier Chare *RYTON* NE40 ....66 B7

Kepier Ct *DHAM* DH1 ....16 F2
Kepier Crs *DHAM* DH1 ....17 M1
Kepier Gdns *MLFD/PNYW* SR4 ...104 E7
Kepier Hts *DHAM* DH1 ....16 F2
Kepier Ter *DHAM* DH1 ....16 F2
Kepier Vls *DHAM* DH1 ....16 F2
Keppel St *DUN/TMV* NE11 ....9 H5
  SSH NE33 ....3 H7
Kepwell Bank Top *PRUD* NE42 ....80 D2
Kepwell Rd *PRUD* NE42 ....80 C1
Kepwell Rd Bottom *PRUD* NE42 ...80 C1
Kerry Cl *BLYTH* NE24 ....31 G6
Kerryhill Dr *DHAM* DH1 ....156 D1
Keston Dr *CRAM* NE23 ....33 H5
Kestrel Cl *WASHS* NE38 ....116 C4
Kestrel Dr *ASHGTN* NE63 ....23 H4
Kestrel Ms *WICK/BNPF* NE16 .....84 E5
Kestrel Pl *LGB/KIL* NE12 ....57 H3
Kestrel Wy *DUN/TMV* NE11 ....86 C6
Kestrel Wy *HAR/WTLS* NE34 ......75 F7
  NSHW NE29 ....2 B6
Keswick Av
  CLDN/WHIT/ROK SR6 ....106 C1
Keswick Dr *TYNE/NSHE* NE30 .....51 F7
Keswick Gdns *WLSD/HOW* NE28 ..59 J7
Keswick Gv *WD/WHPE/BLK* NE5 ..68 E3
Keswick Pl *PLEE/EAS* SR8 ....175 F4
  STLY/ANP DH9 ....126 B3
Keswick St *GATE* NE8 ....10 E6
Keswick Ter *RDHAMSE* DH6 ....160 D1
Kettering Pl *CRAM* NE23 ....33 J7
Kettlewell Ter *TYNE/NSHE* NE30 ...2 F1
Ketton Cl *LGB/KIL* NE12 ....57 H4
Kew Gdns *WBAY* NE26 ....50 D5
Keyes Gdns *JES* NE2 ....56 E7
Kibblesworth Bank
  DUN/TMV NE11 ....100 B7
Kidd Av *RDHAMSE* DH6 ....170 C7
Kidderminster Dr
  WD/WHPE/BLK NE5 ....54 A7
Kidderminster Rd
  SWCK/CAS SR5 ....105 F2
Kidland Cl *ASHGTN* NE63 ....24 B1
Kidlandlee Gn
  WD/WHPE/BLK NE5 ....54 E6
Kidlandlee Pl
  WD/WHPE/BLK NE5 ....54 E6
Kielder Av *CRAM* NE23 ....37 J2
Kielder Cl *BLYTH* NE24 ....34 D2
  LGB/KIL NE12 ....47 J5
  WD/WHPE/BLK NE5 ....54 E6
Kielder Dr *ASHGTN* NE63 ....23 J2
  TRIM TS29 ....182 D7
Kielder Gdns *JRW* NE32 ....89 J1
  STKFD/GP NE62 ....23 C4
Kielder Pl *MONK* NE25 ....49 K4
Kielder Rd
  BW/LEM/TK/HW NE15 ....67 K4
  MONK NE25 ....49 K4
Kielder Ter *TYNE/NSHE* NE30 .....61 F4
Kielder Wy *GOS/KPK* NE3 ....56 B3
Kier Hardie Av *STLY/ANP* DH9 ...126 D2
Kilburn Dr *PLEE/EAS* SR8 ....175 G1
Kilburne Cl *LGB/KIL* NE12 ....58 A7
Kilburn Gdns *NSHW* NE29 ....60 B7
Kilchurn *CON/LDGT* DH8 ....122 D4
Kildale *HLS* DH4 ....117 G6
Killiebrigs
  BW/LEM/TK/HW NE15 ....65 K1
Killin Cl *WD/WHPE/BLK* NE5 ......54 A6
Killingworth Av *SMOOR* NE27 .....48 C5
Killingworth Dr *LGB/KIL* NE12 ....47 H7
  SUNDSW SR3 ....119 H2
Killingworth La *LGB/KIL* NE12 ....48 C6
Killingworth Pl *CNUT* NE1 ....5 J5
Killingworth Rd *GOS/KPK* NE3 ....57 F5
  LGB/KIL NE12 ....58 A1
Killingworth Wy *CRAM* NE23 ......48 A4
  LGB/KIL NE12 ....47 G5
Kiln Ri *WICK/BNPF* NE16 ....98 E1
Kilnshaw Pl *GOS/KPK* NE3 ....56 D1
Kimberley *WASHS* NE38 ....117 J1
Kimberley Av *NSHW* NE29 ....60 C4
Kimberley Gdns *JES* NE2 ....71 G3
Kimberley St *BLYTH* NE24 ....31 F6
  MLFD/PNYW SR4 ....105 K7
Kingarth Av
  CLDN/WHIT/ROK SR6 ....92 C7
Kingdom Pl *NSHW* NE29 ....2 C7
King Edward Bridge Arches
  CNUT NE1 ....10 B1
King Edward Pl *GATE* NE8 ....11 L5
King Edward Rd
  BYK/HTN/WLK NE6 ....71 H2
  MLFD/PNYW SR4 ....105 F7
  RYTON NE40 ....67 G2
  SEA/MUR SR7 ....150 E2
  TYNE/NSHE NE30 ....61 G3
King Edward St *GATE* NE8 ....11 L6
Kingfisher Cl *ASHGTN* NE63 ....24 A5
Kingfisher Rd *LGB/KIL* NE12 ....57 G3
Kingfisher Wy *BLYTH* NE24 ....35 G3
  WLSD/HOW NE28 ....59 J4
King George Av *DUN/TMV* NE11 ...9 G9
King George Rd *GOS/KPK* NE3 ....55 J4
  HAR/WTLS NE34 ....75 J4
King George's Rd *NWBGN* NE64 ..19 F7
Kingham Ct *LGB/HTN* NE7 ....57 F6
King James Hospital Bungalows
  GATE (off Sunderland Rd) NE8 ...11 L5
King James St *GATE* NE8 ....11 H5
King John's Ct *PONT/DH* NE20 ....42 C5
King John St *BYK/HTN/WLK* NE6 ...6 F1
King John Ter *BYK/HTN/WLK* NE6 ..6 E1
Kings Av *CLDN/WHIT/ROK* SR6 ...92 E7
  HEBB NE31 ....73 H6
  MPTH NE61 ....20 D3
Kingsbridge *LGB/KIL* NE12 ....47 H5
Kings Cl *GATE* NE8 ....11 L5
Kingsdale Av *BLYTH* NE24 ....30 C7
Kingsdale Rd *LGB/KIL* NE12 ....57 J3
King's Dr *WBAY* NE26 ....50 E4
King's Gdns *BLYTH* NE24 ....30 E6
Kings Gv *DHAM* DH1 ....168 B5
Kingsland *JES* NE2 ....70 E3
King's La *CLSW/PEL* DH2 ....114 D7
Kingsley Av *GOS/KPK* NE3 ....56 D7
  HAR/WTLS NE34 ....90 E1

MONK NE25 ....50 D5
Kingsley Cl *SWCK/CAS* * SR5 ....106 A4
Kingsley Pl *BYK/HTN/WLK* NE6 ....6 F1
  DUN/TMV NE11 ....9 H6
  WICK/BNPF NE16 ....85 F4
  WLSD/HOW NE28 ....59 H7
Kingsley Ter *ELS/FEN* NE4 ....4 C7
Kings Mdw
  ELS/FEN (off Brunel Ter) NE4 .....9 J1
Kingsmere *CLS/BIR/GTL* DH3 ...115 J7
Kingsmere Gdns
  BYK/HTN/WLK NE6 ....72 C7
Kings Pk *STKFD/GP* NE62 ....29 F1
King's Pl *MLFD/PNYW* SR4 ....106 A6
King's Rd *BDLGTN* NE22 ....29 K4
  CNUT NE1 ....5 J4
  CON/LDGT DH8 ....122 D7
  LGB/KIL NE12 ....57 J1
  WBAY NE26 ....50 D3
  WNGT TS28 ....183 J2
Kings Rd North
  WLSD/HOW NE28 ....58 D6
Kings Rd South
  WLSD/HOW NE28 ....58 D7
The King's Rd *SWCK/CAS* SR5 ...106 A3
King's Ter *MLFD/PNYW* SR4 ......105 K6
Kingston Av
  BDN/LAN/SAC DH7 ....155 F6
  BYK/HTN/WLK NE6 ....7 K7
  SEA/MUR SR7 ....150 C2
Kingston Cl *WBAY* NE26 ....50 D1
Kingston Dr *WBAY* NE26 ....50 D2
Kingston Gn *BYK/HTN/WLK* NE6 ...7 K7
Kingston Ms *HLS* DH4 ....132 A2
Kingston Pk *GOS/KPK* NE3 ....55 J5
Kingston Park Av *GOS/KPK* NE3 ..55 C4
Kingston Park Rd *DIN/WO* NE13 ..55 H2
  GOS/KPK NE3 ....55 K3
Kingston Rd *GATE* NE8 ....11 K7
Kingston Ter
  CLDN/WHIT/ROK SR6 ....106 D3
King St *BLYTH* NE24 ....31 G6
  CLDN/WHIT/ROK SR6 ....106 D1
  CNUT NE1 ....5 M8
  FELL NE10 ....13 K5
  GATE NE8 ....10 B8
  RDHAMSE DH6 ....170 C1
  RDHAMSE DH6 ....173 J4
  SSH NE33 ....3 G7
  SUND SR1 ....14 E4
  TYNE/NSHE NE30 ....61 F4
Kingsway *BDN/LAN/SAC* DH7 ...154 B3
  BLYTH NE24 ....35 G1
  ELS/FEN NE4 ....69 J5
  HLH DH5 ....132 D7
  PONT/DH NE20 ....43 D3
  SSH NE33 ....75 K1
  TYNE/NSHE NE30 ....61 G2
  WICK/BNPF NE16 ....98 E2
Kingsway Av *GOS/KPK* NE3 ....56 C3
Kingsway North
  DUN/TMV NE11 ....86 C6
Kingsway Rd *SWCK/CAS* SR5 ...104 E1
Kingsway South
  DUN/TMV NE11 ....100 D1
Kingswood Av *JES* NE2 ....56 D7
Kingswood Cl *BOLCOL* NE35 ......90 C3
Kingswood Dr *PONT/DH* NE20 ....42 E5
Kingswood Gv
  MLFD/PNYW SR4 ....118 D4
Kingswood Rd *CRAM* NE23 ....33 J7
King Ter *STLY/ANP* DH9 ....126 B2
Kinlett *WASHS* NE38 ....117 J1
Kinley Rd *DHAM* DH1 ....158 A4
Kinloch Ct *CLSW/PEL* DH2 ....129 H6
Kinloss Sq *CRAM* NE23 ....33 J7
Kinnaird Av
  BW/LEM/TK/HW NE15 ....68 E5
Kinross Cl *FELL* NE10 ....13 M4
Kinross Dr *GOS/KPK* NE3 ....55 J5
  STLY/ANP DH9 ....127 F1
Kinver Dr *WD/WHPE/BLK* NE5 ....54 A7
Kiphill Ct *STLY/ANP* DH9 ....112 E6
Kipling Av *BOLCOL* NE35 ....91 F4
  HEBB NE31 ....73 H5
  WICK/BNPF NE16 ....85 F4
Kipling Cl *STLY/ANP* DH9 ....126 E1
Kipling St *SWCK/CAS* SR5 ....106 A4
Kipling Wk *GATE* NE8 ....11 K4
Kira Dr *DHAM* DH1 ....156 D1
Kirby Av *DHAM* DH1 ....156 B4
Kirby Cl *HAR/WTLS* NE34 ....74 D7
Kirkbride Pl *CRAM* NE23 ....33 J7
Kirkdale Gn *ELS/FEN* NE4 ....4 E8
Kirkdale St *HLH* DH5 ....147 J6
Kirkfield Gdns *STLY/ANP* DH9 ...125 G2
Kirkham Av *GOS/KPK* NE3 ....55 G3
Kirkham Rd *DHAM* DH1 ....156 C3
Kirkharle Dr *MPTH* NE61 ....21 J2
Kirkheaton Pl
  WD/WHPE/BLK NE5 ....69 G3
Kirkland Hl *PLEE/EAS* SR8 ....174 B1
Kirklands *DHAM* DH1 ....47 J4
Kirkland Wk *SMOOR* NE27 ....49 G6
Kirklea Rd *HLH* DH5 ....132 D7
Kirkleatham Gdns
  BYK/HTN/WLK NE6 ....71 K1
Kirkley Av *HAR/WTLS* NE34 ....76 A5
Kirkley Cl *GOS/KPK* NE3 ....56 B4
Kirkley Dr *ASHGTN* NE63 ....24 A3
  PONT/DH NE20 ....43 G2
Kirkley Ldg
  GOS/KPK (off Park Av) NE3 .....56 B4
Kirkley Rd *SMOOR* NE27 ....49 H7
Kirklinton Rd *TYNE/NSHE* NE30 ..50 E7
Kirknewton Cl *HLH* DH5 ....132 D7
Kirkside *HLS* DH4 ....132 C1
Kirkston Av
  BW/LEM/TK/HW NE15 ....68 B4
Kirkstone *CLS/BIR/GTL* DH3 .....115 J3
Kirkstone Av *JRW* NE32 ....90 B1
  PLEE/EAS SR8 ....175 H4
  SWCK/CAS SR5 ....106 C2
  TYNE/NSHE NE30 ....50 E7

Kirkstone Cl *HLH* DH5 ....132 D7
Kirkstone Dr *DHAM* DH1 ....157 K4
Kirkstone Gdns *LGB/HTN* NE7 ....57 G7
Kirkstone Rd *FELL* NE10 ....13 H6
Kirk St *BYK/HTN/WLK* NE6 ....6 F1
  CON/LDGT DH8 ....122 E4
Kirk Vw *HLS* DH4 ....132 B3
Kirkwall Cl *SWCK/CAS* SR5 ......104 E4
Kirkwood *ASHGTN* NE63 ....47 J4
Kirkwood Av *MLFD/PNYW* SR4 ..118 C4
Kirkwood Cl *CRAM* NE23 ....39 H6
Kirkwood Dr *GOS/KPK* NE3 ....55 K5
Kirkwood Gdns *FELL* NE10 ....13 L7
Kirton Av *ELS/FEN* NE4 ....69 J5
Kirton Park Ter *NSHW* NE29 ......60 E3
  TYNE/NSHE NE30 ....60 E3
Kirton Wy *CRAM* NE23 ....33 J7
Kismet St *SWCK/CAS* SR5 ....106 A3
Kitchener Rd
  CLDN/WHIT/ROK SR6 ....76 E7
Kitchener St
  LWF/SPW/WRK NE9 ....11 J9
  MLFD/PNYW SR4 ....119 K2
Kitchener Ter
  ASHBK/HED/RY SR2 ....121 F4
  JRW NE32 ....73 K6
  TYNE/NSHE NE30 ....61 G3
Kitching Rd *PLEE/EAS* SR8 ....174 B1
Kitswell Rd *BDN/LAN/SAC* DH7 ..140 A3
Kittiwake Cl *BLYTH* NE24 ....35 G4
  NSHW NE29 ....59 J3
Kittiwake Dr *WASHS* NE38 ....116 B3
Kittiwake St *DUN/TMV* NE11 ......86 D6
Kitty Brewster Rd *BLYTH* NE24 ...30 B6
Knaresborough Cl
  BDLGTN NE22 ....28 D4
Knaresborough Rd
  SEA/MUR SR7 ....149 H5
Knaresdale *CLS/BIR/GTL* DH3 ...115 K5
Knarsdale Av *NSHW* NE29 ....60 B4
Knarsdale Pl
  WD/WHPE/BLK NE5 ....68 C2
Kneller Cl *STLY/ANP* DH9 ....126 D1
Knightsbridge *GOS/KPK* NE3 ......56 C4
  SUNDSW SR3 ....119 J6
Knightside Gdns
  DUN/TMV NE11 ....85 K6
Knitsley La *CON/LDGT* DH8 ......138 C7
Knivestone Ct *LGB/KIL* NE12 .....48 A5
Knobbyends La *BLAY* NE21 ....83 H4
Knoll Ri *DUN/TMV* NE11 ....85 K5
Knollside Cl *SUNDSW* SR3 ....133 K2
The Knoll *ASHBK/HED/RY* SR2 ...14 A7
Knott Memorial Flats
  TYNE/NSHE NE30 ....61 H3
Knott Pl *BW/LEM/TK/HW* NE15 ...68 E6
Knoulberry *WASHS* NE37 ....102 C7
Knoulberry Rd *WASHS* NE37 .....102 C7
Knowledge Hl *BLAY* NE21 ....83 K3
Knowle Pl *LGB/KIL* NE12 ....57 H5
Knowsley Ct
  WD/WHPE/BLK NE5 ....55 F5
Knox Cl *BDLGTN* NE22 ....29 K4
Knox La *BDN/LAN/SAC* DH7 .....152 D6
Knox Rd *BDLGTN* NE22 ....29 H6
Knox Sq *SWCK/CAS* SR5 ....106 A2
Kristin Av *JRW* NE32 ....74 A7
Kyffin Vw *HAR/WTLS* NE34 ....76 B6
Kyle Cl *ELS/FEN* NE4 ....4 F9
Kyloe Av *MONK* NE25 ....40 A6
Kyloe Cl *GOS/KPK* NE3 ....54 E7
Kyloe Ct *WD/WHPE/BLK* NE5 ....54 E7
Kyloe Vls *WD/WHPE/BLK* NE5 ...54 E7
Kyo Bog La *WYLAM* NE41 ....81 H3
Kyo Heugh Rd *STLY/ANP* DH9 ...125 J1
Kyo La *RYTON* NE40 ....81 K5
  STLY/ANP DH9 ....125 K2
Kyo Rd *STLY/ANP* DH9 ....125 H2

L

Laburnam Pk
  BDN/LAN/SAC DH7 ....166 E7
Laburnam Rd
  CLDN/WHIT/ROK SR6 ....106 D2
Laburnam Ter *STLY/ANP* DH9 ...125 G2
Laburnum Av *BLYTH* NE24 ....31 F6
  BYK/HTN/WLK NE6 ....72 B3
  CON/LDGT DH8 ....122 B3
  DHAM DH1 ....16 A4
  FELL NE10 ....13 J9
  WLSD/HOW NE28 ....72 D1
Laburnum Ct *LGB/KIL* NE12 ....47 J5
Laburnum Crs *DUN/TMV* NE11 ..100 C7
  SEA/MUR SR7 ....150 A2
  TRIM TS29 ....183 G6
Laburnum Gdns *FELL* NE10 ....12 C5
  JRW NE32 ....73 J2
Laburnum Gv
  CLDN/WHIT/ROK SR6 ....92 A3
  HAR/WTLS NE34 ....75 K6
  HEBB NE31 ....89 G1
  SWCK/CAS SR5 ....104 E5
  WICK/BNPF NE16 ....84 E5
  WICK/BNPF NE16 ....99 F2
Laburnum Rd *BLAY* NE21 ....84 A2
Laburnum Sq *TRIM* TS29 ....183 G6
Laburnun Ter *ASHGTN* * NE63 ...23 K2
Laburnun St *STKFD/GP* * NE62 ..22 E6
Lacebark *HLS* DH4 ....131 H1
  SUNDSW SR3 ....133 J3
Ladock Cl *ASHBK/HED/RY* SR2 ..121 G6
Lady Anne Rd *RDHAMSE* DH6 ...158 D7
Ladybank *WD/WHPE/BLK* NE5 ....53 K7
Ladyhaugh Dr *WICK/BNPF* NE16 ..98 E1
Ladykirk Rd *ELS/FEN* NE4 ....69 J6
Ladyrigg *PONT/DH* NE20 ....43 D5
Ladysmith Ct *ASHGTN* NE63 ......23 K2
Lady's Piece La *RDHAMSE* DH6 ..158 D3
Lady's Wk *MPTH* NE61 ....20 C4
  SSH NE33 ....3 C5
Ladywell Rd *BLAY* NE21 ....84 A2
  CON/LDGT DH8 ....123 H7

Ladywell Wy *PONT/DH* NE20 ......43 F2
Ladywood Pk *HLS* DH4 ....117 H6
Laet St *NSHW* NE29 ....2 E3
Laindon Av
  CLDN/WHIT/ROK SR6 ....106 D1
Laing Gv *WLSD/HOW* NE28 ....59 J7
Laing St *CON/LDGT* DH8 ....123 F3
Laith Rd *GOS/KPK* NE3 ....55 J5
Lake Av *BLAY* NE21 ....84 C3
Lake Av *HAR/WTLS* NE34 ....76 C5
Lake Bank Ter *WNGT* TS28 ....183 K5
Lake Ct *SUNDSW* SR3 ....134 A1
Lakeland Dr *PLEE/EAS* SR8 ......175 F3
Lake Rd *HLH* DH5 ....132 C7
Lakeside *BLAY* NE21 ....84 D3
  HAR/WTLS NE34 ....76 D5
Lake Vw *HEBB* NE31 ....73 F7
  WNGT TS28 ....183 K5
Laleham Ct *GOS/KPK* NE3 ....55 H3
Lambden Cl *NSHW* NE29 ....60 C7
Lambert Rd *WASHN* NE37 ....102 B6
Lambeth Pl *GATE* NE8 ....11 K7
Lambley Av *TYNE/NSHE* NE30 ...51 F7
Lambley Cl *WICK/BNPF* NE16 ....98 E3
Lambley Crs *HEBB* NE31 ....89 F1
Lambourn Av *LGB/KIL* NE12 ......57 J3
  NSHW NE29 ....60 B6
Lambourne Cl *HLS* DH4 ....131 G4
Lambourne Rd
  ASHBK/HED/RY SR2 ....120 C3
Lamb St *BYK/HTN/WLK* NE6 ......72 C6
Lambton Av *CON/LDGT* DH8 .....123 H7
  WICK/BNPF NE16 ....8 A3
Lambton Cl *RYTON* NE40 ....66 B7
Lambton Ct *PLEE/EAS* SR8 ....174 D7
  SUNDSW SR3 ....119 G2
  WASHS NE38 ....116 A6
Lambton Dr *HLH* DH5 ....147 K6
Lambton Rd *HEBB* NE31 ....73 H4
  JES NE2 ....5 L1
Lambton St *GATE* NE8 ....10 F1
  SUND SR1 ....14 F3
Lambton Ter *JRW* NE32 ....89 K1
Lambton Wk *DHAM* DH1 ....16 C4
Lampeter Cl
  WD/WHPE/BLK NE5 ....55 F7
Lamport St *HEBB* NE31 ....72 E4
Lampton Ct *BDLGTN* NE22 ....29 J4
Lanark Cl *NSHW* NE29 ....60 A2
Lanark Dr *JRW* NE32 ....90 C1
Lancashire Dr *DHAM* DH1 ....158 A6
Lancaster Ct *GOS/KPK* NE3 ....55 H3
Lancaster Dr *WLSD/HOW* NE28 ..59 F3
Lancaster Hl *PLEE/EAS* SR8 ......174 C2
Lancaster Rd *CON/LDGT* DH8 ...137 F1
  DUN/TMV NE11 ....8 E6
Lancaster Ter
  CLS/BIR/GTL DH3 ....129 K5
Lancastrian Rd *CRAM* NE23 ....38 B3
Lancefield Av
  BYK/HTN/WLK NE6 ....72 E7
Lancet Ct *GATE* NE8 ....11 H3
Lanchester Av
  LWF/SPW/WRK NE9 ....101 K2
Lanchester Cl *FELL* NE10 ....88 E6
Lanchester Gn *BDLGTN* NE22 ....29 F4
Lanchester Pk *WASHS* NE38 .....117 G4
Lanchester Rd
  BDN/LAN/SAC DH7 ....125 J7
Lancing Ct *GOS/KPK* NE3 ....55 G3
Landsdowne Crs
  RDHAMSE DH6 ....180 C3
Landsdowne Gdns
  STKFD/GP NE62 ....23 G5
Landsdowne Rd
  RDHAMSE DH6 ....180 C7
Landseer Cl *STLY/ANP* DH9 ......126 D1
Landseer Gdns *HAR/WTLS* NE34 ..91 H2
  LWF/SPW/WRK NE9 ....11 M8
Lane Cnr *HAR/WTLS* NE34 ....75 G6
Lanercost *WASHS* NE38 ....116 E1
Lanercost Av *BLAY* NE21 ....83 K2
Lanercost Dr
  WD/WHPE/BLK NE5 ....69 F3
Lanercost Gdns
  BW/LEM/TK/HW NE15 ....67 F1
  FELL NE10 ....87 J6
Lanercost Rd *NSHW* NE29 ....60 C5
Langdale *MONK* NE25 ....50 C4
Langdale Cl *CON/LDGT* DH8 .....123 K3
  LGB/KIL NE12 ....57 J1
Langdale Crs *DHAM* DH1 ....157 K4
Langdale Dr *CRAM* NE23 ....37 G2
Langdale Gdns
  BYK/HTN/WLK NE6 ....72 C5
  WLSD/HOW NE28 ....59 J6
Langdale Pl *PLEE/EAS* * SR8 .....175 F4
Langdale Rd *HLS* DH4 ....117 J6
  LWF/SPW/WRK NE9 ....87 G7
Langdale St *HLH* DH5 ....147 K6
Langdale Wy *BOL* NE36 ....91 G4
Langdon Cl *NSHW* NE29 ....60 D1
Langdon Gdns *STLY/ANP* DH9 ...125 G2
Langdon Rd
  WD/WHPE/BLK NE5 ....68 B1
Langford Dr *BOLCOL* NE35 ....90 C2
Langham Av *NSHW* NE29 ....60 A2
Langham Rd
  BW/LEM/TK/HW NE15 ....68 D6
Langholm Rd *BOL* NE36 ....91 H4
Langhorn Cl *BYK/HTN/WLK* NE6 ..6 F4
Langhurst *ASHBK/HED/RY* SR2 ..120 E6
Langleeford Av
  WD/WHPE/BLK NE5 ....54 E7
Langley Av *BDN/LAN/SAC* DH7 ..141 G3
  BLYTH NE24 ....30 D6
  FELL NE10 ....88 D6
  MONK NE25 ....50 B6
  SMOOR NE27 ....49 J7
Langley Cl *WASHS* NE38 ....116 D2
Langley Crs *BDN/LAN/SAC* DH7 ..167 J5
Langley Dr *PLEE/EAS* SR8 ....174 B6
Langley La *BDN/LAN/SAC* DH7 ..141 K9
Langley Rd *ASHGTN* NE63 ....23 J2
  BYK/HTN/WLK NE6 ....72 B5
  DHAM DH1 ....156 D3
  NSHW NE29 ....60 B4

SUNDSW SR3 ....120 B4
WD/WHPE/BLK NE5 ....68 D3
Langley St HLS DH4 ....132 B1
Langley Tarn NSHW NE29..........2 D4
Langley Ter JRW NE32 ....89 K1
STLY/ANP DH9 ....125 J3
Langport Rd
ASHBK/HED/RY SR2 ....120 D3
Langton Cl MLFD/PNYW SR4 ......14 A5
Langton Ct PONT/DH NE20 ....42 D5
Langton Dr CRAM NE23 ....33 J5
Langton Lea DHAM DH1 ....169 K5
Langton Ter LGB/HTN NE7 ....71 H1
Langwell Ter MPTH NE61 ....21 K1
Lanivet Cl ASHBK/HED/RY SR2 ...121 F6
Lannerwood NSHW NE29............2 C4
Lansbury Cl CLS/BIR/GTL DH3 ...101 H7
Lansbury Dr CLS/BIR/GTL DH3....101 H7
SEA/MUR SR7 ....149 H5
Lansbury Gdns HEBB NE10 ....13 K8
Lansbury Wy SWCK/CAS SR5 ......105 F4
Lansdowne
ASHBK/HED/RY SR2 ....120 E7
Lansdowne Gdns FELL NE10 ....6 D1
Lansdowne Rd LGB/KIL NE12 ......57 K2
Lansdowne St MLFD/PNYW SR4 ....14 A3
Lansdowne Ter NSHW NE29 ....2 B1
Lansdowne Ter West
NSHW NE29 ....2 A1
Lanthwaite Rd
LWF/SPW/WRK NE9 ....87 G7
Lanton St HLS DH4 ....132 B1
Lapford Dr CRAM NE23.............33 J6
Lapwing Cl BLYTH NE24 ....35 C3
WASHS NE38 ....116 B3
Lapwing Ct WICK/BNPF NE16 ......112 A1
L'arbre Crs WICK/BNPF NE16 ......84 D5
Larch Av CLDN/WHIT/ROK SR6.....93 G3
HAR/WTLS NE34 ....76 A6
HLS DH4 ....132 B6
Larch Cl LWF/SPW/WRK NE9 .....101 K3
Larches Rd DHAM DH1 ....156 B6
The Larches BDN/LAN/SAC DH7...165 C2
ELS/FEN (off Park Rd) NE4 ....9 K1
WICK/BNPF NE16 ....97 K6
Larchlea PONT/DH NE20 ....42 E7
Larchlea South PONT/DH NE20....42 E7
Larch Rd BLAY NE21 ....84 B1
Larch St CON/LDGT DH8 ....123 F4
Larch Ter STLY/ANP DH9 ....111 J5
Larchwood WASHS NE38 ....116 D5
Larchwood Av
BYK/HTN/WLK NE6 ....72 A3
DIN/WO NE13 ....46 C4
GOS/KPK NE3 ....55 K4
Larchwood Dr ASHGTN NE63 ......23 J4
Larchwood Gdns
DUN/TMV NE11 ....86 B7
Larchwood Gv
ASHBK/HED/RY SR2 ....120 C4
Larkfield Crs HLS DH4 ....131 J2
Larkfield Rd
ASHBK/HED/RY SR2 ....120 C3
Lark Rise Cl LGB/HTN * NE7 ......57 K7
Larkspur Cl STLY/ANP DH9 ....112 B6
Larkspur Rd WICK/BNPF NE16.....84 B6
Larkspur Ter JES NE2 ....70 E2
Larriston Pl CRAM NE23 ....38 C2
Lartington Cl CLS/BIR/GTL DH3...145 J2
Lartington Gdns GOS/KPK NE3 ....57 F5
Larwood Ct STLY/ANP DH9 ....125 G4
Lascelles Av HAR/WTLS NE34 .....75 J6
Laski Gdns FELL NE10 ....13 L7
Lassells Rigg PRUD NE42 ....80 D1
Latimer St TYNE/NSHE NE30 ......61 H2
Laude Bank BDN/LAN/SAC DH7...153 F5
Lauderdale Av
WLSD/HOW NE28 ....58 D6
Launceston Cl DIN/WO NE13 ......55 H2
Launceston Dr SUNDSW SR3 ......119 C3
Laura St SUND SR1 ....14 F6
Laurel Av DHAM DH1 ....17 L3
GOS/KPK NE3 ....56 A4
LGB/KIL NE12 ....58 C1
SEA/MUR SR7 ....150 C1
Laurel Ct CLSW/PEL DH2 ....129 H2
TYNE/NSHE NE30 ....2 F2
Laurel Crs BYK/HTN/WLK NE6 .....72 B2
RDHAMSE DH6 ....172 B7
STLY/ANP DH9 ....114 B7
TRIM TS29 ....182 E6
Laurel Dr ASHGTN NE63 ....23 J4
CON/LDGT DH8 ....123 K4
Laurel Gv ASHBK/HED/RY SR2 ...120 C4
Laurel Rd BLAY NE21 ....84 B2
Laurel St BW/LEM/TK/HW NE15 ...53 F7
WLSD/HOW NE28 ....72 E2
Laurel Wy RYTON NE40 ....82 C1
Laurelwood Gdns
DUN/TMV NE11 ....86 B7
Lauren Ct PLEE/EAS SR8 ....162 D5
Laurens Ct WASHN NE37 ....103 F5
Lavender Ct ASHGTN NE63 ....23 J4
Lavender Gdns
BDN/LAN/SAC DH7 ....143 J5
JES NE2 ....70 C2
Lavender Gv SWCK/CAS SR5 .....104 E4
Lavender La HAR/WTLS NE34 ......75 F6
Lavender Rd WICK/BNPF NE16 ....84 E6
Lavender Rw
LWF/SPW/WRK NE9 ....87 H7
Laverick La
FELL (off Newcastle Rd) NE10 ....89 H5
Laverock Ct BYK/HTN/WLK NE6 ....7 G7
Laverock Hall Rd BLYTH NE24 .....34 C4
Laverock Pl BLYTH NE24 ....34 D4
GOS/KPK NE3 ....55 H5
Lavington Rd HAR/WTLS NE34 ....75 J3
Lawe Rd SSH NE33 ....3 J4
Lawmill Wy WD/WHPE/BLK NE5 ...69 F1
Lawn Ct
ASHGTN (off Green La) NE63 ......23 J4
Lawn Dr BOL NE36 ....90 D6
Lawnside SEA/MUR SR7 ....150 B2
The Lawns HLH DH5 ....148 B7

Lawnswood HLH DH5 ....147 J1
Lawrence Av BLAY NE21 ....84 A1
HAR/WTLS NE34 ....91 H1
Lawrence Ct BLAY NE21 ....84 A1
Lawrence Ct SUND SR1 ....15 H5
Lawson Av JRW NE32 ....74 A7
Lawson Crs
CLDN/WHIT/ROK SR6 ....106 D1
Lawson Rd RDHAMSE DH6 ....180 A2
Lawson's St TRIM TS29 ....183 F7
Lawson St NSHW NE29 ....2 D5
WLSD/HOW NE28 ....72 E2
Lawson Ter DHAM DH1 ....16 A4
ELS/FEN NE4 ....69 J7
HLH DH5 ....148 A7
Laws St CLDN/WHIT/ROK SR6 ....106 D1
Laxford Ct SUNDSW SR3 ....133 K2
Layburn Gdns
HAR/WTLS * NE34 ....74 E7
Layburn Gdns
BW/LEM/TK/HW NE15 ....68 C3
Layburn Pl PLEE/EAS SR8 ....174 D3
Layfield Rd GOS/KPK NE3 ....56 C1
Laygate SSH NE33 ....75 G3
Laygate Pl SSH NE33 ....75 G2
Laygate St SSH NE33 ....75 F2
Lea Av JRW NE32 ....90 A2
Leabank BW/LEM/TK/HW NE15 ...68 B3
Leadgate Rd CON/LDGT DH8 .....123 H8
Lead La BW/LEM/TK/HW NE15 ...108 C2
CON/LDGT DH8 ....108 C1
Lead Rd CHPW NE17 ....95 C1
RYTON NE40 ....82 C3
Leafield Crs HAR/WTLS NE34 .....76 A3
Lea Gn CLS/BIR/GTL DH3 ....116 A5
Leagreen Ct GOS/KPK NE3 ....56 A4
Leaholme Crs BLYTH NE24 ....34 E1
Lea La PLEE/EAS SR8 ....162 C3
Leam Gdns FELL NE10 ....88 E4
Leamington St
MLFD/PNYW SR4 ....14 A6
Leam La FELL NE10 ....88 C7
LWF/SPW/WRK NE9 ....102 B1
Leamside FELL NE10 ....88 B6
JRW NE32 ....74 A7
Leander Av CLS/BIR/GTL DH3 ...115 K7
STKFD/GP NE62 ....23 C5
Leander Ct STKFD/GP NE62 ......23 H5
Leander Dr BOLCOL NE35 ....90 C4
Leaplish WASHS NE38 ....117 H4
Lea Riggs HLS DH4 ....146 D6
Leaway PRUD NE42 ....80 B2
Leazes Cl DHAM DH1 ....16 E3
Leazes Crs CNUT NE1 ....5 H5
Leazes La CNUT NE1 ....5 J5
DHAM DH1 ....16 E3
Leazes Pde JES NE2 ....4 F4
Leazes Park Rd CNUT NE1 ....5 H5
Leazes Pkwy
BW/LEM/TK/HW NE15 ....66 C2
Leazes Pl DHAM DH1 ....16 E3
Leazes Ri PLEE/EAS SR8 ....175 C4
Leazes Rd DHAM DH1 ....16 E3
Leazes Ter CNUT NE1 ....5 H4
The Leazes HAR/WTLS NE34 ......75 K5
SUND SR1 ....14 B5
Leazes Vw ROWG NE39 ....97 F3
Lecondale FELL NE10 ....88 B7
Ledbury Rd
ASHBK/HED/RY SR2 ....120 D3
Leech Ct PLEE/EAS SR8 ....163 C5
Leechmere Rd
ASHBK/HED/RY SR2 ....120 C4
Leechmere Wy
ASHBK/HED/RY SR2 ....121 F6
Lee Cl WASHS NE38 ....117 K1
Leeds St CLDN/WHIT/ROK SR6 ...106 D3
Lee Hill Ct BDN/LAN/SAC DH7 ...140 B4
Leeholme HLH DH5 ....147 J1
Leeholme Ct STLY/ANP DH9 .....125 J4
Leeman's La RDHAMSE DH6 .....179 F6
Leeming Gdns
LWF/SPW/WRK NE9 ....87 H6
Leesfield Dr BDN/LAN/SAC DH7 ...167 H7
Leesfield Gdns
BDN/LAN/SAC DH7 ....167 G7
Leesfield Rd
BDN/LAN/SAC DH7 ....167 H7
Lees St STLY/ANP DH9 ....112 D7
Lee St CLDN/WHIT/ROK SR6 .....106 D1
SWCK/CAS SR5 ....106 B4
Legg Av BDLGTN NE22 ....30 A3
Legges Dr DIN/WO NE13 ....36 C2
Legion Gv
BW/LEM/TK/HW NE15 ....68 D4
Legion Rd
BW/LEM/TK/HW NE15 ....68 D4
Leicester Cl WLSD/HOW NE28 ....58 C5
Leicestershire Dr DHAM DH1 ....158 A6
Leicester St BYK/HTN/WLK NE6 ....7 L6
Leighton Rd
ASHBK/HED/RY SR2 ....120 D4
Leighton St BYK/HTN/WLK NE6 ....6 D5
SSH NE33 ....3 L9
Leith Ct HAR/WTLS NE34 ....75 G6
Leith Gdns STLY/ANP DH9........112 B5
Leland Pl MPTH NE61 ....20 B6
Lemington Gdns
WD/WHPE/BLK NE5 ....69 G4
Lemington Rd
BW/LEM/TK/HW NE15 ....67 J4
Lemon St SSH NE33 ....75 F5
Lena Av MONK NE25 ....50 C5
Lenin Ter STLY/ANP DH9 ....126 E2
Leominster Rd
ASHBK/HED/RY SR2 ....120 C4
Leopold St JRW NE32 ....73 K5
Lesbury Av ASHGTN NE63 ....23 K3
SMOOR NE27 ....49 C6
STKFD/GP NE62 ....23 F4
WLSD/HOW NE28 ....59 H7
Lesbury Cha GOS/KPK NE3.........56 B4
Lesbury Cl CLSW/PEL DH2 ......129 F6
Lesbury Rd BYK/HTN/WLK NE6 ...71 H2

Lesbury St
BW/LEM/TK/HW NE15 ....68 B5
WLSD/HOW NE28 ....74 A2
Leslie Av HEBB NE31 ....73 G6
Leslie Crs GOS/KPK NE3 ....56 C7
Leslies Vw MPTH NE61 ....20 C3
Letch Av SEA/MUR SR7 ....162 B1
Leven Av CLSW/PEL DH2 ....129 H6
Levens Wk CRAM NE23 ....38 A1
Levisham Cl SUNDSW SR3 ....120 C7
Lewis Crs ASHBK/HED/RY SR2 ....15 J8
Lewis Dr ELS/FEN NE4.............4 A5
Lexington Ct
BDN/LAN/SAC DH7 ....167 H6
Leybourne Av LGB/KIL NE12 ......57 K1
Leyburn Cl CLSW/PEL DH2 ......114 D5
HLS DH4 ....132 A6
Leyburn Dr LGB/HTN NE7 ....57 G7
Leyburn Gv HLS DH4 ....132 A6
Leyburn Pl CLS/BIR/GTL DH3 ...101 H7
Leyfield Cl SUNDSW SR3 ....134 A2
Leyland Cl RDHAMSE DH6 ....180 B1
Leyton Pl GATE NE8 ....11 K8
Liburn Cl BOL NE36 ....91 F4
Lichfield Av BYK/HTN/WLK NE6 ....7 M8
Lichfield Cl ASHGTN NE63 ....24 B5
CLS/BIR/GTL DH3 ....145 H2
GOS/KPK NE3 ....55 H3
Lichfield Wy SWCK/CAS SR5 ....106 A2
Lidcombe Cl SUNDSW SR3 ......120 B7
Liddell Cl CLDN/WHIT/ROK SR6 ...14 F1
TYNE/NSHE NE30 ....61 H4
Liddell Ter GATE NE8 ....10 C6
Liddle Av RDHAMSE DH6 ....158 C7
Liddle Cl PLEE/EAS SR8 ....174 C2
Liddle Ct ELS/FEN NE4 ....4 D6
Liddle Rd ELS/FEN NE4 ....4 D6
Lieven St DIN/WO NE13 ....46 A5
Liffey Rd HEBB NE31 ....89 H1
Lightbourne Rd
BYK/HTN/WLK NE6 ....72 C5
Lightwood Av
BW/LEM/TK/HW NE15 ....68 E7
Lilac Av BYK/HTN/WLK NE6 .....143 H5
BLYTH NE24 ....31 F6
CLDN/WHIT/ROK SR6 ....93 F1
DHAM DH1 ....156 C4
HAR/WTLS NE34 ....75 K6
LGB/KIL NE12 ....58 B2
SUNDSW SR3 ....120 B6
Lilac Cl WD/WHPE/BLK NE5 ......53 K6
Lilac Ct ASHGTN NE63 ....23 J4
Lilac Crs TRIM TS29 ....183 G6
WICK/BNPF NE16 ....97 J7
Lilac Gdns LWF/SPW/WRK NE9 ...87 F6
WICK/BNPF NE16 ....84 E6
Lilac Gv CLSW/PEL DH2 ....129 C2
Lilac Pk BDN/LAN/SAC DH7 .....167 G1
Lilac Pl CON/LDGT DH8 ....123 K4
Lilac Rd BYK/HTN/WLK NE6 ......72 C2
Lilac Sq HLS DH4 ....131 G4
Lilac St MLFD/PNYW SR4 ....104 E7
Lilac Ter RDHAMSE DH6 ....173 H4
Lilburn Cl BYK/HTN/WLK NE6......7 H8
CLSW/PEL DH2 ....129 G7
Lilburne Cl SUND SR1 ....15 H4
Lilburn Gdns GOS/KPK NE3 ......57 F6
Lilburn Pl SWCK/CAS SR5 ....106 A4
Lilburn Rd SMOOR NE27 ....49 C7
Lilburn St NSHW NE29.............2 A2
Lilian Av ASHBK/HED/RY SR2 ....120 E6
WLSD/HOW NE28 ....72 C2
Lilley Gv SWCK/CAS SR5 ....105 F4
Lily Av BDLGTN NE22 ....29 H6
JES NE2 ....70 E2
Lily Bank WLSD/HOW NE28 ......72 D1
JES NE2 ....70 E2
Lily Gdns STLY/ANP DH9 ....111 G6
Lily St MLFD/PNYW SR4 ....14 B3
Lily Ter WD/WHPE/BLK NE5 ......54 E7
Lilywhite Ter HLH DH5 ....148 A6
Lime Av HLS DH4 ....132 A6
Limecragg Av DHAM DH1 ....157 J6
Limecroft JRW NE32 ....90 A3
Lime Gv PRUD NE42 ....80 B1
RYTON NE40 ....66 B6
Limekiln La WLSD/HOW NE28 ....73 F1
Limekiln Rd WLSD/HOW NE28 ...73 F1
Lime Pk BDN/LAN/SAC DH7 .....167 G6
The Limes ASHBK/HED/RY SR2 ....16 A4
HLS DH4 ....117 K6
Limestone La PONT/DH NE20 ....42 B3
Lime St BLAY NE21 ....84 B3
CNUT NE1 ....6 C5
MLFD/PNYW SR4 ....14 A4
STLY/ANP DH9 ....126 B4
Limetrees Gdns
LWF/SPW/WRK NE9 ....87 F5
Limewood Gv DIN/WO NE13 ......46 B4
Linacre Cl DIN/WO NE13 ....55 F4
Linacre Ct PLEE/EAS SR8 ....174 C5
Linbridge Dr
WD/WHPE/BLK NE5 ....68 C2
Linburn WASHS NE38 ....116 C5
Lincoln Av SUNDSW SR3 ....120 A6
WLSD/HOW NE28 ....58 C7
Lincoln Gn GOS/KPK NE3 ....56 B1
Lincoln Ct CON/LDGT DH8 ......137 F1
Lincoln Rd CRAM NE23 ....33 J6
DHAM DH1 ....156 E2
HAR/WTLS NE34 ....76 B4
Lincolnshire Cl DHAM DH1 .....157 K6
Lincoln St GATE NE8 ....10 F6
MLFD/PNYW SR4 ....105 K6
Lincrest Ct
WD/WHPE/BLK
(off Linhope Rd) NE5 ....68 D1
Lindale Av WICK/BNPF NE16 .....84 E7
Lindale Rd ELS/FEN NE4 ....69 J5
Lindean Pl CRAM NE23 ....38 A2
Lindell Ter RDHAMSE DH6 ......182 D2
Linden Av ELS/FEN NE4 ....69 H4
GOS/KPK NE3 ....56 C1
Linden Ct STKFD/GP NE62 ....23 G7
Linden Gdns
ASHBK/HED/RY SR2 ....120 C3
Linden Gv DUN/TMV NE11 ....9 J7

HLS DH4 ....132 B7
RDHAMSE DH6 ....180 C7
Linden Ms BDN/LAN/SAC DH7 ...154 B3
Linden Pk BDN/LAN/SAC DH7 ...167 G6
BLAY NE21 ....84 B2
GOS/KPK NE3 ....56 C6
LGB/KIL NE12 ....57 K3
MONK NE25 ....39 J5
Linden Wy PONT/DH NE20 ....42 E7
Lindesfarne DHAM DH1 ....169 J5
Lindfield Av WD/WHPE/BLK NE5...69 F2
WASHS NE38 ....116 C2
Lindisfarne Av CLS/BIR/GTL DH3..129 K4
Lindisfarne Cl HLS DH4 ....131 K6
JES NE2 ....57 F7
MPTH NE61 ....20 E7
MPTH NE61 ....21 K1
WD/WHPE/BLK NE5 ....68 D2
Lindisfarne Ct JRW NE32 ....74 D5
Lindisfarne Dr GATE NE8 ....11 H3
Lindisfarne La MPTH NE61 ....20 D7
Lindisfarne Pl WLSD/HOW NE28 ...59 F7
Lindisfarne Recess JRW NE32 ....74 D7
Lindisfarne Rd DHAM DH1 ......156 E4
HEBB NE31 ....89 G1
JES NE2 ....71 F1
Lindisfarne Ter
TYNE/NSHE NE30 ....60 E3
Lindom Av CLS/BIR/GTL DH3 ....129 K4
Lindon Rd STLY/ANP DH9 ....126 C3
Lindrick Ct FELL NE10 ....88 E5
Lindsay Av BLYTH NE24 ....30 E6
Lindsay Cl ASHBK/HED/RY SR2 ...15 H7
Lindsay Rd ASHBK/HED/RY SR2 ...15 H7
Lindsay St HLH DH5 ....148 A2
Lindsey Cl CRAM NE23 ....37 K2
Lindum Rd LWF/SPW/WRK NE9 ...11 H8
Lingdale DHAM DH1 ....158 A6
Lingdale Av
CLDN/WHIT/ROK SR6 ....92 E6
Lingey Gdns FELL NE10 ....88 E4
Lingey La FELL NE10 ....88 D5
Lingfield HLH DH5 ....147 J2
Lingfield Rd CLDN/WHIT/ROK SR6..122 E4
Lingholme CLSW/PEL DH2 ....129 C3
Lingmell WASHN NE37 ....102 D7
Lingshaw FELL NE10 ....13 L9
Linhope Av GOS/KPK NE3 ....55 K3
Linhope Rd WD/WHPE/BLK NE5 ...68 D1
Link Av BDLGTN NE22 ....28 D5
Link Rd WD/WHPE/BLK NE5 ......69 J1
Links Av TYNE/NSHE NE30 ....51 G7
WBAY NE26 ....50 D7
Links Dr CON/LDGT DH8 ....122 E2
Links Gn GOS/KPK NE3 ....56 D4
Links Rd BLYTH NE24 ....35 H3
TYNE/NSHE NE30 ....51 G7
WBAY NE26 ....35 K7
The Links DHAM DH1 ....158 A5
TRIM (off St. Pauls Rd) TS29 ...183 F7
Links Vw ASHGTN NE63 ....24 C5
BLYTH NE24 ....34 E3
Linkway JRW NE32 ....90 B3
Linley Hl WICK/BNPF NE16 ......98 C1
Linnel Dr BW/LEM/TK/HW NE15 ..68 C4
Linnet Ct ASHGTN NE63 ....23 H3
Linnet Gv SWCK/CAS SR5 ......105 G4
Linnheads PRUD NE42 ....80 B3
Linskell ASHBK/HED/RY SR2 ....120 E6
Linskill Pl TYNE/NSHE NE30 .....61 F3
Linskill St TYNE/NSHE NE30 .....2 F2
Linskill Ter TYNE/NSHE NE30 ....61 F4
Linslade Wk CRAM NE23 ....38 A2
Lintfort CLS/BIR/GTL DH3 ......115 K7
Linthorpe Rd GOS/KPK NE3 ......56 C3
TYNE/NSHE NE30 ....61 F1
Linton Rd LWF/SPW/WRK NE9 ...101 F2
WBAY NE26 ....41 H7
Lintonville Rd ASHGTN NE63 .....23 J1
Lintzford Gdns
BW/LEM/TK/HW NE15 ....68 C4
ROWG NE39 ....97 F5
Lintzford La ROWG NE39 ....96 D5
Lintzford Rd ROWG NE39 ....96 C5
Lintz Green La ROWG NE39 ......96 E6
Lintz La WICK/BNPF NE16 ......111 F2
Lintz Ter WICK/BNPF NE16 ....97 H3
Linum Pl ELS/FEN NE4 ....69 J3
Linwood Pl GOS/KPK NE3 ....56 C1
Lion Wk NSHW NE29 ....2 C6
Lisa Av MLFD/PNYW SR4 ....118 E1
Lisburn Ter MLFD/PNYW SR4 ....106 A6
Lisle Gv WLSD/HOW NE28 ....59 J7
Lisle Rd HAR/WTLS NE34 ....75 K4
Lisle St WLSD/HOW NE28 ....72 D1
Lismore Av SSH NE33 ....75 G4
Lismore Pl
BW/LEM/TK/HW NE15 ....69 C5
Lister Av DUN/TMV NE11 ....9 G6
RYTON NE40 ....82 B4
Lister Cl HLH DH5 ....147 G2
Lister Pl PLEE/EAS SR8 ....174 B2
Litchfield La BLAY NE21 ....83 K3
Litchfield Rd DHAM DH1 ....156 E1
Little Bedford St NSHW NE29 ....2 F3
Littlebridge Ct DHAM DH1 ......156 B3
Littleburn Cl HLS DH4 ....132 A6
Littleburn La
BDN/LAN/SAC DH7 ....167 K5
Littleburn Rd
BDN/LAN/SAC DH7 ....167 K6
Little Dene
JES (off Lodore Rd) NE2 ....70 C3
Littledene LWF/SPW/WRK NE9 ...87 F5
Little Eden PLEE/EAS SR8 ......174 E3
Littleton La RDHAMSE DH6 .....159 C7
Little Villiers St SUND * SR1 .....14 F4
Little Wy BW/LEM/TK/HW NE15 ...68 F7
Littondale WLSD/HOW NE28 .....58 B6
Livingstone Pl SSH NE33..........3 H6
Livingstone Rd SUND SR1 ....14 C4
Livingstone St
CON/LDGT * DH8 ....123 J7
Livingstone Vw
TYNE/NSHE NE30 ....61 C3

Lizard La
CLDN/WHIT/ROK SR6 ....92 E2
HAR/WTLS NE34 ....76 C5
Lloyd Av HLH DH5 ....147 F4
Lloyd Ct DUN/TMV NE11 ....11 H4
Lobban Av HEBB NE31 ....89 F1
Lobelia Cl WD/WHPE/BLK NE5 ....54 A7
Lobley Gdns DUN/TMV NE11 ......86 A6
Lobley Hill Rd DUN/TMV NE11 ....86 A6
Lobleyhill Rd WICK/BNPF NE16 ...98 B5
Local Av RDHAMSE DH6 ....171 F1
Lochcraig Pl CRAM NE25 ....38 A2
Lochmaben Ter SWCK/CAS SR5 ..106 D3
Lockerbie Rd CRAM NE23 ....38 A2
Lockhaugh Rd ROWG NE39 ......97 H2
Locksley Cl NSHW NE29 ....59 K1
Locomotion Wy LGB/KIL NE12 ...47 H4
NSHW NE29 ....2 C6
Locomotive Ct
PRUD (off South Rd) NE42 ....80 C2
Lodge Cl ROWG NE39 ....110 C1
Lodgeside Meadow
SUNDSW SR3 ....134 B2
The Lodges Rd
LWF/SPW/WRK NE9 ....100 C2
Lodore Gv JRW NE32 ....90 B1
Lodore Rd JES NE2 ....56 D7
Logan Rd BYK/HTN/WLK NE6 .....72 B2
Logan St HLH DH5 ....147 K5
Lola St HLH DH5 ....45 K4
Lombard Dr CLS/BIR/GTL DH3 ...115 J7
Lombard St SUND SR1 ....15 H4
Lomond Ct SUNDSW * SR3 ......134 A1
Lomond Pl CLSW/PEL DH2 ......129 H6
London Av WASHN NE37 ....102 D4
Londonderry St SEA/MUR SR7 ...151 F3
SUNDSW SR3 ....120 A7
Londonderry Ter SUNDSW SR3 ..120 B7
Longacre HLS DH4 ....132 A7
WASHS NE38 ....117 G5
Long Acres DHAM DH1 ....17 J1
Long Bank CLS/BIR/GTL DH3 ....101 J6
LWF/SPW/WRK NE9 ....101 J4
Longborough Ct LGB/HTN NE7 ...57 G6
Long Burn Dr CLSW/PEL DH2 ...129 F5
Longclose Bank STLY/ANP DH9 ..109 K4
Long Close Rd ROWG NE39 ......110 B1
Long Dl CLSW/PEL DH2 ....129 F5
Longdean Cl HEBB NE31 ....72 E6
Longdean Pk CLS/BIR/GTL DH3 ..129 J1
Long Dr MPTH NE61 ....26 D1
Long Edge BDN/LAN/SAC DH7 ..141 J5
Longedge La CON/LDGT DH8 ....137 H5
Longfield Rd
CLDN/WHIT/ROK SR6 ....106 D2
Longfield Ter
BYK/HTN/WLK NE6 ....72 B7
Long Gair BLAY NE21 ....83 J4
Long Garth DHAM DH1 ....156 A5
Long Headlam
BYK/HTN/WLK NE6 ....7 G5
Longhirst FELL NE10 ....88 C5
LGB/KIL NE12 ....47 K5
WD/WHPE/BLK NE5 ....68 D1
Longhirst Dr DIN/WO NE13 ....46 B4
Longhirst Rd MPTH NE61 ....21 K1
Longlands Dr HLH DH5 ....147 H1
Longleat Gdns MPTH NE61 ....21 J1
SSH NE33 ....3 K6
Longley St ELS/FEN NE4 ....4 D5
Long Meadow La RYTON NE40 ...82 B1
Longmeadows PONT/DH NE20 ...42 D6
SUNDSW SR3 ....133 C1
Longnewton St SEA/MUR SR7 ...150 E3
Longniddry WASHN NE37 ....102 E2
Longniddry Ct
LWF/SPW/WRK NE9 ....100 E2
Longridge Av LGB/HTN NE7 ......57 K7
WASHS NE38 ....116 C4
Longridge Dr WBAY NE26 ....50 C2
Long Ridge Rd RYTON NE40 ......82 E2
Longridge Sq
ASHBK/HED/RY SR2 ....120 D4
Longridge Wy CRAM NE23 ....38 A2
STKFD/GP NE62 ....29 C3
Longrigg FELL NE10 ....88 B5
Long Rigg WICK/BNPF NE16 ......84 E3
Longrigg Rd WICK/BNPF NE16 ...84 E3
Long Rw SSH NE33 ....2 F6
Longsdale Av BLYTH NE24 ....30 A6
Longshank La
CLS/BIR/GTL DH3 ....101 G7
Longston Av TYNE/NSHE NE30 ...51 F6
Longstone
LWF/SPW/WRK
(off Pimlico Ct) NE9 ....101 F1
Longstone Cl LGB/KIL NE12 ......48 A5
Longstone Sq
WD/WHPE/BLK NE5 ....68 B2
Longwood Cl WICK/BNPF NE16 ...99 F2
Lonnen Av ELS/FEN NE4 ....69 H4
Lonnen Dr WICK/BNPF NE16 .....84 E4
The Lonnen HAR/WTLS NE34 .....76 B7
Lonsdale CLS/BIR/GTL DH3 .....116 A5
Lonsdale Av
CLDN/WHIT/ROK SR6 ....92 E6
Lonsdale Ct
JES (off West Jesmond Av) NE2 ...70 E1
Lonsdale Gdns
WLSD/HOW NE28 ....59 J6
Lonsdale Rd
CLDN/WHIT/ROK SR6 ....106 E3
Lonsdale Ter JES NE2 ....70 E1
Loraine Ter
WD/WHPE/BLK NE5 ....68 B5
Lord Byrons Wk SEA/MUR SR7 ..135 F6
Lordenshaw
WD/WHPE/BLK NE5 ....68 B5
Lord Nelson St HAR/WTLS NE34 ..75 F5
Lord St SEA/MUR SR7 ....150 E2
SSH NE33 ....75 J2
SUNDSW SR3 ....120 B7
Lorimers Cl PLEE/EAS SR8 ......174 C5
Lorne St HLH DH5 ....160 A1
Lorne Ter ASHBK/HED/RY SR2 ...14 D8
Lorrain Rd HAR/WTLS NE34 .....91 H2
Lorton Av TYNE/NSHE NE30 .....50 E5

Lorton Rd LWF/SPW/WRK NE9 ....101 G1
Losh Ter BYK/HTN/WLK NE6 ....72 B6
Lossiemouth Rd NSHW NE29 ....59 K5
Lothian Ct WD/WHPE/BLK NE5 ....55 G7
Lotus Cl WD/WHPE/BLK NE5 ....53 K7
Lotus Pl ELS/FEN NE4 ....69 H4
Loudon St HAR/WTLS NE34 ....75 G6
Loud Ter STLY/ANP DH9 ....125 F3
Loud View Ter STLY/ANP DH9 ....125 F4
Loughborough Av
ASHBK/HED/RY SR2 ....120 C3
Loughrigg Av CRAM NE23 ....37 K2
Louie Ter LWF/SPW/WRK NE9 ....87 G7
Louis Av CLDN/WHIT/ROK SR6 ....106 D2
Loup St BLAY NE21 ....84 A1
Louvain Ter STKFD/GP NE62 ....23 F6
Lovaine Av MONK NE25 ....50 E5
Lovaine Pl NSHW NE29 ....2 C3
Lovaine Pl West NSHW NE29 ....2 B3
Lovaine Rw TYNE/NSHE NE30 ....61 H2
Lovaine St
BW/LEM/TK/HW NE15 ....67 G3
CLSW/PEL DH2 ....128 C1
Lovaine Ter NSHW NE29 ....2 C1
Love Av CRAM NE23 ....47 H2
Love La CNUT * NE1 ....6 A7
Loveless Gdns FELL NE10 ....13 L9
Lovett Wk GATE NE8 ....10 B3
Lowbiggin WD/WHPE/BLK NE5 ....54 C4
Low Chare CLS/BIR/GTL DH3 ....129 K4
Low Church St STLY/ANP DH9 ....125 H2
Low Cl PRUD NE42 ....80 E1
Lowdham Av NSHW NE29 ....60 C6
Lowdon Ct
JES (off Richardson Rd) NE2 ....5 G2
Low Downs Rd HLH DH5 ....147 K2
Low Dyke St TRIM TS29 ....183 F7
Lower Dundas St
CLDN/WHIT/ROK SR6 ....14 F1
Lower Rudyerd St NSHW NE29 ....2 E3
Lowerson Av HLS DH4 ....131 J2
Lowery La STLY/ANP DH9 ....127 H5
Lowe's Barn Bank DHAM DH1 ....168 A3
Lowes Ct DHAM DH1 ....168 B2
Lowes Fall DHAM DH1 ....168 B2
Lowes Ri DHAM DH1 ....168 B3
Loweswater Av HLH DH5 ....160 B1
Loweswater Cl BLYTH NE24 ....30 B5
Loweswater Rd
WD/WHPE/BLK NE5 ....69 F3
Loweswood Cl LGB/HTN NE7 ....71 G2
Lowes Wynd DHAM DH1 ....168 B2
Lowfield Ter BYK/HTN/WLK NE6 ....72 B7
Lowfield Wk WICK/BNPF NE16 ....84 E5
Low Flatts Rd CLSW/PEL DH2 ....129 H1
Low Fold BYK/HTN/WLK NE6 ....6 E5
Low Friar St CNUT NE1 ....5 J7
Lowgate BW/LEM/TK/HW NE15 ....67 F2
Low Gosforth Ct GOS/KPK NE3 ....56 D1
Low Gn DHAM DH1 ....169 G4
Low Haugh PONT/DH NE20 ....43 H2
Low Heworth La FELL NE10 ....13 G5
Low Heyworth La FELL NE10 ....13 G5
Lowhills Rd PLEE/EAS SR8 ....174 C2
Lowland Cl SUNDSW SR3 ....134 A2
Lowland Rd BDN/LAN/SAC DH7 ....167 G6
Low La HAR/WTLS NE34 ....75 G7
Low Meadow
CLDN/WHIT/ROK SR6 ....92 A3
Low Moor Rd
BDN/LAN/SAC DH7 ....153 K3
Lownds Ter BYK/HTN/WLK NE6 ....7 M4
Low Quay BLYTH NE24 ....31 H7
Lowrey's La LWF/SPW/WRK NE9 ....87 F7
Low Rd DHAM DH1 ....169 G4
Low Rw PLEE/EAS SR8 ....162 C5
SUND SR1 ....14 C5
Lowry Gdns HAR/WTLS NE34 ....91 H2
Lowry Rd CLDN/WHIT/ROK SR6 ....92 E7
Low Station Rd HLS DH4 ....146 B6
Low Stobhill MPTH NE61 ....20 E6
Low St SUND SR1 ....15 H3
Lowther Cl ASHGTN NE63 ....24 B4
PLEE/EAS SR8 ....174 E3
Lowther Ct PLEE/EAS SR8 ....184 C1
Lowthian Crs BYK/HTN/WLK NE6 ....7 M6
Low Well Gdns FELL * NE10 ....12 F6
Low West Av ROWG NE39 ....96 E4
Lucknow St SUND SR1 ....15 J3
Lucock St HAR/WTLS NE34 ....75 F6
Ludlow Av NSHW NE29 ....60 C2
Ludlow Ct GOS/KPK NE3 ....55 J3
Ludlow Dr MONK NE25 ....49 K5
Ludlow Rd ASHBK/HED/RY SR2 ....120 D4
Luffness Dr HAR/WTLS NE34 ....91 K1
Luke Av RDHAMSE DH6 ....181 H2
Luke Crs SEA/MUR SR7 ....149 G5
Luke's La HEBB NE31 ....89 H2
Luke St TRIM TS29 ....182 D7
Luke Ter RDHAMSE DH6 ....182 D1
Lulsgate SWCK/CAS SR5 ....104 E4
Lulworth Av JRW NE32 ....74 B6
Lulworth Ct SUNDSW SR3 ....119 G7
Lulworth Gdns
ASHBK/HED/RY SR2 ....120 C3
Lumley Av HAR/WTLS NE34 ....76 B5
WICK/BNPF NE16 ....85 F3
Lumley Cl WASHS NE38 ....116 D1
Lumley Ct BDLGTN NE22 ....29 J4
HEBB NE31 ....73 H3
SUNDSW SR3 ....119 G7
Lumley Dr CON/LDGT DH8 ....123 J7
PLEE/EAS SR8 ....174 E7
Lumley Gdns GATE NE8 ....11 L6
Lumley New Rd
CLS/BIR/GTL DH3 ....130 B5
HLS DH4 ....131 F6
Lumley Rd DHAM DH1 ....156 D2
Lumley's La PSHWF NE43 ....80 A6
Lumley St HLS DH4 ....132 B5
MLFD/PNYW SR4 ....106 A7
Lumley Ter CLS/BIR/GTL DH3 ....129 K5
JRW NE32 ....89 K1
Lumley Wk DUN/TMV NE11 ....9 J6
Lumsden's La MPTH NE61 ....20 D4
Lumsden Sq SEA/MUR SR7 ....149 G5
Lund Av DHAM DH1 ....156 B3
Lund's La CON/LDGT DH8 ....124 D7
Lunedale Av
CLDN/WHIT/ROK SR6 ....92 C7
Lunedale Dr CLS/BIR/GTL DH3 ....145 J2
Lunedale St HLH DH5 ....147 K6
Lupin Cl WD/WHPE/BLK NE5 ....54 A6
Luss Av JRW NE32 ....90 C1
Lutterworth Cl LGB/KIL NE12 ....57 H4
Lutterworth Dr LGB/KIL NE12 ....57 G4
Lutterworth Rd
ASHBK/HED/RY SR2 ....120 C3
LGB/KIL NE12 ....57 H5
Luxembourg Rd
MLFD/PNYW SR4 ....105 H5
Lychgate Ct GATE NE8 ....11 H2
Lydbury Cl CRAM NE23 ....33 J6
Lydcott WASHS NE38 ....117 K2
Lydford Ct HLS DH4 ....132 A4
WD/WHPE/BLK NE5 ....55 G4
Lydford Wy CLS/BIR/GTL DH3 ....115 K3
Lyncroft ASHGTN NE63 ....23 J3
Lyncroft Rd NSHW NE29 ....60 C4
Lyndale CRAM NE23 ....33 J6
Lyndhurst Av CLS/BIR/GTL DH3 ....129 J1
JES NE2 ....70 D1
LWF/SPW/WRK NE9 ....101 F1
Lyndhurst Cl BLAY NE21 ....83 J4
Lyndhurst Crs
LWF/SPW/WRK NE9 ....101 G1
Lyndhurst Dr DHAM DH1 ....168 A1
LWF/SPW/WRK NE9 ....101 G1
Lyndhurst Gdns JES NE2 ....70 D1
Lyndhurst Gv
LWF/SPW/WRK NE9 ....101 G1
Lyndhurst Rd ASHGTN NE63 ....24 B4
LGB/KIL NE12 ....57 K3
STLY/ANP DH9 ....126 B1
Lyndhurst St SSH NE33 ....3 K8
Lyndhurst Ter
MLFD/PNYW SR4 ....105 J5
Lyndon Cl BOL NE36 ....91 F5
Lyndon Dr BOL NE36 ....91 F5
Lyndon Gv BOL NE36 ....91 F5
Lyndon Wk BLYTH NE24 ....30 B6
Lyne Cl CLSW/PEL DH2 ....115 F6
Lyne's Dr BDN/LAN/SAC DH7 ....167 J5
Lyne Ter MPTH NE61 ....18 B1
Lynfield WBAY NE26 ....50 C1
Lynfield Ct WD/WHPE/BLK NE5 ....55 F7
Lynfield Pl WD/WHPE/BLK NE5 ....55 F7
Lynford Gdns
ASHBK/HED/RY SR2 ....120 C3
Lynholm Gv LGB/KIL NE12 ....57 K3
Lynmouth Pl LGB/HTN NE7 ....57 H7
Lynmouth Rd NSHW NE29 ....60 A5
Lynndale Av BLYTH NE24 ....30 C7
Lynnholme Gdns
LWF/SPW/WRK NE9 ....11 J8
Lynn Rd NSHW NE29 ....60 B3
WLSD/HOW NE28 ....72 C2
Lynn St BLYTH NE24 ....31 F7
Lynnwood Av ELS/FEN NE4 ....4 B6
Lynnwood Ter ELS/FEN NE4 ....4 B6
Lyntgrove ASHBK/HED/RY SR2 ....121 F6
Lynthorpe ASHBK/HED/RY SR2 ....121 F6
Lyn-Thorpe Gv
CLDN/WHIT/ROK SR6 ....106 E1
Lynton Av JRW NE32 ....74 C6
Lynton Ct HLS DH4 ....132 A4
Lynton Pl WD/WHPE/BLK NE5 ....55 F7
Lynton Wy WD/WHPE/BLK NE5 ....55 F7
Lynwood Av BLAY NE21 ....84 A1
MLFD/PNYW SR4 ....118 E4
Lynwood Cl PONT/DH NE20 ....42 E7
Lyons Av HLH DH5 ....148 A6
Lyons La HLH DH5 ....148 B7
Lyon St HEBB NE31 ....73 F5
Lyric Cl NSHW NE29 ....59 K2
Lysdon Av MONK NE25 ....40 A2
Lyster Cl SEA/MUR SR7 ....134 E6
Lytchfeld FELL NE10 ....13 L9
Lytham Cl CON/LDGT DH8 ....122 E2
CRAM NE23 ....37 K2
WASHN NE37 ....102 E3
WLSD/HOW NE28 ....59 G3
Lytham Dr MONK NE25 ....50 B4
Lytham Gra HLS DH4 ....131 J3
Lytham Gn FELL NE10 ....13 M3
Lytham Pl BYK/HTN/WLK NE6 ....7 L7
Lythe Wy LGB/KIL NE12 ....57 J4

M

Mabel St BLAY NE21 ....84 A1
Macadam St GATE NE8 ....10 C9
Mackintosh Ct DHAM DH1 ....17 K2
Maclynn Cl SUNDSW SR3 ....133 J1
Macmerry Cl SWCK/CAS SR5 ....104 D5
Macmillan Gdns FELL NE10 ....13 K7
Maddison Ct SUND SR1 ....15 J3
Maddison St BLYTH NE24 ....31 G6
Maddox Rd LGB/KIL NE12 ....57 K4
Madeira Av WBAY NE26 ....50 D2
Madeira Cl WD/WHPE/BLK NE5 ....54 A6
Madeira Ter SSH NE33 ....75 H2
Madras St HAR/WTLS NE34 ....74 E7
Mafeking Pl NSHW NE29 ....59 K1
Mafeking St
LWF/SPW/WRK NE9 ....11 J8
MLFD/PNYW SR4 ....105 K7
Magdalene Av DHAM DH1 ....157 K5
Magdalene Ct DHAM DH1 ....17 G2
Magdalene Hts DHAM DH1 ....17 G2
Magdalene St DHAM DH1 ....17 H2
Magdelene Pl
MLFD/PNYW SR4 ....105 K6
Magenta Crs
WD/WHPE/BLK NE5 ....54 A6
Maglona St SEA/MUR SR7 ....150 E3
Magnolia Cl ELS/FEN NE4 ....69 H4
Magnolia Dr ASHGTN NE63 ....23 J4
Magpie Ct ASHGTN NE63 ....23 H3
Maiden La RYTON NE40 ....82 B2
Maiden Law HLS DH4 ....146 D1
Maiden St ELS/FEN NE4 ....9 M1
Maidstone Cl SUNDSW SR3 ....133 H1
Main Crs WLSD/HOW NE28 ....58 B6
Main Rd DIN/WO NE13 ....45 F2
RYTON NE40 ....66 D6
WYLAM NE41 ....65 H5
Mainsforth Ter
ASHBK/HED/RY SR2 ....15 J8
Mainsforth Ter West
ASHBK/HED/RY SR2 ....15 H9
Mains Park Rd
CLS/BIR/GTL DH3 ....129 K5
Mainstone Cl CRAM NE23 ....38 B2
Main St CON/LDGT DH8 ....123 H5
PONT/DH NE20 ....43 G3
RYTON NE40 ....66 B7
Main St North CRAM NE23 ....48 A1
Maitland Vls
NWBGN (off Maitland Ter) NE64 ....25 F1
Makendon St HEBB NE31 ....73 G4
Malaburn Wy SWCK/CAS SR5 ....106 A4
Malaga Cl WD/WHPE/BLK NE5 ....53 K6
Malaya Dr BYK/HTN/WLK NE6 ....72 C6
Malcolm Av RDHAMSE DH6 ....181 G4
Malcolm St BYK/HTN/WLK NE6 ....6 D4
SEA/MUR SR7 ....150 D2
Malden Cl CRAM NE23 ....38 A2
Maling Pk MLFD/PNYW SR4 ....105 F6
Malings Cl SUND SR1 ....15 J5
Maling St BYK/HTN/WLK NE6 ....6 D7
Mallard Cl ASHGTN NE63 ....23 K5
WASHS NE38 ....116 B2
Mallard Ldg FELL * NE10 ....12 C8
Mallard Wy BLYTH NE24 ....35 H4
HLS DH4 ....146 E2
WLSD/HOW NE28 ....59 J4
Mallowburn Crs GOS/KPK NE3 ....55 G6
Malmo Cl NSHW NE29 ....59 K5
Malone Gdns CLS/BIR/GTL DH3 ....101 K7
Malory Pl GATE NE8 ....11 H4
Maltby Cl WASHS NE38 ....117 F2
The Maltings WNGT TS28 ....183 K2
Malton Cl BLYTH NE24 ....30 D7
BW/LEM/TK/HW NE15 ....68 C5
Malton Crs NSHW NE29 ....60 C6
Malton Gdns WLSD/HOW NE28 ....58 D7
Malvern Cl ASHGTN NE63 ....24 A4
PLEE/EAS SR8 ....174 C5
Malvern Ct BW/LEM/TK/HW NE15 ....67 K4
DUN/TMV NE11 ....86 A6
Malvern Crs SEA/MUR SR7 ....150 B1
TRIM TS29 ....183 F6
Malvern Gdns
CLDN/WHIT/ROK SR6 ....106 E2
DUN/TMV NE11 ....86 A5
Malvern Rd NSHW NE29 ....60 A2
WASHS NE38 ....116 D3
WBAY NE26 ....41 G3
WLSD/HOW NE28 ....59 H7
Malvern St ELS/FEN NE4 ....4 C8
SSH NE33 ....75 G4
Malvern Ter STLY/ANP DH9 ....126 E2
Malvern Vls DHAM DH1 ....17 K3
Malvins Close Rd BLYTH NE24 ....30 E7
Malvins Rd BLYTH NE24 ....30 D6
Manchester St MPTH NE61 ....20 D4
Mandale Crs TYNE/NSHE NE30 ....50 E6
Mandarin Cl WD/WHPE/BLK NE5 ....53 K6
Mandarin Ldg FELL NE10 ....12 C8
Mandarin Wy WASHS NE38 ....104 A7
Mandela Cl STLY/ANP DH9 ....126 B2
SUND SR1 ....15 J5
Mandela Wy DUN/TMV NE11 ....8 C3
Mandeville WASHN NE37 ....103 G5
Manet Gdns HAR/WTLS NE34 ....75 H7
Mangrove Cl WD/WHPE/BLK NE5 ....53 K6
Manila St ASHBK/HED/RY SR2 ....120 E2
Manisty Ter PLEE/EAS SR8 ....162 D5
Manley Vw ASHGTN NE63 ....24 C3
Mann Crs SEA/MUR SR7 ....149 J4
Manningford Cl CRAM NE23 ....38 B3
Manningford Dr SUNDSW SR3 ....133 J2
Manor Av LGB/HTN NE7 ....57 J5
Manor Chare CNUT NE1 ....5 M7
Manor Cl GOS/KPK NE3 ....56 D6
Manor Ct BDN/LAN/SAC DH7 ....140 D6
SSH NE33 ....75 J2
Manor Dr LGB/HTN NE7 ....57 J5
NWBGN NE64 ....19 G7
STLY/ANP DH9 ....125 H2
Manorfields LGB/KIL NE12 ....57 K4
Manor Gdns FELL NE10 ....13 M8
LGB/HTN NE7 ....57 J5
Manor Gra BDN/LAN/SAC DH7 ....140 D5
Manor Gv BW/LEM/TK/HW NE15 ....67 H4
HLS DH4 ....118 D7
LGB/HTN NE7 ....57 J5
Manor Hall Cl SEA/MUR SR7 ....134 E7
Manor House Cl
BYK/HTN/WLK NE6 ....7 H6
Manor House Rd JES NE2 ....71 F2
Manor Pl LGB/HTN NE7 ....57 J5
Manor Rd CON/LDGT DH8 ....109 J5
LGB/HTN NE7 ....57 J6
STLY/ANP* DH9 ....112 D7
TYNE/NSHE NE30 ....61 H2
WASHN NE37 ....103 F5
Manor Ter BLAY NE21 ....84 A5
Manor Vw NWBGN NE64 ....19 G7
WASHN NE37 ....103 F5
Manor Vw East WASHN NE37 ....103 G5
Manor Wk LGB/HTN NE7 ....57 J5
Manor Wy PLEE/EAS SR8 ....175 F4
Manorway TYNE/NSHE NE30 ....61 H2
Mansell Crs PLEE/EAS SR8 ....175 F3
Mansell Pl GOS/KPK NE3 ....55 J5
Manse St CON/LDGT DH8 ....122 E3
Mansfield Ct BOL NE36 ....90 E5
Mansfield Crs
CLDN/WHIT/ROK SR6 ....106 E2
Mansfield St ELS/FEN NE4 ....4 E6
Manston Cl SUNDSW SR3 ....133 H2
Manx Sq SWCK/CAS SR5 ....106 B2
Maple Av DHAM DH1 ....17 L3
DUN/TMV NE11 ....9 J9
MONK NE25 ....50 D6
SUNDSW SR3 ....120 B6
WICK/BNPF NE16 ....97 H7
Maplebeck Cl SUNDSW SR3 ....133 H2
Maple Cl BW/LEM/TK/HW NE15 ....68 C5
Maple Ct BDN/LAN/SAC DH7 ....166 E7
MONK NE25 ....40 A2
Maple Crs BLYTH NE24 ....30 B6
SEA/MUR SR7 ....150 D4
Mapledene Rd GOS/KPK NE3 ....55 K4
Maple Gdns CON/LDGT DH8 ....122 C3
Maple Gv CLDN/WHIT/ROK SR6 ....93 F3
FELL NE10 ....12 E8
GATE NE8 ....86 E5
HAR/WTLS NE34 ....75 K6
PRUD NE42 ....80 B2
STLY/ANP DH9 ....126 B4
Maple Pk BDN/LAN/SAC DH7 ....167 G1
Maple Rd BLAY NE21 ....84 A2
Maple Rw WICK/BNPF NE16 ....85 F2
Maple St ASHGTN NE63 ....24 A2
CON/LDGT DH8 ....123 F4
ELS/FEN NE4 ....4 F9
JRW NE32 ....73 J4
STLY/ANP DH9 ....126 B3
Maple Ter ELS/FEN NE4 ....4 E9
HLS DH4 ....131 J2
Maplewood BYK/HTN/WLK NE6 ....72 A3
CLSW/PEL DH2 ....129 H3
Maplewood Av SWCK/CAS SR5 ....105 K2
Maplewood Ct
BDN/LAN/SAC DH7 ....154 A3
Maplewood Dr RDHAMSE DH6 ....160 E6
Maplewood St HLS DH4 ....131 G6
Mapperley Dr
BW/LEM/TK/HW NE15 ....68 C4
Marblet Ct DUN/TMV NE11 ....86 B5
Marbury Cl SUNDSW SR3 ....133 H1
March Rd CRAM NE23 ....47 H2
Marcia Av
CLDN/WHIT/ROK SR6 ....106 D2
Marconi Wy WICK/BNPF NE16 ....85 F3
Marcross Cl WD/WHPE/BLK NE5 ....67 K1
Marcross Dr SUNDSW SR3 ....133 H2
Mardale WASHN NE37 ....102 D6
Mardale Gdns
LWF/SPW/WRK NE9 ....101 G2
Mardale Rd WD/WHPE/BLK NE5 ....69 F2
Mardale St HLH DH5 ....147 K6
Marden Av TYNE/NSHE NE30 ....51 G6
Marden Cl MPTH NE61 ....20 B6
Marden Ct WBAY NE26 ....40 E1
Marden Crs WBAY NE26 ....51 G5
Marden Rd South MONK NE25 ....50 E5
Marden Ter TYNE/NSHE NE30 ....51 G6
Mareburn Crs FELL NE10 ....12 F7
Maree Cl SUNDSW SR3 ....133 J2
Margaret Alice St
MLFD/PNYW SR4 ....105 J6
Margaret Ct RDHAMSE DH6 ....180 A2
Margaret Dr LGB/KIL NE12 ....58 C2
Margaret Gv HAR/WTLS NE34 ....74 E6
Margaret Rd WBAY NE26 ....51 G5
Margaret St
ASHBK/HED/RY SR2 ....121 F4
SEA/MUR SR7 ....150 E2
Margaret Ter ROWG NE39 ....96 E4
TRIM TS29 ....183 F6
Margery La DHAM DH1 ....16 B5
Marguerite Ct MLFD/PNYW SR4 ....14 B4
Marian Ct GATE NE8 ....10 C5
Marian Dr FELL NE10 ....13 M3
Marian Wy HAR/WTLS NE34 ....91 K1
PONT/DH NE20 ....42 D7
Maria St ELS/FEN NE4 ....69 J7
SEA/MUR SR7 ....150 E1
SUNDSW SR3 ....120 A7
Marie Curie Dr ELS/FEN NE4 ....4 B8
Marigold Av FELL NE10 ....11 M3
Marigold Ct MLFD/PNYW SR4 ....14 A3
Marigold Crs HLS DH4 ....131 G4
Marigold Wk HAR/WTLS NE34 ....75 F6
Marina Av
CLDN/WHIT/ROK SR6 ....106 C1
Marina Ct CLDN/WHIT/ROK SR6 ....106 D2
Marina Dr MONK NE25 ....49 K5
SSH NE33 ....3 L7
Marina Gv
CLDN/WHIT/ROK SR6 ....106 D2
Marina Ter CLDN/WHIT/ROK SR6 ....93 F3
Marina View WLSD/HOW NE28 ....73 H1
Marina Vw HEBB NE31 ....73 F5
Marine Ap SSH NE33 ....3 L8
Marine Av WBAY NE26 ....50 E3
Marine Dr ASHBK/HED/RY SR2 ....121 F6
HEBB NE31 ....89 J1
JRW NE32 ....89 J2
Marine Gdns WBAY NE26 ....50 E4
Mariners Cottages SSH NE33 ....3 L7
Mariners' La TYNE/NSHE NE30 ....61 G3
Mariners Point
TYNE/NSHE NE30 ....61 H3
Mariner Sq SUND SR1 ....15 K2
Mariners Whf
CNUT (off Quayside) NE1 ....6 C7
Marine St NWBGN NE64 ....19 H7
Marine Ter BLYTH NE24 ....31 F7
Marine Wk
CLDN/WHIT/ROK SR6 ....107 F3
Marion St ASHBK/HED/RY SR2 ....15 H9
Maritime Crs PLEE/EAS SR8 ....163 G6
Maritime St SUND * SR1 ....14 E5
Maritime Ter SUND SR1 ....14 D5
Marius Av
BW/LEM/TK/HW NE15 ....66 B1
Mariville East
ASHBK/HED/RY SR2 ....135 G2
Mariville West
ASHBK/HED/RY SR2 ....135 G2
Market Crs WNGT TS28 ....183 K5
Market La CNUT NE1 ....5 K7
WICK/BNPF NE16 ....84 E3
Market Pl DHAM DH1 ....16 D3
HLH DH5 ....132 D7
SSH NE33 ....3 G7
Market Sq JRW NE32 ....73 K4
SUND SR1 ....14 E4
Market St CNUT NE1 ....5 K6
CON/LDGT DH8 ....122 D3
CRAM NE23 ....47 G1
HLH DH5 ....148 A3
Market Wy DUN/TMV NE11 ....86 D6
Markham Av
CLDN/WHIT/ROK SR6 ....93 G4
Markham St
ASHBK/HED/RY SR2 ....121 F4
Markington Dr
ASHBK/HED/RY SR2 ....135 F1
Markle Gv HLH DH5 ....147 G3
Mark Ri HLH DH5 ....147 K3
Mark's La HLS DH4 ....146 C4
Marlboro Av WICK/BNPF NE16 ....85 F4
Marlborough Ap GOS/KPK NE3 ....56 C3
Marlborough Av GOS/KPK NE3 ....56 B4
Marlborough Ct GOS/KPK NE3 ....55 H3
HLH DH5 ....147 H2
Marlborough Crs CNUT NE1 ....5 H8
Marlborough Rd
MLFD/PNYW SR4 ....118 D3
WASHN NE37 ....103 G4
Marlborough St North
SSH NE33 ....75 H3
Marlborough St South
SSH NE33 ....75 H3
Marleen Av BYK/HTN/WLK NE6 ....7 H1
Marleen Ct BYK/HTN/WLK NE6 ....7 H1
Marlene Av RDHAMSE DH6 ....179 K1
Marley Crs SWCK/CAS SR5 ....105 K2
Marlfield Ct WD/WHPE/BLK NE5 ....55 F7
Marlow Dr SUNDSW SR3 ....133 H2
Marlowe Gdns GATE NE8 ....11 H5
Marlowe Pl HLH DH5 ....147 H1
Marlow Pl LGB/KIL NE12 ....57 J4
Marlow St BLYTH NE24 ....31 F7
Marmion Rd BYK/HTN/WLK NE6 ....72 B3
Marmion Ter MONK NE25 ....50 D4
Marne St HLS DH4 ....131 K1
Marondale Av
BYK/HTN/WLK NE6 ....72 B4
Marquis Av WD/WHPE/BLK NE5 ....54 A5
Marquis Ct PRUD NE42 ....64 E7
Marr Rd HEBB NE31 ....73 H6
Marsden Av
CLDN/WHIT/ROK SR6 ....93 F2
Marsden Cl HLS DH4 ....132 A7
Marsden Gv
LWF/SPW/WRK NE9 ....101 K2
Marsden La HAR/WTLS NE34 ....76 B4
WD/WHPE/BLK NE5 ....54 E7
Marsden Rd
CLDN/WHIT/ROK SR6 ....91 K4
HAR/WTLS NE34 ....75 K4
Marshall St
CLDN/WHIT/ROK SR6 ....106 D1
Marshall Ter DHAM DH1 ....17 M2
Marshall Wallis Rd SSH NE33 ....75 G3
Marsham Cl
BW/LEM/TK/HW NE15 ....68 C4
CLDN/WHIT/ROK SR6 ....92 A2
Marsham Rd
WD/WHPE/BLK * NE5 ....54 C7
Marsh Ct DUN/TMV NE11 ....9 M9
Marske Ter BYK/HTN/WLK NE6 ....7 M5
Marston LGB/KIL NE12 ....47 K5
Martello Gdns LGB/HTN NE7 ....71 K1
Martin Ct WASHS NE38 ....116 B4
Martindale Av
CLDN/WHIT/ROK SR6 ....92 C7
Martindale Pk HLH DH5 ....147 H1
Martindale Wk WNGT TS28 ....183 K2
Martin Rd WLSD/HOW NE28 ....73 H1
Marwell Dr WASHN NE37 ....103 G3
Marwood Gv PLEE/EAS SR8 ....174 D7
Mary Agnes St GOS/KPK NE3 ....56 A5
Mary Av CLS/BIR/GTL DH3 ....101 H7
Mary Crs RDHAMSE DH6 ....181 G6
Maryhill Cl ELS/FEN NE4 ....69 J7
Mary Magdalene Bungalows
JES (off Claremont Rd) NE2 ....4 E1
Mary's Pl BYK/HTN/WLK NE6 ....72 D5
Mary St BLAY NE21 ....83 J2
SEA/MUR SR7 ....151 F1
SUND SR1 ....14 D6
SUNDSW SR3 ....120 A6
Mary Ter WD/WHPE/BLK NE5 ....68 E1
Masefield Av WICK/BNPF NE16 ....85 F3
Masefield Cl STLY/ANP DH9 ....113 F7
Masefield Dr HAR/WTLS NE34 ....90 E2
Masefield Pl GATE NE8 ....11 H4
Maslin Gv PLEE/EAS SR8 ....174 B7
Mason Rd WLSD/HOW NE28 ....58 C6
Mason St BYK/HTN/WLK NE6 ....7 G6
CON/LDGT DH8 ....123 F5
Master's Crs PRUD NE42 ....80 B2
Mast La TYNE/NSHE NE30 ....51 F6
Matamba Ter MLFD/PNYW SR4 ....14 A5
Matanzas St
ASHBK/HED/RY SR2 ....120 E3
Matfen Av SMOOR NE27 ....49 H6
Matfen Cl BLYTH NE24 ....30 E7
BW/LEM/TK/HW NE15 ....68 C5
Matfen Dr SUNDSW SR3 ....133 H1
Matfen Gdns WLSD/HOW NE28 ....59 H5
Matfen Pl ELS/FEN NE4 ....4 A2
GOS/KPK NE3 ....56 A4
Mather Rd ELS/FEN NE4 ....4 E9
Mathesons Gdns MPTH NE61 ....20 D5
Matlock Gdns
WD/WHPE/BLK NE5 ....54 D7
Matlock Rd JRW NE32 ....74 A6
Matlock Sq MPTH NE61 ....18 C2
Matlock St SUND SR1 ....14 E3
Matterdale Rd PLEE/EAS SR8 ....175 G4
Matthew Bank JES NE2 ....56 E7
Matthew Cl BYK/HTN/WLK NE6 ....6 F4
Matthew Rd BLYTH NE24 ....35 H2
Maudlin Pl WD/WHPE/BLK NE5 ....69 H2
Maudlin St HLH DH5 ....148 A2
Mauds La SUND SR1 ....15 H4
Maud St BW/LEM/TK/HW NE15 ....68 A5
CLDN/WHIT/ROK SR6 ....106 E1
Maughan St BLYTH NE24 ....31 H7
Maureen Ter SEA/MUR SR7 ....150 D1
Maurice Rd WLSD/HOW NE28 ....72 D3
Mautland St HLS DH4 ....132 C6
Mavin St DHAM DH1 ....16 F6
Maxton Cl SUNDSW * SR3 ....133 H2
Maxwell St GATE NE8 ....10 D9
MLFD/PNYW SR4 ....105 K6
SSH NE33 ....3 H9
May Av BLAY NE21 ....84 A5
RYTON NE40 ....66 E5

Maydown Cl SWCK/CAS SR5 ...104 D5
Mayfair Gdns GATE NE8 ...11 K7
  HAR/WTLS NE34 ...75 J4
  PONT/DH NE20 ...43 H3
Mayfair Rd JES NE2 ...70 D1
Mayfield MPTH NE61 ...20 C6
  WICK/BNPF NE16 ...85 F7
Mayfield Av
  BW/LEM/TK/HW NE15 ...67 G2
  CRAM NE23 ...38 D2
Mayfield Ct
  CLDN/WHIT/ROK SR6 ...106 D2
Mayfield Dr
  CLDN/WHIT/ROK SR6 ...92 B3
Mayfield Gdns
  BW/LEM/TK/HW * NE15 ...67 G2
  JRW NE32 ...73 J5
  WLSD/HOW NE28 ...58 B7
Mayfield Gv MLFD/PNYW SR4 ...118 E4
Mayfield Pl DIN/WO NE13 ...46 A4
Mayfield Rd GOS/KPK NE3 ...56 B6
  MLFD/PNYW SR4 ...104 D7
Mayfield Ter
  WD/WHPE/BLK NE5 ...69 J2
May Gv CLDN/WHIT/ROK SR6 ...93 F1
May Lea BDN/LAN/SAC DH7 ...143 G7
Maynard's Rw DHAM DH1 ...17 J3
Mayo Dr SUNDSW SR3 ...133 J2
Mayoral Wy DUN/TMV NE11 ...100 D3
Mayorswell Cl DHAM DH1 ...16 F2
Mayorswell Fld DHAM * DH1 ...16 F2
Mayorswell St DHAM DH1 ...16 F2
Maypole Cl SWCK/CAS SR5 ...106 B4
May St BLAY NE21 ...83 K3
  CLS/BIR/GTL DH3 ...115 J1
  DHAM DH1 ...16 A5
  MLFD/PNYW SR4 ...14 B4
  SSH NE33 ...75 H2
Mayswood Rd
  CLDN/WHIT/ROK SR6 ...106 D2
Maythorne Dr RDHAMSE DH6 ...161 G3
Maywood Cl GOS/KPK NE3 ...55 J6
Mazine Ter RDHAMSE DH6 ...172 D1
McAnany Av HAR/WTLS NE34 ...75 H6
McClaren Wy HLS DH4 ...118 D7
McCracken Cl GOS/KPK NE3 ...56 C2
McCracken Dr DIN/WO NE13 ...46 C2
McCutcheon Ct
  BYK/HTN/WLK NE6 ...7 L9
McErlane Sq HLS NE10 ...13 K5
McEwan Gdns ELS/FEN NE4 ...4 B7
McGuiness Av PLEE/EAS SR8 ...175 F1
McIntyre Rd HEBB NE31 ...73 H4
McKendrick Vls
  WD/WHPE/BLK NE5 ...69 H2
McNally Pl DHAM DH1 ...17 J2
McNamara Ct
  (off Mcnamara Rd) WLSD/HOW NE28 ...59 H7
McNamara Rd WLSD/HOW NE28 ...59 G7
Meacham Wy WICK/BNPF NE16 ...84 E7
Mead Av LGB/KIL NE12 ...58 A2
Mead Crs LGB/KIL NE12 ...58 A2
Meadowbank
  BDN/LAN/SAC DH7 ...154 A3
  CRAM NE23 ...47 G1
Meadow Bank Dr
  STKFD/GP NE62 ...22 E7
Meadow Brook Dr CHPW NE17 ...95 J5
Meadowbrook Dr FELL NE10 ...88 E5
Meadow Cl BLAY NE21 ...83 H3
  CRAM NE23 ...39 G6
  DUN/TMV NE11 ...8 F6
  HLH DH5 ...147 J1
  LGB/KIL* NE12 ...57 H4
  RDHAMSE DH6 ...180 C7
  RYTON NE40 ...67 F6
Meadow Ct BDLGTN NE22 ...28 E5
  PONT/DH NE20 ...43 G4
Meadowdale Crs BDLGTN NE22 ...28 D5
  WD/WHPE/BLK NE5 ...55 H7
Meadow Dr CLSW/PEL DH2 ...129 F5
  DIN/WO NE13 ...46 C1
  SUNDSW SR3 ...133 F2
Meadowfield ASHGTN NE63 ...24 C3
  CON/LDGT DH8 ...122 D4
  MONK NE25 ...50 B4
  PONT/DH NE20 ...43 G4
Meadowfield Av GOS/KPK NE3 ...56 A4
Meadowfield Crs RYTON NE40 ...66 C7
Meadowfield Dr
  CLDN/WHIT/ROK SR6 ...92 B3
Meadowfield Gdns
  BYK/HTN/WLK NE6 ...72 C2
Meadowfield Pk South
  PSHWF NE43 ...79 G7
Meadowfield Rd GOS/KPK NE3 ...56 B6
  PSHWF NE43 ...79 G7
Meadowfield Wy
  STLY/ANP DH9 ...112 A6
Meadow Gdns SUNDSW SR3 ...120 B3
Meadow Gra CLDN/WHIT/ROK SR6 ...131 G5
Meadow Gv MLFD/PNYW SR4 ...118 E1
Meadow La DUN/TMV NE11 ...8 F6
  RYTON NE40 ...66 C7
Meadow Laws HAR/WTLS NE34 ...76 A4
Meadow Ri CON/LDGT DH8 ...123 G5
  LWF/SPW/WRK NE9 ...87 J7
  WD/WHPE/BLK NE5 ...55 H7
Meadow Rd
  BW/LEM/TK/HW NE15 ...68 B4
  MONK NE25 ...50 B5
  WBAY NE26 ...40 E2
  WLSD/HOW NE28 ...73 H1
Meadows Crest PSHWF NE43 ...94 A2
Meadowside
  ASHBK/HED/RY SR2 ...120 B2
Meadows La HLS DH4 ...146 E4
The Meadows GOS/KPK NE3 ...55 K4
  HLS DH4 ...131 F4
  HLS DH4 ...146 D5
  RYTON NE40 ...67 F6
  WICK/BNPF NE16 ...111 J2
Meadow St HLH DH5 ...147 F4
Meadowsweet Cl BLYTH NE24 ...34 E3
Meadow V ASHBK/HED/RY SR2 ...14 D9
Meadowvale PONT/DH NE20 ...42 C7

Meadow Vw
  BOLCOL (off Foxhomes) NE35 ...90 B4
  CON/LDGT DH8 ...138 D1
  MONK NE25 ...40 A2
  STLY/ANP DH9 ...111 F5
  SUNDSW SR3 ...133 F2
Meadow Wy
  BDN/LAN/SAC DH7 ...140 B5
Meadow Well Wy NSHW NE29 ...60 C6
Mead Wk BYK/HTN/WLK NE6 ...72 B5
Mead Wy LGB/KIL NE12 ...58 B2
Meadway Dr LGB/KIL NE12 ...58 B3
Means Dr CRAM NE23 ...47 H4
Medburn Av TYNE/NSHE NE30 ...51 G7
Medburn Rd
  BW/LEM/TK/HW NE15 ...67 K4
  MONK NE25 ...40 B6
Medham Cl FELL NE10 ...88 A6
Medina Cl SUNDSW SR3 ...133 J2
Mediterranean Village
  WICK/BNPF
  (off Metrocentre) NE16 ...8 B4
Medlar Cl HLS DH4 ...131 H2
Medomsley Gdns
  LWF/SPW/WRK NE9 ...102 A1
Medomsley Rd CON/LDGT DH8 ...123 F4
Medomsly St MLFD/PNYW SR4 ...106 A6
Medway JRW NE32 ...90 A2
Medway Av HEBB NE31 ...89 G1
Medway Cl PLEE/EAS SR8 ...174 D6
Medway Crs GATE NE8 ...11 L7
Medway Gdns
  MLFD/PNYW SR4 ...119 H2
  TYNE/NSHE NE30 ...60 E3
Medway Pl CRAM NE23 ...33 J6
Megstone
  LWF/SPW/WRK
  (off Pimlico Ct) NE9 ...101 F1
Megstone Av CRAM NE23 ...38 B3
Megstone Ct LGB/KIL NE12 ...48 A5
Melbeck Dr CLSW/PEL DH2 ...114 E4
Melbourne Ct GATE NE8 ...10 F1
Melbourne Crs MONK NE25 ...50 C6
Melbourne Gdns
  HAR/WTLS NE34 ...90 D1
Melbourne Pl MLFD/PNYW SR4 ...119 J2
Melbourne St CNUT NE1 ...5 M7
Melbury MONK NE25 ...50 A3
Melbury Ct
  CLDN/WHIT/ROK SR6 ...106 D2
Melbury Rd LGB/HTN NE7 ...71 C2
Melbury St SEA/MUR SR7 ...150 E3
Meldon Av GOS/KPK NE3 ...55 K3
  HAR/WTLS NE34 ...75 J5
  RDHAMSE DH6 ...170 D1
Meldon Ct RYTON NE40 ...82 A1
Meldon Gdns DUN/TMV NE11 ...86 A7
  STKFD/GP NE62 ...23 F5
Meldon Rd MLFD/PNYW SR4 ...105 K6
Meldon St WLSD/HOW NE28 ...74 A2
Meldon Ter BYK/HTN/WLK NE6 ...6 F1
Meldon Wy BLAY NE21 ...83 H4
  DHAM DH1 ...169 J5
  STLY/ANP DH9 ...125 K3
Melgarve Dr SUNDSW SR3 ...133 J2
Melkington Ct
  WD/WHPE/BLK NE5 ...55 F7
Melkridge Pl CRAM NE23 ...38 A3
Mellendean Cl
  WD/WHPE/BLK NE5 ...55 F7
Melling Rd CRAM NE23 ...38 A2
Melmerby Cl GOS/KPK NE3 ...56 D3
Melness Rd DIN/WO NE13 ...46 A4
Melock Ct
  DIN/WO (off Melness Rd) NE13 ...46 A4
Melrose Av BDLGTN NE22 ...29 K5
  HEBB NE31 ...89 G1
  SEA/MUR SR7 ...149 F6
  SMOOR NE27 ...39 K7
  TYNE/NSHE NE30 ...50 E7
Melrose Cl
  BW/LEM/TK/HW NE15 ...68 C5
  GOS/KPK NE3 ...46 B7
Melrose Ct BDLGTN NE22 ...29 K4
Melrose Crs SEA/MUR SR7 ...135 F7
Melrose Gdns
  CLDN/WHIT/ROK SR6 ...106 E2
  WLSD/HOW NE28 ...59 J6
Melrose Gv JRW NE32 ...74 C7
Melrose Ter NWBGN NE64 ...25 F2
Melsonby Cl SUNDSW SR3 ...133 H1
Meltham Ct WD/WHPE/BLK NE5 ...67 J1
Meltham Dr SUNDSW SR3 ...133 J2
Melton Av BYK/HTN/WLK NE6 ...72 B6
Melton Crs WBAY NE26 ...41 G4
Melton Dr MONK NE25 ...40 A2
Melvaig Cl SUNDSW SR3 ...133 J2
Melville Av BLYTH NE24 ...35 F2
Melville Gdns MONK NE25 ...50 A5
Melville Gv LGB/HTN NE7 ...57 G7
Melville St CLS/BIR/GTL DH3 ...129 J5
Melvin Pl WD/WHPE/BLK NE5 ...69 F1
Melvyn Gdns
  CLDN/WHIT/ROK SR6 ...106 E2
Membury Cl SUNDSW SR3 ...133 J2
Memorial Av PLEE/EAS SR8 ...163 F4
Mendip Av CLSW/PEL DH2 ...129 H5
Mendip Cl ASHGTN NE63 ...24 A4
  PLEE/EAS SR8 ...174 C4
Mendip Dr WASHS NE38 ...116 D3
Mendip Gdns DUN/TMV NE11 ...86 B3
Mendip Ter STLY/ANP DH9 ...126 E2
Mendip Wy LGB/KIL NE12 ...57 K4
Menvill Pl SUND SR1 ...15 H5
Mercantile Rd HLS DH4 ...147 F1
Mercia Wy
  BW/LEM/TK/HW NE15 ...68 C6
Meredith Gdns GATE * NE8 ...11 H5
Mere Dr DHAM DH1 ...156 C2
Mere Knolls Rd
  CLDN/WHIT/ROK SR6 ...92 E7
Mereside FELL NE10 ...88 C5
Merevale Cl WASHN NE37 ...103 G3
Merganser Ldg FELL * NE10 ...12 C8
Meridan Wy LGB/HTN NE7 ...57 K7
Merlay Dr DIN/WO NE13 ...45 F3
Merle Gdns BYK/HTN/WLK NE6 ...7 G7

MPTH NE61 ...20 B3
Merle Ter MLFD/PNYW SR4 ...105 K5
Merley Ga MPTH NE61 ...20 E7
Merlin Cl SEA/MUR SR7 ...135 J7
Merlin Ct BDN/LAN/SAC DH7 ...165 F2
  FELL NE10 ...12 C1
Merlin Crs WLSD/HOW NE28 ...59 H7
Merlin Dr CLS/BIR/GTL DH3 ...115 K7
Merlin Pl LGB/KIL NE12 ...57 G3
Merlin Wy SMOOR NE27 ...59 J1
Merrington Cl SUNDSW SR3 ...133 H2
Merrion Cl SUNDSW SR3 ...133 H1
Merryfield Gdns
  CLDN/WHIT/ROK SR6 ...106 E2
Mersey Pl GATE NE8 ...11 M6
Mersey Rd GATE NE8 ...11 M7
  HEBB NE31 ...89 G1
Mersey St CHPW NE17 ...95 J4
  CON/LDGT DH8 ...123 K2
Merton Ct ELS/FEN NE4 ...69 H7
Merton Rd BYK/HTN/WLK NE6 ...13 H1
  PONT/DH NE20 ...43 G3
Merton Sq BLYTH NE24 ...31 G6
Messenger Bank
  CON/LDGT DH8 ...122 C1
Metcalfe Crs SEA/MUR SR7 ...149 G5
Metcalfe Rd CON/LDGT DH8 ...123 H6
Methven Wy CRAM NE23 ...33 J5
The Mews BLAY NE21 ...84 C2
  CNUT* NE1 ...5 J5
  DHAM (off Low Rd East) DH1 ...169 G4
  FELL NE10 ...13 M9
  HLS DH4 ...146 D1
  SUNDSW SR3 ...119 F7
  TYNE/NSHE NE30 ...60 E2
Michaelgate BYK/HTN/WLK NE6 ...7 G1
Mickle Cl WASHN NE37 ...102 C7
Mickleton Cl CLS/BIR/GTL DH3 ...145 J1
  CON/LDGT DH8 ...123 F6
Mickleton Gdns SUNDSW SR3 ...120 B4
Middle Cl WASHS NE38 ...116 D5
Middle Dr DIN/WO NE13 ...54 D1
  PONT/DH NE20 ...42 D7
Middle Engine La
  WLSD/HOW NE28 ...59 H5
Middlefield CLSW/PEL DH2 ...114 E7
Middlegarth
  WD/WHPE/BLK NE5 ...69 H1
Middle Ga MPTH NE61 ...20 D7
  WD/WHPE/BLK NE5 ...68 B2
Middle Gn MONK NE25 ...50 A5
Middleham Cl CLSW/PEL DH2 ...114 E5
Middleham Rd SWCK/CAS SR5 ...105 J2
Middleham Rd DHAM DH1 ...156 E2
Middles Rd STLY/ANP DH9 ...126 A4
Middle St BYK/HTN/WLK NE6 ...72 B5
  CON/LDGT DH8 ...123 F5
  SUND SR1 ...14 E4
  TYNE/NSHE NE30 ...61 H5
Middle St East
  BYK/HTN/WLK NE6 ...72 C5
Middleton Av ELS/FEN NE4 ...69 J5
  ROWG NE39 ...97 H4
Middleton Cl SEA/MUR SR7 ...134 E4
Middleton St BLYTH NE24 ...31 G7
Middlewood Pk ELS/FEN NE4 ...69 J3
Middlewood Rd
  BDN/LAN/SAC DH7 ...140 B5
Middridge Rd
  BDN/LAN/SAC DH7 ...153 K3
Midfield Dr
  CLDN/WHIT/ROK SR6 ...106 E4
Midgley Dr SUNDSW SR3 ...133 J2
Midhill Cl BDN/LAN/SAC DH7 ...167 G5
Midhurst Av HAR/WTLS NE34 ...75 K3
Midhurst Cl SUNDSW SR3 ...133 H1
Midhurst Rd LGB/KIL NE12 ...57 K3
Midmoor Rd MLFD/PNYW SR4 ...105 J6
Midsomer Cl SUNDSW SR3 ...133 H2
Midway BYK/HTN/WLK NE6 ...72 C5
Milbanke Cl CLSW/PEL DH2 ...115 F5
Milbank Ter RDHAMSE DH6 ...173 H4
  WNCT TS28 ...184 A6
Milburn Dr
  BW/LEM/TK/HW NE15 ...69 F5
Milburn Rd ASHGTN NE63 ...23 K2
Milburn Ter STKFD/GP NE62 ...23 H7
Mildmay Rd JES NE2 ...70 D1
Milecastle Ct
  WD/WHPE/BLK NE5 ...68 B1
Mile End Rd SSH NE33 ...3 G4
Milfield Av SMOOR NE27 ...49 H6
  WLSD/HOW NE28 ...58 E6
Milford Gdns GOS/KPK NE3 ...56 B1
Milford Rd
  BW/LEM/TK/HW NE15 ...69 G6
Military Rd TYNE/NSHE NE30 ...61 F4
Milk Market CNUT NE1 ...6 A7
Millais Gdns HAR/WTLS NE34 ...91 G2
Millbank
  SSH (off Station Rd) NE33 ...3 G9
Mill Bank SWCK/CAS SR5 ...106 C1
Millbank Ct DHAM * DH1 ...16 A1
Millbank Pl BDLGTN NE22 ...29 H6
Millbank Rd BDLGTN NE22 ...29 H5
  BYK/HTN/WLK NE6 ...72 C7
Millbeck Gv HLH DH5 ...147 G2
Millbrook NSHW NE29 ...60 C5
Millbrook Rd CRAM NE23 ...33 J6
Millburngate DHAM DH1 ...16 C3
Millburn St MLFD/PNYW SR4 ...14 A3
Mill Cl NSHW NE29 ...60 C5
Mill Ct CHPW NE17 ...95 H7
  HLS DH4 ...131 G5
Mill Crs HEBB NE31 ...88 E1
Milldale SEA/MUR SR7 ...135 F7
Milldale Av BLYTH NE24 ...30 C9
Mill Dam SSH NE33 ...2 F8
Mildene Av TYNE/NSHE NE30 ...61 G2
Mill Dene Vw JRW NE32 ...73 K6
Mill Dyke Cl MONK NE25 ...50 A3
Millennium Wy SWCK/CAS SR5 ...14 D1
Miller Gdns CLSW/PEL DH2 ...128 D3
Millers Dene
  BYK/HTN/WLK
  (off Shields Rd) NE6 ...72 B3
Millers Hi HLS DH4 ...132 A1
Millershill La CON/LDGT DH8 ...137 K7

Miller's La WICK/BNPF NE16 ...85 F3
Millers Rd BYK/HTN/WLK NE6 ...7 H3
Miller St GATE NE8 ...10 C7
Miller Ter SUNDSW SR3 ...120 A6
Mill Farm Rd ROWG NE39 ...96 C7
Millfield BDLGTN NE22 ...29 G7
  BDN/LAN/SAC DH7 ...140 B4
  WBAY NE26 ...41 G3
Millfield Av GOS/KPK NE3 ...55 J7
Millfield Cl
  BW/LEM/TK/HW NE15 ...67 H3
Millfield Ct BDLGTN NE22 ...29 G6
Millfield East BDLGTN NE22 ...29 G6
Millfield Gdns BLYTH NE24 ...31 F5
  FELL NE10 ...12 B8
  TYNE/NSHE NE30 ...61 G2
Millfield Gv TYNE/NSHE NE30 ...61 G2
Millfield La
  BW/LEM/TK/HW NE15 ...67 H3
Millfield North BDLGTN NE22 ...29 G6
Millfield Rd WICK/BNPF NE16 ...85 F6
Millfield South BDLGTN NE22 ...29 G7
Millfield West BDLGTN NE22 ...29 G6
Millford FELL NE10 ...88 C7
Millford Wy RDHAMSE DH6 ...180 B2
Mill Gv HAR/WTLS NE34 ...76 B7
  TYNE/NSHE NE30 ...61 G2
Millgrove Vw GOS/KPK NE3 ...55 K7
Mill Hi HLH DH5 ...147 G2
  PLEE/EAS SR8 ...174 A2
Mill Hill Rd SUNDSW SR3 ...133 K1
  WD/WHPE/BLK NE5 ...68 D5
Mill House Ct DHAM DH1 ...17 M3
Milling Ct GATE NE8 ...10 B4
Mill La BDN/LAN/SAC DH7 ...167 F2
  BLAY NE21 ...83 K5
  BW/LEM/TK/HW NE15 ...52 B7
  CLDN/WHIT/ROK SR6 ...93 F1
  CLSW/PEL DH2 ...144 C4
  CON/LDGT DH8 ...108 E2
  CRAM NE23 ...38 D7
  DHAM DH1 ...17 M2
  DHAM DH1 ...17 L9
  ELS/FEN NE4 ...4 C7
  HEBB NE31 ...89 F2
  NSHW NE29 ...2 E4
  RDHAMSE DH6 ...170 C1
  SPEN DL16 ...177 K7
  STLY/ANP DH9 ...114 D4
Milne Ct BDLGTN NE22 ...29 F5
Millom Ct PLEE/EAS SR8 ...174 B7
Millom Pl LWF/SPW/WRK NE9 ...87 H7
Mill Race Cl CHPW NE17 ...95 H7
Mill Ri GOS/KPK NE3 ...56 E6
Mill Rd BDN/LAN/SAC DH7 ...167 K5
  CHPW NE17 ...95 H5
  GATE NE8 ...6 B9
  SEA/MUR SR7 ...135 F7
Mills Gdns WLSD/HOW NE28 ...58 D7
Millside MPTH NE61 ...20 D5
Mill St MLFD/PNYW SR4 ...14 A5
Mill Vw BOL NE36 ...90 E5
  FELL NE10 ...87 J5
Mill View Av
  CLDN/WHIT/ROK SR6 ...106 D2
Millview Dr TYNE/NSHE NE30 ...61 G2
Mill View Ri PRUD NE42 ...64 D2
Mill Wy BW/LEM/TK/HW NE15 ...64 D3
Millway LWF/SPW/WRK NE9 ...11 K9
  WBAY NE26 ...41 G3
Milner Crs BLAY NE21 ...83 J3
Milner St SSH NE33 ...3 L9
Milne Wy GOS/KPK NE3 ...55 K4
Milrig Cl SUNDSW SR3 ...133 J2
Milsted Cl SUNDSW SR3 ...133 H1
Milsted Ct WD/WHPE/BLK NE5 ...67 J1
Milton Av HEBB NE31 ...73 G5
  HLH DH5 ...147 J1
Milton Cl JES NE2 ...6 A3
  SEA/MUR SR7 ...150 C1
  STLY/ANP DH9 ...127 F1
Milton Gn JES NE2 ...6 A3
Milton Gv ASHGTN NE63 ...24 B3
  NSHW NE29 ...60 D4
  PRUD NE42 ...80 B3
  RDHAMSE DH6 ...173 J4
Milton Pl JES NE2 ...6 A3
  LWF/SPW/WRK NE9 ...102 A4
  NSHW NE29 ...60 D4
Milton Rd WICK/BNPF NE16 ...85 F4
Milton Sq GATE NE8 ...11 J4
Milton St JES NE2 ...73 K3
  MLFD/PNYW SR4 ...106 A6
  RYTON NE40 ...82 A3
  SSH NE33 ...75 H2
Milton Ter NSHW NE29 ...60 D4
Milvain Av ELS/FEN NE4 ...69 J5
Milvain St GATE NE8 ...11 H6
Milverton Ct GOS/KPK NE3 ...55 G4
Mimosa Dr HEBB NE31 ...89 G1
Mimosa Pl ELS/FEN NE4 ...69 H3
Mindrum Ter
  BYK/HTN/WLK NE6 ...72 B7
  NSHW NE29 ...60 B6
Minehead Gdns SUNDSW SR3 ...120 A6
Minerva Cl WD/WHPE/BLK NE5 ...54 A6
Mingary Cl HLH DH5 ...147 F4
Minorca Cl SUND SR1 ...15 H5
Minorca Pl GOS/KPK NE3 ...55 K7
Minskip Cl SUNDSW SR3 ...133 H2
Minster Ct GATE NE8 ...11 L4
Minster Gv WD/WHPE/BLK NE5 ...53 K7
Minster Pde JRW NE32 ...74 A4
Minting Pl CRAM NE23 ...38 A2
Minton La NSHW NE29 ...2 B4
Minton Sq MLFD/PNYW SR4 ...105 J6
Mirk La GATE NE8 ...5 M9
Mirlaw Rd CRAM NE23 ...38 A3
Mistletoe Rd JES NE2 ...70 E2
Mistletoe St DHAM DH1 ...16 A4
Mitcham Crs LGB/HTN NE7 ...57 H7

Mitchell Av JES NE2 ...70 E1
  MONK NE25 ...50 B5
Mitchell Cl PLEE/EAS SR8 ...174 C2
Mitchell Dr ASHGTN NE63 ...24 C2
Mitchell Gdns HAR/WTLS NE34 ...75 K4
Mitchell St BYK/HTN/WLK NE6 ...72 D6
  DHAM DH1 ...16 B3
  STLY/ANP DH9 ...126 B3
Mitford Av BLYTH NE24 ...34 E1
  MONK NE25 ...39 K5
  MPTH NE61 ...21 J1
Mitford Cl DHAM DH1 ...169 J5
  WASHS NE38 ...116 D2
Mitford Ct PLEE/EAS SR8 ...174 E6
Mitford Dr ASHGTN NE63 ...23 K3
  RDHAMSE DH6 ...158 D7
Mitford Gdns DUN/TMV NE11 ...86 A7
  STKFD/GP NE62 ...23 F5
  WLSD/HOW NE28 ...59 H5
Mitford Pl GOS/KPK NE3 ...56 A4
Mitford Rd HAR/WTLS NE34 ...75 J5
  MPTH NE61 ...20 A5
Mitford St
  CLDN/WHIT/ROK SR6 ...106 E1
  WLSD/HOW* NE28 ...74 A1
Mitford Ter JRW NE32 ...89 K2
Mitford Wy DIN/WO NE13 ...45 F3
Mithras Gdns
  BW/LEM/TK/HW NE15 ...66 A1
Mitre Pl SSH NE33 ...75 F3
Moat Gdns FELL NE10 ...88 E4
Moatside Ms
  DHAM (off Saddler St) DH1 ...16 D4
Moffat Av JRW NE32 ...74 C7
Moffat Cl NSHW NE29 ...60 A2
Moffatt Vls
  SSH (off Imeary St) NE33 ...75 H2
Moine Gdns
  CLDN/WHIT/ROK SR6 ...106 E2
Molineux Cl BYK/HTN/WLK NE6 ...6 E4
Molineux Ct BYK/HTN/WLK NE6 ...6 E4
Molineux St BYK/HTN/WLK NE6 ...6 E4
Mollyfair Cl RYTON NE40 ...66 B7
Monarch Rd ELS/FEN NE4 ...9 J2
Monarch Wy SUNDSW SR3 ...133 G2
Mona St STLY/ANP DH9 ...112 D7
Moncreiff Ter PLEE/EAS SR8 ...162 D5
Monday Crs ELS/FEN NE4 ...4 E4
Monday Pl ELS/FEN NE4 ...4 E4
Money Slack DHAM DH1 ...168 C5
Monkchester Gn
  BYK/HTN/WLK NE6 ...7 L7
Monkchester Rd
  BYK/HTN/WLK NE6 ...7 L8
Monk Ct GATE NE8 ...11 H3
  PLEE/EAS SR8 ...174 C7
Monkdale Av BLYTH NE24 ...34 C1
Monkhouse Av
  TYNE/NSHE NE30 ...60 E1
Monkridge WBAY NE26 ...40 E1
  WD/WHPE/BLK NE5 ...67 K1
Monkridge Gdns DUN/TMV NE11 ...9 H9
Monks Av MONK NE25 ...50 B6
Monks' Crs DHAM DH1 ...157 G6
Monks Rdg MPTH NE61 ...20 B6
Monks Rd MONK NE25 ...50 A6
Monkstone Av
  TYNE/NSHE NE30 ...61 G2
Monkstone Cl TYNE/NSHE NE30 ...61 G2
Monkstone Crs
  TYNE/NSHE NE30 ...61 G2
Monk St CLDN/WHIT/ROK SR6 ...106 D4
Monksway JRW NE32 ...74 C5
Monks Wy TYNE/NSHE NE30 ...61 G1
Monks Wd NSHW NE29 ...60 D2
Monkswood Sq SUNDSW SR3 ...134 B1
Monkton FELL NE10 ...12 E9
Monkton Av HAR/WTLS NE34 ...74 D7
Monkton La HEBB NE31 ...89 G2
  JRW NE32 ...73 H7
Monkton Rd JRW NE32 ...73 K4
Monkton Ter JRW NE32 ...73 K5
Monmouth Gdns
  WLSD/HOW NE28 ...59 J6
Monroe Pl WD/WHPE/BLK NE5 ...69 H1
Mons Av HEBB NE31 ...73 G6
Montagu Av GOS/KPK NE3 ...70 A1
Montagu Ct GOS/KPK NE3 ...70 A1
Montague Ct
  LWF/SPW/WRK
  (off Lindum Rd) NE9 ...11 H8
Montague St
  BW/LEM/TK/HW NE15 ...68 B5
  CLDN/WHIT/ROK SR6 ...106 D2
Monteigne Dr RDHAMSE DH6 ...180 A2
Monterey SUNDSW SR3 ...133 J2
  WASHN NE37 ...103 F2
Montfalcon Cl PLEE/EAS SR8 ...174 D4
Montford Cl SUNDSW * SR3 ...133 H2
Montpellier Pl GOS/KPK NE3 ...55 K7
Montpellier Ter
  ASHBK/HED/RY SR2 ...120 E2
Montrose Cl MONK NE25 ...40 A2
Montrose Crs
  LWF/SPW/WRK NE9 ...11 M9
Montrose Dr FELL NE10 ...12 E9
Montrose Gdns SUNDSW SR3 ...120 A3
Monument MI CNUT NE1 ...5 K6
Monument Vw
  BDN/LAN/SAC
  (off Brookside) DH7 ...143 H4
  HLS DH4 ...117 J6
Moor Cl NSHW NE29 ...60 B5
  SUND SR1 ...15 J4
Moor Ct CLDN/WHIT/ROK SR6 ...92 E4
  JES (off Westfield) NE2 ...70 B1

Moor Crs DHAM DH1 ....17 M1
GOS/KPK NE3 ....56 C7
RDHAMSE DH6 ....172 B3
Moor Crest Ter NSHW * NE29....60 D2
Moorcroft Cl
BW/LEM/TK/HW NE15 ....68 B4
Moorcroft Rd
BW/LEM/TK/HW NE15 ....68 C4
Moordale Av BLYTH NE24....34 C1
Moore Av DUN/TMV NE11 ....9 H8
HAR/WTLS NE34 ....75 J5
Moore Crs South HLH DH5....147 H1
Moor Edge BDN/LAN/SAC DH7 ....167 G7
Moor Edge Rd SMOOR NE27 ....49 G5
Moor End
GOS/KPK (off High St) NE3 ....56 C7
Moore St GATE NE8 ....11 K5
STLY/ANP DH9....126 C2
Moore Street Vls GATE NE8 ....11 K5
Moorfield JES NE2....56 D7
Moorfield Gdns
CLDN/WHIT/ROK SR6 ....92 A4
Moorfields MPTH NE61....20 E7
Moorfoot Av CLSW/PEL DH2 ....129 J5
Moorfoot Gdns DUN/TMV NE11 ....86 A5
Moorhead WD/WHPE/BLK NE5 ....69 J2
Moorhill DUN/TMV NE11 ....100 C7
Moorhouse Cl HAR/WTLS * NE34....75 H6
Moorhouse Est ASHGTN NE63 ....24 B1
Moorhouse La ASHGTN NE63....24 B2
Moorhouses Rd NSHW NE29 ....60 A2
Moorland Av BDLGTN NE22 ....30 A3
Moorland Ct BDLGTN NE22 ....30 A3
Moorland Crs BDLGTN NE22....30 A3
BYK/HTN/WLK NE6....7 L3
CON/LDGT DH8 ....136 E2
Moorland Dr BDLGTN NE22 ....30 A4
Moorlands CON/LDGT DH8....122 C2
DHAM DH1 ....17 L2
JRW NE32....90 B3
PRUD NE42 ....80 E3
Moorlands Crs CON/LDGT DH8 ....122 D3
The Moorlands STLY/ANP DH9....111 G5
Moorland Vw CHPW NE17 ....95 H5
Moorland Vls BDLGTN NE22....30 A3
Moorland Wy CRAM NE23 ....32 E6
Moor La BOL NE36....91 J4
CLDN/WHIT/ROK SR6 ....92 C4
HAR/WTLS NE34 ....75 J5
PONT/DH NE20 ....42 D5
WD/WHPE/BLK NE5 ....55 H6
WNGT TS28....183 K4
Moor La East HAR/WTLS NE34....75 K5
Moormill La DUN/TMV NE11 ....100 E7
Moor Park Ct NSHW NE29 ....60 A3
Moor Park Rd NSHW NE29....59 K3
Moor Pl GOS/KPK NE3....56 C7
Moor Rd PRUD NE42 ....80 E4
Moor Rd North GOS/KPK NE3 ....56 D6
Moor Rd South JES NE2 ....56 D7
Moorsburn Dr HLS DH4....132 A6
Moors Cl HLS DH4 ....131 K7
Moorsfield HLS DH4 ....131 K7
Moorside
LGB/KIL
(off Great Lime Rd) NE12....47 H7
WASHN NE37 ....102 D6
Moorside North ELS/FEN NE4 ....69 J2
Moorside Rd SUNDSW SR3....133 H2
Moorside South ELS/FEN NE4....4 A1
Moorsley Rd HLH DH5....159 F1
Moor St RDHAMSE DH6....182 E1
SUND SR1 ....15 H4
Moor Ter SUND SR1 ....15 J5
Moorvale La
WD/WHPE/BLK NE5 ....69 J1
Moor Vw CLDN/WHIT/ROK SR6 ....92 E4
Moorview CON/LDGT DH8 ....122 E3
Moor Vw LGB/KIL NE12....47 J5
Moor View Cl MPTH NE61 ....21 H2
Moorview Crs
WD/WHPE/BLK NE5 ....69 J1
Moor View Ter STLY/ANP DH9....125 G4
Moorway WASHN NE37....102 D7
Moorway Dr
BW/LEM/TK/HW NE15....68 C4
Moraine Crs CHPW NE17 ....95 H7
Moralee Cl LGB/HTN NE7 ....57 K7
Moran St CLDN/WHIT/ROK SR6 ....106 D1
Moray Cl CLS/BIR/GTL DH3....115 K5
PLEE/EAS SR8 ....174 D5
Moray St CLDN/WHIT/ROK SR6 ....106 D3
Morcott Gdns NSHW NE29....2 A5
Morden St CNUT NE1 ....5 J5
Mordey Cl ASHBK/HED/RY SR2 ....15 H7
Moreland Rd HAR/WTLS NE34....91 H1
Moreland St
CLDN/WHIT/ROK SR6 ....106 D3
Morgan St SWCK/CAS SR5 ....106 B3
Morgans Wy BLAY NE21 ....83 J2
Morland Av WASHS NE38 ....117 G3
Morland Gdns
LWF/SPW/WRK NE9....11 M9
Morley Av FELL NE10....13 L4
Morley Ct BYK/HTN/WLK NE6 ....7 G3
Morley Hill Rd
WD/WHPE/BLK NE5 ....68 D3
Morley La BDN/LAN/SAC DH7....176 C1
Morley Ter FELL NE10 ....12 C8
HLS DH4 ....131 J7
Morningside
BDN/LAN/SAC DH7 ....143 H4
WASHS NE38 ....116 A6
Mornington Av GOS/KPK NE3 ....55 K7
Morpeth Av DIN/WO NE13 ....46 C2
HAR/WTLS NE34 ....75 J4
JRW NE32....89 K1
MPTH NE61 ....21 H1
Morpeth Cl STKFD/GP NE62 ....22 E7
WASHS NE38 ....116 C2
Morpeth Dr SUNDSW SR3....133 H1
Morpeth Rd ASHGTN NE63....23 F1
STKFD/GP* NE62 ....22 E6
Morpeth St JES NE2 ....4 F1
PLEE/EAS SR8 ....175 G2
Morpeth Ter NSHW NE29 ....60 B6
Morris Av HAR/WTLS NE34 ....91 F1
Morris Crs BOLCOL NE35....90 E4
RDHAMSE DH6 ....172 B6
Morris Gdns FELL NE10....13 M8
Morrison Rd MPTH NE61 ....20 D4
Morrison St GATE NE8....10 A4
Morris Rd WICK/BNPF NE16....85 F4
Morris St CLS/BIR/GTL DH3....115 H2
GATE NE8 ....10 A7
Morston Dr
BW/LEM/TK/HW NE15 ....68 C5
Mortimer Av NSHW NE29 ....60 B4
WD/WHPE/BLK NE5 ....54 E7
Mortimer Cha CRAM NE23 ....33 H4
Mortimer Rd HAR/WTLS NE34....75 J4
SSH NE33 ....75 H3
Mortimer St CON/LDGT DH8....122 D4
MLFD/PNYW SR4 ....105 K6
Morton Cl WASHS NE38....117 F2
Morton Sq PLEE/EAS SR8 ....174 D3
Morton St BYK/HTN/WLK NE6 ....7 J5
SSH NE33 ....3 J5
Morton Wk SSH NE33 ....3 H5
Morval Cl SUNDSW SR3....133 H2
Morwick Cl CRAM NE23 ....38 A3
Morwick Pl WD/WHPE/BLK NE5 ....69 H2
Morwick Rd NSHW NE29 ....60 B2
Mosley St CNUT NE1 ....5 K7
Moss Bank LWF/SPW/WRK NE9....101 H2
Moss Cl BW/LEM/TK/HW NE15 ....68 A3
Moss Crs RYTON NE40....66 C7
Mossdale DHAM DH1....158 A5
Moss Side LWF/SPW/WRK NE9 ....101 H2
Mossway CLSW/PEL DH2 ....114 D7
Motcombe Wy CRAM NE23 ....33 J5
Moulton Pl WD/WHPE/BLK NE5 ....69 G1
Mountbatten Av HEBB NE31....73 G7
Mount Cl LGB/KIL NE12....47 K5
MLFD/PNYW SR4 ....105 F7
MONK NE25 ....50 B6
Mountfield Gdns GOS/KPK NE3....55 K6
Mountford Rd MONK NE25 ....40 A1
Mount Gv MLFD/PNYW SR4 ....120 A2
Mount Joy Crs DHAM DH1 ....16 F7
Mount La LWF/SPW/WRK NE9....102 A5
Mount Park Dr
BDN/LAN/SAC DH7 ....140 B4
Mount Pleasant
BDN/LAN/SAC DH7 ....141 G4
BLAY* NE21 ....83 K3
CLS/BIR/GTL DH3 ....115 J1
HLH DH5....132 D7
STLY/ANP DH9....111 G5
SWCK/CAS SR5....106 A4
Mount Pleasant Ct
BW/LEM/TK/HW NE15 ....67 F1
Mount Pleasant Gdns GATE NE8....11 J6
Mount Rd CLS/BIR/GTL DH3....115 K1
LWF/SPW/WRK NE9 ....102 A5
MLFD/PNYW SR4 ....119 K2
Mountside CON/LDGT DH8....122 D1
Mountside Gdns
DUN/TMV NE11....85 K5
Mount Stewart St
SEA/MUR SR7 ....150 E3
Mount Ter SSH NE33 ....3 H8
The Mount
BW/LEM/TK/HW NE15 ....66 E1
CON/LDGT DH8 ....122 D1
RYTON NE40 ....66 E6
Mount Vw BDN/LAN/SAC DH7 ....140 B4
WICK/BNPF NE16 ....85 F4
Mourne Gdns DUN/TMV NE11 ....86 A6
Moutter Cl PLEE/EAS SR8....175 F2
Mowbray Cl ASHBK/HED/RY SR2....14 F8
Mowbray Rd
ASHBK/HED/RY SR2 ....15 G8
LGB/KIL NE12....57 K2
NSHW NE29 ....60 B4
SSH NE33 ....75 J2
Mowbray St BYK/HTN/WLK NE6 ....6 C4
DHAM DH1 ....16 A3
Mowlam Dr STLY/ANP DH9....126 E1
Mozart St SSH NE33 ....3 K9
Muirfield MONK NE25 ....50 B4
SSH NE33 ....75 K2
Muirfield Cl CON/LDGT DH8 ....122 E2
Muirfield Dr FELL NE10....87 K6
WASHN NE37 ....102 E3
Muirfield Rd LGB/HTN NE7....57 J5
Mulben Cl ELS/FEN NE4 ....69 J7
Mulberry RDHAMSE DH6 ....180 D7
Mulberry Gdns FELL NE10 ....12 B4
Mulberry Gv WICK/BNPF NE16 ....111 J2
Mulberry St FELL NE10....12 B5
Mulcaster Gdns
WLSD/HOW NE28 ....58 C7
Mulgrave Dr
CLDN/WHIT/ROK SR6 ....15 H1
Mulgrave Ter GATE NE8 ....10 F2
Mulgrave Vls GATE NE8 ....10 F3
Mullen Dr RYTON NE40....66 E7
Mullen Gdns WLSD/HOW NE28 ....58 C6
Mullen Rd WLSD/HOW NE28 ....58 C6
Mull Gv JRW NE32....90 C1
Muncaster Ms PLEE/EAS SR8....174 B7
Mundella Ter BYK/HTN/WLK NE6 ....6 F2
Mundell St STLY/ANP DH9 ....126 B3
Mundle Av BLAY NE21....84 A6
Mundles La BOL NE36....91 G5
Munslow Rd SUNDSW SR3 ....119 G6
Muriel St STLY/ANP DH9 ....126 C4
Murphy Gv
ASHBK/HED/RY SR2 ....120 E7
Murray Av HLS DH4....131 J6
Murray Ct CON/LDGT DH8 ....122 D2
Murrayfield CRAM NE23....39 G6
Murrayfield Dr
BDN/LAN/SAC DH7 ....167 F7
Murrayfield Rd
WD/WHPE/BLK NE5 ....55 H7
Murrayfields SMOOR NE27 ....59 F1
Murray Gdns DUN/TMV NE11 ....9 J8
Murray Rd CLSW/PEL DH2 ....129 H4
WLSD/HOW NE28 ....59 H7
Murray St BLAY NE21 ....84 A1
PLEE/EAS SR8 ....175 H4
Murston Av CRAM NE23 ....33 J5
Murton La HLH DH5....148 C7
NSHW NE29 ....59 J1
Murton St SUND SR1 ....15 G6
Muscott Gv
BW/LEM/TK/HW NE15 ....68 E5
Musgrave Gdns DHAM DH1 ....17 L2
Musgrave Rd
LWF/SPW/WRK NE9 ....87 F6
Musgrave Ter BYK/HTN/WLK NE6....7 M4
Muswell Hl
BW/LEM/TK/HW NE15 ....68 E6
Mutual St WLSD/HOW NE28....72 D1
Mylord Crs LGB/KIL NE12 ....47 H4
Myrella Crs
ASHBK/HED/RY SR2 ....120 C4
Myreside Pl LGB/KIL NE12 ....57 H3
Myrtle Av CLDN/WHIT/ROK SR6....93 F3
DUN/TMV NE11 ....9 H9
Myrtle Buildings
ASHGTN
(off Woodhorn Rd) NE63....23 K1
Myrtle Crs LGB/KIL NE12....57 K1
Myrtle Gv HAR/WTLS NE34....75 K7
JES NE2 ....70 E1
LWF/SPW/WRK NE9 ....101 F1
SUNDSW SR3 ....120 B7
WLSD/HOW NE28 ....73 F2
Myrtle Rd BLAY NE21 ....84 A3
Myrtles CLSW/PEL DH2 ....129 H2
Myrtle St ASHGTN NE63 ....23 K1

N

Nafferton Pl
WD/WHPE/BLK NE5 ....69 G3
Nailsworth Cl BOLCOL NE35....90 C2
Nairn Cl CLS/BIR/GTL DH3....115 K4
WASHN NE37 ....102 E3
Nairn Rd CRAM NE23....38 C1
Nairn St JRW NE32....90 C1
Naisbitt Av PLEE/EAS SR8....175 F2
Nansen Cl WD/WHPE/BLK * NE5 ....68 D1
Nansen St CON/LDGT * DH8 ....123 G4
Napier Rd SEA/MUR SR7....135 G7
WICK/BNPF NE16 ....84 E3
Napier St HAR/WTLS NE34 ....75 F5
JES NE2 ....6 A4
JRW NE32....73 K4
Napier Wy BLAY NE21 ....84 C2
Narvik Wy NSHW NE29 ....59 K5
Nash Av HAR/WTLS NE34 ....91 H1
Naters St WBAY NE26 ....51 G5
Natley Av BOL NE36 ....91 J5
Navan Cl STKFD/GP NE62 ....23 K5
Navenby Cl GOS/KPK NE3....56 D2
Naworth Av TYNE/NSHE NE30....60 E1
Naworth Ct PLEE/EAS SR8 ....174 C7
Naworth Dr WD/WHPE/BLK NE5....54 C7
Naworth Ter JRW NE32 ....74 B7
Nawton Av SWCK/CAS SR5....106 C3
Nayland Rd CRAM NE23 ....38 B1
Naylor Av BLAY NE21....84 B6
Naylor Pl WBAY NE26 ....40 E1
Neale St CLDN/WHIT/ROK SR6 ....106 D2
PRUD NE42 ....80 D1
Nearlane Cl DIN/WO NE13 ....46 C1
Neasdon Crs TYNE/NSHE NE30 ....61 F1
Neasham Rd SEA/MUR SR7 ....135 G6
Nedderton Cl
WD/WHPE/BLK NE5 ....53 K6
Needham Pl CRAM NE23 ....38 C1
Neill Dr WICK/BNPF NE16 ....99 F3
Neilson Rd FELL NE10 ....11 M3
Neil St HLH DH5 ....148 B7
Nelson Av CRAM NE23 ....32 E7
GOS/KPK NE3 ....56 A5
SSH NE33 ....3 L7
Nelson Cl ASHBK/HED/RY SR2 ....15 G7
ASHGTN NE63 ....24 A3
PLEE/EAS SR8 ....175 H2
Nelson Crs NSHW NE29....60 B7
Nelson Dr CRAM NE23....38 B2
Nelson Rd BYK/HTN/WLK NE6 ....72 D7
CRAM NE23 ....32 E6
MONK NE25....49 K4
STKFD/GP NE62....23 G6
Nelson St ASHBK/HED/RY SR2 ....121 F7
CLS/BIR/GTL DH3 ....129 J5
CNUT NE1....5 J6
CON/LDGT DH8 ....123 J3
CON/LDGT DH8 ....123 F5
DUN/TMV NE11....9 G5
GATE NE8 ....10 F1
HLH DH5....147 K5
SEA/MUR SR7 ....135 H7
SSH* NE33 ....3 G7
WASHS NE38 ....117 G2
Nelson Ter NSHW NE29....60 B7
Nelson Wy CRAM NE23....32 D5
Nenthead Cl CLS/BIR/GTL DH3....145 J1
Neptune Rd
BW/LEM/TK/HW NE15 ....68 B5
WLSD/HOW NE28 ....72 D1
Nesbit Rd PLEE/EAS SR8....175 F5
Nesburn Rd MLFD/PNYW SR4 ....120 A2
Nesham Pl HLH DH5 ....132 C7
Nesham Ter SUND SR1 ....15 J3
Ness Ct BLAY NE21....83 J2
Nest Rd FELL NE10....12 D3
Netherburn Rd SWCK/CAS SR5 ....106 C3
Netherby Dr
WD/WHPE/BLK NE5 ....69 G3
Netherdale BDLGTN NE22 ....28 D5
Nether Farm Rd FELL NE10 ....13 H6
Nether Riggs BDLGTN NE22....29 F6
Netherton LGB/KIL NE12 ....47 J4
Netherton Av NSHW NE29 ....60 B3
Netherton Cl
BDN/LAN/SAC DH7 ....154 A3
CLSW/PEL DH2 ....129 F5
Netherton Gdns DIN/WO NE13 ....46 B3
Netherton Gv NSHW NE29 ....60 B3
Netherton La BDLGTN NE22....28 C4
Nettleham Rd SWCK/CAS SR5 ....106 C3
Nettles La SUNDSW SR3 ....134 B1
Nevile Sq MPTH NE61 ....18 C2
Nevilledale Ter DHAM DH1....16 A5
Neville Dene DHAM DH1....168 A1
Neville Rd
BW/LEM/TK/HW NE15 ....68 B4
MLFD/PNYW SR4 ....105 K6
PLEE/EAS SR8 ....174 D3
Neville's Cross Bank
DHAM DH1 ....168 B2
Neville's Cross Rd HEBB NE31 ....73 H6
Neville Sq DHAM DH1 ....168 B3
Neville St CNUT NE1 ....5 H8
DHAM DH1 ....16 C4
Nevill Rd PSHWF NE43 ....79 H5
Nevinson Av HAR/WTLS NE34 ....91 H1
Nevis Cl WBAY NE26 ....50 B1
Nevis Gv BOL NE36 ....91 F5
New Acres BDN/LAN/SAC DH7 ....155 F7
Newacres Rd STLY/ANP DH9 ....126 C5
Newark Cl PLEE/EAS SR8 ....174 D3
Newark Crs SEA/MUR SR7 ....135 G7
Newark Dr CLDN/WHIT/ROK SR6....93 F4
Newark Sq NSHW NE29 ....2 A5
Newarth Cl
BW/LEM/TK/HW NE15 ....68 B4
Newbiggin La
BDN/LAN/SAC DH7 ....139 H4
CON/LDGT DH8 ....138 E4
WD/WHPE/BLK NE5 ....54 D6
Newbiggin Rd ASHGTN NE63....24 A4
Newbold Av SWCK/CAS SR5 ....106 C3
Newbold St BYK/HTN/WLK NE6....7 K6
Newbolt Ct GATE NE8 ....11 K4
Newbottle La HLS DH4 ....146 C1
Newbottle St HLS DH4 ....132 B5
Newbridge Av SWCK/CAS SR5 ....106 C3
Newbridge Bank
CLS/BIR/GTL DH3 ....130 A2
Newbridge Banks
CLSW/PEL DH2 ....128 A3
New Bridge St CNUT NE1 ....5 M5
New Bridge St West CNUT NE1 ....5 L5
Newbrough Crs JES NE2 ....70 E1
Newburgh Av MONK NE25....39 K6
New Burn Av RDHAMSE DH6 ....180 A2
Newburn Av SWCK/CAS SR5....106 C3
Newburn Bridge Rd BLAY NE21 ....67 G5
Newburn Ct SSH NE33 ....75 H2
Newburn Crs HLS DH4 ....132 B6
Newburn Rd
BW/LEM/TK/HW NE15 ....67 G2
STLY/ANP DH9....112 E6
Newbury LGB/KIL NE12 ....47 K5
Newbury Av GATE NE8 ....10 C8
Newbury Cl
BW/LEM/TK/HW NE15 ....68 B4
Newbury Dr CON/LDGT DH8 ....108 E7
Newbury St SSH NE33....75 H4
SWCK/CAS SR5....106 C2
Newby Cl BDLGTN NE22 ....29 J3
Newby La RDHAMSE DH6....159 F4
Newby Pl LWF/SPW/WRK NE9....101 H1
Newcastle Av PLEE/EAS SR8 ....175 G2
Newcastle Bank
CLS/BIR/GTL DH3 ....101 H6
Newcastle Rd BLYTH NE24....34 E3
BOL NE36....89 J5
CLS/BIR/GTL DH3 ....129 J2
DHAM DH1 ....168 A1
HAR/WTLS NE34 ....74 D6
SWCK/CAS SR5....92 A7
Newcastle St NSHW NE29 ....2 C2
New Cross Rd WNGT TS28 ....183 J3
New Dr SEA/MUR SR7 ....135 H6
New Durham Rd
ASHBK/HED/RY SR2 ....14 B6
STLY/ANP DH9....125 J4
New Elvet DHAM DH1 ....16 E4
Newfield Wk WICK/BNPF * NE16....85 F6
New Front STLY/ANP DH9 ....125 H3
New Front St STLY/ANP DH9 ....112 B5
Newgate Ml
CNUT (off Eldon Sq) NE1 ....5 J6
Newgate St CNUT NE1 ....5 J7
MPTH NE61 ....20 D4
New George St SSH NE33....75 G3
New Grange Ter
CLSW/PEL DH2 ....128 D3
New Green St SSH NE33 ....75 G2
Newham Av DIN/WO NE13....46 A5
Newhaven Av SWCK/CAS SR5 ....106 C3
Newholme Est WNGT TS28....184 A6
Newhouse Av
BDN/LAN/SAC DH7 ....165 G1
Newhouse Rd
BDN/LAN/SAC DH7 ....165 G2
Newington Ct
SWCK/CAS SR5....106 C3
Newington Rd
BYK/HTN/WLK NE6....6 C4
JES NE2 ....6 B3
New King St NWBGN NE64 ....19 G7
Newland Ct HAR/WTLS NE34 ....75 G6
Newlands CON/LDGT DH8 ....122 D2
Newlands Av BLYTH NE24 ....35 F2
GOS/KPK NE3 ....56 C1
MONK NE25....50 B6
SUNDSW SR3....120 B3
Newlands Pl BLYTH NE24....35 F2
Newlands Rd BLYTH NE24 ....35 F2
DHAM DH1 ....157 K5
JES NE2 ....56 D7
Newlands Rd East
SEA/MUR SR7 ....135 H7
Newlands Rd West
SEA/MUR SR7 ....135 G6
Newlyn Crs NSHW NE29 ....60 C5
Newlyn Dr CRAM NE23 ....33 H7
JRW NE32....74 B5
Newlyn Rd GOS/KPK NE3 ....55 J5
Newman Pl GATE NE8....11 J7
Newman Ter GATE NE8....11 J7
Newmarch St JRW NE32....73 J4
Newmarket St CON/LDGT DH8 ....123 F4
Newmarket Wk SSH NE33 ....3 J9
New Mills ELS/FEN NE4....4 E4
Newminster Cl HLS DH4 ....131 K5
New Phoenix Yd MPTH NE61 ....20 D5
Newport Gv SUNDSW SR3 ....120 A6
New Quay NSHW NE29 ....2 E4
Newquay Gdns
LWF/SPW/WRK NE9 ....101 F3
New Queen St NWBGN NE64 ....19 G7
New Ridley Rd PSHWF NE43 ....79 H5
Newriggs WASHS NE38....117 G4
New Rd BOLCOL NE35 ....90 E4
DUN/TMV NE11....86 B6
FELL NE10 ....88 E7
STLY/ANP DH9....113 K7
WICK/BNPF NE16 ....97 J6
Newsham Cl
WD/WHPE/BLK NE5 ....53 K6
Newsham Rd BLYTH NE24 ....34 E2
Newstead Ct WASHS NE38 ....116 E1
Newstead Ri CON/LDGT DH8 ....122 C2
Newstead Rd HLS DH4 ....132 A5
Newsteads Cl MONK NE25 ....50 B4
Newsteads Dr MONK NE25 ....50 A4
Newstead Sq SUNDSW SR3 ....134 A1
New Strangford Rd
SEA/MUR SR7 ....150 D1
New St DHAM DH1....16 B3
MLFD/PNYW SR4 ....104 E7
Newton Av TYNE/NSHE NE30 ....51 F6
WLSD/HOW NE28 ....59 H7
Newton Cl
BW/LEM/TK/HW NE15 ....68 C4
Newton Dr DHAM DH1 ....156 C4
Newton Gv HAR/WTLS NE34 ....74 E6
Newton Pl LGB/HTN NE7....71 H1
Newton Rd LGB/HTN NE7....57 G7
Newton St BDN/LAN/SAC DH7....155 F1
DUN/TMV NE11....9 H5
GATE NE8 ....10 C7
New Vls
JES (off Hunters Rd) NE2....4 E1
New York Rd NSHW NE29 ....59 K1
SMOOR NE27....49 G6
New York Wy SMOOR NE27....59 J2
Nicholas Av
CLDN/WHIT/ROK SR6 ....93 F4
Nicholas St HLH DH5 ....148 A3
Nichol Ct ELS/FEN * NE4....69 H6
Nicholson Cl SUND SR1....15 H5
Nicholson Ter LGB/KIL NE12....58 A1
Nichol St ELS/FEN NE4 ....69 H6
Nickleby Chare DHAM DH1 ....16 A9
Nidderdale Av HLH DH5 ....147 J6
Nidderdale Cl BLYTH NE24 ....30 C6
Nidsdale Av BYK/HTN/WLK NE6 ....72 C4
Nightingale Cl
MLFD/PNYW SR4 ....118 E2
Nightingale Pl STLY/ANP DH9 ....127 F2
Nile Cl BW/LEM/TK/HW NE15....68 A3
Nile Ct GATE NE8 ....11 K5
Nile St CON/LDGT DH8....123 F5
NSHW NE29....2 D2
SSH NE33 ....2 F9
SUND SR1....15 G4
Nilverton Av
ASHBK/HED/RY SR2 ....120 D3
Nimbus Ct SUNDSW SR3 ....134 A1
Nine Lands HLS DH4 ....132 A7
Ninth Av BLYTH NE24 ....35 F1
BYK/HTN/WLK NE6....7 G1
CLSW/PEL DH2 ....129 H4
MPTH NE61 ....21 F6
Ninth Rw ASHGTN NE63 ....23 H1
Ninth St PLEE/EAS SR8 ....175 H3
Nissan Wy WASHN NE37 ....103 K6
Nixon St GATE NE8....6 C9
Nixon Ter BLYTH NE24....35 H1
Noble's Bank Rd
ASHBK/HED/RY SR2 ....15 J7
Noble St ASHBK/HED/RY SR2....15 J8
ELS/FEN NE4 ....9 G1
FELL* NE10....12 D5
PLEE/EAS SR8 ....162 E4
Noble Ter ASHBK/HED/RY SR2....15 J8
Noel Av BLAY NE21 ....84 A6
Noel St STLY/ANP DH9....112 E7
Noel Ter BLAY NE21 ....84 B5
GATE (off Sunderland Rd) NE8 ....12 A5
Noirmont Wy SUNDSW SR3 ....133 J1
Nookside MLFD/PNYW SR4 ....119 H2
Nookside Ct MLFD/PNYW SR4....119 G2
The Nook NSHW NE29....2 A2
Nora St HAR/WTLS NE34....75 G6
MLFD/PNYW SR4 ....119 K2
Norburn La BDN/LAN/SAC DH7 ....142 E5
Norburn Pk BDN/LAN/SAC DH7 ....143 F7
Norbury Gv BYK/HTN/WLK NE6....7 K7
Nordale Wy BLYTH NE24....30 C6
Norfolk Av CLS/BIR/GTL DH3 ....115 J5
SUNDSW SR3 ....119 K6
Norfolk Cl ASHGTN NE63....23 G1
SEA/MUR SR7 ....135 G6
Norfolk Dr WASHN NE37....103 F3
Norfolk Gdns WLSD/HOW NE28....59 G6
Norfolk Rd CON/LDGT DH8....137 G1
GATE NE8 ....6 C9
HAR/WTLS NE34 ....76 C4
Norfolk Sq BYK/HTN/WLK NE6 ....6 F5
Norfolk St SUND SR1....14 F4
TYNE/NSHE NE30 ....2 E1
Norfolk Wk PLEE/EAS SR8 ....174 D2
Norfolk Wy
BW/LEM/TK/HW NE15....68 C4
Norham Av HAR/WTLS NE34 ....76 A3
Norham Av North
HAR/WTLS NE34 ....76 A3
Norham Av South
HAR/WTLS NE34 ....76 A3
Norham Cl BLYTH NE24....30 E7
DIN/WO NE13 ....46 A4
MPTH NE61 ....27 F1
Norham Ct HLS DH4 ....131 F6
Norham Dr MPTH NE61 ....21 F7
PLEE/EAS SR8 ....174 C7
WD/WHPE/BLK NE5 ....54 C7
Norham Gdns STKFD/GP NE62 ....23 G4
Norham Pl JES NE2 ....70 E2
Norham Rd ASHGTN NE63 ....23 K3
DHAM DH1 ....156 D2
GOS/KPK NE3 ....56 B4
MONK NE25....50 D4
NSHW NE29....60 A5
Norham Rd North NSHW NE29 ....59 K2

Norham Ter JRW NE32 73 K7
Norhurst WICK/BNPF NE16 84 C7
Norland Rd
BW/LEM/TK/HW NE15 68 D6
Norley Av SWCK/CAS SR5 106 C3
Norma Crs WBAY NE26 51 G5
Norman Av SUNDSW SR3 120 B7
Normanby Cl SEA/MUR SR7 135 G6
Normanby Ct
CLDN/WHIT/ROK SR6 15 H1
Normandy Crs HLH DH5 132 D7
Norman Rd ROWG NE39 97 G4
Norman Ter WLSD/HOW NE28 73 K1
Normanton Ter ELS/FEN NE4 4 D6
Normount Rd ELS/FEN NE4 69 J6
Northampton Rd
PLEE/EAS SR8 174 D2
Northamptonshire Dr
DHAM DH1 158 A6
North Ap CLSW/PEL DH2 129 H3
North Av GOS/KPK NE3 56 B6
HAR/WTLS NE34 75 J5
LGB/KIL NE12 57 K4
PLEE/EAS SR8 175 G3
STKFD/GP NE62 22 E6
WD/WHPE/BLK NE5 68 D1
North Bailey DHAM DH1 16 D5
Northbourne Rd HEBB NE31 73 J5
Northbourne St ELS/FEN NE4 4 A9
GATE NE8 11 H7
North Brancepeth Cl
BDN/LAN/SAC DH7 167 K4
North Bridge St
CLDN/WHIT/ROK SR6 14 E1
SWCK/CAS SR5 14 E2
North Burns CLS/BIR/GTL DH3 129 J3
North Church St
TYNE/NSHE NE30 61 F4
North Cliff
CLDN/WHIT/ROK
(off Roker Ter) SR6 107 F2
North Cl BYK/HTN/WLK NE6 7 G3
HAR/WTLS NE34 75 K5
RYTON NE40 66 E6
Northcote WICK/BNPF NE16 84 E7
Northcote Av SUND SR1 15 G6
WD/WHPE/BLK NE5 68 A2
Northcote St ELS/FEN NE4 4 D6
SSH NE33 75 H3
North Crs PLEE/EAS SR8 162 D6
WASHS NE38 116 E5
North Cft LGB/KIL NE12 58 A3
North Cross St CON/LDGT DH8 123 J3
GOS/KPK NE3 56 C5
Northdene CLS/BIR/GTL DH3 101 J7
Northdene Av SEA/MUR SR7 135 K6
North Dr CLDN/WHIT/ROK SR6 91 J3
CLS/BIR/GTL DH3 115 K7
HEBB NE31 72 E6
North Durham St SUND SR1 15 H4
North Eastern Ct DUN/TMV NE11 8 F8
North End BDN/LAN/SAC DH7 167 F5
DHAM DH1 156 C6
Northern Wy SWCK/CAS SR5 106 A3
North Farm BDLGTN NE22 28 A5
North Farm Av
MLFD/PNYW SR4 119 F4
North Farm Rd HEBB NE31 73 F6
Northfield BDLGTN NE22 30 D2
Northfield Cl WICK/BNPF NE16 84 D7
Northfield Dr LGB/KIL NE12 47 H7
MLFD/PNYW SR4 119 F4
Northfield Gdns
HAR/WTLS NE34 75 K3
Northfield Rd GOS/KPK NE3 56 B6
SSH NE33 75 K2
Northfield Vw CON/LDGT DH8 123 G4
Northgate LGB/KIL NE12 47 K5
North Gra PONT/DH NE20 43 G2
North Gv CLDN/WHIT/ROK SR6 106 E2
RYTON NE40 67 F6
North Guards
CLDN/WHIT/ROK SR6 92 E4
North Hall Rd MLFD/PNYW SR4 119 H2
North Hvn SEA/MUR SR7 135 H7
North Hylton Rd
SWCK/CAS SR5 106 A3
North Jesmond Av JES NE2 70 E1
North King St TYNE/NSHE NE30 61 F4
Northlands BLAY NE21 83 K3
Northlands Pk TRIM TS29 182 D7
Northlands Rd MPTH NE61 20 D3
North La BOL NE36 91 G5
HLH DH5 148 C3
Northlea
BW/LEM/TK/HW * NE15 68 C3
Northlea Rd SEA/MUR SR7 135 G7
North Leech MPTH NE61 20 B3
North Magdalene
CON/LDGT DH8 109 H5
North Mason Ldg DIN/WO NE13 44 E1
North Mdw PRUD NE42 64 A6
North Milburn St
MLFD/PNYW SR4 14 A3
North Moor Av TRIM TS29 182 E7
North Moor Ct SUNDSW SR3 119 J5
North Moor La SUNDSW SR3 119 J5
Northmoor Rd
BYK/HTN/WLK NE6 7 M1
North Moor Rd SUNDSW SR3 119 J5
Northolt Av CRAM NE23 38 C1
North Pde WBAY NE26 51 F4
North Railway St
SEA/MUR * SR7 150 E1
North Ravensworth St
MLFD/PNYW SR4 14 A3
North Rdg BDLGTN NE22 28 D5
MONK NE25 50 A4
North Rd BOL NE36 91 G5
BOLCOL NE35 90 C3
CLS/BIR/GTL DH3 115 J7
DHAM DH1 16 C3
HLH DH5 147 H3
NSHW NE29 60 D2
PONT/DH NE20 43 G1
SEA/MUR SR7 135 K6
STLY/ANP DH9 111 G6
WLSD/HOW NE28 72 D1
WNGT TS28 183 J2
North Road Head DHAM DH1 16 B3
North Seaton Rd ASHGTN NE63 23 K3
NWBGN NE64 25 F2
Northside Pl MONK NE25 40 B6
North Stead Dr CON/LDGT DH8 122 C2
North St BLAY NE21 83 J2
CLDN/WHIT/ROK SR6 92 A3
CNUT NE1 5 K5
HLH DH5 147 G3
HLS DH4 132 B3
JRW NE32 73 K4
RDHAMSE DH6 178 E5
SSH NE33 3 G6
SUNDSW SR3 120 A6
SWCK/CAS SR5 106 C4
North Ter JES NE2 5 H2
SEA/MUR SR7 135 K7
SUNDSW SR3 120 A6
WLSD/HOW NE28 73 G1
Northumberland Av
BDLGTN NE22 28 E5
GOS/KPK NE3 56 A6
LGB/KIL NE12 57 K3
NWBGN NE64 25 F2
Northumberland Cl
ASHGTN NE63 23 G1
Northumberland Dock Rd
WLSD/HOW NE28 74 A2
Northumberland Gdns JES NE2 71 G3
WD/WHPE/BLK NE5 53 K7
Northumberland Pl
PLEE/EAS SR8 174 C2
TYNE/NSHE* NE30 2 D1
Northumberland Rd
BW/LEM/TK/HW NE15 68 A5
CNUT NE1 5 K5
RYTON NE40 66 E5
Northumberland Sq NSHW NE29 2 D2
Northumberland St CNUT NE1 5 K5
PLEE/EAS SR8 175 G2
WLSD/HOW NE28 72 E1
Northumberland Ter
BYK/HTN/WLK NE6 6 D5
TYNE/NSHE NE30 61 H3
Northumberland Vls
WLSD/HOW NE28 73 G1
Northumberland Wy
WASHN NE37 103 F3
WASHS NE38 117 G3
Northumbrian Rd CRAM NE23 33 J7
Northumbrian Wy
LGB/KIL NE12 47 J7
NSHW NE29 2 C6
Northumbria Pl STLY/ANP DH9 112 E7
North Vw BYK/HTN/WLK NE6 6 E4
CLDN/WHIT/ROK SR6 106 D2
CON/LDGT DH8 122 D3
DHAM DH1 17 K2
DIN/WO NE13 45 F2
HAR/WTLS NE34 75 K3
HLH DH5 148 C7
JRW NE32 73 J5
LGB/KIL NE12 57 K2
NWBGN NE64 25 F2
SWCK/CAS SR5 105 G4
WBAY NE26 51 G5
WICK/BNPF NE16 84 E5
WLSD/HOW NE28 72 E1
North View Ter GATE * NE8 12 A5
North Walbottle Rd
WD/WHPE/BLK NE5 67 J1
Northway
BW/LEM/TK/HW NE15 53 F7
LWF/SPW/WRK NE9 11 L9
STKFD/GP* NE62 23 F6
Northwood Ct SWCK/CAS SR5 106 C3
Northwood Rd SEA/MUR SR7 135 H7
Norton Av RDHAMSE DH6 180 A2
SEA/MUR SR7 135 G6
Norton Cl CLSW/PEL DH2 129 F6
Norton Rd SWCK/CAS SR5 106 A2
Norton Wy
BW/LEM/TK/HW NE15 68 C5
Norway Av MLFD/PNYW SR4 119 J2
Norwich Av DIN/WO NE13 46 B4
Norwich Cl ASHGTN NE63 24 C3
CLS/BIR/GTL DH3 145 H1
Norwich Rd DHAM DH1 156 E2
Norwood Av BYK/HTN/WLK NE6 71 H2
GOS/KPK NE3 46 C7
Norwood Gdns
LWF/SPW/WRK NE9 11 J8
Norwood Rd
BW/LEM/TK/HW NE15 68 B3
DUN/TMV NE11 9 L9
Nottingham Pl PLEE/EAS SR8 174 C2
Nottinghamshire Rd
DHAM DH1 157 K6
Nuneaton Wy
WD/WHPE/BLK NE5 53 K6
Nunnykirk Cl PRUD NE42 64 A7
Nuns La CNUT NE1 5 J7
GATE NE8 11 G2
Nuns Moor Crs ELS/FEN NE4 69 J4
Nuns Moor Rd ELS/FEN NE4 69 J4
Nuns' Rw DHAM DH1 157 G6
Nun St CNUT NE1 5 J6
Nunwick Gdns NSHW NE29 60 A4
Nunwick Wy LGB/KIL NE7 57 K7
Nursery Cl SUNDSW SR3 120 A4
Nursery Ct CHPW NE17 95 H7
Nursery Gdns PLEE/EAS SR8 166 E6
Nursery La CLDN/WHIT/ROK SR6 92 A3
Nursery Pk ASHGTN NE63 24 A4
Nursery Rd SUNDSW SR3 120 A4
Nutley Pl BW/LEM/TK/HW NE15 68 E6
Nye Dene SWCK/CAS SR5 105 F4

O

Oakapple Cl BDLGTN NE22 29 F5
Oak Av DHAM DH1 17 L4
DIN/WO NE13 45 G2
DUN/TMV NE11 9 G9
HAR/WTLS NE34 76 A6
Oak Crs CLDN/WHIT/ROK SR6 93 G3
CLSW/PEL DH2 144 B5
Oakdale BDLGTN NE22 28 B6
Oakdale Cl
BW/LEM/TK/HW NE15 68 B5
Oakdale Rd CON/LDGT DH8 123 G4
Oakenshaw
BW/LEM/TK/HW NE15 68 B5
Oakerside Dr PLEE/EAS SR8 174 D6
Oakes Pl ELS/FEN NE4 4 F6
Oakeys Rd STLY/ANP DH9 112 D5
Oakfield Av WICK/BNPF NE16 85 F6
Oakfield Cl SUNDSW SR3 133 G1
WICK/BNPF NE16 85 F6
Oakfield Crs RDHAMSE DH6 180 B2
Oakfield Dr LGB/KIL NE12 48 B6
WICK/BNPF NE16 85 F6
Oakfield Gdns
BW/LEM/TK/HW NE15 69 H6
WLSD/HOW NE28 58 B7
Oakfield Gra DIN/WO NE13 45 F2
Oakfield La CON/LDGT DH8 122 C6
Oakfield North RYTON NE40 66 D6
Oakfield Pk PRUD NE42 80 D2
Oakfield Rd DUN/TMV NE11 86 A6
GOS/KPK NE3 56 B7
WICK/BNPF NE16 84 D7
Oakfields WICK/BNPF NE16 97 K6
Oakfield Ter FELL NE10 13 J6
GOS/KPK NE3 56 B6
PRUD NE42 80 D2
Oakfield Wy CRAM NE23 39 G7
Oakgreen Flats
BDN/LAN/SAC DH7 167 G6
Oak Gv WLSD/HOW NE28 73 F1
Oakham Av WICK/BNPF NE16 84 D6
Oakham Dr DHAM DH1 158 A4
Oakham Gdns NSHW NE29 60 C6
Oakhurst Dr GOS/KPK NE3 70 A1
Oakhurst Ter LGB/KIL NE12 57 K3
Oakland Rd JES NE2 70 D1
MONK NE25 50 B5
Oaklands GOS/KPK NE3 56 C7
PONT/DH NE20 42 E5
WICK/BNPF NE16 8 A7
Oaklands Ct PONT/DH NE20 43 F5
Oaklands Crs SWCK/CAS SR5 106 A3
Oaklands Ter MLFD/PNYW SR4 120 A1
Oakland Ter ASHGTN * NE63 23 J2
MPTH NE61 18 C1
Oak La CON/LDGT DH8 108 C7
Oak Lea BDN/LAN/SAC DH7 143 G7
Oaklea CLSW/PEL DH2 129 G3
Oakleigh Gdns
CLDN/WHIT/ROK SR6 92 A2
Oakley Cl CRAM NE23 47 H1
Oakley Dr CRAM NE23 38 D1
Oakmere Cl HLS DH4 131 K1
Oakridge WICK/BNPF NE16 84 D6
Oakridge Rd
BDN/LAN/SAC DH7 155 F7
Oak Rd NSHW NE29 59 J3
PLEE/EAS SR8 162 E6
Oak Sq GATE NE8 10 A5
The Oaks ASHBK/HED/RY SR2 15 G8
BDN/LAN/SAC DH7 165 G2
RHTLP TS27 184 D6
RYTON NE40 82 D3
Oak St BDN/LAN/SAC DH7 154 B2
CON/LDGT DH8 123 F5
HLS DH4 131 G6
JRW NE32 73 J4
PSHWF NE43 79 J4
SUND SR1 15 K5
Oak Ter
BDN/LAN/SAC
(off Holmside) DH7 142 C1
CLSW/PEL DH2 114 C7
SEA/MUR SR7 149 H5
STLY/ANP DH9 125 G2
STLY/ANP DH9 127 F4
Oaktree Av WLSD/HOW NE28 72 C2
Oaktree Gdns MONK NE25 50 C6
Oakville ASHGTN NE63 24 C3
Oakway Ct BDN/LAN/SAC DH7 167 K6
Oakwellgate GATE NE8 6 A9
Oakwood BDN/LAN/SAC DH7 140 D6
FELL NE10 88 A7
HEBB NE31 72 E4
RDHAMSE DH6 161 G3
Oakwood Av DIN/WO NE13 46 C4
LWF/SPW/WRK NE9 101 G2
NWBGN NE64 19 F7
Oakwood Cl
LWF/SPW/WRK NE9 102 B3
Oakwood Gdns DUN/TMV NE11 86 B7
Oakwood Pl
WD/WHPE/BLK NE5 69 G2
Oakwood St
ASHBK/HED/RY SR2 14 B7
Oatens Bank
BW/LEM/TK/HW NE15 64 A1
Oates St MLFD/PNYW SR4 106 A7
Oatfield Cl ASHGTN NE63 23 H3
Oatlands Rd MLFD/PNYW SR4 119 J2
Oatlands Wy DHAM DH1 156 D1
Oban Av WLSD/HOW NE28 59 H6
Oban Gdns BYK/HTN/WLK NE6 7 G7
Oban St FELL NE10 12 A6
JRW NE32 90 C1
Oban Ter FELL NE10 12 A6
Obelisk La DHAM DH1 16 A2
Ocean Rd ASHBK/HED/RY SR2 121 F4
SSH NE33 3 H6
Ocean Vw ASHBK/HED/RY SR2 121 F7
WBAY NE26 51 F4
Ochiltree Ct WBAY NE26 41 G2
Octavia Cl BDLGTN NE22 28 E4
Octavia Ct WLSD/HOW NE28 59 G6
Octavian Wy DUN/TMV NE11 100 C2
Odinel Ct PRUD NE42 80 D1
Offerton Cl MLFD/PNYW SR4 104 D7
Offerton La MLFD/PNYW SR4 104 D7
Offerton St MLFD/PNYW SR4 106 A7
Office Pl HLH DH5 147 K5
Office Row
RDHAMSE (off Front St) DH6 173 J3
Office St PLEE/EAS SR8 163 G5
Ogden St MLFD/PNYW SR4 106 A7
Ogle Av DIN/WO NE13 46 A5
MPTH NE61 20 C5
Ogle Dr BLYTH NE24 34 E1
Ogle Gv JRW NE32 89 J1
O'hanlon Crs WLSD/HOW NE28 58 C6
Oil Mill Rd BYK/HTN/WLK NE6 72 D4
Okehampton Dr HLS DH4 132 A3
Okehampton Sq
SWCK/CAS SR5 106 A2
Old Brewery Sq PRUD NE42 63 G7
Old Coronation St SSH NE33 3 G8
Old Course Rd
CLDN/WHIT/ROK SR6 92 A4
Old Durham Rd GATE NE8 11 H6
LWF/SPW/WRK NE9 87 H7
Old Elvet DHAM DH1 16 E4
Old Farm Ct WICK/BNPF NE16 99 F3
Oldfield Rd BYK/HTN/WLK NE6 13 H1
Old Fold Rd FELL NE10 11 M4
The Old Forge
BDN/LAN/SAC DH7 176 D2
PSHWF NE43 62 A6
Oldgate MPTH NE61 20 D5
Old George Yd CNUT * NE1 5 K7
Old Hall Rd CON/LDGT DH8 123 H6
Old Main St RYTON NE40 82 A1
Old Mill La CLS/BIR/GTL DH3 145 G2
Old Mill Rd ASHBK/HED/RY SR2 15 K7
SWCK/CAS SR5 106 A2
Old Station Ct PONT/DH NE20 42 E6
Oldstead Gdns
MLFD/PNYW SR4 119 J2
Old Vicarage Wk
BYK/HTN/WLK * NE6 7 H5
Old Well La BLAY NE21 83 K3
Oley Mdw CON/LDGT DH8 108 C7
Olive Gdns LWF/SPW/WRK NE9 87 G6
Olive Pl ELS/FEN NE4 69 H4
Oliver Crs RDHAMSE DH6 171 H4
Oliver Pl DHAM DH1 168 B3
Oliver St BW/LEM/TK/HW NE15 69 F6
SEA/MUR SR7 135 H7
STLY/ANP DH9 126 C3
Olive St CLSW/PEL DH2 128 E6
SSH NE33 75 F5
SUND SR1 14 D6
Ollerton Dr
BW/LEM/TK/HW NE15 66 D1
Ollerton Gdns FELL NE10 87 J5
Olney Cl CRAM NE23 38 E1
Olympia Av STKFD/GP NE62 22 E6
Olympia Gdns MPTH NE61 20 D4
Olympia Hl MPTH NE61 20 D3
O'Neil Dr PLEE/EAS SR8 174 E5
Ongar Wy LGB/KIL NE12 57 H3
Onslow Gdns
LWF/SPW/WRK NE9 87 F7
Onslow St MLFD/PNYW SR4 105 J6
The Open CNUT * NE1 5 J5
Oram Cl MPTH NE61 21 F5
Orange Gv CRAM NE23 38 C7
WICK/BNPF NE16 8 A9
Orchard Av ROWG NE39 97 F4
Orchard Cl HAR/WTLS NE34 75 F6
LGB/KIL NE12 48 B7
MPTH NE61 21 F5
PRUD NE42 80 D2
ROWG NE39 97 F5
STLY/ANP DH9 128 A1
Orchard Ct RYTON NE40 66 E6
RYTON NE40 82 B3
Orchard Dene ROWG NE39 97 F4
Orchard Dr DHAM DH1 17 G1
Orchard Gdns
CLDN/WHIT/ROK SR6 92 E4
CLS/BIR/GTL DH3 129 J6
LWF/SPW/WRK NE9 101 G1
WLSD/HOW NE28 58 C7
Orchard Hl PRUD NE42 80 C1
Orchard-leigh
BW/LEM/TK/HW NE15 68 B5
Orchard Pk CLS/BIR/GTL DH3 115 J2
Orchard Pl JES NE2 71 F2
Orchard Priory DHAM * DH1 16 B5
Orchard Rd ROWG NE39 97 F4
WICK/BNPF NE16 8 A9
The Orchards BLYTH NE24 30 D6
Orchard St CLS/BIR/GTL DH3 115 J2
CLSW/PEL DH2 114 E7
CNUT NE1 5 K8
MLFD/PNYW SR4 105 K6
Orchard Ter CLS/BIR/GTL DH3 129 J6
The Orchard
BW/LEM/TK/HW NE15 68 B5
CLS/BIR/GTL
(off Picktree La) DH3 129 K3
DHAM DH1 156 C1
MPTH NE61 27 J1
NSHW
(off South Preston Gv) NE29 2 C2
WICK/BNPF NE16 85 G5
Orchid Cl ASHGTN NE63 23 J3
Ord Ct ELS/FEN NE4 69 H4
Orde Av WLSD/HOW NE28 59 G7
Ordley Cl BW/LEM/TK/HW NE15 68 C5
Ord St ELS/FEN NE4 10 A1
Ord Ter STKFD/GP * NE62 23 H5
Oriel Cl CLDN/WHIT/ROK SR6 106 D4
Orkney Dr ASHBK/HED/RY SR2 120 D6
Orlando Rd NSHW NE29 60 B4
Ormesby Rd
CLDN/WHIT/ROK SR6 106 D2
Ormiscraig
BW/LEM/TK/HW NE15 68 C5
Ormiston BW/LEM/TK/HW NE15 68 C5
Ormonde Av
BW/LEM/TK/HW NE15 68 E5
Ormonde St JRW NE32 73 K4
MLFD/PNYW SR4 119 K1
Ormskirk Cl
BW/LEM/TK/HW NE15 68 B5
Ormskirk Gv CRAM NE23 38 D1
Ormston St CRAM NE23 33 H4
Orpen Av HAR/WTLS NE34 91 G1
Orpine Ct ASHGTN NE63 23 J3
Orpington Av BYK/HTN/WLK NE6 7 L3
Orpington Rd CRAM NE23 38 D1
Orr Av SUNDSW SR3 134 B1
Orton Cl ELS/FEN * NE4 69 J7
Orwell Cl HAR/WTLS NE34 91 F2
PLEE/EAS SR8 174 C6
Orwell Gdns STLY/ANP DH9 126 C3
Osbaldeston Gdns
GOS/KPK NE3 56 B7
Osborne Av JES NE2 70 E3
SSH NE33 75 H2
Osborne Cl BDLGTN NE22 29 J4
Osborne Gdns NSHW NE29 60 E3
WBAY NE26 50 D4
Osborne Rd JES NE2 70 E3
SWCK/CAS SR5 104 E6
Osborne St
CLDN/WHIT/ROK SR6 106 D3
SSH NE33 3 L9
Osborne Ter GATE NE8 10 D5
JES NE2 5 M2
Osborne Vls JES NE2 70 E3
Osier Ct STKFD/GP NE62 23 J6
Oslo Cl NSHW NE29 59 K6
Osman Cl ASHBK/HED/RY SR2 15 G7
Osprey Cl BDN/LAN/SAC DH7 165 F2
Osprey Dr BLYTH NE24 35 G3
NSHW NE29 59 J4
Osprey Wy HAR/WTLS NE34 74 E7
Oswald Cl DHAM DH1 17 M4
Oswald Ct DHAM DH1 16 E6
Oswald Rd HLH DH5 147 K3
MPTH NE61 20 E3
Oswald St MLFD/PNYW SR4 106 A6
Oswald Ter
ASHBK/HED/RY SR2 121 F4
GATE NE8 10 D6
PLEE/EAS SR8 162 E5
Oswald Ter South
SWCK/CAS SR5 105 G4
Oswald Wk GOS/KPK NE3 56 E5
Oswestry Pl CRAM NE23 38 D1
Oswin Av LGB/KIL NE12 58 A2
Oswin Ct LGB/KIL NE12 58 A1
Oswin Ter NSHW NE29 60 B5
Otley Cl CRAM NE23 38 E1
Otterburn Av MONK NE25 49 K5
Otterburn Cl LGB/KIL NE12 58 B2
Otterburn Ct
GATE (off Fourth St) NE8 10 C6
Otterburn Crs HLS DH4 132 A6
Otterburn Dr ASHGTN NE63 23 H3
Otterburn Gdns DUN/TMV NE11 86 A5
HAR/WTLS NE34 75 J5
LWF/SPW/WRK NE9 100 E1
WICK/BNPF NE16 85 F5
Otterburn Gv BLYTH NE24 34 D1
Otterburn Rd NSHW NE29 60 D3
Otterburn Ter JES NE2 70 E2
Otterburn Vls JES * NE2 70 E2
Otterburn Vls South JES * NE2 70 E3
Otter Burn Wy PRUD NE42 80 A3
Ottercap Cl
BW/LEM/TK/HW NE15 68 B5
Otterington WASHS NE38 117 J2
Ottershaw
BW/LEM/TK/HW NE15 68 C5
Otto Ter ASHBK/HED/RY SR2 14 B7
Ottovale Crs BLAY NE21 83 J3
Ottringham Cl
BW/LEM/TK/HW NE15 68 B5
Oulton Cl CRAM NE23 38 E1
Ousby Ct DIN/WO NE13 55 H3
Ouseburn Cl
ASHBK/HED/RY SR2 121 F5
Ouseburn Rd BYK/HTN/WLK NE6 6 D2
CNUT NE1 6 C5
Ouselaw DUN/TMV NE11 100 D7
Ouse St CNUT NE1 6 D6
Ouslaw La DUN/TMV NE11 100 B7
Ousterley Ter STLY/ANP DH9 127 F5
Ouston Cl FELL NE10 88 E5
Ouston La CLSW/PEL DH2 115 F7
Ouston St
BW/LEM/TK/HW NE15 68 D6
Outputs La CON/LDGT DH8 137 K4
Outram St HLH DH5 132 C6
Oval Park Vw FELL NE10 12 D9
The Oval BDLGTN NE22 29 J5
BLYTH NE24 34 D4
BYK/HTN/WLK NE6 7 K9
CLSW/PEL DH2 115 F4
CLSW/PEL DH2 144 C1
DIN/WO NE13 54 D2
HLS DH4 132 A7
LGB/KIL NE12 57 K4
Overdale Ct STKFD/GP NE62 22 E7
Overdene
BW/LEM/TK/HW NE15 68 D4
SEA/MUR SR7 150 A3
Overfield Rd GOS/KPK NE3 55 K5
Overhill Ter GATE NE8 10 D5
Overton Cl
BW/LEM/TK/HW NE15 68 B5
Overton Rd NSHW NE29 60 C2
Ovingham Cl WASHS NE38 117 H1
Ovingham Gdns DIN/WO NE13 46 B3
Ovingham Rd WYLAM NE41 65 G5
Ovington Gv
WD/WHPE/BLK NE5 69 G3
Ovington Vw PRUD NE42 80 B3
Owen Brannigan Dr
CRAM NE23 47 H2
Owen Ct
JES (off Richardson Rd) NE2 5 G2
Owen Dr BOL NE36 91 F4
Owengate DHAM DH1 16 D4
Owen St HAR/WTLS NE34 75 F6
Owlet Cl BLAY NE21 83 J3
Oxbridge St
ASHBK/HED/RY SR2 121 F4
Oxclose Rd WASHS NE38 117 G2
Oxford Av CRAM NE23 38 D1
SSH NE33 75 H3
WASHN NE37 102 D5
WLSD/HOW NE28 58 C7
Oxford Cl SUNDSW SR3 119 K6
Oxford Crs HEBB NE31 73 H5
Oxford Pl CLS/BIR/GTL DH3 115 J5
Oxford Rd STKFD/GP NE62 23 G6

Oxfordshire Dr DHAM DH1 ....157 K6
Oxford Sq MLFD/PNYW SR4 ......105 J6
Oxford St BLYTH NE24 ....31 H7
  CNUT NE1.......5 L5
  MLFD/PNYW SR4 ....105 J6
  SEA/MUR SR7 ....150 B1
  SSH NE33 ....75 H5
  TYNE/NSHE NE30 ....61 H5
  WBAY NE26 ....51 F4
Oxford Ter GATE NE8 ....10 F5
Oxley St CON/LDGT DH8 ....122 D3
Oxnam Crs JES NE2 ....4 E2
Oxted Cl CRAM NE23 ....38 E1
Oxted Pl BYK/HTN/WLK NE6 ....12 F1
Oyston St SSH NE33 ....3 G8
Ozanan Cl CRAM NE23 ....47 H2

P

Pacific Hall SEA/MUR SR7 ....134 E7
Packham Rd MLFD/PNYW SR4 ....119 G1
Paddock Cl
  CLDN/WHIT/ROK SR6 ....91 J5
  HLS DH4 ....131 H2
  PRUD NE42 ....80 E2
Paddock Hl PONT/DH NE20 ....43 H2
Paddock La SUNDSW SR3 ....120 C7
Paddock Ri ASHGTN NE63 ....23 H3
The Paddock ASHGTN * NE63 ....24 D3
  BDN/LAN/SAC DH7 ....140 B5
  BLYTH NE24 ....30 E7
  BW/LEM/TK/HW NE15 ....67 H2
  CRAM NE23 ....38 E2
  DIN/WO NE13 ....54 D2
  FELL NE10 ....88 B6
  HLS DH4 ....118 D7
  LGB/KIL
  (off Garth Thirtytwo) NE12 ....48 A6
  PSHWF NE43 ....79 C7
  STLY/ANP DH9 ....112 A6
Paddock Wd PRUD NE42 ....80 E2
Pader Cl DIN/WO NE13 ....46 B4
Padgate Rd MLFD/PNYW SR4 ....119 G1
Padstow Cl
  ASHBK/HED/RY SR2 ....121 F6
Padstow Rd NSHW NE29 ....60 C6
Page Av HAR/WTLS NE34 ....75 J4
Page St HEBB NE31 ....73 H4
Paignton Av ELS/FEN NE4 ....69 J6
  MONK NE25 ....50 B5
Paignton Sq SUNDSW SR3 ....119 J4
Painshawfield Rd PSHWF NE43 ....79 F7
Paisley Sq SUNDSW SR3 ....119 J4
Palace Buildings
  BOLCOL (off North Rd) NE35 ....90 D4
Palace Gn DHAM DH1 ....16 D4
Palace Rd BDLGTN NE22 ....29 K4
Palace St ELS/FEN NE4 ....4 E8
Palatine Vw DHAM DH1 ....16 B4
Palermo St MLFD/PNYW SR4 ....105 K5
Paley St SUND SR1 ....14 C4
Palgrove Rd MLFD/PNYW SR4 ....119 C1
Palgrove Sq MLFD/PNYW SR4 ....119 G1
Pallinsburn Ct
  WD/WHPE/BLK NE5 ....55 F7
Pallion New Rd
  MLFD/PNYW SR4 ....105 K5
Pallion Pk MLFD/PNYW SR4 ....105 K5
Pallion Rd MLFD/PNYW SR4 ....105 K7
Pallion Subway
  MLFD/PNYW SR4 ....105 J5
Palm Av ELS/FEN NE4 ....69 H4
  HAR/WTLS NE34 ....76 A6
Palmer Crs HEBB NE31 ....73 H5
Palmer Gdns FELL NE10 ....88 E4
Palmer Rd PLEE/EAS SR8 ....174 B5
  STLY/ANP DH9 ....111 G5
Palmers Garth DHAM DH1 ....16 E5
Palmers Gn LGB/KIL NE12 ....58 B1
Palmer's Hill Rd
  CLDN/WHIT/ROK SR6 ....14 F2
Palmerston Av
  BYK/HTN/WLK NE6 ....7 M2
Palmerston Rd
  MLFD/PNYW SR4 ....119 F3
Palmerston St CON/LDGT DH8 ....123 F5
Palmerston Wk GATE NE8 ....10 B4
Palmer St JRW NE32 ....73 J4
  STLY/ANP DH9 ....126 B2
Palm Lea BDN/LAN/SAC DH7 ....167 F6
Palmstead Rd
  MLFD/PNYW SR4 ....119 G1
Palmstead Sq
  MLFD/PNYW SR4 ....119 G1
Palm St BDN/LAN/SAC DH7 ....154 B2
  CON/LDGT DH8 ....123 F4
Palm Ter STLY/ANP DH9 ....127 F4
Pan Bank
  SSH (off Commercial Rd) NE33 ....75 F2
Pancras Rd SUNDSW SR3 ....119 J4
Pandon CNUT NE1 ....5 M7
Pandon Bank CNUT NE1 ....5 M6
Pangbourne Cl
  BW/LEM/TK/HW NE15 ....68 A3
Pankhurst Gdns FELL NE10 ....13 K8
Pankhurst Pl STLY/ANP DH9 ....127 F3
Pann La SUND SR1 ....14 E4
Panns Bank SUND SR1 ....14 F3
The Parade ASHBK/HED/RY SR2 ....15 K6
  BYK/HTN/WLK NE6 ....72 C6
  CLSW/PEL DH2 ....128 C1
  WICK/BNPF
  (off Metrocentre) NE16 ....8 B4
Paradise Crs PLEE/EAS SR8 ....162 E5
Paradise La PLEE/EAS SR8 ....162 E5
Paradise Rw CRAM NE23 ....38 C2
Paradise St PLEE/EAS SR8 ....175 J4
Paradise Yd
  BW/LEM/TK/HW
  (off Scotswood Rd) NE15 ....8 B1
Park Av BDLGTN NE22 ....30 A3
  BLAY NE21 ....84 A2
  CLDN/WHIT/ROK SR6 ....106 E2
  CON/LDGT DH8 ....123 C4
  DUN/TMV NE11 ....8 A5
  GOS/KPK NE3 ....55 K3

  HAR/WTLS NE34 ....75 K7
  PRUD NE42 ....80 E3
  RDHAMSE DH6 ....180 B4
  SMOOR NE27 ....49 H6
  SUNDSW SR3 ....120 B7
  TYNE/NSHE NE30 ....61 G3
  WBAY NE26 ....50 E4
  WLSD/HOW NE28 ....72 D1
Park Chare WASHS NE38 ....117 F1
Park Cl BDN/LAN/SAC DH7 ....154 C3
  ELS/FEN NE4 ....4 D8
  STLY/ANP DH9 ....125 J4
Park Ct GATE NE8 ....11 G2
Park Crs SMOOR NE27 ....49 H6
  TYNE/NSHE NE30 ....61 F4
Park Crs East TYNE/NSHE NE30 ....61 G3
Parkdale Ri WICK/BNPF NE16 ....84 D5
Park Dr BDN/LAN/SAC DH7 ....154 B3
  BLYTH NE24 ....34 D3
  GOS/KPK NE3 ....56 C1
  LGB/KIL NE12 ....58 A2
  MPTH NE61 ....20 E6
  MPTH NE61 ....27 J5
  WICK/BNPF NE16 ....8 A9
Parker Av GOS/KPK NE3 ....56 B7
Parker Ct DUN/TMV NE11 ....8 F4
Park Farm Vls BLYTH NE24 ....34 E5
Park Fld RYTON NE40 ....66 E6
Park Field Ter WBAY NE26 ....41 F2
Park Gdns WBAY NE26 ....50 E4
Park Ga CLDN/WHIT/ROK SR6 ....106 E2
Park Gv SMOOR NE27 ....49 H6
  WASHN NE38 ....103 F4
Parkham Cl CRAM NE23 ....33 H6
Parkhead STLY/ANP DH9 ....125 C5
Parkhead Gdns BLAY NE21 ....83 K4
Park Head Rd LGB/HTN NE7 ....71 G1
Park Hl RDHAMSE DH6 ....180 B5
Parkhouse Av
  BDN/LAN/SAC DH7 ....155 F6
Parkhouse Av SWCK/CAS SR5 ....105 F5
Park House Cl RDHAMSE DH6 ....158 C7
Park House Rd DHAM DH1 ....168 B3
Parkhurst Rd MLFD/PNYW SR4 ....119 F2
Parkin Gdns FELL NE10 ....88 A5
Parkland BLAY NE21 ....67 J3
  LGB/KIL NE12 ....57 K4
Parkland Av BLAY NE21 ....83 K4
Parkland Ct SEA/MUR SR7 ....135 H7
Parklands FELL NE10 ....88 E4
  PONT/DH NE20 ....42 D7
  ROWG NE39 ....110 B1
Parklands Ct FELL NE10 ....88 E3
Parklands Wy FELL NE10 ....88 E3
Parkland Ter SEA/MUR SR7 ....135 H7
Park La BLAY NE21 ....83 K4
  PLEE/EAS SR8 ....175 H5
  PRUD NE42 ....80 D3
  SEA/MUR SR7 ....149 G5
  SMOOR NE27 ....49 H6
  SUND SR1 ....14 E6
Park Lea
  CON/LDGT (off Park Rd) DH8 ....122 E4
  SUNDSW SR3 ....133 F1
Park Lea Rd
  CLDN/WHIT/ROK SR6 ....106 E2
Parkmore Rd MLFD/PNYW SR4 ....118 E2
Park Pde CLDN/WHIT/ROK SR6 ....106 E3
  WBAY NE26 ....50 E4
Park Pl CLS/BIR/GTL DH3 ....129 K2
Park Pl West
  ASHBK/HED/RY SR2 ....14 F7
Park Ri BW/LEM/TK/HW NE15 ....68 A4
Park Rd ASHBK/HED/RY SR2 ....14 F7
  ASHGTN 23 H2
  BDLGTN NE22 ....29 G5
  BW/LEM/TK/HW NE15 ....67 J3
  CON/LDGT DH8 ....122 D4
  ELS/FEN NE4 ....9 K1
  GATE NE8 ....11 K2
  HEBB NE31 ....73 G6
  JRW NE32 ....73 J5
  MONK NE25 ....39 K5
  MPTH NE61 ....18 C2
  PLEE/EAS SR8 ....175 G2
  ROWG* NE39 ....97 F3
  SMOOR NE27 ....49 H6
  STLY/ANP DH9 ....126 B2
  TRIM TS29 ....183 F7
  WBAY NE26 ....50 E4
  WLSD/HOW NE28 ....72 D1
Park Rd Central
  CLS/BIR/GTL DH3 ....129 K4
Park Rd East ASHGTN NE63 ....23 J1
Park Rd North
  CLS/BIR/GTL DH3 ....129 J2
Park Rd South
  CLS/BIR/GTL DH3 ....129 K5
Park Rw FELL NE10 ....12 C7
  SWCK/CAS SR5 ....106 A3
Parkshiel HAR/WTLS NE34 ....75 K7
Parkside BDLGTN NE22 ....30 A3
  BDN/LAN/SAC DH7 ....141 H2
  BDN/LAN/SAC DH7 ....143 H5
  BW/LEM/TK/HW NE15 ....67 G2
  DHAM DH1 ....16 B3
  DUN/TMV NE11 ....9 F4
  HEBB NE31 ....72 E7
  STLY/ANP DH9 ....112 A5
  TYNE/NSHE NE30 ....61 H1
  WLSD/HOW NE28 ....59 F7
Parkside Av BLAY NE21 ....83 K3
  LGB/HTN NE7 ....57 H5
Parkside Crs SEA/MUR SR7 ....150 D1
  TYNE/NSHE NE30 ....61 H2
The Parks CLS/BIR/GTL DH3 ....130 A6
Parkstone Cl MLFD/PNYW SR4 ....118 E4
Park St CON/LDGT DH8 ....122 E3
  SEA/MUR SR7 ....149 G5
Park St South SWCK/CAS SR5 ....105 G4
Park Ter BDLGTN NE22 ....29 J3
  CON/LDGT DH8 ....123 K3
  JES NE2 ....5 J2
  PLEE/EAS SR8 ....175 H4
  SWCK/CAS SR5 ....105 K3
  TYNE/NSHE NE30 ....61 G4
  WICK/BNPF NE16 ....84 E3
  WICK/BNPF NE16 ....97 J7

  WLSD/HOW NE28 ....72 D1
Park Vw ASHGTN NE63 ....23 H1
  BLAY NE21 ....84 A4
  BLYTH NE24 ....31 H7
  BYK/HTN/WLK NE6 ....72 C6
  CLSW/PEL DH2 ....144 E4
  CON/LDGT DH8 ....123 H4
  CRAM (off Burradon Rd) NE23 ....47 J3
  HLH DH5 ....147 K5
  JRW NE32 ....73 K7
  MONK NE25 ....40 A5
  WBAY NE26 ....50 E4
  WICK/BNPF NE16 ....97 K7
  WLSD/HOW NE28 ....72 D1
Parkway GOS/KPK NE3 ....55 G4
  STKFD/GP NE62 ....23 F6
  WASHS NE38 ....116 E1
  WICK/BNPF NE16 ....84 C7
Park Wood Av
  BDN/LAN/SAC DH7 ....155 F6
Parkwood Av PRUD NE42 ....81 F1
Parliament St CON/LDGT DH8 ....122 E5
Parmeter St STLY/ANP DH9 ....126 C3
Parmontley St
  BW/LEM/TK/HW NE15 ....68 D6
Parnaby St CON/LDGT DH8 ....122 E5
Parnell St HLS DH4 ....131 K7
Parry Dr CLDN/WHIT/ROK SR6 ....92 E3
Parson Rd WYLAM NE41 ....65 H5
Parson's Av BYK/HTN/WLK NE6 ....72 B6
Parsons Gdns DUN/TMV NE11 ....9 H5
Parsons Rd PLEE/EAS SR8 ....174 E1
  WASHN NE37 ....102 D6
Partick Rd MLFD/PNYW SR4 ....119 F2
Partick Sq MLFD/PNYW SR4 ....119 F2
Partnership Ct SEA/MUR SR7 ....134 E5
Partridge Cl WASHN NE38 ....116 B3
The Pastures BLYTH NE24 ....35 F3
  MPTH NE61 ....20 B6
  PSHWF NE43 ....79 F4
Pathside JRW NE32 ....89 K2
Patience Av DIN/WO NE13 ....46 C1
Patina Cl BW/LEM/TK/HW NE15 ....68 A3
Paton Rd SUNDSW SR3 ....119 K4
Paton Sq SUNDSW SR3 ....119 K4
Patrick Crs RDHAMSE DH6 ....160 D1
Patterdale Cl BOL NE36 ....91 C5
  DHAM DH1 ....158 B5
Patterdale Gdns LGB/HTN NE7 ....57 H7
Patterdale Gv SWCK/CAS SR5 ....106 C1
Patterdale Ms CON/LDGT DH8 ....123 K3
Patterdale Rd BLYTH NE24 ....30 C6
Patterdale St HLH DH5 ....147 K6
Patterdale Ter GATE NE8 ....11 C8
Patterson St BLAY NE21 ....68 C7
Pattinson Gdns FELL NE10 ....12 A4
  LWF/SPW/WRK NE9 ....11 L9
Pattinson Rd WASHS NE38 ....103 K7
Patton Wk RDHAMSE DH6 ....173 F7
Patton Wy MPTH NE61 ....21 J2
Pauline Av
  CLDN/WHIT/ROK SR6 ....106 D2
Pauline Gdns
  BW/LEM/TK/HW NE15 ....68 A4
Pauls Gn HLH DH5 ....147 K2
Paulsway JRW NE32 ....73 F7
The Pavilion WICK/BNPF NE16 ....84 D3
Pawston Rd ROWG NE39 ....82 C7
Paxford Cl LGB/HTN NE7 ....57 F5
Paxton Ter MLFD/PNYW SR4 ....106 A6
Peacock Cl DUN/TMV NE11 ....86 B5
Peacock St West
  MLFD/PNYW SR4 ....105 K7
Pea Flatts La CLS/BIR/GTL DH3 ....145 K1
Peareth Ct GATE NE8 ....11 G2
Peareth Gv
  CLDN/WHIT/ROK SR6 ....106 E2
Peareth Hall Rd
  LWF/SPW/WRK NE9 ....102 B4
  WASHN NE37 ....102 D3
Peareth Rd
  CLDN/WHIT/ROK SR6 ....106 E1
Pear Lea BDN/LAN/SAC DH7 ....167 F6
Pearl Rd SUNDSW SR3 ....119 K4
Pearson Pl JRW NE32 ....74 A3
  TYNE/NSHE NE30 ....2 F1
Pearson St SSH NE33 ....3 J4
  STLY/ANP DH9 ....112 D6
Peart Cl RDHAMSE DH6 ....170 D1
Peartree Bungalows
  CHPW NE17 ....95 J7
Peartree Gdns
  BYK/HTN/WLK NE6 ....72 B2
Peary Cl WD/WHPE/BLK NE5 ....54 B2
Pease Av BW/LEM/TK/HW NE15 ....69 G5
Peasemoor Rd
  MLFD/PNYW SR4 ....119 F1
Pease Rd PLEE/EAS SR8 ....174 A2
Pecket Cl BLYTH NE24 ....34 C2
Peebles Cl NSHW NE29 ....59 K2
Peebles Rd SUNDSW SR3 ....119 J4
Peel Av DHAM DH1 ....157 J6
Peel La CNUT NE1 ....5 H8
Peel St ASHBK/HED/RY SR2 ....15 C7
Peggy's Wicket STLY/ANP DH9 ....113 K6
Pegwood Rd MLFD/PNYW SR4 ....119 G1
Peile Pk CON/LDGT DH8 ....122 C1
Pelaw Av CLSW/PEL DH2 ....129 H2
  NWBGN NE64 ....19 F4
  STLY/ANP DH9 ....112 E6
Pelaw Bank CLS/BIR/GTL DH3 ....129 J3
Pelaw Crs CLSW/PEL DH2 ....129 H2
Pelaw Grange Ct
  CLS/BIR/GTL DH3 ....115 J6
Pelaw Leazes La DHAM DH1 ....16 F3
Pelaw Pl CLSW/PEL DH2 ....129 H2
Pelaw Rd CLSW/PEL DH2 ....129 H2
Pelaw Sq CLSW/PEL DH2 ....129 H2
  MLFD/PNYW SR4 ....105 G6
Pelaw Wy FELL NE10 ....13 K7
Peldon Cl LGB/HTN NE7 ....57 H5
Pelham Ct GOS/KPK NE3 ....55 C1
Peltondale Av BLYTH NE24 ....34 C1

Pelton Fell Rd CLSW/PEL DH2 ....129 G3
Pelton La CLSW/PEL DH2 ....129 F1
Pelton Ms CLSW/PEL DH2 ....128 C1
Pelton Rd MLFD/PNYW SR4 ....119 G2
Pemberton Av CON/LDGT DH8 ....122 C7
Pemberton Bank HLH DH5 ....148 A7
Pemberton Cl SWCK/CAS SR5 ....106 B4
Pemberton Gdns SUNDSW SR3 ....120 B3
Pemberton Rd CON/LDGT DH8 ....122 B5
Pemberton St HLH DH5 ....147 K4
Pembroke Av BYK/HTN/WLK NE6 ....7 L2
  CLS/BIR/GTL DH3 ....115 K5
  SUNDSW SR3 ....134 A1
Pembroke Ct GOS/KPK NE3 ....55 H5
Pembroke Dr PONT/DH NE20 ....42 C4
Pembroke Gdns ASHGTN NE63 ....24 C4
  WLSD/HOW NE28 ....59 J6
Pembroke Pl PLEE/EAS SR8 ....174 C2
Pembroke Ter SSH NE33 ....75 C4
Pendeford MLFD/PNYW SR4 ....117 J2
Pendle Cl WASHS NE38 ....116 D3
Pendleton Dr CRAM NE23 ....33 G6
Pendower Wy
  BW/LEM/TK/HW NE15 ....69 G5
Penfold Cl LGB/HTN * NE7 ....57 J6
Penhale Dr
  ASHBK/HED/RY SR2 ....121 F6
Penhill Cl CLDN/WHIT/ROK SR6 ....114 E5
Penistone Rd MLFD/PNYW SR4 ....118 E2
Penman Pl NSHW NE29 ....2 C4
Penman Sq MLFD/PNYW SR4 ....119 F2
Pennant Sq MLFD/PNYW SR4 ....105 G7
Pennine Ct STLY/ANP DH9 ....125 H4
  PLEE/EAS SR8 ....174 C4
Pennine Dr ASHGTN NE63 ....24 A4
Pennine Gdns DUN/TMV NE11 ....86 A5
  STLY/ANP DH9 ....126 E2
Pennine Gv BOL NE36 ....91 F5
Pennine Wy LGB/KIL NE12 ....57 G4
Penn Sq MLFD/PNYW SR4 ....105 G7
Penn St ELS/FEN NE4 ....9 L2
Pennycross Rd
  MLFD/PNYW SR4 ....118 E2
Pennycross Sq
  MLFD/PNYW SR4 ....118 E1
Pennyfine Cl NSHW NE29 ....60 D2
Pennyfine Rd WICK/BNPF NE16 ....99 G2
Pennygate Sq
  MLFD/PNYW SR4 ....118 E1
Pennygreen Sq
  MLFD/PNYW SR4 ....118 E1
Pennymore Sq
  MLFD/PNYW SR4 ....118 E2
Pennywell Rd
  MLFD/PNYW SR4 ....119 G2
Penrith Av TYNE/NSHE NE30 ....50 E7
Penrith Gdns
  LWF/SPW/WRK NE9 ....101 H1
  SWCK/CAS SR5 ....106 C1
Penrith Rd HEBB NE31 ....73 H7
  SWCK/CAS SR5 ....106 C1
Penryn Av SEA/MUR SR7 ....149 J5
Penryn Wy BDN/LAN/SAC DH7 ....167 H6
Pensford Ct GOS/KPK NE3 ....55 C5
Penshaw Cl BDN/LAN/SAC DH7 ....154 A3
Penshaw Gn
  WD/WHPE/BLK NE5 ....55 H7
Penshaw La HLS DH4 ....117 K6
Penshaw Vw
  BDN/LAN/SAC DH7 ....143 J6
  FELL NE10 ....88 E4
  HEBB NE31 ....73 F7
  JRW NE32 ....73 K7
Penshaw Wy CLS/BIR/GTL DH3 ....116 A2
Pensher St FELL NE10 ....11 M5
  MLFD/PNYW SR4 ....106 A7
Pensher St East FELL NE10 ....12 A5
Pent Ct
  RYTON (off Lead Rd) NE40 ....82 C3
Pentland Cl ASHGTN NE63 ....24 A5
  CRAM NE23 ....33 H6
  NSHW NE29 ....60 D1
  PLEE/EAS SR8 ....174 B5
  WASHS NE38 ....116 D3
Pentland Gdns DUN/TMV NE11 ....9 J9
Pentland Gv LGB/KIL NE12 ....57 H1
Pentlands Ter STLY/ANP DH9 ....126 E2
Pentridge Cl CRAM NE23 ....38 D1
Penwood Rd MLFD/PNYW SR4 ....119 G1
Pen-y-Ghent Wy WASHN NE37 ....102 C7
Penzance Bungs
  SEA/MUR SR7 ....149 J4
Penzance Rd MLFD/PNYW SR4 ....119 F2
Peppercorn Ct CNUT * NE1 ....5 M8
Percival St MLFD/PNYW SR4 ....105 K6
Percy Av WBAY NE26 ....50 D4
Percy Ct NSHW NE29 ....60 B7
Percy Crs NSHW NE29 ....60 B7
Percy Gdns CON/LDGT DH8 ....123 H6
  DUN/TMV NE11 ....86 A5
  LGB/KIL NE12 ....57 K2
  MONK NE25 ....50 E5
  STKFD/GP NE62 ....23 G5
  TYNE/NSHE NE30 ....61 H2
Percy La DHAM DH1 ....168 B1
Percy Lonnen PRUD NE42 ....80 D1
Percy Pk TYNE/NSHE NE30 ....61 H2
Percy Park Rd TYNE/NSHE NE30 ....61 H2
Percy Rd WBAY NE26 ....51 F4
Percy Scott St HAR/WTLS NE34 ....91 C1
Percy Sq DHAM DH1 ....168 B3
Percy St BLYTH NE24 ....31 H6
  BW/LEM/TK/HW NE15 ....68 A5
  CNUT NE1 ....5 J5
  CRAM NE23 ....38 C2
  HLH DH5 ....148 A4
  JRW NE32 ....74 A4
  LGB/KIL NE12 ....58 B1
  RDHAMSE DH6 ....172 C6
  SSH NE33 ....3 J9
  TYNE/NSHE NE30 ....61 H3
  WLSD/HOW NE28 ....72 E1
Percy St South BLYTH NE24 ....31 H7
Percy Ter ASHBK/HED/RY SR2 ....168 B1
  DHAM DH1 ....168 B1
  MONK NE25 ....50 C4
Percy Ter South
  ASHBK/HED/RY SR2 ....120 E5

Percy Vls
  TYNE/NSHE
  (off Lovaine Rw) NE30 ....61 J2
Percy Wy BW/LEM/TK/HW NE15 ....67 J2
Peregrine Pl LGB/KIL NE12 ....57 G3
Perivale Rd MLFD/PNYW SR4 ....119 G1
Perrycrofts SUNDSW SR3 ....134 A3
Perry St GATE NE8 ....11 H4
Perth Av JRW NE32 ....90 B1
Perth Cl NSHW NE29 ....60 A2
  WLSD/HOW NE28 ....59 H6
Perth Ct SUNDSW SR3 ....119 J5
Perth Gdns WLSD/HOW NE28 ....59 H6
Perth Rd SUNDSW SR3 ....119 J5
Perth Sq SUNDSW SR3 ....119 K4
Pesspool La RDHAMSE DH6 ....161 G5
Peterborough Cl GATE NE8 ....10 F4
Peterborough Rd DHAM DH1 ....157 F3
  GATE NE8 ....10 F4
Peter's Bank STLY/ANP DH9 ....111 J7
Petersfield Rd
  MLFD/PNYW SR4 ....119 F2
Petersham Rd
  MLFD/PNYW SR4 ....105 G7
Peth Bank BDN/LAN/SAC DH7 ....140 C5
Petherton Ct GOS/KPK NE3 ....55 G4
Peth Gn HLH DH5 ....148 A7
Peth La BDN/LAN/SAC DH7 ....141 F4
  RYTON NE40 ....67 F5
Pethside BDN/LAN/SAC DH7 ....140 D5
Petrel Cl SSH * NE33 ....3 G6
Petrel Wy BLYTH NE24 ....35 H3
Petterll WASHS NE38 ....116 C5
Petterson Dl RDHAMSE DH6 ....180 D6
Petwell Crs PLEE/EAS SR8 ....162 D5
Petwell La PLEE/EAS SR8 ....162 E4
Petworth Cl SSH NE33 ....3 K6
Petworth Gdns MPTH NE61 ....21 J2
Pevensey Cl NSHW NE29 ....60 D1
Pheonix Ct CON/LDGT DH8 ....122 C4
Philadelphia La HLS DH4 ....132 A2
Philip Av RDHAMSE DH6 ....180 A1
Philiphaugh WLSD/HOW NE28 ....72 D3
Philip Pl ELS/FEN NE4 ....4 D4
Philipson St BYK/HTN/WLK NE6 ....72 B5
Philip Sq SUNDSW SR3 ....119 J4
Philip St ELS/FEN NE4 ....4 D4
Phillips Av WICK/BNPF NE16 ....84 E4
Phoenix Cl BDN/LAN/SAC DH7 ....153 K3
Phoenix Cha NSHW NE29 ....59 K2
Phoenix House
  SUND (off Union St) SR1 ....14 E4
Phoenix Rd MLFD/PNYW SR4 ....105 J4
  WASHS NE38 ....102 A7
Phoenix Wy HLS DH4 ....147 F1
Piccadilly SUNDSW SR3 ....119 J6
Pickard Cl PLEE/EAS SR8 ....175 F4
Pickard St MLFD/PNYW SR4 ....106 A6
Pickering Rd MLFD/PNYW SR4 ....118 E3
Pickering Sq MLFD/PNYW SR4 ....119 F2
Pickersgill Ct MLFD/PNYW SR4 ....119 F5
Pickhurst Rd MLFD/PNYW SR4 ....119 F5
Pickhurst Sq MLFD/PNYW SR4 ....119 F5
Picktree La CLS/BIR/GTL DH3 ....129 K3
  WASHS NE38 ....116 A6
Picktree Ldg CLS/BIR/GTL DH3 ....115 K6
Pickwick Cl DHAM DH1 ....16 A9
Pier Pde SSH NE33 ....3 L5
Pier Rd TYNE/NSHE NE30 ....61 J3
Pier Vw CLDN/WHIT/ROK SR6 ....107 F3
Pike Hl CON/LDGT DH8 ....108 A7
Pikestone Cl WASHS NE38 ....116 C3
Pikesyde STLY/ANP DH9 ....110 D7
Pilgrim Cl SWCK/CAS SR5 ....106 C4
Pilgrim St CNUT NE1 ....5 K6
Pilgrims' Wy DHAM DH1 ....157 G6
Pilgrimsway JRW NE32 ....74 C5
  LWF/SPW/WRK NE9 ....11 K9
Pilgrims Wy MPTH NE61 ....20 B3
Pilton Rd WD/WHPE/BLK NE5 ....54 D7
Pimlico DHAM DH1 ....16 C6
Pimlico Rd HLH DH5 ....148 A7
  MLFD/PNYW SR4 ....119 F2
Pinders Wy RDHAMSE DH6 ....171 G1
Pine Av DHAM DH1 ....17 J4
  DIN/WO NE13 ....45 G2
  GOS/KPK NE3 ....55 K3
  HAR/WTLS NE34 ....76 A6
  STKFD/GP NE62 ....22 D6
  WICK/BNPF NE16 ....97 H7
Pinedale Dr RDHAMSE DH6 ....160 E2
Pinegarth PONT/DH NE20 ....42 D7
Pine Lea BDN/LAN/SAC DH7 ....167 F6
Pine Pk BDN/LAN/SAC DH7 ....167 G1
Pine Rd BLAY NE21 ....84 A2
The Pines
  ELS/FEN (off Park Rd) NE4 ....9 K1
  RYTON NE40 ....82 D3
Pine St BDN/LAN/SAC DH7 ....154 B2
  CLS/BIR/GTL DH3 ....115 J1
  CLSW/PEL DH2 ....128 A2
  JRW NE32 ....73 J5
  MLFD/PNYW SR4 ....105 K6
  STLY/ANP DH9 ....126 B3
Pinesway SUNDSW SR3 ....120 B3
Pinetree BDN/LAN/SAC DH7 ....165 J3
Pinetree Centre
  CLS/BIR/GTL
  (off Durham Rd) DH3 ....115 J3
Pinetree Gdns MONK NE25 ....50 C6
Pinetree Wy WICK/BNPF NE16 ....85 F2
Pine View Vls
  BDN/LAN/SAC DH7 ....165 J3
Pinewood HEBB NE31 ....72 E4
Pinewood Av CRAM NE23 ....33 H6
  DIN/WO NE13 ....46 C4
  GOS/KPK NE3 ....46 C4
  WASHS NE38 ....116 C5
Pinewood Cl BYK/HTN/WLK NE6 ....72 A2
  DIN/WO NE13 ....55 H4
Pinewood Dr MPTH NE61 ....20 B3
Pinewood Gdns DUN/TMV NE11 ....86 A7
Pinewood Rd SWCK/CAS SR5 ....105 K3
Pinewood Sq SWCK/CAS SR5 ....105 K3
Pinewood St HLS DH4 ....131 G6
Pinewood Vls HAR/WTLS NE34 ....76 A5
Pink La CNUT * NE1 ....5 H8
Pinner Pl BYK/HTN/WLK NE6 ....7 L8

Pinner Rd *MLFD/PNYW* SR4 ....119 G1
Pintail Ct
  HAR/WTLS (off Clive St) NE34 .....74 E7
Piper Rd *PRUD* NE42 ....64 B6
Pipershaw *WASHN* NE37 ....102 B7
Pipe Track La *ELS/FEN* NE4 ....69 H7
Pipewellgate *GATE* NE8 ....10 D1
Pitcairn Rd *MLFD/PNYW* SR4 ....119 G1
Pithouse La *CON/LDGT* DH8 ....109 H6
  HLS DH4 ....146 B5
Pit La *BDN/LAN/SAC* DH7 ....166 C5
  DHAM DH1 ....156 D1
Pittington La *DHAM* DH1 ....158 B4
Pittington Rd *HLH* DH5 ....158 D1
Pitt St *CON/LDGT* DH8 ....123 F5
  ELS/FEN NE4 ....4 F5
Pixley Dell *CON/LDGT* DH8 ....138 D1
Plains Rd *SUNDSW* SR3 ....119 K4
Plaistow Sq *MLFD/PNYW* SR4 ....105 G7
Plaistow Wy *CRAM* NE23 ....33 H6
Plane Ct *CON/LDGT* DH8 ....123 G5
Planesway *FELL* NE10 ....88 A7
Planet Pl *LGB/KIL* NE12 ....47 J7
Planetree Av *ELS/FEN* NE4 ....69 H3
Plane Tree Ct *SUNDSW* * SR3 ....133 J1
Plantation Av *RDHAMSE* DH6 ....159 G6
  WICK/BNPF NE16 ....84 E4
Plantation Gv *FELL* NE10 ....13 M4
Plantation Rd
  MLFD/PNYW SR4 ....105 J6
Plantation Sq
  MLFD/PNYW SR4 ....105 J6
Plantation St *CON/LDGT* DH8 ....123 K3
  WLSD/HOW NE28 ....72 D3
The Plantation
  LWF/SPW/WRK NE9 ....87 G7
Plantation Vw *MLFD/PNYW* SR4 ....127 K1
Plantation Wk *RDHAMSE* DH6 ....160 E2
Plawsworth Gdns
  LWF/SPW/WRK NE9 ....101 J2
Plawsworth Rd
  BDN/LAN/SAC DH7 ....143 H5
Pleasant Vw
  BDN/LAN/SAC DH7 ....141 G4
  CON/LDGT DH8 ....122 B3
Plenmeller Pl *WICK/BNPF* NE16 ....98 E2
Plessey Av *BLYTH* NE24 ....35 G1
Plessey Crs *MONK* NE25 ....51 F5
Plessey Gdns *NSHW* NE29 ....60 B5
Plessey Rd *BLYTH* NE24 ....31 H7
Plessey Ter *LGB/HTN* NE7 ....71 H1
Plough Rd *SUNDSW* SR3 ....133 K2
Plover Cl *BLYTH* NE24 ....35 G1
Plover Dr *WICK/BNPF* NE16 ....112 A1
Ploverfield Cl *ASHGTN* NE63 ....23 J3
Plover Ldg
  CLS/BIR/GTL
  (off Durham Rd) DH3 ....101 J7
Plunkett Rd *STLY/ANP* DH9 ....111 G5
Plunkett Ter *CLSW/PEL* DH2 ....128 D3
Plymouth Cl *SEA/MUR* SR7 ....150 A2
Plymouth Sq *SUNDSW* SR3 ....119 J4
Point Pleasant Ter
  WLSD/HOW NE28 ....73 G1
Polden Cl *PLEE/EAS* SR8 ....174 B5
Polden Crs *NSHW* NE29 ....50 C7
Polebrook Rd
  MLFD/PNYW SR4 ....105 G7
Polgrade Ct
  HLS (off Wynyard St) DH4 .....131 G1
Police Houses
  CON/LDGT
  (off Watling St) DH8 ....123 J3
  NWBGN (off Woodlea) NE64 .....19 F7
Pollard St *SSH* NE33 ....3 J6
Polmuir Rd *SUNDSW* SR3 ....119 J4
Polmuir Sq *SUNDSW* * SR3 ....119 J4
Polpero Cl *CLS/BIR/GTL* DH3 .....115 K3
Polworth Cl *ASHBK/HED/RY* SR2 ....121 F7
Polton Sq *MLFD/PNYW* SR4 ....105 G7
Polwarth Crs *GOS/KPK* NE3 ....56 C2
Polwarth Dr *GOS/KPK* NE3 ....56 C1
Polwarth Rd *GOS/KPK* NE3 ....56 C1
Polworth Sq *SUNDSW* SR3 ....119 K4
Ponds Ct *CON/LDGT* DH8 ....122 E5
Pont Bungalows
  CON/LDGT DH8 ....123 J2
Pontefract Rd
  MLFD/PNYW SR4 ....119 F3
Ponteland Cl *NSHW* NE29 ....60 A3
  WASHN NE38 ....116 B2
Ponteland Rd
  BW/LEM/TK/HW NE15 ....53 F6
  DIN/WO NE13 ....54 E3
  ELS/FEN NE4 ....4 C2
  PONT/DH NE20 ....43 J3
  WD/WHPE/BLK NE5 ....55 F4
Ponthaugh *ROWG* NE39 ....97 H2
Pont La *CON/LDGT* DH8 ....109 H7
Pontop Pike La *STLY/ANP* DH9 .....124 E1
Pontop Sq *MLFD/PNYW* SR4 ....105 G7
Pontop St *HLH* DH5 ....147 F4
Pontopsyde *STLY/ANP* DH9 ....110 E7
Pontop Vw *CON/LDGT* DH8 ....123 H7
  ROWG NE39 ....97 F3
Pont St *ASHGTN* NE63 ....23 K1
Pont Vw *PONT/DH* NE20 ....43 H2
Poole Cl *CRAM* NE23 ....38 D1
Poole Rd *MLFD/PNYW* SR4 ....105 G7
Pooley Cl *WD/WHPE/BLK* NE5 ....69 F2
Pooley Rd *WD/WHPE/BLK* NE5 ....69 F2
Poplar Av *BLYTH* NE24 ....31 F5
  BYK/HTN/WLK * NE6 ....72 B2
  DIN/WO NE13 ....45 C2
  WICK/BNPF NE16 ....97 H7
Poplar Buildings
  ASHGTN
  (off Woodhorn Rd) NE63 ....23 K1
Poplar Crs *CLS/BIR/GTL* DH3 .....115 H1
  DUN/TMV NE11 ....9 G9
  GATE NE8 ....10 E4
Poplar Dr *CLDN/WHIT/ROK* SR6 ....93 F5
  DHAM DH1 ....157 H6
Poplar Gv *ASHBK/HED/RY* SR2 ....120 C6
  BDLGTN NE22 ....29 H5
  HAR/WTLS NE34 ....75 K6
Poplar Lea *BDN/LAN/SAC* DH7 ....167 F6

Poplar Rd *BLAY* NE21 ....84 A3
  DHAM DH1 ....158 A5
The Poplars
  ELS/FEN (off De Grey St) NE4 .....9 K1
  GOS/KPK NE3 ....56 C7
  HLH DH5 ....148 D7
  SWCK/CAS SR5 ....105 K3
Poplar St *CLS/BIR/GTL* DH3 ....129 J4
  STLY/ANP DH9 ....126 B3
Popplewell Gdns
  LWF/SPW/WRK NE9 ....101 G1
Popplewell Ter *NSHW* NE29 ....60 E2
Porchester Dr *CRAM* NE23 ....38 D1
Porlock Ct *CRAM* NE23 ....33 G6
Porlock Rd *JRW* NE32 ....74 B6
Portadown Rd
  MLFD/PNYW SR4 ....119 F3
Portberry St *SSH* NE33 ....75 F3
Portberry Wy *SSH* NE33 ....75 F3
Porchester Gv *BOLCOL* NE35 ....90 C4
Portchester Rd
  MLFD/PNYW SR4 ....119 G1
Portchester Sq
  MLFD/PNYW SR4 ....119 G1
Porter Ter *SEA/MUR* SR7 ....149 H5
Porthcawl Dr *WASHN* NE37 ....102 E3
Portia St *ASHGTN* NE63 ....24 A1
Portland Av *SEA/MUR* SR7 ....150 B1
Portland Gdns *CRAM* NE23 ....38 D1
  LWF/SPW/WRK NE9 ....101 F3
  TYNE/NSHE NE30 ....60 E2
Portland Rd
  BW/LEM/TK/HW NE15 ....67 G1
  JES NE2 ....6 A3
  SUNDSW SR3 ....119 K4
Portland Sq *SUNDSW* SR3 ....119 K3
Portland St *BLYTH* NE24 ....31 F6
  ELS/FEN NE4 ....4 B8
  FELL NE10 ....13 H6
Portland Ter *JES* NE2 ....5 M2
Portman Ms *JES* NE2 ....6 B4
Portman Pl *BYK/HTN/WLK* NE6 ....12 E1
Portman Sq *MLFD/PNYW* SR4 .....119 G1
Portmeads Rd
  CLS/BIR/GTL DH3 ....115 K2
Portobello La
  CLDN/WHIT/ROK SR6 ....106 D4
Portree Sq *SUNDSW* SR3 ....119 J5
Portrush Cl *WASHN* NE37 ....102 E5
Portrush Rd *MLFD/PNYW* SR4 .....105 G7
Portrush Wy *LGB/HTN* NE7 ....57 J5
Portslade Rd *MLFD/PNYW* SR4 ....119 F2
Portsmouth Rd
  MLFD/PNYW SR4 ....119 F1
  NSHW NE29 ....60 A5
Portsmouth Sq
  MLFD/PNYW SR4 ....119 F1
Portugal Pl *WLSD/HOW* NE28 .....72 D2
Postern Crs *MPTH* NE61 ....20 C6
Post Office La *NSHW* NE29 ....60 E1
Post Office St *BLYTH* NE24 ....31 H6
Potterhouse La *DHAM* DH1 ....156 A1
The Potteries *SSH* NE33 ....75 J2
Potter Pl *STLY/ANP* DH9 ....127 F2
Potters Bank *DHAM* DH1 ....16 A8
Potters Cl *DHAM* DH1 ....168 B3
Potter Sq *SUNDSW* SR3 ....119 J4
Potter St *JRW* NE32 ....73 J4
  WLSD/HOW NE28 ....73 J2
Pottersway *LWF/SPW/WRK* NE9 ....87 G6
Pottery Bank
  BYK/HTN/WLK NE6 ....13 H1
  MPTH NE61 ....20 C3
Pottery La *CNUT* NE1 ....10 B1
  MLFD/PNYW SR4 ....104 E6
Pottery Rd *SWCK/CAS* SR5 ....106 A4
Pottery Yd *HLS* DH4 ....132 C7
Potto St *RDHAMSE* DH6 ....173 J4
Potts St *BYK/HTN/WLK* NE6 ....7 G4
Powburn Cl *CLSW/PEL* DH2 ....129 G6
Powburn Gdns *ELS/FEN* NE4 ....69 J3
Powis Rd *SUNDSW* SR3 ....119 K4
Powis Sq *SUNDSW* SR3 ....119 K4
Powys Pl *ELS/FEN* NE4 ....4 D4
Poynings Cl *WD/WHPE/BLK* NE5 ....55 G5
Praetorian Dr *WLSD/HOW* NE28 ....72 D2
Prebends Fld *DHAM* DH1 ....157 G5
The Precinct
  BLAY (off Wesley Ct) NE21 ....84 B1
Prefect Pl *LWF/SPW/WRK* NE9 ....87 C5
Premier Rd *SUNDSW* SR3 ....119 J4
Prendwick Av *HEBB* NE31 ....89 F1
Prendwick Cl *CLSW/PEL* DH2 .....129 C7
Prengarth Av
  CLDN/WHIT/ROK SR6 ....106 D2
Prensgarth Wy *HAR/WTLS* NE34 ....90 D1
Prescot Rd *MLFD/PNYW* SR4 .....105 G7
Press La *SUND* SR1 ....14 F4
Prestbury Av *CRAM* NE23 ....33 G6
Prestbury Rd *MLFD/PNYW* SR4 ....118 E2
Prestdale Av *BLYTH* NE24 ....30 C7
Presthope Rd
  MLFD/PNYW SR4 ....118 E2
Preston Av *TYNE/NSHE* NE30 ....60 E1
Preston North Rd *NSHW* NE29 .....60 D1
Preston Pk *NSHW* NE29 ....60 D1
Preston Rd *ASHBK/HED/RY* SR2 ....15 J9
Preston Ter *NSHW* NE29 ....60 D2
Preston Towers
  NSHW (off Preston Rd) NE29 ....60 E3
Preston Wd *TYNE/NSHE* NE30 .....60 E1
Prestwick Av *NSHW* NE29 ....60 A3
Prestwick Av *NSHW* NE29 ....60 A3
Prestwick Cl *WASHN* NE37 ....102 E3
Prestwick Dr *FELL* NE10 ....88 E5
Prestwick Gdns *GOS/KPK* NE3 ....55 K6
Prestwick Rd *MLFD/PNYW* SR4 ....105 G7
Pretoria Av *MPTH* NE61 ....20 D5
Pretoria Sq *SUNDSW* SR3 ....119 J4
Pretoria St
  BW/LEM/TK/HW NE15 ....68 E7
Price St *HEBB* * NE31 ....72 E4
  MPTH NE61 ....20 C4
Priestburn Cl
  BDN/LAN/SAC DH7 ....165 G1
Priestclose Rd *PRUD* NE42 ....80 D2
Priestfield Cl *SUNDSW* SR3 ....133 K2

Priestfield Gdns
  WICK/BNPF * NE16 ....97 H7
Priestley Ct *HAR/WTLS* NE34 ....90 E1
Priestley Gdns *FELL* NE10 ....13 L8
Priestly Crs *MLFD/PNYW* SR4 ....14 A2
Priestman Av *CON/LDGT* DH8 .....122 C6
Priestman Ct *MLFD/PNYW* SR4 ....105 H7
Primary Gdns
  ASHBK/HED/RY SR2 ....15 J7
Primate Rd *SUNDSW* SR3 ....119 J4
Primrose Av *HAR/WTLS* NE34 .....75 F6
  PLEE/EAS SR8 ....175 G3
Primrose Cl *CRAM* NE23 ....47 G1
Primrose Ct *ASHGTN* NE63 ....23 H4
Primrose Crs
  CLDN/WHIT/ROK SR6 ....106 D2
  HLS DH4 ....131 G4
Primrose Gdns
  WLSD/HOW NE28 ....58 C6
Primrose Hl
  LWF/SPW/WRK NE9 ....87 G7
Primrose Prec
  CLDN/WHIT/ROK SR6 ....106 D2
Primrose St *MLFD/PNYW* SR4 .....104 E7
Primrose Ter *CLS/BIR/GTL* DH3 ....115 K2
  JRW NE32 ....74 A7
Prince Albert Ter *JES* * NE2 ....6 A5
Prince Charles Av
  RDHAMSE DH6 ....179 K2
Prince Consort La *HEBB* NE31 .....73 F5
Prince Consort Rd *GATE* NE8 .....10 F3
  HEBB NE31 ....72 E5
  JRW NE32 ....74 A5
Prince Consort Wy *NSHW* NE29 ....2 C7
Prince Edward Gv
  HAR/WTLS NE34 ....76 C5
Prince Edward Rd
  HAR/WTLS NE34 ....75 J6
Prince Edward Rd East
  HAR/WTLS NE34 ....76 C5
Prince George Av
  CLDN/WHIT/ROK SR6 ....106 D1
Prince of Wales Cl
  HAR/WTLS NE34 ....75 J6
Prince Philip Cl
  BW/LEM/TK/HW NE15 ....69 G6
Prince Rd *WLSD/HOW* NE28 ....58 D7
Princes Av *CLDN/WHIT/ROK* SR6 ....92 E7
  GOS/KPK NE3 ....56 B4
Princes Cl *GOS/KPK* NE3 ....56 B2
Prince's Gdns *BLYTH* NE24 ....30 E6
  CLDN/WHIT/ROK SR6 ....92 E7
Prince's Meadow *GOS/KPK* NE3 ....56 A5
Princes Pk *DUN/TMV* NE11 ....86 B7
Princes Pk *GOS/KPK* NE3 ....56 B1
Princess Av *CON/LDGT* DH8 ....122 D2
Princess Ct *PRUD* NE42 ....64 D7
Princess Dr *GATE* NE8 ....9 G6
Princess Louise Rd *BLYTH* NE24 ....31 G7
Princess Mary Ct *JES* NE2 ....70 D2
Princess Rd *SEA/MUR* SR7 ....150 D1
Princess Sq *CNUT* NE1 ....5 K5
Princess St *ASHBK/HED/RY* SR2 ....14 D7
  FELL NE10 ....13 J6
  WICK/BNPF NE16 ....99 F3
Princes' St *DHAM* DH1 ....16 A2
  HLS DH4 ....131 J2
  STLY/ANP DH9 ....125 H2
  TYNE/NSHE NE30 ....61 F3
Princess Wy *PRUD* NE42 ....64 C7
Prince St *SUND* SR1 ....14 E4
Princesway *DUN/TMV* NE11 ....86 C6
Princetown Ter *SUNDSW* SR3 .....119 J4
Princeway *TYNE/NSHE* NE30 ....61 H2
Pringle Cl *BDN/LAN/SAC* DH7 .....166 D3
Pringle Gv *BDN/LAN/SAC* DH7 ....166 E3
Pringle Pl *BDN/LAN/SAC* DH7 .....166 E3
Prinn Pl *WICK/BNPF* NE16 ....99 F3
Priors Cl *DHAM* DH1 ....156 B7
Priors Gra *RDHAMSE* DH6 ....158 E4
Prior's Ter *TYNE/NSHE* NE30 ....61 H3
Priors Wk *MPTH* NE61 ....20 C6
Priors Wy *WLSD/HOW* NE28 ....73 G1
Priory Av *MONK* NE25 ....50 D5
Priory Cl *CON/LDGT* DH8 ....122 C2
Priory Ct *BDN/LAN/SAC* DH7 .....143 H6
  GATE NE8 ....11 G2
Priory Flats
  DHAM (off Priory Rd) DH1 .....156 C4
Priory Gra *BLYTH* NE24 ....30 E6
Priory Gn *BYK/HTN/WLK* NE6 ....7 G6
Priory Gv *MLFD/PNYW* SR4 ....119 K1
Priory Pl *DIN/WO* NE13 ....46 A4
  STKFD/GP NE62 ....23 C5
  JRW NE32 ....74 A3
Priory Wy *WD/WHPE/BLK* NE5 .....54 D6
Proctor Sq *SUNDSW* SR3 ....119 K4
Proctor St *BYK/HTN/WLK* NE6 .....72 C6
Promenade
  ASHBK/HED/RY SR2 ....121 G3
  NWBGN NE64 ....25 C1
  SEA/MUR SR7 ....135 K7
  SSH NE33 ....61 K7
  WBAY NE26 ....50 E3
The Promenade
  CON/LDGT DH8 ....123 F3
Prospect Av *MONK* NE25 ....39 K5
  WLSD/HOW NE28 ....58 D7
Prospect Av North
  WLSD/HOW NE28 ....58 D6
Prospect Ct *ELS/FEN* NE4 ....4 D6
Prospect Crs *HLH* DH5 ....160 B1
Prospect Gdns *BOL* NE36 ....90 E5
Prospect Pl *BDN/LAN/SAC* DH7 ....166 D2
  CON/LDGT DH8 ....123 F4
  ELS/FEN NE4 ....4 D6
Prospect Rw *SUND* SR1 ....15 J3
Prospect St *NWBGN* NE64 ....19 G3
Prospect Ter
  BDN/LAN/SAC DH7 ....166 D2
  TYNE/NSHE NE30 ....61 G4
Prospect Vw *HLS* DH4 ....146 C6
Providence Cl *DHAM* DH1 ....16 E2
Providence Rw *DHAM* DH1 ....16 E2
Provident St *CLSW/PEL* DH2 ....128 C1
Provost Gdns
  BW/LEM/TK/HW NE15 ....69 H7

Prudhoe Gv *JRW* NE32 ....89 J1
Prudhoe St *MLFD/PNYW* SR4 .....105 K6
  NSHW NE29 ....2 D4
Prudhoe Ter *TYNE/NSHE* NE30 ....61 H2
Pudding Chare *CNUT* NE1 ....5 K8
Purbeck Gdns *CRAM* NE23 ....38 D1
Purbeck Rd *LGB/KIL* NE12 ....57 H4
Purley *WASHS* NE38 ....117 J2
Purley Cl *WLSD/HOW* NE28 ....59 H6
Purley Gdns *GOS/KPK* NE3 ....55 K6
Purley Rd *SUNDSW* SR3 ....119 J4
Purley Sq *SUNDSW* SR3 ....119 J4
Putney Sq *MLFD/PNYW* SR4 .....119 F2
Pykerley Ms
  MONK (off Pykerley Rd) NE25 ....50 C4
Pykerley Rd *MONK* NE25 ....50 C4

Q

The Quadrant *NSHW* NE29 ....60 C5
  SUND SR1 ....15 J3
Quality Rw *BYK/HTN/WLK* NE6 ....6 D6
Quality Row Rd
  WICK/BNPF NE16 ....84 E3
Quantock Cl *LGB/KIL* NE12 ....57 H4
  NSHW NE29 ....50 C7
Quantock Pl *PLEE/EAS* SR8 ....174 B4
Quarry Bank Ct *ELS/FEN* NE4 ....4 E7
Quarry Crs *BDN/LAN/SAC* DH7 ....155 F6
Quarryfield Rd *GATE* NE8 ....6 B9
Quarryheads La *DHAM* DH1 ....16 B6
Quarry House La *DHAM* DH1 .....168 A1
  HLH DH5 ....147 G4
Quarry La *HAR/WTLS* NE34 ....76 A1
Quarry Rd
  BW/LEM/TK/HW * NE15 ....68 C3
  HEBB NE31 ....73 G6
  STLY/ANP DH9 ....112 D7
  SUNDSW SR3 ....120 B7
Quarry Rw *FELL* NE10 ....12 C6
Quarry St *SUNDSW* SR3 ....120 A7
Quay Rd *BLYTH* NE24 ....31 H6
Quayside *BLYTH* NE24 ....31 H6
  CNUT NE1 ....5 M8
The Quay *HLH* DH5 ....147 K5
Quay Vw *WLSD/HOW* NE28 ....73 H1
Queen Alexandra Br
  MLFD/PNYW SR4 ....106 A5
Queen Alexandra Rd
  ASHBK/HED/RY SR2 ....120 E4
  NSHW NE29 ....60 D3
  SEA/MUR SR7 ....150 E2
  SUNDSW SR3 ....120 B3
Queen Alexandra Rd West
  NSHW NE29 ....60 C3
Queen Anne Ct
  BYK/HTN/WLK NE6 ....7 G3
Queen Elizabeth Av
  LWF/SPW/WRK NE9 ....87 H7
Queen Elizabeth Dr *HLH* DH5 .....160 C1
Queen Elizabeth II Br *CNUT* NE1 ....10 D1
Queens Av *CLDN/WHIT/ROK* SR6 ....92 E7
Queensberry St
  MLFD/PNYW SR4 ....14 B4
Queensbridge *LGB/KIL* NE12 ....57 F3
Queensbury Dr
  WD/WHPE/BLK NE5 ....67 K1
Queensbury Rd *SEA/MUR* SR7 .....150 D1
Queen's Ct
  BW/LEM/TK/HW NE15 ....67 J2
  GATE NE8 ....10 A6
  GOS/KPK NE3 ....46 B7
Queen's Crs *HEBB* NE31 ....73 F7
  MLFD/PNYW SR4 ....120 A1
  WLSD/HOW NE28 ....58 C7
Queen's Dr *WBAY* NE26 ....50 E4
  WICK/BNPF NE16 ....85 F7
Queen's Gdns *BLYTH* NE24 ....30 E6
Queens Gv *DHAM* DH1 ....168 B3
Queensland Av *HAR/WTLS* NE34 ....74 C7
Queens La *CNUT* * NE1 ....5 K8
Queensmere *CLS/BIR/GTL* DH3 ....115 J7
Queens Pl *NWBGN* NE64 ....19 C7
Queen's Rd *BDLGTN* NE22 ....29 K4
  BW/LEM/TK/HW NE15 ....67 J2
  CON/LDGT DH8 ....122 E2
  CRAM NE23 ....38 C7
  JES NE2 ....71 F2
  SWCK/CAS SR5 ....106 B4
  WBAY NE26 ....41 G2
  WBAY NE26 ....50 D3
  WD/WHPE/BLK NE5 ....68 E1
  WNGT TS28 ....183 J3
Queen's Ter *JES* NE2 ....71 F2
  WLSD/HOW NE28 ....72 D1
Queen St *ASHBK/HED/RY* SR2 ....121 F6
  CLSW/PEL DH2 ....128 A2
  CNUT NE1 ....5 M8
  CON/LDGT DH8 ....123 F5
  GATE NE8 ....10 A7
  HLH DH5 ....147 K3
  NWBGN NE64 ....19 G7
  SEA/MUR SR7 ....150 D1
  SSH NE33 ....61 K7
  SUND SR1 ....14 D3
  TYNE/NSHE NE30 ....2 F1
Queen St East *SUND* SR1 ....15 H4
Queens Wy *CON/LDGT* DH8 ....122 C2
Queensway *ELS/FEN* NE4 ....69 H3
  GOS/KPK NE3 ....56 B1
  HLH DH5 ....147 J1
  MPTH NE61 ....20 B6
  PONT/DH NE20 ....43 F7
  TYNE/NSHE NE30 ....61 H2
Queensway North
  DUN/TMV NE11 ....10 A9
Queen Victoria Rd *CNUT* NE1 ....5 J4
Queen Victoria St *FELL* NE10 ....13 H6
Quentin Av *GOS/KPK* NE3 ....55 H5
Quetlaw Rd *RDHAMSE* DH6 ....182 D1
Quilstyle Rd *RDHAMSE* DH6 ....182 D1
Quinn Cl *PLEE/EAS* SR8 ....174 E5
Oulton Cl *WD/WHPE/BLK* NE5 ....55 F6

R

Rabbit Banks Rd *GATE* NE8 ....10 D2
Raby Av *PLEE/EAS* SR8 ....163 F4
Raby Cl *HLS* DH4 ....131 J6
Raby Crs *BYK/HTN/WLK* NE6 ....7 G5
Raby Cross *BYK/HTN/WLK* NE6 ....7 G7
Raby Dr *SUNDSW* SR3 ....119 G7
Raby Gdns *JRW* NE32 ....73 K7
  WICK/BNPF NE16 ....97 G5
Raby Rd *DHAM* DH1 ....156 D2
  WASHS NE38 ....116 B1
Raby St *BYK/HTN/WLK* NE6 ....7 G5
  GATE NE8 ....11 H7
  MLFD/PNYW SR4 ....14 A6
Raby Wy *BYK/HTN/WLK* NE6 ....7 G7
Rachel Cl *ASHBK/HED/RY* SR2 ....120 C7
Rackly Wy *CLDN/WHIT/ROK* SR6 ....93 F4
Radcliffe Cottages
  BW/LEM/TK/HW
  (off Hexham Rd) NE15 ....67 F1
Radcliffe Pl *WD/WHPE/BLK* NE5 ....69 H1
Radcliffe Rd *SWCK/CAS* SR5 ....105 G4
Radcliffe St *CLS/BIR/GTL* DH3 .....115 J3
Radlett Rd *SWCK/CAS* SR5 ....105 H3
Radnor Gdns *WLSD/HOW* NE28 ....59 J7
Radnor St *CNUT* NE1 ....5 M4
Radstock Pl *LGB/KIL* NE12 ....57 J3
Rae Av *WLSD/HOW* NE28 ....58 D6
Raeburn Av *WASHS* NE38 ....117 G3
Raeburn Gdns
  LWF/SPW/WRK NE9 ....11 M9
Raeburn Rd *HAR/WTLS* NE34 ....91 H2
  SWCK/CAS SR5 ....105 G2
Raglan Av *ASHBK/HED/RY* SR2 ....120 E3
Raglan Pl *WICK/BNPF* NE16 ....97 K7
Raglan St *CON/LDGT* DH8 ....123 F5
Railway Cl *DHAM* DH1 ....170 B1
Railway Pl *CON/LDGT* DH8 ....122 E4
Railway Rw *SUND* SR1 ....14 B5
Railway St *BDN/LAN/SAC* DH7 ....140 C5
  CON/LDGT DH8 ....123 J3
  DUN/TMV NE11 ....9 M2
  ELS/FEN NE4 ....9 M2
  HEBB NE31 ....73 H4
  HLH DH5 ....147 K5
  HLS DH4 ....132 B5
  JRW NE32 ....73 J4
  NSHW * NE29 ....2 D2
  STLY/ANP DH9 ....125 J4
  STLY/ANP DH9 ....127 G5
  SUND SR1 ....15 J5
Railway Ter *ELS/FEN* NE4 ....9 L2
  NSHW NE29 ....2 D2
Raine Gv *SUND* SR1 ....15 H6
Rainford Av
  ASHBK/HED/RY SR2 ....120 E3
Rainhill Cl *WASHN* NE37 ....103 G4
Rainhill Rd *WASHN* NE37 ....103 G4
Rainton Cl *FELL* NE10 ....88 E6
Rainton Gv *HLH* DH5 ....147 H2
Rainton St *HLS* DH4 ....146 A7
  MLFD/PNYW SR4 ....106 A7
  SEA/MUR SR7 ....150 E2
Rainton Vw *HLS* DH4 ....146 C6
Rake La *NSHW* NE29 ....60 A1
Raleigh Cl *SSH* NE33 ....75 F3
Raleigh Rd *SWCK/CAS* SR5 ....105 H3
Ralph Av *ASHBK/HED/RY* SR2 ....120 E6
Ralph St *HEBB* NE31 ....73 H4
Ramilies *ASHBK/HED/RY* SR2 ....134 D1
Ramilies Rd *SWCK/CAS* SR5 ....105 G2
Ramona Av *RDHAMSE* DH6 ....181 F6
The Ramparts
  BW/LEM/TK/HW NE15 ....68 C3
Ramsay Rd *CHPW* NE17 ....95 H3
Ramsay St *BLAY* NE21 ....83 K3
  RDHAMSE DH6 ....179 K7
Ramsay Ter *CON/LDGT* DH8 ....123 H7
Ramsey Cl *DHAM* DH1 ....17 M3
  PLEE/EAS SR8 ....174 E2
Ramsey St *CLS/BIR/GTL* DH3 ....129 J5
Ramsgate Rd *SWCK/CAS* SR5 .....105 J2
Ramshaw Cl
  BDN/LAN/SAC DH7 ....153 K3
  LGB/HTN NE7 ....58 A7
Ramside Vw *DHAM* DH1 ....158 A4
Randolph St *JRW* NE32 ....74 A4
Rangoon Rd *SWCK/CAS* SR5 ....105 G2
Ranmere Rd
  BW/LEM/TK/HW NE15 ....68 E6
Ranmore Cl *CRAM* NE23 ....38 C1
Rannoch Av *CLSW/PEL* DH2 ....129 H6
Rannoch Cl *FELL* NE10 ....88 E4
Rannoch Rd *SWCK/CAS* SR5 ....105 G2
Ranson Crs *HAR/WTLS* NE34 ....74 D6
Ranson St *MLFD/PNYW* SR4 ....120 A2
Raphael Av *HAR/WTLS* NE34 ....91 G1
Rathmore Gdns
  TYNE/NSHE NE30 ....60 E1
Ratho Ct *FELL* NE10 ....88 A6
Ravenburn Gdns
  BW/LEM/TK/HW NE15 ....68 D5
Raven Ct *BDN/LAN/SAC* DH7 .....165 G2
Ravenna Rd *SWCK/CAS* SR5 ....105 F2
Ravensbourne Av *BOL* NE36 ....91 H4
Ravenscar Cl *WICK/BNPF* NE16 ....84 C7
Ravenscourt Pl *GATE* * NE8 ....10 C6
Ravenscourt Rd *SWCK/CAS* SR5 ....105 G3
Ravensdale Gv *BLYTH* NE24 ....30 C7
Ravens Hill Dr *ASHGTN* NE63 ....23 C7
Ravenshill Rd
  WD/WHPE/BLK NE5 ....68 B2
Ravenside Rd *CON/LDGT* DH8 .....122 D4
Ravenside Ter *CON/LDGT* DH8 ....122 C6
Ravenstone *WASHN* NE37 ....102 D6
Ravenswood Cl *LGB/KIL* NE12 .....58 A2
Ravenswood Gdns
  LWF/SPW/WRK NE9 ....101 F2
Ravenswood Rd
  BYK/HTN/WLK NE6 ....71 J2
  SWCK/CAS SR5 ....105 G2
Ravenswood Sq
  SWCK/CAS SR5 ....105 F2

Ravensworh St
 MLFD/PNYW SR4 ....14 A4
Ravensworth
 ASHBK/HED/RY SR2 ....134 D1
Ravensworth Av HLS DH4 ....131 H6
 LWF/SPW/WRK NE9 ....101 J3
Ravensworth Cl
 WLSD/HOW NE28 ....73 H1
Ravensworth Ct GOS/KPK * NE3...55 H3
 RDHAMSE DH6 ....160 E2
Ravensworth Rd
 CLS/BIR/GTL DH3 ....115 H1
 DUN/TMV NE11 ....9 J6
Ravensworth St
 WLSD/HOW NE28 ....73 H1
Ravensworth Ter DHAM DH1 .....16 F3
 DUN/TMV NE11 ....9 J7
 JRW NE32 ....89 K1
 SSH NE33 ....75 G4
Rawdon Rd SWCK/CAS SR5 ....105 J2
Rawling Ct GATE NE8 ....10 C7
Rawiston Wy
 WD/WHPE/BLK NE5 ....55 C7
Rawmarsh Rd SWCK/CAS SR5 ...105 G2
Raydale SWCK/CAS SR5 ....105 J2
Raydale Av WASHN NE37 ....102 D5
Raylees Gdns DUN/TMV NE11 .....86 A5
Rayleigh Dr DIN/WO NE13 ....46 B2
Rayleigh Gv GATE NE8 ....10 D9
Raynes Cl MPTH NE61 ....20 B6
Raynham Cl CRAM NE23 ....38 A5
Raynham Ct SSH NE33 ....3 H9
Rayn Ter RDHAMSE DH6 ....182 D2
Readhead Av SSH NE33 ....75 J2
Readhead Dr
 BYK/HTN/WLK NE6 ....72 B7
Readhead Rd HAR/WTLS NE34 ....75 H4
Reading Rd HAR/WTLS NE34 ....75 H4
 SWCK/CAS SR5 ....105 G2
Reading Sq SWCK/CAS SR5 ....105 G2
Rea Pl GOS/KPK NE3 ....56 A5
Reasby Gdns RYTON NE40 ....66 D6
Reavley Av BDLGTN NE22 ....30 A3
Reay Crs BOLCOL NE35 ....91 F4
Reay Gdns WD/WHPE/BLK NE5 ...68 E1
Reay St FELL NE10 ....13 L3
Rectory Bank BOL NE36 ....90 D5
Rectory Ct WICK/BNPF NE16 ....85 F5
Rectory Dene MPTH NE61 ....20 D6
Rectory Gn BOL NE36 ....90 D5
Rectory Gv GOS/KPK NE3 ....56 D5
Rectory La BLAY NE21 ....83 K3
 WICK/BNPF NE16 ....85 F6
Rectory Pk MPTH NE61 ....20 D6
Rectory Pl GATE NE8 ....10 D5
Rectory Rd FELL NE10 ....12 B9
 GATE NE8 ....10 D6
 GOS/KPK NE3 ....56 D6
 HLH DH5 ....147 K5
Rectory Rd East FELL NE10 ....87 K5
Red Admiral Ct DUN/TMV NE11 ...86 B5
Red Barnes CNUT NE1 ....6 B6
Red Berry Wy HAR/WTLS NE34 ....75 F7
Redburn Ct HLS DH4 ....132 A7
Redburn Rd
 WD/WHPE/BLK NE5 ....54 D6
Redby Cl CLDN/WHIT/ROK SR6 ..106 D3
Redcar Rd BYK/HTN/WLK NE6 .....71 K2
 SWCK/CAS SR5 ....105 J3
 WLSD/HOW NE28 ....59 J7
Redcar Sq SWCK/CAS SR5 ....105 J3
Redcliffe Wy
 WD/WHPE/BLK NE5 ....55 F7
Redditch Sq SWCK/CAS SR5 ....105 H2
Rede Av HEBB NE31 ....73 F5
Redemarsh FELL NE10 ....88 B5
Redesdale Av BLAY NE21 ....83 H4
 GOS/KPK NE3 ....56 A5
Redesdale Cl LGB/KIL NE12 ....57 J2
Redesdale Gdns DUN/TMV NE11...9 H9
Redesdale Gv NSHW NE29 ....60 A4
Redesdale Pl BLYTH NE24 ....30 D7
Redesdale Rd CLSW/PEL DH2 ....129 C6
 NSHW NE29 ....60 A4
 SWCK/CAS SR5 ....105 G2
Rede St DUN/TMV NE11 ....86 C7
 JRW NE32 ....73 J6
Redewater Gdns
 WICK/BNPF NE16 ....84 E6
Redewater Rd ELS/FEN NE4 ....69 J3
Redwood Cl
 WD/WHPE/BLK NE5 ....68 E2
Red Firs BDN/LAN/SAC DH7 ......167 G6
Redford Pl LGB/KIL NE12 ....47 J4
Red Hall Dr LGB/HTN NE7 ....57 K7
Redheugh Bridge Rd
 ELS/FEN NE4 ....10 A1
Redheugh Ct GATE NE8 ....9 M7
Redheugh Rd MONK NE25 ....49 K4
Redhill CLDN/WHIT/ROK SR6 ....92 E4
Redhill Dr WICK/BNPF NE16 ....98 C1
Redhill Rd SWCK/CAS SR5 ....105 H2
Redhills La DHAM DH1 ....156 B7
Red Hills Ter DHAM DH1 ....156 B7
Redhills Wy HLH DH5 ....147 K6
Redhouse Cl
 BDN/LAN/SAC DH7 ....143 J6
Red House Dr MONK NE25 ....50 A3
Red House Farm BDLGTN NE22 ...28 C6
Red House Gdns
 BDLGTN
 (off Netherton La) NE22 ....28 D6
Red House Rd HEBB NE31 ....73 H5
Redland Av GOS/KPK NE3 ....55 H4
Red Lion La WASHN NE37 ....102 A3
Redmayne Ct FELL NE10 ....12 B7
Redmires Cl CLSW/PEL DH2 ....114 C3
Redmond Rd SWCK/CAS SR5 ......105 J2
Redmond Sq SWCK/CAS SR5 ......105 J2
Rednam Pl WD/WHPE/BLK NE5 ...69 G1
Red Row BDLGTN NE22 ....29 J3
Redruth Gdns
 LWF/SPW/WRK NE9 ....101 F3
Redruth Sq SWCK/CAS SR5 ....105 H3
Redshank Cl WASHS NE38 ....116 B4
Redshank Dr BLYTH NE24 ....35 G3

Redstart Ct
 ROWG
 (off South Sherburn) NE39 ....97 K4
Red Wk LGB/HTN NE7 ....71 G1
Redwell Ct HAR/WTLS NE34 ....76 C4
 PRUD NE42 ....80 D2
Redwell La HAR/WTLS NE34 ....76 D4
Redwell Rd PRUD NE42 ....80 E2
Redwing Cl WASHS NE38 ....116 B3
Redwood BDN/LAN/SAC DH7 .....165 G3
 BDN/LAN/SAC DH7 ....167 G6
Redwood Cl HLH DH5 ....147 J5
 LGB/KIL NE12 ....47 J5
Redwood Ct CON/LDGT DH8 ......122 E3
 LGB/KIL NE12 ....47 J4
Reed Av LGB/KIL NE12 ....47 J4
Reedham Ct
 WD/WHPE/BLK NE5 ....55 F6
Reedling Ct SWCK/CAS SR5 ....105 J4
Reedside RYTON NE40 ....67 F6
Reedsmouth Pl
 WD/WHPE/BLK NE5 ....69 F3
Reed St SSH NE33 ....75 F3
 TYNE/NSHE NE30 ....61 F4
Reedswood Crs CRAM NE23 ....38 E3
Reestones Pl GOS/KPK NE3 ....55 H5
Reeth Rd SWCK/CAS SR5 ....105 H3
Reeth Sq SWCK/CAS SR5 ....105 H3
Reeth Wy
 BW/LEM/TK/HW NE15 ....66 E2
Reform Pl
 DHAM (off North Rd) DH1 ....16 C3
Regal Rd MLFD/PNYW SR4 ....106 A6
Regency Ct
 JES (off Jesmond Rd) NE2 ....71 F3
 NSHW (off Ritson Cl) NE29 ....60 C3
 SEA/MUR SR7 ....150 E1
Regency Dr SUNDSW SR3 ....120 B6
 WICK/BNPF NE16 ....84 D6
Regency Gdns NSHW NE29 ....60 C4
Regent Av GOS/KPK NE3 ....56 B5
Regent Ct GATE NE8 ....11 G3
 SSH NE33 ....75 G2
Regent Dr WICK/BNPF NE16 ....98 D1
Regent Farm Rd GOS/KPK NE3 ....56 A4
Regent Rd ASHBK/HED/RY SR2 ...135 C2
 GOS/KPK NE3 ....56 C5
 JRW NE32 ....74 A5
 WLSD/HOW NE28 ....58 C7
Regents Ct WLSD/HOW NE28.......58 A6
Regents Dr PRUD NE42 ....64 E7
 TYNE/NSHE NE30 ....61 G2
Regents Pk WLSD/HOW NE28 ......58 A7
Regent St BLYTH NE24 ....31 C5
 HLH DH5 ....147 K3
 STLY/ANP DH9 ....125 H2
Regent Ter
 ASHBK/HED/RY SR2 ....121 F4
 GATE NE8 ....10 F3
 NSHW NE29 ....60 C3
Reginald St BOLCOL NE35 ....90 D4
 GATE NE8 ....11 M6
 MLFD/PNYW SR4 ....105 K6
Regina Sq SWCK/CAS SR5 ....105 H2
Reid Av WLSD/HOW NE28 ....58 D7
Reid Park Cl JES NE2 ....71 F1
Reid Park Rd JES NE2 ....71 F1
Reid's La CRAM NE23 ....39 F7
Reid St MPTH NE61 ....20 E5
Reigate Sq CRAM NE23 ....38 C1
Rekendyke La SSH NE33 ....75 F2
Relley Cl BDN/LAN/SAC DH7 ......167 G1
Relly Pth DHAM DH1 ....168 B2
Relton Av BYK/HTN/WLK NE6 ....7 K8
Relton Cl HLS DH4 ....146 D1
Relton Ter CLS/BIR/GTL DH3 ....129 J5
 MONK NE25 ....50 C4
Rembrandt Av HAR/WTLS NE34 ...91 G2
Remscheid Wy ASHGTN NE63 ....23 J4
Remus Av
 BW/LEM/TK/HW NE15 ....65 K1
Remus Cl DIN/WO NE13 ....46 B4
Rendel St DUN/TMV NE11 ....9 G5
Rendle Rd BYK/HTN/WLK NE6 .....72 D7
Renforth St DUN/TMV NE11 ....9 H7
Renfrew Cl NSHW NE29 ....60 A2
Renfrew Rd SWCK/CAS SR5 ....105 H2
Rennie Rd SWCK/CAS SR5 ....105 H2
Rennie Sq SWCK/CAS SR5 ....105 H2
Rennington FELL NE10 ....88 B7
Rennington Av
 TYNE/NSHE NE30 ....61 G1
Rennington Cl MPTH NE61 ....27 F1
Rennington Pl
 WD/WHPE/BLK NE5 ....69 H1
Renny's La DHAM DH1 ....17 M2
Renny St DHAM DH1 ....17 G2
Renoir Gdns HAR/WTLS NE34 ......91 H2
Renwick Av GOS/KPK NE3 ....55 J4
Renwick Rd BLYTH NE24 ....31 F7
Renwick St BYK/HTN/WLK NE6 .....6 F4
Resida Cl BW/LEM/TK/HW NE15 ...68 A3
Retford Rd SWCK/CAS SR5 ....105 H2
Retford Sq SWCK/CAS SR5 ....105 H2
The Retreat ASHBK/HED/RY SR2 .135 F4
Revell Ter WD/WHPE/BLK NE5 .....69 H2
Revelstoke Rd SWCK/CAS SR5 ...105 F2
Revesby St SSH NE33 ....75 G5
Reynolds Av HAR/WTLS NE34 ......91 H1
 LGB/KIL NE12 ....47 H7
 WASHS NE38 ....117 G2
Reynolds Ct STLY/ANP DH9 ....126 D1
Reynolds Rd PLEE/EAS SR8.........175 J4
Rheims Ct MLFD/PNYW SR4 ....105 H6
Rheydt Av WLSD/HOW NE28 ....72 B1
Rhodesia Rd SWCK/CAS SR5 ......105 H2
Rhodes St BYK/HTN/WLK NE6 .....72 C5
Rhondda Rd SWCK/CAS SR5 ......105 G2
Rhuddlan Ct
 WD/WHPE/BLK NE5 ....55 F6
Rhyl Sq SWCK/CAS SR5 ....105 J2
Ribbledale Gdns LGB/HTN NE7 ....57 H7
Ribble Rd SWCK/CAS SR5 ....105 H2
Ribblesdale HLS DH4 ....117 K7
Ribblesdale Av BLYTH NE24 ....30 C6
Richard Av MLFD/PNYW SR4 ......120 A2
Richard Browell Rd
 BW/LEM/TK/HW NE15 ....67 F2

Richard Hollon Ct
 MPTH (off New Market) NE61 ....20 D5
Richardson Av HAR/WTLS NE34 ...74 D7
Richardson Rd JES NE2 ....4 F2
Richardson St
 BYK/HTN/WLK NE6 ....71 J3
 WLSD/HOW NE28 ....72 E1
Richardson Ter
 ASHBK/HED/RY SR2 ....135 G1
Richard St BLYTH NE24 ....31 G7
 HLH DH5 ....147 K5
Richmond Av FELL NE10 ....88 E3
 WASHS NE38 ....103 F7
Richmond Cl BDLGTN NE22 ....28 E4
Richmond Ct
 LWF/SPW/WRK
 (off Kells La) NE9 ....101 F1
Richmond Gdns
 WLSD/HOW NE28 ....59 G7
Richmond Gv NSHW NE29 ....60 C5
Richmond Ms JES NE2 ....71 F4
Richmond Pk WLSD/HOW NE28 ...58 A7
Richmond Pl
 CLS/BIR/GTL
 (off Durham Rd) DH3 ....115 J4
Richmond Rd DHAM DH1 ....156 E2
 HAR/WTLS NE34 ....75 C5
Richmond St SWCK/CAS SR5 ....14 D2
Richmond Ter FELL NE10 ....12 D8
 GATE NE8 ....10 F6
 RDHAMSE DH6 ....160 D6
 WBAY NE26 ....50 D2
Richmond Wy CRAM NE23 ....38 B5
 PONT/DH NE20 ....42 C4
Rickaby St SUND SR1 ....15 J2
Rickgarth FELL NE10 ....88 B7
Rickleton Av CLS/BIR/GTL DH3 ...129 K2
Rickleton Wy WASHS NE38..........116 B3
Riddell Av
 BW/LEM/TK/HW NE15 ....69 G6
Ridding Ct BDN/LAN/SAC DH7 ...165 G3
Ridding Rd BDN/LAN/SAC DH7 ...165 G2
Riddings Rd SWCK/CAS SR5 ....105 H2
Riddings Sq SWCK/CAS SR5 ....105 H2
Ridgely Dr PONT/DH NE20 ....43 J3
Ridge Ter BDLGTN NE22 ....28 E5
The Ridge RYTON NE40 ....66 E7
Ridge Wy MONK NE25 ....40 B7
Ridgeway ASHBK/HED/RY SR2 ...134 C1
 ASHGTN NE63 ....24 C3
 ELS/FEN NE4 ....69 J3
 FELL NE10 ....13 M9
 STKFD/GP NE62 ....23 G5
Ridgeway Crs SUNDSW SR3 ....120 B3
The Ridge Wy GOS/KPK NE3 ....55 K6
The Ridgeway HAR/WTLS NE34 ....91 K1
Ridgewood Crs GOS/KPK NE3 ......57 F5
Ridgewood Gdns GOS/KPK NE3 ...56 E5
Ridgewood Vls GOS/KPK NE3 ......56 E5
Ridley Av ASHBK/HED/RY SR2 ....121 F7
 BLYTH NE24 ....31 H7
 WLSD/HOW NE28 ....59 J6
 GOS/KPK NE3 ....56 D5
Ridley Gdns WICK/BNPF NE16 .....84 E3
Ridley Gv HAR/WTLS NE34 ....76 A4
Ridley Mill Rd PSHWF NE43 ....79 F7
Ridley Pl CNUT NE1 ....5 K4
Ridley St BLYTH NE24 ....31 H6
 GATE NE8 ....10 D7
 STLY/ANP DH9 ....112 D7
 SWCK/CAS SR5 ....106 B3
Ridley Ter ASHBK/HED/RY SR2 ....15 J8
 CON/LDGT DH8 ....123 K3
 FELL NE10 ....12 F7
Ridsdale Av WD/WHPE/BLK NE5 ...68 B7
Ridsdale Cl MONK NE25 ....39 K5
 WLSD/HOW NE28 ....58 E6
Rievaulx WASHS NE38 ....116 E3
Riga Sq SWCK/CAS SR5 ....105 G2
The Riggs HLH DH5 ....132 D7
Rignall WASHS NE38 ....117 J1
Riley St JRW NE32 ....73 J4
Ringlet Cl DUN/TMV NE11 ....9 L9
Ringmore Ct
 ASHBK/HED/RY SR2 ....120 C4
Ringway STKFD/GP NE62 ....23 F5
 SWCK/CAS SR5 ....104 E5
Ringwood Dr CRAM NE23 ....38 C1
Ringwood Gn LGB/KIL NE12 ....57 J3
Ringwood Rd SWCK/CAS SR5 .....105 H2
Ringwood Sq SWCK/CAS SR5 .....105 H2
Rink St BLYTH NE24 ....31 H6
Ripley Av NSHW NE29 ....60 C6
Ripley Cl BDLGTN NE22 ....28 D4
Ripley Dr CRAM NE23 ....38 A5
Ripley Ter BYK/HTN/WLK NE6 ....7 M4
Ripon Cl CRAM NE23 ....38 A5
Ripon Ct BDN/LAN/SAC DH7 ......143 G5
Ripon Gdns JES NE2 ....71 G3
 WLSD/HOW NE28 ....59 G7
Ripon Rd DHAM DH1 ....156 E1
Ripon St CLDN/WHIT/ROK SR6 ...106 E4
 GATE NE8 ....10 F6
Ripon Ter SEA/MUR SR7 ....149 H5
The Rise BLAY NE21 ....67 J7
 CON/LDGT DH8 ....137 F2
 GATE (off Duncan St) NE8 ....11 L6
 GOS/KPK NE3 ....56 C5
 PONT/DH NE20 ....42 D7
 WBAY NE26 ....41 G4
Rishton Sq SWCK/CAS SR5 ....105 G2
Ritson Av BDN/LAN/SAC DH7 .....155 F6
Ritson Cl NSHW NE29 ....60 C3
Ritson's Rd CON/LDGT DH8 ....122 D2
Ritson St CLDN/WHIT/ROK SR6 ..106 E1
 CON/LDGT DH8 ....122 D3
 STLY/ANP DH9 ....126 C1
River Bank STKFD/GP NE62 ....23 J5

River Bank East STKFD/GP NE62...23 J6
Riverbank Rd SWCK/CAS SR5 .....105 H3
Riverdale SWCK/CAS SR5 ....105 F5
River Dr SSH NE33 ....3 G5
River La RYTON NE40 ....66 E5
Rivermead Wy WASHS NE38 ....117 G5
Riversdale CHPW NE17 ....95 H7
Riversdale Av STKFD/GP NE62 .....23 G6
Riversdale Rd
 GATE (off Askew Rd) NE8 ....10 B5
Riversdale Ter
 ASHBK/HED/RY SR2 ....14 A8
 STKFD/GP* NE62 ....23 G6
Riverside Wy
 BW/LEM/TK/HW NE15 ....67 K5
Riverside CON/LDGT DH8 ....122 C1
 PONT/DH NE20 ....43 G3
Riverside Av STKFD/GP NE62 ....22 D6
Riverside Ct DUN/TMV NE11 ....9 J5
Riverside Pk MLFD/PNYW SR4....105 F6
Riverside Rd SWCK/CAS SR5 ......105 J3
Riverside Wy BLAY NE21 ....84 C1
 ROWG NE39 ....97 F5
 WICK/BNPF NE16 ....84 C1
River Vw BLAY NE21 ....83 K2
 CHPW NE17 ....95 H7
 ELS/FEN NE4 ....69 H7
 TYNE/NSHE NE30 ....61 G4
River View Cl BDLGTN NE22 ....29 K5
Roachburn Rd
 WD/WHPE/BLK NE5 ....68 C1
Robertson Rd SWCK/CAS SR5 ....105 F2
Robertson Sq SWCK/CAS SR5 ....105 F2
Robert Sq SEA/MUR SR7 ....151 F2
Roberts St
 BW/LEM/TK/HW NE15 ....68 C7
Roberts Ter JRW NE32 ....73 K6
Robert St MLFD/PNYW SR4 ....106 A6
 SEA/MUR SR7 ....151 F2
 SSH NE33 ....75 H2
 SUNDSW SR3 ....120 B7
Robert Westall Wy NSHW NE29 .....2 C7
Robin Cl HLH DH5 ....147 F5
Robin Gv SWCK/CAS SR5 ....105 G4
Robin La HLH DH5 ....146 E6
Robinson Gdns
 CLDN/WHIT/ROK * SR6 ....93 F3
 WLSD/HOW NE28 ....59 J7
Robinson St SSH * NE33 ....3 J9
Robinson Ter
 ASHBK/HED/RY SR2 ....15 J9
Robsheugh Pl
 WD/WHPE/BLK NE5 ....69 G3
Robson Av PLEE/EAS SR8 ....174 E3
Robson Crs RDHAMSE DH6 ....180 A1
Robson Pl ASHBK/HED/RY SR2 ...135 C1
Robson St BYK/HTN/WLK NE6 ....6 E4
 CON/LDGT* DH8 ....123 C4
 LWF/SPW/WRK NE9 ....87 F7
Rochdale Rd SWCK/CAS SR5 ......105 H2
Rochdale St HLH DH5 ....147 K6
 WLSD/HOW NE28 ....72 C2
Rochdale Wy SWCK/CAS SR5 .....105 H2
Roche Ct WASHS NE38 ....116 E2
Rochester Cl ASHGTN NE63 ....24 C3
Rochester Gdns DUN/TMV NE11 ...9 J8
Rochester Rd DHAM DH1 ....156 E2
Rochester St
 BYK/HTN/WLK NE6 ....72 C6
Rochford Gv CRAM NE23 ....38 A6
Rochford Rd SWCK/CAS SR5 ......105 G2
Rockcliffe SSH NE33 ....75 K2
Rockcliffe Gdns
 BW/LEM/TK/HW NE15 ....68 D4
Rockcliffe St WBAY NE26 ....51 G4
Rockcliffe Wy
 LWF/SPW/WRK NE9 ....101 J3
Rocket Wy LGB/KIL NE12 ....58 B2
Rock Gv LWF/SPW/WRK NE9 ....87 F7
Rockhope WASHS NE38 ....116 B6
Rockingham Rd
 SWCK/CAS SR5 ....105 G2
Rockingham Sq
 SWCK/CAS SR5 ....105 G2
Rock Lodge Rd
 CLDN/WHIT/ROK SR6 ....106 E2
Rockmore Rd BLAY NE21 ....84 A3
Rock Ter BDN/LAN/SAC DH7 ......166 E2
 JES NE2 ....6 A4
Rockville CLDN/WHIT/ROK SR6 ...106 E1
Rockwood Hill Est RYTON NE40 ...82 A4
Rockwood Hill Rd RYTON NE40....82 A4
Rodin Av HAR/WTLS NE34 ....91 H2
Rodney Cl
 ASHBK/HED/RY * SR2 ....134 C1
 TYNE/NSHE NE30 ....61 H3
Rodney St BYK/HTN/WLK NE6 ....6 F5
Rodney Wy WBAY NE26 ....50 B2
Rodridge Pk WNGT TS28 ....184 A5
Rodsley Av GATE NE8 ....10 F7
Rodwell St TRIM TS29 ....182 E6
Roeburn Av SWCK/CAS SR5 ....55 K7
Roedean Rd SWCK/CAS SR5 ......105 J2
Roehedge FELL NE10 ....88 D6
Rogerley Ter STLY/ANP DH9 ....125 G2
Rogers Cl PLEE/EAS SR8 ....175 H4
Rogerson Ter
 WD/WHPE/BLK NE5 ....54 C7
Roger St BYK/HTN/WLK NE6 ....6 E4
Rogues La ROWG NE39 ....82 C6
Rokeby Av
 BW/LEM/TK/HW NE15 ....68 B5
Rokeby Dr GOS/KPK NE3 ....55 K6
Rokeby Sq DHAM DH1 ....168 B3
Rokeby St
 BW/LEM/TK/HW NE15 ....68 B5
 MLFD/PNYW SR4 ....14 A3
Rokeby Ter BYK/HTN/WLK NE6 ....71 J2
Rokeby Vw
 LWF/SPW/WRK NE9 ....101 G3
Roker Av CLDN/WHIT/ROK SR6 ...14 F1
 MONK NE25 ....50 C6
Roker Baths Rd
 CLDN/WHIT/ROK SR6 ....106 E3
Rokerby Av WICK/BNPF NE16 ....85 G6

Roker Park Rd
 CLDN/WHIT/ROK SR6 ....106 E3
Roker Park Ter
 CLDN/WHIT/ROK SR6 ....107 F3
Roland Burn Wy ROWG NE39 ....97 F5
Roland Rd WLSD/HOW NE28 ....73 G1
Rollesby Ct WD/WHPE/BLK NE5 ...55 F6
Rolling Mill Rd JRW NE32 ....73 J3
Romaldskirk Cl
 MLFD/PNYW SR4 ....119 F1
Roman Av BYK/HTN/WLK NE6 ....7 L3
 CLS/BIR/GTL DH3 ....129 K4
Roman Forum
 WICK/BNPF
 (off Metrocentre) NE16 ....8 B5
Roman Rd SSH NE33 ....3 J5
The Roman Wy
 WD/WHPE/BLK NE5 ....68 B2
Romany Dr CON/LDGT DH8 ....122 E5
Romford Cl CRAM NE23 ....38 A5
Romford Pl LWF/SPW/WRK NE9 ...11 K9
Romford St MLFD/PNYW SR4 ......105 K7
Romilly St SSH NE33 ....3 J8
Romley Gv FELL NE10 ....89 F5
Romney Av
 ASHBK/HED/RY SR2 ....120 E3
 HAR/WTLS NE34 ....91 H1
 WASHS NE38 ....117 G2
Romney Cl HLS DH4 ....132 A2
Romney Dr DHAM DH1 ....158 A4
Romney Gdns
 LWF/SPW/WRK NE9 ....11 M9
Romsey Cl CRAM NE23 ....38 C1
Romsey Dr BOLCOL NE35 ....90 C4
Romsey Gv
 BW/LEM/TK/HW NE15 ....68 A3
Ronald Dr
 BW/LEM/TK/HW NE15 ....68 C1
Ronald Gdns HEBB NE31 ....73 F7
Ronaldsay Cl
 ASHBK/HED/RY SR2 ....120 E6
Ronald Sq
 CLDN/WHIT/ROK SR6 ....106 D2
Rookery Cl BLYTH NE24 ....30 D7
Rookery La WICK/BNPF NE16 ....98 C1
The Rookery WICK/BNPF * NE16....97 K7
Rookswood MPTH NE61 ....20 E7
Rookswood Gdns ROWG NE39 .....97 F7
Rookwood Dr DIN/WO NE13 ....46 C1
Rookwood Rd
 WD/WHPE/BLK NE5 ....68 C1
Roosevelt Rd DHAM DH1 ....17 K1
Ropery La CLS/BIR/GTL DH3........129 K5
 HEBB NE31 ....73 G1
 WLSD/HOW NE28 ....73 G1
Ropery Rd GATE NE8 ....9 L6
 MLFD/PNYW SR4 ....106 A5
The Ropery MLFD/PNYW NE6...........7 J9
Ropery Wk SEA/MUR SR7 ....150 E2
Rosalie Ter ASHBK/HED/RY SR2...15 H9
Rosalind Av BDLGTN NE22 ....29 G6
Rosalind St ASHGTN NE63 ....23 K1
Rosamond Pl BLYTH NE24 ....31 H7
Rosa St SSH NE33 ....3 K9
Rose Av HLS DH4 ....131 H6
 STLY/ANP DH9 ....126 B2
 WICK/BNPF NE16 ....85 F5
Rosebank Cl
 ASHBK/HED/RY SR2 ....120 E6
Rosebay Rd BDN/LAN/SAC DH7...167 K6
Roseberry Cres RDHAMSE DH6 ...172 B4
Roseberry Gra LGB/KIL NE12 ....58 C1
Roseberry St STLY/ANP DH9 ....113 H7
Roseberry Vls CLSW/PEL DH2 ....128 C2
Rosebery Av BLYTH NE24 ....31 F7
 GATE NE8 ....11 J7
 NSHW NE29 ....60 D7
 SSH NE33 ....75 J2
Rosebery Crs JES NE2 ....6 B1
Rosebery Pl JES NE2 ....6 C1
Rosebery St SWCK/CAS SR5 ....106 C4
Rosebery Ter CON/LDGT DH8 .....123 F5
Roseby Rd PLEE/EAS SR8 ....175 G3
Rose Ct BDN/LAN/SAC DH7 ....153 F7
 PLEE/EAS SR8 ....174 C2
Rose Crs BDN/LAN/SAC DH7 ......143 J5
 CLDN/WHIT/ROK SR6 ....93 F2
Rosedale BDLGTN NE22 ....28 E5
 WLSD/HOW NE28 ....58 B6
Rosedale Av
 CLDN/WHIT/ROK SR6 ....92 E6
 CON/LDGT DH8 ....122 D2
Rosedale Ct WD/WHPE/BLK NE5...68 B2
Rosedale Crs HLS DH4 ....131 K5
Rosedale Rd DHAM DH1 ....158 A5
 RYTON NE40 ....82 B1
Rosedale St HLH DH5 ....147 H7
 SUND SR1 ....14 E5
Rosedale Ter
 CLDN/WHIT/ROK SR6 ....106 E1
 JES NE2 ....6 A3
 PLEE/EAS SR8 ....175 C3
 TYNE/NSHE NE30 ....61 F4
Roseden Ct LGB/KIL NE12 ....57 J3
Rosedene Vls CRAM NE23 ....38 E2
Rose Gdns WLSD/HOW NE28 ....58 D6
Rosegill WASHN NE37 ....102 D7
Rosehill WLSD/HOW NE28 ....73 C1
Rosehill Rd WLSD/HOW NE28 ....73 H1
Rose Hill Wy
 WD/WHPE/BLK NE5 ....69 G3
Rose Lea BDN/LAN/SAC DH7 ......143 G7
Roselea
 CLDN/WHIT/ROK SR6 ....106 E1
Rosemary La PLEE/EAS SR8 ....162 C6
Rosemary Rd SWCK/CAS SR5 .....105 H2
Rosemary Ter BLYTH NE24 ....35 H1
Rosemount DHAM DH1 ....156 E1
 MLFD/PNYW SR4 ....118 C1
 MPTH NE61 ....20 E6
 WD/WHPE/BLK NE5 ....55 F5
Rosemount Av FELL NE10 ....13 M9
Rosemount Cl WASHN NE37 ....102 E3
Rosemount Ct BOL NE36 ....91 F5
Rosemount Wy LGB/HTN NE7 ......57 J5
 MONK NE25 ....50 A4
Roseneath Ct ASHGTN NE63 ....23 K2

Rose St GATE NE8 ......10 A4
  HEBB NE31 ......73 F6
  MLFD/PNYW SR4 ......14 B4
  TRIM TS29 ......182 C2
Rose St West HLS DH4 ......117 K6
Rose Ter WD/WHPE/BLK NE5 ......69 J2
Roseville St MLFD/PNYW SR4 ......14 A8
Rosewell Pl WICK/BNPF NE16 ......98 C1
Rosewood LGB/KIL NE12 ......48 B6
Rosewood Av GOS/KPK NE3 ......56 C4
Rosewood Crs
  BYK/HTN/WLK NE6 ......72 B2
  WBAY NE26 ......41 G4
Rosewood Gdns ASHBK/HED/RY SR2 ......55 K6
  LWF/SPW/WRK NE9 ......87 H6
Rosewood Sq MLFD/PNYW SR4 ......118 E4
Rosewood Ter WLSD/HOW NE28 ......73 J1
Rosewood Wk BDN/LAN/SAC
  (off Broom La) DH7 ......155 F7
Roseworth Av GOS/KPK NE3 ......56 C4
Roseworth Crs GOS/KPK NE3 ......56 C4
Roseworth Ter WICK/BNPF NE16 ......85 F5
Roslin Pk BDLGTN NE22 ......29 H5
  BDLGTN NE22 ......29 J5
Roslin Wy CRAM NE23 ......38 B5
Ross CLSW/PEL DH2 ......115 G4
Ross Av DUN/TMV NE11 ......9 C6
Rosse Cl WASHN NE37 ......102 C5
Rossendale Pl LGB/KIL NE12 ......57 F4
Ross Gv CRAM NE23 ......38 A1
Ross Lea HLS DH4 ......131 J3
Rosslyn Av ASHBK/HED/RY SR2 ......121 F1
  GOS/KPK NE3 ......55 J5
Rosslyn St MLFD/PNYW SR4 ......106 A7
Ross St SWCK/CAS SR5 ......106 C4
Ross Wy GOS/KPK NE3 ......55 K2
  WBAY NE26 ......50 C2
Rosyth Rd SWCK/CAS SR5 ......105 J2
Rosyth Sq SWCK/CAS SR5 ......105 J2
Rotary Pkwy ASHGTN NE63 ......23 J1
  NSHW NE29 ......60 C7
Rothay Pl WD/WHPE/BLK NE5 ......69 G1
Rothbury ASHBK/HED/RY SR2 ......134 D1
  FELL NE10 ......13 J5
  GOS/KPK NE3 ......56 B4
  JRW NE32 ......73 H7
  PLEE/EAS SR8 ......175 G2
Rothbury Cl CLSW/PEL DH2 ......129 G6
  LGB/KIL NE12 ......47 J3
  TRIM TS29 ......182 D7
Rothbury Gdns DUN/TMV NE11 ......86 A7
  WLSD/HOW NE28 ......59 H7
Rothbury Rd DHAM DH1 ......156 D2
  SWCK/CAS SR5 ......105 H2
Rothbury Ter BYK/HTN/WLK NE6 ......6 F1
  NSHW NE29 ......60 A3
Rotherfield Cl CRAM NE23 ......38 C1
Rotherfield Gdns
  LWF/SPW/WRK NE9 ......101 G3
Rotherfield Rd SWCK/CAS SR5 ......105 G2
Rotherfield Sq SWCK/CAS SR5 ......105 G2
Rotherham Rd HLH DH5 ......147 G2
Rotherham Rd SWCK/CAS SR5 ......105 J2
Rothlea Gdns STKFD/GP NE62 ......23 C5
Rothley WASHS NE38 ......117 H4
Rothley Av ASHGTN NE63 ......23 K3
  WD/WHPE/BLK NE5 ......69 G4
Rothley Cl GOS/KPK NE3 ......56 D5
  PONT/DH NE20 ......43 F2
Rothley Ct SWCK/CAS SR5 ......105 K1
Rothley Gdns TYNE/NSHE NE30 ......50 E7
Rothley Gv MONK NE25 ......39 K5
Rothley Wy WBAY NE26 ......50 C2
Rothsay CLSW/PEL DH2 ......115 F5
Rothwell Rd GOS/KPK NE3 ......56 C5
  SWCK/CAS SR5 ......105 G2
Roundhill Av WD/WHPE/BLK NE5 ......69 G1
Roundstone Cl LGB/HTN NE7 ......57 K6
The Roundway LGB/KIL NE12 ......57 H3
Rowan Av WASHS NE38 ......116 E5
Rowanberry Rd LGB/KIL NE12 ......57 H4
Rowan Cl BDLGTN NE22 ......29 F4
  MLFD/PNYW SR4 ......119 F1
Rowan Ct BDN/LAN/SAC DH7 ......165 F5
  BLYTH NE24 ......35 F1
Rowan Dr DHAM DH1 ......157 F1
  GOS/KPK NE3 ......55 J4
  HLH DH5 ......147 J4
  PONT/DH NE20 ......43 G2
Rowan Gv PRUD NE42 ......80 B2
Rowan Lea BDN/LAN/SAC DH7 ......167 G6
Rowan Tree Av DHAM DH1 ......157 H5
Rowantree Rd
  BYK/HTN/WLK NE6 ......72 C2
Rowanwood Gdns
  DUN/TMV NE11 ......86 A7
Rowell Cl SUNDSW SR3 ......134 C1
Rowes Ms BYK/HTN/WLK NE6 ......7 H9
Rowlandson Crs FELL NE10 ......12 D8
Rowlandson Ter FELL * NE10 ......12 D8
Rowland Sq SEA/MUR SR7 ......149 G5
Rowley Bank CON/LDGT DH8 ......136 E2
Rowley Cl BDN/LAN/SAC DH7 ......166 D3
Rowley Crs BDN/LAN/SAC DH7 ......165 G1
Rowley Dr BDN/LAN/SAC DH7 ......167 G2
Rowley Link
  BDN/LAN/SAC DH7 ......165 G1
Rowley St BLYTH NE24 ......31 G7
Rowntree Wy NSHW NE29 ......2 C6
Rowsley Rd JRW NE32 ......74 A6
Roxburgh Cl BLAY NE21 ......83 J4
Roxburgh Pl BYK/HTN/WLK NE6 ......6 F2
Roxburgh St
  CLDN/WHIT/ROK SR6 ......106 D3
Roxburgh Ter WBAY NE26 ......50 E4
Roxby Gdns NSHW NE29 ......60 C5
Roxby Wynd WNGT TS28 ......183 K2
Royal Crs ELS/FEN NE4 ......69 J3
Royal Rd STLY/ANP DH9 ......112 C7
The Royalty ASHBK/HED/RY SR2 ......14 B6

Roydon Av
  ASHBK/HED/RY SR2 ......120 E3
Royle St ASHBK/HED/RY SR2 ......121 F4
Royston Ter BYK/HTN/WLK NE6 ......72 C7
Ruabon Cl CRAM NE23 ......38 B5
Rubens Av HAR/WTLS NE34 ......91 H1
Ruby St HLS DH4 ......132 B5
Rudby Cl GOS/KPK NE3 ......56 D2
Rudchester Pl
  WD/WHPE/BLK NE5 ......69 G3
Ruddock Sq BYK/HTN/WLK NE6 ......7 G7
Rudyard Av
  ASHBK/HED/RY SR2 ......120 E3
Rudyerd Ct NSHW NE29 ......2 E5
Rudyerd St NSHW NE29 ......2 D2
Rugby Gdns
  LWF/SPW/WRK NE9 ......101 K2
Ruislip Pl CRAM NE23 ......38 A5
Ruislip Rd MLFD/PNYW SR4 ......118 E1
Runcie Rd RDHAMSE DH6 ......180 A2
Runcorn ASHBK/HED/RY SR2 ......120 C7
Runcorn Rd SWCK/CAS SR5 ......105 G2
Runhead Est RYTON NE40 ......67 F6
Runnymede
  ASHBK/HED/RY SR2 ......120 D7
Runnymede Gdns CHPW NE17 ......95 H6
Runnymede Rd PONT/DH NE20 ......42 D5
  SWCK/CAS SR5 ......105 H2
  WICK/BNPF NE16 ......84 E6
Runnymede Wy GOS/KPK NE3 ......55 J6
  SWCK/CAS SR5 ......105 H2
Runswick Av LGB/KIL NE12 ......57 F4
Runswick Cl SUNDSW SR3 ......120 C7
Rupert Sq SWCK/CAS SR5 ......105 J2
Rupert St CLDN/WHIT/ROK SR6 ......93 F1
Rushall Pl LGB/KIL NE12 ......57 H4
Rushey Gill BDN/LAN/SAC DH7 ......167 F6
Rushford ASHBK/HED/RY SR2 ......120 D7
Rushie Av
  BW/LEM/TK/HW NE15 ......69 G6
Rushley Crs BLAY NE21 ......84 A1
Rushsyde Cl WICK/BNPF NE16 ......84 C7
Rushton Av
  ASHBK/HED/RY SR2 ......120 E3
Rushyrig WASHN NE37 ......102 C7
Ruskin Av ASHGTN NE63 ......24 B2
  CLSW/PEL DH2 ......128 E4
  DUN/TMV NE11 ......9 H6
  DUN DH5 ......160 B1
  LGB/KIL NE12 ......57 J1
Ruskin Cl PRUD NE42 ......80 B3
  STLY/ANP DH9 ......127 F1
Ruskin Crs HAR/WTLS NE34 ......91 F1
  RDHAMSE DH6 ......172 B6
Ruskin Dr BOLCOL NE35 ......90 E4
  LGB/HTN NE7 ......72 A1
Ruskin Rd CLS/BIR/GTL DH3 ......115 J2
  LWF/SPW/WRK NE9 ......87 H5
  WICK/BNPF NE16 ......84 E4
Russel Crs TRIM TS29 ......183 G6
Russell Av HAR/WTLS NE34 ......76 A5
Russell Cl CON/LDGT DH8 ......123 C4
Russell Ct GATE NE8 ......10 A5
Russell Sq BDN/LAN/SAC DH7 ......165 F4
  JRW NE32 ......74 A4
  NSHW NE29 ......2 D2
  SSH NE33 ......3 H7
  SUND SR1 ......15 G3
Russell Ter BDLGTN NE22 ......29 F6
  JES NE2 ......6 A5
Russell Wy WICK/BNPF
  (off Metrocentre) NE16 ......8 B4
Ruswarp Dr SUNDSW SR3 ......134 B1
Rutherford Av SEA/MUR SR7 ......135 F7
Rutherford Pl STKFD/GP NE62 ......22 E6
Rutherford Pl MPTH NE61 ......20 C6
Rutherford Rd SWCK/CAS SR5 ......105 F2
  WASHN NE37 ......103 G4
Rutherford Sq SWCK/CAS SR5 ......105 F2
Rutherford St BLYTH NE24 ......35 G1
  CNUT NE1 ......5 H7
  GATE NE8 ......59 K7
Rutherglen Rd SWCK/CAS SR5 ......105 J2
Rutland Av BYK/HTN/WLK NE6 ......72 C4
  SUNDSW SR3 ......119 K7
Rutland Pl CON/LDGT DH8 ......137 G1
  NSHW NE29 ......60 C4
  WASHN NE37 ......103 F3
Rutland Rd CON/LDGT DH8 ......137 G1
  HEBB NE31 ......89 H1
  WLSD/HOW NE28 ......58 D7
Rutland Sq CLS/BIR/GTL DH3 ......115 H1
Rutland St ASHGTN * NE63 ......23 J2
  HAR/WTLS* NE34 ......75 F5
  MLFD/PNYW SR4 ......105 K6
  MONK NE25 ......40 A5
Ryal Cl BLYTH NE24 ......30 D7
Ryal Ter BYK/HTN/WLK NE6 ......72 B6
Rydal FELL NE10 ......13 J7
Rydal Av HLH DH5 ......160 B1
  STLY/ANP DH9 ......126 B3
  TYNE/NSHE NE30 ......50 E7
Rydal Cl BDN/LAN/SAC DH7 ......143 G5
  BOL NE36 ......91 G4
  LGB/KIL NE12 ......48 B6
Rydal Crs BLAY NE21 ......83 K4
  PLEE/EAS SR8 ......175 F4
Rydale Ct TRIM TS29 ......183 F6
Rydal Gdns HAR/WTLS NE34 ......75 J5
Rydal Ms WLSD/HOW NE28 ......123 K3
Rydal Mt NWBGN NE64 ......24 E7
  PLEE/EAS SR8 ......162 E5
  SWCK/CAS SR5 ......104 E5
Rydal Rd BW/LEM/TK/HW NE15 ......68 B3
  CLSW/PEL DH2 ......129 H6
  GOS/KPK NE3 ......56 D5
Rydal St GATE NE8 ......10 E6
Ryde Pl CRAM NE23 ......38 C1
Ryde Ter DUN/TMV NE11 ......9 J5
Rye Cl BW/LEM/TK/HW NE15 ......67 G2
Ryedale CLDN/WHIT/ROK SR6 ......93 F5
  DHAM DH1 ......158 A6
  WLSD/HOW NE28 ......58 B5
Ryedale Cl ASHGTN NE63 ......23 H3
Rye HI ELS/FEN NE4 ......4 E8

Ryehill Vw HLH DH5 ......147 F4
Ryelands Wy DHAM DH1 ......156 D1
Ryemount Rd
  ASHBK/HED/RY SR2 ......120 D7
Rye View Rd
  ASHBK/HED/RY SR2 ......121 F6
Ryhope Gdns
  WD/WHPE/BLK NE5 ......69 G3
Ryhope Rd ASHBK/HED/RY SR2 ......14 F9
Ryhope St ASHBK/HED/RY SR2 ......120 E7
Rymers Cl PLEE/EAS SR8 ......162 B6
Ryton Ct SSH NE33 ......75 H2
Ryton Crs SEA/MUR SR7 ......150 B1
  STLY/ANP* DH9 ......112 D6
Ryton Hall Dr RYTON NE40 ......66 E5
Ryton Ter BYK/HTN/WLK NE6 ......72 B7

S

Sackville Rd BYK/HTN/WLK NE6 ......71 J2
  SUNDSW SR3 ......119 J3
Sacriston Av SUNDSW SR3 ......119 K3
Sacriston La
  BDN/LAN/SAC DH7 ......155 F1
Saddleback WASHN NE37 ......102 D5
Saddler St DHAM DH1 ......16 D4
Saffron Pl BYK/HTN/WLK NE6 ......72 C6
Sage Cl BW/LEM/TK/HW NE15 ......68 A3
St Agnes' West House
  RYTON NE40 ......66 A7
St Aidan's Av
  ASHBK/HED/RY SR2 ......121 F5
  DHAM DH1 ......156 B4
  LGB/KIL NE12 ......58 E1
St Aidan's Cl NSHW NE29 ......60 B2
St Aidan's Crs DHAM DH1 ......156 B7
  MPTH NE61 ......20 E7
  STLY/ANP DH9 ......125 H4
St Aidan's Rd SSH NE33 ......3 J5
  WLSD/HOW NE28 ......72 C2
St Aidan's St CON/LDGT DH8 ......122 E3
  GATE NE8 ......10 D6
St Aidan's Ter HLS DH4 ......132 C1
St Albans Cl ASHGTN NE63 ......24 C3
  CLS/BIR/GTL DH3 ......145 J1
St Alban's Crs
  BYK/HTN/WLK NE6 ......71 K1
St Albans Pl TYNE/NSHE NE30 ......61 H3
St Alban's St
  ASHBK/HED/RY SR2 ......120 E3
St Alban's Ter GATE NE8 ......10 F7
St Albans Vw SMOOR NE27 ......49 G7
St Aldwyn Rd SEA/MUR SR7 ......135 H7
St Aloysius Vw HEBB NE31 ......73 F5
St Andrews HLS DH4 ......131 K7
St Andrews Av WASHN NE37 ......102 D5
St Andrew's Cl CON/LDGT DH8 ......122 D3
  MONK NE25 ......50 B4
St Andrews Ct NSHW NE29 ......60 D2
St Andrew's Crs
  CON/LDGT DH8 ......122 D3
St Andrew's Dr
  LWF/SPW/WRK NE9 ......100 E2
St Andrew's Gdns
  CON/LDGT DH8 ......122 C3
St Andrew's La PRUD NE42 ......63 H7
St Andrew's Rd CON/LDGT DH8 ......122 C3
  STLY/ANP DH9 ......112 D5
St Andrew's Sq SEA/MUR SR7 ......149 K4
St Andrew's St CNUT NE1 ......5 H6
  HEBB NE31 ......72 E4
St Andrew's Ter
  CLDN/WHIT/ROK SR6 ......106 E3
St Annes Ct DHAM DH1 ......16 C3
St Ann's Cl CNUT NE1 ......6 C6
St Ann's St CNUT NE1 ......6 B7
St Ann's Yd
  CNUT (off Breamish St) NE1 ......6 C6
St Anselm Crs NSHW NE29 ......60 A3
St Anselm Rd NSHW NE29 ......60 A3
St Anthony's Rd
  BYK/HTN/WLK NE6 ......7 M6
St Anthonys Wk
  BYK/HTN/WLK NE6 ......13 G1
St Asaph Cl LGB/HTN NE7 ......57 K6
St Aubyn's Wy STLY/ANP DH9 ......113 F7
St Austell Cl
  WD/WHPE/BLK * NE5 ......55 G6
St Austell Gdns
  LWF/SPW/WRK NE9 ......101 F3
St Barnabas HLS DH4 ......131 K4
St Barnabas Wy
  ASHBK/HED/RY SR2 ......15 J8
St Bartholomews Cl
  ASHGTN NE63 ......18 B7
St Bede Crs RDHAMSE DH6 ......172 B7
St Bede's Cl DHAM DH1 ......168 B1
St Bede's Ct BDN/LAN/SAC DH7 ......140 B3
St Bede's Dr GATE NE8 ......11 H5
St Bedes Pk ASHBK/HED/RY SR2 ......14 F7
St Bedes Pl BLYTH NE24 ......34 D3
St Bedes Rd BLYTH NE24 ......34 D3
St Bedes Ter
  ASHBK/HED/RY SR2 ......14 F7
St Bedes Wk SMOOR NE27 ......58 E1
St Bedes Wy
  BDN/LAN/SAC DH7 ......167 K5
St Brandon's Gv
  BDN/LAN/SAC DH7 ......167 F6
St Buryan Crs
  WD/WHPE/BLK NE5 ......55 G6
St Catherine's Ct
  SWCK/CAS SR5 ......105 H4
St Catherines Gv JES NE2 ......6 B1
St Chad's Crs SUNDSW SR3 ......119 F7
St Chad Sq RDHAMSE DH6 ......172 A7
St Chad's Rd SUNDSW SR3 ......119 F7
St Chad's Vls BOL NE36 ......91 H5
St Christophers Cl
  ASHGTN NE63 ......18 B7
St Christopher's Rd
  ASHBK/HED/RY SR2 ......120 A4
Saint Ct SUNDSW SR3 ......134 A2
St Cuthbert Av
  CLS/BIR/GTL DH3 ......129 K4

St Cuthbert Rd RDHAMSE DH6 ......172 B7
St Cuthbert's Av
  CON/LDGT DH8 ......122 C2
  DHAM DH1 ......156 B4
  HAR/WTLS NE34 ......76 A3
St Cuthberts Cl PRUD NE42 ......80 C2
St Cuthberts Ct BLYTH NE24 ......31 H6
  GATE NE8 ......10 D3
St Cuthberts Dr
  BDN/LAN/SAC DH7 ......143 C5
  FELL NE10 ......13 C9
St Cuthberts Pk
  WICK/BNPF NE16 ......98 E5
St Cuthbert's Pl GATE * NE8 ......10 D5
St Cuthbert's Rd GATE NE8 ......10 D4
  HLS DH4 ......132 B4
  LGB/KIL NE12 ......58 D1
  PLEE/EAS SR8 ......174 E5
  WD/WHPE/BLK NE5 ......69 F4
  WICK/BNPF NE16 ......98 E6
  WLSD/HOW NE28 ......59 F7
St Cuthbert's Ter
  MLFD/PNYW SR4 ......14 A3
St Cuthberts Wk
  BDN/LAN/SAC DH7 ......167 K5
  BLAY NE21 ......84 B1
  RDHAMSE DH6 ......170 C1
  SMOOR NE27 ......58 E1
St Davids Cl ASHGTN * NE63 ......18 B7
St David's Wy WBAY NE26 ......50 D1
St Ebba's Wy CON/LDGT DH8 ......108 E3
St Edmund's Dr FELL NE10 ......13 G9
St Edmund's Rd GATE NE8 ......11 H5
St Etienne Ct FELL NE10 ......12 D6
St Gabriel's Av
  BYK/HTN/WLK NE6 ......71 J7
  MLFD/PNYW SR4 ......105 K7
St George's Av SSH NE33 ......75 J3
St George's Cl JES NE2 ......70 E1
St Georges Ct FELL NE10 ......13 M9
St Georges Crs MONK NE25 ......50 D5
  NSHW NE29 ......2 A2
St George's Est WASHS NE38 ......116 E5
St George's Pl
  BW/LEM/TK/HW NE15 ......68 C6
  CON/LDGT DH8 ......122 E4
St George's Rd
  BW/LEM/TK/HW NE15 ......68 B6
  TYNE/NSHE NE30 ......51 F6
St George's Ter BOL NE36 ......91 H5
  BW/LEM/TK/HW NE15 ......68 C6
  CLDN/WHIT/ROK SR6 ......107 F3
  JES NE2 ......70 E1
St George's Wy
  ASHBK/HED/RY SR2 ......14 E7
St Giles Cl DHAM DH1 ......17 J3
St Godric's Cl DHAM DH1 ......156 D2
St Godrics Ct DHAM DH1 ......16 C3
St Godric's Dr HLS DH4 ......146 D6
St Helen's Crs
  LWF/SPW/WRK NE9 ......86 E7
St Heliers Wy STLY/ANP DH9 ......113 F7
St Hilda's Wy WLSD/HOW NE28 ......59 G7
St Hilda St SSH NE33 ......3 H8
St Hilds Ct DHAM DH1 ......17 M2
St Hild's La DHAM DH1 ......17 L3
St Ignatius Cl
  ASHBK/HED/RY SR2 ......15 H8
St Ives Cl CON/LDGT DH8 ......123 K3
St Ives Wy WD/WHPE/BLK NE5 ......55 G6
St James Bvd CNUT * NE1 ......5 H6
St James Ct GATE NE8 ......11 M6
St James' Crs
  BW/LEM/TK/HW NE15 ......69 H7
St James Gdns
  BW/LEM/TK/HW * NE15 ......69 H6
St James' Rd
  BW/LEM/TK/HW NE15 ......69 H6
  GATE NE8 ......11 K4
St James Sq GATE NE8 ......11 K3
St James' St CNUT NE1 ......5 H5
  GOS/KPK NE3 ......56 D5
St James' Ter NSHW NE29 ......60 B7
St Johns SUND SR1 ......15 J2
St John's Av HEBB NE31 ......73 F6
St John's Cl WBAY NE26 ......50 D1
St Johns Ct ELS/FEN * NE4 ......69 J7
St John's Crs BDLGTN NE22 ......29 K3
  RDHAMSE DH6 ......180 A2
St John's Gn NSHW NE29 ......60 B7
St John's Ms
  BDN/LAN/SAC DH7 ......141 H2
St John's Pl BDLGTN NE22 ......29 K3
  CLS/BIR/GTL DH3 ......115 J2
  FELL NE10 ......12 C7
  WBAY NE26 ......50 D1
St John's Rd BDLGTN NE22 ......29 K4
  BDN/LAN/SAC DH7 ......167 K6
  DHAM DH1 ......168 B1
  ELS/FEN NE4 ......69 J7
St John's St NSHW NE29 ......60 B7
St John's Ter BOL NE36 ......91 J5
  JRW NE32 ......73 K4
  NSHW NE29 ......60 B7
St John St CNUT NE1 ......5 J7
St Johns V MLFD/PNYW SR4 ......118 E2
St Johns Wk ELS/FEN NE4 ......4 A9
  NSHW NE29 ......60 B7
St Joseph's Cl DHAM DH1 ......17 L2
St Josephs Ct
  CLS/BIR/GTL (off Mount Rd) DH3 ......115 J1
  HEBB NE31 ......89 F1
St Joseph's Wy JRW NE32 ......89 K3
St Jude's Ter SSH NE33 ......75 G2
St Julien Gdns LGB/HTN NE7 ......71 K2
  WLSD/HOW NE28 ......59 K7
St Lawrence Cl RDHAMSE DH6 ......159 F4
St Lawrence Rd
  BYK/HTN/WLK NE6 ......6 F2
  RDHAMSE DH6 ......158 E4
St Lawrence Sq
  BYK/HTN/WLK NE6 ......6 F2
St Leonard's Wk MPTH NE61 ......20 A3
St Lucia Cl ASHBK/HED/RY SR2 ......15 G8
  WBAY NE26 ......50 C1

St Lukes Cl ASHGTN NE63 ......18 C7
St Luke's Rd MLFD/PNYW SR4 ......105 G6
St Luke's Ter MLFD/PNYW SR4 ......60 B7
St Luke's Ter MLFD/PNYW SR4 ......105 K6
St Margaret's Av
  SWCK/CAS SR5 ......104 E4
St Margaret's Cl DHAM * DH1 ......16 B4
St Margaret's Dr
  STLY/ANP DH9 ......112 A3
St Margarets Garth DHAM DH1 ......16 B4
St Margarets Ms DHAM DH1 ......16 B4
St Margaret's Rd
  BW/LEM/TK/HW NE15 ......69 F7
St Margargets Av LGB/KIL NE12 ......57 K4
St Marks Crs MLFD/PNYW SR4 ......14 A5
St Mark's Rd MLFD/PNYW SR4 ......14 A5
St Mark's Rd North
  MLFD/PNYW SR4 ......106 A6
St Mark's St BYK/HTN/WLK NE6 ......7 G3
  MLFD/PNYW SR4 ......20 C4
  MPTH NE61 ......20 C4
St Mark's Wy SSH NE33 ......75 G2
St Martin's Cl WBAY NE26 ......50 D2
St Marys Av HAR/WTLS NE34 ......75 K5
  WBAY NE26 ......50 D2
St Marys Cl CLSW/PEL DH2 ......129 H5
  CON/LDGT DH8 ......122 D3
  DHAM DH1 ......169 G4
  PLEE/EAS SR8 ......162 B6
St Marys Ct GATE NE8 ......11 H3
St Mary's Crs CON/LDGT DH8 ......122 C3
St Marys Dr ASHGTN NE63 ......18 B7
  BLYTH NE24 ......34 D2
  HLS DH4 ......146 D6
  RDHAMSE DH6 ......170 C1
St Marys Gn WICK/BNPF * NE16 ......85 F5
St Mary's Pl
  BW/LEM/TK/HW NE15 ......67 G1
  CNUT NE1 ......5 K4
St Mary's Rd DHAM DH1 ......157 K5
St Mary's St CON/LDGT DH8 ......122 D3
St Mary's Ter BOL NE36 ......91 H5
  FELL NE10 ......13 G7
St Mary's Vw SUND SR1 ......14 D4
St Mary's Wy SUND SR1 ......14 D4
St Mary's Wynd WBAY NE26 ......41 H4
St Mathews La PRUD NE42 ......80 D2
St Matthews Vw SUNDSW SR3 ......120 A3
St Michaels HLS DH4 ......131 K7
St Michael's Av MONK NE25 ......40 B2
  SSH NE33 ......75 H2
St Michael's Av North SSH NE33 ......75 H2
St Michaels Mt
  BYK/HTN/WLK NE6 ......7 H6
St Michael's Rd
  BYK/HTN/WLK NE6 ......7 L3
St Michaels Wy SUND SR1 ......14 C4
  WICK/BNPF NE16 ......8 B6
St Monica Gv DHAM DH1 ......168 B1
St Nicholas Av GOS/KPK NE3 ......56 C6
  SUNDSW SR3 ......120 B3
St Nicholas Chambers
  CNUT * NE1 ......5 K8
St Nicholas Cl ASHGTN NE63 ......18 B7
St Nicholas Dr DHAM DH1 ......156 A5
St Nicholas Rd BOL NE36 ......90 E5
St Nicholas' St CNUT NE1 ......5 K7
St Nicholas Ter PLEE/EAS SR8 ......162 E5
St Omers Rd DUN/TMV NE11 ......9 G4
St Oswald Av BYK/HTN/WLK NE6 ......7 L3
St Oswalds Av
  BYK/HTN/WLK * NE6 ......7 L4
St Oswald's Dr DHAM DH1 ......168 B5
St Oswald's Gn
  BYK/HTN/WLK NE6 ......7 L3
St Oswald's Rd HEBB NE31 ......73 H4
  WLSD/HOW NE28 ......59 F6
St Oswin's Pl CON/LDGT DH8 ......122 D3
  TYNE/NSHE NE30 ......61 H3
St Oswin's St SSH NE33 ......75 H4
St Patricks Cl FELL NE10 ......12 D8
St Patricks Wk FELL NE10 ......12 D8
St Pauls Ct GATE
  (off Derwentwater Rd) NE8 ......10 B6
St Pauls Dr HLS DH4 ......117 G6
St Paul's Gdns MONK NE25 ......40 B2
St Pauls Pl ELS/FEN NE4 ......4 D7
St Paul's Rd JRW NE32 ......74 B4
St Peter's Av HAR/WTLS NE34 ......75 J5
St Peters Ct BYK/HTN/WLK NE6 ......7 H7
St Peter's Rd BYK/HTN/WLK NE6 ......7 H8
  WLSD/HOW NE28 ......59 F6
St Peters Vw
  CLDN/WHIT/ROK SR6 ......15 G1
St Peters' Wy
  CLDN/WHIT/ROK SR6 ......15 G2
St Peter's Whf
  BYK/HTN/WLK NE6 ......7 H9
St Philips Cl ELS/FEN NE4 ......4 E6
St Philips Wy ELS/FEN * NE4 ......4 E6
St Ronan's Dr WBAY NE26 ......40 E1
St Ronan's Rd MONK NE25 ......50 D5
St Ronans Vw
  LWF/SPW/WRK NE9 ......101 G3
St Simon St HAR/WTLS NE34 ......76 E7
St Stephen's Cl MONK NE25 ......39 J5
St Stephen's Wy NSHW NE29 ......74 B1
St Stevens Cl HLS DH4 ......117 G6
St Thomas Cl PLEE/EAS SR8 ......162 B6
St Thomas' Crs CNUT NE1 ......5 J4
St Thomas Ms PRUD NE42 ......80 D2
St Thomas' St CNUT NE1 ......5 J4
  LWF/SPW/WRK NE9 ......87 G1
  SUND SR1 ......14 F4
St Thomas Ter CNUT NE1 ......5 J4
St Vincent Ct GATE NE8 ......11 K5
St Vincents Cl
  BW/LEM/TK/HW NE15 ......68 C3
St Vincent's Pl WBAY NE26 ......50 D1
St Vincent St
  ASHBK/HED/RY SR2 ......15 G7
  GATE NE8 ......11 K5
  SSH NE33 ......75 J2
St Vincent's Wy WBAY NE26 ......50 D1
Salcombe Av JRW NE32 ......74 B6
Salcombe Cl SEA/MUR SR7 ......150 B2

Salcombe Gdns	
LWF/SPW/WRK NE9	101 F3
Salem Av CON/LDGT DH8	123 H7
Salem HI ASHBK/HED/RY SR2	15 G8
Salem Rd ASHBK/HED/RY SR2	15 G7
Salem St ASHBK/HED/RY SR2	15 G7
JRW NE32	74 A4
SSH NE33	3 G6
Salem Ter South	
ASHBK/HED/RY SR2	15 G8
Salem Ter ASHBK/HED/RY SR2	15 G7
Salisbury Av NSHW NE29	60 D5
Salisbury CI ASHGTN NE63	24 B5
CLS/BIR/GTL DH3	145 H2
CON/LDGT DH8	108 E7
CRAM NE23	37 K2
Salisbury Gdns JES NE2	71 G3
Salisbury PI SSH NE33	3 L7
Salisbury Rd DHAM DH1	157 F2
Salisbury St ASHBK/HED/RY SR2	15 G4
CON/LDGT DH8	123 C4
FELL NE10	13 J6
SSH NE33	3 K8
STLY/ANP DH9	126 B2
Salkeld Gdns	
LWF/SPW/WRK NE9	11 J8
Salkeld Rd LWF/SPW/WRK NE9	87 C6
Sallyport Crs CNUT NE1	5 M7
Salmon St SSH NE33	3 J5
Saltburn Gdns WLSD/HOW NE28	59 K7
Saltburn Rd SUNDSW SR3	119 G3
Saltburn Sq SUNDSW SR3	119 G3
Salterfen La	
ASHBK/HED/RY SR2	121 G6
Salterfen Rd	
ASHBK/HED/RY SR2	121 G6
Salters CI CLS/BIR/GTL DH3	56 E4
Salters' La GOS/KPK NE3	57 F4
HLH DH5	133 J5
LGB/KIL NE12	57 G1
RDHAMSE DH6	160 E7
SEA/MUR SR7	148 E2
TRIM TS29	182 C5
Salters' Rd GOS/KPK NE3	56 A6
Saltmeadows Rd GATE NE8	6 D9
Saltwell PI GATE NE8	10 C7
Saltwell Rd GATE NE8	10 C7
Saltwell Rd South	
LWF/SPW/WRK NE9	86 E6
Saltwell St GATE NE8	10 D7
Saltwell Vw LWF/SPW/WRK NE9	10 F9
Salvin St RDHAMSE DH6	178 C5
Samson CI LGB/KIL NE12	47 H7
Sancroft Dr HLH DH5	147 H1
Sandalwood HAR/WTLS NE34	91 H1
Sandalwood Sq	
MLFD/PNYW SR4	118 E4
Sanderling CI RYTON NE40	67 F7
Sanderson Rd JES NE2	70 E1
Sanderson St ELS/FEN NE4	9 H1
Sandfield Rd BDLGTN NE22	30 D2
TYNE/NSHE NE30	51 F6
Sandford Av CRAM NE23	33 H6
Sandford Rd CON/LDGT DH8	122 B3
Sandgate CNUT NE1	6 A7
STLY/ANP DH9	125 K3
Sandgrove	
CLDN/WHIT/ROK SR6	92 A3
Sandhill CNUT NE1	5 L8
Sandholm CI WLSD/HOW NE28	59 H5
Sandhurst Av TYNE/NSHE NE30	51 F7
Sandmartin CI ASHGTN NE63	24 A5
Sandmere PI	
BW/LEM/TK/HW NE15	68 E6
Sandmere Rd	
ASHBK/HED/RY SR2	120 E5
Sandoe Gdns	
BW/LEM/TK/HW NE15	69 F6
Sandon CI SMOOR NE25	48 E4
Sandown CI SMOOR NE27	40 A7
Sandown Gdns GATE NE8	10 B8
SUNDSW SR3	119 K6
WLSD/HOW NE28	59 H6
Sandpiper CI BLYTH NE24	35 G3
RYTON NE40	67 F7
Sand Point Rd	
CLDN/WHIT/ROK SR6	107 F4
Sandray CI CLS/BIR/GTL DH3	115 K5
Sandridge NWBGN NE64	19 H7
Sandringham Av LGB/KIL NE12	57 J4
Sandringham Ct	
FELL (off Sheriffs CI) NE10	12 A8
Sandringham Dr BLYTH NE24	35 F4
MONK NE25	49 K5
STLY/ANP DH9	125 H2
WICK/BNPF NE16	84 E5
Sandringham Gdns NSHW NE29	60 E3
Sandringham Rd	
CLDN/WHIT/ROK SR6	106 D3
GOS/KPK NE3	56 E6
WD/WHPE/BLK* NE5	68 C3
Sandringham Ter	
CLDN/WHIT/ROK SR6	106 E3
Sandringham Wy	
PONT/DH NE20	42 E5
Sandsay CI ASHBK/HED/RY SR2	120 D6
The Sands Flats DHAM DH1	16 E2
Sands Rd WICK/BNPF NE16	84 E3
Sandstone CI HAR/WTLS NE34	90 D1
Sandwell Dr HLS DH4	117 H6
Sandwich Rd NSHW NE29	60 D1
Sandy Chare	
CLDN/WHIT/ROK SR6	92 E4
Sandy Crs BYK/HTN/WLK NE6	7 M9
Sandyford Av PRUD NE42	81 F1
Sandyford Pk JES NE2	6 B1
Sandyford Rd CNUT NE1	5 L3
JES NE2	5 L4
Sandy La ASHGTN NE63	24 D5
DIN/WO NE13	45 H3
GOS/KPK NE3	46 E5
LWF/SPW/WRK NE9	101 K4
Sandypath La WICK/BNPF NE16	97 J6
Sandysykes PRUD NE42	80 B2
Sans St South SUND* SR1	15 G5
Sarabel Av STKFD/GP NE62	22 E6
Sargent Av HAR/WTLS NE34	91 H2
Satley Gdns SUNDSW SR3	120 B4
Saturn CI PLEE/EAS SR8	162 D5
Saturn St PLEE/EAS SR8	162 D5
Saunton Ct HLS DH4	132 A4
Saville PI CNUT NE1	5 L5
Saville Rw CNUT NE1	5 K5
Saville St SSH NE33	3 J7
TYNE/NSHE NE30	2 E2
Saville St West NSHW NE29	2 D3
Savory Rd WLSD/HOW NE28	59 H7
Sawmill La DHAM/LAN/SAC DH7	167 F6
Saxilby Dr GOS/KPK NE3	56 D2
Saxon CI CLDN/WHIT/ROK SR6	91 J3
Saxon Crs SUNDSW SR3	119 K3
Saxondale Rd GOS/KPK NE3	55 J5
Saxon Dr TYNE/NSHE NE30	61 G1
Saxon Wy JRW NE32	74 A3
Saxton Gv LGB/KTN NE7	57 G6
Saxton St ASHBK/HED/RY SR2	121 F4
Scafell CLS/BIR/GTL DH3	115 K4
Scafell CI PLEE/EAS SR8	175 F4
Scafell Dr WD/WHPE/BLK NE5	55 F1
Scafell Gdns DUN/TMV NE11	86 A6
Scalby CI GOS/KPK NE3	56 D2
Scales Crs PRUD NE42	81 F2
Scarborough Ct	
BYK/HTN/WLK NE6	7 J5
Scarborough Rd	
BYK/HTN/WLK NE6	7 K5
SUNDSW SR3	119 K6
Scardale Wy DHAM DH1	158 B5
Sceptre CI ELS/FEN* NE4	4 C8
Sceptre PI ELS/FEN NE4	4 C7
Sceptre St ELS/FEN NE4	4 C7
Schalksmuhle Rd BDLGTN NE22	29 F5
Schimel St SWCK/CAS SR5	106 B3
School Ap HAR/WTLS NE34	76 A5
School Av DUN/TMV NE11	9 C9
RDHAMSE DH6	181 G5
STKFD/GP NE62	23 F6
School CI FELL NE10	87 K6
Schoolhouse La	
WICK/BNPF NE16	98 C6
School La ROWG NE39	96 C2
STLY/ANP DH9	126 B3
WICK/BNPF NE16	85 F5
School Loaning	
HAR/WTLS NE34	75 F6
School Rd BDLGTN NE22	29 K3
HLH DH5	147 F4
HEBB NE31	73 C4
PLEE/EAS SR8	163 F5
RDHAMSE DH6	179 K7
SEA/MUR SR7	150 E3
WICK/BNPF NE16	84 E5
School Ter STLY/ANP DH9	126 B2
School Vw HLH DH5	160 C1
HLS DH4	146 C7
Scorer's La CLS/BIR/GTL DH3	130 D7
Scorer St NSHW NE29	2 A2
Scotland Head BLAY NE21	83 J5
Scotland St	
ASHBK/HED/RY SR2	135 G1
Scotswood Rd	
BW/LEM/TK/HW NE15	68 E7
CNUT NE1	5 G9
ELS/FEN NE4	8 A3
Scotswood Vw DUN/TMV NE11	8 C4
WICK/BNPF NE16	8 A3
Scott Av CRAM NE23	33 H7
Scott Ct CLS/BIR/GTL DH3	145 H1
Scott's Ter HLH DH5	147 K4
Scott St CRAM NE23	33 J6
STLY/ANP DH9	126 C1
Scoular Dr ASHGTN NE63	24 C2
Scripton Gill	
BDN/LAN/SAC DH7	167 F6
Scripton Gill Rd	
BDN/LAN/SAC DH7	166 E7
Scripton La DHAM/LAN/SAC DH7	177 F1
Scrogg Rd BYK/HTN/WLK NE6	7 M3
Scruton Av SUNDSW SR3	119 K4
Sea Banks TYNE/NSHE NE30	61 J2
Seaburn Dr HLS DH4	132 A7
Seaburn Gdns	
CLDN/WHIT/ROK SR6	106 E1
LWF/SPW/WRK NE9	101 K2
Seaburn Gv WBAY NE26	41 F2
Seaburn HI	
CLDN/WHIT/ROK SR6	106 E1
Seaburn Ter	
CLDN/WHIT/ROK SR6	106 E1
Seaburn Vw MONK NE25	40 A2
Seacombe Av TYNE/NSHE NE30	51 F6
Seacrest Av TYNE/NSHE NE30	51 F7
Sea Crest Rd NWBGN NE64	19 G6
Seafield PI BLYTH NE24	35 G2
Seafields CLDN/WHIT/ROK SR6	92 E7
Seafield Ter SSH NE33	3 K6
Seafield Vw TYNE/NSHE NE30	61 H2
Seaforth Rd SUNDSW SR3	120 A3
Seaforth St BLYTH NE24	31 G6
Seaham CI HAR/WTLS NE34	76 B5
Seaham Gdns	
LWF/SPW/WRK NE9	101 J3
Seaham Rd HLH DH5	132 D7
Seaham St SEA/MUR SR7	151 F3
SUNDSW SR3	120 A7
Sea La CLDN/WHIT/ROK SR6	106 E1
Sea Rd CLDN/WHIT/ROK SR6	106 D1
SSH NE33	3 L5
Seascale PI	
LWF/SPW/WRK NE9	101 H1
Seaside La PLEE/EAS SR8	162 D5
Seaton Av BLYTH NE24	34 E3
HLH DH5	132 E7
NWBGN NE64	25 H1
Seaton CI FELL NE10	88 D6
Seaton Crs MONK NE25	40 C6
MONK NE25	50 C4
SEA/MUR SR7	134 E6
Seaton Gv SEA/MUR SR7	134 D7
Seaton La SEA/MUR SR7	134 E6
Seaton Pk SEA/MUR SR7	135 F7
Seaton PI BYK/HTN/WLK NE6	12 F2
DIN/WO NE13	46 A3
Seaton Rd SMOOR NE27	49 J5
Seatonville Crs MONK NE25	50 D3
Seatonville Rd MONK NE25	50 C6
Sea Vw ASHBK/HED/RY SR2	135 G1
MPTH NE61	18 D2
PLEE/EAS SR8	162 C6
Sea View Gdns	
CLDN/WHIT/ROK SR6	106 E2
PLEE/EAS SR8	175 H2
Sea View Pk	
CLDN/WHIT/ROK SR6	92 D4
CRAM NE23	38 E2
Sea View Rd	
ASHBK/HED/RY SR2	120 E4
Sea View Rd West	
ASHBK/HED/RY SR2	120 E4
Sea View St	
SUNDSW SR3	121 F4
Sea View Wk	
SEA/MUR SR7	149 K4
Sea Wy SSH NE33	3 M7
Second Av ASHGTN NE63	23 K2
BLYTH NE24	35 F1
BYK/HTN/WLK NE6	7 G1
CLSW/PEL DH2	115 H6
CLSW/PEL DH2	129 H5
DUN/TMV NE11	86 C6
MPTH NE61	21 F6
NSHW NE29	59 K6
Second St CON/LDGT DH8	123 H1
CON/LDGT DH8	123 J2
GATE NE8	10 C5
Sedgeletch Rd HLS DH4	131 J6
Sedgemoor LGB/KIL NE12	47 K5
Sedgemoor Av	
BW/LEM/TK/HW NE15	68 C7
Sedley Rd WLSD/HOW NE28	72 D2
Sedling Rd WASHS NE38	116 D4
Sefton Av BYK/HTN/WLK NE6	71 H2
Sefton Ct CRAM NE23	33 J6
Sefton Sq SUNDSW SR3	119 J3
Selborne Gdns CON/LDGT DH8	122 D1
JES NE2	6 C1
Selbourne CI CRAM NE23	37 K2
Selbourne St SSH NE33	3 K8
Selby CI CRAM NE23	37 K2
Selby Gdns BYK/HTN/WLK NE6	72 B3
CON/LDGT DH8	122 C6
WLSD/HOW NE28	58 D7
Selby Sq SUNDSW SR3	119 J3
Selina PI CLDN/WHIT/ROK SR6	106 E4
Selkirk CI CLS/BIR/GTL DH3	101 J7
Selkirk Gv CRAM NE23	33 J6
Selkirk St JRW NE32	90 C1
Selkirk Wy NSHW NE29	60 A2
Selsdon Av MLFD/PNYW SR4	118 E4
Selsey Ct FELL NE10	88 A6
Selwood CI HAR/WTLS NE34	75 H6
Selwyn Av MONK NE25	50 B6
Serlby CI WASHN NE37	102 E4
Seton Av HAR/WTLS NE34	74 D7
Setting Stones WASHS NE38	116 C6
Sevenoaks Dr	
MLFD/PNYW SR4	118 C3
Seventh Av ASHGTN NE63	24 A3
BLYTH NE24	35 F1
BYK/HTN/WLK NE6	7 G1
CLSW/PEL DH2	129 H4
MPTH NE61	21 F6
Seventh Rw ASHGTN NE63	23 H1
Seventh St PLEE/EAS SR8	175 H3
Severn Av HEBB NE31	89 C1
Severn CI PLEE/EAS SR8	174 D6
Severn Dr JRW NE32	90 A2
Severn Gdns GATE NE8	11 L7
Severus Rd ELS/FEN NE4	69 J4
Seymour CI CRAM NE23	24 D2
Seymour Sq SUNDSW SR3	119 J3
Seymour St CON/LDGT DH8	123 F5
DUN/TMV NE11	9 J5
NSHW NE29	2 C4
PLEE/EAS SR8	175 J4
Seymour Ter HLH DH5	148 A7
Shadfen Crs MPTH NE61	21 J2
Shadforth CI PLEE/EAS SR8	174 B6
Shadon Wy CLS/BIR/GTL DH3	116 A2
Shaftesbury Av	
ASHBK/HED/RY SR2	120 E7
HAR/WTLS NE34	74 C6
JRW NE32	74 B5
WBAY NE26	50 D2
Shaftesbury Crs RHTLP TS27	175 K6
SUNDSW SR3	119 K3
TYNE/NSHE NE30	50 E6
Shaftesbury Gv	
BYK/HTN/WLK NE6	6 E2
Shaftesbury Rd RHTLP TS27	175 K5
Shafto CI CON/LDGT DH8	123 H7
Shafto Ct RYTON NE40	82 B1
Shaftoe Rd SUNDSW SR3	119 J4
Shaftoe Sq SUNDSW SR3	119 H4
Shaftoe Wy DIN/WO NE13	44 B2
Shafto St	
BW/LEM/TK/HW NE15	68 C6
WLSD/HOW NE28	59 C7
Shaftsbury Dr	
BDN/LAN/SAC DH7	177 F1
Shaftsbury Wk GATE NE8	10 C5
Shakespeare Av HEBB NE31	73 C5
Shakespeare St HLH DH5	147 H1
JRW* NE32	73 K3
RDHAMSE DH6	182 D1
SEA/MUR SR7	150 E1
SSH* NE33	75 H2
SWCK/CAS SR5	106 A2
WASHN NE38	73 H1
Shakespeare Ter	
ASHBK/HED/RY SR2	14 C7
PLEE/EAS SR8	162 C6
Shalcombe CI SUNDSW SR3	134 A1
Shallcross ASHBK/HED/RY SR2	14 B8
Shallon Ct ASHGTN NE63	23 J3
Shalstone WASHN NE37	103 H4
Shamrock CI	
BW/LEM/TK/HW NE15	68 A3
Shandon Wy GOS/KPK NE3	55 J5
Shanklin PI CRAM NE23	37 K2
Shannon CI SWCK/CAS SR5	104 E4
Shannon Ct GOS/KPK NE3	55 C3
Shap CI WASHS NE38	117 F3
Shap La WD/WHPE/BLK NE5	68 C2
Shap Rd TYNE/NSHE NE30	50 E7
Sharnford CI SMOOR NE27	49 F4
Sharon Av RDHAMSE DH6	181 G6
Sharon CI LGB/KIL NE12	47 H7
Sharp Crs DHAM DH1	17 M1
Sharpendon St HEBB * NE31	73 G4
Sharpley Dr SEA/MUR SR7	134 C7
Shaw Av HAR/WTLS NE34	75 F7
Shawbrow CI LGB/HTN NE7	58 A7
Shawdon CI WD/WHPE/BLK NE5	55 F5
Shaw Gdns FELL NE10	13 L8
Shaw La CON/LDGT DH8	109 F2
Shaw St SEA/MUR SR7	150 E1
Shaw Wood CI DHAM DH1	156 B6
Shearlegs Rd GATE NE8	11 K2
Shearwater	
CLDN/WHIT/ROK SR6	93 F1
Shearwater Av LGB/KIL NE12	57 G3
Shearwater CI	
WD/WHPE/BLK NE5	55 F6
Shearwater Wy BLYTH NE24	35 G3
Sheelin Av CLSW/PEL DH2	129 J5
Sheen Ct HLS DH4	146 D6
Sheen Ct WD/WHPE/BLK NE5	55 F5
Sheepfolds North	
SWCK/CAS SR5	14 E2
Sheepfolds Rd SWCK/CAS SR5	14 E2
Sheepfolds South	
SWCK/CAS SR5	14 E2
Sheep HI WICK/BNPF NE16	97 K7
Sheepwash Av STKFD/GP NE62	22 E6
Sheepwash Bank	
STKFD/GP NE62	22 E6
Sheldon Gv CRAM NE23	33 H6
GOS/KPK NE3	69 K1
Sheldon Rd HAR/WTLS NE34	75 K2
Sheldon St JRW NE32	73 K4
Shelford Gdns	
BW/LEM/TK/HW NE15	68 C4
Shellbark HLS DH4	131 H1
Shelley Av BOLCOL NE35	90 E4
HAR/WTLS NE34	76 B6
HLH DH5	160 C1
LWF/SPW/WRK NE9	102 A4
Shelley Ct CLSW/PEL DH2	128 E4
Shelley Dr GATE NE8	11 J4
Shelley Gdns CLSW/PEL DH2	129 F4
Shelley Rd	
BW/LEM/TK/HW NE15	67 H4
Shelley St SEA/MUR SR7	150 E1
Shepherd St MLFD/PNYW SR4	106 A6
Shepherds Wy BOL NE36	90 E5
Shepherd Wy WASHS NE38	117 G4
Sheppard Ter SWCK/CAS SR5	105 F4
Sheppey Ct SUNDSW * SR3	134 A1
Shepton Cottages	
WICK/BNPF NE16	99 G2
Sheraton FELL NE10	88 C7
Sheraton St JES NE2	4 F1
Sherborne Av NSHW NE29	60 B2
Sherburn Gra North JRW NE32	73 J6
Sherburn Gra South JRW NE32	73 J6
Sherburn Gv HLS DH4	132 A6
Sherburn Park Dr ROWG NE39	97 H2
Sherburn Rd DHAM DH1	17 M3
Sherburn Road Flats DHAM DH1	17 J2
Sherburn Ter CON/LDGT DH8	123 C9
Sherburn Vw WFELL NE10	88 D6
Sherfield Dr LGB/KIL NE7	57 J7
Sheridan Dr STLY/ANP DH9	127 F1
Sheridan Gn WASHS NE38	116 C5
Sheridan St MLFD/PNYW SR4	105 K6
Sheriff Mt North	
LWF/SPW/WRK NE9	11 K9
Sheriffs CI LWF/SPW/WRK NE9	11 M8
Sheriff's Moor Av HLH DH5	160 B3
Sheringham Av NSHW NE29	60 B3
Sheringham CI SUNDSW SR3	134 A1
Sheringham Dr CRAM NE23	37 K2
Sheringham Gdns	
BW/LEM/TK/HW NE15	66 D1
Sherringham Av GOS/KPK NE3	55 J5
Sherwood CI CON/LDGT DH8	108 C7
SMOOR NE27	49 K7
WASHS NE38	117 F2
Sherwood Ct SUNDSW * SR3	134 A1
Sherwood PI GOS/KPK NE3	46 C7
Sherwood Vw WLSD/HOW NE28	58 C6
Shetland Ct SUNDSW * SR3	134 A1
Shibdon Bank BLAY NE21	84 B2
Shibdon Crs BLAY NE21	84 B2
Shibdon Park Vw BLAY NE21	84 B2
Shibdon Rd BLAY NE21	84 A1
Shibdon Wy BLAY NE21	84 D2
Shield Av WICK/BNPF NE16	85 F3
Shield Ct JES * NE2	6 A3
Shieldfield La JES NE2	6 A5
Shield Rd CLDN/WHIT/ROK SR6	92 C7
Shieldrow La STLY/ANP DH9	125 J4
Shields Rd DHAM DH1	16 D3
BYK/HTN/WLK NE6	7 H3
CLDN/WHIT/ROK SR6	92 B6
CLS/BIR/GTL DH3	129 K2
FELL NE10	13 G7
HAR/WTLS NE34	91 K1
MONK NE25	50 D7
MPTH NE61	21 F7
Shields Rd West	
BYK/HTN/WLK NE6	6 D5
Shield St JES NE2	6 A4
Shiel Gdns CRAM NE23	37 K2
Shillaw PI CRAM NE23	37 K2
Shilmore Rd GOS/KPK NE3	55 K5
Shilton CI HAR/WTLS NE34	76 A6
Shincliffe Av SWCK/CAS SR5	105 G3
Shincliffe Gdns	
LWF/SPW/WRK NE9	101 J2
Shincliffe La DHAM DH1	169 J3
Shinwell Crs RDHAMSE DH6	172 B4
Shinwell Ter RDHAMSE DH6	182 D1
SEA/MUR SR7	149 G5
Shipcote La GATE NE8	11 G7
Shipcote Ter GATE NE8	11 H7
Shipley Av ELS/FEN NE4	69 J5
Shipley PI BYK/HTN/WLK NE6	6 C5
Shipley Ri BYK/HTN/WLK NE6	7 G5
Shipley Rd TYNE/NSHE NE30	61 G3
Shipley St	
BW/LEM/TK/HW NE15	68 C5
Shipley Wk BYK/HTN/WLK * NE6	6 C5
Shipton CI BOLCOL NE35	90 C5
Shire Cha DHAM * DH1	156 E1
Shire Farm Gv ASHGTN NE63	23 G5
Shirlaw CI WD/WHPE/BLK NE5	54 C6
Shirley Gdns SUNDSW SR3	120 B3
Shirwood Av WICK/BNPF NE16	84 E7
Shop Spouts BLAY NE21	84 A1
Shoreham Ct GOS/KPK NE3	55 C5
Shoreham Sq SUNDSW SR3	119 J3
Shorestone Av	
TYNE/NSHE NE30	51 F6
Shore St CLDN/WHIT/ROK SR6	106 D4
Short Gv SEA/MUR SR7	149 F5
Shortridge St SSH * NE33	3 K6
Shortridge Ter JES NE2	71 F2
Shot Factory La CNUT NE1	10 B1
Shotley Av SWCK/CAS SR5	106 C3
Shotley Ct ASHGTN NE63	23 H3
Shotley Gdns	
LWF/SPW/WRK NE9	11 J9
Shotley Grove Rd	
CON/LDGT DH8	122 B2
Shotton Av BLYTH NE24	35 G4
Shotton Bank PLEE/EAS SR8	174 A7
Shotton La CRAM NE23	32 C5
MPTH NE61	32 A7
PLEE/EAS SR8	174 B6
RDHAMSE DH6	173 J4
Shotton Rd PLEE/EAS SR8	175 G3
Shotton Wy FELL NE10	89 C6
Shrewsbury CI LGB/KIL NE12	57 K6
PLEE/EAS SR8	174 C5
Shrewsbury Crs SUNDSW SR3	119 K3
Shrewsbury Dr SMOOR NE27	48 D3
Shrewsbury St DUN/TMV NE11	9 H8
SEA/MUR SR7	150 E3
Shrewsbury Ter SEA/MUR SR7	75 G4
Shrigley Gdns GOS/KPK NE3	55 K5
Shropshire Dr DHAM DH1	157 K7
Shunner CI WASHN NE37	102 C7
Sibthorpe St NSHW NE29	2 E3
Side CNUT NE1	5 L8
Side Cliff Rd	
CLDN/WHIT/ROK SR6	106 D2
Sidegate DHAM DH1	16 C2
Sidgate	
CNUT (off Eldon Sq) NE1	5 J5
Sidlaw Av CLSW/PEL DH2	129 G5
NSHW NE29	60 D1
Sidlaw Ct ASHGTN NE63	24 A4
Sidmouth CI HLS DH4	132 A3
SEA/MUR SR7	150 A2
Sidmouth Rd	
LWF/SPW/WRK NE9	101 F2
NSHW NE29	60 A4
Sidney Gv ELS/FEN NE4	4 C5
GATE NE8	10 C6
Sidney St BLYTH NE24	31 F7
BOLCOL NE35	90 D4
NSHW NE29	2 D2
Sidney Ter STLY/ANP DH9	112 B6
Silent Bank RDHAMSE DH6	171 H4
Silkey's La NSHW NE29	2 A3
Silksworth CI SUNDSW SR3	119 K6
Silksworth Gdns	
LWF/SPW/WRK NE9	101 J3
Silksworth Hall Dr	
SUNDSW SR3	133 K1
Silksworth La SUNDSW SR3	120 A5
Silksworth Rd SUNDSW SR3	133 C1
Silksworth Rw SUND SR1	14 B4
Silksworth Ter SUNDSW SR3	120 A7
Silksworth Wy SUNDSW SR3	133 H1
Silkwood CI CRAM NE23	33 H6
Silloth Av WD/WHPE/BLK NE5	68 C3
Silloth Dr WASHN NE37	102 E3
Silloth PI TYNE/NSHE NE30	51 F7
Silloth Rd SUNDSW SR3	119 H4
Silver Cts BDN/LAN/SAC DH7	167 G6
Silverdale SUNDSW SR3	134 A3
Silverdale Av FELL NE10	89 F5
Silverdale Dr BLAY NE21	83 H3
Silverdale Rd CRAM NE23	33 H6
Silverdale Ter GATE NE8	11 G8
Silverdale Wy HAR/WTLS NE34	90 D1
WICK/BNPF NE16	98 D1
Silver Fox Wy SMOOR NE27	59 G2
Silverhill Dr WD/WHPE/BLK NE5	68 C4
The Silverlink North	
SMOOR NE27	59 G1
The Silverlink SMOOR NE27	59 J3
Silver Lonnen	
WD/WHPE/BLK NE5	69 F3
Silvermere Dr RYTON NE40	67 F7
Silverstone LGB/KIL NE12	48 A6
Silverstone Rd WASHN NE37	103 G5
Silver St CON/LDGT DH8	122 D3
DHAM DH1	16 D3
SUND SR1	15 J2
TYNE/NSHE NE30	61 H3
Silverwood Gdns	
DUN/TMV NE11	86 B7
Simonburn Av ELS/FEN NE4	69 J3
NSHW NE29	60 D1
Simonburn La ASHGTN NE63	24 B3
Simon PI DIN/WO NE13	46 A4
Simonside PRUD NE42	80 B3
WBAY NE26	41 G4
Simonside Av STKFD/GP NE62	23 G5
WLSD/HOW NE28	59 H6
Simonside CI MPTH NE61	20 B6
Simonside Rd BLAY NE21	84 A3
SUNDSW SR3	119 H3
Simonside Ter	
BYK/HTN/WLK NE6	71 H3

NWBGN NE64 ....19 F7
Simonside Vw JRW NE32 ....74 A7
PONT/DH NE20 ....43 F2
Simonside Wy LGB/KIL NE12 ....48 B5
Simpson Ct ASHGTN NE63 ....24 C2
Simpson St BLYTH NE24 ....31 G6
MLFD/PNYW SR4 ....14 A2
NSHW NE29 ....60 C5
WBAY NE26 ....51 G5
Simpson Ter JES NE2 ....6 A5
Sinclair Dr CLS/BIR/GTL DH3 ....115 K6
Sinclair Gdns MONK NE25 ....40 A5
Sinderby Cl GOS/KPK NE3 ....56 D2
Sir Godfrey Thomson Ct
FELL NE10 ....12 B7
Six-mile Br DIN/WO NE13 ....46 C1
Sixth Av ASHGTN NE63 ....24 A3
BLYTH NE24 ....35 F1
BYK/HTN/WLK NE6 ....7 G2
MPTH NE61 ....21 F6
Sixth St PLEE/EAS SR8 ....175 H3
Skafell Ct STLY/ANP DH9 ....125 H4
Skaylock Dr WASHS NE38 ....116 C3
Skelder Av LGB/KIL NE12 ....57 H4
Skelton Ct GOS/KPK NE3 ....55 J2
Skerne Cl PLEE/EAS SR8 ....174 D6
Skerne Gv CON/LDGT DH8 ....123 K2
Skiddaw Cl PLEE/EAS SR8 ....175 F4
Skiddaw Ct STLY/ANP DH9 ....125 G4
Skiddaw Dr
CLDN/WHIT/ROK * SR6 ....92 C7
Skiddaw Pl
LWF/SPW/WRK NE9 ....101 H1
Skinnerburn Rd ELS/FEN NE4 ....10 A2
Skipsey Ct NSHW NE29 ....60 B7
Skipton Cl BDLGTN NE22 ....28 D4
CRAM NE23 ....33 J6
Skirlaw Cl WASHS NE38 ....117 F2
Ski Vw SUNDSW SR3 ....119 K6
Skye Ct SUNDSW SR3 ....133 K1
Skye Gv JRW NE32 ....90 C2
Slaidburn Rd STLY/ANP DH9 ....112 D7
Slake Rd JRW NE32 ....74 B3
Slaley WASHS NE38 ....117 G5
Slaley Cl FELL NE10 ....88 E5
Slaley Ct BDLGTN NE22 ....29 G5
SUNDSW SR3 ....134 A1
Slatyford La
WD/WHPE/BLK NE5 ....68 E3
Sled La WYLAM NE41 ....81 J1
Sledmere Cl PLEE/EAS SR8 ....174 E3
Sleekburn Av BDLGTN NE22 ....29 K3
Slingsby Gdns LGB/HTN NE7 ....57 K7
Sloane Ct JES NE2 ....5 L3
Smailes La ROWG NE39 ....96 E3
Smailes St STLY/ANP DH9 ....126 C2
Smallholdings
ASHGTN
(off Woodhorn Demesne) NE63 ....18 E6
Smallhope Dr
BDN/LAN/SAC DH7 ....140 C5
Smeaton Ct WLSD/HOW NE28 ....73 J2
Smeaton St WLSD/HOW NE28 ....73 J2
Smillie Cl PLEE/EAS SR8 ....174 E3
Smillie Rd PLEE/EAS SR8 ....175 F1
Smithburn Rd FELL NE10 ....12 E9
Smith Cl RDHAMSE DH6 ....170 B1
Smithfield DHAM DH1 ....156 C1
Smith Gv ASHBK/HED/RY SR2 ....134 E1
Smith St ASHBK/HED/RY SR2 ....135 F1
SSH NE33 ....75 F3
Smith Ter GATE NE8 ....9 M6
Smithyford
LWF/SPW/WRK NE9 ....101 G4
Smithy La DUN/TMV NE11 ....100 E4
Smithy St SSH NE33 ....3 G7
Smyrna Pl SUND SR1 ....15 H5
Snaith Ter WNGT TS28 ....183 J3
Snipes Dene ROWG NE39 ....97 G2
Snowdon Ct STLY/ANP DH9 ....125 G4
Snowdon Gdns DUN/TMV NE11 ....86 A6
Snowdon Gv BOL NE36 ....91 F5
Snowdon Pl PLEE/EAS SR8 ....174 B5
Snowdrop Av PLEE/EAS SR8 ....175 G3
Snow's Green Rd
CON/LDGT DH8 ....122 C1
Soane Gdns HAR/WTLS NE34 ....91 H1
Softley Pl
BW/LEM/TK/HW NE15 ....68 D4
Solingen Est BLYTH NE24 ....35 H2
Solway Av TYNE/NSHE NE30 ....50 E7
Solway Rd HEBB NE31 ....73 G7
Solway Sq SUNDSW SR3 ....119 J3
Solway St BYK/HTN/WLK NE6 ....7 H8
Somerford
LWF/SPW/WRK NE9 ....102 B3
Somersby Dr GOS/KPK NE3 ....55 J5
Somerset Cl ASHGTN NE63 ....23 G1
Somerset Gdns
WLSD/HOW NE28 ....58 C7
Somerset Gv NSHW NE29 ....60 B2
Somerset Pl ELS/FEN NE4 ....4 D7
Somerset Rd CON/LDGT DH8 ....137 F1
HEBB NE31 ....89 H1
SUNDSW SR3 ....119 H3
Somerset Sq SUNDSW SR3 ....119 H3
Somerset St SUNDSW * SR3 ....120 A5
Somerton Ct GOS/KPK NE3 ....55 G4
Sophia St SEA/MUR SR7 ....150 E1
Sophy St SWCK/CAS SR5 ....106 B3
Sorley St MLFD/PNYW SR4 ....106 A7
Sorrel Cl ASHGTN NE63 ....23 J3
ELS/FEN* NE4 ....69 H4
Sorrel Gdns HAR/WTLS NE34 ....91 J1
Soulby Ct DIN/WO NE13 ....55 H2
Sourmilk Hill La
LWF/SPW/WRK NE9 ....87 G6
Souter Rd GOS/KPK NE3 ....56 A5
Souter Vw CLDN/WHIT/ROK SR6 ....93 F2
South Ap CLSW/PEL DH2 ....129 J5
South Av HAR/WTLS NE34 ....75 K6
South Bailey DHAM DH1 ....16 C6
South Bend GOS/KPK NE3 ....56 B1
South Bents Av
CLDN/WHIT/ROK SR6 ....92 E6
South Benwell Rd
BW/LEM/TK/HW NE15 ....69 G7
Southburn Cl HLS DH4 ....132 A7
South Burns CLS/BIR/GTL DH3 ....129 J3
South Cliff
CLDN/WHIT/ROK
(off Roker Ter) SR6 ....107 F3
South Cl HAR/WTLS NE34 ....75 K6
HLH DH5 ....160 C1
RYTON NE40 ....66 E7
Southcote WICK/BNPF NE16 ....84 E7
South Crs BOLCOL NE35 ....90 D4
DHAM DH1 ....16 A1
SEA/MUR SR7 ....151 F1
WASHS NE38 ....116 D6
South Cft LGB/KIL NE12 ....58 A3
Southcroft WASHS NE38 ....117 F5
South Cross St CON/LDGT DH8 ....123 J3
South Dene HAR/WTLS NE34 ....75 F6
South Dock SUND SR1 ....15 L2
South Dr CLDN/WHIT/ROK SR6 ....91 K3
DIN/WO NE13 ....36 D2
DIN/WO NE13 ....54 D2
HEBB NE31 ....72 E7
South Durham Ct SUND SR1 ....15 H5
South East Vw PLEE/EAS SR8 ....175 H3
South Eldon St SSH NE33 ....75 F4
Southend Av BLYTH NE24 ....34 E1
Southend Rd
LWF/SPW/WRK NE9 ....87 H7
SUNDSW SR3 ....119 J4
Southern Cl ASHGTN NE63 ....24 D2
Southern Rd BYK/HTN/WLK NE6 ....72 B7
Southern Wy RYTON NE40 ....66 E7
Southey St SSH * NE33 ....75 H3
South Farm BDLGTN NE22 ....28 A6
Southfield CLSW/PEL DH2 ....114 E7
Southfield Gdns
WICK/BNPF NE16 ....85 G5
Southfield La CHPW NE17 ....110 B3
Southfield Rd HAR/WTLS NE34 ....75 K3
LGB/KIL NE12 ....57 J4
WICK/BNPF NE16 ....85 G6
Southfields CRAM NE23 ....47 G1
Southfield Wy DHAM DH1 ....156 B5
South Foreshore SSH NE33 ....61 K7
Southfork
BW/LEM/TK/HW NE15 ....68 A3
South Frederick St SSH NE33 ....75 F4
Southgate LGB/KIL NE12 ....47 K6
South Grange Pk
SEA/MUR SR7 ....135 F5
South Gv RYTON NE40 ....67 F7
South Hetton Rd HLH DH5 ....160 C1
South Hill Crs
ASHBK/HED/RY SR2 ....14 B7
South Hill Rd GATE NE8 ....10 B6
Southhill Rd HAR/WTLS NE34 ....76 A5
Southlands JRW NE32 ....90 B3
LGB/HTN NE7 ....71 G1
TYNE/NSHE NE30 ....61 F2
South La BOL NE36 ....91 G5
South Lea BDN/LAN/SAC DH7 ....155 G1
South Magdalene
CON/LDGT DH8 ....109 H5
South Market St HLH DH5 ....148 A4
Southmayne Rd
MLFD/PNYW SR4 ....119 H2
Southmead Av
WD/WHPE/BLK NE5 ....69 F2
South Mdw STLY/ANP DH9 ....111 F6
South Moor Rd STLY/ANP DH9 ....126 C3
South Nelson Rd CRAM NE23 ....32 E7
South Newsham Rd
BLYTH NE24 ....34 E4
South Pde FELL NE10 ....13 L4
RDHAMSE DH6 ....172 C6
WBAY NE26 ....51 F4
South Preston Gv NSHW NE29 ....2 B2
South Preston Ter NSHW NE29 ....2 C2
South Railway St
SEA/MUR SR7 ....150 E1
South Rdg ASHGTN NE63 ....24 D3
GOS/KPK NE3 ....56 B2
South Riggs BDLGTN NE22 ....29 F6
South Rd CHPW NE17 ....95 H4
DHAM DH1 ....168 D4
PRUD NE42 ....80 D2
South Rw GATE NE8 ....6 D9
South Sherbourne ROWG NE39 ....97 G3
South Shore Rd GATE NE8 ....6 B8
South Side PLEE/EAS SR8 ....162 C6
South St CLSW/PEL DH2 ....129 H3
CNUT NE1 ....5 J9
DHAM DH1 ....16 C5
GATE NE8 ....11 H6
GOS/KPK NE3 ....56 A5
HLH DH5 ....147 F4
HLS DH4 ....132 B4
ROWG NE39 ....96 B1
SMOOR NE27 ....49 H5
SUND SR1 ....14 E4
South Ter BDN/LAN/SAC DH7 ....165 J1
DHAM DH1 ....156 B4
PLEE/EAS SR8 ....175 G3
SEA/MUR SR7 ....151 F1
SWCK/CAS SR5 ....106 B4
WLSD/HOW NE28 ....73 G1
South Vw ASHGTN NE63 ....23 J1
BDN/LAN/SAC DH7 ....167 H7
BLYTH NE24 ....34 E3
CLDN/WHIT/ROK SR6 ....106 D2
CLS/BIR/GTL DH3 ....115 K2
CON/LDGT DH8 ....122 C3
DHAM DH1 ....17 K3
HLH DH5 ....160 C2
JRW NE32 ....73 J5
MPTH NE61 ....21 J2
RDHAMSE (off Front St) DH6 ....173 J3
RHTLP TS27 ....184 C2
SEA/MUR SR7 ....150 A3
STKFD/GP NE62 ....22 E6
STLY/ANP DH9 ....111 K4
WASHS NE38 ....117 G5
WD/WHPE/BLK NE5 ....68 C3
South View Gdns
STLY/ANP DH9 ....125 J4
South View Rd
MLFD/PNYW SR4 ....118 E1
South View Ter HLS DH4 ....131 K7
WICK/BNPF NE16 ....85 F4
South Vw West
BYK/HTN/WLK NE6 ....6 D4
Southward WBAY NE26 ....41 G3
Southward Cl WBAY NE26 ....41 G3
Southward Wy MONK NE25 ....40 B7
Southway BDN/LAN/SAC DH7 ....140 B4
BW/LEM/TK/HW NE15 ....68 C4
LWF/SPW/WRK NE9 ....87 H6
PLEE/EAS SR8 ....174 D5
Southwick Rd SWCK/CAS SR5 ....14 E1
SWCK/CAS SR5 ....106 B4
Southwold Gdns SUNDSW SR3 ....119 K6
Southwold Pl CRAM NE23 ....37 K2
South Woodbine St SSH NE33 ....3 K7
Southwood Gdns GOS/KPK NE3 ....55 K6
Sovereign Ct ELS/FEN NE4 ....4 D8
JES NE2 ....71 F3
Sovereign Pl ELS/FEN NE4 ....4 C8
Spa Dr CON/LDGT DH8 ....108 C7
Spalding Cl LGB/HTN NE7 ....57 J6
Spanish Battery
TYNE/NSHE NE30 ....61 J3
Sparkwell Cl HLS DH4 ....132 A3
Spartylea WASHS NE38 ....117 H5
Spa Well Cl BLAY NE21 ....83 K4
Spa Well Dr SWCK/CAS SR5 ....105 G3
Speedwell Ct ASHGTN NE63 ....23 H4
Spelter Works Rd
ASHBK/HED/RY SR2 ....121 F4
Spelvit La MPTH NE61 ....20 C6
Spen Burn ROWG NE39 ....96 C1
Spencer Cl STLY/ANP DH9 ....127 F1
Spencer Ct BLYTH NE24 ....30 D5
Spencer Dr MPTH NE61 ....21 J2
Spencer Gv WICK/BNPF NE16 ....84 E4
Spencer Rd BLYTH NE24 ....30 D5
Spencers Bank
WICK/BNPF NE16 ....84 E3
Spencer St BYK/HTN/WLK NE6 ....7 H1
CON/LDGT DH8 ....123 F5
NSHW NE29 ....2 D3
Spence Ter NSHW NE29 ....2 B2
Spenfield Rd
WD/WHPE/BLK NE5 ....55 H7
Spen La ROWG NE39 ....96 C1
RYTON NE40 ....82 B5
Spen Rd ROWG NE39 ....96 B1
Spenser St JRW NE32 ....73 K3
Spen St STLY/ANP DH9 ....126 C2
Spetchells PRUD * NE42 ....80 D1
Spinneyside Gdns
DUN/TMV NE11 ....85 K5
Spinney Ter BYK/HTN/WLK NE6 ....7 M5
The Spinney CRAM NE23 ....47 J1
LGB/HTN (off Newton Pl) NE7 ....71 H1
MPTH NE61 ....20 E7
PLEE/EAS SR8 ....162 B5
WASHS NE38 ....117 F4
Spire Hollin PLEE/EAS SR8 ....174 D4
Spire Rd WASHN NE37 ....103 H6
Spires La BYK/HTN/WLK NE6 ....7 H5
Spital Crs NWBGN NE64 ....24 E2
Spital Rd NWBGN NE64 ....24 E2
Spital Ter GOS/KPK NE3 ....56 C5
Split Crow Rd GATE NE8 ....11 J7
Spohr Ter SSH NE33 ....75 H2
Spoors Cottages
WICK/BNPF NE16 ....84 E6
Spoor St DUN/TMV NE11 ....9 H6
Spout La WASHN NE37 ....103 F5
WASHS NE38 ....103 F7
Springbank Rd JES NE2 ....6 C2
SUNDSW SR3 ....119 H3
Springbank Sq SUNDSW SR3 ....119 H3
Springdale Av TRIM TS29 ....183 G6
Springfield NSHW * NE29 ....2 C1
PRUD NE42 ....63 G7
Springfield Av
LWF/SPW/WRK NE9 ....101 J4
Springfield Cl PRUD NE42 ....63 H7
Springfield Crs SEA/MUR SR7 ....150 D2
Springfield Gdns
CLS/BIR/GTL DH3 ....129 J2
WLSD/HOW NE28 ....58 B7
Springfield Gv MONK NE25 ....50 C6
Springfield Pk DHAM DH1 ....156 B6
Springfield Pl
LWF/SPW/WRK NE9 ....87 G6
Springfield Rd BLAY NE21 ....83 K2
HLS DH4 ....132 B4
WD/WHPE/BLK NE5 ....69 G2
Springfield Ter FELL NE10 ....12 B9
PLEE/EAS SR8 ....163 G6
Spring Garden Cl SUND SR1 ....15 G4
Spring Gdns NSHW NE29 ....2 B2
Springhill Gdns
BW/LEM/TK/HW NE15 ....69 H5
Springhill Wk MPTH NE61 ....20 C6
Springhouse Cl CON/LDGT DH8 ....108 E4
Springhouse La
CON/LDGT DH8 ....108 E5
Spring Pk BDLGTN NE22 ....29 G6
Springside BDN/LAN/SAC DH7 ....143 H5
The Springs CLS/BIR/GTL DH3 ....115 K3
Spring St ELS/FEN * NE4 ....4 F5
Springsyde Cl WICK/BNPF NE16 ....84 C7
Spring Ter NSHW NE29 ....2 C1
Springwell Av
BDN/LAN/SAC DH7 ....154 B3
BYK/HTN/WLK NE6 ....7 L8
DHAM DH1 ....156 B6
JRW NE32 ....74 A5
LWF/SPW/WRK NE9 ....101 J3
Springwell Cl
BDN/LAN/SAC * DH7 ....154 B3
Springwell Rd DHAM DH1 ....156 B6
JRW NE32 ....73 K6
LWF/SPW/WRK NE9 ....102 A2
MLFD/PNYW SR4 ....119 H3
Springwood HEBB NE31 ....72 E4
The Square STKFD/GP NE62 ....22 E6
WICK/BNPF (off Front St) NE16 ....85 F5
Squires Gdns FELL NE10 ....87 K5
Stack Garth BDN/LAN/SAC DH7 ....167 H5
Stadium Rd GATE NE8 ....11 M2
Stadium Wy SWCK/CAS SR5 ....14 D1
Stafford Gv
ASHBK/HED/RY SR2 ....134 E1
SWCK/CAS SR5 ....106 B3
Stafford Pl PLEE/EAS SR8 ....174 C3
Staffordshire Dr DHAM DH1 ....158 A6
Staffords La
CLDN/WHIT/ROK SR6 ....93 F4
Stafford St SUND SR1 ....15 J2
Stafford Vls
LWF/SPW/WRK NE9 ....102 B4
Stagshaw LGB/KIL NE12 ....47 J4
Staindrop FELL NE10 ....88 C7
Staindrop Rd DHAM DH1 ....156 E3
Staindrop Ter STLY/ANP DH9 ....125 H3
Staines Rd BYK/HTN/WLK NE6 ....7 K9
Stainmore Dr CLS/BIR/GTL DH3 ....145 J2
Stainton Dr FELL NE10 ....12 D7
Stainton Gv
CLDN/WHIT/ROK SR6 ....92 C7
Stainton St East SSH NE33 ....75 H2
Stainton Wy PLEE/EAS SR8 ....174 D4
Staithes Av LGB/KIL NE12 ....57 J4
Staithes La MPTH NE61 ....20 E4
Staithes Rd WASHS NE38 ....117 J3
Staithes St BYK/HTN/WLK NE6 ....72 D5
Staith La BLAY NE21 ....67 J7
Staiths Rd DUN/TMV NE11 ....9 J5
Stakeford Crs STKFD/GP NE62 ....23 H6
Stakeford La STKFD/GP NE62 ....23 G6
Stalks Rd DIN/WO NE13 ....46 B3
Stamford Av MONK NE25 ....40 B6
SUNDSW SR3 ....119 K3
Stamfordham Av NSHW NE29 ....60 B5
Stamfordham Cl
WLSD/HOW NE28 ....72 C1
Stamfordham Ms
WD/WHPE/BLK NE5 ....69 H2
Stamfordham Rd
PONT/DH NE20 ....52 B2
WD/WHPE/BLK NE5 ....53 H4
Stampley Cl BLAY NE21 ....83 J3
Stamps La SUND SR1 ....15 J3
Stancley Rd PRUD NE42 ....80 E2
Standfield Gdns FELL NE10 ....88 E4
Standish St STLY/ANP DH9 ....126 B2
Stanelaw Wy STLY/ANP DH9 ....112 D5
Staneway FELL NE10 ....102 A1
Stanfield Ct LGB/HTN NE7 ....58 A7
Stanfield Gdns FELL * NE10 ....88 E4
Stanhope WASHS NE38 ....116 B1
Stanhope Cl
BDN/LAN/SAC DH7 ....167 H6
DHAM DH1 ....156 E2
HLS DH4 ....147 G1
Stanhope Gdns STLY/ANP DH9 ....125 H3
Stanhope Pde SSH NE33 ....75 H3
Stanhope Rd
CLDN/WHIT/ROK SR6 ....106 E1
HAR/WTLS NE34 ....75 F5
JRW NE32 ....74 B6
SSH NE33 ....75 H4
Stanhope St ELS/FEN NE4 ....4 D5
SSH NE33 ....3 H6
Stanhope Wy ELS/FEN NE4 ....4 E5
Stanley Cl RDHAMSE DH6 ....170 C1
Stanley Crs PRUD NE42 ....80 E1
Stanley Gdns CON/LDGT DH8 ....123 F4
LWF/SPW/WRK NE9 ....101 J3
Stanley Gv BDLGTN NE22 ....29 H5
LGB/HTN NE7 ....57 G7
Stanley St BLYTH NE24 ....31 H6
CON/LDGT DH8 ....123 F4
ELS/FEN* NE4 ....4 A9
HAR/WTLS NE34 ....75 F6
JRW NE32 ....74 A4
NSHW NE29 ....2 D3
SEA/MUR SR7 ....135 H7
SWCK/CAS SR5 ....105 F4
WLSD/HOW NE28 ....59 H7
Stanley St West NSHW NE29 ....2 C3
Stanmore Rd
BYK/HTN/WLK NE6 ....71 J2
Stannerford Rd RYTON NE40 ....66 A6
Stannington Av
BYK/HTN/WLK NE6 ....6 E2
Stannington Gdns
ASHBK/HED/RY SR2 ....120 C4
Stannington Gv
ASHBK/HED/RY SR2 ....120 C4
Stannington Pl
BYK/HTN/WLK NE6 ....6 F2
PONT/DH NE20 ....43 G1
Stannington Rd NSHW NE29 ....60 A5
Stannington Station Rd
MPTH NE61 ....27 G7
Stannington St BLYTH NE24 ....31 H7
Stansfield St
CLDN/WHIT/ROK SR6 ....106 E4
Stanstead Cl SWCK/CAS SR5 ....104 E5
Stanton Av BLYTH NE24 ....34 D2
HAR/WTLS NE34 ....75 J4
Stanton Cl FELL NE10 ....89 F5
Stanton Dr MPTH NE61 ....21 H2
Stanton Rd SMOOR NE27 ....49 G7
TYNE/NSHE NE30 ....60 D1
Stanton St ELS/FEN NE4 ....4 D5
Stanway Dr LGB/HTN NE7 ....57 G7
Stanwick St TYNE/NSHE NE30 ....61 H2
Stapeley Vw GOS/KPK NE3 ....55 H5
Stapleford Cl
WD/WHPE/BLK NE5 ....69 F2
Staple Rd JRW NE32 ....74 A4
Stapylton Dr
ASHBK/HED/RY SR2 ....120 B2
Starbeck Av JES NE2 ....6 A2
Starbeck Ms JES * NE2 ....6 A2
Stardale Av BLYTH NE24 ....34 C1
Stargate Cl BDN/LAN/SAC DH7 ....153 K3
Stargate La RYTON NE40 ....67 G7
Starlight Crs MONK NE25 ....39 K5
Starling Wk WICK/BNPF NE16 ....99 F3
Startforth Cl CLS/BIR/GTL DH3 ....145 J1
Station Ap BOL NE36 ....91 J4
DHAM DH1 ....16 B3
LGB/KIL NE12 ....57 K4
SSH* NE33 ....3 H6
Station Av BDN/LAN/SAC DH7 ....165 H2
BDN/LAN/SAC DH7 ....167 H6
HLH DH5 ....147 K5
Station Bank DHAM DH1 ....16 C3
PSHWF NE43 ....79 J2
RYTON NE40 ....66 E5
Station Crs SEA/MUR SR7 ....135 H7
Station Est East SEA/MUR SR7 ....149 F5
Station Est North
SEA/MUR SR7 ....149 F5
Station Est South
SEA/MUR SR7 ....149 F5
Station Field Rd STLY/ANP DH9 ....112 D5
Station La CLS/BIR/GTL DH3 ....115 H2
CLSW/PEL DH2 ....128 D1
DHAM DH1 ....17 G2
WNGT TS28 ....183 K5
Station Rd ASHBK/HED/RY SR2 ....135 G1
ASHGTN NE63 ....23 J1
BDLGTN NE22 ....29 H5
BDN/LAN/SAC DH7 ....140 C5
BDN/LAN/SAC DH7 ....166 E1
BDN/LAN/SAC DH7 ....167 H6
BOLCOL NE35 ....90 C2
BW/LEM/TK/HW NE15 ....66 B1
BW/LEM/TK/HW NE15 ....67 H4
CLS/BIR/GTL DH3 ....129 J4
CLSW/PEL DH2 ....129 J4
CRAM NE23 ....38 B1
CRAM NE23 ....39 G7
CRAM NE23 ....47 F1
DIN/WO NE13 ....55 F4
FELL NE10 ....13 L3
GOS/KPK NE3 ....56 E5
HEBB NE31 ....73 F5
HLH DH5 ....147 K5
HLS DH4 ....117 H6
HLS DH4 ....131 J1
HLS DH4 ....132 B6
HLS DH4 ....146 C7
LGB/KIL NE12 ....47 H5
LGB/KIL NE12 ....57 K3
LWF/SPW/WRK NE9 ....86 E7
NSHW NE29 ....60 B6
PLEE/EAS SR8 ....163 G5
PRUD NE42 ....80 C1
RDHAMSE DH6 ....158 D2
RDHAMSE DH6 ....173 G3
RHTLP TS27 ....185 H2
ROWG NE39 ....97 H4
SEA/MUR SR7 ....135 F7
SEA/MUR SR7 ....149 F5
SMOOR NE27 ....49 F6
SSH NE33 ....3 G8
STLY/ANP DH9 ....112 D7
STLY/ANP DH9 ....113 J6
STLY/ANP DH9 ....125 H4
SWCK/CAS SR5 ....106 C1
TRIM TS29 ....182 E5
TYNE/NSHE NE30 ....51 G6
WASHS NE38 ....117 H2
WBAY NE26 ....51 F5
WLSD/HOW NE28 ....58 B5
WLSD/HOW NE28 ....73 J2
WNGT TS28 ....183 K5
WYLAM NE41 ....65 H5
Station Rd North LGB/KIL NE12 ....57 K2
Station St BDN/LAN/SAC DH7 ....165 F4
BLYTH NE24 ....31 G6
RDHAMSE DH6 ....160 E6
SUND SR1 ....14 E4
Station Ter TYNE/NSHE NE30 ....61 H3
Station Vw BDN/LAN/SAC DH7 ....165 H2
HLH DH5 ....147 K5
Staveley Rd
CLDN/WHIT/ROK SR6 ....92 C7
PLEE/EAS SR8 ....175 F4
Stavordale St SEA/MUR SR7 ....150 E2
Stavordale St West
SEA/MUR SR7 ....150 E3
Stavordale Ter
LWF/SPW/WRK NE9 ....11 K9
Staward Av MONK NE25 ....40 A6
Staward Ter BYK/HTN/WLK NE6 ....72 B7
Staynebrigg FELL NE10 ....88 C6
Stead La BDLGTN NE22 ....29 H5
The Steads MPTH NE61 ....20 E7
Stead St WLSD/HOW NE28 ....59 J7
Steavenson St RDHAMSE DH6 ....180 A3
Stedham Cl WASHN NE37 ....103 G3
Steel St CON/LDGT DH8 ....123 F4
Steep Hl SUNDSW SR3 ....119 F6
Stella Bank BLAY NE21 ....67 H6
Stella Hall BLAY NE21 ....67 J7
Stella La BLAY NE21 ....67 H7
Stella Rd BLAY NE21 ....67 J7
Stephenson Cl HLH DH5 ....148 A4
Stephenson Ct TYNE/NSHE NE30 ....2 F2
Stephenson Rd
BYK/HTN/WLK NE6 ....71 H2
PLEE/EAS SR8 ....174 D1
WASHN NE37 ....103 G3
Stephenson St GATE NE8 ....10 C8
SEA/MUR SR7 ....149 H5
TYNE/NSHE NE30 ....2 E1
WLSD/HOW NE28 ....73 K2
Stephenson Ter
BW/LEM/TK/HW
(off Hexham Rd) NE15 ....67 F1
FELL NE10 ....12 C9
Stephenson Wy BLAY NE21 ....83 K4
STKFD/GP NE62 ....29 G2
Stephens Rd SEA/MUR SR7 ....149 G5
Stephen St BLYTH NE24 ....31 G6
BYK/HTN/WLK NE6 ....6 D5
CON/LDGT DH8 ....123 F4
Stepney Bank CNUT NE1 ....6 C5
Stepney La CNUT NE1 ....6 A6
Stepney Rd JES NE2 ....6 B4
Sterling Cottages FELL NE10 ....12 A9
Sterling St MLFD/PNYW SR4 ....106 A7
Steward Crs HAR/WTLS NE34 ....76 B4
Stewart Av
ASHBK/HED/RY SR2 ....134 E1
Stewart Dr BOL NE36 ....91 F5
WNGT TS28 ....183 K2
Stewart St MLFD/PNYW SR4 ....106 A7
PLEE/EAS SR8 ....162 E5
SEA/MUR SR7 ....151 F2
SUNDSW SR3 ....120 A7
Stileford FELL NE10 ....13 K9
Stirling Av JRW NE32 ....74 C7

ROWG NE39 ....97 G4
Stirling Cl *WASHS* NE38 ....117 H2
Stirling Dr *BDLGTN* NE22 ....29 J4
NSHW NE29 ....60 A2
Stirling La *ROWG* NE39 ....97 G4
St Leonards Cl *PLEE/EAS* SR8 ....174 C5
St Michaels Wy *SUND* SR1 ....14 C5
Stobart St *BDN/LAN/SAC* DH7 ....143 G1
SWCK/CAS SR5 ....14 D1
Stobhill Vls *MPTH* NE61 ....20 E6
Stockerley Br *CON/LDGT* DH8 ...139 G2
Stockerley La
BDN/LAN/SAC DH7 ....139 G2
Stockerley Rd *CON/LDGT* DH8 ...123 H6
Stockholm Cl *WASHS* NE38 ....59 K5
Stockley Av *SWCK/CAS* SR5 ....105 G3
Stockley Cl *BDN/LAN/SAC* DH7 ...167 H1
Stockley Gv *BDN/LAN/SAC* DH7 ..176 D4
Stockley La *BDN/LAN/SAC* DH7 ...176 C4
Stockley Rd *WASHS* NE38 ....103 H3
Stocksfield Av
WD/WHPE/BLK NE5 ....69 G4
Stockton Rd
ASHBK/HED/RY SR2 ....14 E8
ASHBK/HED/RY SR2 ....135 F2
DHAM DH1 ....16 E7
NSHW NE29 ....2 A6
PLEE/EAS SR8 ....162 B7
SEA/MUR SR7 ....135 F5
SUND SR1 ....14 D6
Stockton St *SEA/MUR* SR7 ....135 H7
Stockwell Gn
BYK/HTN/WLK NE6 ....72 B3
Stoddart St *HAR/WTLS* NE34 ......75 C5
JES NE2 ....6 B4
Stoker Av *WASHN* NE34 ....74 D7
Stoker Crs *RDHAMSE* * DH6 ......182 D2
Stoker Ter *ROWG* NE39 ....96 C2
Stokesley Gv *LGB/HTN* NE7 ....57 G7
Stokoe Dr *ASHGTN* NE63 ....24 C2
Stokoe St *CON/LDGT* * DH8 ....122 E3
Stone Br *DHAM* DH1 ....168 A3
Stone Cellar Rd *WASHN* NE37 ....102 D3
Stonechat Pl *LGB/KIL* NE12 ....57 G3
Stonecroft Gdns *LGB/HTN* NE7 ...57 K7
Stonecross *ASHGTN* NE63 ....23 H3
Stonefold Cl
WD/WHPE/BLK NE5 ....55 F7
Stonegate
BW/LEM/TK/HW NE15 ....64 D2
Stonehaugh Wy *PONT/DH* NE20 ...42 C7
Stonehills
FELL (off Shields Rd) NE10 ....13 M5
Stoneleigh *MPTH* NE61 ....27 J2
Stoneleigh Av *LGB/KIL* NE12 ....57 G3
Stoneleigh Cl *HLS* DH4 ....132 A6
Stone Rw *CLSW/PEL* DH2 ....128 A2
Stonesdale *HLS* DH4 ....117 G6
Stone St *FELL* NE10 ....87 J6
Stoneygate Gdns *FELL* NE10 ......12 F6
Stoneygate La *FELL* NE10 ....12 E6
Stoneyhurst Av
BW/LEM/TK/HW NE15 ....69 F4
Stoneyhurst Rd *GOS/KPK* NE3 .....56 E6
Stoney La *LWF/SPW/WRK* NE9 ...102 B4
SWCK/CAS SR5 ....106 A4
Stoneylea Cl *RYTON* NE40 ....82 A1
Stoneylea Rd
WD/WHPE/BLK NE5 ....68 D3
Stonybank Wy *PSHWF* NE43 ....79 J4
Stonyflat Bank *PRUD* NE42 ....80 C2
Stonyheap La *CON/LDGT* DH8 ....124 D5
Stony La *STLY/ANP* DH9 ....114 A6
Store Farm Rd *NWBGN* NE64 ....18 E7
Store St *BW/LEM/TK/HW* NE15 ....68 A5
CON/LDGT DH8 ....123 F4
Storey Crs *NWBGN* NE64 ....19 F7
Storey La *BLAY* NE21 ....67 J7
Stormont St *NSHW* NE29 ....2 B3
Stotfold Cl *SEA/MUR* SR7 ....134 E7
Stothard St *JRW* NE32 ....74 A4
Stotts Rd *BYK/HTN/WLK* NE6 ......72 C3
Stowe Gdns *MPTH* NE61 ....21 J1
Stowell St *CNUT* NE1 ....5 H7
Stowell Ter *FELL* NE10 ....12 F7
The Stow *LGB/KIL* NE12 ....57 G5
Straker St *JRW* NE32 ....74 B5
Straker Ter *HAR/WTLS* NE34 ....75 F6
The Strand *SUNDSW* SR3 ....119 J6
Strangford Rd *SEA/MUR* SR7 .....150 C1
Strangways St *SEA/MUR* SR7 .....150 E2
Stranton Ter
CLDN/WHIT/ROK SR6 ....106 C3
Stratfield Rd *MLFD/PNYW* SR4 ...105 J6
Stratford Av
ASHBK/HED/RY SR2 ....120 C3
Stratford Cl *CRAM* NE23 ....37 K1
LGB/KIL NE12 ....48 A6
Stratford Gdns
CON/LDGT * DH8 ....123 F3
LWF/SPW/WRK NE9 ....87 F6
Stratford Gv *BYK/HTN/WLK* NE6 ...6 C3
Stratford Grove Ter
BYK/HTN/WLK NE6 ....6 C3
Stratford Gv West
BYK/HTN/WLK NE6 ....6 C3
Stratford Rd *BYK/HTN/WLK* NE6 ...6 C3
Stratford Vls *BYK/HTN/WLK* NE6 ...6 D2
Strathearn Wy *GOS/KPK* NE3 ......55 K3
Strathmore Av *ROWG* NE39 ....97 G4
Strathmore Cl *STLY/ANP* DH9 ....113 F7
Strathmore Crs *ELS/FEN* NE4 ......69 J1
Strathmore Rd *GOS/KPK* NE3 .....56 C3
LWF/SPW/WRK NE9 ....11 M9
ROWG NE39 ....97 F4
SUNDSW SR3 ....119 J4
Strathmore Sq *SUNDSW* SR3 ....119 J4
Stratton Cl *ASHBK/HED/RY* SR2 ..121 C6
Stratus Ct *SUNDSW* SR3 ....134 A1
Strawberry Gdns
WLSD/HOW NE28 ....58 C0
Strawberry La *CNUT* NE1 ....4 E6
DHAM DH1 ....169 H6
Street Gate Pk *WICK/BNPF* NE16 ..99 C2
Stretton Cl *HLS* DH4 ....146 D1
Stretton Wy *SMOOR* NE27 ....48 E4
Stridingedge *WASHN* NE37 ....102 C7

Strothers Rd *ROWG* NE39 ....82 B7
Stuart Cl *GOS/KPK* NE3 ....55 F4
Stuart Gdns
BW/LEM/TK/HW NE15 ....66 E1
Stuart Ter *FELL* NE10 ....12 D5
Stubbs Av *WICK/BNPF* NE16 ....84 E4
Studdon Wk *GOS/KPK* NE3 ....55 H5
Studland Cl *NSHW* NE29 ....60 D1
Studley Gdns
LWF/SPW/WRK NE9 ....87 F7
MONK NE25 ....50 E5
Studley Ter *ELS/FEN* NE4 ....4 A3
Studley Vls *LGB/KIL* NE12 ....58 A3
Sturdee Gdns *JES* NE2 ....56 E7
Styford Gdns
BW/LEM/TK/HW NE15 ....68 C4
Success Rd *HLS* DH4 ....131 K2
Sudbury Wy *CRAM* NE23 ....37 K1
Suddick St *SWCK/CAS* SR5 ....106 B4
Suez St *TYNE/NSHE* NE30 ....2 E1
Suffolk Cl *ASHGTN* NE63 ....23 C1
Suffolk Gdns *HAR/WTLS* NE34 ....76 C4
WLSD/HOW NE28 ....59 G6
Suffolk Pl *CLS/BIR/GTL* DH3 ......115 K5
GATE NE8 ....6 C9
Suffolk Rd *HEBB* NE31 ....89 H1
Suffolk St *ASHBK/HED/RY* SR2 ....15 H8
JRW NE32 ....73 K5
Suffolk Wk *PLEE/EAS* SR8 ....174 D2
Suffolk Wy *DHAM* DH1 ....156 E1
Sugley Dr
BW/LEM/TK/HW NE15 ....68 B5
Sugley La *BW/LEM/TK/HW* NE15 ..68 B5
Sulgrave Rd *WASHN* NE37 ....103 H4
Sullivan Wk *HEBB* NE31 ....73 G6
Summerdale *CON/LDGT* DH8 ......108 C2
Summerfield *STLY/ANP* DH9 ....128 A1
Summerfield Rd
LWF/SPW/WRK NE9 ....11 H9
Summerhill *ASHBK/HED/RY* SR2 ...14 B6
BLAY NE21 ....83 K1
JRW NE32 ....90 B3
SUNDSW SR3 ....119 F7
Summerhill Av *GOS/KPK* NE3 ......56 D1
Summerhill Gv *ELS/FEN* NE4 ....4 A5
Summerhill Rd *HAR/WTLS* NE34 ...75 K4
Summerhill St *ELS/FEN* NE4 ....4 A5
Summerhill Ter *CNUT* NE1 ....5 C8
Summerhouse Farm *HLH* DH5 ....147 C3
Summerhouse La *ASHGTN* NE63 ..18 D7
Summerson St *HLH* DH5 ....148 A4
Summerson Wy *BDLGTN* NE22 ....29 K4
Summer St *BLYTH* NE24 ....31 G6
Summerville *DHAM* DH1 ....16 B5
Sunbury Av *JES* NE2 ....70 E1
Sunderland Av *PLEE/EAS* SR8 ....175 G2
Sunderland Hwy *WASHS* NE38 ...102 B7
Sunderland Rd *BOL* NE36 ....91 J5
CLDN/WHIT/ROK SR6 ....92 B4
DHAM DH1 ....17 K2
FELL NE10 ....13 G7
GATE NE8 ....11 H3
HAR/WTLS NE34 ....75 J4
HLS DH4 ....132 C4
PLEE/EAS SR8 ....163 G7
SEA/MUR SR7 ....162 C3
SSH NE33 ....75 H3
SWCK/CAS SR5 ....106 A3
Sunderland Road Vls *FELL* NE10 ..13 H8
Sunderland St *CNUT* NE1 ....5 H8
HLH DH5 ....132 C6
Sundew Rd *LWF/SPW/WRK* NE9 ...87 J7
Sundridge Dr *FELL* NE10 ....88 E5
Sunholme Dr *WLSD/HOW* NE28 ...58 C5
Sunlea Av *TYNE/NSHE* NE30 ....51 G7
Sunniside *WICK/BNPF* NE16 ....84 C7
Sunnilaws *HAR/WTLS* NE34 ....76 A7
Sunningdale *MONK* NE25 ....50 B5
SSH NE33 ....75 J2
Sunningdale Av
BYK/HTN/WLK NE6 ....72 C5
WLSD/HOW NE28 ....72 E1
Sunningdale Cl *FELL* NE10 ....87 K5
Sunningdale Dr *WASHN* NE37 ....102 E3
Sunningdale Rd *SUNDSW* SR3 ...119 H3
Sunnirise *HAR/WTLS* NE34 ....76 A7
Sunnirise *MLFD/PNYW* SR4 ....104 E7
NSHW NE29 ....60 B5
Sunniside Ct *WICK/BNPF* NE16 ....99 F3
Sunniside Dr *HAR/WTLS* NE34 .....76 A7
Sunniside Gdns
BW/LEM/TK/HW NE15 ....69 F5
Sunniside La
CLDN/WHIT/ROK SR6 ....92 B2
Sunniside Rd
WICK/BNPF NE16 ....85 F7
Sunniside Ter
CLDN/WHIT/ROK SR6 ....92 A2
Sunnybank Av
BW/LEM/TK/HW NE15 ....69 H6
Sunnybanks
BDN/LAN/SAC DH7 ....140 B4
Sunny Blunts *PLEE/EAS* SR8 .....174 D6
Sunny Brae *RYTON* * NE40 ....82 B4
Sunnybrow *SUNDSW* SR3 ....119 K6
Sunnycrest
BYK/HTN/WLK NE6 ....72 B5
Sunny Ter *STLY/ANP* DH9 ....112 C7
Sunnyway *WD/WHPE/BLK* NE5 ....69 G1
Sunrise La *HLS* DH4 ....132 B6
Surrey Av *SUNDSW* SR3 ....134 A1
Surrey Cl *ASHGTN* NE63 ....23 C1
Surrey Crs *CON/LDGT* DH8 ....137 C3
Surrey Pl *ELS/FEN* NE4 ....4 D7
HLS DH4 ....132 A1
Surrey Rd *HEBB* NE31 ....89 H1
NSHW NE29 ....60 B4
Surrey St *HLS* DH4 ....132 A1
JRW NE32 ....73 J3
Surtees Av *RDHAMSE* DH6 ....180 A2
Surtees Dr *DHAM* DH1 ....156 B7
Surtees Pl *CON/LDGT* DH8 ....122 C2
Surtees Rd *PLEE/EAS* SR8 ....175 F4
Sussex Gdns *WLSD/HOW* NE28 ...59 G7
Sussex Pl *WASHN* NE37 ....103 H3
Sussex Rd *CON/LDGT* DH8 ....137 C1

Sussex St *BLYTH* NE24 ....31 H6
JRW NE32 ....73 J3
Sutherland Av *ELS/FEN* NE4 ....69 J4
NWBGN NE64 ....25 F1
Sutherland Ct *HAR/WTLS* NE34 ...91 H2
Sutherland Gra *HLS* DH4 ....132 B3
Sutherland Gv *RDHAMSE* DH6 ...173 H3
Sutherland Pl *DHAM* DH1 ....17 M5
Sutherland St
CLDN/WHIT/ROK SR6 ....106 D3
SEA/MUR SR7 ....135 H7
Sutton Cl *HLS* DH4 ....131 J1
Sutton Ct *WLSD/HOW* NE28 ....58 B5
The Sutton Est
JES (off Barrack Rd) NE2 ....4 F4
Sutton Pl
MLFD/PNYW SR4
(off Midmoor Rd) SR4 ....105 J6
Sutton St *BYK/HTN/WLK* NE6 ......7 M1
DHAM DH1 ....16 B3
Sutton Wy *HAR/WTLS* NE34 ....76 B6
Swainby Cl *GOS/KPK* NE3 ....55 H4
Swaledale *CLDN/WHIT/ROK* SR6 ...93 F5
WLSD/HOW NE28 ....58 B5
Swaledale Av *BLYTH* NE24 ....30 C7
Swaledale Cl *HLS* DH4 ....147 H7
Swaledale Crs *HLS* DH4 ....117 J6
Swaledale Gdns *LGB/HTN* NE7 ...57 H7
MLFD/PNYW SR4 ....119 K1
Swallow Cl *ASHBK/HED/RY* SR2 ...24 A4
BDN/LAN/SAC DH7 ....165 F1
The Swallows *WLSD/HOW* NE28 ...59 G3
Swallow Tail Ct *HAR/WTLS* NE34 ..75 F7
Swallow Tail Dr *DUN/TMV* NE11 ...9 M9
Swalwell Bank
WICK/BNPF NE16 ....84 E3
Swalwell Cl *PRUD* NE42 ....80 C2
Swan Av *WLSD/HOW* * NE28 ....59 F7
Swan Dr *GATE* NE8 ....9 K6
Swan Rd *BYK/HTN/WLK* NE6 ....7 H4
PLEE/EAS SR8 ....174 A5
WASHS NE38 ....117 H3
Swansfield *MPTH* NE61 ....20 C6
Swan St *GATE* * NE8 ....11 G1
STLY/ANP DH9 ....125 G1
SWCK/CAS SR5 ....106 C4
Swanton Cl *WD/WHPE/BLK* NE5 ...55 F6
Swards Rd *FELL* NE10 ....88 A5
Swarland Av *LGB/HTN* NE7 ....57 H5
Swarland Rd *MONK* NE25 ....40 A6
Swarth Ct *WASHN* NE37 ....102 C7
Sweetbriar Cl *MPTH* NE61 ....20 B3
Sweetbriar Wy *BLYTH* NE24 ....34 E3
Sweethope Av *ASHGTN* NE63 ......24 A3
Sweethope Dene *MPTH* NE61 .....20 F7
Swiftden Dr *MLFD/PNYW* SR4 .....118 E2
Swinbourne Gdns *WBAY* NE26 ....50 D3
Swinbourne Ter *JRW* NE32 ....89 K1
Swinburn Cl *GATE* NE8 ....10 F1
JRW NE32 ....74 C5
Swinburn Rd *MONK* NE25 ....40 A6
Swindale Dr *LGB/KIL* NE12 ....47 J6
Swindon Rd *SUNDSW* SR3 ....119 H3
Swindon Sq *SUNDSW* SR3 ....119 J3
Swindon St *HEBB* NE31 ....73 F5
Swinton Ter *BYK/HTN/WLK* NE6 ...71 H2
Swing Br *CNUT* NE1 ....5 L8
Swinhoe Gdns *DIN/WO* NE13 ....46 B2
Swinhope *WASHS* NE38 ....116 C6
Swinley Gdns
BW/LEM/TK/HW NE15 ....68 D5
Swinside Dr *DHAM* DH1 ....157 K5
Swinton Cl *MPTH* NE61 ....21 F7
The Swirle *CNUT* NE1 ....5 K6
Sycamore Av *BLYTH* NE24 ....31 F5
DIN/WO NE13 ....45 C2
HAR/WTLS NE34 ....75 K7
MONK NE25 ....50 D5
PONT/DH NE20 ....43 F5
STKFD/GP NE62 ....22 E6
Sycamore Cl *GATE* NE8 ....20 E1
Sycamore Dr *RHTLP* TS27 ....185 G2
SWCK/CAS SR5 ....106 B2
Sycamore Gv *FELL* NE10 ....12 E6
LWF/SPW/WRK NE9 ....87 F6
PRUD NE42 ....80 A2
Sycamore Rd *BLAY* NE21 ....84 A2
CLDN/WHIT/ROK SR6 ....93 F3
CLSW/PEL DH2 ....144 A5
The Sycamores
ASHBK/HED/RY SR2 ....120 E3
ELS/FEN (off Park Rd) NE4 ....9 K1
WICK/BNPF NE16 ....112 A1
Sycamore St *ASHGTN* NE63 ....23 K1
BW/LEM/TK/HW NE15 ....53 F7
WLSD/HOW NE28 ....72 E2
Sydenham Ter
MLFD/PNYW SR4 ....120 A1
SSH NE33 ....3 K7
Sydney Ct *GATE* NE8 ....10 F2
Sydney Gdns *CON/LDGT* DH8 ....123 H7
HAR/WTLS NE34 ....90 D1
Sydney Gv *WLSD/HOW* NE28 ......58 C5
Sydney St *HLS* DH4 ....131 C5
STLY/ANP DH9 ....114 A7
Syke Rd *WICK/BNPF* NE16 ....97 H7
Sylvan Cl *MPTH* NE61 ....20 B6
Sylverton Gdns *SSH* NE33 ....75 K2
Sylvia Ter *STLY/ANP* DH9 ....112 D6
Symington Gdns *SUNDSW* SR3 ..119 K6
Syon St *TYNE/NSHE* NE30 ....61 H2
Syron *WICK/BNPF* NE16 ....84 C7
Syston Cl *HLS* DH4 ....146 D1

T

Taberna Cl
BW/LEM/TK/HW NE15 ....66 A1
Tadcaster Rd *SUNDSW* SR3 ......119 C5
Tadema Rd *SSH* NE33 ....75 K1
Tail-upon-End La
RDHAMSE DH6 ....180 A1
Talbot Cl *WASHS* NE38 ....117 F2

Talbot Gn *WD/WHPE/BLK* NE5 .....68 D3
Talbot Pl *SEA/MUR* SR7 ....150 E1
Talbot Rd *CLDN/WHIT/ROK* SR6 ..106 E2
HAR/WTLS NE34 ....75 C5
Talgarth *WASHS* NE38 ....117 K1
Talisman Cl *RDHAMSE* DH6 ....170 C1
Talley Ct *WASHS* NE38 ....116 E1
Tamar Cl *NSHW* NE29 ....60 A2
PLEE/EAS SR8 ....174 D5
Tamar Ct *HLH* DH5 ....160 B1
Tamerton Dr *CLS/BIR/GTL* DH3 ...115 K4
Tamerton St *MLFD/PNYW* SR4 ...105 K7
Tamworth Rd *ELS/FEN* NE4 ....4 C5
Tamworth Sq *SUNDSW* SR3 ....119 C5
Tanbark *HLS* DH4 ....131 H1
Tanfield Gdns *HAR/WTLS* NE34 ...76 B5
Tanfield Pl *LWF/SPW/WRK* NE9 ..101 J3
Tanfield Rd
BW/LEM/TK/HW NE15 ....68 E5
LWF/SPW/WRK NE9 ....101 J3
SUNDSW SR3 ....119 H5
Tanfield St *MLFD/PNYW* SR4 .....105 J6
Tangmere Cl *CRAM* NE23 ....38 D1
Tankerville Pl *JES* NE2 ....70 E2
Tankerville Ter *JES* NE2 ....70 E2
Tanmeads *CLSW/PEL* DH2 ....144 A4
Tanners' Bank *TYNE/NSHE* NE30 ..61 G4
Tantobie Rd
BW/LEM/TK/HW NE15 ....68 E5
Tarlton Crs *FELL* NE10 ....12 B8
Tarn Cl *PLEE/EAS* SR8 ....175 F4
Tarn Dr *ASHBK/HED/RY* SR2 ....121 F6
Tarragon Wy *HAR/WTLS* NE34 .....91 H1
Tarrington Cl *WLSD/HOW* NE28 ...59 H5
Tarset Dr *PRUD* NE42 ....80 D2
Tarset Rd *MONK* NE25 ....49 K4
Tarset St *CNUT* NE1 ....6 C6
Tasmania Rd *HAR/WTLS* NE34 .....90 D1
Tasman Rd *SUNDSW* SR3 ....119 G6
Tate Av *RDHAMSE* DH6 ....181 F6
Tate St *BYK/HTN/WLK* NE6 ....31 H6
Tatham St *SUND* SR1 ....15 G5
Tatham St Back *SUND* SR1 ....15 G5
Tattershall *ASHBK/HED/RY* SR2 ..120 B2
Taunton Av *JRW* NE32 ....74 C6
NSHW NE29 ....60 B1
Taunton Cl *WLSD/HOW* NE28 ......59 H5
Taunton Pl *CRAM* NE23 ....33 H7
Taunton Rd *SUNDSW* SR3 ....119 H5
Tavistock Ct *HLS* DH4 ....132 A4
Tavistock Pl *JRW* NE32 ....74 B6
SUND SR1 ....14 F5
Tavistock Rd *JES* NE2 ....70 E1
Tavistock Sq *SUNDSW* SR3 ....120 A6
Taylor Av *ASHGTN* NE63 ....24 D2
BDN/LAN/SAC DH7 ....155 C6
DIN/WO NE13 ....46 C3
ROWG NE39 ....97 H4
Taylor Gdns *FELL* NE10 ....13 K5
WBAY NE26 ....41 G2
Taylor Gv *WNGT* TS28 ....183 J2
Taylor St *BLYTH* NE24 ....30 C6
CON/LDGT DH8 ....123 F5
SSH NE33 ....75 F4
STLY/ANP DH9 ....125 G2
Taynton Gv *CRAM* NE23 ....39 C6
Tay Rd *SUNDSW* SR3 ....119 G4
Tay St *CHPW* NE17 ....95 J4
HLH DH5 ....160 B1
Teal Av *BLYTH* NE24 ....35 F5
Teal Cl *WASHS* NE38 ....116 B3
Team St *GATE* NE8 ....9 L5
Teasdale St *ASHBK/HED/RY* SR2 ...15 J8
CON/LDGT * DH8 ....123 G4
Tebay Dr *WD/WHPE/BLK* NE5 .....55 D3
Tedco Business see Cl *PLEE/EAS* SR8 ...174 D6
Tees Ct *HAR/WTLS* NE34 ....75 C5
Tees Crs *STLY/ANP* DH9 ....126 D2
Teesdale Av *HLS* DH4 ....117 J6
Teesdale Gdns *LGB/HTN* NE7 .....57 H7
Teesdale Gv *LGB/KIL* NE12 ....57 K2
Teesdale Pl *BLYTH* NE24 ....30 B6
Tees Rd *HEBB* NE31 ....89 C1
Tees St *HLH* DH5 ....160 C1
PLEE/EAS SR8 ....175 H3
SEA/MUR SR7 ....135 K7
Tees Ct *PLEE/EAS* SR8 ....174 D5
Teindland Cl *ELS/FEN* NE4 ....69 J7
Tel-el-Kebir Rd
ASHBK/HED/RY SR2 ....120 E2
Telford Cl *DHAM* DH1 ....169 J2
SMOOR NE27 ....48 E4
Telford Ct *WLSD/HOW* NE28 ....74 A1
Telford Rd *SUNDSW* SR3 ....119 H4
Telford St *GATE* NE8 ....10 D9
WLSD/HOW NE28 ....74 A1
Temperance Ter
BDN/LAN/SAC DH7 ....154 E7
Tempest Rd *SEA/MUR* SR7 ....150 E1
Tempest St *BLAY* NE21 ....67 J7
SUNDSW * SR3 ....120 A7
Templar St *CON/LDGT* DH8 ....122 D3
Temple Gn *GATE* NE8 ....10 B7
HAR/WTLS NE34 ....75 J6
Temple Park Rd
HAR/WTLS NE34 ....75 H5
Temple St *CNUT* NE1 ....5 D8
FELL NE10 ....12 D5
SSH NE33 ....75 F4
Temple St West *SSH* NE33 ....75 F3
Temple Town *SSH* NE33 ....75 F3
Tenbury Crs *LGB/KIL* NE12 ....57 J3
NSHW NE29 ....60 A2
Tenby Rd *SUNDSW* SR3 ....119 G6
Tenby Sq *CRAM* NE23 ....33 J7
Ten Flds *HLH* DH5 ....147 J3
Tennant St *HAR/WTLS* NE34 ....74 E7
HEBB NE31 ....73 H5
Tennison Gdns
WD/WHPE/BLK NE5 ....55 F7
Tennyson Av *BOLCOL* NE35 ....91 F4
Tennyson Crs *WICK/BNPF* NE16 ..84 E4
Tennyson Rd *CLSW/PEL* DH2 ....128 E4

Tyne Tunnel (Pedestrian)

Tennyson St *SSH* NE33 ....3 K8
SWCK/CAS SR5 ....106 A3
Tennyson Ter *NSHW* NE29 ....2 D4
Tenter Garth
BW/LEM/TK/HW
(off Hexham Rd) NE15 ....66 E1
Tenter Ter *DHAM* DH1 ....16 C3
Tenth Av *BLYTH* NE24 ....35 F2
BYK/HTN/WLK NE6 ....7 G1
DUN/TMV NE11 ....100 D3
MPTH NE61 ....21 F7
Tenth Av West *DUN/TMV* NE11 ...100 C2
Tenth St *PLEE/EAS* SR8 ....175 H3
Tern Cl *BLYTH* NE24 ....35 H3
Terrace Pl *CNUT* NE1 ....5 F3
The Terrace *CON/LDGT* DH8 ......122 C1
RDHAMSE (off Front St) DH6 ..173 J3
Terrier Cl *BDLGTN* NE22 ....29 J5
Territorial La *DHAM* DH1 ....16 E4
Tetford Pl *LGB/KIL* NE12 ....57 J3
Teviot *WASHS* NE38 ....116 B3
Teviotdale Gdns *LGB/HTN* NE7 ...57 H7
Teviot St *GATE* NE8 ....11 K7
HLH DH5 ....160 B1
Teviot Wy *JRW* NE32 ....73 J9
Tewkesbury *LGB/KIL* NE12 ....47 K5
Tewkesbury Rd
BW/LEM/TK/HW NE15 ....68 A4
Thackeray Rd *SUNDSW* SR3 ......119 H4
Thames Crs *HLS* DH4 ....131 J7
STLY/ANP DH9 ....126 D3
Thames Gdns *WLSD/HOW* NE28 ..72 D2
Thames Rd *HEBB* NE31 ....73 H7
PLEE/EAS SR8 ....174 D5
SUNDSW SR3 ....119 G6
Thames St *GATE* NE8 ....11 K7
HLH DH5 ....160 B1
Thanet Rd *SUNDSW* SR3 ....119 H5
Tharsis Rd *HEBB* NE31 ....73 F6
Thatcher Cl *WICK/BNPF* NE16 .....84 E7
Theatre Pl *NSHW* NE29 ....2 D3
Thelma St *MLFD/PNYW* SR4 ....14 A6
Theme Rd *SUNDSW* SR3 ....119 G6
Theresa St *BLAY* NE21 ....84 A1
The Sands *DHAM* DH1 ....16 E1
The Tyne Tunnel (Pedestrian)
WLSD/HOW NE28 ....73 K2
Thieves Bank *MPTH* NE61 ....23 F4
Third Av *ASHGTN* NE63 ....24 A2
BLYTH NE24 ....35 F1
BYK/HTN/WLK NE6 ....7 G2
CLSW/PEL DH2 ....115 H7
DUN/TMV NE11 ....86 D6
MPTH NE61 ....21 F6
NSHW NE29 ....59 K5
Third St *CON/LDGT* DH8 ....123 J2
PLEE/EAS SR8 ....175 H4
Thirkeld Pl *HLS* DH4 ....117 J7
Thirlington Cl
WD/WHPE/BLK NE5 ....55 F7
Thirlmere *CLDN/WHIT/ROK* SR6 ..92 A3
CLS/BIR/GTL DH3 ....116 A4
FELL NE10 ....13 J7
Thirlmere Av *CLSW/PEL* DH2 .....129 H6
HLH DH5 ....160 B1
TYNE/NSHE NE30 ....50 E7
Thirlmere Cl *LGB/KIL* NE12 ....48 B6
Thirlmere Ct *HEBB* NE31 ....73 H6
Thirlmere Crs *BLAY* NE21 ....83 K4
HLS DH4 ....131 K1
Thirlmere Rd *PLEE/EAS* SR8 ......175 F3
Thirlmere Wy *BLYTH* NE24 ....30 C5
WD/WHPE/BLK NE5 ....69 F2
Thirlmoor *WASHN* NE37 ....102 C7
Thirlmoor Pl *STKFD/GP* NE62 ......23 C5
Thirlwell Gv *JRW* NE32 ....89 J1
Thirlwell Rd *GATE* NE8 ....6 C9
Thirsk Rd *SUNDSW* SR3 ....119 H4
Thirston Dr *CRAM* NE23 ....38 D2
Thirston Pl *NSHW* NE29 ....60 B3
Thirston Wy *GOS/KPK* NE3 ....55 H5
Thistle Av *RYTON* NE40 ....66 C7
Thistlecroft *HLH* DH5 ....147 H1
Thistledon Av *WICK/BNPF* NE16 ..84 E7
Thistle Rd *BDN/LAN/SAC* DH7 ...168 A6
SUNDSW SR3 ....119 G5
Thistley Cl *BYK/HTN/WLK* NE6 ....72 A3
Thistley Gn *FELL* NE10 ....13 M1
Thomas Hawksley Pk
SUNDSW SR3 ....120 A3
Thomas St *ASHBK/HED/RY* SR2 ..135 F1
CON/LDGT DH8 ....122 C6
LWF/SPW/WRK NE9 ....101 K4
PLEE/EAS SR8 ....163 F4
SSH NE33 ....3 H7
STLY/ANP DH9 ....127 H4
WICK/BNPF NE16 ....84 E7
Thomas St North
CLDN/WHIT/ROK SR6 ....14 C1
Thomas St South
ASHBK/HED/RY SR2 ....135 F1
SWCK/CAS SR5 ....106 A4
Thompson Av *LGB/KIL* NE12 ....47 J5
Thompson Crs *SWCK/CAS* SR5 ..105 F4
Thompson Gdns
WLSD/HOW NE28 ....72 D2
Thompson Pl *FELL* NE10 ....12 C7
Thompson Rd *SWCK/CAS* SR5 ...106 C3
Thompson St *BLYTH* NE24 ....31 G5
HAR/WTLS * NE34 ....75 F6
PLEE/EAS * SR8 ....175 H2
Thorburn St
CLDN/WHIT/ROK SR6 ....106 D1
Thornbank Cl *SUNDSW* SR3 ......134 A3
Thornbridge *WASHS* NE38 ....117 J1
Thornbury Av *CRAM* NE23 ....39 C6
Thornbury Cl *BOLCOL* NE35 ....90 C3
DIN/WO NE13 ....55 F4
Thornbury Dr *MONK* NE25 ....50 A3
Thornbury St *MLFD/PNYW* SR4 ..106 A6
Thorncliffe Pl *NSHW* NE29 ....60 C5
Thorn Cl *DIN/WO* NE13 ....46 A4
Thorndale Pl *BLYTH* NE24 ....30 C6
Thorndale Rd
BW/LEM/TK/HW NE15 ....68 D6
DHAM DH1 ....158 A0

SUNDSW SR3 ...... 119 C5
Thorne Av FELL NE10 ...... 13 M8
Thorne Brake FELL NE10 ...... 88 C5
Thornehill Gdns STKFD/GP NE62 ...... 23 C5
Thorne Rd SUNDSW SR3 ...... 119 C5
Thornes CI PLEE/EAS SR8 ...... 175 C5
Thorne Sq SUNDSW SR3 ...... 119 C5
Thorne Ter BYK/HTN/WLK NE6 ...... 7 M3
Thorneyburn CI HLS DH4 ...... 132 A5
Thorneyburn PI BLYTH NE24 ...... 30 D7
Thorney Close Rd
SUNDSW SR3 ...... 119 H5
Thorneyford PI PONT/DH NE20 ...... 43 G2
Thorneyholme Ter
STLY/ANP DH9 ...... 126 C1
Thornfield Gv
ASHBK/HED/RY SR2 ...... 120 E4
Thornfield PI ROWG NE39 ...... 97 G2
Thornfield Rd CON/LDGT DH8 ...... 122 C6
GOS/KPK NE3 ...... 56 B6
Thorngill WASHN NE37 ...... 102 D7
Thornhaugh Av
WICK/BNPF NE16 ...... 84 D6
Thornhill CI DUN/TMV NE11 ...... 9 K3
MONK NE25 ...... 40 A6
Thornhill Crs
ASHBK/HED/RY SR2 ...... 14 C6
Thornhill Gdns
ASHBK/HED/RY SR2 ...... 14 C9
Thornhill Pk
ASHBK/HED/RY SR2 ...... 14 C8
PONT/DH NE20 ...... 43 G2
Thornhill Reach SEA/MUR SR7 ...... 135 H4
Thornhill Rd LGB/KIL NE12 ...... 57 K4
PONT/DH NE20 ...... 43 G2
RDHAMSE DH6 ...... 173 H4
Thornhill St HLS DH4 ...... 132 B7
Thornhill Ter
ASHBK/HED/RY SR2 ...... 14 C7
Thornholme Av
HAR/WTLS NE34 ...... 76 B5
Thornholme Rd
ASHBK/HED/RY SR2 ...... 14 B9
Thornhope CI WASHS NE38 ...... 103 H7
Thornlaw North
RDHAMSE DH6 ...... 172 A6
Thornlea MPTH NE61 ...... 27 J2
Thornlea Gdns
LWF/SPW/WRK NE9 ...... 87 F5
Thornlea Gv
BDN/LAN/SAC DH7 ...... 140 A4
Thornleigh Gdns
CLDN/WHIT/ROK SR6 ...... 92 A2
Thornleigh Rd JES NE2 ...... 70 D2
Thornley Av CRAM NE23 ...... 38 D2
FELL NE10 ...... 88 D6
Thornley CI BDN/LAN/SAC DH7 ...... 167 G1
WICK/BNPF NE16 ...... 98 E1
Thornley La BLAY NE21 ...... 83 J6
ROWG NE39 ...... 97 J1
Thornley Rd
WD/WHPE/BLK NE5 ...... 68 C2
Thornley Vw ROWG NE39 ...... 97 H3
Thornton CI HLS DH4 ...... 117 J7
MPTH* NE61 ...... 21 F7
RDHAMSE DH6 ...... 172 B3
Thornton Ct
CNUT (off Forth PI) NE1 ...... 5 H8
WASHS NE38 ...... 116 E1
Thornton Crs BLAY NE21 ...... 84 A1
Thornton Lea CLSW/PEL DH2 ...... 114 D7
Thornton St CNUT NE1 ...... 5 H8
Thorntree Av DIN/WO NE13 ...... 37 G7
Thorn Tree Dr BDLGTN NE22 ...... 29 F4
Thorntree Dr
BW/LEM/TK/HW NE15 ...... 68 C4
MONK NE25 ...... 49 K5
Thorntree Gdns ASHGTN NE63 ...... 24 C3
Thorntree Ter STLY/ANP DH9 ...... 113 F7
Thorntree Wy BLYTH NE24 ...... 30 B7
Thornwood Gdns
DUN/TMV NE11 ...... 86 B7
Thorp CI MPTH NE61 ...... 20 E3
Thorp CI BLYTH NE24 ...... 34 D2
Thorpe CI ELS/FEN NE4 ...... 4 D5
Thorpe Dr RYTON NE40 ...... 67 F6
Thorpeness Rd SUNDSW SR3 ...... 119 C5
Thorpe Rd PLEE/EAS SR8 ...... 162 C6
Thorpe St PLEE/EAS SR8 ...... 163 F4
PLEE/EAS* SR8 ...... 175 H1
Threap Gdns WLSD/HOW NE28 ...... 59 C6
Three Rivers Dr BOL NE36 ...... 90 E5
Threlkeld Gv
CLDN/WHIT/ROK SR6 ...... 92 C1
Thrift St NSHW* NE29 ...... 2 C4
Thristley Gdns
ASHBK/HED/RY SR2 ...... 120 C3
Throckley Av HAR/WTLS NE34 ...... 75 F5
Thropton Av BLYTH NE24 ...... 34 E2
LGB/HTN NE7 ...... 57 H5
Thropton CI DHAM DH1 ...... 169 J5
FELL NE10 ...... 88 C5
Thropton Ct BLYTH NE24 ...... 30 E7
Thropton Crs GOS/KPK NE3 ...... 56 B4
Thropton PI NSHW NE29 ...... 60 B3
Thropton Ter LGB/HTN NE7 ...... 71 H1
Thrush Gv SWCK/CAS SR5 ...... 105 C4
Thurlston HLS DH4 ...... 132 A3
Thursby Av TYNE/NSHE NE30 ...... 51 F7
Thurso CI SUNDSW SR3 ...... 119 F5
Tiberius St WLSD/HOW NE28 ...... 72 D2
Tilbeck Sq SUNDSW SR3 ...... 134 A1
Tilbury CI HLS DH4 ...... 132 A2
Tilbury Gdns SUNDSW SR3 ...... 119 C5
Tilbury Gv MONK NE25 ...... 50 E6
Tilbury Rd SUNDSW SR3 ...... 119 C6
Tileshed La BOL NE36 ...... 91 G3
Till Av BLAY NE21 ...... 83 K2
Tilley Rd WASHS NE38 ...... 116 B1
Tillmouth Av MONK NE25 ...... 40 A6
Tillmouth Gdns ELS/FEN NE4 ...... 69 C5
Tillmouth Park Rd
BW/LEM/TK/HW NE15 ...... 67 F2
Till St BYK/HTN/WLK NE6 ...... 7 H8
Tilson Wy GOS/KPK NE3 ...... 55 K4
Timber Beach Rd
SWCK/CAS SR5 ...... 105 H4
Timber Rd PLEE/EAS SR8 ...... 175 H1

Times Sq
CNUT (off Scotswood Rd) NE1 ...... 5 H9
Timlin Gdns WLSD/HOW NE28 ...... 59 K7
Tindal CI ELS/FEN NE4 ...... 4 E6
Tindale Av CRAM NE23 ...... 38 D2
Tindale St CON/LDGT DH8 ...... 123 J5
Tindal St ELS/FEN NE4 ...... 4 F7
Tinmill PI CON/LDGT DH8 ...... 122 D4
Tintagel CI CRAM NE23 ...... 33 H7
SUNDSW SR3 ...... 119 F5
Tintagel Dr SEA/MUR SR7 ...... 135 J7
Tintern WASHS NE38 ...... 116 E3
Tintern CI HLS DH4 ...... 132 A5
Tintern Crs BYK/HTN/WLK NE6 ...... 6 F7
NSHW NE29 ...... 60 B2
Tintern St MLFD/PNYW SR4 ...... 14 A5
Tiree CI BDN/LAN/SAC DH7 ...... 167 H5
Tiree CI SUNDSW * SR3 ...... 134 A1
Tirril PI WD/WHPE/BLK NE5 ...... 68 E2
Titan Rd BYK/HTN/WLK NE6 ...... 72 C5
Titchfield Rd WASHS NE38 ...... 116 E2
Titchfield Ter ASHGTN NE63 ...... 23 K3
Titian Av HAR/WTLS NE34 ...... 91 C2
Titlington Gv HEBB NE31 ...... 89 F1
Tiverton Av ELS/FEN NE4 ...... 69 J6
NSHW NE29 ...... 60 A1
Tiverton CI HLS DH4 ...... 132 A3
WLSD/HOW NE28 ...... 59 H5
Tiverton Gdns
LWF/SPW/WRK NE9 ...... 101 F2
Tiverton PI CRAM NE23 ...... 33 H7
Tiverton Sq SUNDSW SR3 ...... 119 C5
Toberty Gdns FELL NE10 ...... 13 L8
Toft Crs SEA/MUR SR7 ...... 149 H5
Togstone PI WD/WHPE/BLK NE5 ...... 69 G2
Toll Bar Rd ASHBK/HED/RY SR2 ...... 120 D5
Toll Bridge Rd BLAY NE21 ...... 84 D1
Tollerton Dr SWCK/CAS SR5 ...... 104 D4
Tollgate Flds HLS DH4 ...... 146 C7
Tollgate Rd ROWG NE39 ...... 110 B3
Toll House Rd DHAM DH1 ...... 156 A7
Tolls CI MONK NE25 ...... 50 A4
Toll Sq TYNE/NSHE NE30 ...... 3 G1
Tomlea Av BDLGTN NE22 ...... 29 K5
Tonbridge Av NSHW NE29 ...... 60 C5
Toner Av HEBB NE31 ...... 89 F1
Topaz St SEA/MUR SR7 ...... 150 B1
Topcliffe CLDN/WHIT/ROK SR6 ...... 15 H1
Torcross Wy CRAM NE23 ...... 33 H7
Toronto Rd SUNDSW SR3 ...... 119 H4
Toronto Sq SUNDSW SR3 ...... 119 H4
Torquay Gdns
LWF/SPW/WRK NE9 ...... 101 F2
Torquay Rd SUNDSW SR3 ...... 119 H4
Torrens Rd SUNDSW SR3 ...... 119 H4
Torrington CI HLS DH4 ...... 132 A3
Torver CI DIN/WO NE13 ...... 46 A4
Torver Crs CLDN/WHIT/ROK SR6 ...... 92 C7
Torver PI LWF/SPW/WRK NE9 ...... 101 H1
Torver Wy TYNE/NSHE NE30 ...... 50 D7
Tosson PI ASHGTN NE63 ...... 24 A2
NSHW NE29 ...... 60 B5
Tosson Ter BYK/HTN/WLK NE6 ...... 71 J2
Totnes Dr CRAM NE23 ...... 33 H7
Toward Rd ASHBK/HED/RY SR2 ...... 15 C9
SUND SR1 ...... 14 F6
Toward St BYK/HTN/WLK NE6 ...... 6 E4
Tower Bank BDN/LAN/SAC DH7 ...... 125 C7
Tower Ct DUN/TMV NE11 ...... 9 J6
Tower Gdns RYTON NE40 ...... 66 E6
Tower PI ASHBK/HED/RY SR2 ...... 120 C4
Tower Rd BDN/LAN/SAC DH7 ...... 125 J7
STLY/ANP DH9 ...... 125 C5
WASHN NE37 ...... 103 C6
Towers Av JES NE2 ...... 56 E7
Towers CI BDLGTN NE22 ...... 29 C6
Towers PI HAR/WTLS NE34 ...... 74 C6
Tower St West
CNUT NE1 ...... 5 M7
PLEE/EAS SR8 ...... 163 G4
Tower St West
ASHBK/HED/RY SR2 ...... 15 H9
The Towne Ga
BW/LEM/TK/HW NE15 ...... 66 A1
Townend Ct HAR/WTLS NE34 ...... 75 C6
Townfield Gdns
BW/LEM/TK/HW NE15 ...... 67 H3
Town Hall MPTH * NE61 ...... 20 C4
Townley Flds ROWG NE39 ...... 97 H3
Townley Rd ROWG NE39 ...... 97 F3
Townsend Crs MPTH NE61 ...... 20 B7
Townsend Rd SUNDSW SR3 ...... 119 C6
Townsville Av MONK NE25 ...... 50 B6
Towton LGB/KIL NE12 ...... 47 K5
Toynbee WASHS NE38 ...... 117 J1
Tracey Av BOL NE36 ...... 91 F4
Trafalgar Rd WASHN NE37 ...... 103 C4
Trafalgar Sq SUND SR1 ...... 15 J4
Trafalgar St CNUT NE1 ...... 5 M6
CON/LDGT DH8 ...... 123 F5
Trafford LWF/SPW/WRK NE9 ...... 101 C3
Trafford Rd SWCK/CAS SR5 ...... 106 A4
Trafford Wk
WD/WHPE/BLK NE5 ...... 54 C7
Trajan Av SSH NE33 ...... 3 J4
Trajan Wk
BW/LEM/TK/HW NE15 ...... 65 K1
Tranwell CI GOS/KPK NE3 ...... 55 C5
MPTH NE61 ...... 21 J2
Travers St HLS DH4 ...... 132 A1
Treby St MLFD/PNYW SR4 ...... 106 A6
Tredegar Av WD/WHPE/BLK NE5 ...... 55 F6
Treecone CI SUNDSW SR3 ...... 134 A2
Treen Crs SEA/MUR SR7 ...... 149 J5
Trefoil Rd STLY/ANP DH9 ...... 112 B6
Tregoney Av SEA/MUR SR7 ...... 149 J5
Treherne Rd JES NE2 ...... 56 D7
Trent Av HEBB NE31 ...... 89 C1
Trent DI CON/LDGT DH8 ...... 123 K2
Trent Dr JRW NE32 ...... 90 A2
Trent Gdns GATE NE8 ...... 11 M7
Trentham Gdns MPTH NE61 ...... 21 J1
Trenton Av WASHS NE38 ...... 103 H7
Trent Rd SUNDSW SR3 ...... 119 C5
Trent St HLH DH5 ...... 160 A1

Trevarren Dr
ASHBK/HED/RY SR2 ...... 121 F6
Trevelyan Av BDLGTN NE22 ...... 29 H5
BLYTH 34 E1
Trevelyan Dr
WD/WHPE/BLK NE5 ...... 54 E7
Trevelyan PI PLEE/EAS SR8 ...... 174 C5
Trevethick St GATE NE8 ...... 10 C8
Trevone PI CRAM NE23 ...... 39 H6
Trevone Sq SEA/MUR SR7 ...... 149 J5
Trevor Gv CLDN/WHIT/ROK SR6 ...... 92 A4
Trevor Ter TYNE/NSHE NE30 ...... 60 E3
Trewhitt Rd BYK/HTN/WLK NE6 ...... 71 J3
Tribune PI LWF/SPW/WRK NE9 ...... 87 H6
Trident Rd SUNDSW SR3 ...... 120 A7
Trimdon St West
MLFD/PNYW SR4 ...... 14 A3
Trinity Buildings
TYNE/NSHE NE30 ...... 3 G2
Trinity Chare
CNUT (off Quayside) NE1 ...... 5 M8
Trinity CI NSHW NE29 ...... 2 D4
Trinity Ct GATE NE8 ...... 11 G2
Trinity Ctyd BYK/HTN/WLK NE6 ...... 7 J9
Trinity Gv CRAM NE23 ...... 39 H6
Trinity Pk HLS DH4 ...... 131 G2
Trinity PI NSHW NE29 ...... 2 D4
Trinity Sq GATE NE8 ...... 11 G2
SUND SR1 ...... 15 H4
Trinity St NSHW NE29 ...... 2 D4
SWCK/CAS SR5 ...... 105 K3
Trinity Wk SSH NE33 ...... 75 F2
Trojan Av BYK/HTN/WLK NE6 ...... 7 L2
Tromso St SUNDSW NE29 ...... 59 K5
Trool Ct SUNDSW SR3 ...... 134 A2
Troon CI CON/LDGT DH8 ...... 122 E2
WASHN NE37 ...... 102 E3
Trotter Gv BDLGTN NE22 ...... 29 J5
Trotter Ter ASHBK/HED/RY SR2 ...... 135 F1
Troutbeck Av
BYK/HTN/WLK NE6 ...... 72 B6
Troutbeck Rd
CLDN/WHIT/ROK SR6 ...... 92 C7
PLEE/EAS SR8 ...... 175 F3
Troutdale PI LGB/KIL NE12 ...... 57 F4
Trout's La DHAM DH1 ...... 155 J2
Trowbridge Wy GOS/KPK NE3 ...... 55 K5
Truro Av SEA/MUR SR7 ...... 149 J4
Truro Gv NSHW NE29 ...... 60 B2
Truro Rd SUNDSW SR3 ...... 119 H5
Tuart St CLS/BIR/GTL DH3 ...... 129 J4
Tudor Av NSHW NE29 ...... 60 C4
Tudor Ct PONT/DH NE20 ...... 42 E5
RDHAMSE DH6 ...... 173 J4
Tudor Dr STLY/ANP DH9 ...... 112 B3
Tudor Gra PLEE/EAS SR8 ...... 162 B6
Tudor Rd CLS/BIR/GTL DH3 ...... 129 K2
SSH NE33 ...... 2 F9
Tudor Wk GOS/KPK NE3 ...... 55 H3
Tudor Wy GOS/KPK NE3 ...... 55 C4
WD/WHPE/BLK NE5 ...... 55 F5
Tudor Wynd BYK/HTN/WLK NE6 ...... 71 K2
Tulip St GATE NE8 ...... 12 A6
Tumulus Av BYK/HTN/WLK NE6 ...... 72 C3
Tunbridge Rd SUNDSW SR3 ...... 119 H4
Tundry Wy BLAY NE21 ...... 68 D7
Tuneside FELL NE10 ...... 13 L9
Tunis Rd SUNDSW SR3 ...... 119 H4
Tunstall Av BYK/HTN/WLK NE6 ...... 7 J4
HAR/WTLS NE34 ...... 76 B5
RDHAMSE DH6 ...... 180 A2
Tunstall Bank SUNDSW SR3 ...... 120 C7
Tunstall Gv CON/LDGT DH8 ...... 123 K3
Tunstall Hill CI
ASHBK/HED/RY SR2 ...... 120 C4
Tunstall Pk
ASHBK/HED/RY SR2 ...... 120 C2
Tunstall Rd ASHBK/HED/RY SR2 ...... 14 D6
SUNDSW SR3 ...... 120 B5
Tunstall Ter ASHBK/HED/RY SR2 ...... 14 D6
Tunstall Ter West
ASHBK/HED/RY SR2 ...... 14 C6
Tunstall V ASHBK/HED/RY SR2 ...... 14 D9
Tunstall Vw SUNDSW SR3 ...... 120 B6
Tunstall Village Gn
SUNDSW SR3 ...... 120 C7
Tunstall Village Rd
SUNDSW SR3 ...... 120 B7
Tunstall Vls SUNDSW SR3 ...... 120 B7
Turbinia Gdns LGB/HTN NE7 ...... 71 J1
Turfside FELL NE10 ...... 13 L9
Turnberry CLSW/PEL DH2 ...... 115 F4
MONK NE25 ...... 50 A4
SSH NE33 ...... 75 J2
Turnberry CI CON/LDGT DH8 ...... 122 E2
WASHN NE37 ...... 102 E3
Turnberry Wy GOS/KPK * NE3 ...... 56 E4
Turnbull CI DHAM DH1 ...... 17 L3
Turnbull St SUND SR1 ...... 15 J2
Turner Av HAR/WTLS NE34 ...... 91 H1
Turner CI RYTON NE40 ...... 67 F7
Turner Crs GOS/KPK NE3 ...... 56 A5
Turner St CON/LDGT DH8 ...... 122 D4
Turners Wy MPTH NE61 ...... 20 B5
Turnham Rd SUNDSW SR3 ...... 119 C5
Turn Pk
CLS/BIR/GTL
(off Station Rd) DH3 ...... 129 J4
The Turn MPTH NE61 ...... 26 D1
Turnstone Dr WASHS NE38 ...... 116 B3
Turret Rd BW/LEM/TK/HW NE15 ...... 68 D4
Tuscan CI BDN/LAN/SAC DH7 ...... 166 D3
Tuscan Rd SUNDSW SR3 ...... 119 C5
Tweddle Ter RDHAMSE DH6 ...... 179 K2
Tweed Av CON/LDGT DH8 ...... 123 K2
Tweed CI ASHBK/HED/RY SR2 ...... 121 F6
CLSW/PEL DH2 ...... 115 F6
PLEE/EAS SR8 ...... 174 D5
Tweed Gv
BW/LEM/TK/HW NE15 ...... 68 A4
Tweed St ASHGTN * NE63 ...... 24 A1
ELS/FEN NE4 ...... 4 B7
HEBB NE31 ...... 73 F5

HLH DH5 ...... 160 B1
JRW NE32 ...... 73 J6
WASHS NE38 ...... 117 G2
Tweed Ter STLY/ANP DH9 ...... 126 D3
Tweedy Ter BYK/HTN/WLK NE6 ...... 72 B6
Twelfth Av BLYTH NE24 ...... 35 F1
CLSW/PEL DH2 ...... 129 H3
Twelfth St PLEE/EAS SR8 ...... 175 G3
Twentieth Av BLYTH NE24 ...... 34 E2
Twentyfifth Av BLYTH NE24 ...... 35 F2
Twentyfirst Av BLYTH NE24 ...... 34 E2
Twentysecond Av BLYTH NE24 ...... 34 E2
Twentysixth Av BLYTH NE24 ...... 34 E2
Twentythird Av BLYTH NE24 ...... 34 E2
Twickenham Ct CRAM NE23 ...... 39 G6
Twickenham Rd SUNDSW SR3 ...... 119 G4
Twizell La STLY/ANP DH9 ...... 127 J2
Twizell PI PONT/DH NE20 ...... 43 G2
Twizell St BLYTH * NE24 ...... 35 H1
Twyford CI CRAM NE23 ...... 33 H7
Tyldesley Sq SUNDSW SR3 ...... 119 C5
Tyndal Gdns DUN/TMV NE11 ...... 9 H5
Tyne Ap JRW NE32 ...... 73 J3
Tyne Av CON/LDGT DH8 ...... 123 K3
Tynebank BLAY NE21 ...... 83 K2
Tyne Br GATE NE8 ...... 5 M8
Tynedale Av WBAY NE26 ...... 50 D5
WLSD/HOW NE28 ...... 58 D6
Tynedale CI WYLAM NE41 ...... 65 H5
Tynedale Crs HLS DH4 ...... 117 K7
Tynedale Dr BLYTH NE24 ...... 30 C7
Tynedale Gdns PSHWF NE43 ...... 79 H6
Tynedale Rd HAR/WTLS NE34 ...... 75 J3
Tynedale St HLH DH5 ...... 147 H7
Tynedale Ter LGB/KIL NE12 ...... 57 K4
Tyne Gdns PRUD NE42 ...... 64 B7
WASHN NE37 ...... 103 F4
Tynegate Prec
GATE (off Sunderland Rd) NE8 ...... 11 H3
Tyne Main Rd FELL NE10 ...... 12 A2
Tynemouth CI
BYK/HTN/WLK NE6 ...... 6 F4
Tynemouth Ct
BYK/HTN/WLK NE6 ...... 7 C3
TYNE/NSHE NE30 ...... 61 H3
Tynemouth PI MONK NE25 ...... 50 D5
Tynemouth Rd
BYK/HTN/WLK NE6 ...... 7 G3
JRW NE32 ...... 89 J2
TYNE/NSHE NE30 ...... 61 H3
WLSD/HOW NE28 ...... 73 H1
Tynemouth Sq SUNDSW SR3 ...... 119 H5
Tynemouth Ter
TYNE/NSHE NE30 ...... 61 H3
Tynemouth Wy
BYK/HTN/WLK NE6 ...... 7 G3
Tyne Rd STLY/ANP DH9 ...... 126 C2
Tyne Rd East GATE NE8 ...... 10 B3
STLY/ANP DH9 ...... 126 C2
Tyneside Rd ELS/FEN NE4 ...... 9 M2
Tyne St ASHGTN NE63 ...... 24 A1
BLAY NE21 ...... 83 K3
CNUT NE1 ...... 6 C7
CON/LDGT DH8 ...... 123 G5
FELL NE10 ...... 12 F3
HLH DH5 ...... 160 B1
JRW NE32 ...... 73 K3
SEA/MUR* SR7 ...... 150 E1
TYNE/NSHE NE30 ...... 2 F2
Tyne Ter HAR/WTLS NE34 ...... 75 F4
Tynevale Av BLAY NE21 ...... 83 K3
Tyne Vw BW/LEM/TK/HW NE15 ...... 68 A5
HEBB NE31 ...... 72 E5
Tyne View Av WICK/BNPF NE16 ...... 8 A7
Tyne View Gdns FELL NE10 ...... 13 H5
Tyneview Pk
DUN/TMV
(off Whitley Rd) NE11 ...... 86 D6
Tyne View PI GATE NE8 ...... 9 M5
Tyne View Ter PRUD NE42 ...... 80 D7
WLSD/HOW NE28 ...... 73 K2
Tyne-wear Trail DUN/TMV NE11 ...... 8 D4
Tyne Wear Trail
WICK/BNPF NE16 ...... 85 H7
Tyzack St BDN/LAN/SAC DH7 ...... 143 F1

U

Ugly La CLSW/PEL DH2 ...... 144 A4
Uldale Ct GOS/KPK NE3 ...... 55 J3
Ullerdale CI DHAM DH1 ...... 158 B5
Ullswater Av HLH DH5 ...... 160 B1
JRW NE32 ...... 90 B1
Ullswater CI BLYTH NE24 ...... 30 A6
Ullswater Crs BLAY NE21 ...... 83 K4
Ullswater Dr LGB/KIL NE12 ...... 48 B6
Ullswater Gdns HAR/WTLS NE34 ...... 75 H4
Ullswater Gv SWCK/CAS SR5 ...... 106 C4
Ullswater Rd CLSW/PEL DH2 ...... 129 H6
NWBGN NE64 ...... 24 C2
Ullswater Wy
WD/WHPE/BLK NE5 ...... 69 F2
Ulverstone Ter
BYK/HTN/WLK NE6 ...... 7 M3
Ulverston Gdns
LWF/SPW/WRK NE9 ...... 101 H2
Umfraville Dene PRUD NE42 ...... 80 D1
Underhill
LWF/SPW/WRK
(off Kells La) NE9 ...... 87 G6
Underhill Dr STKFD/GP NE62 ...... 22 E7
Underhill Rd
CLDN/WHIT/ROK SR6 ...... 91 K4
Underwood Gv CRAM NE23 ...... 33 G6
Union Aly SSH NE33 ...... 3 G1
Union Hall Rd
BW/LEM/TK/HW NE15 ...... 68 A3
Union La CLSW/PEL DH2 ...... 144 C1
SUND SR1 ...... 15 H1
Union Quay TYNE/NSHE NE30 ...... 3 G2
Union Rd BYK/HTN/WLK NE6 ...... 7 H4
TYNE/NSHE NE30 ...... 3 H1
Union Stairs TYNE/NSHE NE30 ...... 2 E3
Union St BLYTH NE24 ...... 31 G6
HLH DH5 ...... 147 K4
JES NE2 ...... 6 B5
JRW NE32 ...... 73 K3

MLFD/PNYW SR4 ...... 104 E7
NSHW NE29 ...... 2 E3
SEA/MUR SR7 ...... 150 E2
SSH NE33 ...... 75 F5
SUND SR1 ...... 14 E4
WLSD/HOW NE28 ...... 72 D3
Unity Ter STLY/ANP DH9 ...... 111 K4
STLY/ANP DH9 ...... 111 G7
University Prec
MLFD/PNYW
(off Chester Rd) SR4 ...... 14 A6
Unsworth Gdns
CON/LDGT DH8 ...... 123 F6
Unsworth St CON/LDGT DH8 ...... 123 F5
Uplands MONK NE25 ...... 50 B4
The Uplands CLS/BIR/GTL DH3 ...... 115 K1
GOS/KPK NE3 ...... 55 K6
Uplands Wy
LWF/SPW/WRK NE9 ...... 102 B3
Upper Camden St
TYNE/NSHE NE30 ...... 2 D1
Upper Elsdon St NSHW NE29 ...... 2 C4
Upper Fenwick Gv MPTH NE61 ...... 20 D3
Upper Market St SUND SR1 ...... 14 E5
Upper Norfolk St
TYNE/NSHE NE30 ...... 2 E1
Upper Pearson St
TYNE/NSHE NE30 ...... 2 E1
Upper Prec
BLAY (off Wesley Ct) NE21 ...... 84 B1
Upper Queen St
TYNE/NSHE * NE30 ...... 2 F1
Upper Walworth Wy SUND SR1 ...... 14 D4
Upton St GATE NE8 ...... 10 A6
Urfa Ter SSH NE33 ...... 3 J5
Urswick Ct WD/WHPE/BLK NE5 ...... 55 F5
Urwin St HLH DH5 ...... 148 A5
Ushaw Rd HEBB NE31 ...... 73 H5
Usher Av SWCK/CAS SR5 ...... 106 B4
Usk Av JRW NE32 ...... 90 A1
Usworth Cottages
SWCK/CAS
(off Washington Rd) SR5 ...... 104 B2
Usworth Station Rd
WASHN NE37 ...... 103 G5
Uxbridge Ter FELL NE10 ...... 12 D5

V

Valebrooke Av
ASHBK/HED/RY SR2 ...... 14 C9
Valebrooke Gdns
ASHBK/HED/RY SR2 ...... 14 D8
Valehead MONK NE25 ...... 50 B5
Valentia Av BYK/HTN/WLK NE6 ...... 7 L2
Valeria CI WLSD/HOW NE28 ...... 59 F4
Valerian Av
BW/LEM/TK/HW NE15 ...... 66 B1
Valerian Ct ASHGTN NE63 ...... 23 H4
Valeside BW/LEM/TK/HW NE15 ...... 66 E1
DHAM DH1 ...... 16 A2
Vale St HLH DH5 ...... 160 A1
MLFD/PNYW SR4 ...... 14 A7
Vale St East MLFD/PNYW SR4 ...... 14 A7
Vale Vw BDN/LAN/SAC DH7 ...... 141 H5
Vale Wk JES NE2 ...... 6 D2
Valley Crs BLAY NE21 ...... 83 J2
Valley Dene BDN/LAN/SAC DH7 ...... 165 F1
DUN/TMV NE11 ...... 9 G9
LWF/SPW/WRK NE9 ...... 11 J9
WICK/BNPF NE16 ...... 84 E4
Valley Forge WASHS NE38 ...... 103 F7
Valley Gdns CON/LDGT DH8 ...... 122 C3
LWF/SPW/WRK NE9 ...... 11 J9
MONK NE25 ...... 50 B4
WLSD/HOW NE28 ...... 59 F2
Valley Garth
BDN/LAN/SAC DH7 ...... 153 F7
Valley Gv BDN/LAN/SAC DH7 ...... 140 C5
Valley La HAR/WTLS NE34 ...... 76 C5
Valley Rd CLSW/PEL DH2 ...... 128 C3
MONK NE25 ...... 40 C6
Valley Vw BDN/LAN/SAC DH7 ...... 143 G6
BDN/LAN/SAC DH7 ...... 167 G1
CLS/BIR/GTL DH3 ...... 101 H6
CON/LDGT DH8 ...... 122 B2
CON/LDGT DH8 ...... 123 J4
JES NE2 ...... 71 F2
JRW NE32 ...... 73 K7
PRUD NE42 ...... 80 E3
ROWG NE39 ...... 97 F3
WASHS NE38 ...... 117 G5
WICK/BNPF NE16 ...... 97 H6
Vallum Rd
BW/LEM/TK/HW NE15 ...... 67 G1
BYK/HTN/WLK NE6 ...... 7 M4
Vallum Wy ELS/FEN NE4 ...... 4 E6
Vanborough Ct MONK NE25 ...... 40 A6
Vanburgh Gdns MPTH NE61 ...... 20 B5
Vancouver Dr LGB/HTN NE7 ...... 71 K1
Vane St PLEE/EAS SR8 ...... 163 F5
SUNDSW SR3 ...... 120 A7
WNGT SR28 ...... 184 A6
Vane Ter ASHBK/HED/RY SR2 ...... 15 K7
SEA/MUR SR7 ...... 135 K7
Van Mildert CI PLEE/EAS SR8 ...... 174 C6
Vardy Ter HLS DH4 ...... 118 C7
Vauxhall Rd BYK/HTN/WLK NE6 ...... 72 C3
Vedra St SWCK/CAS SR5 ...... 106 B4
Velville Ct WD/WHPE/BLK NE5 ...... 55 F4
Ventnor Av ELS/FEN NE4 ...... 4 A7
Ventnor Crs LWF/SPW/WRK NE9 ...... 86 E1
Ventnor Gdns
LWF/SPW/WRK NE9 ...... 86 E6
WBAY NE26 ...... 50 E3
Vera St RYTON NE40 ...... 82 B4
Verdun Av HEBB NE31 ...... 73 C5
Vermont WASHN NE37 ...... 103 H5
Vernon CI SSH NE33 ...... 75 F3
Vernon Dr MONK NE25 ...... 50 C5
Vernon St WASHN NE37 ...... 103 C5
Veryan Gdns SUNDSW SR3 ...... 120 B3

Vespasian Av SSH NE33 3 J5
Viador CLS/BIR/GTL DH3 129 J3
Viaduct St WLSD/HOW NE28 73 G1
Vicarage Cl CLSW/PEL DH2 114 E7
SUNDSW SR3 119 K7
Vicarage Ct FELL NE10 13 H8
Vicarage Est WNGT TS28 183 K3
Vicarage Flats
BDN/LAN/SAC DH7 167 G6
Vicarage La MLFD/PNYW SR4 104 E7
Vicarage Rd SUNDSW SR3 120 A7
Vicarage St NSHW NE29 2 C3
Vicarsholme Cl SUNDSW SR3 133 J2
Vicars' La LGB/HTN NE7 57 G5
Vicars Wy LGB/KIL NE12 57 F4
Viceroy St SEA/MUR SR7 150 E1
Victoria Av
ASHBK/HED/RY SR2 120 E4
BDN/LAN/SAC DH7 167 H6
FELL NE10 12 A8
LGB/KIL NE12 57 K3
MLFD/PNYW SR4 105 F7
WLSD/HOW NE28 72 D1
Victoria Av West
ASHBK/HED/RY SR2 120 E4
Victoria Ct GATE NE8 10 A6
Victoria Crs NSHW NE29 2 B4
Victoria Ms BLYTH NE24 35 F1
JES NE2 6 C1
Victoria Pl
BDN/LAN/SAC
(off Blackhouse) DH7 127 J6
SUND (off Murton St) SR1 15 G6
Victoria Rd CON/LDGT DH8 123 F5
GATE NE8 10 A7
SSH NE33 75 G2
WASHN NE37 103 F5
Victoria Rd East HEBB NE31 73 H5
Victoria Rd West FELL NE10 88 E2
HEBB NE31 88 E2
Victoria Sq FELL * NE10 12 C8
JES NE2 5 L2
Victoria St BDN/LAN/SAC DH7 140 B4
CON/LDGT DH8 122 E4
DUN/TMV NE11 9 J6
ELS/FEN NE4 4 F8
HLH DH5 147 K4
NSHW NE29 2 D5
RDHAMSE DH6 173 J4
RYTON NE40 66 B7
SEA/MUR SR7 150 D1
Victoria Ter DHAM DH1 16 B2
JRW NE32 73 J5
WBAY NE26 51 F4
Victor St CLDN/WHIT/ROK SR6 106 E4
CLS/BIR/GTL DH3 129 J4
Victory St MLFD/PNYW SR4 105 J6
Victory St East HLH DH5 148 A4
Victory St West HLH DH5 148 A4
Victory Wy SUNDSW SR3 133 G2
Viewforth Dr SWCK/CAS SR5 106 C2
Viewforth Rd
ASHBK/HED/RY SR2 135 F2
Viewforth Ter SWCK/CAS SR5 106 B2
Viewlands
ASHGTN (off Hirst Yd) NE63 23 K1
View La STLY/ANP DH9 112 D7
View Pk MONK NE25 40 A5
Vigo La CLS/BIR/GTL DH3 130 A1
WASHS NE38 116 B6
Village Centre WASHS NE38 117 F2
Village Ct WBAY NE26 50 D4
Village East RYTON NE40 66 E5
Village Farm
BW/LEM/TK/HW NE15 67 J2
Village Hts GATE NE8 10 D4
Village La WASHS NE38 103 F7
Village Pl BYK/HTN/WLK NE6 7 J6
Village Rd CRAM NE23 38 D2
The Village
ASHBK/HED/RY SR2 135 G1
Villa Pl GATE NE8 10 E5
Villa Real Rd CON/LDGT DH8 123 G3
The Villas BDN/LAN/SAC DH7 141 G3
NWBGN
(off Woodhorn Rd) NE64 19 F7
STLY/ANP DH9 125 G4
Villa Vw LWF/SPW/WRK NE9 87 G6
Villette Brook St
ASHBK/HED/RY SR2 15 G9
Villette Pth ASHBK/HED/RY SR2 15 H9
Villette Rd ASHBK/HED/RY SR2 120 E2
Villiers St SUND SR1 15 G4
Villiers St South SUND SR1 15 G5
Vimy Av HEBB NE31 73 G5
Vincent St PLEE/EAS SR8 163 F5
SEA/MUR SR7 150 E2
Vincent Ter STLY/ANP DH9 125 J4
Vine Cl GATE NE8 10 A5
Vine La CNUT NE1 5 K4
Vine Pl HLS DH4 132 C7
SUND SR1 14 D6
Vine St SSH NE33 75 G5
WLSD/HOW NE28 72 E2
Viola Crs BDN/LAN/SAC DH7 143 H6
CLSW/PEL DH2 115 F4
Viola St WASHN NE37 103 F5
Viola Ter WICK/BNPF * NE16 85 F5
Violet Cl ELS/FEN NE4 69 H7
Violet St HLS DH4 132 B7
MLFD/PNYW SR4 14 B4
MLFD/PNYW SR4 104 E7
Viscount Rd SUNDSW SR3 120 A7
Vivian Crs CLSW/PEL DH2 129 J5
Vivian Sq CLDN/WHIT/ROK SR6 106 D2
Voltage Ter HLS DH4 132 B3
Vulcan Pl BDLGTN NE22 29 G6

W

Waddington St DHAM DH1 16 A3
Wadsley Sq
ASHBK/HED/RY SR2 120 E3
Wagon Wy WLSD/HOW NE28 73 F1
Wagonway Rd HEBB NE31 73 F4
Wagtail Cl BLAY NE21 84 A4
Wagtail La STLY/ANP DH9 126 E6
Wagtail Ter STLY/ANP DH9 127 G5
Wakefield Av HAR/WTLS NE34 76 B6
Wakenshaw Rd DHAM DH1 17 J1
Walbottle Rd
BW/LEM/TK/HW NE15 67 H2
Walden Cl CLSW/PEL DH2 114 D5
Waldo St NSHW NE29 2 E3
Waldridge La CLSW/PEL DH2 129 F5
Waldridge Rd CLSW/PEL DH2 129 H5
Waldron Sq
ASHBK/HED/RY SR2 120 E3
Walkerburn CRAM NE23 38 C5
Walkergate DHAM DH1 16 D3
Walker Gv BYK/HTN/WLK NE6 72 B3
Walker Pl TYNE/NSHE NE30 3 G1
Walker Riverside
BYK/HTN/WLK
(off Wincomblee Rd) NE6 72 D7
Walker Rd BYK/HTN/WLK NE6 7 L9
Walker St RDHAMSE DH6 180 A3
Walker Ter GATE NE8 10 F3
Wallace Gdns
LWF/SPW/WRK NE9 102 A1
Wallace St DUN/TMV NE11 9 J6
HLS DH4 132 B7
JES NE2 4 F2
SWCK/CAS SR5 106 C4
Wallflower Av PLEE/EAS SR8 175 G3
Wallingford Av
ASHBK/HED/RY SR2 120 E4
Wallington Av DIN/WO NE13 46 A3
TYNE/NSHE NE30 60 E1
Wallington Cl BDLGTN NE22 29 J4
Wallington Ct MONK NE25 40 A5
Wallington Dr
BW/LEM/TK/HW NE15 68 C3
Wallington Gv SSH NE33 3 H5
Wallington Rd ASHGTN NE63 24 B3
Wallis St HLS DH4 117 K6
SSH* NE33 3 G7
Wallnook La
BDN/LAN/SAC DH7 154 C2
Wallridge Dr MONK NE25 40 B7
Wallsend Rd NSHW NE29 60 B6
WLSD/HOW NE28 60 A7
Wall St GOS/KPK * NE3 56 A5
Wall Ter BYK/HTN/WLK NE6 7 L3
Walnut Gdns GATE NE8 10 A8
Walnut Pl GOS/KPK NE3 55 K7
Walpole Cl SEA/MUR SR7 150 A2
Walpole Ct MLFD/PNYW SR4 105 K7
Walpole St BYK/HTN/WLK NE6 7 L1
Walsham Cl BLYTH NE24 34 D2
Walsh Av HEBB NE31 73 G4
Walsingham WASHS NE38 116 E3
Walter St JRW NE32 73 K3
Walter Ter ELS/FEN NE4 4 D3
HLH DH5 148 A7
Walter Thomas St
SWCK/CAS SR5 105 K3
Waltham WASHS NE38 117 F2
Waltham Cl WLSD/HOW NE28 58 B7
Waltham Pl WD/WHPE/BLK NE5 69 F2
Walton Av BLYTH NE24 30 E6
NSHW NE29 60 D3
SEA/MUR SR7 150 A2
Walton Cl STLY/ANP DH9 126 E2
Walton Dr STKFD/GP NE62 23 F6
Walton La SUND SR1 15 H3
Walton Pk NSHW NE29 60 D2
Walton Rd WASHS NE38 117 K1
WD/WHPE/BLK NE5 68 E2
Waltons Ter BDN/LAN/SAC DH7 166 E2
Walton Ter WNGT TS28 183 J2
Walwick Av NSHW NE29 60 B4
Walwick Rd MONK NE25 49 K4
Walworth Av HAR/WTLS NE34 76 C5
Walworth Gv JRW NE32 89 K1
Wandsworth Rd
BYK/HTN/WLK NE6 6 E3
Wanebeck WASHS NE38 116 C5
Wanlass Ter DHAM DH1 16 E2
Wanley St BLYTH NE24 31 G6
Wanlock Cl CRAM NE23 38 C5
Wanny Rd BDLGTN NE22 29 H6
Wansbeck Av BLYTH NE24 35 G1
STKFD/GP NE62 23 G5
STLY/ANP DH9 126 D2
TYNE/NSHE NE30 51 G6
Wansbeck Cl CLSW/PEL DH2 115 F6
WICK/BNPF NE16 98 E2
Wansbeck Crs MPTH NE61 21 J2
Wansbeck Gdns
STKFD/GP NE62 23 H5
Wansbeck Gv CON/LDGT DH8 123 J2
MONK NE25 40 A2
Wansbeck Ms ASHGTN NE63 23 H1
Wansbeck Rd ASHGTN NE63 23 G3
CRAM NE23 47 F1
JRW NE32 73 J6
Wansbeck Rd North
GOS/KPK NE3 56 A3
Wansbeck Rd South
GOS/KPK NE3 56 A4
Wansbeck St MPTH NE61 20 E5
Wansbeck Ter STKFD/GP NE62 23 K6
Wansbeck Vw STKFD/GP NE62 23 H5
Wansdyke MPTH NE61 20 B4
Wansfell Av WD/WHPE/BLK NE5 55 H7
Wansford Av
WD/WHPE/BLK NE5 69 F2
Wantage Av NSHW NE29 60 B6
Wantage Rd DHAM DH1 158 A4
Wantage St SSH NE33 75 H4
Wapping St SSH NE33 3 G4
Warbeck Cl WD/WHPE/BLK NE5 55 F4
Warburton Crs
LWF/SPW/WRK NE9 11 K8
Warcop Ct GOS/KPK NE3 55 J3
Ward Ct ASHBK/HED/RY SR2 15 H8
Warden Law La SUNDSW SR3 133 J1
Wardill Gdns
LWF/SPW/WRK NE9 87 H5
Wardle Av SSH NE33 75 J2
Wardle Dr CRAM NE23 47 H1
Wardle Gdns FELL NE10 12 F9
Wardle St GOS/KPK NE3 56 E5
STLY/ANP DH9 126 C4
Wardley Ct FELL NE10 89 F4
Wardley Dr FELL NE10 89 F4
Wardley La FELL NE10 88 E3
Warenford Cl CRAM NE23 38 D4
Warenford Pl
WD/WHPE/BLK NE5 69 G4
Warenmill Cl
BW/LEM/TK/HW NE15 67 K4
Warennes St MLFD/PNYW SR4 105 J6
Warenton Pl NSHW NE29 59 K1
Waring Av WBAY NE26 40 E1
Waring Ter SEA/MUR SR7 150 A2
Wark Av NSHW NE29 60 A4
SMOOR NE27 49 H5
Wark Crs JRW NE32 89 K2
Warkdale Av BLYTH NE24 30 C7
Warkworth Av BLYTH NE24 35 G2
HAR/WTLS NE34 76 B4
WLSD/HOW NE28 58 E6
Warkworth Cl WASHS NE38 116 D2
Warkworth Crs ASHGTN NE63 23 J2
GOS/KPK NE3 56 B4
SEA/MUR SR7 149 K1
Warkworth Dr CLSW/PEL DH2 129 G6
DIN/WO NE13 46 C2
MPTH NE61 21 K2
Warkworth Rd DHAM DH1 156 D2
Warkworth St
BW/LEM/TK/HW NE15 68 A5
Warkworth Ter JRW NE32 89 K1
TYNE/NSHE NE30 61 H2
Warnham Av
ASHBK/HED/RY SR2 120 E4
Warnhead Rd BDLGTN NE22 29 H5
Warren Av BYK/HTN/WLK NE6 72 C3
Warren Cl HLS DH4 132 A3
Warren Ct ASHGTN NE63 23 J3
Warrenmor FELL NE10 13 K9
Warren Sq SUND SR1 15 J2
Warren St PLEE/EAS SR8 175 H4
Warrington Rd ELS/FEN NE4 4 D8
GOS/KPK NE3 55 J4
Warton Ter BYK/HTN/WLK NE6 71 J3
Warwick Av CON/LDGT DH8 137 F1
WICK/BNPF NE16 84 E7
Warwick Cl CRAM NE23 39 F7
WICK/BNPF NE16 84 E7
Warwick Ct DHAM DH1 168 B3
GATE NE8 11 G3
GOS/KPK NE3 55 H3
Warwick Dr HLH DH5 147 H2
SUNDSW SR3 119 G7
WASHN NE37 103 F3
WICK/BNPF NE16 85 F7
Warwick Gv BDLGTN NE22 28 D5
Warwick Hall Wk LGB/HTN NE7 71 K1
Warwick Pl PLEE/EAS SR8 174 C2
Warwick Rd HAR/WTLS NE34 75 H4
HEBB NE31 89 H1
WD/WHPE/BLK NE5 68 C3
WLSD/HOW NE28 72 D2
Warwickshire Dr DHAM DH1 157 K7
Warwick St BLYTH NE24 34 D3
GATE NE8 11 G3
JES NE2 6 B3
SWCK/CAS SR5 106 D4
Warwick Ter SUNDSW SR3 120 A6
Wasdale Cl CRAM NE23 38 C5
PLEE/EAS SR8 175 F4
Wasdale Ct
CLDN/WHIT/ROK SR6 92 C7
Wasdale Rd WD/WHPE/BLK NE5 69 F3
Washington Hwy HLS DH4 117 G7
WASHN NE37 102 C5
WASHS NE38 116 E4
Washington Rd SWCK/CAS SR5 104 D2
Washington St
MLFD/PNYW SR4 105 K7
Washingwell La
WICK/BNPF NE16 85 H5
Washingwell Pk
WICK/BNPF NE16 85 G6
Waskdale Crs BLAY NE21 83 K4
Waskerley Cl WICK/BNPF NE16 98 E2
Waskerley Dr RDHAMSE DH6 173 G3
Waskerley Rd WASHS NE38 117 H1
Watch House Cl NSHW NE29 2 C7
Watcombe Cl WASHN NE37 103 H3
Waterbeach Pl
WD/WHPE/BLK NE5 68 E1
Waterbeck Cl CRAM NE23 38 C5
Waterbury Rd GOS/KPK NE3 56 B1
Waterfield Rd BDLGTN NE22 30 D2
Waterford Cl HLH DH5 147 G4
WBAY NE26 41 G2
Waterford Gn ASHGTN NE63 23 K5
Waterford Pk DIN/WO NE13 45 K3
Watergate Rd CON/LDGT DH8 136 E2
Waterloo Pl NSHW NE29 60 E4
SUND SR1 14 E5
Waterloo Rd BLYTH NE24 31 G7
MONK NE25 49 J4
WASHN NE37 103 G4
Waterloo Sq SSH NE33 3 H7
Waterloo St BLAY NE21 83 J3
CNUT NE1 5 H8
Waterlow Cl SWCK/CAS SR5 105 K1
Watermill RYTON NE40 67 F6
Watermill La FELL NE10 12 E8
Water Rw
BW/LEM/TK/HW NE15 67 G4
Waterside Dr DUN/TMV NE11 8 E4
Waterside Pk HEBB NE31 72 E5
Waterson Crs
BDN/LAN/SAC DH7 143 G7
Water St BDN/LAN/SAC DH7 143 H5
ELS/FEN NE4 9 L2
Waterville Pl NSHW NE29 2 C3
Waterville Rd NSHW NE29 60 B6
Waterville Ter NSHW NE29 2 D3
Waterworks Rd SUND SR1 14 B5
Watford Cl SWCK/CAS SR5 105 K1
Watkin Crs SEA/MUR SR7 149 H5
Watling Av SEA/MUR SR7 150 A2
Watling Pl LWF/SPW/WRK NE9 87 H6
Watling St CON/LDGT DH8 123 H1
HAR/WTLS NE34 75 F6
Watling Street Bungalows
CON/LDGT DH8 123 J2
Watling Wy BDN/LAN/SAC DH7 140 B5
Watson Av HAR/WTLS NE34 76 B6
Watson Cl RDHAMSE DH6 173 F7
SEA/MUR SR7 150 A2
Watson Crs TRIM TS29 183 G6
Watson Gdns WLSD/HOW NE28 59 J7
Watson Pl HAR/WTLS NE34 76 B6
Watson St CON/LDGT DH8 122 E3
JRW NE32 74 A3
STLY/ANP DH9 112 D6
WICK/BNPF NE16 97 K7
Watt's La NWBGN NE64 19 G7
Watt's Rd WBAY NE26 50 E3
Watts St SEA/MUR SR7 149 H5
Watt St GATE NE8 10 D9
Wavendon Crs
MLFD/PNYW SR4 119 H2
Waveney Gdns STLY/ANP DH9 126 C3
Waveney Rd PLEE/EAS SR8 174 C6
Waverdale Av
BYK/HTN/WLK NE6 72 C4
Waverdale Wy SSH NE33 75 F5
Waverley Av BDLGTN NE22 29 J4
MONK NE25 50 D5
Waverley Cl BLAY NE21 83 H4
RDHAMSE DH6 173 G3
Waverley Crs
BW/LEM/TK/HW NE15 68 B4
Waverley Dr BDLGTN NE22 29 J4
Waverley Rd ELS/FEN NE4 4 E9
LWF/SPW/WRK NE9 101 G3
Waverley Ter MLFD/PNYW SR4 105 J6
Waverton Cl CRAM NE23 38 C5
Wawn St SSH NE33 75 H2
Wayfarer Rd SWCK/CAS SR5 106 A4
Wayland Sq
ASHBK/HED/RY SR2 120 E5
Wayman St SWCK/CAS SR5 106 C4
Wayside ASHBK/HED/RY SR2 14 A9
BW/LEM/TK/HW NE15 69 F6
RDHAMSE DH6 178 C5
Wealcroft FELL NE10 88 B6
Wealleans Cl ASHGTN NE63 24 D2
Wear Av CON/LDGT DH8 123 K2
Wear Ct HAR/WTLS NE34 75 G6
Weardale Av BLYTH NE24 30 B6
BYK/HTN/WLK NE6 72 C4
CLDN/WHIT/ROK SR6 92 E6
LGB/KIL NE12 57 K2
WASHN NE37 102 E5
WLSD/HOW NE28 58 D6
Weardale Crs HLS DH4 117 K7
Weardale Pk RDHAMSE DH6 173 F7
Weardale St HLH DH5 147 H7
Weardale Ter STLY/ANP DH9 125 J4
Weardale Wy SPEN DL16 177 G7
Wearfield SWCK/CAS SR5 105 J4
Wear Ldg CLS/BIR/GTL DH3 115 J7
Wearmouth Av SWCK/CAS SR5 106 C3
Wearmouth Br SUND SR1 14 E3
Wearmouth Dr SWCK/CAS SR5 106 C3
Wearmouth St
CLDN/WHIT/ROK SR6 106 D4
Wear Rd HEBB NE31 73 G7
STLY/ANP DH9 126 D2
Wearside Dr DHAM DH1 16 E1
Wear St CHPW NE17 95 J4
CON/LDGT DH8 123 G5
HLH DH5 147 K5
HLS DH4 146 D1
JRW NE32 73 K4
MLFD/PNYW SR4 104 E6
SEA/MUR* SR7 150 E1
SUND SR1 15 J5
SWCK/CAS SR5 106 A4
Wear Vw DHAM DH1 16 F2
Weathercock La
LWF/SPW/WRK NE9 87 F7
Weatherside BLAY NE21 83 K3
Webb Av SEA/MUR SR7 149 H4
SEA/MUR SR7 149 K1
Webb Gdns FELL NE10 13 K8
Webb Sq PLEE/EAS SR8 175 F1
Wedgewood Cottages
BW/LEM/TK/HW NE15 68 B5
Wedgwood Rd SEA/MUR SR7 149 K2
Wedmore Rd
WD/WHPE/BLK NE5 68 B1
Weetman St SSH NE33 75 F2
Weetslade Crs CRAM NE23 47 G2
Weetslade Rd CRAM NE23 47 G2
Weetwood Rd CRAM NE23 38 D4
Weidner Rd
BW/LEM/TK/HW NE15 69 H6
Welbeck Gn BYK/HTN/WLK NE6 7 L6
Welbeck Rd BYK/HTN/WLK NE6 7 H6
STKFD/GP NE62 22 E6
Welbeck Ter MPTH NE61 21 K1
Welburn Cl PRUD NE42 64 B6
Weldon Av ASHBK/HED/RY SR2 120 E4
Weldon Crs LGB/HTN NE7 71 H1
Weldon Pl NSHW NE29 60 B2
Weldon Rd CRAM NE23 39 F3
LGB/KIL NE12 57 H4
Weldon Ter CLS/BIR/GTL DH3 129 K5
Weldon Wy GOS/KPK NE3 56 B4
Welfare Cl PLEE/EAS SR8 163 F5
Welfare Crs ASHGTN NE63 24 B2
NWBGN NE64 24 E1
RHTLP TS27 175 K7
Welfare Rd HLH DH5 147 K4
Welford Av GOS/KPK NE3 56 A5
Welford Rd CON/LDGT DH8 122 C7
Welland Cl PLEE/EAS SR8 174 D6
Welland La
CLDN/WHIT/ROK SR6 92 E3
Wellands Cl
CLDN/WHIT/ROK SR6 92 E3
Wellands Ct
CLDN/WHIT/ROK SR6 92 E3
Wellands Dr
CLDN/WHIT/ROK SR6 92 E3
Well Bank Rd WASHN NE37 102 D5
Wellburn Pk JES NE2 71 G2
Wellburn Rd WASHN NE37 102 D4
Well Close Wk WICK/BNPF NE16 84 E6
Well Dean PRUD NE42 80 D1
Wellesley St JRW NE32 73 K6
Wellesley Ter ELS/FEN NE4 4 C6
Wellfield Cl
BW/LEM/TK/HW NE15 66 E2
Wellfield Ct RYTON NE40 82 A2
Wellfield La WD/WHPE/BLK NE5 68 E1
Wellfield Rd ELS/FEN NE4 69 H6
ROWG NE39 96 E3
SEA/MUR SR7 149 G5
WNGT TS28 183 K2
Wellfield Ter FELL NE10 13 M5
Wellhead Ct
ASHGTN
(off Wellhead Ter) NE63 23 G1
Wellhead Dean Rd MPTH NE61 22 E3
Wellhead Ter ASHGTN NE63 23 G1
Wellington Av MONK NE25 49 J4
Wellington Ct FELL NE10 12 B7
GOS/KPK NE3 55 H3
Wellington Dr SSH NE33 3 G5
Wellington La MLFD/PNYW SR4 14 A2
Wellington Rd DUN/TMV NE11 8 D6
STKFD/GP NE62 23 G6
Wellington St BLYTH * NE24 31 H7
ELS/FEN NE4 5 G5
FELL NE10 12 B7
HEBB NE31 73 F6
Well La SMOOR NE27 49 K7
Wellmere Rd
ASHBK/HED/RY SR2 121 F5
Well Ridge Cl MONK NE25 50 A3
Well Ridge Pk MONK NE25 50 A2
Well Rd PSHWF NE43 79 F7
Wells Cl LGB/KIL NE12 57 K6
Wells Crs SEA/MUR SR7 150 A1
Wells Gdns LWF/SPW/WRK NE9 101 F3
Wells Gv HAR/WTLS NE34 76 A4
Wellshede FELL NE10 88 D5
Well St MLFD/PNYW SR4 105 K6
Well Wy MPTH NE61 20 D4
Wellway Ct MPTH NE61 20 D4
Wellwood Gdns MPTH NE61 20 E5
Well Yd
TYNE/NSHE (off Percy St) NE30 61 J3
Welsh Ter STLY/ANP DH9 125 J4
Welton Cl PSHWF NE43 79 H6
Welwyn Av BDLGTN NE22 29 K2
Welwyn Cl SWCK/CAS SR5 104 E5
WLSD/HOW NE28 58 B6
Wembley Av MONK NE25 50 C5
Wembley Rd SWCK/CAS SR5 105 K2
Wendover Cl SWCK/CAS SR5 105 J1
Wendover Wy SWCK/CAS SR5 105 J1
Wenham Sq
ASHBK/HED/RY SR2 120 B2
Wenlock WASHS NE38 116 E2
Wenlock Dr NSHW NE29 60 C2
Wenlock Rd HAR/WTLS NE34 74 E6
Wensley Cl CLSW/PEL DH2 114 E5
Wensleydale WLSD/HOW NE28 58 B5
Wensleydale Av HLS DH4 117 J7
WASHN NE37 102 E5
Wens Leydale Dr LGB/KIL NE12 57 K2
Wensleydale Ter BLYTH NE24 35 H1
Wentworth SSH NE33 75 J2
Wentworth Cl FELL NE10 87 K5
Wentworth Ct PONT/DH NE20 42 E5
Wentworth Dr WASHN NE37 102 E3
Wentworth Gdns MONK NE25 50 A4
Wentworth Gra
GOS/KPK (off the Gv) NE3 56 D6
Wentworth Pl ELS/FEN NE4 4 D8
Wentworth Ter
MLFD/PNYW SR4 14 A4
Werdohl Wy CON/LDGT DH8 123 G2
Werhale Gn FELL NE10 12 D8
Wesley Ct FELL NE10 12 B6
STLY/ANP DH9 125 H2
Wesley Dr LGB/KIL NE12 58 D1
Wesley Gdns CON/LDGT DH8 137 F2
Wesley Gv RYTON NE40 82 A1
Wesley Mt RYTON NE40 82 A1
Wesley St CON/LDGT DH8 123 F5
LWF/SPW/WRK NE9 87 F7
Wesley Ter CON/LDGT DH8 137 G2
PRUD NE42 80 D2
STLY/ANP DH9 125 H3
Wesley Wy
BW/LEM/TK/HW NE15 67 F1
LGB/KIL NE12 58 D1
SEA/MUR SR7 150 A1
Wessex Cl SWCK/CAS SR5 105 K1
Wessington Wy SWCK/CAS SR5 105 J4
West Acre CON/LDGT DH8 122 C2
Westacre Gdns
WD/WHPE/BLK NE5 69 G4
West Acres DIN/WO NE13 45 F2
Westacres Av WICK/BNPF NE16 99 F1
Westacres Crs
BW/LEM/TK/HW NE15 69 G5
West Av CLDN/WHIT/ROK SR6 92 E3
GOS/KPK NE3 56 C6
HAR/WTLS NE34 75 J5
LGB/KIL NE12 57 K4
NSHW NE29 60 B5
PLEE/EAS SR8 163 F4
ROWG NE39 97 F4
SEA/MUR SR7 149 H6
STKFD/GP NE62 23 D6
WASHS NE38 116 D5
WD/WHPE/BLK NE5 68 D1
West Bailey LGB/KIL NE12 47 K5
Westbourne Av
BYK/HTN/WLK NE6 72 B3
GATE NE8 10 E7
GOS/KPK NE3 56 C3
STKFD/GP NE62 23 G4
Westbourne Dr HLS DH4 131 J1
Westbourne Rd SUND SR1 14 B5
West Bridge St BLYTH NE24 31 F3
Westburn Gdns
WLSD/HOW NE28 58 B6
Westburn Ms RYTON NE40 82 A1
Westburn Ter
CLDN/WHIT/ROK SR6 106 E3
Westbury Av
BYK/HTN/WLK NE6 72 B3

Westbury Rd NSHW NE29 ....60 D2
Westcliff Cl PLEE/EAS SR8 ....162 B6
Westcliffe Rd
CLDN/WHIT/ROK SR6 ....107 F1
Westcliffe Wy HAR/WTLS NE34 ....90 D1
West Clifton LGB/KIL NE12 ....47 J5
West Coppers
BW/LEM/TK/HW NE15 ....68 C4
Westcott Av SSH NE33 ....75 J2
Westcott Dr DHAM DH1 ....156 B4
Westcott Rd HAR/WTLS NE34 ....75 G6
PLEE/EAS SR8 ....174 E3
West Ct
DHAM (off Elvet Hill Rd) DH1 ....16 C8
West Crs FELL NE10 ....88 E4
Westcroft CLDN/WHIT/ROK SR6 ....92 E3
Westcroft Rd LGB/KIL NE12 ....58 A2
West Dene Dr TYNE/NSHE NE30 ....60 E2
West Denton Cl
BW/LEM/TK/HW NE15 ....68 B3
West Denton Rd
BW/LEM/TK/HW NE15 ....68 B3
West Denton Wy
WD/WHPE/BLK NE5 ....68 B1
West Dr BDN/LAN/SAC DH7 ....140 B5
BLYTH NE24 ....34 E3
CLDN/WHIT/ROK SR6 ....91 J3
CLSW/PEL DH2 ....129 F5
West End Front St
BDLGTN NE22 ....29 F6
Westerdale HLS DH4 ....117 G6
WLSD/HOW NE28 ....58 B6
Westerdale Pl
BYK/HTN/WLK NE6 ....72 D5
Westerham Cl SWCK/CAS SR5 ....105 K1
Westerhope Gdns
WD/WHPE/BLK NE5 ....69 H2
Westerhope Homes
WD/WHPE/BLK
(off Hillhead Rd) NE5 ....54 C7
Westerhope Rd WASHS NE38 ....117 H1
Westerkirk CRAM NE23 ....38 C4
Western Ap SSH NE33 ....75 G2
Western Av BDN/LAN/SAC DH7 ....165 G1
MONK NE25 ....39 J5
PRUD NE42 ....80 B2
WD/WHPE/BLK NE5 ....68 B2
Western Dr ELS/FEN NE4 ....4 A6
Western Hwy WASHS NE38 ....116 C4
Western Hl ASHBK/HED/RY SR2 ....14 A6
CON/LDGT DH8 ....122 C2
Westernmoor WASHN NE37 ....102 B7
Western Rd JRW NE32 ....73 J4
WLSD/HOW NE28 ....73 H1
Western Ter BOL NE36 ....90 E5
CRAM NE23 ....47 F1
Western Wy BLAY NE21 ....84 C2
BW/LEM/TK/HW NE15 ....52 C2
PONT/DH NE20 ....42 C5
RYTON NE40 ....66 E7
WBAY NE26 ....50 D1
West Farm
BOL (off North Rd) NE36 ....91 G5
West Farm Av LGB/KIL NE12 ....57 F4
West Farm Ct
CON/LDGT (off Manor Rd) DH8 ....109 J4
CRAM* NE23 ....38 C1
West Farm La CON/LDGT DH8 ....109 J4
West Farm Rd
BYK/HTN/WLK NE6 ....7 M3
CLDN/WHIT/ROK SR6 ....92 B4
WLSD/HOW NE28 ....59 G7
West Farm Wynd LGB/KIL NE12 ....57 F5
Westfield GOS/KPK NE3 ....70 B1
MPTH NE61 ....20 C6
Westfield Av DIN/WO NE13 ....46 A3
GOS/KPK NE3 ....56 C7
MONK NE25 ....50 B5
RYTON NE40 ....82 B1
Westfield Ct
JRW (off Borough Rd) NE32 ....73 K5
MLFD/PNYW SR4 ....119 J2
WLSD/HOW NE28 ....72 D3
Westfield Crs NWBGN NE64 ....25 F2
RYTON NE40 ....82 B1
Westfield Dr GOS/KPK NE3 ....56 B7
Westfield Gv GOS/KPK NE3 ....56 B7
MLFD/PNYW SR4 ....119 J2
Westfield La RYTON NE40 ....66 D5
Westfield Pk WLSD/HOW NE28 ....72 C1
Westfield Rd
BW/LEM/TK/HW NE15 ....69 G6
GATE NE8 ....10 E7
Westfields STLY/ANP DH9 ....126 C2
Westfield Ter GATE NE8 ....10 F7
West Ford Rd STKFD/GP NE62 ....23 H5
Westgarth WD/WHPE/BLK NE5 ....54 C6
Westgarth Gv RDHAMSE DH6 ....173 G3
Westgate MPTH NE61 ....20 B6
Westgate Av SUNDSW SR3 ....120 A6
Westgate Cl MONK NE25 ....50 A3
Westgate Gv SUNDSW SR3 ....120 A6
Westgate Hill Ter CNUT NE1 ....5 G8
Westgate Rd CNUT NE1 ....5 G7
ELS/FEN NE4 ....69 J5
West George Potts St SSH NE33 ....75 G2
West Gra SWCK/CAS SR5 ....106 C2
Westgreen STKFD/GP NE62 ....28 E1
West Greens MPTH NE61 ....20 E5
West Gv MLFD/PNYW SR4 ....119 F1
Westheath Av
ASHBK/HED/RY SR2 ....120 E4
West High Horse Cl ROWG NE39 ....97 H1
West Hl MLFD/PNYW SR4 ....119 J2
MPTH NE61 ....20 B6
Westhills STLY/ANP DH9 ....111 J4
Westhills Cl BDN/LAN/SAC DH7 ....143 G3
West Holborn SSH NE33 ....75 F2
Westholme Gdns
BW/LEM/TK/HW NE15 ....69 H5
Westhope Cl HAR/WTLS NE34 ....76 A4
Westhope Rd HAR/WTLS NE34 ....76 A4
West Jesmond Av JES NE2 ....70 E1
Westlands
BW/LEM/TK/HW NE15 ....68 A2
JRW NE32 ....90 B3
LGB/HTN NE7 ....57 G7
TYNE/NSHE NE30 ....61 F1
WBAY NE26 ....40 E2
West La BLAY NE21 ....83 J4
CHPW NE17 ....109 H2
CLS/BIR/GTL DH3 ....129 J5
LGB/KIL NE12 ....57 K1
RDHAMSE DH6 ....161 J3
SEA/MUR SR7 ....162 A2
WICK/BNPF NE16 ....98 A4
West Lawn ASHBK/HED/RY SR2 ....14 D9
West Law Rd CON/LDGT DH8 ....108 D6
West Lawson St NSHW NE29 ....2 C5
West Lea BLAY NE21 ....84 A4
Westleigh Ct MLFD/PNYW SR4 ....105 K7
Westleigh Rd HLS DH4 ....132 A3
Westley Av WBAY NE26 ....41 H7
Westley Cl WBAY NE26 ....41 H7
Westloch Rd CRAM NE23 ....38 C5
Westmacott St
BW/LEM/TK/HW NE15 ....67 G3
West Market St MPTH NE61 ....18 D2
West Mdw WD/WHPE/BLK NE5 ....54 B6
West Meadows Dr
CLDN/WHIT/ROK SR6 ....92 A4
West Meadows Rd
CLDN/WHIT/ROK SR6 ....92 A4
Westminster Av NSHW NE29 ....59 K2
Westminster Crs HEBB NE31 ....89 G2
Westminster Dr
DUN/TMV * NE11 ....85 K6
Westminster St GATE NE8 ....10 D8
Westminster Wy LGB/HTN NE7 ....57 J6
West Moffett St SSH * NE33 ....75 H2
West Moor Dr
CLDN/WHIT/ROK SR6 ....92 A5
Westmoor Dr LGB/KIL NE12 ....57 H1
Westmoor Rd
MLFD/PNYW SR4 ....105 H6
Westmoreland St
WLSD/HOW NE28 ....72 E1
Westmorland Av BDLGTN NE22 ....28 E5
NWBGN NE64 ....25 F2
WASHN NE37 ....103 F3
WLSD/HOW NE28 ....73 K2
Westmorland Gdns
LWF/SPW/WRK NE9 ....87 F7
Westmorland La CNUT NE1 ....5 H8
Westmorland Ri PLEE/EAS SR8 ....174 C2
Westmorland Rd CNUT NE1 ....5 G8
ELS/FEN NE4 ....4 B9
HAR/WTLS NE34 ....76 C4
NSHW NE29 ....59 K3
Westmorland Wk ELS/FEN NE4 ....9 H1
Westmorland Wy CRAM NE23 ....38 A2
West Mt MLFD/PNYW SR4 ....119 J1
Westoe Av SSH NE33 ....75 J2
Westoe Dr SSH NE33 ....75 J2
Westoe Rd SSH NE33 ....3 J9
Westoe Village SSH NE33 ....75 J3
Weston Av WICK/BNPF NE16 ....84 D7
Weston Vw PLEE/EAS SR8 ....174 D3
West Ousterley Rd
STLY/ANP DH9 ....126 E5
Westover Gdns
LWF/SPW/WRK NE9 ....87 F5
West Pde CON/LDGT DH8 ....123 F5
ELS/FEN NE4 ....4 E8
HEBB NE31 ....73 F7
West Pk DUN/TMV NE11 ....9 G6
MPTH NE61 ....20 C6
SUNDSW SR3 ....133 F1
West Park Gdns BLAY NE21 ....84 A3
West Park Rd
CLDN/WHIT/ROK SR6 ....93 F1
LWF/SPW/WRK NE9 ....86 E5
SSH NE33 ....75 G3
West Park Vw CRAM NE23 ....47 F1
West Pastures ASHGTN NE63 ....23 H3
BOL NE36 ....90 A7
West Percy Rd NSHW NE29 ....2 A3
West Percy St NSHW NE29 ....2 C2
Westport Cl SWCK/CAS SR5 ....105 K1
West Quay Rd SWCK/CAS SR5 ....105 K4
West Riggs BDLGTN NE22 ....29 F6
The West Rig GOS/KPK NE3 ....55 J6
West Rd BDLGTN NE22 ....29 K4
CON/LDGT DH8 ....122 C3
PONT/DH NE20 ....43 F3
PRUD NE42 ....80 B2
STLY/ANP DH9 ....111 J5
West Salisbury St BLYTH NE24 ....31 F6
West St SMOOR NE27 ....59 F1
West Stainton St SSH * NE33 ....75 H2
West Stevenson St SSH NE33 ....75 H2
West Stoneycroft LGB/KIL NE12 ....48 A7
West St CLS/BIR/GTL DH3 ....115 J2
CLSW/PEL DH2 ....128 A2
CON/LDGT DH8 ....123 J3
GATE NE8 ....10 F1
HEBB NE31 ....73 G4
RDHAMSE DH6 ....173 H4
RDHAMSE DH6 ....179 F6
ROWG NE39 ....96 B1
SEA/MUR SR7 ....150 E1
STLY/ANP DH9 ....112 B6
SUND SR1 ....14 D5
SUNDSW SR3 ....120 A6
WICK/BNPF NE16 ....84 E5
WLSD/HOW NE28 ....72 C1
West Sunniside SUND SR1 ....14 F4
Westsyde PONT/DH NE20 ....42 C6
West Ter DHAM DH1 ....16 A2
STKFD/GP NE62 ....23 J6
WBAY NE26 ....41 G2
West Thorns Wk
WICK/BNPF NE16 ....84 E6
West Thorp
WD/WHPE/BLK NE5 ....54 D5
West Vallum
BW/LEM/TK/HW NE15 ....68 D4
West Vw ASHGTN NE63 ....23 K2
BDLGTN NE22 ....29 J3
BDN/LAN/SAC
(off Lymington) DH7 ....165 H3
BDN/LAN/SAC DH7 ....167 H7
BLAY NE21 ....84 A1
BW/LEM/TK/HW NE15 ....68 A5
CLDN/WHIT/ROK SR6 ....106 D2
DHAM DH1 ....17 H2
DUN/TMV NE11 ....100 D7
ELS/FEN NE4 ....4 A9
HLS DH4 ....131 K3
LGB/KIL NE12 ....57 K2
MPTH NE61 ....21 J2
STKFD/GP NE62 ....24 E7
STLY/ANP
(off Catchwell Rd) DH9 ....111 F6
SWCK/CAS SR5 ....105 F4
WICK/BNPF NE16 ....97 J7
West Walls CNUT NE1 ....5 H7
West Walpole St SSH NE33 ....75 F2
Westward Ct
WD/WHPE/BLK NE5 ....54 C7
Westward Pl WASHS NE38 ....116 D5
Westway BLAY NE21 ....83 K2
BW/LEM/TK/HW NE15 ....53 F7
West Wy DUN/TMV NE11 ....9 J8
Westway PLEE/EAS SR8 ....174 D5
West Wy SSH NE33 ....75 G4
West Wear St SUND SR1 ....14 E3
Westwell Ct LGB/HTN NE7 ....57 F6
West Wellington St NSHW NE29 ....2 D2
Westwood Av
BYK/HTN/WLK NE6 ....71 H2
Westwood Cl WICK/BNPF NE16 ....97 K6
Westwood Gdns GOS/KPK NE3 ....55 J6
STKFD/GP NE62 ....23 F4
Westwood Rd GOS/KPK NE3 ....56 C1
Westwood St MLFD/PNYW SR4 ....105 K7
Westwood Vw RYTON NE40 ....82 A1
West Wylam Dr PRUD NE42 ....80 E1
West Wynd LGB/KIL NE12 ....47 K6
Wetheral Gdns
LWF/SPW/WRK NE9 ....101 G2
Wetheral Ter
BYK/HTN/WLK NE6 ....72 B7
Wetherburn Av SEA/MUR SR7 ....149 G5
Wetherby Cl CON/LDGT DH8 ....108 D7
Wetherby Gv GATE NE8 ....10 C9
Wetherby Rd
ASHBK/HED/RY SR2 ....121 G5
Wettondale Av BLYTH NE24 ....30 C7
Weybourne Sq
ASHBK/HED/RY SR2 ....120 E4
Weyhill Av NSHW NE29 ....60 B6
Weymouth Dr SEA/MUR SR7 ....150 B2
Weymouth Gdns
LWF/SPW/WRK NE9 ....101 F3
Whaggs La WICK/BNPF NE16 ....85 F6
Whalebone La MPTH NE61 ....20 D5
Whalton Av GOS/KPK NE3 ....56 A4
Whalton Cl FELL NE10 ....88 E5
RDHAMSE DH6 ....170 D1
Whalton Ct HAR/WTLS NE34 ....75 J5
Whaper Sq RDHAMSE DH6 ....182 D2
Wharfdale Pl
BYK/HTN/WLK NE6 ....72 C5
Wharfedale HLS DH4 ....117 J6
WLSD/HOW NE28 ....58 B5
Wharfedale Av WASHN NE37 ....102 D5
Wharfedale Dr SSH NE33 ....75 G4
Wharfedale Gdns BLYTH NE24 ....30 C6
Wharmlands Rd
BW/LEM/TK/HW NE15 ....68 D4
Wharncliffe St SUND SR1 ....14 B5
Wharnley Wy CON/LDGT DH8 ....136 E2
Wharrier St BYK/HTN/WLK NE6 ....72 B7
Wharton St BLYTH NE24 ....34 E2
SSH NE33 ....3 K9
Wheatall Dr
CLDN/WHIT/ROK SR6 ....93 F1
Wheatfield Cl PRUD NE42 ....64 B7
Wheatfield Gv LGB/KIL NE12 ....57 H3
Wheatfield Rd
WD/WHPE/BLK NE5 ....54 D7
Wheatley Gdns BOL NE36 ....90 E5
Wheatley Green La
BDN/LAN/SAC DH7 ....127 H7
Wheatley Ter RDHAMSE DH6 ....182 D1
Wheatleywell La
CLS/BIR/GTL DH3 ....144 D3
Wheatridge MONK NE25 ....39 J4
Wheatsheaf Ct
CLDN/WHIT/ROK SR6 ....107 F4
Whernside Pl CRAM NE23 ....38 C5
Whernside Wk RYTON NE40 ....67 F7
Whickham Av DUN/TMV NE11 ....9 H8
Whickham Bank
WICK/BNPF NE16 ....84 E5
Whickham Cl HLS DH4 ....132 A7
Whickham Gdns
BYK/HTN/WLK NE6 ....7 G7
Whickham Hwy
DUN/TMV NE11 ....85 J5
WICK/BNPF NE16 ....8 C9
Whickham Ldg
WICK/BNPF NE16 ....85 G5
Whickham Pk WICK/BNPF NE16 ....8 A9
Whickham Rd HEBB NE31 ....73 F6
Whickham St
CLDN/WHIT/ROK SR6 ....15 G1
PLEE/EAS SR8 ....162 D5
Whickham St East
CLDN/WHIT/ROK SR6 ....106 E4
Whickham Vw
BW/LEM/TK/HW NE15 ....68 E5
LWF/SPW/WRK NE9 ....87 G7
Whickhope WASHS NE38 ....117 G4
Whinbank PONT/DH NE20 ....43 F7
Whinbrooke FELL NE10 ....88 C6
Whinbush Pl
BW/LEM/TK/HW NE15 ....68 E6
Whindyke RHTLP TS27 ....175 K7
Whinfell Cl CRAM NE23 ....38 D5
Whinfell Rd PONT/DH NE20 ....43 F6
Whinfield Av RDHAMSE DH6 ....173 H4
Whinfield Ter ROWG NE39 ....97 F3
Whinfield Wy ROWG NE39 ....96 E4
Whinham Wy MPTH NE61 ....26 E1
Whinlatter Gdns
LWF/SPW/WRK NE9 ....101 G1
Whinmoor Pl
WD/WHPE/BLK NE5 ....69 J2
Whinney Cl BLAY NE21 ....83 J4
Whinneyfield Rd
BYK/HTN/WLK NE6 ....72 B3
Whinney Hl DHAM DH1 ....16 F7
Whinny La CON/LDGT DH8 ....108 E5
Whinny Pl CON/LDGT DH8 ....137 F2
Whinshaw FELL NE10 ....88 B5
Whinside STLY/ANP DH9 ....112 C7
Whinstone Ms
LGB/KIL (off Station Rd) NE12 ....57 K4
Whistler Gdns HAR/WTLS NE34 ....91 H1
Whitbay Crs LGB/KIL NE12 ....57 J4
Whitbeck Rd
WD/WHPE/BLK NE5 ....68 E2
Whitbourne Cl WASHN NE37 ....103 G3
Whitburn Bents Rd
CLDN/WHIT/ROK SR6 ....93 F5
Whitburn Cl BDN/LAN/SAC DH7 ....154 A3
Whitburn Gdns
LWF/SPW/WRK NE9 ....101 K2
Whitburn Pl CRAM NE23 ....38 C5
Whitburn Rd
CLDN/WHIT/ROK SR6 ....91 K4
Whitburn Rd East
CLDN/WHIT/ROK SR6 ....92 B3
Whitburn St
CLDN/WHIT/ROK SR6 ....14 F1
Whitburn Ter BOL NE36 ....91 H5
CLDN/WHIT/ROK SR6 ....106 D1
Whitby Av CLDN/WHIT/ROK SR6 ....93 F6
Whitby Dr WASHS NE38 ....117 F3
Whitby Gdns WLSD/HOW NE28 ....59 G6
Whitby St TYNE/NSHE NE30 ....61 F4
Whitchurch Cl BOLCOL NE35 ....90 C3
SWCK/CAS SR5 ....105 K1
Whitchurch Rd SWCK/CAS SR5 ....105 K1
Whiteacres MPTH NE61 ....20 E6
Whitebark SUNDSW SR3 ....133 J3
Whitebridge Cl GOS/KPK NE3 ....56 C2
Whitebridge Ct GOS/KPK NE3 ....56 C2
Whitebridge Pk GOS/KPK NE3 ....56 D3
White Cedars
BDN/LAN/SAC DH7 ....167 F7
Whitecliff Cl NSHW NE29 ....60 D2
White Crs RHTLP TS27 ....185 H2
Whitecroft Rd LGB/KIL NE12 ....47 G7
Whitecross Wy
CNUT (off Eldon Sq) NE1 ....5 J5
Whitefield Crs HLS DH4 ....117 J7
MPTH NE61 ....21 J2
Whitefield Gdns RYTON NE40 ....82 B4
Whitefield Gv FELL NE10 ....12 C7
Whitefield Ter
BYK/HTN/WLK NE6 ....71 K2
Whiteford Pl CRAM NE23 ....39 H6
Whitefriars Wy LGB/KIL NE12 ....57 G5
White Gates Dr HLH * DH5 ....148 A6
Whitegates Rd RDHAMSE DH6 ....158 C6
Whitehall Rd
BW/LEM/TK/HW NE15 ....67 H1
GATE NE8 ....10 F6
Whitehall St SSH NE33 ....75 G5
Whitehead St SSH NE33 ....75 F4
Whitehill FELL NE10 ....88 B7
Whitehill Crs CLSW/PEL DH2 ....128 E3
Whitehill Dr FELL NE10 ....87 K6
Whitehill Hall Gdns
CLSW/PEL DH2 ....129 G3
Whitehill Rd CRAM NE23 ....33 G6
White Hill Rd HLH DH5 ....160 B1
Whitehorn Crs
WD/WHPE/BLK NE5 ....69 H1
White Horse Vw
HAR/WTLS NE34 ....76 C5
Whitehouse Av
BDN/LAN/SAC DH7 ....141 G4
Whitehouse Crs
LWF/SPW/WRK NE9 ....102 A1
Whitehouse La
BDN/LAN/SAC DH7 ....154 E7
NSHW NE29 ....60 B2
White House Pl
ASHBK/HED/RY SR2 ....15 J6
White House Rd
ASHBK/HED/RY SR2 ....15 H6
Whitehouse Rd
BW/LEM/TK/HW NE15 ....69 F7
White House Wy FELL NE10 ....88 A7
Whitehouse Wy PLEE/EAS SR8 ....174 A4
RDHAMSE DH6 ....174 A6
Whitelaw Pl CRAM NE23 ....38 D4
White Lea Cl PLEE/EAS SR8 ....175 G5
Whiteleas Wy HAR/WTLS NE34 ....75 G7
Whitelees Ct GOS/KPK NE3 ....55 J3
White Le Head Gdns
STLY/ANP DH9 ....111 J4
Whiteley Cl RYTON NE40 ....82 C3
Whiteley Rd BLAY NE21 ....68 C7
Whitemere Cl
ASHBK/HED/RY SR2 ....120 E4
White Mere Gdns FELL NE10 ....88 E4
Whiteoak Av DHAM DH1 ....157 J6
White Oaks FELL NE10 ....88 A7
White Rocks Gv
CLDN/WHIT/ROK SR6 ....93 F1
Whitesmocks DHAM DH1 ....156 B5
Whitesmocks Av DHAM DH1 ....156 A6
White St BYK/HTN/WLK NE6 ....72 D6
Whitewell La RYTON NE40 ....66 E6
Whitewell Rd BLAY NE21 ....84 A2
Whitfield Dr LGB/KIL NE12 ....57 J4
Whitfield Rd
BW/LEM/TK/HW NE15 ....68 D6
LGB/KIL NE12 ....57 K2
MONK NE25 ....40 A5
Whitfield St CON/LDGT DH8 ....123 G4
Whitgrave Rd
WD/WHPE/BLK NE5 ....55 H7
Whithorn Ct BLYTH NE24 ....30 E7
Whitley Rd LGB/KIL NE12 ....58 A4
MONK NE25 ....49 J4
WBAY NE26 ....51 F5
Whitmore Rd BLAY NE21 ....84 A1
Whittingham Cl ASHGTN NE63 ....23 G3
Whittingham Ct GATE * NE8 ....10 C5
Whittingham Rd
TYNE/NSHE NE30 ....51 G7
WD/WHPE/BLK NE5 ....54 D6
Whittington Gv
WD/WHPE/BLK NE5 ....69 G4
Whittleburn FELL NE10 ....88 B7
Whitton Av BLYTH NE24 ....34 D2
Whitton Gdns NSHW NE29 ....60 B3
Whitton Pl LGB/HTN NE7 ....57 G6
MONK NE25 ....40 A5
Whittonstall WASHS NE38 ....117 H5
Whittonstall Rd CHPW NE17 ....95 G4
Whitton Wy GOS/KPK NE3 ....56 B4
Whitwell Acres DHAM DH1 ....169 J6
Whitwell Ct DHAM DH1 ....17 L1
Whitworth Cl
BYK/HTN/WLK NE6 ....72 C6
GATE NE8 ....86 D5
Whitworth La
BDN/LAN/SAC DH7 ....176 E5
Whitworth Rd PLEE/EAS SR8 ....174 A4
WASHN NE37 ....102 B6
Whorlton Pl
WD/WHPE/BLK NE5 ....54 C7
Whorral Bank MPTH NE61 ....21 F3
Whyndyke FELL NE10 ....88 A7
Whytrigg Cl MONK NE25 ....39 J4
Wicklow Ct STKFD/GP NE62 ....23 K5
Widderburn Sq ASHGTN NE63 ....23 J2
Widdrington Av
HAR/WTLS NE34 ....76 B3
Widdrington Gdns
DIN/WO NE13 ....46 C3
Widdrington Rd BLAY NE21 ....84 A2
Widdrington Ter
NSHW (off West Percy St) NE29 ....2 C2
Widnes Pl LGB/KIL NE12 ....57 J3
Wigeon Cl WASHS NE38 ....116 B4
Wigmore Av BYK/HTN/WLK NE6 ....7 L9
Wilber Ct MLFD/PNYW SR4 ....105 K6
Wilberforce St JRW NE32 ....74 A4
WLSD/HOW NE28 ....72 D3
Wilberforce Wk GATE NE8 ....10 B3
Wilber St MLFD/PNYW SR4 ....105 K6
Wilbury Pl WD/WHPE/BLK NE5 ....69 G1
Wilden Ct SUNDSW SR3 ....120 B4
Wilden Rd WASHS NE38 ....117 H3
Wildshaw Cl CRAM NE23 ....38 D5
Wilfred St BOLCOL NE35 ....90 D5
BYK/HTN/WLK NE6 ....6 D5
CLS/BIR/GTL DH3 ....129 J5
MLFD/PNYW SR4 ....105 J6
Wilfrid St CLS/BIR/GTL DH3 ....115 J3
Wilkes Cl WD/WHPE/BLK * NE5 ....68 D1
Wilkinson Av HEBB NE31 ....89 F1
Wilkinson Rd PLEE/EAS SR8 ....175 F1
Wilkinson Ter
ASHBK/HED/RY SR2 ....134 E1
Wilkwood Cl CRAM NE23 ....38 D4
Willans Buildings DHAM DH1 ....17 J3
Willerby Dr GOS/KPK NE3 ....56 D2
Willerby Gv PLEE/EAS SR8 ....174 C3
William Armstrong Dr
ELS/FEN NE4 ....8 F2
William Cl LGB/KIL NE12 ....58 C2
William Morris Av ROWG NE39 ....96 D3
William Pl DHAM DH1 ....17 J3
Williams Cl STLY/ANP DH9 ....126 E2
Williams Pk LGB/KIL NE12 ....57 J4
Williamson Ter
CLDN/WHIT/ROK SR6 ....14 F1
Williams Rd SEA/MUR SR7 ....149 H5
Williams Ter
ASHBK/HED/RY SR2 ....134 E1
William St BLYTH NE24 ....31 G7
CHPW NE17 ....95 H4
FELL NE10 ....12 D6
GOS/KPK NE3 ....56 E5
HEBB NE31 ....73 F4
MPTH NE61 ....21 K2
RDHAMSE DH6 ....180 A2
SUND SR1 ....14 F3
WICK/BNPF NE16 ....84 E5
William St West HEBB NE31 ....73 F5
NSHW* NE29 ....2 C3
Willington Ter WLSD/HOW NE28 ....59 G7
Willis St HLH DH5 ....147 K3
Willmore St MLFD/PNYW SR4 ....106 A7
Willoughby Dr WBAY NE26 ....50 C2
Willoughby Rd NSHW NE29 ....60 B4
Willow Av BLYTH NE24 ....31 F5
DUN/TMV NE11 ....9 G8
ELS/FEN NE4 ....69 H3
Willowbank Gdns JES NE2 ....56 E7
Willow Bank Rd
ASHBK/HED/RY SR2 ....120 C3
Willow Cl BDN/LAN/SAC DH7 ....167 G6
MPTH NE61 ....21 F5
WICK/BNPF
(off Whaggs La) NE16 ....85 F6
Willow Ct RDHAMSE DH6 ....180 C7
RYTON NE40 ....67 F5
STKFD/GP NE62 ....23 H6
Willow Crs BLYTH NE24 ....34 E3
CON/LDGT DH8 ....123 K4
HLH DH5 ....148 C7
Willowdene LGB/KIL NE12 ....58 A1
Willowfield Av GOS/KPK NE3 ....55 K4
Willow Gdns LGB/KIL NE12 ....47 J5
Willow Gra JRW NE32 ....73 J4
Willow Gv FELL NE10 ....12 D8
HAR/WTLS NE34 ....75 K6
PLEE/EAS SR8 ....175 J5
WLSD/HOW NE28 ....73 F1
Willow Pk BDN/LAN/SAC DH7 ....153 K3
Willow Pl PONT/DH NE20 ....43 G5
Willow Rd BDN/LAN/SAC DH7 ....165 G1
BLAY NE21 ....84 B2
HLS DH4 ....132 A7
Willows Cl DIN/WO NE13 ....46 A4
The Willows
BW/LEM/TK/HW NE15 ....67 F2
DHAM DH1 ....158 A4
ELS/FEN (off Clumber St) NE4 ....9 J2
MPTH NE61 ....20 E5
WASHS NE38 ....117 H2
Willowtree Av DHAM DH1 ....157 H5
Willow Tree Av DHAM DH1 ....169 G4
Willow Vw WICK/BNPF NE16 ....97 J7
Willow Wy PONT/DH NE20 ....43 F7
Wilmington Cl
WD/WHPE/BLK NE5 ....55 F4
Wilson Av BDLGTN NE22 ....30 D2
CLS/BIR/GTL DH3 ....115 J1
Wilson Crs DHAM DH1 ....17 M1

Wilson Dr *BOLCOL* NE35 ....91 F4
Wilson Gdns *GOS/KPK* NE3 ....56 B7
Wilson Pl *PLEE/EAS* SR8 ....174 E2
Wilson's La *LWF/SPW/WRK* NE9 ....87 F7
Wilson St *DUN/TMV* NE11 ....9 H8
  MLFD/PNYW SR4 ....106 A6
  SSH NE33 ....75 G2
  WLSD/HOW NE28 ....72 D1
Wilson St North *SWCK/CAS* SR5 .....14 D2
Wilson Ter *LGB/KIL* NE12 ....57 K1
  SUNDSW SR3 ....120 A6
Wilsway *BW/LEM/TK/HW* NE15 .....66 E1
Wilton Av *BYK/HTN/WLK* NE6 ....7 L8
Wilton Cl *CRAM* NE23 ....38 D5
  MONK NE25 ....49 K4
Wilton Dr *MONK* NE25 ....49 K5
Wilton Gdns North
  BOLCOL NE35 ....90 C2
Wilton Gdns South
  BOLCOL NE35 ....90 C3
Wiltshire Cl *DHAM* DH1 ....157 K6
  SWCK/CAS SR5 ....105 J1
Wiltshire Dr *WLSD/HOW* NE28 ....58 B5
Wiltshire Gdns
  WLSD/HOW NE28 ....58 B7
Wiltshire Rd *NSHW* NE37 ....103 F3
Wiltshire Rd *SWCK/CAS* SR5 ....105 J2
Wimbledon Cl *SWCK/CAS* SR5 ....105 K2
Wimborne Cl *BOLCOL* NE35 ....90 C4
Wimbourne Av
  MLFD/PNYW SR4 ....119 J2
Wimbourne Gn
  WD/WHPE/BLK NE5 ....54 D7
Wimpole Cl *WASHN* NE37 ....103 G5
Wimslow Cl *WLSD/HOW* NE28 ....58 B7
Winalot Av *ASHBK/HED/RY* SR2 ....120 E4
Wincanton Pl *NSHW* NE29 ....60 C6
Winchcombe Pl *LGB/HTN* NE7 ....57 G7
Winchester Av *BLYTH* NE24 ....31 G7
Winchester Cl *ASHGTN* NE63 ....24 B3
  CLS/BIR/GTL DH3 ....145 H1
Winchester Ct *JRW* NE32 ....89 K3
  MLFD/PNYW SR4 ....105 K7
Winchester Dr
  BDN/LAN/SAC DH7 ....177 F1
  PLEE/EAS SR8 ....174 A5
Winchester Rd *DHAM* DH1 ....157 F2
Winchester St *SSH* NE33 ....3 J7
Winchester Ter *ELS/FEN* NE4 ....4 F7
Winchester Wk *BDLGTN* NE22 ....29 F4
Wincomblee Rd
  BYK/HTN/WLK NE6 ....13 K1
Windburgh Dr *CRAM* NE23 ....38 C5
Windermere
  CLDN/WHIT/ROK SR6 ....92 A3
Windermere Av *CLSW/PEL* DH2 .....129 J6
  FELL NE10 ....13 H7
  HLH DH5 ....160 B1
Windermere Cl *CRAM* NE23 ....38 C5
Windermere Crs *BLAY* NE21 ....83 K4
  HAR/WTLS NE34 ....75 J3
  HEBB NE31 ....73 H6
  HLS DH4 ....131 K1
  JRW NE32 ....90 B1
Windermere Gdns
  WICK/BNPF NE16 ....8 B9
Windermere Rd *NWBGN* NE64 ....24 E2
  RDHAMSE DH6 ....161 G1
  SEA/MUR SR7 ....149 K2
  WD/WHPE/BLK NE5 ....69 F3
Windermere St
  ASHBK/HED/RY SR2 ....121 F4
  GATE NE8 ....10 E6
Windermere St West *GATE* NE8 ......10 E6
Windermere Ter *NSHW* NE29 ....2 B1
  STLY/ANP DH9 ....126 B2
Windhill Rd *BW/LEM/TK/HW* NE15 ..13 H1
The Winding *DIN/WO* NE13 ....45 F2
Windlass Ct *HAR/WTLS* NE34 ....75 G6
Windlass La *WASHN* NE37 ....102 E6
Windmill Ct *JES* NE2 ....5 L1
Windmill Gv *BLYTH* NE24 ....30 C6
Windmill Hl *DHAM* DH1 ....16 B9
  SSH NE33 ....75 F2
Windmill Sq *SWCK/CAS* SR5 ....106 C1
Windmill Wy *GATE* NE8 ....10 E3
  HEBB NE31 ....73 G3
  MPTH NE61 ....21 F5
Winds La *SEA/MUR* SR7 ....149 G6
Winds Lonnen Est
  SEA/MUR SR7 ....149 F5
Windsor Av *GATE* NE8 ....10 E7
Windsor Cl *WICK/BNPF* NE16 ....98 E1
Windsor Cottages
  WLSD/HOW NE28 ....59 J6
Windsor Ct *BDLGTN* NE22 ....29 F6
  CRAM NE23 ....33 G6
  FELL (off Sheriffs Cl) NE10 ....12 A8
  GOS/KPK NE3 ....55 J3
Windsor Crs *HEBB* NE31 ....73 H5
  HLH DH5 ....132 D7
  PRUD NE42 ....64 B6
  WBAY NE26 ....51 C5
  WD/WHPE/BLK NE5 ....54 E7
Windsor Dr
  CLDN/WHIT/ROK SR6 ....91 J3
  HLH DH5 ....147 H2
  RDHAMSE DH6 ....160 E1
  STLY/ANP DH9 ....125 H2
  SUNDSW SR3 ....120 A7
  WLSD/HOW NE28 ....59 J7
Windsor Gdns *BDLGTN* NE22 ....29 F6
  FELL NE10 ....12 A8
  HAR/WTLS NE34 ....75 J4
  NSHW NE29 ....60 E3
  WBAY NE26 ....50 D3
Windsor Pk *WLSD/HOW* NE28 ....58 B7

Windsor Pl *PONT/DH* NE20 ....42 D5
  RDHAMSE DH6 ....173 J3
  SMOOR NE27 ....58 E1
Windsor Rd *CLS/BIR/GTL* DH3 ....101 H7
  LWF/SPW/WRK NE9 ....102 A4
  MONK NE25 ....50 C4
  NWBGN NE64 ....25 F1
  SEA/MUR SR7 ....150 A1
Windsor St *TRIM* TS29 ....182 E6
  WLSD/HOW NE28 ....72 D1
Windsor Ter *GOS/KPK* NE3 ....56 E6
  JES NE2 ....5 K2
  PLEE/EAS SR8 ....175 J4
  RDHAMSE DH6 ....160 D6
  SEA/MUR SR7 ....149 J6
  WBAY NE26 ....51 C5
Windsor Wy *GOS/KPK* NE3 ....55 G3
Windt St *DIN/WO* NE13 ....46 A4
Windy Gyle *ASHGTN* NE63 ....24 A1
Windy Nook Rd
  LWF/SPW/WRK NE9 ....87 H6
Windy Ridge Vls *FELL* NE10 ....87 J5
Wingate Cl
  BW/LEM/TK/HW NE15 ....68 C5
  HLS DH4 ....132 B7
Wingate Gdns
  LWF/SPW/WRK NE9 ....101 K1
Wingate La *RDHAMSE* DH6 ....182 D2
Wingate Rd *TRIM* TS29 ....183 F5
Wingrove *ROWG* NE39 ....97 F4
Wingrove Av
  CLDN/WHIT/ROK SR6 ....106 C5
  ELS/FEN NE4 ....4 A4
Wingrove Cl *WNGT* TS28 ....183 K2
Wingrove Gdns *ELS/FEN* NE4 ....4 A4
Wingrove Rd *ELS/FEN* NE4 ....69 J2
Wingrove Rd North
  ELS/FEN NE4 ....69 J3
Wingrove Ter *CON/LDGT* DH8 ....123 K3
Winifred St
  CLDN/WHIT/ROK SR6 ....106 E2
Winifred Ter *SUND* SR1 ....15 G6
Winshields *CRAM* NE23 ....38 D4
Winship Cl *HAR/WTLS* NE34 ....91 G2
Winship St *BLYTH* NE24 ....34 E2
Winship Ter *BW/LEM/TK/HW* NE6 ....7 H5
Winskell Rd *HAR/WTLS* NE34 ....74 D7
Winslade Cl *SUNDSW* SR3 ....120 B6
Winslow Cl *BOLCOL* NE35 ....90 D7
  BYK/HTN/WLK NE6 ....72 C5
  SWCK/CAS SR5 ....105 K1
Winslow Crs *SEA/MUR* SR7 ....150 A1
Winslow Gdns
  LWF/SPW/WRK NE9 ....86 E7
Winslow Pl *BYK/HTN/WLK* NE6 ....72 C5
Winsten *WASHS* NE38 ....116 C5
Winston Crs *MLFD/PNYW* SR4 ....119 J2
Winston Gn *HLS* DH4 ....117 H6
Winton Cl *CRAM* NE23 ....39 H6
Winton Wy *GOS/KPK* NE3 ....55 K5
Wishaw Cl *CRAM* NE23 ....38 D4
Wishaw Ri
  BW/LEM/TK/HW NE15 ....68 C4
Witham Rd *HEBB* NE31 ....89 H1
Witherington Cl *LGB/HTN* NE7 ....58 A7
Withernsea Gv
  ASHBK/HED/RY SR2 ....120 D7
Witney Cl *SWCK/CAS* SR5 ....105 J1
Witney Wy *BOL* NE36 ....90 C5
Witton Av *BDN/LAN/SAC* DH7 ....143 H5
  HAR/WTLS NE34 ....76 A5
Witton Ct *GOS/KPK* NE3 ....55 J4
  SUNDSW SR3 ....120 B4
Witton Gdns *JRW* NE32 ....89 K1
Witton Garth *PLEE/EAS* SR8 ....174 D7
Witton Gv *DHAM* DH1 ....156 A5
  HLS DH4 ....147 F1
Witton Rd *BDN/LAN/SAC* DH7 ....143 G6
  HEBB NE31 ....73 H3
  SMOOR NE27 ....49 H6
Witty Av *HEBB* NE31 ....73 H6
Woburn *WASHS* NE38 ....117 F2
Woburn Cl *CRAM* NE23 ....33 G6
  WLSD/HOW NE28 ....58 B7
Woburn Dr *BDLGTN* NE22 ....29 J4
  SUNDSW SR3 ....134 A1
Woburn Wy *WD/WHPE/BLK* NE5 ....68 E1
Wolmer Rd *BLYTH* NE24 ....35 H2
Wolseley Cl *GATE* NE8 ....10 A5
  RDHAMSE DH6 ....180 A2
Wolseley Gdns *JES* NE2 ....6 C1
Wolseley Ter *MLFD/PNYW* SR4 ......120 A1
Wolsey Cl *HAR/WTLS* NE34 ....75 C5
Wolsey Rd *SEA/MUR* SR7 ....149 K2
Wolsingham Ct *CRAM* NE23 ....38 A1
Wolsingham Dr *DHAM* DH1 ....156 E3
Wolsingham Rd
  BDN/LAN/SAC DH7 ....165 K7
  GOS/KPK NE3 ....56 B6
Wolsingham St *ELS/FEN* NE4 ....9 H1
Wolsingham Ter
  STLY/ANP * DH9 ....125 H3
Wolsley Rd *BLYTH* NE24 ....31 G6
Wolveleigh Ter *GOS/KPK* NE3 ....56 D5
Woodbine Av *PLEE/EAS* SR8 ....175 G2
  WLSD/HOW NE28 ....72 D1
Woodbine Cl *ELS/FEN* NE4 ....4 A8
Woodbine Pl *GATE* NE8 ....10 E5
Woodbine Rd *DHAM* DH1 ....156 B2
  GOS/KPK NE3 ....56 C6
Woodbine St *GATE* NE8 ....10 E5
  SSH NE33 ....3 J5
  SUND SR1 ....15 J5
Woodbine Ter *ASHGTN* * NE63 ......23 F1
  BLYTH NE24 ....35 H1
  FELL NE10 ....11 M7
  MLFD/PNYW SR4 ....105 K5
Woodbine Vls *GATE* NE8 ....10 F5

Woodbrook Av
  WD/WHPE/BLK NE5 ....68 E3
Woodburn *FELL* NE10 ....88 A7
  STLY/ANP DH9 ....112 A6
Woodburn Av *ELS/FEN* NE4 ....69 J2
Woodburn Cl *BLAY* NE21 ....83 J4
Woodburn Dr *HLS* DH4 ....132 A6
  WBAY NE26 ....50 C2
Woodburn Gdns
  DUN/TMV NE11 ....86 A6
Woodburn Sq *WBAY* NE26 ....50 B2
Woodburn St
  BW/LEM/TK/HW NE15 ....68 A5
Woodchurch Cl *LGB/KIL* NE12 ....57 K6
Woodcroft Cl *CRAM* NE23 ....38 B7
Woodcroft Rd *WYLAM* NE41 ....65 C5
Woodend *PONT/DH* NE20 ....42 E7
Woodend Wy *GOS/KPK* NE3 ....55 G2
Woodfield *PLEE/EAS* SR8 ....174 D4
Woodfield Rd *PONT/DH* NE20 ....42 E7
Woodford *LWF/SPW/WRK* NE9 ......101 F4
Woodford Cl *SWCK/CAS* SR5 ....105 K2
Woodgate Gdns *FELL* NE10 ....13 M5
Wood Ga *FELL* NE10 ....13 M4
Wood Gv *BW/LEM/TK/HW* NE15 ....14 B4
Woodhall Spa *HLS* DH4 ....131 J3
Woodhead Rd
  BYK/HTN/WLK NE6 ....7 M1
  PRUD NE42 ....81 F1
Woodhill Dr *MPTH* NE61 ....20 C5
Woodhorn Dr *STKFD/GP* NE62 ....23 F5
Woodhorn Gdns *DIN/WO* NE13 ....46 B3
Woodhorn La *NWBGN* NE64 ....19 C2
Woodhorn Rd *ASHGTN* NE63 ....24 A1
  NWBGN NE64 ....19 F7
Woodhorn Vls *ASHGTN* NE63 ....24 B1
Woodhouses La
  WICK/BNPF NE16 ....84 C6
Woodhurst Gv
  MLFD/PNYW SR4 ....118 E4
Woodland Cl
  BDN/LAN/SAC DH7 ....155 F6
Woodland Ct *CON/LDGT* DH8 ....122 D1
Woodland Crs
  BW/LEM/TK/HW NE15 ....69 F7
  RDHAMSE DH6 ....181 G6
Woodland Dr *MLFD/PNYW* SR4 .....119 J2
Woodland Gra *HLS* DH4 ....131 H6
Woodland Ri *SUNDSW* SR3 ....133 J1
Woodlands *BW/LEM/TK/HW* NE15 ..66 E1
  GOS/KPK NE3 ....56 C7
  NSHW NE29 ....60 E2
  PONT/DH NE20 ....43 F6
  WASHS NE38 ....116 A6
Woodlands Cl *MONK* NE25 ....49 J4
  ROWG NE39 ....96 C2
Woodlands Dr
  CLDN/WHIT/ROK SR6 ....92 A4
Woodlands Gra *LGB/KIL* NE12 ....58 A1
Woodlands Park Dr *BLAY* NE21 ......84 B2
Woodlands Rd *ASHGTN* NE63 ....24 C3
  BDN/LAN/SAC DH7 ....165 G1
  BW/LEM/TK/HW NE15 ....68 B4
  CLDN/WHIT/ROK SR6 ....91 K4
  CON/LDGT DH8 ....122 D1
  ROWG NE39 ....97 F3
Woodlands Ter *FELL* NE10 ....12 B8
  SSH NE33 ....3 K5
Woodlands Vw
  CLDN/WHIT/ROK SR6 ....92 A4
Woodlands Veiw *WNGT* TS28 ....183 J3
Wood La *BDLGTN* NE22 ....29 H5
  BDN/LAN/SAC DH7 ....140 B5
Wood Lea *HLH* DH5 ....147 K1
Woodlea *LGB/KIL* NE12 ....57 K1
Woodlea Cl *HLH* DH5 ....147 K4
Woodlea Ct *NSHW* NE29 ....60 C7
Woodlea Gdns *GOS/KPK* NE3 ....56 E5
Woodlea Sq *NSHW* NE29 ....60 C7
Woodleigh Rd *MONK* NE25 ....50 C5
Woodleigh Vw
  WD/WHPE/BLK NE5 ....55 J9
Woodman St *NE61 ....20 C6
Woodman St *WLSD/HOW* NE28 ......59 K7
Woodmans Wy
  WICK/BNPF NE16 ....98 C1
Woodnansey Cl *PLEE/EAS* SR8 ......174 C3
Woodpack Av *WICK/BNPF* NE16 .....84 D6
Woodside *ASHBK/HED/RY* SR2 ......14 B8
  BDLGTN NE22 ....29 J5
  BLYTH NE24 ....35 H1
  MPTH NE61 ....20 B5
  PONT/DH NE20 ....42 E7
  PRUD NE42 ....80 E2
  RDHAMSE DH6 ....171 H2
Woodside Av
  BDN/LAN/SAC DH7 ....155 F6
  BW/LEM/TK/HW NE15 ....67 C1
  MONK NE25 ....40 A6
Woodside Bank
  CON/LDGT DH8 ....124 D7
Woodside Cl *RYTON* NE40 ....66 D6
Woodside Crs *LGB/KIL* NE12 ....58 A2
Woodside Dr *CON/LDGT* DH8 ....123 J1
Woodside Gdns *DUN/TMV* NE11 .....85 K5
  STLY/ANP DH9 ....127 F4
Woodside La *HLS* DH4 ....146 B7
  RYTON NE40 ....66 D7
Woodside Rd *RYTON* NE40 ....66 D6
Woodside Rd *SUNDSW* SR3 ....133 G1
Woodside Vw
  BDN/LAN/SAC
  (off Daisy Hl) DH7 ....143 G2
Woodside Wk *ROWG* NE39 ....96 E4

Woodside Wy *RYTON* NE40 ....66 D6
  SSH NE33 ....75 F4
Woods Ter *GATE* NE8 ....11 H6
  SEA/MUR SR7 ....149 J5
Woodstock Rd
  BW/LEM/TK/HW NE15 ....68 C6
  LWF/SPW/WRK NE9 ....101 G3
Wood St *CLSW/PEL* DH2 ....114 E7
  CON/LDGT DH8 ....122 C1
  DUN/TMV NE11 ....9 H8
  MLFD/PNYW SR4 ....106 A6
  WICK/BNPF NE16 ....97 J7
Woodthorne Rd *JES* NE2 ....56 E7
Woodvale *PONT/DH* NE20 ....42 E7
Woodvale Dr *HEBB* NE31 ....72 E7
Woodvale Gdns
  LWF/SPW/WRK NE9 ....87 J6
  WYLAM NE41 ....65 C5
Woodvale Rd *BLAY* NE21 ....84 B3
  LGB/KIL NE12 ....47 J5
Wood Vw *BDN/LAN/SAC* DH7 ....154 B2
  TRIM TS29 ....183 G6
Woodville Ct *MLFD/PNYW* SR4 ......119 J2
Woodville Crs
  MLFD/PNYW SR4 ....119 J2
Woodville Rd
  BW/LEM/TK/HW NE15 ....68 B3
Wooler Av *NSHW* NE29 ....60 B6
Wooler Crs *GATE* NE8 ....9 M7
Wooler Sq *ASHBK/HED/RY* SR2 .....120 E3
  DIN/WO NE13 ....46 C2
Woolerton Dr
  BW/LEM/TK/HW NE15 ....68 C4
  LWF/SPW/WRK NE9 ....87 H6
Wooler Wk *JRW* NE32 ....73 J7
Wooley Dr *BDN/LAN/SAC* DH7 .....167 H1
Wooley St *WLSD/HOW* NE28 ....72 D2
Woolmer Ct *LGB/HTN* NE7 ....58 A7
Woolsington Ct
  MLFD/PNYW SR4 ....105 K7
Woolsington Gdns
  DIN/WO NE13 ....54 D2
Woolsington Pk South
  DIN/WO NE13 ....54 D2
Woolsington Rd *NSHW* NE29 ....60 A3
Woolwich Cl *SWCK/CAS* SR5 ....105 K1
Woolwich Rd *SWCK/CAS* SR5 ....105 K1
Wooperton Gdns
  WD/WHPE/BLK NE5 ....69 G4
Worcester Cl *CLS/BIR/GTL* DH3 .....145 H1
Worcester Gn *GATE* NE8 ....10 F4
Worcester Rd *DHAM* DH1 ....156 E2
Worcester St
  ASHBK/HED/RY SR2 ....14 D7
Worcester Ter
  ASHBK/HED/RY SR2 ....14 D7
Worcester Wy *DIN/WO* NE13 ....46 B4
Wordsworth Av *BLYTH* NE24 ....34 E2
  CLSW/PEL DH2 ....128 C5
  HEBB NE31 ....73 C5
  HLH DH5 ....160 C1
  RDHAMSE DH6 ....172 E7
  SEA/MUR SR7 ....149 K5
  WICK/BNPF NE16 ....85 F4
Wordsworth Crs
  LWF/SPW/WRK NE9 ....102 B4
Wordsworth Rd *PLEE/EAS* SR8 ......162 D5
Wordsworth St *GATE* NE8 ....11 J4
Worley Cl *ELS/FEN* NE4 ....4 D6
Worley St *ELS/FEN* NE4 ....4 D6
Worm Hill Ter *WASHS* NE38 ....117 G5
Worsdell Rd *BLYTH* NE24 ....31 G5
Worsley Cl *WLSD/HOW* NE28 ....58 B7
Worswick St *CNUT* NE1 ....5 L6
Worthing Cl *WLSD/HOW* NE28 ....58 B7
Worton Cl *RDHAMSE* DH6 ....173 H3
Wouldhave St *SSH* NE33 ....3 K6
Wraith Ter *ASHBK/HED/RY* SR2 .....134 E1
Wraysbury Ct *GOS/KPK* NE3 ....55 H3
Wreigh St *HEBB* NE31 ....73 F5
Wreken Gdns *FELL* NE10 ....88 E4
Wrekenton Rw
  LWF/SPW/WRK NE9 ....101 J3
Wren Cl *WASHS* NE38 ....116 C3
Wren Gv *SWCK/CAS* SR5 ....105 G4
Wretham Pl *JES* NE2 ....6 A4
Wright Dr *CRAM* NE23 ....47 C2
Wrightson St *CRAM* NE23 ....33 H4
Wright St *BLYTH* NE24 ....31 F6
Wright Ter *HLS* DH4 ....131 J2
Wroxham Ct
  ASHBK/HED/RY SR2 ....120 E4
  WD/WHPE/BLK NE5 ....55 F6
Wroxton *WASHS* NE38 ....116 E3
Wuppertal Ct *JRW* NE32 ....73 K5
Wychcroft Wy
  WD/WHPE/BLK * NE5 ....69 G1
Wych Elm Crs *LGB/HTN* NE7 ....57 J7
Wycliffe Av *GOS/KPK* NE3 ....55 K7
Wycliffe Rd *MLFD/PNYW* SR4 ....119 K2
  SEA/MUR SR7 ....149 K1
Wye Av *JRW* NE32 ....90 A1
Wye Rd *HEBB* NE31 ....89 C1
Wylam Av *MONK* NE25 ....40 C6
Wylam Cl *HAR/WTLS* NE34 ....75 J6
  WASHN NE37 ....103 G4
Wylam Gdns *WLSD/HOW* NE28 ......59 H6
Wylam Gv *SUND* SR1 ....15 H6
Wylam Rd *NSHW* NE29 ....2 A7
  STLY/ANP DH9 ....112 E7
Wylam St *JRW* NE32 ....73 K4
  RDHAMSE DH6 ....180 A3
  STLY/ANP DH9 ....127 G5
Wylam Ter *STLY/ANP* DH9 ....112 D6
Wylam Vw *BLAY* NE21 ....83 K2

Wylam Wood Rd *WYLAM* NE41 ......65 H6
Wynbury Rd
  LWF/SPW/WRK NE9 ....87 G2
Wyncote Ct *LGB/HTN* NE7 ....71 H1
The Wynde *HAR/WTLS* NE34 ....75 G6
  PONT/DH NE20 ....43 F5
Wyndfall Wy *GOS/KPK* NE3 ....56 A7
Wyndham Av *GOS/KPK* NE3 ....55 K7
Wyndham Wy *NSHW* NE29 ....59 K2
The Wynding *BDLGTN* NE22 ....28 E4
  CRAM NE23 ....38 B7
Wyndley Cl *WICK/BNPF* NE16 ....84 D7
Wyndley Pl *GOS/KPK* NE3 ....69 K1
Wyndsail Pl *GOS/KPK* NE3 ....56 A7
The Wynds *BDN/LAN/SAC* DH7 .....165 G2
The Wynd
  BW/LEM/TK/HW NE15 ....67 F2
  CLSW/PEL DH2 ....128 C1
  GOS/KPK NE3 ....56 A6
  LGB/KIL NE12 ....58 A1
  TYNE/NSHE NE30 ....60 E2
Wyndtop Pl *GOS/KPK* NE3 ....56 A7
Wyndways Dr *STLY/ANP* DH9 ....111 G5
Wynn Gdns *FELL* NE10 ....13 H5
Wynyard *CLSW/PEL* DH2 ....129 G4
Wynyard Dr *BDLGTN* NE22 ....29 J3
Wynyard Gdns
  LWF/SPW/WRK NE9 ....101 J5
Wynyard Gv *DHAM* DH1 ....17 J2
Wynyard Sq
  ASHBK/HED/RY SR2 ....120 E3
Wynyard St *DUN/TMV* NE11 ....9 G8
  HLS DH4 ....131 J7
  SEA/MUR SR7 ....150 E3
  SUNDSW SR3 ....120 A7
Wyvern Sq *ASHBK/HED/RY* SR2 ....120 E4

Y

Yardley Cl *SUNDSW* SR3 ....134 A2
Yardley Gv *CRAM* NE23 ....33 G7
Yarmouth Cl *SEA/MUR* SR7 ....150 B2
Yarmouth Dr *CRAM* NE23 ....33 G7
Yatesbury Av
  WD/WHPE/BLK NE5 ....69 F1
Yeadon Ct *GOS/KPK* NE3 ....55 G3
Yeckhouse La
  BDN/LAN/SAC DH7 ....139 J5
Yelverton Ct *CRAM* NE23 ....33 G7
Yelverton Crs
  BYK/HTN/WLK NE6 ....13 G6
Yeoman St *NSHW* NE29 ....2 E4
Yeovil Ct *CRAM* NE23 ....33 G7
Yetholm Av *CLSW/PEL* DH2 ....129 H5
Yetholm Pl *WD/WHPE/BLK* NE5 .....54 A7
Yetholm Rd *GATE* NE8 ....9 M5
Yetlington Dr *GOS/KPK* NE3 ....56 A6
Yewbank Av *DHAM* DH1 ....157 J6
Yewburn Wy *LGB/KIL* NE12 ....57 H4
Yewcroft Av
  BW/LEM/TK/HW NE15 ....68 D5
Yewdale Gdns
  LWF/SPW/WRK NE9 ....101 G1
Yewtree Av *SWCK/CAS* SR5 ....105 K3
Yew Tree Dr *BDLGTN* NE22 ....29 F4
Yewtree Gdns
  BYK/HTN/WLK NE6 ....72 C5
Yewtrees *FELL* NE10 ....13 H6
Yewvale Rd *WD/WHPE/BLK* NE5 .....69 H2
Yoden Av *PLEE/EAS* SR8 ....175 G2
Yoden Crs *PLEE/EAS* SR8 ....175 G2
Yoden Rd *PLEE/EAS* SR8 ....174 E3
Yoden Wy *PLEE/EAS* SR8 ....175 G4
York Av *CON/LDGT* DH8 ....137 F1
  JRW NE32 ....89 K1
  PLEE/EAS SR8 ....175 G3
York Cl *CRAM* NE23 ....33 G7
York Ct
  BYK/HTN/WLK
  (off York Dr) NE6 ....72 C2
York Crs *DHAM* DH1 ....156 E1
  HLH DH5 ....147 J4
Yorkdale Pl *BYK/HTN/WLK* NE6 .....72 C5
York Dr *WLSD/HOW* NE28 ....72 C2
York Gv *BDLGTN* NE22 ....28 D4
York Rd *CLS/BIR/GTL* DH3 ....115 J5
  CON/LDGT DH8 ....122 C2
  PLEE/EAS SR8 ....174 D2
  WBAY NE26 ....51 F4
York Ter *CLS/BIR/GTL* DH3 ....129 K5
  FELL NE10 ....12 D7
  NSHW NE29 ....2 B1
York Wy *HAR/WTLS* NE34 ....76 A5
Yorkwood *HEBB* NE31 ....72 E4
Young Rd *LGB/KIL* NE12 ....58 B1
Young St *DHAM* DH1 ....17 K2

Z

Zetland Dr *MONK* NE25 ....50 D7
Zetland Sq
  CLDN/WHIT/ROK SR6 ....106 E4
Zetland St
  CLDN/WHIT/ROK SR6 ....106 E4
Zion St *SUND* SR1 ....15 H4
Zion Ter *SWCK/CAS* SR5 ....106 C2

Abbeyfields County School
MPTH NE61 .... 20 C5
Abbey Road Industrial Estate
DHAM DH1 .... 156 C1
Abbey Sports Centre
DHAM DH1 .... 156 D1
Abbeywoods Business Park
DHAM DH1 .... 156 C1
Acre Rigg Junior & Infant School
PLEE/EAS SR8 .... 174 C2
Adamsez West Industrial Estate
BLAY NE21 .... 68 D7
Adderlane First School
PRUD NE42 .... 80 E1
Addison Industrial Estate
BLAY NE21 .... 67 H6
Adelaide Row Medical Centre
SEA/MUR SR7 .... 150 E1
Airport Industrial Estate
GOS/KPK NE3 .... 55 H4
Akhurst Preparatory School
JES NE2 .... 71 F1
Albert Elliott County Junior Mixed School
HAR/WTLS NE34 .... 91 G2
Albert Road Surgery
JRW NE32 .... 73 K5
Alexandra Business Park
MLFD/PNYW SR4 .... 105 J5
Algernon Industrial Estate
SMOOR NE27 .... 59 H1
All Saints Business Centre
CNUT NE1 .... 5 H6
All Saints Junior Mixed School
HAR/WTLS NE34 .... 75 F7
Amberley First School
LGB/KIL NE12 .... 48 A5
AMF Bowling
ELS/FEN NE4 .... 4 B6
AMF Bowling
WASHS NE38 .... 116 E1
Amphitheatre
SSH NE33 .... 3 M6
Annfield Plain County Junior Mixed School
STLY/ANP DH9 .... 125 J5
Annfield Plain Cricket Club
STLY/ANP DH9 .... 125 G4
Annfield Plain Infants School
STLY/ANP DH9 .... 125 H4
Appletree Gardens First School
MONK NE25 .... 50 C5
Arbeia Roman Fort & Museum
SSH NE33 .... 3 H4
Archbishop Runcie C of E School
GOS/KPK NE3 .... 56 D4
Archibald First School
GOS/KPK NE3 .... 56 B5
Arcot Hall Golf Club
CRAM NE23 .... 37 J5
Argyle House School
ASHBK/HED/RY SR2 .... 14 C8
Armstrong Industrial Estate
WASHN NE37 .... 102 C4
Armstrong Industrial Park
ELS/FEN NE4 .... 9 K2
Arnison Centre
DHAM DH1 .... 156 C1
The Art Gallery
SUND SR1 .... 14 E5
Arthurs Hill Clinic
ELS/FEN NE4 .... 4 E6
Ascham House School
GOS/KPK NE3 .... 56 C6
Ashburne Medical Centre
ASHBK/HED/RY SR2 .... 15 G9
Ashington Alexandra County First School
ASHGTN NE63 .... 24 B2
Ashington Association Football Club
ASHGTN NE63 .... 23 J1
Ashington Business Centre
ASHGTN NE63 .... 23 K1
Ashington Coulson Park County First School
ASHGTN NE63 .... 24 B3
Ashington County High School
ASHGTN NE63 .... 23 H2
Ashington Cricket Club
ASHGTN NE63 .... 23 J1
Ashington Hirst Park County Middle School
ASHGTN NE63 .... 24 A2
Ashington Hospital
ASHGTN NE63 .... 23 J1
Ashington Leisure Centre
ASHGTN NE63 .... 23 H1
Ashington St Aidans RC Aided First School
ASHGTN NE63 .... 24 A4
Ashington Seaton Hirst County Middle School
ASHGTN NE63 .... 24 C3
Ashleigh School
TYNE/NSHE NE30 .... 2 F1
Ashley Road County JMI School
HAR/WTLS NE34 .... 75 G5
Assembly Rooms
DHAM DH1 .... 16 D4
Astley Community High School
MONK NE25 .... 39 K5
Atkinson House School
CRAM NE23 .... 39 G6
Atkinson Road Primary School
BW/LEM/TK/HW NE15 .... 69 G7
The Avenues Medical Practice
GOS/KPK NE3 .... 56 C7
Aykley Heads Business Centre
DHAM DH1 .... 156 C1
Ayton Primary School
WASHS NE38 .... 116 B3
Backworth Business Park
SMOOR NE27 .... 48 E5
Backworth County First School
SMOOR NE27 .... 48 D4

Backworth Golf Club
SMOOR NE27 .... 48 E5
Bailey Green First School
LGB/KIL NE12 .... 47 J5
Balliol Business Park
LGB/KIL NE12 .... 57 G2
Balliol First School
LGB/KIL NE12 .... 57 H4
Baltic Business Centre
GATE NE8 .... 11 K1
Baltic Industrial Park
GATE NE29 .... 60 C7
Barley Mow Primary School
CLS/BIR/GTL DH3 .... 115 K4
Barmston Medical Centre
WASHS NE38 .... 117 H1
Barmston Village Primary School
WASHS NE38 .... 117 H1
Barnes Junior School
MLFD/PNYW SR4 .... 119 K2
Barnwell Primary School
HLS DH4 .... 117 K6
Barrington Industrial Estate
STKFD/GP NE62 .... 29 G2
Bassington Industrial Estate
CRAM NE23 .... 32 D7
Battle Hill First School
WLSD/HOW NE28 .... 59 F5
BBC North & Radio Newcastle
JES NE2 .... 4 D2
Beaconhill County First School
CRAM NE23 .... 37 K2
Beacon Shopping Centre
NSHW NE29 .... 2 D2
Beamish County School
STLY/ANP DH9 .... 113 H7
Beamish Park Golf Club
STLY/ANP DH9 .... 113 G4
Beamish, The North of England Open Air Museum
STLY/ANP DH9 .... 113 H5
Bebside County Middle School
BLYTH NE24 .... 30 B6
Bede Infant School
FELL NE10 .... 11 M4
Bede Trading Estate
JRW NE32 .... 74 C5
Bedewell Industrial Park
HEBB NE31 .... 73 J5
Bedewell School
HEBB NE31 .... 73 G7
Bedlington Community High School
BDLGTN NE22 .... 29 K4
Bedlingtonshire Golf Club
BDLGTN NE22 .... 29 F7
Bedlington Station County First School
BDLGTN NE22 .... 29 K3
Bedlington Stead County First School
BDLGTN NE22 .... 29 J5
Belford House Sports Club
ASHBK/HED/RY SR2 .... 120 D3
Belle Vue Leisure Centre
CON/LDGT DH8 .... 123 G4
Belle Vue Swimming Centre
CON/LDGT DH8 .... 123 G4
Bells Close Industrial Estate
BW/LEM/TK/HW NE15 .... 68 C6
Bellway Industrial Estate
LGB/KIL NE12 .... 58 B3
Belmont Business Park
DHAM DH1 .... 157 J5
Belmont C of E (Controlled) Junior School
DHAM DH1 .... 157 K6
Belmont Comprehensive School
DHAM DH1 .... 157 K6
Belmont County Infant School
DHAM DH1 .... 157 K6
Belmont Grange Clinic
DHAM DH1 .... 157 K5
Belmont Industrial Estate
DHAM DH1 .... 16 D2
Belmont Industrial Estate
DHAM DH1 .... 157 J4
Belvedere Retail Park
GOS/KPK NE3 .... 55 G4
Benedict Biscop C of E School
SUNDSW SR3 .... 133 H2
Benfield Business Park
BYK/HTN/WLK NE6 .... 72 D4
Benfield Comprehensive School
BYK/HTN/WLK NE6 .... 72 A2
Benfieldside CP School
CON/LDGT DH8 .... 122 C2
Bensham District Clinic
GATE NE8 .... 10 D7
Bensham Synagogue
GATE NE8 .... 10 D6
Bensham Trading Estate
GATE NE8 .... 10 C7
Bentall Business Park
WASHN NE37 .... 103 H6
Benton Park Primary School
LGB/HTN NE7 .... 57 H6
Benton Square Industrial Estate
LGB/KIL NE12 .... 58 D1
Benwell Hill Cricket Club
BW/LEM/TK/HW NE15 .... 69 F4
Bernard Gilpin Primary School
HLH DH5 .... 132 C7
Bessie Surtees House
CNUT NE1 .... 5 L8
Bewicke Health Centre
WLSD/HOW NE28 .... 73 J1
Bewicke Road Industrial Estate
WLSD/HOW NE28 .... 73 J1
Bewick Road Medical Centre
GATE NE8 .... 11 G5
Bexhill Primary School
SWCK/CAS SR5 .... 104 D2

Biddick Hall County Infant School
HAR/WTLS NE34 .... 90 E1
Biddick Hall County Junior School
HAR/WTLS NE34 .... 75 F7
Biddick School
WASHS NE38 .... 117 G3
Bill Quay Cricket Club
FELL NE10 .... 13 M4
Birtley East Primary School
CLS/BIR/GTL DH3 .... 101 J7
Birtley Golf Club
CLS/BIR/GTL DH3 .... 115 K3
Birtley Lane Surgery
CLS/BIR/GTL DH3 .... 115 J2
Birtley St Josephs RC School
CLS/BIR/GTL DH3 .... 115 J2
Birtley Sports Complex
CLS/BIR/GTL DH3 .... 115 J4
Birtley Swimming Pool
CLS/BIR/GTL DH3 .... 115 J3
Bishop Ian Ramsey School
CON/LDGT DH8 .... 109 J4
Blackfell Primary School
WASHN NE37 .... 102 C7
Blackfriars Craft Centre
CNUT NE1 .... 5 H6
Blackfyne Comprehensive School
CON/LDGT DH8 .... 122 E2
Black Gate
CNUT NE1 .... 5 K8
Blackhall Primary School
RHTLP TS27 .... 175 K7
Bladen Street Industrial Estate
JRW NE32 .... 73 J4
Blakelaw Comprehensive School & Leisure Centre
WD/WHPE/BLK NE5 .... 69 G1
Blakelaw Health Centre
WD/WHPE/BLK NE5 .... 69 G1
Blaydon Business Centre
BLAY NE21 .... 84 C1
Blaydon Business Park
BLAY NE21 .... 68 D7
Blaydon Cricket Club
BLAY NE21 .... 84 A2
Blaydon Haugh Industrial Estate
BLAY NE21 .... 84 C1
Blaydon Haughs Industrial Estate
BLAY NE21 .... 68 C7
Blaydon Industrial Park
BLAY NE21 .... 84 B1
Blaydon Rugby Football Club
WICK/BNPF NE16 .... 84 D3
Blaydon Swimming Pool
BLAY NE21 .... 84 C2
Blaydon West Primary School
BLAY NE21 .... 84 A1
Blezard Business Park
DIN/WO NE13 .... 37 G7
Bloemfontein Co Junior Mixed School
STLY/ANP DH9 .... 126 E4
Blyth Delaval County Middle School
BLYTH NE24 .... 35 F2
Blyth Golf Club
BLYTH NE24 .... 34 D3
Blyth New Delaval County First School
BLYTH NE24 .... 34 C3
Blyth Newsham County First School
BLYTH NE24 .... 34 E2
Blyth Plessey Road County First School
BLYTH NE24 .... 31 H7
Blyth Power Station
BLYTH NE24 .... 30 E3
Blyth Spartans AFC
BLYTH NE24 .... 35 C1
Blyth Sports Centre
BLYTH NE24 .... 31 F7
Blyth Tynedale County High School
BLYTH NE24 .... 30 C7
Blyth Tynedale County Middle School
BLYTH NE24 .... 30 C7
Bobby Shafto Caravan Park
STLY/ANP DH9 .... 114 A5
Boker Lane Health Centre
BOLCOL NE35 .... 91 F4
Bolam Business Park
CRAM NE23 .... 32 D7
Boldon Business Park
BOLCOL NE35 .... 90 C4
Boldon Comprehensive School & Leisure Centre
BOLCOL NE35 .... 90 E4
Boldon Golf Club
BOL NE36 .... 91 F6
Boldon Lane Health Centre
HAR/WTLS NE34 .... 75 G7
Bolingbrooke Sports & Recreation Hall
SSH NE33 .... 3 J8
Bothal County Middle School
ASHGTN NE63 .... 23 F1
Bowburn County Infant School
RDHAMSE DH6 .... 180 A3
Bowburn County Junior School
RDHAMSE DH6 .... 180 B2
Bowburn North Industrial Estate
RDHAMSE DH6 .... 179 K2
Bowburn South Industrial Estate
RDHAMSE DH6 .... 179 K3
Bow School
DHAM DH1 .... 16 D7

Bracken Hill Business Park
PLEE/EAS SR8 .... 174 A5
Bradley Workshops Industrial Estate
CON/LDGT DH8 .... 123 H3
Brama Teams Industrial Park
GATE NE8 .... 9 L5
Brancepeth Castle
BDN/LAN/SAC DH7 .... 176 E3
Brancepeth Castle Golf Club
BDN/LAN/SAC DH7 .... 176 E3
Brandling Primary School
FELL NE10 .... 12 C6
Brandon Cricket Club
BDN/LAN/SAC DH7 .... 167 J5
Brandon Modern School
BDN/LAN/SAC DH7 .... 167 G6
Brandon United Football Club
BDN/LAN/SAC DH7 .... 167 H5
The Bridges Shopping Centre
SUND SR1 .... 14 D5
Brighton Avenue Primary School
GATE NE8 .... 10 D6
Brinkburn Industrial Estate
HAR/WTLS NE34 .... 75 H4
Broadway East First School
GOS/KPK NE3 .... 56 D3
Broadway Junior School
MLFD/PNYW SR4 .... 119 H2
Broadwood Junior & Infant School
BW/LEM/TK/HW NE15 .... 68 D4
Brockwell Clinic
CRAM NE23 .... 33 H7
Brockwell County Middle School
CRAM NE23 .... 33 H7
Broomley County First School
PSHWF NE43 .... 79 H7
Brooms RC Primary School
CON/LDGT DH8 .... 123 K3
Browney County Primary School
BDN/LAN/SAC DH7 .... 167 J7
Browns Gallery
JES NE2 .... 70 E1
Brunswick Beech Special School
DIN/WO NE13 .... 46 A3
Brunswick Park Industrial Est
DIN/WO NE13 .... 45 K3
Buddle Industrial Estate
WLSD/HOW NE28 .... 72 C7
Bugatti Industrial Park
NSHW NE29 .... 60 A5
Builder's South Retail Park
BLYTH NE24 .... 31 F6
Bullion Lane Primary School
CLSW/PEL DH2 .... 129 H5
Burnhope Primary School
BDN/LAN/SAC DH7 .... 141 G3
Burnmoor Cricket Club
HLS DH4 .... 131 G3
Burnopfield Primary School
WICK/BNPF NE16 .... 97 H7
Burnside County First School
CRAM NE23 .... 33 J6
Burnside High School
WLSD/HOW NE28 .... 73 J1
Burnside JMI School
STLY/ANP DH9 .... 127 F2
Burnside Primary School
HLS DH4 .... 132 B6
Burradon First School
CRAM NE23 .... 47 J3
Business & Innovation Centre
SWCK/CAS SR5 .... 105 K4
Business Centre
BDN/LAN/SAC DH7 .... 167 K6
Business Enterprise Centre
SSH NE33 .... 75 F2
Byermoor Industrial Estate
WICK/BNPF NE16 .... 98 A6
Byermoor RC Aided Junior & Infant School
WICK/BNPF NE16 .... 98 B6
Bywell Estate Office
PSHWF NE43 .... 78 D1
Byker Business Development Centre
BYK/HTN/WLK NE6 .... 6 E5
Byker Primary School
BYK/HTN/WLK NE6 .... 6 F6
Caedmon Primary School
GATE NE8 .... 10 F6
Cambois County First School
BLYTH NE24 .... 30 E2
Camden Square Secondary School
SEA/MUR SR7 .... 150 D1
Camperdown Industrial Estate
LGB/KIL NE12 .... 47 H5
Carr Hill Infant & Junior School
LWF/SPW/WRK NE9 .... 11 L9
Cartmel Business Centre
FELL NE10 .... 13 L2
Carville First School
WLSD/HOW NE28 .... 72 C4
Cassop Primary School
RDHAMSE DH6 .... 181 D3
Castle Dene Special School
GOS/KPK NE3 .... 57 F6
Castle Eden & Peterlee Golf Club
RHTLP TS27 .... 184 C2
Castle Keep
CNUT NE1 .... 5 L8
Castle Leazes Halls
JES NE2 .... 4 F3
Castleside County Junior & Infant School
CON/LDGT DH8 .... 136 E2
Castleside Industrial Estate
CON/LDGT DH8 .... 137 E2

Castle View School
SWCK/CAS SR5 .... 104 E4
Catchgate Primary School
STLY/ANP DH9 .... 125 G3
Cedars Special School
LWF/SPW/WRK NE9 .... 101 G2
Central County First School
ASHGTN NE63 .... 23 K1
Central First School
WLSD/HOW NE28 .... 73 F1
Central High School
GOS/KPK NE3 .... 56 C6
Central Newcastle High School
JES NE2 .... 5 L1
Central Surgery
SUND SR1 .... 14 F5
Cestria Health Centre
CLSW/PEL DH2 .... 129 F5
Cestria Primary School
CLS/BIR/GTL DH3 .... 129 K4
Chainbridge Road Industrial Estate
BLAY NE21 .... 68 C7
Chantry Middle School
MPTH NE61 .... 20 C4
Chantry Museum
MPTH NE61 .... 20 E5
Chapel House Middle School
WD/WHPE/BLK NE5 .... 67 K1
Chapel Park Shopping Centre
WD/WHPE/BLK NE5 .... 54 B6
Chase School
WICK/BNPF NE16 .... 85 F5
Cherryburn (NT)
PSHWF NE43 .... 79 J3
Cherry Knowle Hospital
ASHBK/HED/RY SR2 .... 134 C7
Chester-le-Street Leisure Centre
CLS/BIR/GTL DH3 .... 129 K4
Chester-le-Street C of E Junior School
CLSW/PEL DH2 .... 129 H3
Chester-le-Street Cricket Club
CLS/BIR/GTL DH3 .... 129 K5
Chester-le-Street Golf Club
CLS/BIR/GTL DH3 .... 130 B5
Chester-le-Street Health Centre
CLS/BIR/GTL DH3 .... 129 K3
Chester Road Surgery
MLFD/PNYW SR4 .... 120 A1
Cheveley Park Medical Centre
DHAM DH1 .... 158 A6
Cheveley Park Primary School
DHAM DH1 .... 158 A5
Cheveley Park Shopping Centre
DHAM DH1 .... 158 A5
Cheviot County Junior Mixed School
HAR/WTLS NE34 .... 76 A3
Cheviot First School
WD/WHPE/BLK NE5 .... 54 E6
Chevyside Middle School
WD/WHPE/BLK NE5 .... 54 E6
Childrens Hospital
SUNDSW SR3 .... 120 A2
Chillingham Industrial Estate
BYK/HTN/WLK NE6 .... 7 H2
Chillingham Road Primary School
BYK/HTN/WLK NE6 .... 7 G1
Choppington County First School
STKFD/GP NE62 .... 28 E1
Chopwell County Primary School
CHPW NE17 .... 95 H4
The Chorister School
DHAM DH1 .... 16 C6
Christ Church C of E Primary School
JES NE2 .... 5 M5
Churchill Playing Fields Track
WBAY NE26 .... 50 D4
Church of England Primary School
WLSD/HOW NE28 .... 73 G1
Church View Medical Centre
SUNDSW SR3 .... 120 A7
City of Newcastle Golf Club
GOS/KPK NE3 .... 56 C3
City of Sunderland College
ASHBK/HED/RY SR2 .... 120 E4
City of Sunderland College
HLS DH4 .... 131 K2
City of Sunderland College
SUND SR1 .... 14 E4
City of Sunderland College
SWCK/CAS SR5 .... 105 H3
City of Sunderland College
SWCK/CAS SR5 .... 106 C3
City Pool
CNUT NE1 .... 5 K4
City Stadium
JES NE2 .... 6 C4
Civic Centre Derwentside DC
CON/LDGT DH8 .... 123 G3
Civil Service Sports Club
LGB/KIL NE12 .... 58 A5
Claremont Footcare Surgery
WBAY NE26 .... 50 C2
Clayton Street Indoor Mini Market
CNUT NE1 .... 5 J7
Cleadon Village C of E Infant School
CLDN/WHIT/ROK SR6 .... 92 B3
Cleadon Village County JMI School
CLDN/WHIT/ROK SR6 .... 91 K3
Cleasewell Hill School
STKFD/GP NE62 .... 23 F6
C of E Junior Mixed & Infant School
CON/LDGT DH8 .... 108 E3

Cold Hesleden
  Industrial Estate
  SEA/MUR SR7 .... 150 A5
Collierley County
  Primary School
  STLY/ANP DH9 .... 110 E6
Collingwood Primary School
  NSHW NE29 .... 60 B5
Collingwood School
  MPTH NE61 .... 21 F6
Community College
  SEA/MUR SR7 .... 135 J7
Community Health Clinic
  RDHAMSE DH6 .... 172 E7
Concordia Leisure Centre
  CRAM NE23 .... 38 A2
Condercum Industrial Estate
  BW/LEM/TK/HW NE15 .... 69 H6
Consett Business Park
  CON/LDGT DH8 .... 123 H3
Consett County Court
  CON/LDGT DH8 .... 123 F5
Consett County Infant School
  CON/LDGT DH8 .... 123 G5
Consett & District Golf Club
  CON/LDGT DH8 .... 123 F2
Consett Medical Centre
  CON/LDGT DH8 .... 123 G5
Consett RC JMI School
  CON/LDGT DH8 .... 123 F4
Coopies Lane Industrial Estate
  MPTH NE61 .... 21 F5
Coquet Park First School
  WBAY NE26 .... 50 E3
Corrymella Scott Gallery
  JES NE2 .... 70 E2
Cotsford Junior School
  PLEE/EAS SR8 .... 175 J3
County Durham
  Health Authority
  PLEE/EAS SR8 .... 174 E4
County Hospital
  DHAM DH1 .... 16 A3
County Junior & Infant School
  BDN/LAN/SAC DH7 ...... 155 G6
County Junior & Infant School
  RDHAMSE DH6 .... 160 D6
County Junior Middle &
  Infant School
  STLY/ANP DH9 .... 127 K1
County Junior Mixed School
  RDHAMSE DH6 .... 172 B6
County Junior Mixed School
  WNGT TS28 .... 183 K3
Cowgate Leisure Centre
  WD/WHPE/BLK NE5 .... 55 H7
Cowgate Primary School
  ELS/FEN NE4 .... 69 J2
Cowpen Crematorium
  BLYTH NE24 .... 30 E6
Coxhoe District Sports Centre
  RDHAMSE DH6 .... 180 C7
Cragside County First School
  CRAM NE23 .... 38 C4
Cragside Primary School
  LGB/HTN NE7 .... 57 G7
Crag Works
  CON/LDGT DH8 .... 123 J1
Craigievar School
  CLDN/WHIT/ROK SR6 .... 106 E2
Cramlington Football Club
  CRAM NE23 .... 38 E2
Crawcrook Medical Centre
  RYTON NE40 .... 66 B7
Crawcrook RC Junior &
  Infant School
  RYTON NE40 .... 66 A7
The Crematorium
  WBAY NE26 .... 41 J7
Crofton Mill Industrial Estate
  BLYTH NE24 .... 35 H1
Crook Hall
  DHAM DH1 .... 16 D1
Crookhill Junior School
  RYTON NE40 .... 67 G6
Crowther Industrial Estate
  WASHS NE38 .... 116 B2
Crowtree Leisure Centre &
  Ice Rink
  SUND SR1 .... 14 D5
Cruddas Park Health Centre
  ELS/FEN NE4 .... 4 D9
Cruddas Park Shopping Centre
  ELS/FEN NE4 .... 4 D9
Cullercoats Primary School
  TYNE/NSHE NE30 .... 51 G6
Dame Allans Boys School
  ELS/FEN NE4 .... 69 J4
Dame Dorothy Street School
  CLDN/WHIT/ROK SR6 ...... 15 G1
Davenport School
  HLH DH5 .... 147 H2
Dawdon Industrial Estate
  SEA/MUR SR7 .... 151 F4
Deaf Hill Primary School
  TRIM TS29 .... 182 E5
Deerness Park Medical Centre
  ASHBK/HED/RY SR2 .... 15 H7
Deerness Sports Centre
  BDN/LAN/SAC DH7 ...... 167 F1
Deerness Valley
  Comprehensive School
  BDN/LAN/SAC DH7 ...... 155 F6
Delaval Primary School
  BW/LEM/TK/HW NE15 .... 69 F6
Delaval Trading Estate
  MONK NE25 .... 39 K3
Delves Lane Industrial Estate
  CON/LDGT DH8 .... 138 C1
Denbigh Community
  First School
  WLSD/HOW NE28 .... 59 J7
Dene House County
  Mixed Modern School
  PLEE/EAS SR8 .... 175 H4
Deneside Junior &
  Infant School
  SEA/MUR SR7 .... 150 B2

Deneside Medical Centre
  SEA/MUR SR7 .... 150 C1
Dental Hospital
  JES NE2 .... 5 H3
Denton Park Middle School
  WD/WHPE/BLK NE5 .... 68 C1
Denton Park Pool
  WD/WHPE/BLK NE5 .... 68 C1
Denton Road Primary School
  BW/LEM/TK/HW NE15 .... 68 D6
Derwentdale Industrial Estate
  CON/LDGT DH8 .... 122 D4
Derwenthaugh
  Industrial Estate
  BLAY NE21 .... 84 D1
Derwent Infant School
  GATE NE8 .... 10 A6
Derwentside College
  BDN/LAN/SAC DH7 ...... 154 A3
Derwentside College
  CON/LDGT DH8 .... 123 F4
Diamond Hall Junior &
  Infant School
  MLFD/PNYW SR4 .... 105 K6
Dinnington Village
  First School
  DIN/WO NE13 .... 45 G2
Dipton Surgery
  STLY/ANP DH9 .... 110 E6
Discovery Museum
  CNUT NE1 .... 5 G8
Donwell Primary School
  WASHN NE37 .... 102 E4
Downhill Primary School
  SWCK/CAS SR5 .... 105 F1
Dragonville Industrial Estate
  DHAM DH1 .... 157 J7
Dragonville Industrial Park
  DHAM DH1 .... 157 J7
Dr Chandys Surgery
  PLEE/EAS SR8 .... 175 H3
The Drive Primary School
  FELL NE10 .... 12 F7
Dr Reg Carrs Surgery
  BLYTH NE24 .... 31 H7
Drum Industrial Estate
  CLSW/PEL DH2 .... 115 H7
Dryburn Hospital
  DHAM DH1 .... 156 B5
Dry Docks
  WLSD/HOW NE28 .... 72 E3
Dubmire County Junior &
  Infant School
  HLS DH4 .... 131 J7
Dubmire Industrial Estate
  HLS DH4 .... 131 K6
Dubmire Industrial Estate
  HLS DH4 .... 147 G1
Dudley Business Centre
  CRAM NE23 .... 38 A6
Dudley Surgery
  CRAM NE23 .... 47 H1
Dunholme School
  DHAM DH1 .... 156 C4
Dunston Activity Centre
  DUN/TMV NE11 .... 9 J7
Dunston Federation
  Football Club
  DUN/TMV NE11 .... 8 F5
Dunston Health Centre
  DUN/TMV NE11 .... 8 F8
Dunston Hill Hospital
  DUN/TMV NE11 .... 8 D9
Dunston Hill Junior &
  Infant School
  DUN/TMV NE11 .... 8 F8
Dunston Industrial Estate
  DUN/TMV NE11 .... 8 E5
Dunston Riverside
  Primary School
  DUN/TMV NE11 .... 9 H5
Dunston Swimming Pool
  DUN/TMV NE11 .... 8 F9
Durham Baths
  DHAM DH1 .... 16 F4
Durham Blue Coat C of E
  (aided) Junior School
  DHAM DH1 .... 156 D3
Durham Business Centre
  BDN/LAN/SAC DH7 ...... 167 K5
Durham Castle
  DHAM DH1 .... 16 D4
Durham Cathedral
  DHAM DH1 .... 16 D5
Durham CCC - County Ground,
  Riverside
  CLS/BIR/GTL DH3 .... 130 A1
Durham City Amateur
  Football Club
  DHAM DH1 .... 157 J5
Durham City Cricket Club
  DHAM DH1 .... 17 G4
Durham City Golf Club
  BDN/LAN/SAC DH7 ...... 168 A7
Durham City Rugby Club
  DHAM DH1 .... 17 H5
Durham County Constabulary
  PLEE/EAS SR8 .... 174 E4
Durham County NHS Trust
  DHAM DH1 .... 155 K2
Durham Crown Court
  DHAM DH1 .... 16 E5
Durham Gilesgate
  Comprehensive School
  DHAM DH1 .... 157 H6
Durham High School
  DHAM DH1 .... 168 C5
Durham Johnston
  Comprehensive School
  DHAM DH1 .... 17 G6
Durham Johnston
  Comprehensive School
  DHAM DH1 .... 156 B7
Durham Light Infantry
  Museum & Durham Art
  DHAM DH1 .... 156 D6

Durham Newton Hall
  County Infant School
  DHAM DH1 .... 156 D3
Durham Road Trading Estate
  CLS/BIR/GTL DH3 .... 115 J6
Durham St Hilds C of E (Aided)
  Primary School
  DHAM DH1 .... 17 M2
Durham School
  DHAM DH1 .... 16 B6
Durham Sixth Form Centre
  DHAM DH1 .... 16 D2
Durken Business Park
  CRAM NE23 .... 39 G6
Earls House Hospital
  DHAM DH1 .... 155 K3
Easington C of E School
  PLEE/EAS SR8 .... 162 B6
Easington Colliery
  Primary School
  PLEE/EAS SR8 .... 162 D5
Easington
  Comprehensive School
  PLEE/EAS SR8 .... 162 B6
Easington District
  Leisure Centre
  SEA/MUR SR7 .... 150 C1
Easington Lane
  Primary School
  HLH DH5 .... 160 C1
East Boldon Junior School
  BOL NE36 .... 91 G5
Eastcliffe Grammar School
  GOS/KPK NE3 .... 56 D1
East Durham
  Community College
  PLEE/EAS SR8 .... 174 E4
East End Pool & Library
  BYK/HTN/WLK NE6 .... 7 G4
East Herrington
  Primary School
  SUNDSW SR3 .... 119 G7
Eastlea First School
  CRAM NE23 .... 33 J7
East Rainton JMI School
  HLH DH5 .... 147 K4
East Riding Clinic
  MPTH NE61 .... 21 F3
Eastwood County
  Middle School
  PRUD NE42 .... 81 F1
Eccles Industrial Estate
  SMOOR NE27 .... 48 E5
Eden Hall Infant School
  PLEE/EAS SR8 .... 175 F3
Edmondsley JMI School
  BDN/LAN/SAC DH7 ...... 143 G1
Eldon Gardens Shopping Centre
  CNUT NE1 .... 5 F5
Eldon Square Shopping Centre
  CNUT NE1 .... 5 G5
Elemore Golf Course
  HLH DH5 .... 159 K1
Elemore Leisure Centre
  HLH DH5 .... 148 B7
Ellison C of E JMI School
  JRW NE32 .... 73 K5
Elswick Park Leisure
  Centre & Pool
  ELS/FEN NE4 .... 4 C9
Elswick Way Industrial Estate
  BOL NE36 .... 91 H4
Elswick Way Industrial Estate
  HAR/WTLS NE34 .... 74 E5
Emmanuel College
  DUN/TMV NE11 .... 85 K7
Emmaville Primary School
  RYTON NE40 .... 66 B7
Empire Theatre
  SUND SR1 .... 14 C4
English Martyrs RC
  Primary School
  SWCK/CAS SR5 .... 105 J3
Epinay Special School
  JRW NE32 .... 74 A5
Eppleton Cricket Club
  HLH DH5 .... 147 K2
Esh C of E Aided
  Primary School
  BDN/LAN/SAC DH7 ...... 153 J4
Esh RC Primary School
  BDN/LAN/SAC DH7 ...... 153 H5
Esh Winning Child
  Health Clinic
  BDN/LAN/SAC DH7 ...... 165 H1
Esh Winning Industrial Estate
  BDN/LAN/SAC DH7 ...... 165 H1
The Evergreen Gallery
  CNUT NE1 .... 5 J8
Ever Ready Industrial Estate
  STLY/ANP DH9 .... 112 B4
Fairfield Industrial Estate
  FELL NE10 .... 13 K3
Farne First School
  WD/WHPE/BLK NE5 .... 54 E7
Farnham Medical Centre
  HAR/WTLS NE34 .... 75 G5
Farrington Court &
  Leisure Centre
  SUNDSW SR3 .... 119 H7
Farrington Infant School
  SUNDSW SR3 .... 119 H6
Farrington Junior School
  SUNDSW SR3 .... 119 H6
Fatfield Junior &
  Infant School
  WASHS NE38 .... 117 H4
Felldyke Primary &
  Infant School
  LWF/SPW/WRK NE9 ...... 101 K2
Fellgate JMI School
  JRW NE32 .... 89 K3
Felling Business Centre
  FELL NE10 .... 12 C3
Felling Pool
  FELL NE10 .... 88 D7
Felling Shore Industrial Estate
  FELL NE10 .... 12 D2

Fellside County Primary School
  WICK/BNPF NE16 .... 84 E6
Fell Tower Medical
  Centre Whereis Building
  LWF/SPW/WRK NE9 ...... 101 F1
Felstead School
  MLFD/PNYW SR4 .... 105 H7
Fenham Pool
  ELS/FEN NE4 .... 69 H3
Finchale County Infant School
  DHAM DH1 .... 157 F2
Finchale Priory
  DHAM DH1 .... 145 J5
Fire Station
  CNUT NE1 .... 5 L6
Fire Station
  SUND SR1 .... 14 B5
Fisher Industrial Estate
  BYK/HTN/WLK NE6 .... 72 D4
Fleming Business Centre
  JES NE2 .... 70 D3
Fordley Clinic
  CRAM NE23 .... 47 G1
Forest Road Industrial Estate
  SSH NE33 .... 3 H8
Fox Cover Industrial Estate
  SEA/MUR SR7 .... 150 E4
Framwellgate Moor
  Comprehensive School
  DHAM DH1 .... 156 C3
Framwellgate Moor Junior &
  Infant School
  DHAM DH1 .... 156 C3
Freeman Hospital
  LGB/HTN NE7 .... 57 G6
Front Street Industrial Estate
  RDHAMSE DH6 .... 160 E2
Front Street Industrial Estate
  RDHAMSE DH6 .... 172 E7
Front Street Industrial Estate
  RDHAMSE DH6 .... 173 J3
Front Street Junior &
  Infant School
  WICK/BNPF NE16 .... 84 E5
Fulwell Grange
  Christian School
  SWCK/CAS SR5 .... 106 C2
Fulwell Junior School
  CLDN/WHIT/ROK SR6 .... 106 E1
Fulwell Medical Centre
  CLDN/WHIT/ROK SR6 .... 106 D1
Fyndoune Community College
  BDN/LAN/SAC DH7 ...... 143 H6
The Gables Medical Group
  BDLGTN NE22 .... 29 K4
Galactic Zoo
  CNUT NE1 .... 5 H8
The Gallery
  CLSW/PEL DH2 .... 144 C1
The Gambling Man Gallery
  TYNE/NSHE NE30 .... 2 F4
Garden Park Surgery
  WLSD/HOW NE28 .... 59 J6
Garesfield Golf Club
  CHPW NE17 .... 95 K1
The Garrick Gallery
  STLY/ANP DH9 .... 126 C1
Gatehouse Industrial Estate
  CON/LDGT DH8 .... 123 F5
Gateshead Area
  Health Authority
  BLAY NE21 .... 84 C2
Gateshead Area
  Health Authority
  DUN/TMV NE11 .... 86 A6
Gateshead Area
  Health Authority
  GATE NE8 .... 10 E4
Gateshead Area
  Health Authority
  GATE NE8 .... 10 A5
Gateshead Area
  Health Authority
  LWF/SPW/WRK NE9 .... 87 J6
Gateshead Area
  Health Authority
  WICK/BNPF NE16 .... 85 F5
Gateshead College
  LWF/SPW/WRK NE9 .... 11 G9
Gateshead Complimentary
  Health Centre
  GATE NE8 .... 10 E6
Gateshead Fell Cricket Club
  LWF/SPW/WRK NE9 .... 87 G6
Gateshead Health Care
  FELL NE10 .... 88 D6
Gateshead Health NHS Trust
  LWF/SPW/WRK NE9 .... 11 J9
Gateshead Hospitals NHS Trust
  GATE NE8 .... 86 D5
Gateshead
  International Stadium
  FELL NE10 .... 12 A2
Gateshead Jewish Boys School
  GATE NE8 .... 10 F5
Gateshead Jewish
  Primary School
  GATE NE8 .... 10 F6
Gateshead Leisure Centre
  GATE NE8 .... 11 G7
Gateshead Little Theatre
  GATE NE8 .... 10 F8
Gateshead Magistrates Court
  GATE NE8 .... 11 G3
Gateshead & South Tyneside
  Health Authority
  SSH NE33 .... 75 H2
Gateshead Talmudical College
  GATE NE8 .... 10 D6

Gibside School
  WICK/BNPF NE16 .... 84 D5
Gilesgate County Junior School
  DHAM DH1 .... 17 L1
Glebe School
  WBAY NE26 .... 50 C1
Glebe Village Primary School
  WASHS NE38 .... 117 H1
Glen Dene School
  PLEE/EAS SR8 .... 162 B5
The Globe Gallery
  TYNE/NSHE NE30 .... 2 E1
Glover Industrial Estate
  WASHN NE37 .... 103 H6
Glynwood Primary School
  LWF/SPW/WRK NE9 .... 87 G7
Goathland Primary School
  LGB/KIL NE12 .... 57 J4
Gosforth Business Park
  LGB/KIL NE12 .... 57 F3
Gosforth Central Middle School
  GOS/KPK NE3 .... 56 C4
Gosforth Cricket Club
  GOS/KPK NE3 .... 56 C6
Gosforth East Middle School
  GOS/KPK NE3 .... 56 D3
Gosforth Golf Club
  GOS/KPK NE3 .... 56 D3
Gosforth High School &
  Leisure Centre
  GOS/KPK NE3 .... 56 C4
Gosforth Industrial Estate
  GOS/KPK NE3 .... 56 D4
Gosforth Memorial
  Health Centre
  GOS/KPK NE3 .... 56 C4
Gosforth Pool
  GOS/KPK NE3 .... 56 C5
Gosforth West Middle School
  GOS/KPK NE3 .... 56 B5
Grainger Market
  CNUT NE1 .... 5 F6
Grange First School
  GOS/KPK NE3 .... 56 B4
Grange Park Primary School
  SWCK/CAS SR5 .... 106 C3
Grangetown Family Dental
  Health Centre
  ASHBK/HED/RY SR2 .... 120 E4
Grangetown Junior &
  Infant School
  ASHBK/HED/RY SR2 .... 121 F3
Greencroft Comprehensive
  Lower School
  STLY/ANP DH9 .... 125 G3
Greencroft
  Comprehensive School
  STLY/ANP DH9 .... 125 G3
Greencroft Industrial Estate
  STLY/ANP DH9 .... 125 G5
Greenesfield Business Centre
  GATE NE8 .... 10 E2
Greenfields Special School
  HEBB NE31 .... 73 H4
Greenland County JMI School
  STLY/ANP DH9 .... 126 B3
Green Lane Industrial Estate
  FELL NE10 .... 13 K7
Greenside Cricket Club
  RYTON NE40 .... 82 B5
Greenside JMI School
  RYTON NE40 .... 82 B5
Grey College
  DHAM DH1 .... 16 B9
Greystoke Surgery
  MPTH NE61 .... 20 D4
Grindon Infants School
  MLFD/PNYW SR4 .... 119 F3
Grove County JMI School
  CON/LDGT DH8 .... 122 C6
The Grove Industrial Estate
  CON/LDGT DH8 .... 122 D6
Guide Post County
  Middle School
  STKFD/GP NE62 .... 23 F3
Guide Post Ringway
  County First School
  STKFD/GP NE62 .... 23 F4
Hadrian JMI School
  SSH NE33 .... 3 H4
Hadrian Park First School
  WLSD/HOW NE28 .... 59 G3
Hadrian Park Middle School
  WLSD/HOW NE28 .... 59 G3
Hadrian School
  BW/LEM/TK/HW NE15 .... 69 G3
Halls of Residence
  MLFD/PNYW SR4 .... 14 A6
Hamsteels County
  Junior & Infant School
  BDN/LAN/SAC DH7 ...... 165 F1
Hancock Museum
  JES NE2 .... 5 K3
Hannington Works
  WICK/BNPF NE16 .... 84 E2
Harelaw Industrial Estate
  STLY/ANP DH9 .... 111 G7
Hare Law School
  STLY/ANP DH9 .... 125 G1
Harlow Green Infant School
  LWF/SPW/WRK NE9 ...... 101 G3
Harraton Primary School
  WASHS NE38 .... 116 D5
Hartlepool Community
  Care NHS Trust
  PLEE/EAS SR8 .... 174 E4
Harton School
  HAR/WTLS NE34 .... 76 A5
Hatfield College
  DHAM DH1 .... 16 D5
Havelock Primary School
  MLFD/PNYW SR4 .... 105 H7
Hawick Crescent
  Industrial Estate
  BYK/HTN/WLK NE6 .... 6 F8
Hawthorn First School
  ASHGTN NE63 .... 23 K4

Hawthorn House
 Medical Centre
 BYK/HTN/WLK NE6 ...... 7 G4
Hawthorn Primary School
 ELS/FEN NE4 ...... 4 D8
Hawthorns Hospital
 PLEE/EAS SR8 ...... 175 F5
Hazlewood Community
 Primary School
 DIN/WO NE13 ...... 46 B4
Headway Theatre
 BLYTH NE24 ...... 31 H6
The Health Centre
 MPTH NE61 ...... 20 E5
Heathfield Senior High
 School & Leisure Centre
 LWF/SPW/WRK NE9 ...... 87 F6
Heaton Manor Lower School
 LGB/HTN NE7 ...... 71 G1
Heaton Manor Upper School
 LGB/HTN NE7 ...... 57 J6
Hebburn Baths
 HEBB NE31 ...... 73 G6
Hebburn Community Centre
 HEBB NE31 ...... 73 F5
Hebrew Synagogue
 WBAY NE26 ...... 50 E4
Heddon-on-the-Wall C of E
 Controlled First School
 BW/LEM/TK/HW NE15 ...... 66 A1
Hedworthfield
 Comprehensive School
 JRW NE32 ...... 89 K3
Heritage Centre
 DHAM DH1 ...... 16 E5
Hermiston Retail Park
 CON/LDGT DH8 ...... 123 F6
Herrington Medical Centre
 HLS DH4 ...... 132 A2
Hertburn Industrial Estate
 WASHN NE37 ...... 103 G6
Hesleden County
 Junior & Infant School
 RHTLP TS27 ...... 185 H2
Hetton Health Centre
 HLH DH5 ...... 147 K4
Hetton Lyons Industrial Estate
 HLH DH5 ...... 148 A5
Hetton Lyons School
 HLH DH5 ...... 147 K6
Hetton Primary School
 HLH DH5 ...... 147 J5
Hetton Secondary School
 HLH DH5 ...... 147 J5
Hetton UDC Swimming Baths
 HLH DH5 ...... 147 J5
Heworth Golf Club
 FELL NE10 ...... 88 E6
Heworth Grange Comprehensive
 School & Leisure Centre
 FELL NE10 ...... 13 H8
High Farm Middle School
 WLSD/HOW NE28 ...... 58 D5
High Fell Special School
 LWF/SPW/WRK NE9 ...... 11 K9
Highfield County Infant School
 HAR/WTLS NE34 ...... 76 A2
Highfield County Middle School
 PRUD NE42 ...... 80 C3
Highfield Hospital
 CLS/BIR/GTL DH3 ...... 129 J2
Highfield Junior &
 Infant School
 ROWG NE39 ...... 96 D3
High Spen Industrial Estate
 ROWG NE39 ...... 82 B7
High Spen Industrial Estate
 ROWG NE39 ...... 97 H2
Hillcrest Day Special School
 CRAM NE23 ...... 38 C2
Hill Top School
 LWF/SPW/WRK NE9 ...... 102 A1
Hillview Clinic
 ASHBK/HED/RY SR2 ...... 120 D4
Hillview Infant School
 ASHBK/HED/RY SR2 ...... 120 D4
Hill View Junior School
 ASHBK/HED/RY SR2 ...... 120 D4
Hilton Primary School
 WD/WHPE/BLK NE5 ...... 69 F1
Hindu Temple
 ELS/FEN NE4 ...... 69 H5
Hirst High School
 ASHGTN NE63 ...... 24 B3
HM Prison
 DHAM DH1 ...... 16 F5
HMS Calliope Cadet
 Training Centre
 GATE NE8 ...... 6 A8
The Hobart Gallery
 GOS/KPK NE3 ...... 56 C6
Hobson Industrial Estate
 WICK/BNPF NE16 ...... 111 J1
Hobson Municipal Golf Club
 WICK/BNPF NE16 ...... 111 K1
Hollyhurst Medical Centre
 BLAY NE21 ...... 83 J3
Holly Park Primary School
 WASHS NE38 ...... 116 B3
Holmside & South
 Moor Hospital
 STLY/ANP DH9 ...... 126 E3
Holy Cross RC Primary School
 WLSD/HOW NE28 ...... 59 H6
Holystone First School
 SMOOR NE27 ...... 48 E7
Holystone Trading Estate
 HEBB NE31 ...... 73 F5
Holywell County First School
 MONK NE25 ...... 40 C6
Hookergate Comprehensive
 School & Leisure Centre
 ROWG NE39 ...... 96 D2
Horden Cotsford County Infant
 School
 PLEE/EAS SR8 ...... 175 J4

Horden & Easington RC
 Primary School
 PLEE/EAS SR8 ...... 175 G1
Horton Grange First School
 BLYTH NE24 ...... 30 B6
Hotspur Primary School
 BYK/HTN/WLK NE6 ...... 6 D4
Houghall College
 DHAM DH1 ...... 17 H8
Houghton Colliery Welfare
 Cricket Club
 HLS DH4 ...... 132 A6
Houghton Health Centre
 HLH DH5 ...... 132 C7
Houghton Kepier School
 HLS DH4 ...... 132 B7
Houghton-le-Spring Golf Club
 HLH DH5 ...... 133 F7
Houghton Sports Centre
 HLS DH4 ...... 132 B6
Howden Gas Works
 WLSD/HOW NE28 ...... 73 J1
Howdon Works
 WLSD/HOW NE28 ...... 73 K1
Howletch Lane Junior &
 Infant School
 PLEE/EAS SR8 ...... 174 C4
Hownsgill Industrial Park
 CON/LDGT DH8 ...... 122 E7
Hudson Road Primary School
 SUND SR1 ...... 15 G6
Hutton Henry C of E School
 WNGT TS28 ...... 184 D6
Hylton Castle
 SWCK/CAS SR5 ...... 105 F3
Hylton Castle Health Centre
 SWCK/CAS SR5 ...... 105 F3
Hylton Castle Junior School
 SWCK/CAS SR5 ...... 104 D3
Hylton Retail Park
 SWCK/CAS SR5 ...... 105 G4
Imex Business Centre
 CLS/BIR/GTL DH3 ...... 115 H1
Inland Revenue
 DHAM DH1 ...... 17 G5
Ivy Road Primary School
 LGB/KIL NE12 ...... 58 A2
Jesmond Pool
 JES NE2 ...... 70 E1
Jewish Boarding School
 GATE NE8 ...... 10 F5
Jewish High School
 GATE NE8 ...... 11 G5
Jewish Infant School
 GATE NE8 ...... 11 G5
John Spence Community
 High School
 TYNE/NSHE NE30 ...... 60 E2
Joseph Swan School
 LWF/SPW/WRK NE9 ...... 100 E2
Jubilee Industrial Estate
 ASHGTN NE63 ...... 23 J4
Jubilee Industrial Estate
 BDLGTN NE22 ...... 29 J4
Jubilee Infant School
 SEA/MUR SR7 ...... 149 J5
Kelloe JMI School
 RDHAMSE DH6 ...... 181 H5
Kelvin Grove Primary School
 GATE NE8 ...... 10 E8
Kenton Comprehensive School
 GOS/KPK NE3 ...... 55 H6
Kenton Lodge
 Residential School
 ELS/FEN NE4 ...... 70 B1
Kenton Park Shopping Centre
 GOS/KPK NE3 ...... 56 A7
Kenton Park Sports Complex
 GOS/KPK NE3 ...... 55 J5
Kepier Clinic
 DHAM DH1 ...... 17 L1
Kibblesworth Primary School
 DUN/TMV NE11 ...... 100 D7
Killingworth Middle School
 LGB/KIL NE12 ...... 47 K5
Killingworth Sports Centre
 LGB/KIL NE12 ...... 47 K6
King Edward Junior &
 Infant School
 TYNE/NSHE NE30 ...... 61 F3
Kingfisher Industrial Estate
 SEA/MUR SR7 ...... 135 G7
King George
 Comprehensive School
 HAR/WTLS NE34 ...... 91 K1
Kingsmeadow
 Comprehensive School
 DUN/TMV NE11 ...... 8 E7
Kings School
 TYNE/NSHE NE30 ...... 61 H3
Kingston Park Primary School
 GOS/KPK NE3 ...... 55 G4
Kingsway First School
 BLYTH NE24 ...... 35 G1
Kitty Brewster Industrial Estate
 BLYTH NE24 ...... 30 B5
Knoplaw First School
 WD/WHPE/BLK NE5 ...... 68 A1
Laing Art Gallery
 CNUT NE1 ...... 5 L5
Lancaster University
 CNUT NE1 ...... 5 K8
Lanchester CP Infant &
 Junior School
 BDN/LAN/SAC DH7 ...... 140 B4
Lanchester Infant School
 BDN/LAN/SAC DH7 ...... 140 B4
Lanchester RC Mixed &
 Infant School
 BDN/LAN/SAC DH7 ...... 140 B4
Langley Moor Primary School
 BDN/LAN/SAC DH7 ...... 167 K4
Langley Park Industrial Estate
 BDN/LAN/SAC DH7 ...... 154 B1
Langley Park Primary School
 BDN/LAN/SAC DH7 ...... 154 B3
Larkspur Primary School
 LWF/SPW/WRK NE9 ...... 101 J1

La Sagesse Convent
 High School
 JES NE2 ...... 56 E7
Laurel Avenue County
 Junior & Infant School
 DHAM DH1 ...... 17 K4
Laygate Lane County
 Infant School
 SSH NE33 ...... 75 G2
Laygate School
 SSH NE33 ...... 75 G2
Leadgate County Junior
 Mixed School
 CON/LDGT DH8 ...... 123 J4
Leadgate Industrial Estate
 CON/LDGT DH8 ...... 124 A5
Leadgate Surgery
 CON/LDGT DH8 ...... 123 J3
Leafield House School
 CLS/BIR/GTL DH3 ...... 115 K3
Leechmere Industrial Estate
 ASHBK/HED/RY SR2 ...... 120 D5
Lemington Clinic
 BW/LEM/TK/HW NE15 ...... 68 B5
Lemington First School
 BW/LEM/TK/HW NE15 ...... 68 B5
Lemington Middle School
 BW/LEM/TK/HW NE15 ...... 68 B3
Lightfoot Leisure Centre
 BYK/HTN/WLK NE6 ...... 72 B7
Linden School
 LGB/KIL NE12 ...... 57 K2
Lindisfarne County
 Primary School
 GATE NE8 ...... 11 H3
Lingey House Primary School
 FELL NE10 ...... 88 D5
Linhope First School
 WD/WHPE/BLK NE5 ...... 68 D1
Littleburn Industrial Estate
 BDN/LAN/SAC DH7 ...... 167 K5
Little Theatre
 CLDN/WHIT/ROK SR6 ...... 92 A3
Live Theatre
 CNUT NE1 ...... 5 M8
Lizard Lane Caravan &
 Camping Site
 CLDN/WHIT/ROK SR6 ...... 92 E2
Lobley Hill Junior &
 Infant School
 DUN/TMV NE11 ...... 86 A7
Longbenton Community College
 LGB/KIL NE12 ...... 57 J3
Longrigg Medical Centre
 FELL NE10 ...... 88 C5
Lord Chancellors Department
 CNUT NE1 ...... 5 J8
Lord Chancellors Department
 GATE NE8 ...... 10 F2
Lord Lawson of Beamish
 School & Leisure Centre
 CLS/BIR/GTL DH3 ...... 115 K3
Louisa Surgery
 STLY/ANP DH9 ...... 126 C1
Low Fell Clinic
 LWF/SPW/WRK NE9 ...... 101 G1
Low Fell Junior & Infant School
 LWF/SPW/WRK NE9 ...... 87 F7
Low Prudhoe Industrial Estate
 PRUD NE42 ...... 65 F6
Low Willington Industrial Estate
 CRK/WIL DL15 ...... 176 A7
Ludworth JMI School
 RDHAMSE DH6 ...... 172 A3
Lumley County Infant School
 CLS/BIR/GTL DH3 ...... 130 C7
Lumley Junior Middle &
 Infant School
 CLS/BIR/GTL DH3 ...... 145 J1
Lynemouth County
 First School
 MPTH NE61 ...... 18 D1
Lynnwood Business Centre
 ELS/FEN NE4 ...... 4 B7
Maiden Law Hospital
 BDN/LAN/SAC DH7 ...... 140 C2
Malvins Close County
 First School
 BLYTH NE24 ...... 30 E6
Manor Walks Shopping Centre
 CRAM NE23 ...... 38 B2
Maplewood School
 SWCK/CAS SR5 ...... 105 J2
Marden Bridge Middle School
 MONK NE25 ...... 50 E5
Marden High School
 TYNE/NSHE NE30 ...... 61 F1
Marine Avenue Medical Centre
 WBAY NE26 ...... 50 D4
Marine Park JMI School
 SSH NE33 ...... 3 K7
Market Hall
 DHAM DH1 ...... 16 D3
Market Place Industrial Estate
 HLH DH5 ...... 132 D6
Marlborough Clinic
 SEA/MUR SR7 ...... 150 E1
Marley Hill Primary School
 WICK/BNPF NE16 ...... 98 E5
Mary Trevelyan Primary School
 ELS/FEN NE4 ...... 9 H1
Maurice Road Industrial Estate
 WLSD/HOW NE28 ...... 72 D3
Maxwell Street Industrial Estate
 SSH NE33 ...... 75 G2
Mayfield Medical Centre
 JRW NE32 ...... 73 J5
McKennas Sports Club
 BDN/LAN/SAC DH7 ...... 165 H2
Meadowfield Clinic
 BDN/LAN/SAC DH7 ...... 167 J6
Meadowfield Industrial Estate
 BDN/LAN/SAC DH7 ...... 167 J7
Meadowfield Industrial Estate
 PONT/DH NE20 ...... 43 G3
Meadowfield Sports Centre
 BDN/LAN/SAC DH7 ...... 167 J6

Meadow Well Primary School
 NSHW NE29 ...... 60 B6
Megabowl
 LGB/KIL NE12 ...... 58 C3
Mercia Retail Park
 DHAM DH1 ...... 156 D1
Metrocentre East
 Business Park
 DUN/TMV NE11 ...... 8 D4
The Metro Centre
 WICK/BNPF NE16 ...... 8 B4
Metro Retail Park
 WICK/BNPF NE16 ...... 85 F2
Mickley County First School
 PSHWF NE43 ...... 79 J3
Middlefields Industrial Estate
 HAR/WTLS NE34 ...... 75 F5
Millbank Industrial Estate
 SSH NE33 ...... 2 F8
Millburngate Shopping Centre
 DHAM DH1 ...... 16 C3
Mitre Industrial Estate
 SSH NE33 ...... 75 F4
Modern Mixed School
 RDHAMSE DH6 ...... 173 H3
Monkhouse Primary School
 TYNE/NSHE NE30 ...... 61 F1
Monkseaton Clinic
 MONK NE25 ...... 50 C5
Monkseaton High School
 MONK NE25 ...... 50 C7
Monkseaton Medical Centre
 MONK NE25 ...... 50 B5
Monkseaton Middle School
 MONK NE25 ...... 50 C5
Monkton Business Park
 HEBB NE31 ...... 89 G2
Monkton County Infant School
 HAR/WTLS NE34 ...... 74 E7
Monkton County Junior
 Mixed School
 HAR/WTLS NE34 ...... 74 D7
Monkton Hall Hospital
 HEBB NE31 ...... 73 H7
Monkton Stadium
 JRW NE32 ...... 73 J7
Monkwearmouth Health Centre
 SWCK/CAS SR5 ...... 14 E1
Monkwearmouth Hospital
 SWCK/CAS SR5 ...... 106 C3
Monkwearmouth Railway
 Station Museum
 SWCK/CAS SR5 ...... 14 E2
Montagu Junior &
 Infant School
 WD/WHPE/BLK NE5 ...... 55 J7
Monument Mall
 Shopping Centre
 CNUT NE1 ...... 5 K5
Moor Edge First School
 LGB/KIL NE12 ...... 47 H6
Mooride Community
 Primary School
 ELS/FEN NE4 ...... 4 D4
Mooride
 Comprehensive School
 CON/LDGT DH8 ...... 122 B7
Mooride County First School
 NWBGN NE64 ...... 19 F7
Mooride County School
 CON/LDGT DH8 ...... 137 F1
Morgan Business Centre
 LGB/KIL NE12 ...... 47 H4
Morpeth Chantry
 Bagpipe Museum
 MPTH NE61 ...... 20 E5
Morpeth Cottage Hospital
 MPTH NE61 ...... 20 D7
Morpeth County Court
 MPTH NE61 ...... 20 D5
Morpeth County First School
 MPTH NE61 ...... 20 E5
Morpeth Golf Club
 MPTH NE61 ...... 20 D7
Morpeth King Edward VI School
 MPTH NE61 ...... 20 D3
Morpeth Newminster
 County Middle School
 MPTH NE61 ...... 20 C4
Morpeth Riverside
 Leisure Centre
 MPTH NE61 ...... 20 D5
Morpeth Stobhillgate
 County First School
 MPTH NE61 ...... 21 F6
Morpeth Town Athletics
 Football Club
 MPTH NE61 ...... 20 B7
Morrison Industrial Estate
 STLY/ANP DH9 ...... 125 J3
Morrison Industrial
 Estate North
 STLY/ANP DH9 ...... 125 J4
Mortimer Comprehensive
 School & Leisure Centre
 HAR/WTLS NE34 ...... 75 H4
Mountbatten Medical Centre
 HEBB NE31 ...... 73 F6
Mountfield Primary School
 GOS/KPK NE3 ...... 55 J5
Mount Oswald Manor &
 Golf Course
 DHAM DH1 ...... 168 C4
Mowden Hall (Newton)
 School Trust
 PSHWF NE43 ...... 62 C4
Mulberry Trading Estate
 FELL NE10 ...... 12 B5
Murton Primary School
 SEA/MUR SR7 ...... 149 J5
Museum of Antiquities
 JES NE2 ...... 5 J3
Music School
 DHAM DH1 ...... 16 D5
National Glasscentre
 CLDN/WHIT/ROK SR6 ...... 15 H2
The Natural Therapy Clinic
 TYNE/NSHE NE30 ...... 2 D1

Nature Reserve
 LGB/KIL NE12 ...... 58 E3
Nelson Health Centre
 NSHW NE29 ...... 2 C2
Nelson Industrial Estate
 CRAM NE23 ...... 32 D5
Nelson Industrial Estate
 CRAM NE23 ...... 33 F6
Nettlesworth Primary School
 CLSW/PEL DH2 ...... 144 A4
Nevilles Cross Primary School
 DHAM DH1 ...... 168 A1
Newbiggin-by-the-Sea
 County Middle School
 NWBGN NE64 ...... 24 E1
Newbiggin Golf Club
 NWBGN NE64 ...... 19 H7
Newbottle Primary School
 HLS DH4 ...... 132 A4
New Brancepeth
 Primary School
 BDN/LAN/SAC DH7 ...... 166 E3
Newburn Hall Motor Museum
 BW/LEM/TK/HW NE15 ...... 67 H3
Newburn Industrial Estate
 BW/LEM/TK/HW NE15 ...... 67 J5
Newburn Leisure Centre
 BW/LEM/TK/HW NE15 ...... 67 G3
Newburn Manor First School
 BW/LEM/TK/HW NE15 ...... 67 H3
Newcastle Antiques &
 Independent Museum
 CNUT NE1 ...... 5 J7
Newcastle Area
 Health Authority
 BW/LEM/TK/HW NE15 ...... 69 F6
Newcastle Area
 Health Authority
 ELS/FEN NE4 ...... 4 C8
Newcastle Arena
 ELS/FEN NE4 ...... 10 A1
Newcastle Business Park
 ELS/FEN NE4 ...... 8 F2
Newcastle Business Park
 ELS/FEN NE4 ...... 9 J3
Newcastle Clinic
 JES NE2 ...... 56 E7
Newcastle College
 ELS/FEN NE4 ...... 4 F9
Newcastle College Concert Hall
 ELS/FEN NE4 ...... 4 F9
Newcastle Falcons
 RFC- Kingston Park
 DIN/WO NE13 ...... 55 F3
Newcastle General Hospital
 ELS/FEN NE4 ...... 4 B5
Newcastle Nuffield Hospital
 JES NE2 ...... 70 E3
Newcastle Playhouse &
 Gulbenkian Studio Theatre
 JES NE2 ...... 5 J3
Newcastle Preparatory School
 JES NE2 ...... 5 L1
Newcastle Racecourse
 GOS/KPK NE3 ...... 46 D6
Newcastle Reform Synagogue
 GOS/KPK NE3 ...... 56 A6
Newcastle Road Baths
 SWCK/CAS SR5 ...... 106 C3
Newcastle United Golf Club
 ELS/FEN NE4 ...... 69 K2
The New City Medical Centre
 SUND SR1 ...... 15 G5
New College Durham
 DHAM DH1 ...... 16 A8
New College Durham
 DHAM DH1 ...... 156 B4
New College Durham
 DHAM DH1 ...... 168 B2
Newgate Shopping Centre
 CNUT NE1 ...... 5 J7
New Herrington
 Industrial Estate
 HLS DH4 ...... 132 A1
Newker Junior & Infant School
 CLSW/PEL DH2 ...... 129 H5
New Seaham Primary School
 SEA/MUR SR7 ...... 135 F6
Newtown Industrial Estate
 CLS/BIR/GTL DH3 ...... 115 J3
New York Industrial Park
 SMOOR NE27 ...... 59 J2
Noble Street Industrial Estate
 ELS/FEN NE4 ...... 9 H1
Norfolk Clinic
 SUND SR1 ...... 14 F4
Norham Community
 High School
 NSHW NE29 ...... 60 B5
North Balkwell Farm
 Industrial Estate
 NSHW NE29 ...... 59 K3
North Biddick Club House
 WASHS NE38 ...... 117 H6
North Blunts Primary School
 PLEE/EAS SR8 ...... 174 E4
Northburn County First School
 CRAM NE23 ...... 33 H6
North Durham
 Community Healthcare
 BDN/LAN/SAC DH7 ...... 140 C2
North Durham Cricket &
 Rugby Club
 GATE NE8 ...... 10 F3
North Durham NHS Trust
 CLS/BIR/GTL DH3 ...... 129 J5
Northern Land & Leisure Centre
 DHAM DH1 ...... 156 C2
Northern Rugby Club
 GOS/KPK NE3 ...... 56 C2
North Fawdon Primary School
 GOS/KPK NE3 ...... 55 K3
Northgate District Hospital
 MPTH NE61 ...... 20 B1

Northgate & Prudhoe NHS Trust
PRUD NE42 .... 80 E4
North Heaton Sports Club
BYK/HTN/WLK NE6 .... 71 J3
North Industrial Estate
CON/LDGT DH8 .... 122 E3
North Industrial Estate
NSHW NE29 .... 59 K4
North Nelson Industrial Estate
CRAM NE23 .... 32 D5
North Sands Business Centre
CLDN/WHIT/ROK SR6 ..... 15 H1
North Seaton Industrial Estate
ASHGTN NE63.............. 24 B4
North Shields Rugby Club
NSHW NE29 .... 60 D2
North Tyne Industrial Estate
LGB/KIL NE12 .... 58 C2
North Tyneside Area
Health Authority
LGB/KIL NE12.............. 47 K6
North Tyneside Area
Health Authority
NSHW NE29 .... 2 C1
North Tyneside Area
Health Authority
WLSD/HOW NE28 .... 58 E7
North Tyneside Area
Health Authority
WLSD/HOW NE28 .... 59 G3
North Tyneside College
WLSD/HOW NE28 .... 59 G5
Northumberland Area
Health Authority
BLYTH NE24 .... 30 D7
Northumberland Area
Health Authority
PRUD NE42 .... 80 E1
Northumberland Business Centre
MPTH NE61 .... 26 E1
Northumberland College of
Arts & Technology
ASHGTN NE63............ 24 A3
Northumberland Community
Health Authority
ASHGTN NE63............. 23 J1
Northumberland County
Cricket Club
JES NE2................... 71 J3
Northumberland Golf Club
GOS/KPK NE3............. 46 C6
Northumberland Mental
Health NHS Trust
CRAM NE23 .... 38 C1
Northumbria Police
STKFD/GP NE62........... 22 E6
Northumbria Sports Centre
WASHN NE37 .... 103 G2
North West Industrial Estate
PLEE/EAS SR8 .... 174 A2
Novacastrians Rugby
Football Club
LGB/HTN NE7............. 57 H6
Number One Industrial Estate
CON/LDGT DH8 .... 123 G2
Oakfield College
ELS/FEN NE4 .... 69 H6
Oakfield Junior School
LWF/SPW/WRK NE9 ..... 101 F2
Oaklea School Clinic
WNGT TS28 .... 183 J2
Oakleigh Gardens School
CLDN/WHIT/ROK SR6 ... 92 B2
Observatory
DHAM DH1 .... 16 B7
Old Fulling Mill & Museum of
Archaeology
DHAM DH1 .... 16 C5
Old Lily Brickworks
ROWG NE39 .... 97 H2
Old Shire Hall
DHAM DH1 .... 16 E4
Old Tyne Iron Works Cottage
BW/LEM/TK/HW NE15 .... 68 B6
Onix Industrial Estate
NSHW NE29 .... 60 A4
The Open University
GOS/KPK NE3............. 56 C4
Oriental Museum
DHAM DH1 .... 16 B9
The Osborne Clinic
JES NE2................... 71 F2
Our Lady of Peace RC School
HLS DH4 .... 117 J1
Our Lady & St Annes
Primary School
ELS/FEN NE4 .... 4 F8
Ouston County Infant School
CLSW/PEL DH2............ 115 F5
Ouston Junior School
CLSW/PEL DH2............ 114 E5
Ovingham C of E First School
PRUD NE42 .... 80 A1
Ovingham Middle School
PRUD NE42 .... 80 A1
Oxclose Community School
WASHS NE38 .... 116 C2
Pallion Health Centre
MLFD/PNYW SR4 .... 105 K7
Pallion Industrial Estate
MLFD/PNYW SR4 .... 105 H6
Pallion Primary School
MLFD/PNYW SR4 .... 105 J5
Pallion Retail Park
MLFD/PNYW SR4 .... 105 J5
Pallion West Industrial Estate
MLFD/PNYW SR4 .... 105 H5
Palmer Community Hospital
JRW NE32 .... 73 K4
Parklands Golfing Complex
GOS/KPK NE3............. 46 E5
Park Road Industrial Estate
CON/LDGT DH8 .... 122 E4
Parkside Infant School
SEA/MUR SR7 .... 150 C3
Parkside Middle School
CRAM NE23 .... 38 C1

Parkside School
WLSD/HOW NE28 .... 58 C5
The Parks Sport &
Leisure Centre
SUNDSW SR3 .... 2 B5
Park View Community School
CLS/BIR/GTL DH3......... 129 K4
Park View
Comprehensive School
CLS/BIR/GTL DH3......... 115 J7
Parkway Medical Centre
WD/WHPE/BLK NE5 .... 68 A1
Parkway School
WD/WHPE/BLK NE5 .... 68 B1
Parsons Industrial estate
WASHN NE37 .... 102 D5
Pattinson Industrial Estate
WASHS NE38 .... 103 K7
Pattinson Industrial Estate
WASHS NE38 .... 117 J3
Pegswood County First School
MPTH NE61 .... 21 K1
Pegswood Industrial Estate
MPTH NE61 .... 21 K1
Pelaw County Infant School
CLSW/PEL DH2............ 129 H2
Pelaw Industrial Estate
FELL NE10................ 13 K6
Pelton County Junior &
Infant School
CLSW/PEL DH2............ 115 F7
Pelton Fell Surgery Building
CLSW/PEL DH2............ 128 E3
Pelton Health Clinic
CLSW/PEL DH2............ 115 F7
Pendower Clinic
BW/LEM/TK/HW NE15 .... 69 F6
Pennywell Business Centre
MLFD/PNYW SR4 .... 119 G1
Pennywell
Comprehensive School
MLFD/PNYW SR4 .... 119 F1
Pennywell Industrial Estate
MLFD/PNYW SR4 .... 118 D3
Pennywell Shopping Centre
MLFD/PNYW SR4 .... 119 F2
Percy Main Cricket Club
NSHW NE29 .... 60 B7
Percy Main Primary School
NSHW NE29 .... 74 B1
Percy St Johns Primary School
NSHW NE29 .... 60 C7
Peterlee College
PLEE/EAS SR8 .... 174 D3
Peterlee Leisure Centre &
Swimming Pool
PLEE/EAS SR8 .... 174 E5
Philadelphia Cricket Club
HLS DH4 .... 132 A2
Phoenix Theatre
BLYTH NE24 .... 31 H7
Pier Works
TYNE/NSHE NE30 .... 61 J3
Plawsworth Road County
Infant School
PONT/DH NE20 .... 43 G2
Plessey Road County
Junior School
BLYTH NE24 .... 31 H7
Point Pleasant Industrial Estate
WLSD/HOW NE28 .... 73 H2
Ponds Court Business Park
CON/LDGT DH8 .... 122 E5
Ponteland County First School
PONT/DH NE20 .... 43 H2
Ponteland County High School
PONT/DH NE20 .... 43 G4
Ponteland County
Middle School
PONT/DH NE20 .... 43 H4
Ponteland Darras
Hall County First School
PONT/DH NE20 .... 42 E6
Ponteland Golf Club
PONT/DH NE20 .... 43 J3
Ponteland Health Centre
PONT/DH NE20 .... 43 G2
Ponteland Leisure Centre
PONT/DH NE20 .... 43 H3
Portberry Street
Industrial Estate
SSH NE33 .... 74 E3
Portland School
SUNDSW SR3 .... 120 A4
Portobello County
Junior Infant School
CLS/BIR/GTL DH3......... 115 K4
Portobello Industrial Estate
CLS/BIR/GTL DH3......... 116 A2
Preston Grange County
Primary School
NSHW NE29 .... 60 C1
Prestwick Industrial Estate
PONT/DH NE20 .... 44 A6
Primrose Community
Association
JRW NE32 .... 73 K7
Primrose Hill Hospital
JRW NE32 .... 74 A7
Prince Bishops
Shopping Centre
DHAM DH1 .... 16 D3
Prince Consort Industrial Estate
WLSD/HOW NE28 .... 72 E4
Princess Louise First School
BLYTH NE24 .... 31 F7
Princess Road Junior School
SEA/MUR SR7 .... 150 D1
Priory Primary School
TYNE/NSHE NE30 .... 61 H2
Priory Theatre
TYNE/NSHE NE30 .... 61 H2
Prospect Business Park
CON/LDGT DH8 .... 123 J4
Prudhoe Castle
PRUD NE42 .... 80 C1
Prudhoe Castle First School
PRUD NE42 .... 80 B2

Prudhoe County High School
PRUD NE42 .... 80 D3
Prudhoe Golf Club
PRUD NE42 .... 81 F1
Prudhoe Health Centre
PRUD NE42 .... 80 E1
Prudhoe Town Football Club
PRUD NE42 .... 65 F7
Prudhoe West County
First School
PRUD NE42 .... 80 C2
Quarrington Hill
Industrial Estate
RDHAMSE DH6............ 181 F4
Queen Elizabeth Hospital
LWF/SPW/WRK NE9 ...... 87 J6
Raby Cross Medical Centre
BYK/HTN/WLK NE6 .... 6 F4
Raich Carter Sports Centre
ASHBK/HED/RY SR2 ...... 15 J9
Rainton Bridge
Industrial Estate
HLS DH4 .... 147 F1
Ramside Hall Golf Club
DHAM DH1 .... 158 B4
Ramside Hall (Hotel)
DHAM DH1 .... 158 B3
Ravenswood Infant &
Primary School
BYK/HTN/WLK NE6 .... 71 J2
Ravensworth Golf Club
LWF/SPW/WRK NE9 ..... 101 H2
Ravensworth Surgery
SSH NE33 .... 75 J2
Ravensworth Terrace
Primary School
CLS/BIR/GTL DH3......... 115 J2
RC JMI School
BDN/LAN/SAC DH7 ...... 143 G4
Recreation Centre
CNUT NE1................. 5 J6
Redesdale First School
WLSD/HOW NE28 .... 58 B6
Red House Junior
Mixed School
SWCK/CAS SR5 .... 105 H3
Red Rose Primary School
CLS/BIR/GTL DH3......... 129 K6
Redwell Hills Clinic
CON/LDGT DH8 .... 124 A3
Regent Farm First School
GOS/KPK NE3............. 56 A4
Regional National
Blood Transfusion Centre
JES NE2.................. 4 E3
Rehabilitation Centre
JES NE2.................. 4 D1
Rekendyke Industrial Estate
SSH NE33 .... 75 F3
Richard Avenue
Primary School
MLFD/PNYW SR4 .... 120 B2
Richard Coates Church of
England Middle School
PONT/DH NE20 .... 43 G2
Richardson Dees First School
WLSD/HOW NE28 .... 73 F1
Rickleton Primary School
WASHS NE38 .... 116 B6
Riverside Business Park
WLSD/HOW NE28 .... 73 J2
Riverside Industrial Estate
BDN/LAN/SAC DH7 ...... 154 B2
Riverside Stadium
CLS/BIR/GTL DH3......... 130 A6
Riverview House
Business Centre
SUND SR1 .... 14 F3
Robins Cinema
DHAM DH1 .... 16 C4
Roman Road Primary School
FELL NE10................ 88 C7
Ronald Moore Gallery
TYNE/NSHE NE30 .... 61 F3
Ropery Walk Primary School
SEA/MUR SR7 .... 151 F1
Roseberry Grange Golf Course
STLY/ANP DH9 .... 128 A2
Roseberry Primary School
CLSW/PEL DH2............ 128 C2
Rowlands Gill Infant School
ROWG NE39 .... 97 H2
Rowlands Gill Junior School
ROWG NE39 .... 97 H2
Rowletch Burn
Industrial Estate
WASHS NE38 .... 115 H2
Royal College of Nursing
CNUT NE1................. 5 K7
Royal Grammar School
JES NE2.................. 5 L2
Royal Industrial Estate
HEBB NE31 .... 73 H3
Royal Quays Outlet Shopping
NSHW NE29 .... 74 C1
Royalty Theatre
ASHBK/HED/RY SR2 ...... 14 B6
Royal Victoria Infirmary
JES NE2.................. 5 H3
Rye Hill Sports Centre
ELS/FEN NE4 .... 4 F8
Ryhope General Hospital
ASHBK/HED/RY SR2 ..... 135 F2
Ryhope Golf Course
ASHBK/HED/RY SR2 ..... 120 E7
Ryhope Health Centre
ASHBK/HED/RY SR2 ..... 120 E7
Ryhope Junior &
Infant School
ASHBK/HED/RY SR2 ..... 120 E7
Ryhope Village C of E
Primary School
ASHBK/HED/RY SR2 ..... 135 F1
Ryton Comprehensive School &
Leisure Centre
RYTON NE40.............. 66 C6
Ryton Golf Club
RYTON NE40.............. 66 B4

Ryton Industrial Estate
BLAY NE21 .... 67 J6
Ryton Junior & Infant School
RYTON NE40.............. 66 C6
Ryton Rugby Club
RYTON NE40.............. 66 C7
Sacred Heart Primary School
ELS/FEN NE4 .... 69 H4
Sacriston Cricket Club
BDN/LAN/SAC DH7 ...... 143 G5
Sacriston Industrial Estate
BDN/LAN/SAC DH7 ...... 143 H5
Sacriston Junior School
BDN/LAN/SAC DH7 ...... 143 H6
Sacriston Swimming Baths
BDN/LAN/SAC DH7 ...... 143 G5
St Aidans College
DHAM DH1 .... 16 B9
St Aidans RC
Comprehensive School
ASHBK/HED/RY SR2 ..... 120 C2
St Albans Medical Group
FELL NE10................ 12 C8
St Aloysius RC Infants School
HEBB NE31 .... 73 G4
St Aloysius RC Junior School
HEBB NE31 .... 73 G4
St Andrews RC Aided
First School
BLYTH NE24 .... 30 E7
St Annes Mixed High School
SSH NE33 .... 75 J3
St Annes RC Primary School
MLFD/PNYW SR4 .... 119 F1
St Anthonys Health Centre
BYK/HTN/WLK NE6 .... 72 B7
St Anthonys RC School
ASHBK/HED/RY SR2 ...... 14 C7
St Augustines RC Infant School
FELL NE10................ 88 B6
St Bede Medical Centre
CLDN/WHIT/ROK SR6 .... 14 F1
St Bedes First School
BDLGTN NE22.............. 28 E5
St Bedes RC
Comprehensive School
BDN/LAN/SAC DH7 ...... 140 B3
St Bedes RC
Comprehensive School
PLEE/EAS SR8 .... 174 D4
St Bedes RC Infants School
JRW NE32 .... 74 A4
St Bedes RC JMI School
JRW NE32 .... 74 A4
St Bedes RC Primary School
BW/LEM/TK/HW NE15 .... 68 D4
St Bedes RC Primary School
SSH NE33 .... 3 H9
St Bedes RC Primary School
WASHN NE37 .... 103 F4
St Benet Biscops RC High School
BDLGTN NE22.............. 28 E6
St Benets Primary RC School
CLSW/PEL DH2............ 115 F5
St Benets RC Primary School
CLDN/WHIT/ROK SR6 .... 106 D3
St Bernadettes RC First School
WLSD/HOW NE28 .... 58 D5
St Catherines RC
Primary School
JES NE2................... 6 B1
St Chads College
DHAM DH1 .... 16 D5
St Charles RC Primary School
GOS/KPK NE3............. 56 B4
St Columbas RC First School
WLSD/HOW NE28 .... 72 C1
St Cuthberts C of E
Junior School
GATE NE8 .... 10 A6
St Cuthberts High School
BW/LEM/TK/HW NE15 .... 69 F5
St Cuthberts RC
Lower School
BW/LEM/TK/HW NE15 .... 69 F5
St Cuthberts RC
Primary School
BW/LEM/TK/HW NE15 .... 67 H1
St Cuthberts RC Primary School
CLS/BIR/GTL DH3......... 129 K5
St Cuthberts RC Primary School
GOS/KPK NE3............. 55 H9
St Cuthberts RC Primary School
NSHW NE29 .... 2 C3
St Cuthberts RC School
SEA/MUR SR7 .... 134 E7
St Cuthberts Walk
Shopping Centre
CLS/BIR/GTL GTL......... 129 J4
St Edmunds RC
Comprehensive School
LWF/SPW/WRK NE9 ..... 101 K1
St Georges Hospital
MPTH NE61 .... 20 E3
St Georges RC Primary School
BW/LEM/TK/HW NE15 .... 68 B6
St Godrics RC Junior &
Infant School
DHAM DH1 .... 156 D3
St Hilda Industrial Estate
SSH NE33 .... 3 G8
St Hildas RC School
SWCK/CAS SR5 .... 106 A3
St Hild & St Bede College
DHAM DH1 .... 17 G3
St James Park
(Newcastle United FC)
CNUT NE1................. 5 H5
St John Bosco RC
Primary School
SWCK/CAS SR5 .... 104 D1
St John Boste RC
Primary School
WASHS NE38 .... 116 C1
St Johns College
DHAM DH1 .... 16 D6
St John Vianney School
WD/WHPE/BLK NE5 ...... 68 B2

St Joseph RC Junior
Primary School
BW/LEM/TK/HW NE15 .... 69 G7
St Joseph's Business &
Training Centre
LGB/KIL NE12 .... 47 K7
St Josephs Infant School
CLS/BIR/GTL DH3......... 115 H1
St Josephs RC School
BDN/LAN/SAC DH7 ...... 155 F7
St Josephs RC School
DHAM DH1 .... 17 L3
St Josephs RC School
MLFD/PNYW SR4 .... 105 K6
St Josephs RC School
SEA/MUR SR7 .... 149 H6
St Josephs School
NSHW NE29 .... 60 C6
St Josephs School
ROWG NE39 .... 96 D3
St Josephs School
WASHS NE38 .... 103 F7
St Lawrence RC
Primary School
BYK/HTN/WLK NE6 .... 7 H5
St Leonards Junior &
Infants School
SUNDSW SR3 .... 120 B6
St Leonards RC
Comprehensive School
DHAM DH1 .... 16 A1
St Margarets C of E
Infants School
DHAM DH1 .... 16 A6
St Margarets C of E
Primary School
DHAM DH1 .... 16 A5
St Marks RC Primary School
WD/WHPE/BLK NE5 .... 54 D6
St Mary Magdalene RC
Primary School
SEA/MUR SR7 .... 135 J7
St Marys College
ELS/FEN NE4 .... 69 H4
St Marys Hospital
MPTH NE61 .... 26 A7
St Marys Junior &
Infant School
STLY/ANP DH9 .... 126 D3
St Marys Primary School
CON/LDGT DH8 .... 122 C4
St Marys RC
Comprehensive School
LGB/HTN NE7............. 57 G5
St Marys RC Primary School
ASHBK/HED/RY SR2 ..... 120 B2
St Marys RC Primary School
JRW NE32 .... 90 B1
St Marys RC Primary School
TYNE/NSHE NE30 .... 50 E7
St Marys RC Primary School
WICK/BNPF NE16 .... 8 A9
St Mary's Roman
Catholic Cathedral
CNUT NE1................. 5 H8
St Matthews RC First School
PRUD NE42 .... 80 C2
St Matthews School
JRW NE32 .... 89 K2
St Michaels Industrial Estate
BYK/HTN/WLK NE6 .... 6 E6
St Michaels RC Primary School
ELS/FEN NE4 .... 9 J1
St Michaels RC School
BDN/LAN/SAC DH7 ...... 153 J5
St Nicholas Cathedral
CNUT NE1................. 5 L8
St Oswalds C E Junior
Mixed & Infant School
HEBB NE31 .... 73 J4
St Oswalds Clinic
FELL NE10................ 12 C8
St Oswalds C of E
Infants School
DHAM DH1 .... 16 E6
St Oswalds RC Infant &
Junior School
LWF/SPW/WRK NE9 ..... 101 J2
St Patricks RC School
ASHBK/HED/RY SR2 ..... 135 F1
St Patricks RC School
BDN/LAN/SAC DH7 ...... 167 K5
St Pauls C of E Primary School
ELS/FEN NE4 .... 4 F8
St Pauls RC First School
CRAM NE23 .... 38 C3
St Peter RC Junior &
Infant School
LWF/SPW/WRK NE9 ...... 87 G6
St Peters JMI School
JRW NE32 .... 74 A3
St Peters RC Middle School
CRAM NE23 .... 38 C4
St Pius RC School
CON/LDGT DH8 .... 122 C6
St Robert of Newminster RC
Comprehensive School
WASHS NE38 .... 117 F1
St Stephens RC Primary School
LGB/KIL NE12............. 57 H3
St Teresas RC Primary School
BYK/HTN/WLK NE6 .... 6 E1
St Thomas More RC (aided)
Comprehensive School
BLAY NE21 .... 83 K1
St Thomas Mores RC School
DHAM DH1 .... 158 A6
St Thomas Street
Business Centre
CNUT NE1................. 5 J5
St Vincents RC Primary School
BYK/HTN/WLK NE6 .... 7 L9
St Wilfreds RC Junior &
Infant School
FELL NE10................ 11 M3
St Wilfrids Middle School
BLYTH NE24 .... 31 F1

St Wilfrids RC
  Comprehensive School
  HAR/WTLS NE34............ 75 H5
Sam Smiths Sports Ground
  BYK/HTN/WLK NE6 .... 72 A2
Sanderson Hospital
  GOS/KPK NE3.................. 56 B6
Sandhaven Caravan &
  Camping Park
  SSH NE33 .... 3 M7
Sands Industrial Estate
  WICK/BNPF NE16 .... 84 E3
Saville Clinic
  CNUT NE1 .... 5 K5
Scotswood Sports Centre
  BW/LEM/TK/HW NE15 ..... 68 D5
Seaburn Centre
  CLDN/WHIT/ROK SR6 .... 93 F7
Seaburn Dene Primary School
  CLDN/WHIT/ROK SR6 .... 92 D1
Seaham College
  SEA/MUR SR7 .... 150 E1
Seaham Comprehensive School
  SEA/MUR SR7 .... 135 F6
Seaham Golf Club
  SEA/MUR SR7 .... 150 E3
Seaham Grange
  Industrial Estate
  SEA/MUR SR7 .... 134 E5
Seaton Delaval Whytrig
  County Middle School
  MONK NE25 .... 39 J4
Seaton Sluice Middle School
  WBAY NE26 .... 40 E1
Sea View Industrial Estate
  PLEE/EAS SR8 .... 175 G2
Sedgeletch Industrial Estate
  HLS DH4 .... 131 J5
Segedunum Business Centre
  WLSD/HOW NE28 .... 72 E2
Segedunum Roman Fort;
  Baths & Museum
  WLSD/HOW NE28 .... 72 E2
Seghill County First School
  CRAM NE23 .... 39 G7
Seghill Industrial Estate
  CRAM NE23 .... 39 G7
Shanklea First School
  CRAM NE23 .... 38 C1
Sherburn Hospital
  DHAM DH1 .... 170 A2
Shieldfield Health Centre
  JES NE2............................. 6 A4
Shield Row Junior &
  Infants School
  STLY/ANP DH9 .... 112 E6
Shincliffe C of E Junior &
  Infant School
  DHAM DH1 .... 169 J5
Shiney Row Primary School
  HLS DH4 .... 131 K1
Shipley Art Gallery
  GATE NE8 .... 11 G7
Shiremoor First School
  SMOOR NE27 .... 49 G6
Shiremoor Middle School
  SMOOR NE27 .... 49 H5
The Shopping Centre
  STLY/ANP DH9 .... 126 D2
The Shopping Centre
  STLY/ANP DH9 .... 126 D3
Shotley Bridge
  General Hospital
  CON/LDGT DH8 .... 122 E1
Shotley Bridge Infant School
  CON/LDGT DH8 .... 108 D7
Shotley Bridge Junior School
  CON/LDGT DH8 .... 108 C7
Shotton Colliery
  Industrial Estate
  RDHAMSE DH6.............. 173 H3
Shotton Colliery
  Primary School
  RDHAMSE DH6.............. 173 H3
Shotton Hall
  Comprehensive School
  PLEE/EAS SR8 .... 174 C6
Shotton Hall Junior School
  PLEE/EAS SR8 .... 174 C6
Shotton RC JMI School
  RDHAMSE DH6.............. 173 G3
The Side Gallery
  CNUT NE1 .... 5 L8
Sidegate Gallery
  WICK/BNPF NE16 .... 99 F2
Silksworth Health Centre
  SUNDSW SR3 .... 120 A7
Silksworth Sports
  Complex Track
  SUNDSW SR3 .... 119 K5
Silverbirch Industrial Estate
  LCB/KIL NE12 .... 47 H5
Silverlink Business Park
  WLSD/HOW NE28 .... 59 J4
Simonside First School
  WD/WHPE/BLK NE5 .... 54 D5
Simonside Industrial Estate
  HAR/WTLS NE34 .... 74 C6
Sir G B Hunter
  Memorial Hospital
  WLSD/HOW NE28 .... 72 E1
Sleekburn Business Centre
  BLYTH NE24 .... 31 F3
Sloping Masonry Business Park
  WLSD/HOW NE28 .... 73 H2
Souter Lighthouse
  CLDN/WHIT/ROK SR6 .... 77 F6
South Benwell Primary School
  ELS/FEN NE4 .... 69 J7
South Cramlington
  Industrial Estate
  CRAM NE23 .... 38 A7
Southdene Medical Centre
  RDHAMSE DH6.............. 173 J3
South Gosforth First School
  JES NE2............................. 56 E6
South Hetton Health Centre
  RDHAMSE DH6.............. 160 E2

South Hetton Industrial Estate
  RDHAMSE DH6.............. 160 E2
South Hetton Primary School
  RDHAMSE DH6.............. 160 E2
South Hylton Primary School
  MLFD/PNYW SR4........... 104 E7
Southlands Middle School
  CRAM NE23 .... 38 C5
Southlands School &
  Swimming Pool
  TYNE/NSHE NE30 .... 60 E2
South Moor Golf Club
  STLY/ANP DH9 .... 126 E4
Southmoor School
  ASHBK/HED/RY SR2 .... 120 E3
South Nelson Industrial Estate
  CRAM NE23 .... 32 E7
Southridge First School
  MONK NE25 .... 50 B3
South Shields FC
  JRW NE32 .... 74 B5
South Shields Golf Club
  HAR/WTLS NE34 .... 76 B6
South Stanley
  Comprehensive School
  STLY/ANP DH9 .... 126 C2
South Stanley County
  Junior Mixed School
  STLY/ANP DH9 .... 126 C2
South Street County
  Primary School
  GATE NE8 .... 11 H6
South Tyneside Area
  Health Authority
  HAR/WTLS NE34 .... 76 A4
South Tyneside College
  HEBB NE31 .... 89 F2
South Tyneside College
  SSH NE33 .... 75 J3
South Tyneside District Hospital
  HAR/WTLS NE34 .... 75 H6
South Tyneside
  Health Care Trust
  HEBB NE31 .... 73 C6
South Tyneside Health
  Care Trust
  SSH NE33 .... 3 K6
South Tyneside
  Magistrates Court
  SSH NE33 .... 3 G9
South Wellfield First School
  MONK NE25 .... 49 K5
South West Industrial Estate
  PLEE/EAS SR8 .... 174 A4
Southwick Health Centre
  SWCK/CAS SR5 .... 106 A4
Southwick Industrial Estate
  SWCK/CAS SR5 .... 105 J3
Springfield Clinic
  GATE NE8 .... 11 H8
Springfield Comprehensive
  School and Leisure Centre
  JRW NE32 .... 73 K6
Spring Gardens Primary School
  NSHW NE29 .... 2 B2
Spring Terrace Health Centre
  NSHW NE29 .... 2 C1
Springwell Health Centre
  SUNDSW SR3 .... 119 J3
Springwell Village
  Primary School
  LWF/SPW/WRK NE9 ..... 102 B4
Stadium Industrial Park
  FELL NE10........................ 11 M2
Stadium Industrial Park
  FELL NE10........................ 12 D6
Stanfield Business Centre
  ASHBK/HED/RY SR2 .... 15 J7
Stanfield Business Centre
  ASHBK/HED/RY SR2 ..... 120 E2
Stanhope County
  Infants School
  SSH NE33 .... 75 G4
Stanhope County
  Junior Mixed School
  SSH NE33 .... 75 F5
Stanhope Parade
  Health Centre
  SSH NE33 .... 75 G3
Stanley Health Centre
  STLY/ANP DH9 .... 126 C1
Stanley RC Junior Mixed &
  Infants School
  STLY/ANP DH9 .... 112 D7
Stannington Children's Hospital
  MPTH NE61 .... 26 B6
Stargate Industrial Estate
  RYTON NE40................... 83 G1
Station Industrial Estate
  PRUD NE42 .... 80 B1
Stella Gill Industrial Estate
  CLSW/PEL DH2............... 128 E2
Stephenson Industrial Estate
  LCB/KIL NE12 .... 47 J7
Stephenson Industrial Estate
  WASHN NE37 .... 103 G3
Stephenson Railway Museum
  SMOOR NE27 .... 59 J3
Stephenson Street
  TYNE/NSHE NE30 .... 2 E2
Stocksfield Cricket Club
  PSHWF NE43 .... 79 G4
Stonelaw County
  Middle School
  CRAM NE23 .... 38 A4
Studio Gallery
  TYNE/NSHE NE30 .... 61 H3
Sulgrave Industrial Estate
  WASHN NE37 .... 103 G4
Sunderland AFC Club Shop
  SUND SR1 .... 14 E4
Sunderland Area
  Health Authority
  ASHBK/HED/RY SR2 .... 14 D9
Sunderland Bowling Centre
  SWCK/CAS SR5 .... 106 C4

Sunderland Counselling
  Services
  MLFD/PNYW SR4........... 119 G1
Sunderland County Court
  SUND SR1 .... 14 F5
Sunderland Eye Infirmary
  ASHBK/HED/RY SR2 ..... 120 D3
Sunderland Football Club
  SWCK/CAS SR5 .... 14 D1
Sunderland High School
  ASHBK/HED/RY SR2 .... 14 E9
Sunderland Museum &
  Winter Gardens
  SUND SR1 .... 14 F5
Sunderland Retail Park
  CLDN/WHIT/ROK SR6 ..... 106 D4
Sunderland Royal Hospital
  MLFD/PNYW SR4........... 105 K7
Sunderland Talmudical College
  GATE NE8 .... 11 G7
Sunderland University
  SUND SR1 .... 14 F4
Swalwell Cricket Club
  BLAY NE21 .... 84 D3
Swan Industrial Estate
  WASHS NE38 .... 117 H2
Talbot House Special School
  BW/LEM/TK/HW NE15 ..... 67 G1
Tanfield Lea County
  Junior Mixed &
  Infants School
  STLY/ANP DH9 .... 112 A5
Tanfield Lea County
  Junior Mixed &
  Infant School
  STLY/ANP DH9 .... 112 B6
Tanfield Lea Industrial Estate
  STLY/ANP DH9 .... 112 C5
Tanfield Lea Industrial
  Estate North
  STLY/ANP DH9 .... 112 A5
Tanfield Lea Industrial
  Estate South
  STLY/ANP DH9 .... 112 C6
Tanfield View Surgery
  STLY/ANP DH9 .... 126 C1
Team Valley Business Centre
  DUN/TMV NE11 .... 86 D6
Team Valley Trading Estate
  DUN/TMV NE11 .... 86 C5
Team Valley Trading Estate
  DUN/TMV NE11 .... 100 D2
Tedco Business Park
  JRW NE32 .... 73 H3
Tedco Business Works
  SSH NE33 .... 3 G8
Temple Park Centre
  HAR/WTLS NE34 .... 75 J7
Theatre Royal
  CNUT NE1 .... 5 K6
The Valley Shopping Village
  DUN/TMV NE11 .... 100 D1
Thomas Bewick Birth
  Place Museum
  PSHWF NE43 .... 79 K2
Thomas Bewick Special School
  WD/WHPE/BLK NE5 .... 68 A1
Thomas Hepburn
  Community School
  FELL NE10........................ 88 A5
Thornhill Comprehensive School
  ASHBK/HED/RY SR2 .... 14 C9
Thornley RC School
  RDHAMSE DH6.............. 172 D7
Thornley Station
  Industrial Estate
  RDHAMSE DH6.............. 173 J6
Thorpe Maternity Hospital
  PLEE/EAS SR8 .... 162 C7
Throckley First School
  BW/LEM/TK/HW NE15 ..... 66 E1
Throckley Industrial Estate
  BW/LEM/TK/HW NE15 ..... 53 F7
Throckley Middle School
  BW/LEM/TK/HW NE15 ..... 66 E1
The Toco Gallery
  JES NE2........................... 70 E1
Toner Avenue County
  Infant School
  HEBB NE31 .... 89 F1
Townend Primary School
  SWCK/CAS SR5 .... 104 D1
Trevelyan College
  DHAM DH1 .... 16 C9
Trimdon Grange Health Clinic
  TRIM TS29..................... 182 D7
Trimdon Grange
  Industrial Estate
  TRIM TS29..................... 182 C7
Trinity Maritime Museum
  CNUT NE1 .... 5 M7
Trinity Medical Centre
  SSH NE33 .... 75 G2
Trinity School
  BLAY NE21 .... 84 C3
Trouts Lane School
  DHAM DH1 .... 155 K2
Tudhoe Colliery
  Primary School
  SPEN DL16 .... 178 C6
Tudhoe Industrial Estate
  SPEN DL16 .... 178 C7
Tynemouth Business Centre
  TYNE/NSHE NE30 .... 61 F4
Tynemouth Castle & Priory
  TYNE/NSHE NE30 .... 61 J3
Tynemouth College
  NSHW NE29 .... 60 D4
Tynemouth Crematorium
  NSHW NE29 .... 60 D3
Tynemouth Cricket Club
  TYNE/NSHE NE30 .... 61 F2
Tynemouth Golf Club
  TYNE/NSHE NE30 .... 61 F1
Tyne Point Industrial Estate
  JRW NE32 .... 74 C5
Tyneside General Hospital
  NSHW NE29 .... 60 C1

Tyneside Golf Club
  RYTON NE40................... 66 D5
Tyneside Retail Park
  NSHW NE29 .... 59 K4
Tyneside Works
  JRW NE32 .... 73 K3
Tyne Tees TV Studios
  CNUT NE1 .... 6 B7
Tyne Theatre & Opera House
  CNUT NE1 .... 5 G7
Tyne Tunnel (Tynemouth)
  Trading Estate
  NSHW NE29 .... 59 K5
Tyneview Primary School
  BYK/HTN/WLK NE6 .... 72 C6
Tyne View Primary School
  GATE NE8 .... 10 B4
University of Durham
  DHAM DH1 .... 16 F5
University Halls of Residence
  SUND SR1 .... 15 G3
University College
  DHAM DH1 .... 16 C4
University for Industry
  SUND SR1 .... 14 E4
University Library
  DHAM DH1 .... 16 C4
University of Durham
  DHAM DH1 .... 16 C8
University of Durham
  DHAM DH1 .... 16 E4
University of Durham
  DHAM DH1 .... 16 E7
University of Durham
  DHAM DH1 .... 16 E9
University of Durham
  DHAM DH1 .... 16 A9
University of Durham
  DHAM DH1 .... 17 G5
University of Durham
  DHAM DH1 .... 17 H8
University of Durham
  DHAM DH1 .... 157 J4
University of Durham
  DHAM DH1 .... 168 D4
University of
  Newcastle Upon Tyne
  CNUT NE1 .... 5 J3
University of
  Newcastle Upon Tyne
  CNUT NE1 .... 5 H5
University of
  Newcastle upon Tyne
  JES NE2............................. 5 L1
University of
  Newcastle upon Tyne
  LGB/HTN NE7.................. 57 J7
University of Northumbria
  at Newcastle
  CNUT NE1 .... 5 L3
University of Northumbria
  at Newcastle
  LGB/HTN NE7.................. 57 J6
University of Northumbria
  Officers Training Corps
  ELS/FEN NE4 .... 4 D3
University of Sunderland
  ASHBK/HED/RY SR2 .... 14 E7
University of Sunderland
  CLDN/WHIT/ROK SR6 ..... 15 C2
University of Sunderland
  CLDN/WHIT/ROK SR6 ..... 106 A4
University of Sunderland
  MLFD/PNYW SR4........... 105 J3
University of Sunderland
  SUND SR1 .... 14 C5
University of Sunderland
  SWCK/CAS SR5 .... 105 F5
University of Sunderland
  WASHN NE37 .... 102 C6
University of Sunderland
  (Library)
  SUND SR1 .... 14 C6
University Technology Park
  ASHBK/HED/RY SR2 .... 14 C6
Ushaw College
  BDN/LAN/SAC DH7 ...... 154 C5
Ushaw Moor Cricket Club
  BDN/LAN/SAC DH7 ...... 166 E1
Ushaw Moor Infant School
  BDN/LAN/SAC DH7 ...... 154 E7
Ushaw Moor Junior School
  BDN/LAN/SAC DH7 ...... 155 F7
Usworth Colliery Junior School
  WASHN NE37 .... 103 G4
Usworth Grange
  Primary School
  WASHN NE37 .... 103 H4
Usworth Secondary School &
  Leisure Centre
  WASHN NE37 .... 103 F3
Valley Road Infant School
  ASHBK/HED/RY SR2 .... 15 J9
Valley Road Junior School
  ASHBK/HED/RY SR2 .... 15 J9
Valley View County
  Infant School
  JRW NE32 .... 73 K7
Vance Business Park
  DUN/TMV NE11 .... 9 L9
Van Mildert College
  DHAM DH1 .... 168 C4
Victoria Industrial Estate
  FELL NE10........................ 88 E1
Victoria Medical Centre
  HEBB NE31 .... 73 F5
Victoria Road Health Centre
  WASHN NE37 .... 103 F5
Viking Gallery
  JRW NE32 .... 73 K4
Viking Industrial Park
  JRW NE32 .... 73 J3
Village Gallery
  WICK/BNPF NE16 .... 85 F5
Wagonway Industrial Estate
  HEBB NE31 .... 73 G3

Walker Comprehensive School and
  Leisure Centre
  BYK/HTN/WLK NE6 .... 72 B5
Walkerdene Special School
  BYK/HTN/WLK NE6 .... 72 B5
Walker Gate Hospital
  BYK/HTN/WLK NE6 .... 72 A3
Walkergate Infant School
  BYK/HTN/WLK NE6 .... 7 M1
Walker Riverside
  Industrial Park
  BYK/HTN/WLK NE6 .... 13 L1
Walker Riverside
  Industrial Park
  BYK/HTN/WLK NE6 .... 72 D6
Wallaw Cinema
  BLYTH NE24 .... 31 G7
Wallsend Business Centre
  WLSD/HOW NE28 .... 72 E2
Wallsend Golf Club
  WLSD/HOW NE28 .... 72 B1
Wallsend Sports Centre
  WLSD/HOW NE28 .... 72 B1
Wansbeck Business Centre
  ASHGTN NE63.................. 23 H1
Wansbeck General Hospital
  ASHGTN NE63.................. 24 C1
Wansbeck St Aidan C of E
  Aided First School
  MPTH NE61 .... 20 B3
Wardley Primary School
  FELL NE10........................ 13 L7
War Memorial
  SUND SR1 .... 14 F6
Washington Albany
  Infants School
  WASHN NE37 .... 102 D6
Washington Football Club
  WASHN NE37 .... 103 F6
Washington Hospital
  WASHS NE38 .... 116 A6
Washington Leisure Centre
  WASHS NE38 .... 116 E2
Washington Old Hall
  WASHS NE38 .... 103 G7
Washington Pit Museum
  WASHN NE37 .... 102 E6
Washington Secondary
  School & Leisure Centre
  WASHN NE37 .... 103 F6
Washington Village
  Primary School
  WASHS NE38 .... 103 G7
Waterhouses JMI School
  BDN/LAN/SAC DH7 ...... 165 G3
Waterloo Medical Group
  BLYTH NE24 .... 31 F6
Waterville Primary School
  NSHW NE29 .... 2 B4
Waterworld
  PRUD NE42 .... 80 E2
Waverley First School
  BW/LEM/TK/HW NE15 ..... 68 C5
Waygood Gallery & Studios
  CNUT NE1 .... 5 K7
Wear Industrial Estate
  WASHS NE38 .... 116 D4
Wearside College
  SUNDSW SR3 .... 119 K3
Wearside Golf Club
  MLFD/PNYW SR4........... 118 B3
Weetslade Industrial Estate
  CRAM NE23 .... 38 A6
Welbeck First School
  ASHGTN NE63.................. 24 C2
Welbeck Primary School
  BYK/HTN/WLK NE6 .... 7 K6
Wellbank Special School
  WASHN NE37 .... 102 D4
Wellfield Comprehensive School
  WNGT TS28................... 183 K2
West Boldon Junior
  Mixed School
  BOL NE36 .... 90 E4
West Chirton (Middle)
  Industrial Estate
  NSHW NE29 .... 59 K3
West Chirton (North)
  Industrial Estate
  NSHW NE29 .... 59 J3
West Chirton (South)
  Industrial Estate
  NSHW NE29 .... 60 A5
West Chirton Trading Estate
  NSHW NE29 .... 60 A4
West Denton First School
  WD/WHPE/BLK NE5 .... 68 A2
West Denton High
  School & Leisure Centre
  WD/WHPE/BLK NE5 .... 68 C1
West Denton Retail Park
  WD/WHPE/BLK NE5 .... 68 E1
Westerhope Clinic
  WD/WHPE/BLK NE5 .... 54 D7
Westerhope First School
  WD/WHPE/BLK NE5 .... 54 C7
Westerhope Golf Club
  WD/WHPE/BLK NE5 .... 54 C6
Westerhope Small
  Business Park
  WD/WHPE/BLK NE5 .... 54 C6
Western First School
  WLSD/HOW NE28 .... 72 C1
Western Infant School
  NSHW NE29 .... 2 B4
Western Middle School
  WLSD/HOW NE28 .... 72 C2
Westfield School
  GOS/KPK NE3.................. 56 B7
West Gate Community College
  ELS/FEN NE4 .... 69 H5
Westgate Hill Primary School
  ELS/FEN NE4 .... 4 C6
West Jesmond Junior School
  JES NE2........................... 70 E2
West Lane Junior &
  Infant School
  BLAY NE21 .... 83 J4

Westlea Junior School
SEA/MUR SR7 .... **134** E7
West Line Industrial Estate
CLSW/PEL DH2.......................... **115** H4
West Moor First School
LGB/KIL NE12 .... **57** J1
Westmoor Middle School
LGB/KIL NE12 .... **57** H1
Westmorland Business Centre
ELS/FEN NE4 .... **5** G8
Westoe Gallery
SSH NE33 .... **3** J9
Westovian Theatre Society
SSH NE33 .... **3** L5
West Rainton Primary School
HLS DH4 .... **146** C6
West Sleekburn County
Middle School
STKFD/GP NE62 .... **24** B7
West Sleekburn
Industrial Estate
STKFD/GP NE62 .... **24** A7
West Walker School
BYK/HTN/WLK NE6 .... **72** C7
Westway Industrial Park
BW/LEM/TK/HW NE15 .... **53** F7

Wheatley Hill Primary School
RDHAMSE DH6.......................... **182** D1
Whickham Comprehensive
School & Leisure Centre
WICK/BNPF NE16 .... **84** E6
Whickham Golf Club
WICK/BNPF NE16 .... **98** C1
Whickham Industrial Estate
WICK/BNPF NE16 .... **84** D3
Whickham Parochial C of E
Junior & Infant School
WICK/BNPF NE16 .... **84** D7
Whickham Thorns Outdoor
Activity Centre
DUN/TMV NE11 .... **8** E7
Whinfield Industrial Estate
ROWG NE39 .... **96** E4
Whitburn Comprehensive
School & Leisure Centre
CLDN/WHIT/ROK SR6 .... **93** G4
Whitburn Cricket Club
CLDN/WHIT/ROK SR6 .... **93** F4
Whitburn Golf Club
HAR/WTLS NE34 .... **76** E6
Whitburn Junior Mixed School
CLDN/WHIT/ROK SR6 .... **92** E4

Whitburn Surgery
CLDN/WHIT/ROK SR6 .... **92** E4
Whitehouse Business Park
RDHAMSE DH6.......................... **174** A6
Whitehouse Industrial Estate
BW/LEM/TK/HW NE15 .... **69** G7
Whitehouse Primary School
NSHW NE29 .... **60** C2
Whitehouse Primary School
NSHW NE29 .... **60** A3
Whitley Bay Cricket Club
MONK NE25 .... **50** E6
Whitley Bay Football Club
MONK NE25 .... **50** E6
Whitley Bay Golf Club
WBAY NE26 .... **50** C1
Whitley Bay High School
MONK NE25 .... **50** C3
Whitley Bay Ice Rink
MONK NE25 .... **50** D6
Whitley Bay Rockcliff RfC
MONK NE25 .... **50** E6
Whitley Lodge First School
WBAY NE26 .... **50** C1
Whitley Memorial School
BDLGTN NE22.......................... **29** G6

Willington High School
WLSD/HOW NE28 .... **59** H5
Winchester House Community
Business Centre
SWCK/CAS SR5 .... **104** D1
Windmill Hills County
Primary School
GATE NE8 .... **10** E4
Windmill Industrial Estate
CRAM NE23 .... **32** C6
Windsor County First School
NWBGN NE64 .... **25** F2
Windy Nook Primary School
FELL NE10.......................... **87** K6
Wingate Grange
Industrial Estate
WNGT TS28.......................... **183** J4
Wingate RC Junior &
Infant School
WNGT TS28.......................... **183** K4
Wingrove Primary School
ELS/FEN NE4 .... **69** J5
Winlaton Park Junior School
BLAY NE21 .... **84** A4
Winlaton Vulcans Rugby Club
BLAY NE21 .... **84** A3

Witherwack Primary School
SWCK/CAS SR5.......................... **105** K1
Witton Gilbert County School
BDN/LAN/SAC DH7 .... **155** F1
Woodhorn Church Museum
ASHGTN NE63.......................... **18** E6
Woodhorn Coliery Mus
ASHGTN NE63.......................... **18** C7
Woodlands Park Health Centre
DIN/WO NE13 .... **46** B4
Woodlea County
Primary School
HLS DH4 .... **131** G6
Workshop Centre
ELS/FEN NE4 .... **4** C8
Wrekenton Health Centre
LWF/SPW/WRK NE9 .... **101** K2
Wylam County First School
WYLAM NE41 .... **65** H5
Yates Jewish School for Girls
GATE NE8 .... **10** F6
The Yemeni School
SSH NE33 .... **75** F2
Yoden Primary School
PLEE/EAS SR8 .... **175** J4

 **Street by Street** QUESTIONNAIRE

Dear Atlas User
Your comments, opinions and recommendations are very important to us. So please help us to improve our street atlases by taking a few minutes to complete this simple questionnaire.

You do NOT need a stamp (unless posted outside the UK). If you do not want to remove this page from your street atlas, then photocopy it or write your answers on a plain sheet of paper.

Send to: The Editor, AA Street by Street, FREEPOST SCE 4598, Basingstoke RG21 4GY

ABOUT THE ATLAS...

Which city/town/county did you buy?

Are there any features of the atlas or mapping that you find particularly useful?

Is there anything we could have done better?

Why did you choose an AA Street by Street atlas?

Did it meet your expectations?

Exceeded ☐   **Met all** ☐   **Met most** ☐   **Fell below** ☐

Please give your reasons

Where did you buy it?

For what purpose? (please tick all applicable)

To use in your own local area ☐   To use on business or at work ☐

Visiting a strange place ☐   In the car ☐   On foot ☐

Other (please state)

LOCAL KNOWLEDGE...

Local knowledge is invaluable. Whilst every attempt has been made to make the information contained in this atlas as accurate as possible, should you notice any inaccuracies, please detail them below (if necessary, use a blank piece of paper) or e-mail us at *streetbystreet@theAA.com*

ABOUT YOU...

Name (Mr/Mrs/Ms)

Address

Postcode

Daytime tel no

E-mail address

Which age group are you in?

Under 25 ☐   25-34 ☐   35-44 ☐   45-54 ☐   55-64 ☐   65+ ☐

Are you an AA member?   YES ☐   NO ☐

Do you have Internet access?   YES ☐   NO ☐

Thank you for taking the time to complete this questionnaire. Please send it to us as soon as possible, and remember, you do not need a stamp (unless posted outside the UK).

MX